Planning for Retirement Needs

Huebner School Series

Walt J. Woerheide, Editor

Individual Medical Expense Insurance
Thomas P. O'Hare

Meeting the Financial Need of Long-Term Care
Burton T. Beam, Jr., and Thomas P. O'Hare

Financial Planning: Process and Environment
Don A. Taylor and C. Bruce Worsham (eds.)

Fundamentals of Insurance Planning
Burton T. Beam, Jr., and Eric A. Wiening

Fundamentals of Financial Planning
David M. Cordell (ed.)

Fundamentals of Income Taxation
James F. Ivers III (ed.)

McGill's Life Insurance
Edward E. Graves (ed.)

McGill's Legal Aspects of Life Insurance
Edward E. Graves and Burke A. Christensen (eds.)

Group Benefits: Basic Concepts and Alternatives
Burton T. Beam, Jr.

Planning for Retirement Needs
David A. Littell and Kenn Beam Tacchino

Fundamentals of Investments for Financial Planning
Walt J. Woerheide and David M. Cordell

Fundamentals of Estate Planning
Constance J. Fontaine

Estate Planning Applications
Ted Kurlowicz

Planning for Business Owners and Professionals
Ted Kurlowicz, James F. Ivers III, and John J. McFadden

Financial Planning Applications
Thomas P. Langdon and William J. Ruckstuhl

Advanced Topics in Group Benefits
Burton T. Beam, Jr., and Thomas P. O'Hare (eds.)

Executive Compensation
John J. McFadden (ed.)

Health and Long-Term Care Financing for Seniors
Burton T. Beam, Jr., and Thomas P. O'Hare

Financial Decisions for Retirement
David A. Littell and Kenn Beam Tacchino

Huebner School Series

Planning for Retirement Needs
Ninth Edition

David A. Littell
Kenn Beam Tacchino

The American College Press/*Bryn Mawr, Pennsylvania*

This publication is designed to provide accurate and authoritative information about the subject covered. While every precaution has been taken in the preparation of this material, the authors and The American College assume no liability for damages resulting from the use of the information contained in this publication. The American College is not engaged in rendering legal, accounting, or other professional advice. If legal or other expert advice is required, the services of an appropriate professional should be sought.

Contents

Students of HS 326

For those of you reading this book in conjunction with The American College's HS 326 course, please note the following:

Due to the constant law and regulatory changes that can affect the content of this course, all students of The American College taking HS 326 are required to check the HS 326 Blackboard site to see if there have been any changes to the content. **Content changes identified on Blackboard may have an impact on the exam for HS 326.**

Preface

This book represents a radical departure from traditional pension literature by focusing primarily on the practical application of the retirement material in a financial services practice. To this end, it includes a feature titled "Your Financial Services Practice" as well as a shorter counterpart called the "Planning Note." In addition, the book is replete with examples and case studies intended to demonstrate how the pension concepts apply in real-world situations. This new practitioner-oriented approach came about for a variety of reasons, perhaps the most important of which is that student feedback indicated a need for change in this direction.

This book is geared to those with little or no experience in the retirement field. The material focuses on the basics that a financial services professional needs to know and deals sparingly with the retirement concepts that are not germane. For example, stock plans are not discussed in great detail because they are not a part of the typical financial services professional's practice. In addition, the amount of detail on any given topic depends on the topic's relevance to our audience. Determining the appropriate plan for the small business is covered in great detail, for example, whereas the question of which funding method the actuary should choose to fund a plan is covered only briefly. In other words, areas such as funding methods and stock plans are discussed in the context of how they apply to the financial services professional. While the material is applicable to the large-, medium-, and small-plan markets, the emphasis is on the small-plan market, where the financial services professional does most of his or her business.

Almost all general statements that one can make about pension material are subject to qualification or exception. If the qualifying remark or exception is of significant magnitude, we have put it into the text as a parenthetical expression. If the qualifying statement or exception would serve to confuse the larger issue, however, we have omitted it so you will not get caught up in the minutia and miss the major point.

It is our sincere hope that this practitioner-oriented approach will speak to your interests and provide both a practical and educational treatment of retirement planning for the business and the business owner as well as for the individual. For those interested in learning more about the topics discussed in other course materials and books prepared by The American College, a related course includes the following:

- HS 352 *Financial Decisions for Retirement,* which goes deeper into the topic of individual retirement planning. In addition to a discussion of determining financial needs and identifying sources of retirement income, this course provides an in-depth look at important issues facing retirees, including the taxation of pension benefits, providing for medical coverage in retirement and housing issues facing the retiree.

The authors would like to acknowledge the help of many individuals who were instrumental in the development of current/former editions of this textbook.

- Current and former faculty members who participated in the drafting of this text, including William J. Ruckstuhl and Edward E. Graves
- Practitioners in the retirement planning field, including Gerald Levinson, Joseph P. Garner, Paul Paleologopoulos, Ken Switzer, and Gary Lyons, who acted more like a coauthor than an adviser
- Our fellow faculty members at The American College, especially Paul Schneider for extensive updates of chapters 15 and 16, Don A. Taylor for compiling the financial calculator keystrokes in chapter 22, Burton T. Beam, Jr., Ted Kurlowicz, and John J. McFadden
- The College's editorial and production staff, especially Wendy de Pinho, Todd Denton, Maria Marlowe, and Evelyn Rice
- Virginia E. Webb, The College's librarian, for help with research
- Dorothy Hoffman for compiling the index
- Stephen Rosen of Stephen H. Rosen & Associates for his actuarial guidance and examples

About the Authors

David A. Littell, JD, is the Joseph E. Bottner Chair in Financial Gerontology and a professor of taxation at The American College. A native of Chicago, David holds a BA in Psychology from Northwestern University and a JD from the Boston University School of Law. At The American College he is responsible for course development in pension and retirement planning. He was previously an attorney with Saul, Ewing, Remick & Saul, and Paul Tanker & Associates, both Philadelphia-based firms.

Kenn B. Tacchino, JD, LLM, is a consultant to The American College and a professor of taxation at Widener University. He is also editor of *The Journal of Financial Service Professionals.* He received his BA from Muhlenberg College, his law degree (JD) from Western New England Law School, and his LLM from Widener University School of Law. Kenn is a member of the American Bar Association and National Council on Aging. He previously worked for Massachusetts Mutual Life Insurance Company, Prentice-Hall, and was formerly a full-time faculty member at The American College.

Planning for Retirement Needs

1

Pension and Retirement Planning Overview

Learning Objectives

An understanding of the material in this chapter should enable you to

1-1. Compare tax-advantaged retirement plans with nonqualified plans and IRAs.

1-2. Identify why tax-advantaged retirement plans are a positive retirement-saving vehicle for employees.

1-3. Explain how tax-advantaged retirement plans benefit employers.

1-4. Explain how tax-advantaged plans benefit business owners.

Chapter Outline

Retirement planning continues to be an important marketplace for the financial services professional. Public consciousness regarding the need for retirement planning has never been higher. The baby-boom generation is marching toward retirement age; and pension benefits are more visible to consumers as employers promote the advantages of employee involvement in 401(k) and 403(b) plans. But this is only part of the story. The retirement market is where the money is; $12 trillion in assets is owned by private retirement plans. Also, Americans are aging. As of the year 2000, one out of every eight Americans was over age 65 and, by the year 2030[1], that figure will increase to one out of five. Considering these demographics, the potential for the growth of the retirement market is nothing short of tremendous.

For financial services professionals, the retirement market offers many attractive and lucrative opportunities to serve clients, including

- setting up qualified plans or other tax-advantaged retirement plans for corporations and other for-profit business entities (chapters 3–5)
- setting up retirement programs for nonprofit organizations (chapter 6)
- modifying existing retirement programs to maximize tax-shelter potential, either by changing the existing plan or by instituting multiple plans (chapters 3–6)
- supplementing existing retirement programs with 401(k) plans (chapter 5)
- updating existing plans to conform with legislative changes (chapters 7–10)
- updating existing plans to conform with changing organizational needs (chapters 7–10)
- designing retirement programs that meet the owner-employee's tax and savings objectives (chapters 7–10)
- advising clients about investment strategies that are appropriate for retirement programs (chapters 11–12)
- selling investment products that are appropriate for retirement programs (chapters 11–12)
- planning for the purchase of life insurance in tax-sheltered plans (chapters 10 and 12)
- setting up nonqualified plans for executives (chapters 15–16)

- selling IRAs and Roth IRAs to clients (chapters 17–18)
- planning for a client's retirement (chapters 19–23)
- planning for the best disposition of a client's retirement benefits (chapters 24–25)

Many financial services professionals choose to specialize in pensions. Others, however, complement their existing practice by providing one or more of these services under the umbrella of comprehensive financial planning. Whether you choose to specialize or offer one or more of these services to clients as part of a comprehensive package, the information in this book should open up a world of opportunity.

THE UNIVERSE OF RETIREMENT PLANNING VEHICLES

The first part of the text focuses on an introduction to the world of employer- and individually sponsored retirement vehicles. Entering this world means exposure to a new vocabulary. Learning and remembering this terminology is facilitated by the organization and categorization of the material. You will find that many plans share similar features and only occasionally have differences. Charts and tables throughout the book will help you remember the material.

Tax-Advantaged Plans of Private Employers

tax-advantaged retirement plans

qualified plans

One way to organize this discussion is to look at the types *of tax-advantaged retirement plans* that can be sponsored by for-profit and nonprofit employers. Most of these are employer-sponsored plans that are referred to as *qualified plans*. Qualified plans are subject to Code Sec. 401(a) and include defined-benefit pension plans, cash-balance plans, money-purchase pension plans, target-benefit plans, profit-sharing plans, 401(k) plans, stock bonus plans, and ESOPs.

All qualified plans are subject to a number of basic requirements, and each type of plan has its own special characteristics. Two other types of tax-advantaged plans available to for-profit entities are referred to as SEPs (simplified employee pensions) and SIMPLEs (savings incentive match plans for employees). These tax-advantaged plans make up the bulk of the retirement market because of their tax advantages, business applications, and special appeal to the business owner. Tax-exempt entities can also sponsor qualified plans, SEPs, and SIMPLEs. In addition, public school systems and those nonprofit organizations qualifying for Code Sec. 501(c)(3) tax-exempt status can sponsor 403(b) plans that are also referred to as tax-sheltered annuities.

Universe of Qualified Plans

- Defined-benefit pension plan
- Cash-balance pension plan
- Money-purchase pension plan
- Target-benefit pension plan

- Profit-sharing plan
- 401(k) plan
- Stock bonus plan
- ESOP (employee stock ownership plan)

All of the employer-sponsored tax-advantaged plans share some characteristics. First, they all provide for deferred compensation. The compensation may be part of an employee's salary that is held for retirement (as in a salary reduction 401(k) plan, SIMPLE, or 403(b) plan), a share of the profits (as in a profit-sharing plan), an employer-provided amount equal to a percentage of salary (as in a money-purchase plan), or the promise of a monthly salary substitute after retirement (as in a defined-benefit plan). In all tax-advantaged plans, the sponsor is required to make contributions to a trust, an insurance contract, or, in the case of a SEP or SIMPLE, an IRA account. Such amounts are held and invested, and distributed only at a later time according to the rules applicable to that plan.

Other Tax-Advantaged Plans Available to Private Employers

- SEPs (simplified employee pensions)
- SIMPLEs (savings incentive match plans for employees)
- 403(b) plans (limited to 501(c)(3) organizations)

What makes tax-advantaged retirement plans special is that the employer takes a tax deduction at the time contributions are made to the plan, even though employees do not have to pay income tax until benefits are paid to them. Under the normal rules that apply to the taxation of compensation, the employer is eligible for a tax deduction only at the time employees are determined to have taxable income. For example, in a nonqualified plan for executives, the taxation of compensation can be deferred, but only at the cost of deferring the employer's deduction until the time taxes are paid. The normal taxation rules are like a seesaw—the employer on one end can be elevated (receive a tax deduction) only if the employee at the other end is touching the ground (paying taxes). Conversely, the employee can be

elevated (avoid paying taxes) only if the employer is on the ground (not receiving a tax deduction). These "laws of tax physics" are suspended, however, if the employer is willing to satisfy the requirements of one of the tax-advantaged retirement plans.

Tax-Advantaged Plan Attributes

- Employer deduction with contribution
- No tax on trust account
- Employee taxed on benefits distributed
- Ability to roll distributions into other tax-deferred plans

A second unique tax advantage is that income on assets held in a trust or an insurance product is not taxed. Retirement investments earn interest and appreciate without being subject to taxation in the year any gain occurs. Although such amounts are not taxed at this level, income is taxed as it is paid out as part of an employee's benefits.

A third advantage has to do with taxation of distributions. As we have discussed, benefits are not taxed until they are distributed from the plan. Unlike nonqualified plans the participant can make an election as to the form of payment at the time benefits are to begin.

The fourth advantage is the ability to roll benefits into other tax-deferred vehicles when the participant becomes eligible to receive the benefit. This typically means that the individual can defer paying taxes until the time that he or she intends to spend the funds—which is usually to support retirement needs.

Qualified plans have some additional special tax rules that are not available in other plans. Currently, only qualified plans allow a portion of the plan's assets to be invested in life insurance. When a qualified plan provides for death benefits paid from the proceeds of a life insurance contract, such amounts are excludible from income to the extent of the pure insurance amount paid (discussed further in chapter 10). In addition, certain distributions from qualified plans may be eligible for special tax treatment (see chapter 25 for further discussion).

In exchange for these tax advantages, the law imposes a large number of requirements. Although the rules are different for each type of plan, there are many similarities. Before we get into the details, it is helpful to get a feeling for what types of requirements are involved.

- *Broad employee participation*—In order for the owners and managers to participate in the tax benefits, the plan must cover a significant number of rank-and-file employees.
- *Vesting*—To make sure that long-service employees who leave prior to the plan's normal retirement age receive some benefits, an employee must be vested in some benefits after he or she has reached a specified number of years of employment. Some types of plans require immediate vesting.
- *Employee communications*—All plans must describe to employees what the terms and conditions of the plan are and to what benefits a participant will be entitled.
- *Nondiscrimination*—All plans have rules regarding the relationship between the level of benefits provided for highly compensated employees and the level of benefits provided to the rank and file.
- *Prefunded*—As has already been mentioned, all plans require that assets be contributed to a funding vehicle—once assets are in the

plan, they are no longer owned by the employer sponsoring the plan. These assets can be used only to pay plan benefits.

- *Plan document*—Plans need to be stated clearly in writing.

Nonqualified versus Tax-Advantaged Plans		
Issue	Nonqualified Plan	Tax-Advantaged Plan
Employer's tax deduction	Deducted at the time employees have taxable income	Deducted at the time contributions are made to the plan.
Tax treatment of earnings	Earnings on assets held to pay benefits are taxed as income to the employer	Earnings are not taxed at the trust level
Back-end tax advantages	Participants can defer tax until distributions are made as long as special rules apply; participants cannot roll benefits into another plan	Participants pay tax upon distribution, but can also continue tax deferral by rolling benefits to another tax-advantaged plan
Coverage	Can limit plan to certain key executives	Must cover a portion of rank-and-file employees
Administrative costs	Lower—few administrative requirements	Higher—significant reporting and administrative obligations

Nonqualified Plans

nonqualified plan

Another very different type of employer-sponsored retirement planning vehicle is the *nonqualified plan*. This term usually refers to deferred-compensation plans other than the tax-advantaged plans described above. Nonqualified plans differ in almost every way from their tax-advantaged counterparts. Unlike tax-advantaged plans, nonqualified plans are generally for only a few key people. There are few design restrictions regarding the benefit structure, vesting requirements, or coverage. In most cases, nonqualified plans do not have separate assets. The employer either pays benefits out of general corporate assets or sets up a side account. Sometimes a trust is set up, but assets must be available to pay the claims of creditors in order to avoid current taxation.

In exchange for the added flexibility in plan design, the tax rules are not as kind to nonqualified plans. A nonqualified plan can be designed to defer the payment of income taxes by the employee until benefits are paid out; however, the employer's tax deduction is deferred to the time of payout as well. This is a disincentive to the corporation because cash payments or qualified plan contributions for the executive would be currently deductible. Because the loss of the tax deduction does not affect nonprofit or governmental entities, Congress has established special limits on the amount of deferred compensation to employees of such entities under Code Sec. 457. Another difference between tax-advantaged and nonqualified plans is that benefits in the latter plans are not as secure. In a nonqualified arrangement, if the entity has financial difficulty, money set aside to pay benefits can be attached by creditors.

Nonqualified Plans

- Can limit to executives
- Few design restrictions
- Employer deduction matched to employee income
- Limited benefit security for participants

IRAs

individual retirement account (IRA)

The final type of plan discussed is the *individual retirement account (IRA)*. As its name implies, this type of plan is generally established not by the employer but by individuals. Although most of the text focuses on employer-sponsored plans, an understanding of both IRAs and Roth IRAs is crucial to this discussion. At times, a business owner or employee will be faced with the choice of participating in a company-sponsored plan or establishing an IRA or Roth IRA. (In some cases, an individual can choose to participate in both.) Understanding the connection between employer-sponsored plans and IRAs is crucial for the following reasons:

1. Many working individuals will have the option of making a $4,000 contribution (for 2007) to a Roth IRA, and some will have the option of choosing instead to make a deductible contribution to a traditional IRA.
2. The IRA is the funding vehicle for the employer-sponsored SEP and SIMPLE. This means that most rules applicable to IRAs will apply to those plans as well.
3. A significant portion of qualified plan and 403(b) benefits paid to terminated employees are rolled over into IRAs. Once the money is in a traditional IRA, many individuals will also have the option to convert to a Roth IRA.

HOW TAX-ADVANTAGED PLANS BENEFIT EMPLOYEES

Tax-advantaged retirement plans make up the bulk of the retirement planning market because of their significant benefits to employees, employers, and business owners. Tax-sheltered plans play a vital role in the retirement security of American workers. Today, approximately half of workers in private industry are covered by a pension plan.[2] The percentage increases with employees of large firms (65 percent of those employed at firms of 100 or more employees), and it is even higher with employees who earn more than $15 an hour (70 percent). Along with Social Security and individual savings, employer-provided pensions have an important effect on the retirement security of Americans.

In addition, employer-provided savings plans—such as 401(k) plans and SIMPLEs—help employees save even more for retirement by providing an easy payroll deduction savings vehicle with tax advantages for the employee. Savings plans have significantly changed the retirement planning landscape. Since 401(k) plans virtually blasted their way onto the scene in 1978, they have grown to the extent that Department of Labor data identified 300,000 401(k) plans covering 37 million active participants, with assets estimated at $1.5 trillion.[3]

Case Study: Saving on a Pretax versus an After-tax Basis

To demonstrate how saving on a tax-deferred basis affects retirement accumulations, let's take the example of William Whitecollar (aged 40), who earns $100,000 and has a marginal state and federal income tax rate of 30 percent. Whitecollar's employer offers him the opportunity to receive an additional $5,000 annually in cash or have that amount contributed to a 401(k) plan on a pretax basis. All invested money earns a 6 percent rate of return.

Under the qualified plan, Whitecollar will save $5,300 by the end of the first year:

Amount contributed	$5,000
plus 6 percent interest	300
Amount saved after one year	$5,300

If Whitecollar invested the cash he received for retirement (individual savings approach), he would have less saved. The culprit would be the individual taxes that Whitecollar (30 percent) would have to pay on the cash and interest earnings:

	Whitecollar
Amount of bonus	$ 5,000.00
minus individual taxes	1,500.00
Amount actually saved	3,500.00
plus 6 percent interest	210.00
Subtotal	3,710.00
minus taxes on interest earned	63.00
Amount saved after one year	$3,647.00

Table 1-1 shows the growth of Whitecollar's retirement savings, both inside and outside of the plan, from ages 40 to 65. With the qualified plan, the number shown assumes accumulation to age 65, and then distribution of the entire amount to Whitecollar with taxation at a 30 percent rate. This assumption allows us to compare after-tax figures at one point in time. However, it doesn't fully represent what will happen. Most taxpayers will continue to take advantage of additional tax-deferred growth by withdrawing funds over time as they are needed.

With this assumption, Whitecollar saves $40,807 more in the qualified plan than he would if he saved on an after-tax basis. This shows us an important trend, but unfortunately, quantifying the tax situation is actually a lot more complicated than it first seems. The comparison of before-tax and after-tax savings depends on how long the pension amount is held in the tax-deferred vehicle and how slowly or quickly it is distributed from the plan. In

---

TABLE 1-1
After-tax Comparison of Retirement Savings Methods*

Participant	Qualified	Individual Savings
Whitecollar at age 65	$207,047	$166,240

*Certain underlying assumptions were made that may affect the actual amount received. The assumptions do not, however, significantly affect the disparity between the savings methods.

---

most cases, the participant takes the benefit slowly over a long period of time. The longer the deferral period, the greater the advantage to the qualified plan. Also, the comparison is affected by the type of investments the individual chooses when saving on an after-tax basis. The previous example assumes that all earnings would be taxed each year, which would be the case if the individual invested in bonds. The tax situation is quite different if assets are invested in equities, with dividends taxed at a lower rate, and the tax on capital appreciation is deferred until the assets are sold. Because the tax situation has become more difficult to quantify today, it is important to look at other reasons why the advantaged plan has value for the participant.

YOUR FINANCIAL SERVICES PRACTICE:
INVESTING THE SPREAD

In the William Whitecollar example, at the end of one year Whitecollar would have $5,300 to invest in a qualified plan and $3,647 to invest using the private savings approach. The $1,653 difference (the spread) represents a significant opportunity to the client. In effect, Whitecollar gets to invest the money that would have been lost in taxation. This is analogous to getting an interest free loan from Uncle Sam which lasts until the time that Whitecollar takes a distribution of the assets during retirement. This "loan" is larger the higher the individual's tax rate, meaning that the tax advantage is the greatest for those in the top tax bracket.

Clients with an understanding of the time value of money should have a greater appreciation of tax-advantaged retirement plans when they view the opportunity as an interest free loan from the government. If this approach doesn't work, clients familiar with poker or other gaming will appreciate the value of betting with "house money.".

A Penny Saved—More Than a Penny Earned?

An individual could accumulate funds in ways other than through a qualified plan, but clearly there are advantages to an employer-sponsored pension program. First we will discuss employer-provided benefits and then separately discuss the opportunity to save additional amounts on a pre-tax basis in 401(k) plans, SIMPLEs, and 403(b) plans.

When the employer funds the plan fully, as in a defined-benefit or profit-sharing plan, the employee is developing assets to provide for retirement without any direct cost. Because the value of this benefit can be significant, it is crucial for prospective employees to carefully evaluate and compare company retirement programs.

Because the employer makes contributions, they are not part of discretionary income and the participant does not feel the same sense of sacrifice that can accompany trying to save a portion of salary. Because of federal ERISA law, these benefits are extremely secure. Assets are held in an irrevocable trust (they no longer can be used by the employer), must be invested according to strict fiduciary scrutiny, and generally offer significant flexibility in the timing and form of benefit payments. Plan participants can benefit from professional management of the trust fund and additional return due to lower investment costs than if each individual was saving separately.

If the plan allows for additional salary deferrals, a participant can benefit simply from a forced savings program through payroll deduction. Also, by saving on a steady ongoing basis, the participant can buy into the investments on a regular basis, which can reduce risk (this investment strategy is commonly referred to as dollar cost averaging). Employee contributions are often matched by the employer. An employer match can be viewed as an instant return on the employee's investment. Finally, some plans offer investment alternatives that are not available individually—for example, a guaranteed investment option that provides for a stated rate of return for a specified time period.

Today, participants in savings plans also benefit from the retirement planning and investment education that they receive from the plan sponsor and related service providers. Employees often attend seminars, receive written information, and utilize software to help them with their retirement planning, as well as use toll-free numbers for additional information and guidance.

Furthermore, there are several other advantages for participating in employer-sponsored retirement plans versus investing on an individual basis:

- Some plans offer participant loans, giving participants a ready source of credit.
- As discussed later in the chapter, qualified plans may offer asset protection from the claims of creditors.
- Investment costs may be lower than with individual investors.

WHY EMPLOYERS NEED TAX-ADVANTAGED RETIREMENT PLANS

In addition to meeting the retirement needs of employees, what other incentives prompt employers to implement a retirement program? Unlike participation in the public retirement program—Social Security—participation in a tax-advantaged or nonqualified retirement program is voluntary. Administrative and funding costs represent a major expenditure (the average cost of providing retirement benefits is 4.3 percent of total payroll, based on 2005 Bureau of Labor Statistics data). So, what is the bottom-line payoff for employers?

The payoff comes in the way retirement plans solve a number of operational problems. Although these solutions do not show up on the balance sheet, the following are key ingredients in a company's fiscal success:

- attraction and retention of employees
- avoidance or appeasement of unions
- employee motivation
- graceful transition in turning over the workforce
- social responsibility
- retirement saving as part of successful compensation planning

Attraction and Retention of Employees

Managers contend that the compelling reason for the salary levels and other employee benefits they offer is local and industry standards. The same logic holds true for private pension programs. In other words, if the local pay scale calls for X amount in salary to attract and retain employees, it also calls for a certain level of retirement benefits. Further, if industry standards in insurance, for example, mandate a certain level of commissions, they also mandate a certain level of retirement benefits. Employers who ignore what the competition is doing with retirement programs soon become noncompetitive.

By meeting competitive standards, retirement programs play an important role in attracting and retaining key employees. An attractive retirement program has a special appeal for employees whose current income needs are being satisfied. Those employees whose skills and knowledge command a high salary are particularly interested in a qualified plan as a means of sheltering their earnings from taxes. These highly compensated employees are usually desired by both employers and their competitors, and the right retirement plan may be the deciding factor in determining which employment opportunity is best.

Retirement plans also attract older employees who are not highly marketable. For example, many capable employees have flocked to federal and state government jobs—even though the salary levels are not equal to those in the private sector—because of their attractive retirement benefits (for example, up to 75 percent of final salary) and their unique plan design (early retirement after 20 years of service).

Perhaps the most important role of retirement plans is not to attract but to retain employees. Well-designed and correctly implemented retirement plans can be the primary reason for staying with a particular company. Benefit formulas can be structured to account for length of service, and benefits can be vested to make it economically desirable for employees to remain instead of joining a competitor. In this age of job-hopping and multiple careers, a soundly structured pension program can be the employer's best recourse against the loss of experienced personnel.

Avoidance or Appeasement of Unions

In 1948, the courts determined that because pensions constitute wages, they are a condition of employment and therefore are negotiable for collective-bargaining purposes.[4] Since then, retirement plans and unions have developed a special relationship.

On one hand, retirement plans have been used to stifle or limit the growth of a union movement. The implementation of a retirement system or the embellishment of an existing system is believed by some managers to be a viable method of forestalling the establishment of a union. While federal law prohibits employers from "union busting," it does not prohibit the employer from competing with unions in trying to meet employee needs. What better way to demonstrate that the employer is looking out for the employee's best interests than to establish a system of retirement benefits?

On the other hand, in unionized companies, retirement benefits and other elements of plan design are always one of the hottest bargaining chips. In these companies, private retirement plans have become a necessary way of life rather than an option. In addition, the laws for and design of some union retirement plans (collectively bargained plans in which more than one employer is required to contribute) have evolved differently from the laws for nonunion plans. (The laws for the so-called *multiemployer pension plans* are beyond the scope of this book. For more information, see Internal Revenue Code Sec. 414(f).)

Employee Motivation

Employee motivation is another reason employers need private retirement plans. Numerous studies have shown that profit-sharing plans and stock ownership plans increase employee identification with the corporation and provide an incentive to increase productivity. A highly visible retirement plan can do wonders for employee morale, improve workers' attitudes toward authority in the work environment, and may be the best management tool available for turning the corner on important projects or getting through crucial times.

Graceful Transition in Turning over the Workforce

Employers face a common problem when dealing with employees who outlast their usefulness. Such employees have been with the company "forever" and are highly compensated, but their current productivity does not **superannuated employees** warrant the high salary. These employees are sometimes called *superannuated employees*. Because it is not considered valid business practice to dismiss long-time employees who are not economically productive (for whatever reason) and because personal affection and respect may keep an employer from demoting these employees, an alternative solution is necessary. The alternative is the proper use of the pension plan. Sound plan structure can make early retirement attractive. In addition, "golden handshakes"—special packages that make early retirement even more appealing—can be offered. If handled properly, a potentially uncomfortable situation can be turned into a mutually beneficial solution through the use of the private retirement program.

Social Responsibility

Some employers implement private retirement programs because of their social desirability. These employers want to provide economic security for retired workers despite the lower profit margin that will result. Although retired workers traditionally rely on Social Security and private savings as well as a company pension, these employers, feel a need to beef up the company pension because they fear for the future existence of Social Security (at least in its current state) and they recognize that we have become a society of spenders and not savers. What is more, the needs of the aged are creeping more and more into the social consciousness, and these employers feel obliged to do their part by instituting forced savings through a retirement program.

Less altruistically, fear of negative public relations stemming from the perception that an employer did not "take care of " employees can stimulate a social conscience. Companies often go to painstaking lengths to be known as a good place to work, and few employers want former employees to be destitute after retirement.

Retirement Saving as Part of Successful Compensation Planning

One question often raised by clients is: "Why not pay retirement benefits out as current compensation and let employees fend for themselves when it comes to saving for retirement?" After all, the funds used to provide for retirement and the funds used to pay salary are both part of the same compensation package. Enlightened employers, however, feel that by committing a certain part of salary to retirement purposes, they not only allow their employees to benefit from the aforementioned tax advantages of a qualified plan, but also provide employees with the most effective compensation package possible. In other words, they maintain a system that meets their employees' financial security needs for both today and tomorrow in the most tax-efficient manner available.

WHY BUSINESS OWNERS NEED TAX-ADVANTAGED RETIREMENT PLANS

Business owners have special needs and concerns when it comes to planning for their retirement and running their business. These include the following:

- tax sheltering as much income as possible
- solving liquidity problems that occur at retirement or death
- sheltering their assets from legal liability and bankruptcy
- avoiding taxes on excess accumulated earnings

Tax Shelter for Business Owners

Qualified plans and other tax-advantaged plans represent one of the best tax shelters available. We have already shown how much more an employee can save for retirement on a pretax versus an after-tax basis. Remember that, in the small-business environment, employers are also employees. Owners of closely held businesses, members of professional corporations, partners, and the self-employed frequently set up retirement plans with the tax sheltering of personal income as their primary motivation. These markets consist of upscale clients who want the greatest possible tax savings from the qualified-plan tax shelter (and who, consequently, make the biggest contributions toward their retirement). Retirement plans are one of the few tax shelters still remaining today. Because their rules are clear, their degree of tax risk is quite low, making them an attractive tax shelter that is not likely to go away.

Note that when the business owner compares saving for retirement through a tax-sheltered vehicle versus after-tax savings, the comparison is not quite the same as for the average employee. The owner may view required contributions for other employees in the qualified environment as a drain on his or her own savings account. For example, if only 50 percent of the contribution to the plan is for the owner's benefit, the owner may feel that he or she is better off taking the entire contribution amount, paying taxes, and saving outside the plan. This is a legitimate concern and may stop some business owners from establishing a plan. However, when working with these clients, be sure to fully consider the following:

- In almost all cases, contributions for the other employees have some value to the business. If contributions to the plan are not made, the employer may have to pay additional cash benefits to employees. Also, other reasons for establishing a plan (discussed above) will come into play, such as employee attraction and retention.

- If the contributions do have some value to the owner, consider quantifying that value when making the mathematical comparison of the qualified plan versus after-tax savings.. For example, take a small-business owner who has $50,000 to save. If the amount is contributed to a qualified plan, assume that he or she will get $30,000 and the employees will get the remaining $20,000. If the owner feels that the contribution for the employees has a value to the business of $10,000, then compare a $40,000 contribution to the plan versus $40,000 saved in an after-tax environment.
- An experienced pension professional may be able to suggest creative ways to limit contributions for other employees. In today's pension environment, there are viable options.

Liquidity Concerns

In addition to functioning as a stable tax shelter, tax-advantaged plans solve liquidity problems that often occur at retirement or death. Small-business owners typically have a difficult time building business or personal liquidity. They are self-achievers and often feel psychologically compelled to reinvest money in their "baby." A common profile of a business owner is someone who initially finds success by investing in himself or herself and the business and who continues to do so throughout his or her lifetime. Because his or her "money "personality" tends to be more that of a spender than of a saver, the savings that occur through a qualified plan may represent the business owner's only available cash at retirement or death. Thus, the qualified plan (along with, for example, a buy-sell agreement) may be essential to the continuation of the business after the owner's death or retirement.

Financial Security Concerns

A third reason that business owners are well served by a tax-advantaged retirement plan is that the plan may provide them with financial security if their business fails. The Bankruptcy Abuse Protection and Consumer Protection Act of 2005 provides sweeping bankruptcy creditor protection for all tax-advantaged plans. Specifically, assets in qualified plans, SEPs, SIMPLEs, 403(b) plans, and 457 plans are exempt from the bankruptcy estate so they cannot be attached by bankruptcy creditors.

Regarding IRAs and Roth IRAs, the maximum amount of the exemption is limited to an aggregate IRA account value of $1 million. However, this million-dollar limit does not apply to SEP or SIMPLE IRAs, or to amounts that are rolled over from qualified plans, 403(b) plans, or 457 plans.

Sweeping pension protection is great news for the small-business owner who can protect himself or herself from complete financial ruin (in case of business failure) by accumulating assets in a tax-advantaged retirement plan. This is also good news for the financial services consultant, who has one more reason to convince the employer to establish a retirement plan.

Accumulated Earnings Tax Concerns

accumulated earnings tax

Qualified plan contributions sometimes offer one other advantage to the small corporation—lowering the business's exposure to the *accumulated earnings tax*. This tax is essentially a penalty tax for C corporations that attempt to reduce the shareholders' tax burden by accumulating earnings instead of paying them out to shareholders. The tax rate on improper accumulations is 15 percent of accumulations that exceed $250,000 ($150,000 for a personal services corporation). Any amounts contributed to a qualified plan will reduce the exposure to the accumulated earnings tax. (For a discussion of the accumulated earnings tax, see Code Secs. 531 through 537.)

CHAPTER REVIEW

Key Terms

tax-advantaged retirement
  plans [1-1]
qualified plans [1-1]
nonqualified plan [1-1]

individual retirement account
  (IRA) [1-1]
superannuated employees [1-3]
accumulated earnings tax [1-4]

Review Questions

Review questions are based on the learning objectives in this chapter. Thus, a [1-3] at the end of a question means that the question is based on learning objective 1-3. If there are multiple objectives, they are all listed.

1. Name all the qualified plans as well as the other tax-advantaged retirement plans. [1-1]

2. What are the tax advantages shared among all tax-advantaged plans, and what makes qualified plans different from the other tax-advantaged plans? [1-1]

3. In exchange for special tax advantages, what common requirements do all tax-advantaged retirement plans share? [1-1]

4. Describe the basic differences between tax-advantaged retirement plans and nonqualified plans. [1-1]

5. Scopes is the owner of Monkey Business, Inc., a small business that trains monkeys for work in films. Scopes would like to save $15,000 a year for retirement. Scopes pays federal and state taxes at the 36 percent marginal rate. [1-2]

    a. Explain to Scopes why he might save more for retirement under a tax-advantaged retirement plan than by taking the $15,000 as extra income and investing it on his own.

    b. Calculate the amount that Scopes will have saved after one year under the qualified plan and individual savings approaches, assuming the amount saved earns a 5 percent return and the earnings are taxable when he saves outside of the plan.

6. Why has the tax comparison between saving in tax-advantaged plans versus saving on an after-tax basis become more complicated in today's tax environment? [1-2]

7. Identify benefits (other than tax advantages) of participating in an employer-sponsored retirement plan. [1-2]

8. RAMCO is a relatively small nonunionized company with 60 "younger" employees. RAMCO is in the competitive computer software market and will soon face a major project of updating its technology to be competitive with the new generation of computers. How can a qualified plan help RAMCO? [1-3]

9. What special personal needs does a qualified plan serve for the owner of the business? [1-4]

NOTES

1. Federal Interagency Forum on Aging-Related Statistics. Older Americans 2000: Key Indicators of Well-Being. Federal Interagency Forum on Aging-Related Statistics, Washington, DC: U.S. Government Printing Office. August 2000.
2. Bureau of Labor Statistics, Employee Benefits in Private Industry 2005.
3. Appendix to September 2003 EBRI Issue Brief identifying U.S. Department of Labor Statistics published in the winter of 2001–02 with data from the 1998 plan year.
4. *Inland Steel Company v. National Labor Relations Board,* 170 F.2d 247.79000.

2

The Retirement Field

Learning Objectives

An understanding of the material in this chapter should enable you to

2-1. Explain how ERISA changed the pension landscape, as well as the major trends in post-ERISA legislation.

2-2. Identify the agencies involved in the regulation of tax-advantaged retirement plans and the role of each of these agencies.

2-3. Describe the types of entities that sponsor retirement plans and the professionals that service these plans.

Chapter Outline

Success in finding clients, planning for clients, and servicing clients starts with an understanding of the boundaries, players, and equipment involved in the retirement field. The retirement field's boundaries are the rules set up by federal legislation and government agencies. The players include your clients, potential clients, support-service companies, and even the inner workings of your own organization. The equipment is the information sources that are available to provide answers when experience fails to provide them. This chapter takes you on a tour of the retirement field and introduces you to the regulatory environment, pension players, and information sources that will become an integral part of your financial services practice.

Because the multifaceted pension industry is largely an outgrowth of the regulatory process, we will explore this complex area first (including the relationship between the financial services professional and the industry-shaping laws) and review the functions of the regulatory agencies. Then, we will discuss the pension prospects—who is involved and to what extent—and the service and financial organizations that serve them, with special emphasis on the insurance industry. We will end by reviewing the sources for pension information—those that provide answers to a client's questions and those that analyze current trends and put pensions in perspective.

THE LEGISLATIVE ENVIRONMENT

Employee Retirement Income Security Act (ERISA)

The passage of the *Employee Retirement Income Security Act (ERISA)* in 1974 marked the beginning of the current retirement-plan era. ERISA represented an intensified commitment by the federal government to oversee the retirement market (especially plans that cover nonhighly compensated employees). Leery of broken retirement promises and plans being used as tax shelters for the wealthy, the federal government decided to protect the retirement interests of all plan participants and implemented ERISA to establish equitable standards and curtail perceived abuses. The text of ERISA has become the pensioner's bible. ERISA's commandments forbid discrimination in favor of the prohibited group (highly compensated employees), restrictive vesting schedules that keep longtime participants from receiving benefits, and inadequate plan funding, which leads to bankrupt plans. In addition, ERISA requires reporting and disclosure of information about retirement plans to the Internal Revenue Service (IRS), the Department of Labor (DOL), the Pension Benefit Guaranty

Corporation (PBGC), and plan participants. In fact, ERISA forces information to be widely disseminated, thereby causing such administrative nightmares that it has become affectionately known as the "full employment in pensions act."

ERISA is composed of four sections known as *titles*. The purpose of the first title is to protect an employee's right to collect benefits. To accomplish this, title I requires employers to report plan information to the federal government and disclose information to participants (reporting and disclosure rules), restricts unlimited employer discretion regarding vesting and plan participation (employers cannot discriminatorily choose whom to cover), implements plan funding standards (employers must set aside sufficient assets to fulfill retirement promises), and lists fiduciary responsibilities (the responsibilities and liabilities of those in charge). Title II amends the Internal Revenue Code, setting forth the necessary requirements for special tax treatment (the plan qualification rules); these requirements are covered in detail in chapters 7 through 10. Title III creates the regulatory and administrative framework necessary for ERISA's ongoing implementation. Responsibilities are divided between the Internal Revenue Service and the Department of Labor, with the IRS having primary jurisdiction for much of the initial and operational administration of pension plans. Title IV establishes the Pension Benefit Guaranty Corporation, an agency that insures pension benefits. The PBGC collects premiums from covered plans (defined-benefit plans only; defined-contribution plans are not insured) and insures a minimum level of benefits for employees if the plan is terminated with insufficient funds.

Four Titles of ERISA

- *Title I*—Amends the labor law to ensure the employee's right to collect promised benefits

- *Title II*— Amends the Internal Revenue Code to condition tax benefits on meeting certain minimum standards

- *Title III*— Creates a regulatory framework for ongoing implementation

- *Title IV*—Establishes the Pension Benefit Guaranty Corporation to insure benefit payments from defined-benefit pension plans

---

The enforcement strategies provided by ERISA are interesting. To enforce title I of ERISA, plan participants, the Department of Labor, and plan fiduciaries can sue to force the payment of appropriate benefits and to require plan representatives to fulfill their jobs. Also, to encourage compliance, errant plan officials can be held personally liable for losses to the plan, fined for certain errors, and in some cases even held criminally liable. It is interesting to note that courts have generally interpreted the enforcement provisions of ERISA to prohibit monetary punitive damages for ERISA claims. Even though ERISA does provide for the award of attorney's fees, the inability to receive punitive damages has probably limited the number of private suits under ERISA over the years.

The strategy for encouraging compliance under the Internal Revenue Code is quite different. Here, both the plan sponsor and the plan participants enjoy special tax treatment in exchange for compliance with the law. Failure to comply can allow the IRS to take away the plan's tax-advantaged status. Because this penalty can harm participants (who are not responsible for ensuring plan compliance), plan disqualification is rarely enforced. In lieu of this terminal penalty, the IRS often negotiates a monetary penalty (payable by the sponsor) and requires that the employer fix any plan defects.[1] Disqualification is not the sole punishment contemplated under the Code. Some plan defects result in a penalty tax. Examples of this will be seen throughout the text.

Unfortunately (or fortunately, depending upon your perspective), ERISA was just the beginning of what has seemed like an endless stream of legislation further regulating private pension plans. From 1974 until today, the only constant has been change. There have been many law changes during this period. (For those interested in a detailed description of the changes over the years, see appendix 1.) For the newcomer to the pension field, the presentation in the appendix may seem overwhelming and confusing. Therefore, an overview of some of the major areas of congressional involvement and a description of the legislative trends over the years appear below.

- *Taxation of pension benefits*—At the time of ERISA, pension benefits were subject to many significant income and estate tax benefits. Over the years, the special tax advantages have been repealed one by one. For example, at one time pension benefits were not subject to estate taxes. Today, all pension assets that remain after the death of the participant are included in the taxable estate. Similarly, many of the special income tax rules have been repealed and, in most cases, pension income is treated as ordinary income (although some rules have been grandfathered).

- *IRAs*—Over the years, IRA rules have swayed with the political breeze. At the time of ERISA, deductible IRA contributions were limited, then IRAs were opened up to virtually everyone, and then, once again, deductible contributions were limited to those who do not participate in an employer-sponsored retirement plan or have relatively low income. However, more recently law changes have expanded the use of the IRA with the introduction of the Roth IRA, an increase in the maximum contribution limits, and an increase in the phaseout ranges.

- *Maximum deductible contributions*—Through the '80s and '90s, the trend was to lower the maximum deductible contribution for highly compensated employees. This was done to raise tax revenue, and maybe also out of a perception that plans inappropriately benefited the highly compensated. Contributions were limited by lowering the maximum allowable contribution for each employee, freezing cost-of-living adjustments on contribution limits; limiting the amount of compensation that can be taken into account; imposing limits on employee contributions; and aggregating plans. This trend had a significant effect on executive compensation and benefit planning, making supplemental executive nonqualified deferred-compensation plans a more and more important part of the retirement planning package. In 2001, there was a significant departure from this trend, with increases in allowable contributions for each participant, the compensation cap, and the maximum deductible contributions. These changes were intended to increase retirement savings and to encourage small businesses to establish retirement plans.

- *Limiting tax deferral*—Tax revenue is also lost the longer pension assets remain in a tax-deferred environment. To speed up the taxation of benefits, Code Sec. 401(a)(9) was introduced in 1986, requiring that distributions from all tax-sheltered plans begin at age 70½ (or, in some cases, at actual retirement, if later). These minimum-distribution rules affect any retiree receiving qualified plan, 403(b), or IRA distributions.

- *Parity*—Over the years, the trend has been toward giving all types of business entities equal access to retirement plan vehicles. With a few minor exceptions, C corporations, S corporations, sole proprietorships, partnerships, and even limited liability companies (LLCs) are all on the same footing.

- *Plans of small businesses*—Apparently, based on the perception that retirement plans of small businesses have treated rank-and-file employees unfairly, today a special set of rules, referred to as the *top-heavy requirements,* applies to the plans of many small businesses. These rules require special minimum contribution and vesting requirements for certain top-heavy plans. Again, the law change in 2001 altered this trend somewhat, simplifying the top-heavy rules and giving the owner the opportunity to accumulate more in a retirement plan.

- *Affiliation requirements*—To ensure that businesses cannot avoid pension coverage requirements by operating separate entities, and to eliminate "double dipping" under the maximum deduction rules, over the years Congress has enacted a series of complex rules requiring the aggregation of related employers. These rules have successfully eliminated loopholes and at the same time have complicated matters for both multinational corporations operating multiple divisions and for the small entrepreneur involved in several businesses.

- *Funding*—ERISA imposed minimum funding requirements for defined-benefit pension plans and established the Pension Benefit Guaranty Corporation (PBGC). This organization ensures that employees in privately sponsored defined-benefit plans will receive at least some of the benefits promised by the plan. At times, the PBGC has run deficits and in response, a number of law changes have required both larger employer contributions and higher PBGC premiums.

- *Employee Stock Ownership Plans (ESOPs)*—To encourage employee stock ownership, in 1981 the Economic Recovery Tax Act (ERTA) provided for a new type of retirement plan vehicle with numerous special tax advantages referred to as an ESOP. Today, some of these provisions have been repealed, but ESOPs still provide significant tax advantages, as well as a mechanism for a plan to purchase stock on a leveraged basis—providing a viable buyer for the small-business owner looking to sell or retire. In fact, ESOP coverage was expanded by the 1996 Act that allowed an S corporation to sponsor an ESOP.

- *Simplification*—One legislative trend that had been consistent from the time of ERISA until 1996 was that each new law made the pension world more complex. However, beginning in 1996, law changes began a trend toward simplification as an attempt to make it easier for the small employer to maintain a tax-advantaged plan. The 1996 law simplified the definition of highly compensated employee and the distribution rules; it eliminated several complex aggregation requirements; and it introduced the SIMPLE, a savings plan alternative to the 401(k) plan with fewer administrative requirements. The 2001 tax law contained additional simplification provisions, making plans (especially 401(k) plans) easier to administer.

One recent law the Pension Protection Act of 2006 is worth noting, since it is the most extensive pension legislation since ERISA. The legislation did not really change recent legislative trends but reinforced them. A large part of the law relates to the funding status of defined benefit plans. The law revises the minimum funding requirements, and has the effect of requiring more accelerated funding for most plans. The law also creates more consequences for plans that are seriously underfunded.

The law includes other provisions that protect plan participants. Plan benefits become more portable by requiring more accelerated vesting for most plans. Also defined contribution plans that invest in employer securities must give most participants the option to elect alternative investments in their accounts.

Another important step was that many of the increased pension limits from previous laws were made permanent. The law tries to improve the pension system by validating the cash balance design, encouraging the practice of allowing automatic enrollment in 401(k) plans, and providing a mechanism to allow participants to receive appropriate investment advice.

REGULATORY AGENCIES

Legislation makes up only part of the regulatory picture. The other part, the administration of the qualified-plan system (and, to a lesser extent, the nonqualified-plan system), is carried out by the Internal Revenue Service, the department that is required to interpret the laws, explain legal fine points, and oversee the day-to-day operations of retirement plans.

The Internal Revenue Service

The IRS plays the most prominent role of all the bureaucratic agencies.

Initial Plan Qualification

In order for an employer to receive favorable tax treatment, the pension plan

---

IRS Regulatory Responsibility

- Qualification letter program
- Audit existing plans
- Interpret legislation

---

must meet the qualification requirements. Plan sponsors may, and usually do, request an IRS advance determination that the plan meets those requirements. Employers send in the plan and appropriate forms requesting IRS approval; the IRS agent checks the plan to see if it meets the guidelines (over time the IRS has developed elaborate rules regarding what provisions may and may not be included); and, if necessary, the IRS and employer enter into negotiations over points at issue. If the plan meets IRS standards, a favorable advance-determination letter—which assures the employer that the plan is qualified and that the first year's contributions will be deductible—is issued. Although the program is voluntary, most employers take advantage of getting "preapproval" that plan contributions are eligible for special tax treatment.

YOUR FINANCIAL SERVICES PRACTICE:
NEW LEGISLATION AS A MARKETING OPPORTUNITY

The constant legislative changes that occur in the retirement area (some might call it overregulation) affect the financial services professional in many ways.

* Continual plan review is necessary to determine what impact the new legislation will have on corporate retirement goals.
* Plans must be updated to reflect law changes.
* Clients rely on additional communication and explanation because pension law becomes increasingly complex and detailed.
* Continued education becomes necessary to keep up with the new laws.

One side effect of this constant federal legislation is the opportunity for financial services professionals to perform a detailed review of the plan and corporate retirement goals. Without legislative change and subsequent plan amendment, employers might ignore their plans, and the plans could become stale and outdated. The financial services professional should capitalize on the opportunity created by legislative change and help the business owner evaluate new retirement goals and strategies.

A second side effect of federal legislation is the need to consider the effect on highly compensated employees. Some of the changes have resulted in the need for secondary nonqualified plans to supplement their retirement Income.

Ongoing Auditing

The IRS monitors retirement plans after initial qualification through periodic planned audits. The purpose of IRS surveillance is to make sure changes in facts or circumstances have not affected plan qualification and plans are used as retirement vehicles rather than as a tax shelter for the prohibited group. Plans chosen for audit are selected from information supplied in the annual 5500 filings, which includes the type and structure of the plan, plan assets, plan liabilities, plan income, and plan funding. In addition, information regarding plan changes, actuarial methods, and distributions to participants and their beneficiaries is required.

The IRS has developed another ongoing enforcement strategy that encourages employers to step forward voluntarily when plan problems are discovered. In exchange for voluntary compliance, the employer is subject to much smaller penalties—usually a set fee—instead of the much larger penalties that could occur if the IRS found the problem upon plan audit. There are a number of different programs that have been coordinated under the Employee Plans Compliance Resolution System (EPCRS). These programs encourage voluntary correction of problems and, in many cases, reward employers for taking reasonable steps to keep their plans in compliance with the law.

Financial Planning Practice

Because the IRS program rewards quality administration, service providers can now tell potential clients how their "quality" services can help to keep the client out of trouble.

Interpretation

One of the major responsibilities of the IRS is to issue numerous communications that further explain the existing laws of the Internal Revenue Code. These communications include the following:

final regulations

- *Final regulations* explain and interpret the various sections of the Internal Revenue Code and deal with legal fine points that are not specifically addressed in the Code. Final regulations are legally enforceable, and the Internal Revenue Service is bound by them. They are originally published in the *Internal Revenue Bulletin* and the *Federal Register* and are later bound together with other regulations in a set of *Internal Revenue Regulations*. Final regulations can also be found in many of the loose-leaf services (discussed later).

proposed regulations

- *Proposed regulations* are sometimes issued right after major legislation to guide practitioners on complex provisions of new laws. Unlike final regulations, proposed regulations will have no legal effect unless they specifically state that they can be relied upon by taxpayers. Still, they are an indication of the IRS's current thinking and are widely followed. Proposed regulations can be changed before they are finalized—often as the result of negative feedback at public hearings.

temporary regulations

- *Temporary regulations* may be issued as an alternative to final regulations, or can be issued simultaneously with proposed regulations. They are binding until they are superseded or withdrawn. This allows individual and corporate taxpayers to rely on the regulations without fear of incurring a Sec. 6661 penalty for substantially understating income tax liability, a protection that is not available to proposed regulations. A great deal of time can pass between when a regulation is proposed and when it becomes final, and temporary regulations are relied on heavily in the interim.

revenue rulings

- *Revenue rulings* are the IRS's interpretations of the provisions of the Internal Revenue Code and regulations as they apply to the factual situations presented by taxpayers. Revenue rulings are replete with valuable examples that clarify complex legal issues and may be used as precedents, thus giving you and your clients a sense of security if you are venturing into an area to which the rulings apply.

private letter rulings

- *Private letter rulings* interpret the law in light of a specific set of circumstances and indicate whether the IRS believes the action to be acceptable. Private letter rulings address only the specific facts presented to the IRS and, because of this, a taxpayer cannot rely upon the guidance provided. Still, they are an important form of guidance, because they address real-life cases that might be similar to your client's situation. (*Planning Note:* If the IRS's position regarding a situation your client is entering into is unclear, you should recommend that the client consider getting a private letter ruling. For a fee, the IRS will issue a ruling that will be binding in the client's situation.)
- *Publications* include general reviews of retirement topics provided by the IRS. Using understandable terms (no legalese), these publications cover a variety of topics. (*Planning Note:* Publications are written to provide a general overview of the tax law on certain subjects. The publications on Keogh plans and qualified retirement plans make good mailers for your clients.)

The Department of Labor (DOL)

Through its Office of Pension and Welfare Benefit Plans (OPWBP), the DOL is heavily involved in the pension arena.

DOL Regulatory Responsibilities

- Protect participants through enforcement of the reporting and disclosure rules
- Oversee plan investments
- Govern actions of fiduciaries
- Interpret legislation

Reporting and Disclosure Rules

The first duty of the DOL is to ensure compliance with the reporting and disclosure rules. The most important disclosure requirement is that the plan provide summary plan descriptions (SPDs) to participants. Failure to comply with this or other reporting and disclosure requirements can result in fines and, in some egregious cases, imprisonment.

Prohibited Transactions

A second duty of the DOL is to oversee plan investments. To ensure that no self-dealing or conflict of interest is involved, ERISA provides that plans cannot have certain dealings with parties who have close relationships with the plan or the company (referred to as parties in interest). Such behavior is referred to as a prohibited transaction. (The responsibility for overseeing prohibited transactions is shared by the IRS, and a separate but similar set of rules for prohibited transactions is also part of the tax law. What constitutes a prohibited transaction is quite complex and will be discussed further in chapter 11.) For now, understand that the goal of the rules is to keep the plan's interests separate from the sponsoring entity's interests, and to ensure that no persons benefit unduly because of their close relationship to the plan. Also note that the statutory scheme prohibits a broad range of behaviors and then carves out a number of statutory exemptions and gives the DOL the authority to issue others.

Fiduciaries

fiduciary

In conjunction with its responsibility to monitor plan investments, the DOL governs the actions of those in charge of running the retirement plans—fiduciaries. A *fiduciary* is a person or corporation that exercises any discretionary authority or control over the management of the plan or plan assets, renders investment advice for a fee, or has any discretionary authority or responsibility in the administration of the plan. Every plan has at least one named fiduciary who is responsible and accountable for operating the plan. Fiduciaries (named or otherwise) invest plan assets (subject to the rules on prohibited transactions), see that plan documents conform to the law, administer plans, and make major decisions regarding plan operation.

The Department of Labor has the means to ensure that fiduciaries uphold their responsibilities; it may sue plan fiduciaries and require a restitution to the plan for any losses that result from breach of fiduciary duty. (In addition, under the tax provisions overseen by the IRS, a fiduciary may be responsible for excise taxes for violation of the prohibited-transaction provisions.) In doing its job of overseeing the fiduciary responsibility rules and the prohibited-transaction rules, the DOL (and, in a subordinate role, the IRS) acts like a police officer on the beat, carefully checking to see that the laws protecting plan participants are not broken.

Interpretation

As we have just seen, like the Internal Revenue Service, the DOL issues numerous communications that create pension rules and explain existing laws. Many of these items parallel IRS publications. The DOL issues final regulations, temporary regulations, and proposed regulations, which perform the same functions as their IRS counterparts. In addition, the DOL issues advisory opinions that are similar to the private letter rulings issued by the IRS. As with IRS private letter rulings, your clients can inquire about the acceptability of their acts or transactions, and only the parties actually involved can safely rely on the opinion. Owing to the DOL's unique responsibilities, not all of its communications are similar to those of the IRS. The DOL issues important communications called *prohibited-transaction exemptions* (PTEs). These exemptions can either be on a class basis (for example, "All banks with FDIC insurance are exempt from . . .") or on a particular transaction basis. (*Planning Note:* The prohibited-transaction exemption is an avenue your client can travel to get approval before taking an investment action that falls into the prohibited-transaction gray area. For example, if your client is a party in interest, he or she can get an exemption from the restrictions on prohibited transactions by applying for a PTE.)

Pension Benefit Guaranty Corporation (PBGC)

Pension Benefit Guaranty Corporation (PBGC)

The PBGC was established under title IV of ERISA as a quasi-governmental corporation. Both the IRS and the Department of Labor are involved to a certain extent with the PBGC, because its board of directors includes the Secretaries of Labor, Treasury, and Commerce. Even though the organization has access to federal government resources, the federal government is not generally liable for any of its obligations or liabilities. This is meaningful, because the PBGC's primary responsibility is to insure participants in and beneficiaries of employee benefit plans against the loss of benefits arising from complete or partial termination of the plan. PBGC insurance coverage applies to most defined-benefit plans of private employers. (The defined-benefit plans of professional services organizations such as physicians, dentists, attorneys, and accountants who have 25 or fewer active participants are exempt from PBGC coverage.) The program does not apply to defined-contribution plans.

PBGC Regulatory Responsibility

- Administer insurance program for defined-benefit plans
- Oversee termination of covered plans
- Interpret legislation

The PBGC operates by collecting compulsory premiums, which are $31 (indexed for 2007) per participant per plan year (more if the plan is underfunded). For such premiums, the PBGC guarantees to pay certain benefits

TABLE 2-1 Review of the Regulatory Environment for Qualified Plans		
IRS	**DOL**	**PBGC**
Initial plan qualification Ongoing auditing through 5500 forms Legal interpretation	Summary plan descriptions Oversee fiduciaries and plan investments Legal interpretation	Insure defined-benefit plans Oversee plan fund solvency Legal interpretation

promised under the plan, in the event that the plan has insufficient assets. The guaranteed benefits are subject to a specified ceiling that is adjusted annually.

In conjunction with its duty to insure benefit payments, the PBGC has the power to investigate anyone who has violated or is about to violate any of the plan termination insurance provisions. It can also initiate a lawsuit in federal court for the enforcement of the provisions of title IV. To help the PBGC identify problems, certain events that would indicate that the plan is in financial difficulty must be reported to the PBGC.

The PBGC has another enforcement tool. If a PBGC investigation reveals that a plan is not funded according to legal standards, or that the plan is unable to meet its benefit payments, or if there is a possible long-run loss that will get out of hand unless the plan is terminated, the PBGC may require the plan to be involuntarily terminated to help cut PBGC losses. The PBGC can also cut its losses by tapping up to 30 percent of the net worth of employers whose plans have terminated, leaving the PBGC liable for payments.

Another function of the PBGC is overseeing plan terminations initiated by the plan sponsor. Today (see chapter 14), an employer can terminate a defined-benefit plan covered by the PBGC insurance program only in limited circumstances. Essentially, the plan must either have sufficient assets to pay all benefits (referred to as a voluntary termination), or the company must virtually be facing liquidation (called a distress termination). When the employer terminates such a plan, it is required to give advance notification to employees and submit the proper forms to the PBGC.

As is the case with the IRS and the DOL's Office of Pension and Welfare Benefit Plans, the PBGC issues various communications that serve as sources of information for the financial services professional: PBGC regulations, news releases, opinion letters, publications, and multiemployer bulletins.

PENSIONS: PROFESSIONALS AND ORGANIZATIONS

While the effect of the regulatory environment on the retirement market is great, these federal laws and agencies are nonetheless only the rules and umpires. Employers sponsoring pension plans plus the expanding service and investment industry are the pension professionals and organizations.

Benefit Associations and Designation Programs

In addition to The American College's CLU, ChFC, and REBC designations and the College's Master of Science in Financial Services with its pension certificate track, several other associations are prominent in the benefits community. These include the following:

- The American Society of Pension Professionals and Actuaries (ASPPA) is an organization for those involved with the consulting, administrative, and design aspects of pension and employee benefit plans. www.aspa.org
- The American Benefits Council is the business community's lobbying arm for pensions and employee benefit plans. www. americanbenefitscouncil.org
- The Employee Benefits Research Institute (EBRI) is the research arm of the pension and employee benefit community. www.ebri.org
- The International Foundation of Employee Benefit Plans is an organization for those involved with benefit consulting. This organization is a cosponsor of the Certified Employee Benefit Specialist (CEBS) designation. www.ifebp.org
- The National Institute of Pension Administrators Educational Foundation, Inc. (NIPA) sponsors the Accredited Pension Administrator (APA) designation. www.nipa.org
- The National Tax-Sheltered Annuity Association (NTSAA) is a relatively new organization representing the interests of those in the 403(b) tax-sheltered annuity marketplace. www.ntsaa.org
- Other groups that focus on specific portions of the pension market include the ESOP Association, www.esopassociation.org, and the Profit-Sharing /401(k) Council of America, www.psca.org.

Plan Sponsors

Retirement plan sponsors constitute one of the most important financial markets today. And because demographics indicate an aging population, which means increased savings for retirement, the plan sponsors' market is possibly *the* most important financial market of tomorrow. Sponsors of retirement plans include corporations, partnerships, and self-employed individuals. According to the Bureau of Labor Statistics, larger employers are most likely to sponsor plans. Almost 70 percent of employees working for companies of 100 or more employees are currently participating in retirement plans, while only 37 percent of those working at companies with fewer than 100 employees are covered. Those who do adopt plans contribute, on average, 4.3 percent of payroll.

Prospects—The Candidates for Pensions

Pension prospects range from business owners and professional corporations needing relief from income tax problems to larger organizations looking to satisfy organizational objectives through retirement plans. Every business owner, whether motivated by tax savings, competitiveness, or a sense of moral obligation to the employees, can be shown the need for a retirement system. The best prospects, however, will be

- businesses in which the owner is an active employee interested in tax savings, such as professional corporations, sole proprietorships, and closely held businesses
- large corporations operating in a competitive labor market looking to change service providers or redesign their programs (most larger employers currently sponsor plans)
- companies and service organizations—large, small, or individually run—that are just turning the corner on financial success
- institutions such as public schools, colleges, hospitals, and charitable organizations
- recently unionized employers or employers staving off union organization
- corporations with one type of retirement plan who may need a supplemental program—a 401(k) arrangement, for example

---

YOUR FINANCIAL SERVICES PRACTICE: RETIREMENT PROSPECTING

Prospecting techniques in the retirement market differ from those in the personal selling market. While prospecting in the retirement market does include the traditional methods of direct mail, preapproach letters combined with phone calls for appointments, and the use of existing clients as referred leads, other unique methods are available. These include (1) developing accountants and attorneys—professionals who are in touch with employers' financial ability to provide retirement benefits—into centers of influence, (2) creating working relationships with banks interested in trust business that complements pension insurance sales, (3) obtaining pension consultants or actuarial firms as referral sources, (4) working with casualty and insurance brokers in the commercial and industrial market whose clients are probably also pension prospects, and (5) obtaining lists of pension prospects in your area. Because plans must file annual forms with the government which are accessible to the public, it is possible to obtain information about ongoing plans in your area. One source is from Judy Diamond Associates at www.freeerisa.com. Another source is from Pension Data Resources, Inc., at www.pensionplanet.com.

Service and Financial Groups

The pension market is replete with organizations that offer to design and implement plans; provide consulting, record-keeping, legal, and actuarial services; furnish employee communications; and oversee plan administration. In short, those in charge of pensions, if desired, can easily farm out the entire process to *third-party administrators (TPAs)*. The same is true regarding the management of the pension plan assets. For those plan administrators who would rather do some or all of their work in-house, there are a variety of computer services, many offered by small, specialized companies.

third-party administrators (TPAs)

The organizations that provide plan services include consulting houses, actuarial firms, insurance companies, administrative consultants, and software companies. In the financial market, there are trust companies, commercial banks, investment houses, asset-management groups, and insurance companies. The major service and financial groups have no particular areas of concentration, but rather offer a myriad of services. For example, consulting houses do not just do consulting and plan installation and administration, they may also offer computer services and investment facilities. Computer software companies may offer consulting services as well as create software.

master and prototype plans

Many financial services organizations sponsor *master and prototype plans*, standardized plans approved and qualified in concept by the Internal Revenue Service, which are then adopted by their customer organizations. The master and prototype plans offer an employer fewer choices in plan design and, thus, can be installed very easily. The use of a master or prototype plan simplifies the task for the financial services professional by setting up an easily understood framework with which to work, known as an *adoption agreement*. An adoption agreement resembles a smorgasbord in many ways—for example, you choose one out of five benefit formulas, one out of three vesting tables, and so on—which simplifies the plan design process and saves time.

INFORMATION

Where do you turn when you need to answer a client's question or find out about the latest law or idea? What sources and references offer necessary information to a pension practitioner? The resources you can call on include primary sources, books, periodicals, loose-leaf services, online databases, and software packages. The following is an analysis of the major items that should be considered for inclusion in your pension library.

Primary Sources and Other Invaluable Resources

primary sources

The most reliable and important sources of information are, of course, the *primary sources*: texts of the laws, the Internal Revenue Code, the example-laden regulations, and many of the numerous agency interpretations. Unlike secondary sources such as books and periodicals, primary sources can be relied on by the practitioner as an accurate and legally enforceable representation of a situation.

Although not binding like primary sources, the IRS and Department of Labor both have publications that explain, usually in plain English, the various rules and regulations. Many of these publications are well written, provide additional guidance on the agency's interpretation of the law, and, best of all, they are free! The IRS has especially good publications on IRAs and the taxation of pension distributions.

A final invaluable source for learning about Congress's meaning of a particular law is to look at the law's statutory history. Generally, the most meaningful of these documents are the committee reports of the Senate, House of Representatives, and Conference Committee (where differences between provisions in the House of Representatives and Senate bills are resolved). For tax legislation, often the joint committee on taxation prepares a report, which is

blue book

known as the *blue book* (available from most loose-leaf services). Blue books are highly regarded in the tax community as understandable resources that explain the legislative intent behind the law.

These primary sources can be found in many places, as discussed below. The easiest way to access most of this material is to go directly to the government Web sites discussed below.

Books

Several outstanding books in the pension field provide in-depth overviews of pensions and retirement plans. These include

- Allen, Melone, Rosenbloom, and Mahoney, *Pension Planning* (a thorough and well-regarded treatment)
- Beam and McFadden, *Employee Benefits* (another good overview of the employee benefits field)
- Canan, *Qualified Retirement Plans and Other Employee Fringe and Welfare Benefit Plans* (comprehensive coverage of the legal requirements)
- Bennett, Bradley, Kaiser and Phillips, Taxation of Distributions from Qualified Plans (a comprehensive and technical treatment of the income and estate tax consequences of qualified plans)
- Choate, *Life and Death Planning for Retirement Benefits* (technical and planning issues related to pension accumulations)
- *The Pension Answer Book Series* (The first edition covered the whole pension field; now, there is a whole series of specialty books covering such topics as 401(k) plans, 403(b) plans, plan investments, and plan distributions)
- A yearly reference book, such as *Tax Facts* (published by National Underwriter, Cincinnati, Ohio), is also an important addition to any pension library

Periodicals

There are innumerable periodicals that report on every angle of pensions and retirement. The employee benefit side of pensions is covered in *Employee Benefit Plan Review* (which contains an excellent listing of benefit-plan service companies), *Benefits Quarterly* (loaded with perceptive articles), and *Pension Benefits* (covers a lot of statistical data). From the investment side of pensions there is *Pensions and Investments*, the newspaper of corporate and institutional investing. The insurance side of pensions is represented by the *Journal of Financial Service Professionals* and *Life Insurance Selling* (the annual reports on pensions are full of good ideas).

Loose-leaf Services

Loose-leaf services are publications that describe the legal and administrative framework of pensions in an up-to-date manner. The term *loose-leaf* refers to the fact that individual pages can be constantly revised to reflect recent happenings and then mailed out to subscribers to replace current pages in a ringed binder. Information about retirement plans, laws, and related areas is always available and current. Commonly used loose-leaf services are the *BNA Pension and Benefits Reporter* (published by the Bureau of National Affairs, Washington, DC), *Pension Plan Guide* (Commerce Clearing House, Chicago, IL), *EBPR Research Reports* (Aspen Publishers, New York, NY), and RIA. Most of these services also provide a weekly bulletin that reports the latest news about retirement plans to keep readers current and informed.

Commercial Electronic Resources

Many of the periodicals and loose-leaf services are now also available through the Internet. For example, CCH and RIA Checkpoint allow online access to pension services as well as a wide array of other products offered by these companies.

Because the world is changing so fast, check with the major publishers to see what is currently available. Publishers include, Aspen Publishers (includes Panel Publishers and Charles D. Spencer) at www.aspenpublishers.com, BNA at www.bna.com, CCH at www.cch.com, and Thomson Publishing Group, (includes RIA and Warren, Gorham & Lamont) at www.thomson.com.

Two different types of commercial electronic resources are also worth considering, Proquest ABI/INFORM (www.proquest.com) links up with leading businesses and management publications and summarizes articles for a quick reference. A controlled vocabulary lets you search for all the information on a specific pension term (for example, 401(k) plans) and lists the various article titles relating to that term. Lexis/Nexis (www.lexisnexis.com) is basically a law library that provides considerable source material. Each service is targeted for a different type of subscriber—Proquest ABI/INFORM for business and insurance and Lexis/Nexis for the legal profession.

Surfing the Net

In addition to the commercial sources just mentioned, there is a rich array of information available on the Internet. Of interest to those in the employee benefit field are the following:

- *Department of Labor Employee Benefits Security Administration* www.dol.gov/ebsa
  This site includes a summary of laws and regulations in the pension and benefits area governed by the DOL. It also includes the full text of bills and statutes. It is an in-depth resource for free access to primary source materials.

- *U.S. Government Printing Office*
  www.access.gpo.gov
  In this site, you can search the Federal Register for the full text of agency regulations or the U.S. Code for laws.
- *International Foundation of Employee Benefit Plans*
  www.ifebp.org
  Here you will find information about the organization and available services, as well as the latest industry news.
- *Benefits Link*
  www.benefitslink.com
  A commercial site that includes laws and regulations, articles, discussion groups, and lists of service providers.
- *Plansponsor*
  www.plansponsor.com
  Another commercial site that provides up-to-the-minute industry news.
- *IRS*
  www.irs.gov
  This site contains tax regulations and IRS publications and forms.
- *Employee Benefit Research Institute*
  www.ebri.org
  Here you will find many useful statistics and studies. This site also has links to other employee benefit Web sites.

Every day, a massive amount of new information becomes available on the Internet. Also, consider using a search engine such as Google, Yahoo, or AltaVista to locate

- Web pages for the organizations and publishing companies discussed in this chapter
- advertisements for other service providers in the benefits area

Software

A wide variety of software packages that enable financial services practitioners to do their jobs more efficiently is available from insurance companies and pension vendors. Software packages are available for client illustrations, pension administration, portfolio management, form preparation, plan document preparation, and distribution planning, as well as for number crunching in a variety of other areas.

CHAPTER REVIEW

Key Terms

Employee Retirement Income
    Security Act (ERISA) [2-1]
final regulations [2-2]
proposed regulations [2-2]
temporary regulations [2-2]
revenue rulings [2-2]
private letter rulings [2-2]
fiduciary [2-2]

Pension Benefit Guaranty
    Corporation (PBGC) [2-2]
third-party administrators
    (TPAs) [2-3]
master and prototype plans [2-3]
primary sources [2-3]
blue book [2-3]

Review Questions

Review questions are based on the learning objectives in this chapter. Thus, a [2-3] at the end of a question means that the question is based on learning objective 2-3. If there are multiple objectives, they are all listed.

1. What were the major reforms instituted by the Employee Retirement Income Security Act of 1974 (ERISA)? [2-1]

2. What have been the post-ERISA legislative trends with regard to the following areas? [2-1]
   a. maximum deductible contributions
   b. limiting tax deferral
   c. parity between various business entities
   d. funding
   e. simplification

3. What effect does new legislation in the retirement area have on the financial services professional? [2-1]

4. What is the role of the Internal Revenue Service with regard to the retirement market? [2-2]

5. Your client, Dr. Sandra Scalpel, would like to fund her qualified money-purchase plan using 50 percent of her retirement account to purchase universal life insurance. As the rule currently stands, the IRS allows 50 percent of the account balance to be used to purchase whole life insurance and only 25 percent of the account to be used to purchase term insurance. The IRS has informally indicated that universal life policies are subject to the

25 percent (not the 50 percent) funding limitation. No regulations or other formal guidance is dispositive on this issue. What can be done to solve this uncertainty in the law that would enable Dr. Scalpel to use 50 percent of her retirement account to purchase universal life insurance? [2-2]

6.   What is the role of the Department of Labor in the pension process? [2-2]

7.   What are the types of organizations involved in providing consulting and investment services to retirement plans? [2-3]

8.   What resources are available to assist the financial services professional with technical research and to help the financial services professional keep abreast of changes in the pension field? [2-3]

NOTE

1.   The IRS currently has several formal programs for substituting plan disqualification with a monetary penalty. The programs can apply upon an IRS audit or can be voluntarily entered into by employers who discover that qualification violations have occurred.

3

Preliminary Concerns

Learning Objectives

An understanding of the material in this chapter should enable you to

3-1. Describe the fact-finding process for helping an employer select the appropriate tax-advantaged retirement plan.

3-2. Identify the rule differences between defined-benefit and defined-contribution plans.

3-3. Compare the defined-benefit with the defined-contribution plan approach.

3-4. Compare plans in the pension category with those in the profit-sharing category.

3-5. Define the term "Keogh" plan and calculate the maximum allowable deduction under a defined-contribution plan

---

Chapter Outline

One of the most promising and lucrative opportunities in the retirement market is the chance to design a client's retirement program. Financial services professionals who act as consultants in this area provide a valuable service that not only leads to the sale of retirement-plan products, but also to the investment of their client's retirement assets. Furthermore, financial services professionals who bring technical expertise to the retirement-decision process gain the confidence of clients and may be entrusted with sales opportunities in other areas of the business. Conversely, financial services professionals who desire only to manage plan assets or sell investment products find themselves at a competitive disadvantage if they cannot offer the technical expertise expected.

For these reasons, it is essential that financial services professionals learn how to select the most appropriate retirement plan or plans for their clients. The study of this process starts with the selection of the most appropriate tax-advantaged plan for your client (chapters 3–6). We discuss the design of plan features, such as the plan's eligibility and vesting provisions, in chapters 7–10. Next, a thorough review of the issues involved in investing plan assets precedes a brief discussion of the various administrative issues involved with maintaining retirement plans. Before moving on to individual retirement planning we also discuss supplemental nonqualified plans, generally for executives (chapters 15 and 16), and the role of individual retirement plans.

In order to choose the best retirement plan, you must identify the client's needs and objectives, understand the various plan options, and match the client's needs and objectives with the proper tax-advantaged retirement plan or plans.

IDENTIFYING NEEDS AND OBJECTIVES

When advising a client on retirement-plan choices, your initial step is to focus the client on the important issues he or she faces, both personally and professionally. In addition, you need to discern the organization's needs and objectives that are relevant to plan selection. The device used to accomplish these steps is a pension planning fact finder (found at the end of this chapter). Although this seven-step fact finder gives you one perspective on the task, other choices in fact finding may work better for you. In any case, you should use this fact finder or an alternative to

- guide the client toward focusing on important issues
- gather the information necessary for you to make insightful recommendations
- provide a systematic approach for solving the client's retirement puzzle

- serve as a due diligence checklist that will ensure the selection of the most appropriate plan
- record your dealings with the client for liability protection

Understanding the Fact Finder

Even basic information about the company will impact the plan design. For example, the type of entity may limit the type of plan that can be established. Another key issue is whether or not the entity has any related entities. Under the rules that apply to tax-advantaged retirement plans, certain related employers have to be aggregated to determine whether a plan satisfies coverage requirements. Because the rules are quite complex it is best to write down all related companies that fit the description in the fact finder, and then have a qualified tax expert carefully analyze the aggregation issues.

Step 1 of the fact finder helps you begin to identify organizational needs, the foundation for proper plan choice. The important comparative analysis that is started in step 2 (involving the interplay between these factors) requires additional discussion with the client to establish the relative desirability of each objective. For example, when an employer has the multiple objectives of attracting and retaining key employees, avoiding an annual financial commitment to fund the plan, and providing tax shelter for top executives, you must gauge which need is most important and to what degree the other needs will have to be subordinated in order to choose the best plan for your client.

Step 3 lists the primary and secondary reasons for establishing the plan, and is a culmination of steps 1 and 2. It forces your client to set priorities on the motives for establishing the plan. Motives can be disparate even in similarly structured organizations, but several generalizations about motives can be made:

- Large organizations typically want to meet the needs of the business while getting the most for the employees out of a given expenditure.
- Small organizations, such as closely held businesses, are particularly concerned with providing tax shelter and extensive retirement benefits to owners and key employees.
- Some organizations (both large and small) desire to adequately provide for rank-and-file employees; others want to favor key employees and will only grudgingly meet the minimum statutory requirements for other employees; and still others fall somewhere between these two polar viewpoints.
- Some organizations establish plans to attract and retain key employees or to motivate employees, and they want the most cost-effective system to meet those goals.

- Some organizations are interested in resolving problems with older, unproductive employees and in creating a graceful transition out of the workforce.
- In today's world, more and more employers want to form a retirement savings partnership with employees and want employer contributions to primarily match employee contributions.

The first three steps provide some insight into the type of plan to be chosen. Steps 4 and 5 (discussing cost objectives and cash flow) are, however, perhaps the most important determinants of the type of plan the client will adopt. The price tag the client can comfortably live with is sometimes a product of the client's objectives (what he or she wants to provide) and sometimes a product of the economics of the situation (what he or she can afford). What clients can afford will vary according to what they want and what they consider a cost-effective price. When considering cost objectives, the organization's ability to make the economic commitment year in and year out should be carefully studied. Some industries have fluctuating profits that ebb and flow with certain uncontrollable economic conditions, while others are fairly stable. In other words, it is not just a question of how much, but also how consistently a certain payment level can be maintained or how much flexibility is needed in order to meet benefit commitments. Carefully examine the following issues before deciding on a price range:

- annual variations in profits
- future cash needs for capital expansion
- potential changes in the prospect's industry over the next 5 years
- length of time until the principals retire
- tax-shelter needs of owner-employees

Step 6 (distinguishing between personal and organizational goals) helps you to better understand the priorities laid out in step 3 and the cost objectives laid out in step 4 by differentiating between the client's personal needs and corporate objectives. You may find that, in the small-plan market, the client's personal needs are of the utmost importance and, as the size of the company grows, the organizational needs become more central to the decision-making process.

Step 7 (analyzing the company's census) is perhaps the most important step in the fact-finding process. A thorough understanding of the ages and salary levels of the people who will be covered by the plan is essential for making the correct plan choice and in establishing the best possible plan design. For example, if all the members of the firm are "older" (by pension standards, over age 45), then it may be desirable to put in a defined-benefit plan that accounts for past service (discussed later). If, however, salary levels are low and employees are young, a more basic plan, such as a simplified employee pension plan, may be desirable.

YOUR FINANCIAL SERVICES PRACTICE:
INFORMATION GATHERING

The pension planning fact finder is just the jumping-off point in your quest to identify your client's needs and objectives. The initial interview should be followed by open communication lines that allow the client's concerns to be more clearly developed over time. The following points typify what can happen in this intervening time:

- Frequently, the person you speak with will not correctly represent the desires of the entire body of authority within the organization. The company will need time to sort out its collective feelings and come up with a response. Try not to get involved in the infighting that may occur, and try to remain as diplomatic and neutral as possible.
- The company's attorney or accountant should be brought into the process in the early stages. A common problem is that the attorney or accountant may resent playing the subordinate role (even though he or she may know little about pension plans). Once again, the solution is diplomacy.

Choosing between a Qualified Plan and the Other Tax-Sheltered Options

Chapters 4 and 5 discuss the various types of qualified plans. Chapter 6 addresses those tax-advantaged plans that are not categorized as qualified plans. For the for-profit employer, the other types of plans available include the SEP and the SIMPLE. The nonprofit employer that is a 501(c)(3) organization also has the option to sponsor a 403(b) tax-sheltered annuity plan.

As we have already begun to discuss (and as described in detail in later chapters), establishing and maintaining a qualified plan requires a significant amount of documentation, government reporting, and employee communication. For the small business, these requirements can be quite onerous. SEPs and SIMPLEs are intended to provide the small business with some less complicated options. Plan documents are less complicated, and there are fewer IRS reporting requirements. Simplicity translates into lower administrative expenses and less time spent operating the plan. However, in exchange for simplicity is a rigidity in plan design. These plans have less flexibility than qualified plans in most regards. The important differences include

- *Coverage.* While the qualified plan rules provide significant flexibility in the number and makeup of the employees covered by the plan, the SEP and SIMPLE eligibility requirements are set in stone.
- *Vesting.* Contributions must be fully and immediately vested in the contributions to SEPs and SIMPLEs, while qualified plans can have a vesting schedule.
- *Contributions.* In some cases in a qualified plan, benefits or contributions can be different for different classes of employees. This is not the case in SEPs and SIMPLEs, where all participants must receive essentially the same level of benefits.
- *Maximum contributions.* In most regards, the limits are lower for SEPs and SIMPLEs than for qualified plans.

The SEP is the appropriate plan option when the employer is going to fund all of the plan benefits. In a SEP, as in a profit-sharing plan, the employer can make contributions annually (or more often) on a discretionary basis. When the employer wants to allow employees the opportunity to make additional contributions on a pretax basis (making it similar to a 401(k) plan), then the SIMPLE is the appropriate choice.

The 403(b) tax-sheltered annuity is a unique retirement planning vehicle. Only tax-exempt 501(c)(3) organizations and public school systems are allowed to sponsor such plans. At one time, there were relatively few rules governing these plans. However, over time, the situation has evolved, and more and more of the rules that apply to qualified plans now also apply to 403(b) plans. One type of plan that still operates quite differently from the way a qualified plan does is the 403(b) plan that involves only employee pretax contributions. This type of plan is not subject to many of the requirements of ERISA (as long as certain requirements are met). With this type of arrangement, the employer has little involvement; the service provider works directly with the employees. When the employer makes contributions to a 403(b) plan, then the plan operates very much like a qualified plan. (The distinctions between the plans are covered further in chapter 6.)

CHOOSING BETWEEN A DEFINED-BENEFIT AND A DEFINED-CONTRIBUTION PLAN

defined-benefit plan

Assuming the employer is going to choose from among the qualified plan options, the first consideration is whether the employer wants a plan of the defined-benefit or defined-contribution type. All qualified plans fall into one of those two categories and each category represents a different philosophy of retirement planning. This philosophy is reflected in the definition of each term. A *defined-benefit plan* specifies the benefits each employee receives at retirement. In most plans, the benefit is stated as a percentage of preretirement salary, which is payable for the participant's remaining life. Under a defined-benefit plan, the contributions required by the employer vary depending upon what is needed to pay the promised benefit, and the amount of annual funding is determined each year by the plan's actuary.

In many ways, the defined-benefit plan looks like an insurance solution to the retirement problem. The risk that is being insured is the loss of income due to the inability to work any longer. Another risk is that an individual will outlive his or her money in retirement. The traditional defined-benefit plan addresses both of these issues. The amount of the benefit is tied to what will be lost—employment income. To address the issue of longevity, in the traditional plan, the benefit is payable for the retired employee's entire life. It is interesting to note that this plan design is due in part to the fact that the first defined-benefit plans were funded with insurance products, although today many "self-fund" the promised benefits.

defined-contribution plan

In a *defined-contribution plan,* on the other hand, employer contributions are allocated to the accounts of individual employees. This approach is similar to a personal savings approach in which an individual opens a bank account and makes regular contributions, and the account grows based on the rate of investment return. Because of this characteristic, defined-contribution plans are sometimes called *individual account plans.* One way to look at these dissimilar approaches is to say that defined-benefit plans provide a fixed predetermined benefit that has an uncertain cost to the employer, whereas defined-contribution plans have a predetermined cost to the employer and provide a variable benefit to employees (based upon the rate of return).

Qualified Plan Categories

Defined-Benefit Plans	Defined-Contribution Plans
• Defined-benefit pension plan • Cash-balance pension plan	• Money-purchase pension plan • Target-benefit pension plan • Profit-sharing plan • 401(k) plan • Stock bonus plan • ESOP

All qualified plans fall into either the defined-benefit or the defined-contribution category. The names of the various qualified plans and the categories into which they fall are listed below. Note, however, that two types of plans are referred to as *hybrid plans*. First is the *cash-balance plan*, which is a defined-benefit plan that has some of the characteristics of a plan using the defined-contribution approach. Second is the *target-benefit plan,* which is a defined-contribution plan that has some of the characteristics of a defined-benefit plan. These distinctions will become more clear in the next two chapters, where the plans are discussed in more detail. Also note that the SEP, the SIMPLE, and the 403(b) tax-sheltered annuity plan all use a defined-contribution approach and share the same strengths and limitations of other defined-contribution plans (in comparison to the defined-benefit approach).

Rule Differences

Because of their vastly different natures, there are a number of important rule differences that apply to defined-benefit and defined-contribution plans. First is how the maximum contribution and benefit rules of Code Sec. 415 apply. Code Sec. 415(b) limits the maximum annual benefit that can be provided in a defined-benefit plan. The rule allows payment of a life annuity beginning at age 65 in the amount of the lesser of 100 percent of the highest consecutive 3-year average compensation or $180,000 (as indexed in 2007, with no actuarial reductions if benefits begin as early as age 62). If payments begin before age 62, the dollar limit is reduced to reflect early commencement. The dollar limit is also increased to reflect commencement after age 65. If the form of payment is other than a life annuity, the benefit generally must be actuarially adjusted.

In a defined-contribution plan, the maximum contribution each year is limited under Code Sec. 415(c). The rule is that the maximum annual additions for any participant for the year cannot exceed the lesser of $45,000 (indexed for 2007) or 100 percent of salary. Annual additions include all employer contributions, employee contributions (of any type), and forfeitures that are allocated to the participant's account. There is one exception: catchup salary deferral contributions made for those individuals over age 50 are not counted under the limit.

Compensation under Code Sec. 415 includes taxable wage income as well as salary deferral contributions to all types of tax-sheltered plans as well as pretax contributions to cafeteria plans and fringe benefit programs. Compensation cannot exceed the cap stated in Code Sec. 417. In 2007, the compensation cap is $225,000.

All defined-contribution plans of related employers are added together to determine whether the annual additions limit of Code Sec. 415(c) has been satisfied Similarly, defined-benefit plans are aggregated to determine whether Code Sec. 415(b) has been satisfied. This means if an individual participated in two defined-contribution plans of a single or related employers, the maximum annual addition for 2007 would be the lesser of 100 percent of compensation or $45,000. Related employers generally means aggregated under the controlled group, affiliated service group, or leased employees rules (discussed in chapter 7), except that under the parent-subsidiary rules, aggregation exists if the parent owns more than 50 percent of the subsidiary (instead of the 80 percent or more rule that normally applies).

The next rule difference has to do with the PBGC. As mentioned in chapter 2, the PBGC insurance program guarantees certain benefit payments from most privately sponsored defined-benefit plans (with the exception of plans with fewer than 25 participants sponsored by professional services organizations). In a defined-benefit plan, the amount of assets never exactly matches the promised benefits, and the PBGC program is there to provide assistance if the company is in financial trouble and the plan does not have sufficient assets to pay the promised benefits. This program does not cover defined-contribution plans because the plan's assets always match the promised benefits owed to participants.

TABLE 3-1
Rule Differences

Defined-Benefit Plans	Defined-Contribution Plans
Code Sec. 415(b) limits the maximum allowable benefit payable from the plan—lesser of 100% of salary or a specified dollar limit.	Code Sec. 415(c) limits the maximum allowable annual contributions—the lesser of 100 percent of salary or a specified dollar limit
Generally subject to the PBGC insurance program	Not subject to the PBGC insurance program
Must satisfy the minimum-participation rule of Code Sec. 401(a)(26)	Not subject to the minimum-participation rule
Deductible contribution based on actuarial calculations	Deductible contribution limited to 25% of aggregate compensation
Longer vesting schedule allowed—5-year cliff or 7-year graded	More accelerated vesting—3-year cliff or 6-year graded

minimum-participation rule

Another important rule difference is that defined-benefit plans are subject to a special coverage provision referred to as the *minimum-participation rule,* which is discussed in detail in chapter 7. Defined-contribution plans are not subject to this rule.

Another distinction is the way the maximum deductible contribution is calculated. In defined-contribution plans, the maximum deductible contribution is 25 percent of aggregate compensation of all covered participants. In a defined-benefit plan, the limit is based on actuarial calculations and is not limited to a specific percentage of compensation.

Beginning in 2007, defined-benefit plans and defined-contribution plans become subject to separate vesting rules. Defined-contribution plans are required to have more accelerated vesting schedules than defined-benefit plans. Defined-contribution plans must use a vesting schedule as favorable as either a 3-year cliff (participants become fully vested after 3 years of service) or a 6-year graded schedule (participants must be 20 percent vested after 2 years and earn an additional 20 percent for each additional year of service). Defined-benefit plans can choose a more extended schedule—either 5-year cliff vesting or 7-year graded vesting. This distinction is discussed further in chapter 9.

Comparing the Defined-Benefit and Defined-Contribution Approaches

Because defined-benefit plans typically describe benefits as a percentage of final-average compensation, benefits can be geared to replace a specified percentage of salary for the long-service employee. Also, defined-benefit plans can provide benefits based on past service (that is, years worked before the plan was initiated), while defined-contribution plans cannot. This means that benefits can accumulate more quickly for the older employee in a defined-benefit plan. Such plans reward those employees who continue employment until retirement, because benefits are usually tied to both length of service and final income.

In defined-benefit plans, the burden of providing an adequate retirement income is placed solely on the employer, because the employer promises to fund the plan sufficiently to pay promised benefits. This means the risk of the investment experience is on the employer; contributions will increase if investment experience is worse than expected and will decrease if performance is better than expected. Even though the employer is responsible to make required contributions, it is important to note that there is generally some funding flexibility in defined-benefit plans. There is, typically, some range (as determined with the help of an actuary) from the required minimum to the maximum allowable deductible contribution.

Also, defined-benefit plans generally provide for a built-in "preretirement" inflation factor by tying benefit payments to salary levels received just prior to retirement. However, defined-benefit plans generally do not increase automatically for inflation occurring after retirement—although it is not unusual for an employer to provide periodic ad hoc benefit increases for retirees. This makes the defined-benefit plan unique, because defined-contribution plans cannot imitate this inflation protection.

Tying benefits to final-average salary does have one down side. When a participant changes jobs, the benefit can be reduced significantly because of the loss of the highest years of salary in the calculation. This means the benefit is not as portable as in a defined-contribution plan where benefits accrue more ratably over the years. This lack of portability ties the employee to the employer, which has a benefit for the employer who offers the defined-benefit plan.

For these reasons, employers looking to (1) maximize benefits for older workers, (2) give long-term employees (including key people) a secure and specified retirement income, and (3) tie employees to the company through the benefit program will be interested in the defined-benefit plan. Still, the defined-benefit plan is only an option if the company is in the financial position and competitive posture to be able to meet the financial obligation of maintaining this type of plan.

Plans in the defined-contribution category are significantly different. From the perspective of both the employer and the employee, such plans look and feel more like deferred-compensation plans. A specified amount is set aside for the employee's benefit, which is paid out at termination of employment (as long as the participant is "vested") or, in some cases, even earlier.

This means that defined-contribution plans do not provide a retirement benefit that is closely tied to the individual's retirement needs (as in a defined-benefit plan). This does not mean that defined-contribution plans will not provide adequate retirement income; it is just much harder to pinpoint the benefit. Also, in a very real way, the employee is at more risk because the benefit is tied to the plan's investment return. In other words, if stock market prices fall drastically, it is the employee who must worry in a defined-contribution plan, but the employer who must worry in a defined-benefit plan.

With a defined-contribution plan, the employer's cost is determinable and will not vary with the plan's investment return. Also, these plans cost less to administer as there are fewer administrative functions. The cost is higher with a defined-benefit plan primarily because the sponsor needs to hire an actuary to determine the cost of providing benefits. The actuary has to make multiple calculations as required by funding, accounting, and PBGC rules.

Employees can more easily follow the growth of their benefits with a defined-contribution plan and can more readily appreciate the value of the cost of the plan to the employer. Defined benefits can have great value, but the cost of the benefit to the employer is not as transparent.

Defined-contribution plans may also allow employees to direct the investments in their individual accounts. As well, the participant's benefit is stated as a single account balance and lump-sum distributions are generally allowed—which is not always the case in a defined-benefit plan.

This account balance is more portable should an employee switch jobs. The lump-sum value can be rolled over to an IRA or to the new employer's plan. Because the benefit grows with annual contributions and investment experience, a participant is not penalized by changing employers, as can be the case with a defined-benefit plan.

Easily determinable costs appeal to employers whose financial positions dictate caution (typically organizations with volatile cash flow). What is more, key employees tend to feel more comfortable about individual accounts that they invest, portable benefits, and the lump-sum distributions traditionally offered under defined-contribution plans. As a result of this employer and key-employee appeal, defined-contribution plans have become a hot ticket for financial services professionals in the pension field.

TABLE 3-2 **Types of Plans Compared**	
Defined-Benefit Plans	**Defined-Contribution Plans**
Defines the benefit	Defines the employer's contribution
Contributions not attributed to specified employees	All contributions allocated to individual employee accounts
Employer assumes risk of preretirement inflation, investment performance, and adequacy of retirement income	Employee assumes risk of preretirement inflation, investment performance, and adequacy of retirement income
Can provide benefits based on past service	Cannot provide benefits for past service
Costly to administer	Lower administrative costs
Can be difficult to communicate both the amount of benefits and the value of benefit (amount it costs the employer)	Easy to communicate the amount of employer contributions and the "bank-account" type accumulation
Unpredictable costs	Predictable costs

The Realities of the Marketplace Today

A look at the contrast between the defined-benefit and the defined-contribution approach would not be complete without a discussion of the realities of today's marketplace. Even though the defined-benefit approach still has the strengths that have been mentioned, few small businesses today are maintaining defined-benefit plans. The 2006 Bureau of Labor Statistics National Compensation Survey identified fewer than 10 percent of employers in private industry with 99 employees or less offering a defined-benefit plan.

This does not mean, however, that defined-benefit plans are not an important part of the retirement planning landscape. The same study revealed one third of workers in mid-size and large companies in private industry (100 or more employees) are covered by defined-benefit plans. Also, in the small-plan marketplace, the pension industry has begun to recognize that defined-benefit plans could play an important role for the older business owner who has not accumulated enough for retirement, has a strong cash flow, and is looking for a significant tax shelter. With the number of aging baby boomers today, we may see more defined-benefit plans installed.

Nevertheless, defined-contribution products have become the bread-and-butter sale for those who deal in qualified deferred compensation. The defined-contribution approach appears to appeal both to senior managers, who are looking for simplicity and contribution certainty, and to employees, who like that they can more easily understand the plan and appreciate that benefits are more portable. The number of employees in the private sector covered by defined-contribution plans has grown to over 50 million. In the small-plan market, almost all plans being installed are 401(k) plans and SIMPLEs (see the 2003 *EBRI Small Employer Retirement Survey*).

Multiple Plans—Combining Defined-Benefit and Defined-Contribution Plans

Defined-benefit plans and defined-contribution plans are not mutually exclusive, and two or more plans can be set up for any one employer. If defined-benefit and defined-contribution plans are used together, restrictions apply to the overall deduction limits.

Today, a combination defined-benefit and defined-contribution plan is typically used in a larger company to provide a comprehensive benefits package. A defined-benefit/defined-contribution combination may be appropriate in the small-plan marketplace as well, when the business owner is looking to maximize benefits and deductible contributions. Theoretically, a plan sponsor could contribute the maximum Code Sec. 415(c) amount to a defined-contribution plan on behalf of the owner and fund the Code Sec. 415(b) maximum allowable benefit in a defined-benefit plan for the owner as well. In practice, this may be beneficial in some cases, but this type of arrangement could run up against the maximum deductible contribution limits. When a sponsor maintains both a defined-benefit and a defined-contribution plan, the maximum deductible contribution will be the greater of the cost of funding the defined-benefit plan or 25 percent of aggregate compensation, with one exception: A matching contribution to a 401(k) plan of up to 6 percent of compensation will not count under the multiple-plan deduction limits. For a more in-depth discussion of the deduction limits, see chapter 11.

Under this rule, if the contribution to the defined-benefit plan exceeds 25 percent of compensation, the employer cannot make contributions to a defined-contribution plan.

CHOOSING BETWEEN A PENSION PLAN AND A PROFIT-SHARING PLAN

All qualified plans fall into either the defined-benefit or defined-contribution categories. Similarly, all plans are also classified as either pension plans or profit-sharing plans. As you can see in the chart below, both types of defined-benefit plans, along with target-benefit and money-purchase plans, are categorized as pension plans. All other defined-contribution plans are profit-sharing plans.

Qualified Plan Categories

Pension Plans	Profit-Sharing Plans
• Defined-benefit pension plan	• Profit-sharing plan
• Cash-balance pension plan	• 401(k) plan
• Money-purchase pension plan	• Stock bonus plan
• Target-benefit pension plan	• ESOP

pension plan category
profit-sharing plan category

The most important difference between a plan in the *pension plan category* and one in the *profit-sharing plan category* concerns the employer's commitment to the plan. Under a pension plan, the organization is legally required to make annual payments to the plan because the plan's main purpose is to provide a retirement benefit. Under a profit-sharing-type plan, however, an organization is not required to make annual contributions. The reasoning here seems to be that profit-sharing plans are not necessarily intended to provide retirement benefits as much as to provide a sharing of profits on a tax-deferred basis.

Consistent with this rationale, the law generally allows that profit-sharing-type plans may be written to permit distributions during employment. The plan can distribute funds accumulated under the plan after a fixed number of years, the attainment of a stated age, or upon the prior occurrence of some event such as layoff, illness, financial hardship, disability, retirement, death, or severance of employment. The IRS has interpreted "a fixed number of years" to mean that:

- Distributions can be made of any contributions that have been held in the plan for 2 years or more.
- Any participant who has 5 or more years of plan participation can receive a distribution of his or her entire account balance.

Note that salary deferral contributions to 401(k) plans are subject to special, more restrictive in-service withdrawal limitations (discussed in chapter 5).

Pension plans are meant to provide retirement income or at least provide for deferral of income until termination of employment. Because of this principle, for many years pension plans could only allow distributions upon termination of employment or attainment of normal retirement age. The Pension Protection Act of 2006 amended this rule somewhat to recognize a recent trend of older workers choosing to stay in the workforce but to cut back the number of hours employed. Since this group may need to begin receiving retirement benefits prior to retiring, the law now allows pension plans to begin payments as early as age 62.

TABLE 3-3 **Differences between Pension and Profit-Sharing Plans**		
Characteristic	**Pension Plan**	**Profit-Sharing Plan**
Employer commitment to annual funding	Yes	No
Withdrawal flexibility for employees	None	After 2 years
Investment in company stock	Limited to 10%	Unlimited

A final distinction between pension and profit-sharing plans concerns the ability of these plans to invest in company stock. Plans in the pension category can invest only up to 10 percent of plan assets in employer stock. Plans in the profit-sharing category, on the other hand, have no restrictions; all plan assets can be used to purchase employer stock (although this is seldom the case). See table 3-3 for a summary of plan differences.

KEOGH PLANS

Keogh plans

In addition to categorizing plans either as defined-benefit or defined-contribution, or as pension or profit-sharing, qualified plans are categorized by the type of business organization they serve. Today, all types of businesses choose from among the same group of qualified plans. Historically, that was not always true. At one time, plans for partnerships and self-employed persons were governed by separate statutory provisions, and plans for such organizations were referred to as *Keogh plans*. Unfortunately, the name still sticks—generally creating more confusion than information. Today, a sole proprietor does not establish a Keogh plan; he or she establishes a profit-sharing, defined-benefit, or other plan from the array of tax-advantaged retirement plans. And, except as described below, the rules for sole proprietorships and partnerships are entirely the same as for corporate entities, and the same considerations regarding plan choice and plan design apply.

There is, however, one remaining distinction between plans of sole proprietorships and partnerships[1] and corporate plans: The self-employed person's contribution or benefit is based on net earnings instead of salary. This creates some complications because net earnings can be determined only after taking into account all appropriate business deductions, including

---

TABLE 3-4
Keogh Deduction Work Sheet

Step I: Self-employed person's work sheet

1. Plan contribution as a decimal (for example, 25% would be 0.25) _____

2. Rate in Line 1 plus 1, shown as a decimal (for example, 0.25 plus 1 would be 1.25) _____

3. Divide Line 1 by Line 2. This is the self-employed contribution rate. (For example, 0.25 ÷ 1.25 = .20) _____

Step II: Figure the deduction

1. Enter the self-employed contribution rate from Line 3 of Step I. _____

2. Enter the amount of net earnings that the business owner has from Schedule C (Form 1040) or Schedule F (Form 1040). $_____

3. Enter the deduction for self-employment tax from the front page of Form 1040. $_____

4. Subtract Line 3 from Line 2 and enter the amount. $_____

5. Multiply Line 4 by Line 1. $_____

6. Multiply $225,000 (2007 compensation cap) by Line 1. $_____

7. Enter the smaller of line 5 or 6. $_____

8. Enter the smaller of line 7 or $45,000 (the maximum allocation allowed for 2007).

Total $_____

---

the deduction for the retirement contribution—thus, the amount of net earnings and the amount of the deduction are dependent on each other.

If a defined-benefit plan is used, an actuary is needed to straighten out the confusion and to determine the plan contribution amount itself. However, if a defined-contribution plan is used, it will be necessary to calculate the maximum deduction for the client (see table 3-4).

This means that a sole proprietor or partner with a profit-sharing plan or money-purchase pension plan can only contribute 20 percent of compensation (not 25 percent of compensation as with a corporate plan). Further complicating matters is the fact that self-employed individuals get a deduction for income tax purposes equal to one-half of their Social Security self-employment tax on their federal tax return. Also, the contribution amount still cannot exceed the Code Sec. 415(c) annual limit. Fortunately, these complications can be eliminated if you follow the formula in table 3-4.

ADDITIONAL PRELIMINARY CONCERNS

Before we study the menu of qualified plans, it should be noted that choosing the best retirement plan is not as simple as picking one type of plan from the menu. The plan's design must also be considered in order to make the proper choice. This is because qualified plans are principally differentiated by only one design feature—their benefit formulas. The many other design choices, however, also affect your plan choice. To put it another way, plan choice is a function of plan design, and plan design is a function of plan choice. (The plan-design details that help you to make a more informed decision are presented in chapters 7 through 10.)

A second consideration when choosing a qualified plan is the makeup of the entire benefits package. For example, if there is a nonqualified plan for key employees, the choice of a qualified plan for all employees should be dovetailed with the nonqualified plan to reach the desired result. When group life and group disability plans are involved, other considerations arise. As a general rule, the choice of a retirement plan should reflect the fact that it is only one part of a benefits package. Special care should be taken to ensure that benefits are not duplicated under the different employee benefit plans.

Example: The professional corporation of Davis and Wickstrom is primarily interested in providing tax-sheltered savings for key employees and minimizing costs attributable to rank-and-file employees. Davis and Wickstrom asks you to help choose the best retirement plan for them. A defined-benefit plan designed with a benefit formula that is integrated with Social Security, and with restrictive eligibility and vesting provisions, is the preferable choice. But if you had only considered the menu of retirement plans without noting the design features, you might have chosen a 401(k) plan instead. At first blush, the

401(k) seems to be a likely fit because it allows tax-sheltered savings for key employees and minimizes costs attributable to the rank and file. On closer inspection, however, you will see that 401(k) plans may not provide enough tax shelter for the principals because such plans must be designed to meet a special nondiscrimination test known as the *actual deferral percentage test*. (See chapter 5.)

PENSION PLANNING FACT FINDER

Client's Name _____

Address _____

_____

_____

Phone Numbers _____

_____

Key Contacts Name _____

Title _____   Phone No._____

Name _____

Title _____   Phone No._____

Name _____

Title _____   Phone No._____

Client's Attorney _____   Phone No._____

Client's Accountant _____   Phone No._____

Employer Identification Number _____

Fiscal Year _____

Accounting Method (circle one)
    Cash
    Accrual
Business Structure (circle one)
    C Corp.
    S Corp.
    Municipal Corp.
    Partnership
    Limited Liability Company
    Sole Proprietorship
    Exempt Organization
    Professional Corp.
    Government Agency
State of Incorporation or Domicile _____
Date of Incorporation or Establishment _____
Were there any predecessor entities? (circle one)   Yes   No
Describe Relationship:

Affiliated Entities
Identify (1) other entities that the owners of this entity own in full or in part, (2) other entities that this entity owns in full or in part, (3) other entities that own this entity in full or in part, and (4) other entities that work with this entity to provide a single product or service. Describe in detail the chain of ownership and how the entities work together.
Name_____
Address_____
_____
Phone No._____
Describe Relationship: _____
_____

Step 1: Set retirement priorities.

Listed below are some typical concerns that organizations have when instituting a retirement program. Grade each of these concerns by scoring 1 for very valuable, 2 for valuable, 3 for moderately valuable, and 4 for least valuable.

1. To what extent is it important to use a qualified plan as a tax shelter for owner-employees and key employees?   [1] [2] [3] [4]

2. To what extent is it important to maximize benefits for long-service employees by including service prior to the inception of the plan?   [1] [2] [3] [4]

3. To what extent is it important to place the risk of investing plan assets with the employee?   [1] [2] [3] [4]

4. To what extent is it important to institute a plan that is easily communicated to employees?   [1] [2] [3] [4]

5. To what extent is it important to institute a plan that is administratively convenient?   [1] [2] [3] [4]

6. To what extent is it important to institute a plan that has predictable costs?   [1] [2] [3] [4]

7. To what extent is it important to avoid an annual financial commitment?   [1] [2] [3] [4]

8. To what extent is it important to allow employees (including owner-employees) to withdraw funds?   [1] [2] [3] [4]

9. To what extent is it important to minimize plan costs by limiting benefits for lower-paid employees?   [1] [2] [3] [4]

10. To what extent is it important to create a market for employer stock?   [1] [2] [3] [4]

11. To what extent is it important that the plan be able to borrow to purchase employer stock?   [1] [2] [3] [4]

12. To what extent is it important to attract key employees?   [1] [2] [3] [4]

13. To what extent is it important to retain experienced personnel?   [1] [2] [3] [4]

14. To what extent is it important to motivate the workforce?   [1] [2] [3] [4]

15. To what extent is it important to encourage the retirement of superannuated employees?   [1] [2] [3] [4]

16. To what extent is it important to give participants the opportunity to save additional amounts on a pretax basis?   [1] [2] [3] [4]

17. To what extent is it important that employer contributions be made only for employees who elect to contribute?   [1] [2] [3] [4]

18. To what extent is it important that benefits for those who terminate prior to retirement be portable?   [1] [2] [3] [4]

19. To what extent is it important for participants with a salary deferral option to be able to choose between tax-deferred and tax-free withdrawals?   [1] [2] [3] [4]

Step 2: Discuss with the client the interplay between various factors in step 1. For example:

		Yes	No
1.	Does the desire to provide tax shelter for owner-employees and key employees outweigh the need to cut costs attributable to lower-paid employees?	[Y]	[N]
2.	Does the desire to provide tax shelter for owner-employees and key employees outweigh the need to have an easily communicated and administratively convenient plan?	[Y]	[N]
3.	Does the need to provide tax shelter for owner-employees and key employees outweigh the need to have predictable costs and payment flexibility?	[Y]	[N]
4.	Is it more important to retain employees than to attract employees?	[Y]	[N]
5.	Is it more important to motivate employees than to attract or retain them?	[Y]	[N]
6.	Is it more important to provide an adequate retirement standard of living than to cut plan costs?	[Y]	[N]
7.	Is it more important to provide an adequate retirement standard of living than to have predictable costs?	[Y]	[N]
8.	Is it more important to provide an adequate standard of living during retirement than to avoid an annual commitment to funding the plan?	[Y]	[N]

9. Is it more important to provide an adequate standard of living during retirement than to allow employees (including owner-employees) to withdraw funds?   [Y]   [N]

10. Is it more important to provide an adequate standard of living during retirement than to have administrative convenience and an easily communicated plan?   [Y]   [N]

11. Is it more important that contributions go only to employees who elect to participate than to provide retirement benefits to all workers?   [Y]   [N]

Additional Comments

Step 3: List the primary reason(s) for establishing the plan and the secondary reason(s) for establishing the plan.

Primary   1.

2.

3.

Secondary   1.

2.

3.

Step 4: Discuss the employer's cost objectives. Discuss the price range that is desired both now and in the future.

Step 5: (A) What are the current and future cash-flow situations

  (1) for the company

  (2) for the industry in general

(B) Attach balance sheets from the last 3 years.

(C) Attach appropriate profit and loss statements.

Step 6: Distinguish between the personal needs that the plan will satisfy for the principals and the organizational goals that are sought.

Step 7: Analyze the company's census (list of employees).

  1. What percentage of employees can be expected to turn over before retirement?

  _____% leave before they complete one year of service

  _____% leave between their first and second years of service

  _____% leave between their second and third years of service

  _____% leave between their third and fourth years of service

  _____% leave between their fourth and fifth years of service

  _____% leave between their fifth and sixth years of service

_____% leave between their sixth and seventh years of service

_____% leave with more than seven years of service

_____% are "lifers" with the company

2. What groups of employees exist?

    _____salaried employees

    _____hourly paid employees

    _____collective-bargaining unit employees

    _____leased employees

3. To what extent are part-time employees used?

    _____part-time employees are used

    _____no part-time employees are used

    _____part-time employees work less than 500 hours

    _____part-time employees work between 500 and 999 hours

    _____part-time employees work 1000 or more hours

4. How many offices (profit centers) are there?
    _____number of different locations

5. What benefit programs do chief competitors offer?

6. Attach employee census.

7. Attach other group benefit plans.

8. Identify other related employers and the relationship to this one. The list should include any entities with interrelated ownership and other entities that work together with this one to produce a product. Describe in detail the chain of ownership and how the entities work together.

CHAPTER REVIEW

Key Terms

defined-benefit plan [3-2]

defined-contribution plan [3-2]

minimum-participation rule [3-2]

pension plan category [3-4]

profit-sharing plan category [3-4]

Keogh plans [3-5]

Review Questions

Review questions are based on the learning objectives in this chapter. Thus, a [3-3] at the end of a question means that the question is based on learning objective 3-3. If there are multiple objectives, they are all listed.

1. June Jones is thinking of installing a retirement plan for her budding flower business. June has indicated that she knows nothing about retirement plans and would like to speak with her financial advisor on the issue. What steps should the advisor take to help June focus on the important issues facing both her and the business and to gather the appropriate information that would enable the advisor to make recommendations? [3-1]

2. What are two typical stumbling blocks that financial services professionals face when helping to plan a client's retirement program? [3-1]

3. Answer these client questions about Code Sec. 415. [3-2]
   a. Can a defined-benefit plan pay the owner $180,000 a year for life beginning at age 60?
   b. I've heard that in 2007, an owner aged 50 or older can actually receive an allocation in a 401(k) plan of $50,000. Is this correct?
   c. Is it true that, if an individual works for a company and participates in two defined-contribution plans with that employer, up to $45,000 can be allocated to the participant in each plan.

4. Sam Doyle, owner of Doyle's Furniture, Inc., has requested a qualified plan that (1) provides an adequate pension for his employees, regardless of what the stock market does, (2) takes care of employees who have been with him for a long time, (3) provides a pension that reflects his employees' salaries at retirement, and (4) ties his long-service employees to the company. Should Doyle's Furniture, Inc., use a defined-benefit or a defined-contribution plan? Explain. [3-3]

5. What advantages are available to the employer under a defined-contribution plan? [3-2]

6. Indicate whether the following statements describe a defined-benefit plan or a defined-contribution plan: [3-3]
    a. Benefits accrue based on all years of salary.
    b. Benefit costs are less predictable.
    c. Administrative costs are lower.
    d. Plan assets are allocated to individual accounts for each participant.
    e. Annual additions for any participant cannot exceed the limits of Code Sec. 415(c).
    f. It can provide benefits based on past service.

7. Under what circumstances is it desirable to use a combination defined-benefit plan and defined-contribution plan? [3-3]

8. What are three basic differences between plans that fall into the pension family and plans that fall into the profit-sharing family? [3-4]

9. Faye is a sole proprietor with a qualified profit-sharing plan that enables her to contribute 25 percent of earned income. Faye's net earnings from schedule C are $100,000. Faye's deduction for one-half of her self-employment tax is $7,200. What is the maximum deduction that Faye is allowed to take under her profit-sharing plan for the year? [3-5]

NOTE

1. Limited-liability companies that are taxed as partnerships are subject to the same limitations as those that apply to partnerships.

4

Defined-Benefit, Cash-Balance, Target-Benefit, and Money-Purchase Pension Plans

Learning Objectives

An understanding of the material in this chapter should enable you to

4-1. Identify the types of benefit formulas available in a defined-benefit plan

4-2. Identify the key components in a unit-benefit formula. Also identify the appropriate candidate for a defined-benefit plan.

4-3. Describe the basic features of a cash-balance plan. Also describe why large employers choose to convert traditional defined-benefit plans to a cash-balance arrangement

4-4. Describe the features of a money-purchase plan and why this plan design is not often chosen today

4-5. Explain how a target-benefit plan is different than a defined-benefit plan, and why this plan design has fallen out of favor.

Chapter Outline

TARGET-BENEFIT PENSION PLANS 4.19
CHAPTER REVIEW 4.21

In order to help your client choose the best retirement plan, you first need to examine the menu of tax-advantaged plans. The next two chapters preview the full range of qualified plans, and chapter 6 will examine SEPs, SIMPLEs, and 403(b) plans. You will assess each plan's strengths and weaknesses, focus on the objectives that each plan serves for your client, and discuss the typical candidates for each type of plan.

The various types of qualified plans are explained in part by the characteristics of the categories they fall under (defined-benefit versus defined-contribution, and pension versus profit-sharing) and in part by their benefit or contribution formula. In chapter 3, you learned a significant amount about each type of category, as you learned how each plan was categorized. The one remaining piece of the puzzle is the plan's benefit or contribution formula. Let's take a closer look at the various types of retirement plans and their benefit (contribution) formulas.

DEFINED-BENEFIT PENSION PLANS

A defined-benefit pension plan falls within both the defined-benefit and pension categories. Knowing this means you already know that defined-benefit plans have the following characteristics:

- The maximum benefit that a person can receive each year is limited by Code Sec. 415(b) .
- Assets are not allocated to individual accounts.
- The employer assumes responsibility for preretirement inflation, income adequacy, and investment results.
- The benefit formula can be designed to consider past service.
- The older business owner can provide the maximum tax-shelter potential available under a qualified plan.
- They are more costly to administer than defined-contribution plans because, among other things, they require the services of an actuary.
- The benefit formula and value of the benefit may be more difficult to communicate than in defined-contribution plans.
- The employer's future costs are not precisely known.
- Annual employer contributions are required.

- Participants may not take in-service withdrawals prior to age 62.
- Investment in the sponsoring company's stock is limited to 10 percent of the plan's assets.

Let's take a closer look at defined-benefit pension plans from a design standpoint by examining the various types of benefit formulas that are used.

The Unit-Benefit Formula

unit-benefit formula

The most frequently used defined-benefit formula is the *unit-benefit formula* (also known as the percentage-of-earnings-per-year-of-service formula). This formula uses both service and salary in determining the participant's pension benefit. A unit-benefit formula might read this way: "Each plan participant will receive a monthly pension commencing at normal retirement date and paid in the form of a life annuity equal to 1.5 percent of final-average monthly salary multiplied by years of service. Service is limited to a maximum of 30 years."

Example:	Larry Novenstern is retiring after 25 years of service with his employer. Larry's final-average monthly salary is $5,000. To determine Larry's benefit, multiply 1.5 percent by the $5,000 final-average monthly salary by 25 (the number of years of service). Larry's monthly retirement benefit will be equal to $1,875 paid in the form of a life annuity. (Note that if a different distribution option is chosen, the benefit will be the actuarial equivalent of the life annuity.)

The unit-benefit formula is the most frequently used benefit formula because it best serves a variety of employer goals.

- The goal of retaining and rewarding experienced personnel is achieved because the pension benefit is based, in part, on the years of service an employee works for an employer.
- The goal of rewarding owner-employees and key employees is achieved because the pension benefit is based, in part, on salary, which is higher for owner-employees and key employees.
- The goal of providing the desired income-replacement ratio can be achieved through proper design of the benefit formula. The *income-replacement ratio* represents the amount of an employee's gross income that will be replaced under the retirement plan. Employers

income-replacement ratio

believe that there is no need to replace 100 percent of an employee's final-average salary in order to provide the desired standard of living at retirement for several reasons:

- Social Security benefits and private savings will fund part of the needed retirement benefit.
- The preretirement standard of living can be maintained at retirement on a lower income because the employee pays less in taxes in the retirement years (such as no Social Security taxes).
- The preretirement standard of living can be maintained at retirement on a lower income because the employee has reduced living expenses (no work-related expenses such as transportation and clothing; self-supporting children; paid-up home mortgage; and so on).

For these reasons, employers generally choose an income replacement of between 40 and 60 percent of final-average salary for employees who have spent their career with the employer, and something less for employees who have not spent as long with the employer.

Example:	The Cooper Corporation would like to provide a 60 percent income-replacement ratio for long-service employees and would like to provide a proportionately reduced income-replacement ratio for shorter-service employees. In order to accomplish these goals, the Cooper Corporation should choose a benefit formula that reads:

> "Each plan participant will receive a monthly pension commencing at normal retirement date and paid in the form of a life annuity equal to 2 percent of final-average monthly salary multiplied by years of service. Service is limited to a maximum of 30 years."

Under this benefit formula, the long-service employees will be provided with a 60 percent income-replacement ratio, and employees with fewer than 30 years of service will be provided with an equitably reduced income-replacement ratio. In addition, by placing the years-of-service cap at 30 years, the Cooper Corporation will never have to fund for benefits higher than 60 percent of average monthly salary.

Through the use of this benefit formula, the Cooper Corporation has achieved several goals:

- The goal of providing for a graceful transition in the workforce is achieved because the use of a years-of-service cap (in the example above, 30 years) discourages employment beyond the stated period. If the employer desires a more rapid turnover of older employees, a lower service cap can be used. If the employer wants to retain experienced personnel, however, a longer service cap may be used, or the employer may choose not to cap service at all.
- The goal of providing the most cost-effective defined-benefit plan possible is achieved because the unit-benefit formula is more cost-effective than other types of defined-benefit formulas. Cost-effectiveness can be defined in this case as getting the most value for each pension dollar by achieving employer goals at the least possible cost. To the extent permitted by law, the employer can reward employees with long service and/or high compensation and avoid paying disproportionate benefits for other employees.

The reason that unit-benefit formulas are the most cost-effective means of spending defined-benefit dollars can be best understood by examining the alternative defined-benefit formulas.

Other Defined-Benefit Formulas

flat-percentage-of-earnings formula

Under an alternative defined-benefit formula called the *flat-percentage-of-earnings formula* (on IRS forms, it is called a fixed-benefit formula), the benefit is related solely to salary and does not reflect an employee's service.

Example: Such a benefit formula may read:

"Each plan participant will receive a monthly pension benefit equal to 40 percent of the final-average monthly salary commencing at normal retirement date and paid in the form of a life annuity."

This formula is generally not cost-effective, however, because it provides a disproportionate benefit to employees hired later in their careers, which is costly to fund. At one time, these formulas were quite popular with small businesses when the owner was significantly older than the rank-and-file employees. The owner could accrue a full benefit over a short period of time while benefits for other employees accrued over a much longer period of time. Realizing that this was discriminatory, the IRS passed regulations that now require a flat-percentage-of-earnings formula to have a 25-year minimum period of service in order for the participants to receive the full benefits promised. For those with less than 25 years of service, the benefit will be proportionately reduced.

Example: Use the 40 percent retirement benefit from the previous example and apply a pro rata reduction for those with less than 25 years of service. If Debbie had final-average compensation of $100,000 and 10 years of service, her benefit would be $16,000 (40 percent of $100,000 multiplied by 10/25).

---

flat-amount-per-year-of-service formula

A second alternative to the unit-benefit formula is a formula that relates the pension benefit solely to service but does not reflect an employee's salary. This type of formula, called a *flat-amount-per-year-of-service formula,* might read: "Each plan participant will receive a monthly pension benefit commencing at normal retirement date and paid in the form of a life annuity equal to $10 for every year worked."

Flat-amount-per-year-of-service formulas are relatively uncommon except in union-negotiated plans. When used in union plans, a flat-amount-per-year-of-service formula may relate the benefit to the actual hours a participant worked. For example, participants working 1,000 hours might receive half as much as participants working 2,000 hours.

TABLE 4-1 Defined-Benefit Plan Formulas *	
Formula	Example
Unit-benefit Flat-percentage of-earnings Flat-amount-per-year of service Flat-amount	2% of FAC* times years of service 50% of FAC* $ 30 per month times years of service $450 per month
*Final-average compensation	

flat-amount formula

A third alternative to the unit-benefit formula is the *flat-amount formula* (called a flat-benefit formula on IRS forms). The flat-amount formula provides the same monthly benefit for each participant. This formula treats all employees alike and does not account for differences in earnings or service. A flat-amount formula might read: "Each plan participant will receive a $200-a-month pension benefit commencing at normal retirement date and paid in the form of a life annuity." As with the flat-amount-per-year-of-service formula, this formula is found primarily in union plans. (See table 4-1 for examples of the four types of benefit formulas.)

Elements of the Unit-Benefit Formula

We will take a closer look at the specific elements of the unit-benefit formula because it is the most common. If a plan has a unit-benefit formula, that formula may read as follows:

Example:	A participant will be entitled to a life annuity, beginning at the normal retirement age, in the amount of 1.5 percent of final-average compensation times years of service. Normal retirement age is the later of age 65 or 5 years of plan participation.

Each of the factors in this benefit formula affects the ultimate value of the benefit. These factors include the definition of compensation under the plan, the definition of final-average compensation, the definition of years of service, the form of benefit, and the age at which benefits can begin. Each of these factors is discussed more fully below.

The Definition of Compensation

One of the most important elements of the defined-benefit formula is the amount of compensation used in the benefit formula. This is a function of both the definition of compensation and the definition of "average" (or final-average) compensation. The most comprehensive definition of compensation includes all wages that are included in taxable income, plus any pretax salary deferrals under a 401(k) (or 403(b)) plan or SIMPLE. A less comprehensive definition can be selected, but must undergo scrutiny under rules that prohibit discrimination in favor of highly compensated employees. As a way to keep plan costs both predictable and under control, many employers choose base salary as the definition of compensation—excluding any extra pay such as bonuses, overtime, or commissions. Under the nondiscrimination rules, this definition would be a problem only if the rank-and-file employees received significant additional pay while the highly compensated did not.

final-average compensation

Just as meaningful is how *final-average compensation* is defined. Benefits could simply be based on the participant's final year (or highest year) of compensation—but this, too, could result in both higher and more unpredictable plan costs. It is more common to choose a definition such as the average of the final 3 (or 5) years' salary, or the average of the highest

3 (or 5) years' consecutive salary. Averaging the highest few years of salary serves the dual purpose of leveling off any abnormal years of compensation while providing a benefit that is tied to the individual's highest salary (providing preretirement inflation protection).

As with all types of qualified plans, compensation is capped at $225,000 (as indexed for 2007), meaning that compensation used for a particular year in the formula can not exceed that year's compensation cap.

Service

past service

Another important element of the defined-benefit formula is the definition of service. Many times years of service in the benefit formula only include years of active plan participation in which the participant earns a minimum of 1,000 hours of service. However, years of service could also include years of service prior to eligibility for the plan and/or service with the employer prior to plan inception.

This ability to provide for past service in the benefit structure is unique to defined-benefit plans. This feature can be particularly important to clients who are setting up a new plan for the benefit of long-service employees or to maximize the plan's tax-shelter potential for owner-employees and key employees. A plan that takes into consideration past service can provide the same benefit accrual for prior years or provide a smaller rate of accrual.

Form of Benefit

normal form of benefit payment

In a defined-benefit plan, the form of payment specified in the benefit formula is an essential characteristic of the plan benefit. The most common form of payment is a life annuity (meaning that payments continue only for as long as the participant lives). However, some plans will use a different form, such as a life annuity with a certain period of payments (typically 5 to 10 years)—meaning that the benefit will be payable for the longer of either life or the specified time period.

The form of payment has a direct effect on the value of the benefit. For example, a life annuity with 10-year certain payments of $1,000 a month is more valuable than a straight life annuity of $1,000 a month. This is significant when participants have the option to receive the benefit in other forms, because the optional forms of payment are almost always the actuarial equivalent of the normal form of payment. For example, if the life annuity with 10-year certain payments were converted to a single-sum benefit, the participant would receive more than if the conversion were based on the straight life annuity. (If this concept seems confusing, the discussion in chapter 26 regarding forms of payment should help to clarify.)

Finally, note that providing a benefit as a life annuity is very different from a defined-contribution plan, where the benefit is based on the account balance. With a defined-contribution plan, if the participant elects to receive a life annuity, the amount of the benefit payment will be based on the annuity that can be "purchased" with the single-sum amount. Another way of saying this is that in the defined-contribution plan, the normal form of payment is a single-sum amount.

Normal Retirement Age

Because defined-benefit plans generally provide benefits in the form of a life annuity, another factor that directly affects the value of the benefit is the date at which benefits can begin. The earlier the retirement age, the longer the payout period and the more valuable (and costly) the benefit. (This subject is discussed more in chapter 9.)

Elements of the Unit-Benefit Formula

Compensation	Base pay, taxable income, or some other nondiscriminatory definition
Final-average compensation	Typically takes the average of the highest 3–5 years of compensation
Years of service	Can count years of participation or years of service, even service prior to the plan set-up
Form of benefit	Typically a life annuity, or a life annuity with period certain
Normal retirement age	Typically 65 but can be age 62 or younger

Candidates for This Type of Plan

Unlike defined-contribution plans, defined-benefit plans can be designed to ensure that benefits replace a specified portion of the participant's preretirement income. But this type of plan comes with a fairly high price tag. Although there may be mitigating factors, such as integration of the plans with Social Security (see integration, chapter 8) and lower costs owing to better-than-expected investment return, defined-benefit plans remain expensive to fund. Also, the actuarial calculations involved make them costly to administer.

For the older business owner, the defined-benefit pension plan is a way to shelter larger amounts than can generally be contributed to a defined-contribution plan. This is because the time to fund for the benefit is short and the annual contributions required to fund the plan will be more significant. At the same time, the older business owner can create a significant retirement benefit over a short period of time, because past service can be factored into the retirement computation.

**YOUR FINANCIAL SERVICES PRACTICE:
DEFINED-BENEFIT PLANS FOR THE SMALL BUSINESS OWNER**

The defined-benefit plan may be a great fit for the business owner in his or her late 40s or early 50s, who has not accumulated sufficient assets for retirement. Unlike defined-contribution plans, there is no specific annual dollar limit (currently $45,000 in 2007) for contributions to defined-benefit plans. The law allows for the funding of a life annuity beginning at age 62 in the amount of the lesser of 100 percent of the final 3 years of salary or $180,000 (as indexed in 2007). Without specific facts, it is hard to identify the exact contribution amount required. But clearly for the 50-year-old owner who establishes a plan providing the maximum benefit, the cost could easily exceed $100,000 a year, significantly more than the maximum contribution to the defined-contribution plan.

A better way of looking at the issue may be to determine how much the individual needs to accumulate for retirement. If that amount exceeds the amount that can be accumulated—assuming $45,000 annual contributions plus investment return—over the remaining period to retirement, then a defined-benefit plan may be appropriate. Remember that with a defined-benefit plan, as long as certain requirements are met, the plan can pay out the present value of a $180,000 life annuity. The exact value depends on interest rates at the time of the distribution. Also, the maximum amount is indexed for inflation and will continue to increase over time. Given these uncertainties, it is still likely that the present value would be almost $2 million.

The Fact Finder

Candidates for defined-benefit pension plans fill out step 1 of the fact finder (see chapter 3) by grading the following as "very valuable":

- To what extent is it important to use a qualified plan as a tax shelter for owner-employees and key employees?
- To what extent is it important to maximize benefits for long-service employees by including service prior to the inception of the plan?

Candidates for a defined-benefit pension plan frequently grade these goals as "least valuable":

- placing the investment risk with the employee
- avoiding an annual financial commitment
- instituting a plan that has predictable costs

- instituting a plan that is administratively convenient
- instituting a plan that is easily communicated to employees

In addition, defined-benefit pension plan candidates fill out step 2 of the fact finder by answering "yes" to these questions: Is it more important to provide an adequate retirement standard of living than to cut plan costs? Is it more important to provide an adequate retirement standard of living than to have predictable costs? Is it more important to provide an adequate standard of living during retirement than to have administrative convenience and an easily communicated plan?

**YOUR FINANCIAL SERVICES PRACTICE:
GETTING MORE OUT OF DEFINED-BENEFIT PLANS
FOR LITTLE OR NO COST**

Surprisingly, many large- and medium-sized organizations find that employee enthusiasm about the firm's defined-benefit plan is low. However, because of the relative complexity of the defined-benefit plan, employees will not appreciate the plan without significant communication. Ways to improve the employee's appreciation of the plan would be to

- issue frequent and informative benefit statements
- rework the summary plan description (see chapter 13)
- set up periodic meetings to review benefits
- demonstrate how favorably an employee's defined-benefit plan compares with other retirement plans
- provide more general retirement planning seminars
- publicize the percentage of employee payroll used to fund the defined-benefit plan and the approximate cost of funding each participant's benefit

---

CASH-BALANCE PENSION PLANS

The cash-balance concept is a relatively new idea in pension plan design, with the first plan introduced in 1984. In its short history, it has been used primarily by large, and in some cases midsize, corporations as an alternative to the traditional defined-benefit plan. In fact, many of the cash-balance plans in existence today started as traditional defined-benefit plans that were later amended. The cash-balance plan is generally motivated by two factors: first, the selection of a benefit design that mirrors the defined-contribution approach, and second, cost savings.

cash-balance plan

The *cash-balance plan* is often referred to as a hybrid plan because it is a defined-benefit plan that is designed to look like a defined-contribution plan. As a defined-benefit plan, it has some level of funding flexibility and is subject to minimum funding requirements and the PBGC insurance program. At the same time, the defined-contribution-like design means it is easier to explain the benefit formula and also that the plan will provide a more portable benefit for today's mobile workforce.

The heart of the cash-balance plan is the benefit structure. As in the defined-contribution plan, the benefit is stated as an account balance that increases with contributions and investment experience. However, in a cash-balance plan the account is hypothetical. Annual credits (referred to as pay credits) are a bookkeeping credit only—no actual contributions are allocated to participants' accounts. Investment credits are also hypothetical and are based either on a rate specified in the plan or on an external index referenced in the plan. To the participants, however, this plan looks like a traditional defined-contribution "account balance" plan. When an individual terminates employment, the benefit payout is based on the value of the participant's hypothetical account. The following example illustrates how a cash-balance formula might appear.

Example: The participant is entitled to a single-sum benefit that is based on a pay credit of 5 percent of compensation each year. The credited amounts will accumulate with interest. Interest will be credited annually using the 30-year Treasury rate as of the valuation date.

Most typically, the contribution credit is stated as a percentage of the individual's current year's pay (for example, 5 percent of salary), or as a formula that considers both salary and years of service to reward those with longer service. For example, a formula can assign credits of 3 percent of salary for those with less than 5 years of service, 6 percent for those with 10 or more years of service, and 9 percent for 20-year veterans. Credits given for investment experience can be stated as a fixed, predetermined rate, a floating rate (based on some external index outside the control of the employer), or a combination of a fixed and floating rate, such as the rate of 30-year Treasury bonds. Also, because this is a defined-benefit plan, contribution and interest credits can be made for past years of service.

From the employer's perspective, this plan is still a defined-benefit plan. Contributions are required in the amount necessary to satisfy the minimum funding requirements. Under these rules, the employer has a degree of flexibility in determining the required contribution. Also, as in any defined-benefit plan, the employer is ultimately responsible for making contributions necessary to pay promised benefits—meaning that the sponsor is "on the hook" for the plan's investment experience. If trust assets earn a higher rate of return, then expected future contributions are reduced, and vice versa.

From the employee's perspective, the cash-balance design looks mostly like a defined-contribution plan. The only similarity to the defined-benefit approach is that benefits are guaranteed by the PBGC and the investment credits are not affected adversely by downturns in the market. In other ways, the cash-balance plan mirrors the strengths and weaknesses of the defined-contribution plan. Benefits accrue (depending on the formula) more evenly over the participant's career, meaning that benefits are not lost if the employee decides to change jobs. A cash-balance plan, like a defined-contribution plan, is easy to communicate. The contribution and interest credits are both easy to follow and may be more appreciated than a traditional defined-benefit plan. Similarly, the cash-balance plan does not have many of the strengths of the traditional defined-benefit approach. Benefits do not replace a specified percentage of preretirement income, and because benefits are not based on final salary, the benefit is not inflation adjusted up to the time benefits begin.

Advantages and Disadvantages

The fact that the cash-balance plan looks like a defined-contribution plan makes the plan easier for participants to understand. But the more interesting question is, looking at the plan as a defined-contribution substitute does it offer anything that a defined-contribution plan does not? The answer is yes. A cash-balance plan formula can establish credits for past service; in some circumstances, this is a big advantage over the defined-contribution plan.

From the participant's perspective, an actual defined-contribution plan will often result in a larger accumulation than the cash-balance plan. In an account plan, assets are generally invested with a long-term investment horizon. Participants sharing in the investment experience of a long-term stock-oriented portfolio will usually be better off than if they are credited with a small but steady rate of return. In a defined-contribution plan, benefits are fully funded at all times and are outside the reach of the employer's creditors. However, if a cash-balance plan is matched with a defined-contribution plan, such as a 401(k) plan, the participant has both the security of the fixed return in the cash-balance arrangement and the upside potential of the asset growth in the defined-contribution plan.

From the employer's perspective, the cash-balance approach offers some flexibility in funding (as compared to a money-purchase pension plan with a fixed contribution) and also the potential for cost savings. If plan assets, on average, outperform the promised rate of return, the employer will benefit through lower required contributions.

Legal Issues

Cash-balance plans have had a short but rough history. The earliest cash-balance plans were overfunded, large-company, defined-benefit plans that were converted to cash-balance arrangements. The conversion allowed the sponsor to switch to a defined-contribution type approach and seamlessly use the excess assets to fund future benefit promises. Under a cash-balance conversion, the former defined-benefit promise usually is frozen at the current accrued benefit level, and the benefit is stated as its single-sum equivalent. Benefits accruing after the change simply increase the total account balance.

Several large employers who converted traditional defined-benefit plans to cash-balance plans received bad publicity afterward. There were two primary issues: (1) a lack of communication—employees did not understand the change and (2) older employees were not fully informed that their overall benefits would be lower than they were under the old plan. In response, other employers converting to the cash-balance approach protected older employees by grandfathering the old benefit formula or giving them a larger annual credit under the new formula. Congress responded to the controversy by amending ERISA to require full disclosure to participants of any plan amendment that reduces future benefit accruals.

On another legal front, employees have filed a number of age discrimination suits arguing that cash-balance plans inherently discriminate against older workers. The argument is that since pay credits for older workers accrue interest for a shorter period of time, the monthly retirement accruals for an older worker will be smaller than for a younger one. Several courts have looked favorably on this argument.

However, Congress thought differently, and the Pension Protection Act of 2006 validated the cash-balance approach. The law clarifies that a cash-balance plan that provides an accrued benefit based on an accumulated account balance can demonstrate nondiscrimination if all participants with the same salary and years of service are similarly situated—regardless of age. For example, if all participants receive a pay credit of 5 percent of compensation, the plan will satisfy the nondiscrimination requirement.

The Pension Protection Act of 2006 added other new rules for cash-balance arrangements. The law provides that cash-balance plans must fully vest participants once they have attained 3 years of service. This is in contrast to the 5-year cliff vesting or 7-year graded vesting options available for other defined-benefit plans. The law also imposes limits on investment credits. The credit can not exceed a "market rate of return." The rules, however, do allow a plan to provide for a reasonable minimum guaranteed rate of return, or for a rate of return that is equal to the greater of a fixed or variable rate of return. Also, the investment credit cannot be less than zero.

The Pension Protection Act also clarifies several other issues that have been litigated in the past. First, a lump-sum benefit payment from a cash-balance plan can simply equal the hypothetical account balance. The plan does not have to look to the interest rate used to calculate lump-sum benefits in traditional defined-benefit plans.

The law also clarifies the process for converting traditional defined-benefit plans into cash-balance formulas. The key issue is the appropriate method of calculating the accrued benefit under the plan. Under the new law, each participant's benefits after the conversion must equal the sum of the pre-conversion benefit under the prior plan formula and the post-conversion benefit under the hybrid formula. In addition, a special conversion rule preserves the value of early retirement subsidies associated with benefits accrued under the prior formula.

Candidates for This Type of Plan

The Pension Protection Act has eliminated much of the legal uncertainty surrounding cash-balance arrangements. In doing so, we may very well see a return to large and midsize employers converting traditional defined-benefit plans into cash-balance arrangements. The conversion allows the employer to switch to a defined-contribution approach, and potentially limit benefits and funding exposure. Clearly the funding obligation for cash-balance plans is less volatile than with traditional defined-benefit plans as both pay credits, and investment credits are relatively predictable. As we will discuss in chapter 14, in many cases defined-benefit plans that are underfunded are not allowed to terminate. However, in most cases a cash-balance amendment would be allowed and can be used as a way to reduce future benefit accruals (as compared with the defined-benefit formula).

Cash-balance plans should also find a place as new plans—especially in the small-plan market—for one important reason: the maximum contribution on behalf of the owner can exceed the Sec. 415(c) dollar limitation. For older business owners looking to shelter a significant amount of income, the cash-balance arrangement becomes an alternative to a traditional defined-benefit plan design. With this design, the sponsor can (as long as the nondiscrimination rules are satisfied) make large contributions for the owner-employees while providing contributions as the level percentage of compensation for rank-and-file employees. The down side to the cash-balance plan will be that this approach has many of the headaches of a defined-benefit plan: PBGC premiums, administrative costs, and satisfaction of the minimum funding requirements. However, the minimum-funding rules do allow for more funding flexibility than with a traditional money-purchase or target-benefit plan.

YOUR FINANCIAL SERVICES PRACTICE:
PENSION PROTECTION ACT TAKES CASH-BALANCE PLANS OUT
OF LEGAL LIMBO

Employee lawsuits arguing that cash-balance plans discriminate against older employees and the IRS's reluctance to give determination letters for cash-balance plans have put these plans in legal limbo for a number of years. The Pension Protection Act of 2006 eliminates this uncertainty and gives support to the cash-balance concept. With this law change, cash-balance conversions and new cash-balance plans may be back in favor. Under the new rules:

- The accrued benefit as well as single sum payouts can be based on a hypothetical account balance that consists of pay and investment credits.
- Benefits of equal present value are considered nondiscriminatory regardless of the ages of the participants.
- Participants with 3 or more years of vesting service must be 100 percent vested.
- The rate used for investment credits can not exceed a reasonable market rate of return or be less than zero.
- With plan conversions the benefit accrual must be equal to the accrual under the old formula plus the accrual under the cash-balance formula.
- With plan conversions early retirement subsidies have to be considered in calculating accrued benefits.

MONEY-PURCHASE PENSION PLANS

A money-purchase pension plan falls within both the defined-contribution and pension categories. Knowing this means you already know that money-purchase pension plans have the following characteristics:

- The maximum annual additions for individual participants are limited by Code Sec. 415(c).
- Participants in the plan have individual accounts that are similar to bank accounts.
- Participants assume the risk of preretirement inflation, investment performance, and adequacy of retirement income.
- The plan can not provide for past service.
- Administrative costs are relatively low.
- The plan is easily communicated to employees.
- The plan has predictable employer costs.
- The employer is required to fund the plan annually.
- Participants may not take in-service withdrawals prior to age 62.

- The employer can deduct up to 25 percent of compensation.
- Investments in company stock are limited to 10 percent of the plan's assets.

money-purchase
pension plan

Under a *money-purchase pension plan*, the company's annual contributions are based on a percentage of each participant's compensation. For example, the money-purchase contribution formula may provide that annual contributions will equal 10 percent of compensation for each participant (if Karen Lamb earns $40,000, the annual contribution placed in her account is $4,000). Money-purchase plan benefits for each employee are the amounts that can be provided by the sums contributed to the employee's individual account plus investment earnings. For example, if Karen Lamb worked for 20 years and her salary remained at $40,000, at retirement she would have $80,000 plus accumulated interest of $58,876 (assuming a 5 percent annual rate) in her account. The term *money-purchase* arose because the participant's account is traditionally used to purchase an annuity that provides monthly retirement benefits.

A money-purchase plan is used to provide a fixed contribution and, therefore, gives employees the sense that it is a substantial and permanent retirement plan. Typically, these organizations provide between 3 and 12 percent of compensation as the annual contribution. Self-employed people provide another market for money-purchase plans (they like the money-purchase plan's simplicity). For example, a self-employed person may express a desire to tax-shelter 15 percent of his or her earned income for retirement.

Advantages and Disadvantages

Money-purchase pension plans can be likened to the station wagons of the retirement fleet because of their dependable annual contributions and simple, basic design. The major advantages of money-purchase pension plans are the predictable costs for the employer (because contributions are based on employee compensation, the employer contribution is basically a percentage of payroll), administrative ease, and understandability for the employees. Corporate objectives, such as competitiveness, attraction, and retention of key employees, can be met within the money-purchase framework without being prohibitively expensive for the employer.

One major drawback of a money-purchase plan (or, for that matter, any defined contribution plan) is that contributions are based on the participant's salary for each year of his or her career, rather than on the salary at retirement. Given a stable inflationary environment, this may not have a negative effect on the adequacy of retirement income. If inflation spirals in the years prior to retirement, however, the chances of achieving an adequate income-replacement ratio are diminished. Take, for example, someone who earned an average middle-class income and whose career spanned the 1950s, 1960s, and 1970s. In 1950, this person earned $2,000 and received a 10 percent money-purchase contribution of $200. In 1960, the employee earned $12,000 and received a 10 percent money-purchase contribution of $1,200. In 1970, the employee earned $24,000 and received a $2,400 contribution. During the 1970s, double-digit inflation hit, and salary levels increased to account for the increased cost of living. If the participant retired in 1980, he or she would be at a disadvantage because only part of the plan contributions would account for the inflationary period right before retirement. What's more, most of the annual contributions would be based on deflated salaries that accrued before the inflationary spiral. If a defined-benefit plan were chosen that calculated benefits based on final average compensation, the participant would have received some inflation protection through the operation of the benefit formula.

A second drawback, also applicable to all defined-contribution plans, is the inability to provide an adequate retirement program for older participants. Those who enter money-purchase pension plans later in their careers have less time to accumulate sufficient assets.

However, money-purchase pension plans can work, given the right set of circumstances.

Example 1:   New employee Bill Nelson is 55 years old and has no other retirement funds except Social Security. Nelson earns $50,000 annually and plans to retire at age 65. The money-purchase pension formula calls for 10 percent of salary to be deposited in Nelson's account each year. The account earns 10 percent annually. Under this accumulation scheme, Nelson will have $79,687 at age 65. Even after combining this with Social Security, Nelson's income will not be adequate to continue his preretirement standard of living.

Example 2:   New employee Gloria Benson is 35 years old and has no other retirement funds except Social Security. Benson earns $50,000 annually and plans to retire at age 65. The money-purchase formula calls for 10 percent of salary to be deposited in Benson's account each year. The account earns 10 percent annually. Under this accumulation scheme, $822,470 will be amassed at retirement. Combined with Social Security, Benson's income is likely to be adequate during the retirement years to maintain the same standard of living.

Candidates for money-purchase plans are businesses with

- a steady cash flow
- young, well-paid key employees
- a stable workforce (low turnover)
- the need for easily communicated employee benefits

Money-purchase candidates disclose on the fact finder that it is less important to provide an adequate retirement standard of living than to have predictable costs, and that it is more important to have administrative convenience and an easily communicated plan than to provide an adequate retirement standard of living.

TARGET-BENEFIT PENSION PLANS

target-benefit pension plan

A *target-benefit pension plan* is a money-purchase pension plan that has a specialized benefit structure. As a money-purchase plan it is a defined-contribution plan in the pension category, and all of the characteristics described above that apply to the money-purchase plan apply to the target plan as well. What makes the structure of a target-benefit plan unique is that contributions are determined in a way that is similar to a defined-benefit plan. For that reason we often refer to a target plan as a hybrid plan design—it is a defined-contribution plan that in some ways looks like a defined-benefit plan.

A defined-benefit plan has a specified benefit formula and the actuary then determines the required contribution to fund the targeted benefit. Similarly, a target-benefit pension plan identifies a targeted benefit at retirement, and contributions are made in the amount necessary to fund the targeted amount. The plan specifies the actuarial method and interest rates used to determine annual contributions so that the amount of contribution can be clearly determined. Unlike a defined-benefit plan, however, the contribution amounts will not change each year based on the value of the plan's assets. Contributions only change to reflect new plan participants and increases in the compensation of existing plan participants. For the sake of convenience and simplicity, the plan is often equipped with a chart indicating contribution levels; an actuary is seldom needed after the plan's inception (see figure 4-1).

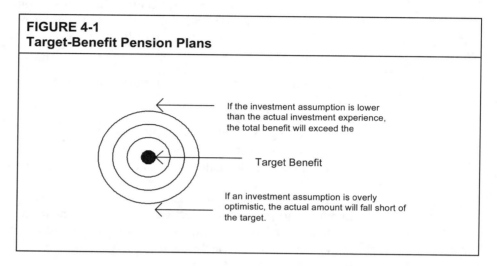

FIGURE 4-1
Target-Benefit Pension Plans

If the investment assumption is lower than the actual investment experience, the total benefit will exceed the

Target Benefit

If an investment assumption is overly optimistic, the actual amount will fall short of the target.

What is fundamentally different about target plans and defined-benefit plans is that with a target plan the contributions are allocated to the participant's account. The participant's benefit will be the value of the account balance and not the promised monthly retirement benefit. The account balance should approximate the amount needed to provide the targeted retirement benefit, but it will be more or less based on the plan's actual investment experience.

TABLE 4-2
Hybrid Plans: Mirrors of Each Other

Target-Benefit Pension Plan	Cash-Balance Pension Plan
Defined-contribution plan	Defined-benefit plan
Not subject to PBGC	Subject to PBGC
Participant entitled to vested account balance	Participant entitled to promised benefit regardless of actual plan assets
Feels like a defined-benefit plan because contributions target a monthly benefit at retirement	Feels like a defined-contribution plan because promised benefit is based on an accumulated hypothetical account balance
Contribution is fixed based on the contribution formula	Contribution is variable based on the actuarial determination

The scheme allows the employer to provide a benefit that attempts to replace a specified portion of the participant's salary without taking on the same risk as a defined-benefit plan. The target-benefit design also can be a good way to provide larger contributions for older, more highly compensated employees. For the business owner with mostly younger employees, this plan design is a way to direct a large percentage of the contribution to the business owner. The plan design, however, is not popular today, since similar results can be had with a profit-sharing plan using an age-weighted or cross-tested contribution formula (discussed in later chapters). The profit-sharing approach is more flexible because the employer is never required to make specific contributions.

CHAPTER REVIEW

Key Terms

unit-benefit formula [4-1]	final-average compensation [4-1]
income-replacement ratio [4-1]	past service [4-2]
flat-percentage-of-earnings formula [4-1]	normal form of benefit payment [4-2]
flat-amount-per-year-of-service formula [4-1]	cash-balance plan [4-3]
flat-amount formula [4-1]	money-purchase pension plan [4-4]
	target-benefit pension plan [4-5]

Review Questions

Review questions are based on the learning objectives in this chapter. Thus, a [4-3] at the end of a question means that the question is based on learning objective 4-3. If there are multiple objectives, they are all listed.

1. Ralph Camdon, the owner of a local tour bus company, would like to establish a defined-benefit plan that helps to retain and reward experienced personnel, that rewards owner-employees and key employees who have high salaries, and that provides an income-replacement ratio of 60 percent for "career" employees. [4-1]
   a. What type of benefit formula should Ralph use in his plan? Explain.
   b. Give an example of how the benefit formula should be written.

2. In what situations are flat-amount-per-year-of-service formulas typically used? [4-1]

3. Describe a flat-amount formula. [4-1]

4. a. Explain how the definitions of *compensation* and *final-average compensation* affect the participant's benefit.
   b. If the normal form of benefit is a life annuity, does this have the same value if the normal form of benefit is a life annuity with 10-year certain payments?
   c. Does a life annuity payable at a normal retirement age of 65 have the same value as a life annuity payable at age 62? [4-2]

5. Why would an employer choose to account for past service in the defined-benefit plan? [4-2]

6. What can the defined-benefit plan offer the older small business owner that a defined-contribution plan cannot? [4-2]

7. Explain the following about cash-balance plans: [4-3]
   a. Is the cash-balance plan a defined-benefit or defined-contribution type of plan?
   b. What makes the cash-balance benefit formula different from a traditional defined-benefit plan?
   c. Why do employers with traditional defined-benefit plans choose to amend them into cash-balance plans?

8. What are the major advantages and disadvantages of a money-purchase plan? [4-4]

9. Dr. Debbie Dwyer runs her own veterinary clinic, Pet Care, Inc. Dr. Dwyer is 56 years old and has never set up a qualified plan for her practice. Dr. Dwyer has two younger employees whom she would like to include in a retirement plan, but she cannot afford to pay too much. In fact, Dr. Dwyer can afford to save only 20 percent of her $100,000 salary. What type of pension plan should Dr. Dwyer adopt? Explain. [4-5]

10. Indicate what type of plan from the pension category you would recommend in each of the following situations: [4-5]
    a. Candidate Able owns a business that has a steady cash flow, young, well-paid key employees, and a low turnover rate. Able's objectives are to adopt a plan that has predictable costs, has a clearly stated contribution for employee security, is administratively convenient, and is easily communicated to employees.
    b. Candidate Baker wants to have a plan that provides for a contribution for himself that is well in excess of the Code Sec. 415(c) annual addition limit. He would like to provide a benefit structure that is similar to the account plan approach of a defined-contribution plan.

c. Candidate Charley has indicated that the following objectives are very important: (1) maximizing benefits for older owner-employees and key employees, (2) maximizing benefits for older employees, (3) maximizing benefits for long-service employees, and (4) providing a predictable pension in retirement that replaces a percentage of the participant's salary.

Profit-Sharing Plans, 401(k) Plans, Stock Bonus Plans, and ESOPs

---

Learning Objectives

An understanding of the material in this chapter should enable you to

---

5-1. Describe the characteristics of a profit-sharing plan that make it a popular plan design.

5-2. Identify the basic features of a 401(k) plan.

5-3. Describe the special nondiscrimination rules and withdrawal restrictions that apply to 401(k) plans.

5-4. Explain the Roth 401(k) tax election, affirmative elections, and the requirements of the plan asset regulations.

5-5. Describe how stock bonus plans and ESOPs differ from profit-sharing plans.

Chapter Outline

Let's turn our attention to qualified plans that are not necessarily intended to provide a pension at retirement. Unlike the pension plans discussed in chapter 4, profit-sharing plans, 401(k) plans, stock bonus plans, and employee stock ownership plans (ESOPs) are often designed to distribute organizational earnings on a tax-sheltered basis with only a partial regard to meeting retirement needs. Historically, these plans have been considered more of a tax shelter for deferred income than a retirement system that will provide an adequate pension in the retirement years. More recently, however, these plans have become an important tool for employers to meet the need for an adequate pension in the following ways:

- They have become part of a comprehensive retirement package that combines these plans with other plans to fund for retirement needs.
- They have become "pensionlike" in their actual application. (for example, regular reoccurring substantial contributions, even if the employer has no profits).

PROFIT-SHARING PLANS IN GENERAL

A profit-sharing plan is a defined-contribution plan that also falls within the profit-sharing category. (*Planning Note:* Do not be confused by the fact that profit sharing is both a category of plan and a type of plan.) Before we begin to discuss the specifics of this plan, we already know the following:

- Employer contributions are discretionary.
- The plan allows for in-service withdrawals.
- The plan can conceivably invest up to 100 percent of its assets in the sponsoring company's stock.
- The maximum annual contribution that an employee can receive is the lesser of 100 percent of compensation or $45,000.
- Participants in the plan have individual accounts that are similar to bank accounts.
- The employee assumes the risk of preretirement inflation, investment performance, and adequacy of retirement income.
- The plan cannot provide for past service.

- Administrative costs are relatively low.
- The plan is easily communicated to employees.
- The employer can deduct up to 25 percent of compensation.

There are two parts to the contribution formula in a profit-sharing plan. One relates to how much the company contributes to the plan and the other applies to how the contribution is allocated among the participants. Let's take a closer look.

Contributions

From the employer's perspective, one of the primary strengths of a profit-sharing plan is that the employer can make contributions on a discretionary basis. In addition, since 1987, an employer can make a contribution to a plan whether or not there are profits. However, there is one limitation: contributions must be "substantial and recurring" over the years or the IRS could determine that the plan has been terminated. The result of this is that all participants become fully vested. (See chapter 14 for a further discussion of this issue.)

Most plans written today specify that the board of directors makes the decision each year as to whether to make contributions and/or how much to contribute. Whether a company actually contributes more in a good financial year is a business decision. However, if the employer is trying to use the plan to motivate participants, there should be a clear relationship between the company's performance and contributions made to the plan.

Another way to address the issue of employee motivation is to write the plan to require a specified contribution. One way to do this is to state the required contribution as a specified percentage of profits or some other objective formula stated in the plan. This approach is appropriate when the employer wants employees to feel they have a clear and determinable stake in the company's performance. Another way is to stipulate that a certain percentage of each participant's salary will be contributed each year. For example, the company will contribute 10 percent of a participant's compensation. This type of contribution requirement allows the employer to use the profit-sharing plan in the same manner as a money-purchase pension plan, in which the corporate goal is typically to provide an adequate pension benefit, not to provide a vehicle for employees to share in company profits.

Allocation Formulas

The heart of a profit-sharing plan is the method of allocating the employer contribution among the participants. This formula must be definite and predetermined. Historically, the most common allocation formula allocates the total contribution so each participant receives a contribution that is the same percentage of compensation (for example, 3 percent or 5 percent). This allocation formula in the plan document would read something like

> "Employer contributions made for the year will be allocated, as of the last day of each plan year, to each participant's account in the proportion that the participant's compensation bears to the total compensation of all eligible participants for the plan year."

YOUR FINANCIAL SERVICES PRACTICE: GETTING THE MOST MILEAGE OUT OF THE PLAN

Employers never enjoy spending money on retirement benefits that employees do not appreciate. Because a profit-sharing plan typically does not require a specified employer contribution, it may be difficult to get employees to appreciate the value of the plan. To get the most out of the plan, the employer should consider taking the following steps:

- Clearly communicate the amount of the contribution and how it was derived.
- Make regular and reoccurring contributions, if at all possible.
- Provide clear and comprehensive benefit statements.
- Identify circumstances that would result in larger employer contributions.

Under this type of allocation formula, for example, if the employer contributed $10,000, total payroll was $100,000, and Alexander earned $25,000, he would have an allocation of $2,500 ($10,000 x $25,000/$100,000). If Barbara earned $30,000, her allocation would be $3,000 ($10,000 x $30,000/$100,000). As you can see, the employer contributed 10 percent of payroll and each participant received an allocation of 10 percent of his or her compensation.

This allocation formula has been popular, in part because it is clear that it satisfies the requirement of Code Sec. 401(a)(4), which requires that contributions or benefits do not discriminate in favor of highly compensated employees. Other ways to allocate contributions include integration with Social Security and newer methods, such as age-weighting and cross-testing. (All of these allocation methods are discussed fully in chapter 8.) As you will see, these allocation formulas add a whole new dimension to the profit-sharing plan, allowing this simple, versatile plan to skew contributions to older (and, not coincidentally, more highly compensated) business owners. Allocation formulas also can be designed to meet any number of other compensation objectives.

> **YOUR FINANCIAL SERVICES PRACTICE:**
> **SWITCHING INVESTMENT CARRIERS**
>
> Frequently, when you are prospecting in the retirement field, you will encounter an established plan that is invested with a competitor. The emergence of new ideas, like cross-testing or age-weighting, can be a useful weapon in fighting the uphill battle of converting already-spoken-for assets. Even if the new design does not fit the needs of these prospective clients, at the very least you will be regarded as someone who is in touch with current trends and who is on the cutting edge of your profession. Future dealings can stem from this favorable impression.

Advantages of a Profit-Sharing Plan to the Business and Business Owner

Even though the profit-sharing plan does not provide the most secure benefit to employees, it is an extremely flexible vehicle that is a very popular choice. Some of the organizational objectives these plans serve are:

discretionary contributions

- allowing *discretionary contributions*—Because the plan can be designed with no predetermined formula, the employer has the option of not making contributions in a given year (for example, the plan may provide that contributions, if any, will be determined annually by the board of directors).
- permitting withdrawal flexibility—Plans can be designed to allow employees to withdraw funds from participant accounts as early as 2 years after they were contributed by the employer.
- controlling benefit costs—Organizations find that adopting a profit-sharing plan is a fiscally responsible move. The organization will not be saddled with cash-flow problems caused by mandatory contributions. Flexibility is especially important for employers with fluctuating profits.
- improving productivity—Another cost advantage is profit sharing's correlation to productivity. Many believe these plans help to increase employee identification with the employer and provide an incentive to employees. This increased productivity can be viewed as a way to maximize the cost-effectiveness of the employer's contributions. The old saying "You have to spend more to get more" applies here, however.

- providing legal discrimination in favor of older owner-employees—The profit-sharing plan can be set up to give (allocate) the majority of the profits to older, high-salaried owner-employees. When used in this manner, the profit-sharing plan makes an excellent tax shelter for the older business owner. This approach also lowers contributions for rank-and-file employees (see chapter 8).

Disadvantages of a Profit-Sharing Plan to the Business and Business Owner

A profit-sharing plan is an extremely versatile vehicle for a small business. However, as compared to other types of plans, there are a few disadvantages. The primary one is that rank-and-file employees might perceive the plan as a hollow benefit if discretionary contributions are not made or if the lion's share of profits goes to the business owner. As discussed above, this problem can be mitigated through good communication with employees.

Profit Sharing Plans: A Summary of the Rules

- **Contributions**—discretionary unless otherwise specified in the plan
- **Allocation formula**—must have a definite and predetermined formula for allocating the contribution among participants. Allocating based on compensation or integration with Social Security is common, with other formulas possible as long as the plan can satisfy a nondiscrimination test.
- **In-service withdrawals**—if allowed by the plan, benefits can be distributed to active participants as long as the participants have met the plan's conditions
- **Maximum contribution**—like other defined contribution plans, the maximum contribution is 25 percent of the payroll of all participants
- **Employer securities**—like other profit-sharing type plans, the plan can invest more than 10 percent of its assets in employer securities
- **Other provisions**—subject to eligibility and vesting requirements that apply to qualified plans

Candidates for Profit-Sharing Plans

Because of the profit-sharing plan's incredible versatility, a large number of companies are candidates for profit-sharing plans. These include businesses with

- cash-flow problems
- less economic stability (for example, new businesses and capital-intensive businesses)
- young, well-paid key employees
- no desire to ensure the adequacy of an employee's retirement income

Candidates for profit-sharing plans fill out the fact finder typically by grading the following as "very valuable":

- placing the investment risk on the employee
- avoiding an annual financial commitment
- allowing employees (including owner-employees) to withdraw funds. (If this is the case, design the plan to allow withdrawals after 2 years; if this is not the case, a profit-sharing plan may still be implemented but withdrawal restrictions should be incorporated.)
- motivating the workforce

YOUR FINANCIAL SERVICES PRACTICE:
LIFE INSURANCE AND PROFIT-SHARING PLANS

Profit-sharing plans have a unique need that can be met through the purchase of life insurance. In addition to using life insurance to fund participants' accounts (discussed in chapter 12), life insurance can be purchased on the client's key people (owner-employees, key employees, and officers) as a general asset of the profit-sharing trust. The profit-sharing trust is permitted to make this purchase because it has an insurable interest in the client's key people. This insurable interest stems from the fact that company profits are generally required to fund the profit-sharing trust and that these people are primarily responsible for these company profits. Here's how it works:

- Insurance contracts are purchased out of unallocated assets given to the trust by the organization.
- The insurance contracts are owned by the trust, which pays the premiums and is also the named beneficiary.
- Because the contracts are not allocated to participant accounts, the percentage limitation applied under the incidental death benefit rules (see chapter 10) is not applicable.
- Upon the death of the insured, the insurance proceeds are paid to the trust and are then typically allocated among participants on the basis of each participant's account balance.

Candidates for a profit-sharing plan typically grade the following goals as "least valuable":

- maximizing benefits for long-service employees by accounting for past service
- providing a specified replacement ratio

Profit-sharing candidates typically answer "yes" to the fact finder question: Is it more important to motivate employees than to attract or retain them? And they typically answer "no" to these fact finder questions: Is it more important to provide an adequate retirement standard of living than to allow employees (including owner-employees) to withdraw funds? Is it more important to provide an adequate retirement standard of living than to have predictable costs?

Candidates for a profit-sharing plan usually put contribution flexibility at the head of their priority list, usually opt for a low income-replacement ratio, and typically come from an organization or industry with an unstable cash-flow history.

With the flexibility in allocation formulas available today, profit-sharing candidates also include those businesses interested in providing a lion's share of the benefits for the key employees while minimizing the cost of benefits for the rank-and-file employee. This can be done quite effectively using the age-weighted and cross-tested allocation formulas discussed briefly above and in more depth in chapter 8. At one time, employers with this goal looked either to the defined-benefit plan or the target-benefit plan. Today, the profit-sharing plan allows for similar skewing of the contribution to the targeted group while maintaining the flexibility of the profit-sharing plan.

YOUR FINANCIAL SERVICES PRACTICE:
PROFIT-SHARING PLANS BECOME EVEN MORE FLEXIBLE

By increasing the maximum deductible contribution limit in profit-sharing plans from 15 percent to 25 percent of compensation, the Economic Growth and Tax Relief Reconciliation Act of 2001 (EGTRRA) eliminated the need for small employers to maintain two defined-contribution plans. Before the law change, a common strategy for the sole proprietor or small-business owner was to establish a 10 percent money-purchase plan and a profit-sharing plan. This strategy enabled the owner to contribute up to 25 percent of compensation while retaining some contribution flexibility. Now this objective can be accomplished within the single more flexible profit-sharing plan. Small businesses that have been maintaining two plans might consider consolidation in order to limit administrative costs.

CASH OR DEFERRED ARRANGEMENTS—401(k) PLANS

cash or deferred arrangement (CODA)

An option that is available under a profit-sharing plan (or a stock bonus plan, which is discussed next) is the *cash or deferred arrangement (CODA)*.

When the CODA option is part of a profit-sharing or stock bonus plan, that plan is usually referred to as a 401(k) plan (401(k) is the section number in the Internal Revenue Code that outlines CODAs). A 401(k) plan allows plan participants to defer taxation on a portion of regular salary or bonuses simply by electing to have such amounts contributed to the plan instead of receiving them in cash. Participants enjoy abundant tax savings. For example, if Simms is in the 28 percent marginal tax bracket and elects to reduce his salary by $6,000, he will save $1,680 in taxes. That is like having Uncle Sam as a contributing partner in Simms's retirement savings. What is more, the money Simms puts in the plan earns tax-deferred interest until retirement. If Simms encounters financial problems, he may decrease his future contributions or discontinue contributions altogether simply by changing his salary reduction agreement (the form that authorizes the employer to reduce the salary and make plan contributions in the amount of the reduction).

Today, almost all large private employers and many midsize companies sponsor such plans (often in addition to sponsoring more a traditional plan such as a defined-benefit or money-purchase pension plan). The plan is starting to expand into the small-plan market as well, and today it is the most popular new plan to install.

401(k) Plan Design

Remember that a 401(k) plan is a profit-sharing (or occasionally a stock bonus) plan that contains a salary deferral (401(k)) feature. This means that, in addition to the salary deferral feature, the plan can also contain a traditional profit-sharing feature, an employer-matching contribution feature, or both; it may even allow for employee after-tax contributions. This means the plan can

stand-alone plan

be as simple as a *stand-alone plan* (salary deferrals only) or as complex as a plan that allows pretax and after-tax employee contributions, employer matching contributions, and employer profit-sharing contributions.

A stand-alone plan (a plan that allows only pretax salary deferrals) can be used by an organization that cannot afford a comprehensive retirement program. The stand-alone plan can be expanded and enhanced in the future as the sponsor's financial strength grows. It can also be established as a supplement to other retirement plans.

The employer that wants to combine salary deferrals with additional employer contributions to the same plan can choose how to spend those dollars—as matching or as profit-sharing contributions. A common practice

matching contribution

today is to choose a *matching contribution* feature in which the plan sponsor agrees to match employee savings to a certain extent. For example, the sponsor might agree to contribute 50 cents to the plan for each dollar the employee saves, up to the first 6 percent of compensation that the participant saves. In this example, the maximum employer match is 3 percent of compensation.

Both the matching percentage and the maximum match must be carefully chosen to meet the employer's objectives and budget. The primary reason for the match is to stimulate plan participation through the offer of an instant return on the participant's savings. Another goal is to create a retirement planning partnership between the employer and the participants. Under this philosophy, an employer is committed to contribute toward an employee's funds for retirement, but only if the employee is willing to save for retirement. Finally, the feature can act as a profit-sharing incentive.

To meet specific employer objectives, the design of the matching contribution can be as straightforward as described above, or more complex—such as a graded formula in which the matching contribution rate varies for different levels of salary deferrals. Under a typical graded formula, the employer contributes 50 cents for each dollar saved by the plan participant, up to 4 percent of covered earnings, plus 25 cents for each dollar saved over 4 percent, but not more than 6 percent of covered earnings. Matching contributions can also be made on a discretionary basis. Because the uncertainty of the employer's contribution might discourage plan participation, it is more common to provide a small, guaranteed matching contribution, which can be made larger at the employer's discretion.

YOUR FINANCIAL SERVICES PRACTICE:
401(k) PLANS FOR THE SMALL BUSINESS

Even with the popularity of 401(k) plans, only a small portion of small businesses sponsor them—meaning there is still a lot of opportunity for the financial services professional. Open doors to new clients with the following points:

- Administration costs are often lower today than before because many organizations have designed simplified "cookie cutter"-type packages.
- If the sponsor already has a profit-sharing plan, point out that a 401(k) feature can be added to that plan, and a second plan is not needed.
- A small employer with a state-of-the-art 401(k) plan can better compete for, and retain, employees.
- The opportunity to design a 401(k) plan to include a safe harbor contribution that eliminates the need for nondiscrimination or top-heavy testing makes it much easier for a small employer to maintain a 401(k) plan.
- A 401(k) feature combined with an age-weighted or cross-tested profit-sharing plan could allow the business owner to maximize his or her own contribution and lower the cost of benefits for rank-and-file employees.
- If employers like the salary deferral concept, but still feel that the plan is too complex, they should consider the SIMPLE IRA (see chapter 6).

The matching contribution can also vary for different groups of employees as long as the nondiscrimination test referred to as the actual contribution percentage test (ACP) can be satisfied. For example, the employer could provide a 50 percent match on the first 6 percent deferred for those employees with less than 5 years of service, a 75 percent match for those with 5 or more years of service, and a 100 percent match for those with 10 or more years of service.

A profit-sharing feature in a 401(k) plan works the same way as in a traditional profit-sharing plan. Contributions are made for eligible participants, regardless of whether they make salary deferral contributions. When the 401(k) plan is the only plan sponsored by the employer, it is not uncommon—in a good year—for the sponsor to make both matching contributions and profit-sharing-type contributions.

Also, note that a 401(k) plan can include employee after-tax contributions in addition to employee pretax salary deferrals. This feature is not that common, but is occasionally included—primarily because employees like the withdrawal flexibility of after-tax contributions. These contributions do not have to be subject to the withdrawal restrictions that apply to pretax contributions (as discussed below). This feature is common in older plans that were converted from after-tax thrift plans. In this case, some employees are more secure with the old way of doing things.

Note that when a plan has more than just salary deferrals, it must have separate bookkeeping accounts for each type of contribution. This requirement is due in part to the fact that the accounts attributable to employer matching and profit-sharing contributions are subject to the same rules that apply to a traditional profit-sharing plan, while the salary deferral account is subject to the special rules described below.

Salary Deferral Limitations

The heart of the 401(k) plan is the salary deferral feature. In most plans, participants are allowed to make salary deferral elections from their regular paycheck. Often the deferral amount is expressed as a percentage of pay or as a specified dollar amount. Occasionally, the plan will also allow for salary deferral elections of extraordinary pay, like bonuses. Another option is for **automatic enrollment** the employer to provide for *automatic enrollment* in which a specified amount is withdrawn from each paycheck unless the individual elects out of the deferral option. More and more employers are choosing automatic enrollment because it often has a positive effect on the plan's participation rate. Also, the Pension Protection Act of 2006 eliminated several legal impediments to this approach.

Regardless of the methodology for making the salary reduction, salary deferral amounts can never exceed a specified limit for a calendar year. For 2007, the limit is $15,500. In addition, the maximum salary deferral is increased for those individuals who have attained age 50 by the end of the current year. For 2007, the additional allowable contribution is $5,000.

It is important to understand that this maximum salary deferral limit to a 401(k) plan applies to the individual. This means that all salary deferral contributions made by that individual to any 401(k) plan, Code Sec. 403(b) annuity, simplified employee pension (SEP), or savings incentive match plan for employees (SIMPLE) will be treated as one plan under the rules. This is even true for an individual who works for a number of unrelated employers.

Example:	Ina Thrifty, aged 52, is a doctor doing research for Drug Co., which maintains a 401(k) plan. For 2007, Ina plans to make the maximum $20,500 salary deferral contribution ($15,500 plus the $5,000 catch-up). Ina is also in a group medical practice (which is unrelated to Drug Co.). The practice also has a 401(k) plan. Unfortunately, Ina cannot make any salary deferral contributions to that plan because the maximum deferral limit applies to all plans in which she participates.

Special Rules That Apply to 401(k) Salary Deferrals

The 401(k) salary deferral part of the profit-sharing plan is subject to a number of special rules:

- 401(k) salary reductions are immediately 100 percent vested and cannot be forfeited.
- In-service withdrawals can be made only if an individual has attained age 59½ or has a financial hardship.
- Salary deferral contributions are considered plan assets and must be contributed to the trust within a reasonable time period.
- An extra nondiscrimination test called the *actual deferral percentage (ADP) test* applies to salary deferral amounts.

Vesting

Technically, amounts contributed to the plan under a salary deferral election are considered employer contributions—even though they are made at the election of the participant. Still, such amounts are treated somewhat differently from how other employer contributions are treated. Normally, employer contributions can be subject to a vesting schedule, meaning that if the employee leaves the company before working for a designated period of time, some or all benefits are forfeited (as discussed further in chapter 9). The portion of the participant's account that is made up of employee salary deferrals (and investment experience thereon) must be nonforfeitable at all times. In other words, employee salary deferral contributions to a 401(k) plan are always 100 percent vested. This makes sense because participants were entitled to receive such amounts at the time they elected to make the salary deferral. When the plan has employer profit-sharing accounts, such accounts can be subject to a vesting schedule under the normal rules. Employer-matching contributions are subject to the more accelerated vesting rules that apply to top-heavy plans. (These will be discussed more fully in chapter 9.)

In-service Withdrawals

A regular profit-sharing plan can allow employees the option of withdrawing the entire account upon 5 years of plan participation or withdrawing contributions 2 years after they are made. However, under a 401(k) plan, withdrawals from the salary deferral election account are restricted.[1] The plan must provide that no distributions from the salary deferral account will be made before separation from service unless the employee either has attained age 59½ or has incurred a financial hardship (referred to as a hardship withdrawal). A *financial hardship* is defined as a financial need that is "necessary in light of immediate and heavy financial needs of the participant or his or her beneficiary" at a time when no other resources are reasonably available to meet this need.

financial hardship

The regulations provide a safe harbor method for determining hardship so plan administrators do not have to make difficult hardship determinations on a case-by-case basis. Under the safe harbor rules, the following specific circumstances constitute hardships:

- medical expenses
- purchase of a principal residence for the participant
- payment of up to 12 months of tuition and related expenses for postsecondary education for a participant, his or her spouse, children, or dependents
- payment of amounts necessary to prevent the eviction of the participant from his or her principal residence or from foreclosure on his or her mortgage
- payments for burial or funeral expenses for the participant's deceased parent, spouse, children, or dependents.
- expenses for the repair of damage to the participant's principal residence

The rules also provide a safe harbor method for determining whether "other resources are reasonably available to meet the need." An employee will be deemed to lack "other reasonable resources" if the following conditions are met:

- The employee must obtain all distributions (including distributions of ESOP dividends) other than hardship distributions and all nontaxable loans available under all plans maintained by the employer.
- The plan must provide that the employee's elective deferral contributions and nondeductible contributions will be suspended for 6 months after the distribution.

Example:	Employee Adams makes elective contributions from January 2006 to June 2006. In June 2006, Adams takes a hardship distribution from the plan. Adams cannot make elective deferral contributions to her 401(k) plan until January 2007 (after the 6-month waiting period has elapsed).

Most employers choose to adopt both safe harbor provisions so they do not have to examine an employee's financial condition. A plan does not have to allow for hardship withdrawals, and some employers choose instead to allow loans because loans can be made without tax consequences. A hardship withdrawal will generally be taxed as ordinary income, as well as be subject to the Section 72(t) 10 percent penalty tax for those who have not yet attained age 59½.

Regardless of whether the general approach or the safe harbor method is elected, distributions are limited to the amount necessary to meet the financial need. This amount can include amounts necessary to pay taxes on the withdrawal. Generally, only the portion of the salary deferral account that represents employee salary deferral contributions can be withdrawn; earnings cannot. However, withdrawals under more liberal provisions can be allowed from the profit-sharing or matching contribution accounts.

Segregating Plan Assets

Department of Labor regulations interpreting the definition of plan assets (including 401(k) plans) have clarified that salary deferral contributions are plan assets, and that they are required to be segregated (contributed to the trust) on the earliest reasonable date. The regulations go on to stipulate that a reasonable date can generally not be later than the 15th business day of the month following the month in which such amounts are withheld from wages. Examples in the regulations do indicate that, in many cases, plan assets can be reasonably expected to be segregated well before the expiration of the 15-day period.

Actual Deferral Percentage Test

actual deferral percentage (ADP) test

401(k) plans are subject to a special nondiscrimination test known as the *actual deferral percentage (ADP) test,* which

- ensures that higher-paid employees do not use the 401(k) plan to stockpile contributions that otherwise would have produced needed tax revenue
- forces employers to design the 401(k) plan so it attracts participation by lower-paid employees by making the amount that higher-paid employees can tax shelter conditional on the amount that the lower-paid employees actually tax shelter

In order to pass the ADP test, one of two requirements must be satisfied:

- *the 125 percent requirement*—Under this requirement, the average of the actual deferral percentages (ADPs) for highly compensated employees for the current year cannot be more than 125 percent of the average ADPs for nonhighly compensated employees in the previous year.
- *the 200 percent/2 percent difference requirement*—Under this requirement, the average of the ADPs for highly compensated employees for the current year cannot be more than 200 percent of the average ADPs for nonhighly compensated employees in the previous year, and the difference between the deferral percentages for the two groups cannot be more than 2 percent.

highly compensated employees (HCEs)

The first step in performing the ADP test is to determine the *highly compensated employees (HCEs)*. Highly compensated employees include

- individuals who are 5-percent owners during the current or previous year and
- individuals who earned over the earnings limit in the preceding year. In 2006 and 2007, the earnings limit is $100,000. (The employer can elect to limit this group to employees whose compensation puts them in the top 20 percent of payroll.)

The second step is determining the ADP for each employee who is eligible to participate in the plan. The ADP is simply the individual's salary deferral amounts for the year divided by compensation earned for the year. The final step is determining the average for the nonhighly compensated group for the previous year. Remember that all participants eligible to make salary deferrals are included, meaning that those who do not make salary deferrals have ADPs of zero.

Once the average of the ADPs for the nonhighly compensated employees for the prior year is determined, the maximum average of the ADPs for the highly compensated employees for the current year can be determined. In general, if the ADP for the nonhighly compensated group is less than 2 percent, the 200 percent limit applies. If the ADP for the nonhighly compensated group is at least 2 percent and not more than 8 percent, the 2 percent spread limit applies. If the ADP for the nonhighly compensated group is 9 percent or more, the 125 percent limit applies (see table 5-2).

TABLE 5-2
Maximum ADP Limits for Highly Compensated Employees

ADP of Nonhighly Compensated Group	ADP Limit
1%	2%
2%	4%
3%	5%
4%	6%
5%	7%
6%	8%
7%	9%
8%	10%
9%	11.25%
10%	12.50%
11%	13.75%
12%	15%
13%	16.25%
14%	17.50%
15%	18.75%
16%	20%

Case Study: Medical Group Professional Corporation

Now that we have laid out the rules, let's examine the application of the ADP test in a case study . The Medical Group Professional Corporation has a 401(k) plan and wants to know what the maximum deferral percentage for HCEs will be for 2007. At the end of 2006, the census data are as follows:

Employees	Salary	Percentage Contributed
Dr. Ben Casey (CEO/75% owner)	$80,000	8%
Dr. Roberta Stone (V.P./25% owner)	80,000	8%
Dr. Mel Practice	150,000	6%
Dr. Frank Burns (treasurer)	20,000	5%
Dr. Ruth Rosenhauser	125,000	8%
Dr. Julius Miller	40,000	8%
Nancy Doe	40,000	5%
Joe Jones	25,000	5%
Sally Crowe	25,000	5%
Jack Dixon	20,000	5%

The first step in the ADP test is to determine who falls into the highly compensated group and who is not a member of that group.

- Dr. Ben Casey and Dr. Roberta Stone are highly compensated employees because they are more-than-5-percent owners.
- Dr. Mel Practice and Dr. Ruth Rosenhauser are highly compensated employees because they receive annual compensation in excess of $100,000 (the indexed number in the look-back year—2006) and are members of the top-paid group (the top 20 percent of the employer's payroll).
- Dr. Frank Burns, Dr. Julius Miller, Nancy Doe, Joe Jones, Sally Crowe, and Jack Dixon are not highly compensated employees.

The second step necessary to perform the ADP test is to determine the deferral percentage for the nonhighly compensated group.

Nonhighly Compensated	Percentage Contributed
Dr. Frank Burns	5.0%
Dr. Julius Miller	8.0%
Nancy Doe	5.0%
Joe Jones	5.0%
Sally Crowe	5.0%
Jack Dixon	5.0%
Average Percent Deferred	5.5%

This means that in 2007, the maximum average ADP for the highly compensated group will be 7.5 percent. (As discussed above, if the deferral percentage for the nonhighly compensated employee group is between 2 and

8 percent, the allowable spread is 2 percent.) Looking at the 2006 data, the average of the ADPs for the highly compensated is on track.

Highly Compensated	Percentage Contributed
Dr. Ben Casey	8.0%
Dr. Roberta Stone	8.0%
Dr. Mel Practice	6.0%
Dr. Ruth Rosenhauser	8.0%
Average Percent Deferred	7.5%

Satisfying the ADP Test

The Small Business Job Protection Act of 1996 greatly simplified 401(k) testing by allowing employers to pass the ADP test using the nonhighly compensated deferral percentage from the previous year. This change means the employer knows the maximum deferral percentage for the highly compensated group at the beginning of the plan year and can appropriately limit contributions by the highly compensated so the test is satisfied. The law went further and provided for other relief from the rigors of the ADP test. The following are all provisions that a 401(k) plan sponsor will want to consider when planning strategies to satisfy the test.

Current-Year Testing—Prior to the Small Business Job Protection Act, the maximum ADP for the highly compensated employees was determined by looking at the ADP percentage for the nonhighly compensated employees for the current year. Under the law, employers can elect the old method of performing the test. Occasionally, current-year testing provides a better result for an employer than look-back testing. This may be particularly true in the first year of plan operation. In the first year, the ADP for the nonhighly compensated group (under look-back testing) is deemed to be 3 percent. If the employer elects instead to use current-year testing, the actual ADP for the nonhighly compensated group may be substantially higher, allowing larger contributions by the highly compensated. (Note that if an employer elects current-year testing, it can only change the election in limited circumstances.)

401(k) SIMPLE—As described more fully in chapter 6, an employer can establish a plan called a SIMPLE that is funded with IRA accounts. However, an employer can instead elect an amendment that adopts essentially the same rigid design restrictions within the 401(k) plan. The result is relief from the ADP test and top-heavy testing (described in chapter 10). This option has not been popular, however, because an employer willing to adopt these design restrictions would prefer the SIMPLE IRA, a plan that is much easier to maintain. A much better option for the sponsor who wants the flexibility of the 401(k) plan is the 401(k) safe harbor design.

401(k) Safe Harbor—A plan is deemed to satisfy the ADP test if a safe harbor contribution is made either to the 401(k) plan or other defined contribution plan of the sponsor. If a plan makes such contributions, the plan will also avoid being considered a top-heavy plan (discussed in chapter 10). In most cases, plans with a safe harbor contribution also avoids the ACP nondiscrimination test that applies to matching contributions.

There are two types of contributions that can satisfy the safe harbor. One option is to make a nonelective contribution for all eligible nonhighly compensated employees (NHCE) in the amount of 3 percent of compensation. This option permits the HCEs to maximize salary deferral and catch-up contributions and also allows the employer to design any type of additional matching contribution or additional profit-sharing contributions.

As an alternative, the employer can make a matching contribution for NHCEs. The basic matching contribution is 100 percent of the first 3 percent of compensation that the participant elects to defer. In addition, a 50 percent match is made on the next 2 percent of compensation deferred.

Example:	Employee Candice elects to defer 8 percent of her $100,000 compensation. The company contributes the basic safe harbor matching contribution. Candice will receive a $4,000 matching contribution, 100 percent of the first 3 percent deferred, and 50 percent of the next 2 percent deferred.

The sponsor can choose a different matching contribution (referred to as an enhanced match) as long as the enhanced formula provides an aggregate amount of matching contributions at least equal to the aggregate amount of matching contributions that would have been provided under the basic matching formula. For example, the sponsor could choose instead to match 100 percent of the first 4 percent of compensation.

Under either matching option, the plan can make matching contributions at a lower rate for highly compensated employees (HCEs), but the rate cannot be higher than that for NHCEs. A matching contribution is also deemed to satisfy the ACP test as long as the match is limited to the first 6 percent of compensation that participants elect to defer. This last requirement limits the matching contribution, but the plan can still be designed to include profit-sharing contributions.

All safe harbor contributions must be fully vested and are subject to the hardship withdrawal provisions that apply to salary deferral contributions.

However, under the regulations, these contributions cannot be withdrawn upon a financial hardship because they are not subject to an election by the employee. In other words, they can only be withdrawn at termination of employment or attainment of age 59½.

In most cases, the employer must adopt a safe harbor contribution provision prior to the beginning of the plan year. Plan participants must be given notice at least 30 days and no more than 90 days before the beginning of each plan year of the safe harbor contributions that will be made during the year.

Correcting Excess Contributions—In addition to these options, the law also gives plans the option to correct a failure of the ADP test after the year ends. There are a number of complex correction methods that create another safety net for satisfying the ADP test.

Other 401(k) Plan Issues and Requirements

Plans with Matching Contributions

actual contribution percentage (ACP) test

If a 401(k) plan has matching contributions, after-tax employee contributions, or both, the plan generally must satisfy another nondiscrimination test referred to as the *actual contribution percentage (ACP) test*. This test operates in essentially the same manner as the ADP test. In many cases, the results of the ACP test are essentially the same as those for the ADP test. (The test is discussed in detail in chapter 8.) However, the ACP test can become more problematic if the matching contribution is complex—for example, employees with more than 10 years of service receive a 100 percent match while other employees receive a 50 percent match. On the practical side, the ADP and ACP tests require that the highly compensated be aware of the possibility that their contributions may be limited, and that the plan design must involve the input of the plan administrator or someone very familiar with the operation of these rules.

Roth 401(k)

Beginning in 2006, 401(k) plans (as well as 403(b) plans) may allow participants to treat some or all of their salary deferral contributions as Roth contributions. If the election is made, the contributions will be made on an after-tax basis and will be subject to the same tax treatment as Roth IRAs at the time of the distribution. This means that the participant would have the option to forgo tax deferral in exchange for tax-free treatment upon distribution.

Plan participants who like the tax treatment of the Roth IRA may be very interested in having this feature added to their own 401(k) (or 403(b)) plan for two reasons. First, the 401(k) plan salary deferral limit ($15,500 in 2007) is significantly higher than the Roth IRA limit ($4,000 in 2007). Second, a Roth 401(k) does not have the income phaseout rules that apply for eligibility for a Roth IRA. Individuals at all income levels can contribute to a Roth 401(k).

At the same time, employers should have a clear mandate from employees that they want this feature because it will add administrative complexity to the plan. The plan will have to keep separate accounts for all Roth 401(k) contributions.

From the 401(k) plan's perspective, Roth 401(k) contributions are characterized as salary deferral contributions. Salary deferral limits, nonforfeitability rules, distribution restrictions, and nondiscrimination testing rules remain the same (and apply to both pre-tax and Roth salary deferrals in aggregate). Because participants can only elect Roth treatment on salary deferral contributions, the election does not affect employer matching or profit-sharing contributions.

Qualifying distributions from Roth 401(k) plans will generally be subject to the same tax-free treatment as Roth IRAs. However, there are some important differences in the tax treatment of these two different accounts. These differences are addressed in detail in chapter 24.

Cafeteria Plans

A popular use of 401(k) plans is to include them as one of the available benefits under a cafeteria plan. In fact, the 401(k) plan is the only type of qualified plan that can be part of a cafeteria plan. The term *cafeteria plan* stems from the fact that these plans allow employees to pick from a menu of benefit choices. More specifically, the benefit dollars in a cafeteria plan are flexible; employees can take them in cash, allocate them to pay for certain welfare benefits (such as life insurance, health insurance, or child care), place them in a 40l(k) plan, or do a combination of any of these three. To the extent that an employee elects to spend benefit dollars on tax-advantaged benefits like a 401(k) plan, there is no current taxation. For this reason, employees may wish to contribute to 401(k) plans in lieu of other benefits available in the cafeteria plan (such as group life insurance in excess of $50,000) that are taxable.

Other Employee Benefit Plans

Many employee benefit plans (including pension plans, group life insurance, and disability insurance) calculate benefits based on the participant's compensation. For example, in a group life insurance plan, the employee's beneficiaries may be entitled to a benefit of two times compensation. When an employer installs a 401(k) plan, benefits under other plans may be reduced if salary reduction elections reduce the definition of compensation under those plans. Unless the employer is exceptionally concerned about costs, it will not want to reduce the definition of compensation because this indirectly penalizes employees for making salary deferrals. Sometimes the employer forgets to review the effect of salary deferrals on other employee benefits, and benefits are accidentally reduced. The advisor should be sure to discuss this issue with the employer when the plan is installed.

Note that salary deferral elections do not adversely affect Social Security benefits. Salary deferrals are considered wages for calculating benefits (as well as for determining Social Security taxes).

Plan Asset Regulations

Sponsors of 401(k) plans must be aware that Department of Labor regulations interpreting the definition of plan assets have clarified that salary deferral contributions are plan assets, and that they are required to be segregated (contributed to the trust) on the earliest reasonable date. The regulations go on to clarify that a reasonable date cannot be later than the 15th business day of the month following the month in which such amounts are withheld from wages. However, examples in the regulations indicate that in most cases, plan assets can be reasonably expected to be segregated well before the end of the 15-day period.

Affirmative Elections

As mentioned above, one way to encourage plan participation is to have an automatic enrollment provision. This design feature provides that all eligible employees automatically make the default salary deferral election unless they opt out of the plan via an affirmative election or elect a different deferral amount. Studies have shown that this type of provision can improve plan participation because some employees will take the course requiring the least amount of action. Although automatic enrollment has been authorized by DOL regulations for a number of years, before the Pension Protection Act of 2006, there were a number of unresolved issues. State garnishment laws prohibited such provisions in some states, and there has been some uncertainty about the fiduciary's liability for the investment of automatic enrollment accounts.

The Pension Protection Act of 2006 has resolved the uncertain legal status by explicitly protecting automatic enrollment against state interference. The act also clarifies the fiduciary issue by stating that ERISA 404(c) (which protects fiduciaries) can apply, even though participants are not making affirmative investment choices (see chapter 11 for a further discussion of this issue). The act requires that automatic enrollment is accompanied by a notice explaining the participant's right to elect out of the plan or to change the rate of contribution, the time periods for making elections, and how contributions will be invested in the absence of any contrary direction by the participant.

Beginning in 2008, the Pension Protection Act also establishes a "qualified automatic enrollment feature" that acts as a third type of safe harbor design—meaning that a plan meeting the requirements will not have to satisfy the ADP or ACP test or satisfy top-heavy testing. A qualified automatic enrollment feature can allow automatic deferrals of up to 10 percent of compensation, but as a minimum must require an automatic deferral of 3 percent of compensation for the first year of eligibility, 4 percent during the second year; 5 percent during the third year; and 6 percent during the fourth year and thereafter. The employer is required to make a 3 percent nonelective contribution for each eligible nonhighly compensated employee or a 100 percent matching contribution on up to one percent of salary deferred and a 50 percent match on up to the next 5 percent deferred.

Additional Design Considerations

Because 401(k) plans only succeed when employees elect to make salary deferrals, many 401(k) plans encourage employee participation through matching contributions, employee investment direction, participant loan programs, and hardship withdrawals. While these features are discussed in other parts of this book, it is helpful to understand how they tie in specifically to the 401(k) plan environment.

- *Matching contributions*—Most 401(k) plans contain some sort of matching employer contributions to encourage employee participation. A common formula is a 50 percent match up to 6 percent of compensation deferred.
- *Employee investment direction*—Because employees perceive salary deferrals as "their own money," most 401(k) plans now give participants the right to direct the investment of at least the salary deferral account. This trend is extremely widespread, and it is rare to find a 401(k) plan that is designed otherwise.
- *Participant loans*—Employees may be reluctant to make salary deferrals unless they can access funds in case of an emergency. Participant loan programs are quite common in 401(k) plans because they allow at least limited access without tax consequences.
- *Hardship withdrawals*—Another way for employees to access funds is through hardship withdrawals. Most 401(k) plans allow either loans or hardship withdrawals, and in some cases both options.

401(k) Plans: Contribution Limits for 2007

- **Salary deferral limit**—Salary deferral contributions made at the election of the participant are limited to $15,500. The limit is increased to $20,500 for participants over age 50. Note that this limit applies to all salary deferral plans (including SIMPLEs and 403(b) plans) to which a participant contributes, even with an unrelated employer.

- **Maximum allocation**—As with other defined-contribution plans, the maximum allocation to a single participant (counting all types of contributions except catch-up salary deferrals for those over age 50) cannot exceed $45,000. If the individual participates in other defined contribution plans sponsored by the same (or related) employer, then both plans are aggregated in determining the $45,000 limit.

- **Employer deduction limit**—The employer's deductible contribution is limited to 25 percent of all covered payroll. This limit rarely affects an individual participant because it is an aggregate limit. Also, salary deferral contributions are not counted when determining the 25 percent limit.

- **Nondiscrimination tests**—The nondiscrimination tests that apply to salary deferral contributions (the ADP test) and to matching employer contributions (ACP test) can, in some cases, result in lowering the allowable contribution for one or more highly compensated employees. These tests have no effect on nonhighly compensated employees. The tests can also be avoided in some cases by using a safe harbor contribution.

STOCK BONUS PLANS AND EMPLOYEE STOCK OWNERSHIP PLANS (ESOPs)

Stock bonus plans and ESOPs are variations of profit-sharing plans and are similar in many ways:

stock bonus plans

- *Stock bonus plans,* ESOPs, and profit-sharing plans are all defined-contribution plans and all fall into the profit-sharing (not pension) category.
- Contributions need not be fixed and need not be made every year.
- The allocation formulas used under a profit-sharing plan may be used under either a stock bonus plan or an ESOP.

- The amount of deductible employer contributions allowed (25 percent) is the same for all three types of plans.
- Contributions for all three types of plans are usually, but are not legally required to be, based on profits.

Stock bonus plans and ESOPs differ from profit-sharing plans, however, in three important ways:

- Both stock bonus plans and ESOPs typically invest plan assets primarily in the employer's stock (in fact, an ESOP is required to invest primarily in employer stock). Profit-sharing plans, on the other hand, are usually structured to diversify investments and do not concentrate investments in employer stock (even though they are legally permitted to do so).
- Both stock bonus plans and ESOPs are chosen because they provide a market for employer stock. This, in turn, generates capital for the corporation and helps finance a company's growth. Profit-sharing plans, however, are not viewed as a way to finance company operations but are more concerned with providing tax-favored deferred compensation that can be used for retirement purposes.
- Stock bonus plans and ESOPs are required to allow distributions to participants in the form of employer stock. Profit-sharing plans can allow this option, but often do not. This creates a distinct advantage for participants in a stock bonus plan or an ESOP because they receive a tax break inasmuch as the unrealized appreciation (gain in value) is not taxed until the stock is sold. (See chapter 24 for a complete discussion of this rule.)

Stock Bonus Plans

Technically, a stock bonus plan is a plan that allows distributions in employer stock. Some or all of the plan's investments can be held in employer stock from time to time. Stock bonus plans have recently given way in popularity to ESOPs, however, because ESOPs allow the plan to borrow to purchase the securities. If this feature is not needed, the stock bonus plan may still be the right choice because it is subject to fewer legal restrictions. Let's take a closer look at ESOPs.

Employee Stock Ownership Plans

ESOPs enjoy the same advantages as stock bonus plans and offer an extra advantage to your clients—they can be used to allow the employer to

leveraged ESOP

borrow in order to provide contributions. (When an ESOP is used for this function, it is also known as a *leveraged ESOP*.) Under this technique, known as leveraging, the plan trustee acquires a loan from the bank and uses the borrowed funds to purchase employer stock. Generally, the employer guarantees repayment of the loan, and the purchased stock is held as collateral. The result is that the plan receives the full proceeds of the bank loan immediately and pays the loan off with the employer's tax-deductible contributions to the ESOP. The collateralized stock is placed in a suspense account. The employer makes annual (deductible) contributions to the plan, which are used to pay back the bank. As the loan is paid off, the stock is released from the suspense account.

Reasons Candidates Choose Stock Bonus Plans and ESOPs

One major advantage of stock bonus plans and ESOPs is that they give employees a stake in the company through stock ownership. This neatly fits most employers' goals of employee motivation and retention. A second major advantage is the previously mentioned delayed taxation of gain on stock distributions. Enhanced cash flow is a third advantage. Cash flow is enhanced because the employer makes a cashless contribution to the retirement plan. A fourth—and perhaps most important—advantage of stock ownership plans is that they help to create a market for employer stock. This is especially important if the organization's stock is not publicly traded. The leveraging advantage associated with ESOPs is also enticing to organizations.

The major disadvantage of stock ownership plans is the possibility of the employer's stock falling drastically in value and, therefore, cutting the availability of retirement funds. Without any diversity of investment, participants are exposed to potential disaster. There is, however, some relief available for ESOP participants. The law requires that once an ESOP

YOUR FINANCIAL SERVICES PRACTICE:
LIFE INSURANCE AND ESOPs

Special arrangements must be made in advance for the corporation to buy back stock from a terminated employee or from a deceased employee's estate without creating a cash-flow crunch. Typically, this is accomplished through the sale of life insurance to the ESOP. For example, the ESOP could purchase life insurance on the lives of its principal employees. At the death of any one of these employees, the life insurance proceeds are used to buy back the stock transferred from the deceased employee's estate.

participant attains age 55 and completes at least 10 years of participation, the participant may elect (between the ages of 55 and 60) to diversify the retirement benefit by moving up to 50 percent of his or her account balance into other investments. (For more information, see Code Sec. 401(a)(28).)

A second disadvantage of stock ownership plans is that if the stock is not readily tradable on an established market, the employer is required to offer a repurchase option (also known as a put option). This option must be available for a minimum of 60 days following the distribution of the stock and, if the option is not exercised in that period, for an additional 60-day period in the following year. The repurchase option creates administrative and cash-flow problems for employers.

Candidates for ESOPs and stock bonus plans are similar to candidates for profit-sharing plans and generally fill out the fact finder in a similar manner. But, unlike the typical profit-sharing candidate, ESOP and stock bonus plan candidates rate as "very valuable" fact finder item 10—creating a market for employer stock. Also, ESOP candidates rate as "very valuable" fact finder item 11—leveraging the purchase of employer stock.

TABLE 5-3
Qualified Plan Scorecard

PENSION
Defined-benefit
Cash-balance
Target-benefit
Money-purchase

KEOGH
Defined-benefit
Cash-balance
Target-benefit
Money-purchase
Profit-sharing
401(k)

CORPORATE
Defined-benefit
Cash-balance
Target-benefit
Money-purchase
Profit-sharing
Stock bonus
ESOP
401(k)

PROFIT-SHARING
Profit-sharing
Stock bonus
ESOP
401(k)

DEFINED-CONTRIBUTION
Target-benefit
Money-purchase
Profit-sharing
Stock bonus
ESOP
401(k)

DEFINED-BENEFIT
Defined-benefit
Cash-balance

CASE STUDY: BAKER MANUFACTURING, INC.

Bill Baker is the president of Baker Manufacturing, Inc., a firm that produces parts for personal computers. Baker Manufacturing has a defined-benefit pension plan for its 40 employees. Bill wants to improve rank-and-file productivity and morale. Business is excellent, but to meet increased sales orders, Bill needs to get more out of his employees. To make matters worse, two of Bill's experienced line workers have just left to work for a competitor. In addition, several of Bill's people have approached him regarding tax-sheltering part of their salary (Bill is also interested). Bill would like to do something extra, but cash flow is a problem. He feels he may need to hold onto profits in case the never-ending new generations of computers require different manufacturing equipment. How would an ESOP help to solve Bill's problems? Would a 401(k) plan offer a solution?   An employee stock ownership plan (ESOP) would be helpful in solving Bill's problems; it would allow him to do something extra without creating cash-flow problems because his ESOP would be leveraged. In addition, employee morale would be improved by the extra benefit provided. Employees would be encouraged not to leave because of their ties to the company's fortunes through the stock itself, and through the amount of stock contributions, which are based on company profits. And, because company profits would be more important to the employees than ever, productivity would likely increase. Bill and his executives could also enjoy the tax advantages of taking distributions of highly productive company stock when they terminate.

A cash or deferred arrangement (401(k) plan) would also be helpful because it would provide something extra for only a minor cost. The executives who wanted to shelter income from taxes would have the opportunity to convert some of their salary into pretax savings (up to the $15,500 maximum in 2007). If Bill provides a matching contribution, the organization's cost would rise slightly, but the paybacks would be increased productivity, better morale, and retention of employees.

CHAPTER REVIEW

Key Terms

discretionary contributions [5-1]
cash or deferred arrangement
    (CODA) [5-2]
stand-alone plan [5-2]

matching contribution [5-2]
automatic enrollment [5-2]
financial hardship [5-3]

actual deferral percentage (ADP) test [5-3]

highly compensated employees (HCEs) [5-3]

actual contribution percentage (ACP) test [5-3]

stock bonus plans [5-5]

leveraged ESOP [5-5]

Review Questions

Review questions are based on the learning objectives in this chapter. Thus, a [5-3] at the end of a question means that the question is based on learning objective 5-3. If there are multiple objectives, they are all listed.

1. Umbrella, Inc., is a business with a cash flow that literally fluctuates with the weather. Umbrella, Inc., would like a qualified plan, despite its erratic cash flow. In addition, the owners of this small business would like to be able to withdraw their funds if they decide to expand the business. What type of qualified plan should Umbrella, Inc., have? Explain. [5-1]

2. Describe the concern about the discretionary nature of the profit-sharing plan and the strategies necessary to ensure that the plan is successful. [5-1]

3. What is an allocation formula? [5-1]

4. Accountants, Inc., has decided to adopt a profit-sharing plan that allocates profits in excess of $10,000 to participants by the ratio that the compensation for a participant bears to the compensation of all participants. Anne with $100,000 in compensation, Bob with $70,000 in compensation, and Cassie with $30,000 in compensation are the plan's only participants. How much will be contributed to each participant's account if Accountants, Inc., has a $30,000 profit? [5-1]

5. In addition to discretionary contributions and withdrawal flexibility, name several other strengths of a profit-sharing plan. [5-1]

6. How can life insurance be used by a profit-sharing trust to protect plan participants from an economic downturn in the event of the death of a key profit maker? [5-1]

7. What is the maximum salary deferral in a 401(k) plan? [5-2]

8. Describe the four types of contributions that can be made to a 401(k) plan. [5-2]

9. How might automatic enrollment help the participation rate in a 401(k) plan? [5-2]

10. Dr. Jones, age 47, works for Mega Hospital and makes a $15,500 salary deferral election to the plan in 2007. If Dr. Jones also has a medical practice that includes a 401(k) plan, what is the maximum salary deferral he can make in that plan? [5-2]

11. Under what circumstances may withdrawals be made from a 401(k) plan? [5-2]

12. ABCO, Inc., has adopted a 401(k) plan whose participants, their compensation, and their percentage contributed are as follows: [5-2]

Eligible Employee	Compensation	2006 Percentage of Compensation Contributed
Abner Anderson (CEO/75% owner)	$150,000	8%
Barbara Bellows (VP/25% owner)	80,000	8%
Cindy Clark (sec/treasurer)	60,000	5%
Don Davidson	40,000	5%
Ellen Ewer	30,000	9%
Frank Fern	20,000	5%
Gary Grant	20,000	5%

In 2007, what will be the maximum deferral percentage for highly compensated employees under the actual deferral percentage test? Explain.

13. What is the effect of making a safe-harbor contribution to a 401(k) plan? [5-2]

14. Why would employees be interested in a Roth 401(k) feature? [5-2]

15. Describe the advantage ESOPs have with regard to borrowing to fund the plan. [5-3]

16. Why should an employer who has an ESOP consider having life insurance on key executives in the plan? [5-3]

NOTE

1. Similar to the vesting rules, the participant's profit-sharing and matching contribution accounts can be subject to the normal withdrawal rules that apply to profit-sharing plans.

6

SEPs, SIMPLEs, and 403(b) Plans

Learning Objectives

An understanding of the material in this chapter should enable you to

6-1. Compare simplified employee pensions (SEPs) to qualified plans and identify when a SEP is a good alternative to a profit-sharing plan.

6-2. Describe the SIMPLE plan and discuss when its use would be appropriate.

6-3. Describe a 403(b) plan with regard to how it can be funded, the applicable legal requirements, and the determination of an individual's maximum contribution.

Chapter Outline

In this chapter, we explore three types of tax-advantaged retirement plans that are not qualified plans covered under Code Sec. 401(a). What is meaningful about these plans is that each has its own unique set of rules. Who can sponsor each type of plan, how much can be contributed, who must participate, vesting provisions, and how contributions are allocated are different from these aspects of qualified plans—and different from each other. You will also see that in some instances, some of the qualified plan rules do apply.

To determine whether the SEP, the SIMPLE, or the 403(b) plan is more appropriate for your client than any of the qualified plan alternatives, this chapter fully explores each type of plan and compares them with qualified plans. At times, the comparisons might be somewhat confusing because at this point in the book you are not yet familiar with all of the rules that apply to qualified plans. Previous chapters have introduced you to the types of qualified plans available, and chapters 7 through 10 will flesh out eligibility, vesting, and limits on contribution formulas, as well as other issues. You may find it helpful to review this chapter after finishing chapter 10.

SEPs

simplified employee pension (SEP)

A *simplified employee pension (SEP)* is a retirement plan that uses an individual retirement account (IRA) or an individual retirement annuity (IRA annuity) as the receptacle for contributions. As its name implies, this type of plan is simpler than a qualified retirement plan, making it, in many cases, attractive to the small business owner.

The documentation, reporting, and disclosure requirements are less cumbersome than for a qualified plan. Trust accounting is also eliminated because separate IRAs are established for each participant and all contributions are made directly to each participant's IRA. Because contributions must be nonforfeitable, the participant's benefit at any time is simply the IRA account balance.

The SEP is often a good choice for the small business because of the reduced administrative tasks and expenses. However, the SEP still has its complications, and the prospective sponsor needs to go in with a clear understanding of the ongoing responsibilities of maintaining such a plan. Also note that there is a tradeoff under the tax rules: in exchange for simplicity is the loss of flexibility. For example, under a SEP, all employees meeting specified requirements must be covered under the plan; the allocation formula may not contain an age-weighting factor (unlike the profit-sharing plans, discussed in chapter 5); and benefits must be fully vested at all times. These requirements are reviewed in more depth below.

Characteristics of the SEP

From a design perspective, the SEP is quite similar to the profit-sharing plan. The employer may, on a discretionary basis, make contributions, which are allocated to participants' accounts. The maximum deductible contribution is the same as for a profit-sharing plan.

Technically, SEPs are subject to the rules contained in IRC Sec. 408(k)—in contrast to qualified plans, which are subject to IRC Sec. 401(a) and related provisions. IRC 408(k) provides some requirements that are unique to SEPs, borrows some of the qualified plan requirements, and states that the investment and distribution provisions for IRAs also apply to SEPs. To learn these rules, it is helpful to group them in these categories.

Requirements Unique to SEPs

Coverage Requirements. SEPs are subject to a very different set of participation requirements from those for qualified retirement plans. The rules require that contributions be made for all employees who have met all three of the following requirements:

- attained age 21
- performed services for the employer for at least 3 of the immediately preceding 5 years
- earned the required minimum compensation ($500 as indexed for 2007)

From a planning perspective, this set of requirements means that the employer can exclude employees with less than 3 years of service, but must cover all employees—including part-time employees earning more than the compensation limit—who have 3 or more years of service. This provision works well for the employer with numerous short-term employees, but is more problematic for the employer with a number of long-term part-time employees.

The rigid coverage rules can also cause problems for companies with related subsidiary companies and for small groups of individuals who own two or more companies. If, in either case, the affiliation constitutes a "controlled group of corporations,"[1] the employees of all the related companies must all be covered under the same plan. This rule generally eliminates the SEP as a viable alternative in the larger corporate setting. The most dangerous problem is that a small employer who is unaware of this rule will establish a plan for one company and forget to cover employees in related companies. The controlled group rules are discussed in more depth in chapter 7.

Allocation Formula. Even though the contribution limits are the same for a SEP as a profit-sharing plan, the allocation formula is more limited. The allocation formula must either allocate contributions as a level percentage of compensation or be integrated with Social Security using the same method as for other defined-contribution plans (see chapter 8 for a more complete description). This means that unlike the profit-sharing plan, the allocation formula cannot use age-weighting or cross-testing (discussed in chapter 8) to skew contributions to older, more highly compensated employees.

Vesting. All contributions to a SEP, either by the employer directly or as an employee contribution (by deferral election), must be immediately and 100 percent vested. From the employer's perspective, this requirement is more onerous than for qualified plans, but remember that employees can be excluded from the plan until they have completed 3 years of employment.

Employee Elective Deferrals. Before 1997, an employer could establish a SEP (often referred to as a SARSEP) that allowed employees the opportunity to make pretax contributions in the same way as in a 401(k) plan (often referred to as a SARSEP). In 1996, the Small Business Job Protection Act replaced the SARSEP with the SIMPLE and prohibited new SARSEPs. However, employers were allowed to continue to sponsor plans that were in effect as of December 31, 1996. The SARSEP was never a very popular plan, but there are still a few remaining SARSEPs in existence today. In a SARSEP, employees can elect to defer up to the same deferral amount allowed in a 401(k) plan. Like the 401(k) plan, the SARSEP is subject to a nondiscrimination rule similar to the ADP test. SARSEPs also are subject to several requirements that do not apply to 401(k) plans, each of which makes the plan less attractive than a 401(k) plan:

- Only an employer with 25 or fewer employees can sponsor a SARSEP.
- At least 50 percent of all eligible employees must participate in the SARSEP.
- The employer may not make matching contributions to encourage employees to contribute to the plan.

Timing of Distribution. Participants must be given the opportunity to withdraw the account balance at any time. This is entirely different from the situation with qualified pension plans, which do not allow distributions until termination of employment, and with qualified profit-sharing plans, in which the employer can choose whether or not to allow in-service withdrawals.

Documentation and Reporting. The supporting plan document is much simpler than with a qualified plan. The IRS supplies Form 5305(SEP) and service providers, such as banks and insurance companies, may also sponsor a SEP prototype document and receive IRS approval. If the IRS form or the prototype document is used, the plan does not have to file Form 5500 annually as long as participants receive (1) either a copy of the plan or a summary of the plan, (2) some general information about SEPs, and (3) annual notice of contributions made on their behalf. When working with SEPs, note that these alternative document and disclosure requirements must be followed exactly or the plan sponsor will be required to file annual Form 5500 reports and meet all other ERISA disclosure requirements.

Qualified Plan Rules That Apply to SEPs

Maximum Contributions. The maximum employer contribution to the SEP is the same as for a profit-sharing plan, that is, 25 percent of the compensation of all employees eligible to participate in the plan. All profit-sharing plans and SEPs sponsored by the same company are aggregated under this rule. The Code Sec. 415(c) maximum allocation limit also applies to the allocation of contributions to each participant. Similarly, the compensation cap that applies to qualified plans also applies to SEPs.

Top-heavy Rules. The same rules that apply to qualified plans apply to SEPs. Although most SEPs will be top-heavy (benefits for key employees will generally equal or exceed 60 percent of total benefits), the top-heavy rules do not have much effect on the SEP. SEPs are already required to have 100 percent immediate vesting, and the minimum contribution requirement for nonkey employees does not have much effect because of the special nondiscrimination rules that apply.

IRA Rules That Apply to SEPs

Investment Restrictions. Because contributions are held in IRA accounts, the limitations that apply to individually sponsored IRAs also apply to SEPs. These rules prohibit investment in life insurance and in collectibles (except for U.S. government gold coins). Similarly, loans cannot be made from a SEP.

Taxation of Distributions. Distributions are taxed in the same way as distributions from IRAs. Distributions are treated as ordinary income and are not eligible for special lump-sum averaging. The penalties for early withdrawals and large distributions apply (as they do with qualified plans). Most distributions can also be rolled over to either an IRA or other tax-advantaged retirement plan to avoid current taxation. Chapter 24 covers the tax treatment of IRA distributions in more detail.

SEP Candidates

Candidates for SEPs fill out the pension planning fact finder by grading as "very valuable" the items regarding the avoidance of an annual financial commitment and by instituting a plan that is administratively convenient. SEP candidates say "no" to the following questions in step 2 of the fact finder: Is it more important to provide an adequate retirement standard of living than to avoid an annual commitment? Is it more important to provide an adequate retirement standard of living than to have administrative convenience and an easily communicated plan?

SEP: A Summary of the Rules

- **Employer contributions**—similar to a profit-sharing plan,
- contributions are discretionary, with a maximum deductible contribution of 25 percent of compensation
- **Allocations**—must allocate based on compensation or integrated with Social Security
- **Eligibility**—must cover all employees aged 21 with 3 years earning more than the current year's dollar limit in the last 5 years
- **Vesting**—full and immediate vesting required
- **Withdrawal restrictions**—withdrawals can be made at any time
- **Investment restrictions**—like other IRAs, cannot invest in life insurance or most collectibles
- **Salary deferral contributions**—not allowed except in grandfathered SARSEP started before 1997
- **Taxation**—like other IRAs, subject to ordinary income tax upon distribution

---

The SEP is a good choice for the small employer with these goals in mind. The coverage rules are easier to work with than those for a qualified plan; shorter-term employees (less than 3 years) can be excluded from the plan, eliminating cost and administrative burdens. However, the SEP is not the right approach when the employer has many long-term part-time employees, because they will have to be covered under the plan. The lack of flexibility in the coverage and vesting requirements typically eliminates larger employers as SEP candidates.

Any employer considering a profit-sharing plan should also consider a SEP, because the maximum deduction limits (25 percent of compensation) and the ability to make discretionary employer contributions are the same. Assuming the coverage requirements discussed above do not cause any problems, the SEP is usually the better choice. The employer should avoid the more complex profit-sharing plan unless the employer really values one or more of the features only available in a profit-sharing plan, including:

- age-weighted or cross-tested allocation formulas that skew contributions to older, more highly compensated employees
- investments in life insurance
- limits on plan withdrawals
- participant loans
- deferred vesting

SIMPLEs

savings incentive match plan for employees (SIMPLE)

Since 1997, employers have had another plan option that allows pre-tax salary deferrals, referred to as the *savings incentive match plan for employees (SIMPLE)*.

Plan Requirements

Like SEPs and SARSEPs, the SIMPLE plan is funded with individual retirement accounts, which means that the following requirements apply to the SIMPLE:

- Participants must be fully vested in all benefits at all times.
- Assets cannot be invested in life insurance or collectibles.
- No participant loans are allowed.

Eligible Employers

Any type of business entity can establish a SIMPLE; however, the business cannot have more than 100 employees (only counting those employees who earned $5,000 or more of compensation). If the employer grows beyond the 100-employee limit, the law does allow the employer to sponsor the plan for an additional 2-year grace period. Also note that to be eligible, the sponsoring employer cannot maintain any other qualified plan, 403(b), or SEP at the same time it maintains the SIMPLE.

Salary Deferral Contributions

In a SIMPLE, all eligible employees have the opportunity to make elective pretax contributions of up to $10,500 (indexed for 2007). As with the 401(k) plan, participants who have attained age 50 before the end of the year can make additional contributions to a SIMPLE. For 2007 the additional amount is $2,500.

Employer Contributions

Unlike the 401(k) plan (or the old SARSEP), there is no nondiscrimination testing, meaning that highly compensated employees can make contributions without regard to the salary deferral elections of the nonhighly compensated employees.

However, in exchange, the SIMPLE has a mandatory employer contribution requirement. This contribution can be made in one of two ways:

1. The employer can make a dollar-for-dollar matching contribution on the first 3 percent of compensation that the individual elects to defer, or
2. The employer can make a 2 percent nonelective contribution for all eligible employees.

If the employer elects the matching contribution, there is one other option. Periodically, the employer can elect a lower match as long as

- the matching contribution is not less than one percent of compensation
- participants are notified of the lower contribution within a reasonable time before the 60-day election period that comes before the beginning of the year

The employer can elect the lower percentage for up to 2 years in any 5-year period, which can even include the first 2 years that the plan is in force.

The employer contribution amount just described is both the minimum required and the maximum employer contribution allowed. In other words, if the employer elects the matching contribution, 3 percent is the maximum match, and nonelective contributions are not allowed. If the employer elects the nonelective contribution, then the 2 percent contribution is the maximum, and matching contributions are not allowed.

Eligibility Requirements

The SIMPLE has eligibility requirements that are different from both the SEP and the qualified plan. The plan must cover any employee who earned $5,000 in any 2 previous years and is reasonably expected to earn $5,000 again in the current year. Employees subject to a collectively bargained agreement can be excluded. Eligible employees must be given the right to make the salary deferral and receive either an employer matching or nonelective contribution. For determining eligibility, compensation is essentially taxable income plus pretax salary deferrals. For a self-employed person, compensation is net earnings (not reduced by salary deferral elections). SIMPLEs can be maintained only on a calendar-year basis, and all employees become eligible to participate as of January 1.

Plan Operations

The sponsoring employer must notify participants that they have the 60-day election period just prior to the calendar year to make a salary deferral election or modify a previous election for the following year. The employee who does make a salary deferral election must be given the option to stop making deferrals at any time during the year. The sponsor can require that the participant wait until the following year to elect back into the plan, or may have a more liberal election modification provision—for example, allowing participants to modify their election at any time.

Every year, prior to the 60-day election period, the trustee must prepare and the employer must distribute a summary plan description (SPD) that includes employer-identifying data, a description of eligibility under the plan, benefits provided, terms of the salary election, and description of the procedures for and effects (tax results) of making a withdrawal. Also, 30 days after the calendar year ends, the trustee must give participants a statement of the year's activity and the closing account balance.[2]

**YOUR FINANCIAL SERVICES PRACTICE:
MARKETING SIMPLEs**

Some financial services professionals choose not to get involved in selling the highly technical qualified plan. These professionals may still want to consider marketing the SIMPLE. With no annual reporting, no individual IRA accounts, and no distribution paperwork, the SIMPLE poses little time-consuming administration. With a SIMPLE, the professional is likely to establish a direct relationship with all the participants, providing an ever-expanding group of individual clients.

The clear and precise disclosure requirements are accompanied by clear penalties for failure to comply. The trustee is fined $50 a day for late distribution of participant statements or the annual summary plan description. The employer is fined $50 a day for late notification to participants of their right to make salary deferral elections.[3] The disclosure requirements and penalty system were probably deemed necessary because there is no direct incentive for the employer to encourage SIMPLE participation (unlike the 401(k) plan, in which highly compensated contribution levels are tied to nonhighly compensated contributions under the ADP nondiscrimination test).

Like SEPs, the plan cannot put any limitations on participant withdrawals. This means that participants have access to funds at any time to spend them or roll them over into another IRA. To discourage participants from spending their SIMPLE accounts, a special tax rule assesses a 25 percent penalty tax (in addition to ordinary income taxes) for amounts withdrawn within 2 years of the date of participation. Other early withdrawals may be subject to the special 10 percent excise tax discussed in chapter 23.

Administrative costs for a SIMPLE should be quite low. At the present time, no annual reporting with the IRS or DOL is required. Also, unlike the 401(k) plan, no ADP test or other nondiscrimination tests must be performed.

Candidates for the SIMPLE

The candidate for the SIMPLE will be the employer looking for a plan that allows participants the right to make pretax contributions and who wants to develop a plan that creates a retirement planning partnership between the employer and employee. The candidate must have 100 or fewer employers and also be looking for a plan with the lowest possible administrative hassle and cost.

The employer considering the SIMPLE will be choosing between the 401(k) plan and the SIMPLE. Feature by feature, the advantage almost always goes to the 401(k) plan. The 401(k) plan is better for maximizing contributions and skewing employer contributions to a targeted group of employees—which are typically two common goals of small plan sponsors. In addition, a 401(k) plan is much more flexible. The plan can be limited to part of the workforce as long as the minimum coverage requirements are met, and matching and profit-sharing contributions can be designed to meet a variety of goals. Finally, employer contributions can increase or decrease over time.

This is not to say, however, that the SIMPLE IRA is not a good retirement plan. It is most likely to appeal to the employer who has never maintained a plan before and who is looking for a low-cost plan with few administrative headaches. With little expense, the employer can have a plan that looks to the employees just like a 401(k) plan. Also, the employer does not have to be concerned about how many employees choose to make salary deferrals because the plan does not have to satisfy a nondiscrimination test.

There are several other advantages that the SIMPLE has over the 401(k) plan regarding the IRA funding vehicle. Participants can withdraw their funds at any time or even change investment vehicles. If money is withdrawn to pay educational expenses, the 10 percent early withdrawal penalty tax will not apply. Also, an employer can terminate the plan quite simply without having to be concerned about making distributions from the trust.

SIMPLE: A Summary of the Rules

- **Limits on sponsorship**—any type of employer as long as there is no other plan and 100 or fewer employers
- **Salary deferral contributions**—eligible participants can defer $10,500 (in 2007)
- **Catch-up election**—participants over age 50 can defer an additional $2,500 (in 2007)
- **Employer contributions**—sponsor must contribute *either* a specified matching *or* nonelective contribution (but not both)
- **Eligibility**—must cover all employees with 2 years of $5,000 or more of compensation
- **Vesting**—full and immediate vesting required
- **Withdrawal restrictions**—eligible for withdrawal at any time, but subject to special 25 percent penalty tax in first 2 years of participation
- **Investment restrictions**—like other IRAs, cannot invest in life insurance or most collectibles
- **Taxation**—like other IRAs, subject to ordinary income tax upon distribution

---

403(b) PLANS

Overview

403(b) plan

The plans we have studied up to this point are not limited to any particular type of industry. For the most part, they are available to any organization. In contrast to other retirement plans, a *403(b) plan* can be sold only to tax-exempt organizations and public schools. Despite these limitations, 403(b) plans represent a separate and lucrative opportunity for financial services professionals, particularly those who sell annuity products. A 403(b) plan, which is also referred to as a tax-sheltered annuity (TSA) or a tax-deferred annuity (TDA), is similar to a 401(k) plan. Like the 401(k) plan, the 403(b) plan

- permits an employee to defer tax on income by allowing before-tax contributions to be made to the employee's individual account
- allows the employer to make matching or nonelective contributions
- can be used in conjunction with, or in lieu of, most other retirement plans

However, 403(b) plans are distinguishable from 401(k) plans both in the market they serve and in their makeup. In this section, we will discuss the distinct market that 403(b) plans serve and analyze the fundamental makeup of a 403(b) plan.

Eligible Sponsors

Sec. 501(c)(3) organizations

A 403(b) program can only be sponsored by either *Sec. 501(c)(3) organizations* (employers that are exempt from tax under Code Sec. 501(c)(3)) or educational institutions of a state or political subdivision of a state. These can include public school districts, community colleges, state colleges, and state universities. Tax-exempt organizations under Code Sec. 501(c)(3) include entities organized and operated exclusively for religious, charitable, scientific, public safety testing, literary, or educational purposes. A state or local government or any of its agencies or instrumentalities can be a qualified employer, but only with regard to employees who perform (or have performed) service, directly or indirectly, for an educational organization. An educational organization is defined as one that maintains a regular faculty and curriculum and has a regularly enrolled body of students in attendance at the place where its educational activities are conducted.

YOUR FINANCIAL SERVICES PRACTICE: COMPLIANCE PROBLEMS

Believe it or not, one of the most common 403(b) compliance problems is an ineligible nonprofit organization adopting a plan. Do not set up a 403(b) plan or even take over the administration of a plan unless the client can produce the IRS document confirming that the entity is a 501(c)(3) organization.

Employee Status

Contributions to a 403(b) annuity plan can only be made on behalf of individuals who are current, former, or retired employees of an eligible employer. This includes employees who receive wages, bonuses, or other compensation reported on Form W-2, but does not include independent contractors. Clergy members are an exception. Even though they are generally considered self-employed for purposes of applying Social Security taxes, the employer may establish a 403(b) account on behalf of a clergy member.

Funding Vehicles

Funding a 403(b) annuity plan can be done either by purchasing an annuity contract from an insurance company or by purchasing shares in a mutual fund. Neither the Code nor the Regulations define what type of annuity contracts can be provided. Therefore, contracts with a wide variety of features may be used. They may be single-premium or annual-premium, provide for fixed variable annuity payments, begin immediately or provide deferred payments, and either include or omit a refund provision. Annuity contracts may also contain incidental life insurance protection. The term *incidental* has essentially the same meaning as in the qualified plan context (see chapter 10 for more detail). The other funding alternative is contributions to custodial accounts invested in regulated investment company stock, whether or not shares are redeemable—more commonly referred to as a mutual fund.

Even though there is some flexibility in the investment vehicles, there is certainly less flexibility than in qualified retirement plans. In qualified plans, assets can be invested directly in stocks, bonds, money instruments, or even more exotic investment alternatives. This distinction is probably less important than it first seems because 403(b) plans are most similar to 401(k) plans. Most 401(k) plans provide individual investment direction, giving participants the option to choose between a number of mutual funds or annuity options. Some 401(k) plans, however, actually offer individual brokerage accounts, which would not be allowed in a 403(b) plan.

Vesting Provisions

Similar to 401(k) plans, salary deferral contributions must be fully vested at all times. Employer contributions can be subject to the vesting schedules available for defined-contribution plans (see chapter 9). However, because of certain rules that at one time applied to 403(b) plans, most plans in existence do not use a deferred vesting schedule.

**YOUR FINANCIAL SERVICES PRACTICE:
THE ANNUITY CONTRACT**

In many ways, the 403(b) contract is more similar to an IRA account than to a pension trust. When employees leave, they can leave benefits in the account, or even transfer them to a 403(b) account with another vendor. Unlike the pension trust, the account can continue as a 403(b) account without the intervention of a plan sponsor. For a terminating employee, this is meaningful primarily for one reason: participant loans. If the 403(b) account is rolled over into an IRA, then loans become unavailable.

Employee Elections to Defer Salary

Tax-sheltered annuity contracts must be purchased by an eligible employer. However, the premiums paid by the employer may either constitute additional compensation for the employee or be indirectly paid by the employee as a reduction in salary. Amounts contributed under salary reduction are excludible from gross income (for federal tax purposes).

Plans that offer salary deferral contributions must offer the opportunity to all employees (regardless of age or years of service), unless such employees are covered under another salary deferral type plan.[4] In addition, the employer may not require a minimum contribution level beyond a de minimis contribution of $200. Nonresident aliens, students who work for their schools, and employees who normally work less than 20 hours per week are excluded from this requirement.

The agreement to defer salary must be legally binding and irrevocable for amounts earned while the agreement is in effect. An individual can change the election prospectively during the year (as often as the plan allows) or end the agreement for amounts not yet earned.

If a Code Sec. 403(b) annuity plan only contains salary deferral contributions, the plan is extremely simple to operate because it is generally not subject to ERISA and is subject to few tax rules that require ongoing compliance. In a salary deferral only plan, it is typical for vendors to solicit employee participation directly with little involvement of the sponsor.

Employer Contributions

Employers may use 403(b) plans as a means of providing additional retirement benefits for their employees. Including employer contributions drastically changes the nature of the plan, subjecting it to ERISA and placing additional fiduciary responsibility on the plan sponsor. Also, a significant number of additional tax rules—which make the 403(b) plan more like a qualified plan—will apply.

As in a 401(k) plan, employer contributions can be made as matching contributions based on employee elections to defer compensation. Another alternative is to make contributions on a nonelective basis, as in a profit-sharing plan or money-purchase pension plan. Typically, such plans provide contributions as a uniform percentage of compensation; however, some flexibility is available in determining the allocation formula. When employer contributions are made, the nondiscrimination requirements of Code Sec. 401(a)(4) will apply to the amount allocated to such contributions.

The following briefly describe the additional rules that apply to a 403(b) plan when the plan contains employer contributions other than salary deferrals. Note, however, that plans maintained by churches are exempt from these requirements and government-sponsored plans are exempt from many of the rules.

- *Coverage requirements:* The employer contribution feature has to satisfy the provisions of Code Sec. 410(b) (discussed in chapter 7).
- *Matching contributions:* The employer contribution must satisfy the average deferral percentage (ADP) test that applies to 401(k) plans (discussed in chapter 8).
- *Nonelective employer contributions:* The allocation of employer contributions must satisfy the nondiscrimination requirements of Code Sec. 401(a)(4) (discussed in chapter 8).
- *Timing of contributions:* Employee salary deferral contributions must be contributed by the 15th day of the month following the month when the employee would have otherwise received the contribution. Employer contributions can be made up to the due date of the employer's tax return (plus extensions) for the tax year ending with or within the plan year.
- *Joint-and-survivor requirements:* The plan will be subject to the qualified joint-and-survivor rules. The plan may, however, be eligible for the exception that applies to profit-sharing plans (see chapter 10).
- *Written plan document:* The written document identifies the named fiduciary, contains procedures for funding and administration, describes benefits and specifies when they will be paid.

Maximum Deferral Limit

The maximum salary reduction contribution made by an individual is subject to the same dollar limitations that apply to 401(k) plans. For 2007, the dollar limit is $15,500. Also, as with the 401(k) plan, additional contributions can be made by individuals who have attained age 50 by the end of the current year. For 2007, the additional allowable contribution is $5,000.

Also remember that the dollar limit applies to all contributions made by the individual to any 403(b) plan, 401(k) plan, simplified employee pension (SEP), or savings incentive match plan for employees (SIMPLE). This is true even if the individual is covered by plans of unrelated employers. For example, a 40-year-old participant deferring $6,000 in a 403(b) plan for 2007 would be able to defer only a maximum of $9,500 under a 401(k) arrangement for 2007.

On top of the normal limit (including the additional contribution allowed by participants over age 50), another special "catch-up" election applies to 403(b) plans. Individuals who have completed at least 15 years of service with most qualified sponsors[5] are eligible for the catch-up election. The otherwise applicable limit ($15,500 for 2007) is increased for such eligible individuals by the smallest of the following amounts:

- $3,000 (which makes the limit $18,500 for 2007)
- $15,000, reduced by increases to the regular limit the individual was allowed during earlier years because of this rule
- $5,000 times the number of years of service with the organization, minus the total elective deferrals made under the plan for the individual during earlier years.

Roth 403(b) Election

As with 401(k) plans, 403(b) plans may allow participants to treat some or all of their salary deferral contributions as Roth contributions. If the election is made, the contributions will be made on an after-tax basis and will be subject to the same tax treatment as Roth IRAs at the time of the distribution. This means that the participant would have the option to forgo tax deferral in exchange for tax-free treatment upon distribution.

From the 403(b) plan's perspective, Roth 403(b) contributions are characterized as salary deferral contributions. Salary deferral limits, nonforfeitability rules, and distribution restrictions remain the same (and apply to both pre-tax and Roth salary deferrals in aggregate). Because participants can only elect Roth treatment on salary deferral contributions, the election does not affect employer matching or nonelective contributions. For a more complete discussion see the Roth 401(k) material in chapter 5.

Code Sec. 415 Limitations

The Code Sec. 415 limitations that apply to qualified defined-contribution plans also apply to Code Sec. 403(b) annuity plans. The annual amount that can be credited to a participant's account, including employer contributions, employee contributions, and forfeitures, cannot exceed the lesser of 100 percent of the employee's compensation from the employer or $45,000 (indexed for 2007).

Loans and Distributions

Similar to 401(k) plans, 403(b) plan benefits are generally distributed at the time of termination of employment. In a plan funded with annuity contracts, salary deferral contributions can only be withdrawn in-service if the participant has attained age 59½ or suffers a financial hardship. When the plan is funded with mutual fund custodial accounts, then the in-service withdrawal restrictions apply to all types of contributions. Distributions are generally subject to ordinary income tax treatment and the 10 percent early withdrawal Sec. 72(t) penalty tax (discussed in chapter 24).

As an alternative to a distribution, loans can be made from 403(b) plans. The maximum amount that can be borrowed without creating a taxable event is the same as with qualified plans (see chapter 9). ERISA-subjected 403(b) plans will have to satisfy the ERISA requirements concerning availability, adequate security, and interest rates that apply to qualified plans (see chapter 9).

Proposed IRS Regulations

In 2004 the IRS issued proposed regulations for 403(b) plans. There had been a lack of guidance, and therefore the rules covered a wide range of areas. However, the proposed regulations have been quite controversial since they make a number of significant changes that would affect the marketplace. For example, the proposed regulations place many more requirements on 403(b) plans that are not subject to ERISA. The rules also prohibit life insurance as an investment alternative. Because of their controversial nature, the IRS has deferred the effective date of the regulations several times. Currently the IRS has indicated that the final regulations will not be effective before January 1, 2008. Since this guidance is likely to change, the text does not reflect the provisions of the proposed regulations.

MINI-CASES

Case One—Facts

Survey, Inc., wishes to establish a qualified plan for its employees. The company is relatively new, and profits fluctuate wildly. The employer would like to reward employees when the company does well and is somewhat concerned that the company has no retirement plan, which might make it difficult to attract experienced people to work there. The company is also concerned about the costs of maintaining the plan.

Case Two—Facts

Near Retirement, Inc., is a closely held company whose original owners are about to retire. The company has a defined-benefit pension plan, which has already served the purpose of providing benefits for the current owners. Assume that the owners do not have family members interested in the business, that the employees have worked for the company for a long time, and that the employees are potential buyers of the company.

Case Three—Facts

Stable, Inc., has had a modest money-purchase pension plan for a long time. Participation in the plan precludes employees from participating in a tax-deferred IRA. The company realizes that the plan is not adequate but has little additional money to provide retirement benefits.

Case Four—Facts

Teeny-Tiny Corp. has four employees. The owner realizes that competing employers are sponsoring 401(k) plans. To compete with the other employers, the owner would like a similar plan, but is not willing to pay the administrative expenses associated with that type of plan.

CHAPTER REVIEW

Key Terms

simplified employee pension
    (SEP) [6-1]
savings incentive match plan for
    employees (SIMPLE) [6-2]

403(b) plan [6-3]
Sec. 501(c)(3) organizations [6-3]

Review Questions

Review questions are based on the learning objectives in this chapter. Thus, a [6-3] at the end of a question means that the question is based on learning objective 6-3. If there are multiple objectives, they are all listed.

1. Describe a simplified employee pension (SEP) plan's similarities to the qualified plan and IRA, as well as the SEP's unique design characteristics. [6-1]

2. What are the major advantages and disadvantages of a SEP? [6-1]

3. In the following situations, identify whether a SEP is appropriate and, if not, what other type of plan the sponsor should consider. [6-1]
   a. Candidate Growthco, Inc., has indicated that it would like to have the option to avoid contributions in certain plan years. Growthco wants to motivate employees, but it is hesitant to use stock ownership as an incentive because the owners want to control all stock.
   b. Candidate Smallco, Inc., has five employees and has indicated that it would like to institute a plan that is administratively convenient and allows the company to skip contributions.
   c. Candidate TAMCO, Inc., would like to provide a plan that encourages participants to save for their own retirement and that allows for discretionary employer contributions. TAMCO would like to accomplish this objective in the most tax-efficient manner possible.
   d. The owner of candidate Transition, Inc., would like to retire and sell the company to the employees. Transition, Inc., employees do not have sufficient funds to purchase the stock outright.

4. Technology, Inc., maintains a SEP. Determine whether the following employees are eligible for the plan as of January 1, 2007. [6-1]
   a. Sally, aged 45, was hired August 15, 2004, on a full-time basis. Sally earns $55,000 a year.
   b. Rich works part-time on an on-and-off basis. He earned $3,000 in 2003, nothing in 2004, $2,500 in 2005, and $1,500 in 2006.

5. Describe the major characteristics of the SIMPLE plan. [6-2]

6. What are the contribution options that the employer has in a SIMPLE? [6-2]

7. What employers are most likely to choose the SIMPLE? [6-2]

8. Identify the market in which 403(b) plans can be used. [6-3]

9. The benefits administrator of Mercy Hospital has asked you to determine which of the following employees would be allowed to participate in the hospital's 403(b) plan. [6-3]

    a.   Dr. Smith, who heads up the hospital's radiology department and is a full-time employee of the hospital

    b.   Dr. Jones, who has admitting privileges at the hospital and is considered an independent contractor

    c.   Gary Green, who is called in by the hospital every summer to clean out the boilers

    d.   Joy Cheerful, who works part-time (500 hours per year) distributing magazines to patients

10. a.   List the two methods that can be used to fund a 403(b) plan.

      b.   How can insurance protection be provided under both of these methods? [6-3]

11.   What is the difference between a 403(b) plan that contains only salary deferral contributions versus one that has additional employer contributions? [6-3]

NOTES

1. The determination of whether a controlled group of corporations exists is governed by IRC Secs. 414(b) and (c). The area is quite complex, but as a rule of thumb, a controlled group exists when one company owns 80 percent or more of another corporation or the same five or fewer individuals have controlling interest in two or more businesses. The rules also apply to partnerships and sole proprietorships. In the small business setting, a common example would be one individual owning two separate businesses.

2. Code Sec. 408(l)

3. Code Sec. 6693(c)(1)

4. Including a Code Sec. 457 plan, a Code Sec. 401(k) plan, a SIMPLE, or another Code Sec. 403(b) annuity plan

5. Including an educational organization, hospital, home health service agency, health and welfare service agency, church, or convention or association of churches (or associated organization)

Coverage, Eligibility, and Participation Rules

Learning Objectives

An understanding of the material in this chapter should enable you to

7-1.   Explain how the adoption agreement can help facilitate the plan design process.

7-2.   Determine whether a qualified plan satisfies the minimum-coverage requirements of Code Sec. 410(b) and the minimum-participation rule of Code Sec. 401(a)(26).

7-3.   Identify planning opportunities under the minimum-coverage rules.

7-4.   Explain the rules for determining when participation must begin.

7-5.   Describe the impact of the controlled group, affiliated service group, and leased employee rules on tax-advantaged retirement plans.

Chapter Outline

Perhaps the most challenging assignment in the retirement field is advising a client about how his or her plan should be designed. In order to design a plan effectively, the financial services professional must

- acquire expertise about the qualification rules
- ascertain the client's objectives
- choose plan provisions that meet the qualification rules and accomplish employer objectives

In addition, both the client's objectives and the qualification rules are constantly evolving and require financial services professionals to monitor client needs and to know the latest laws and regulations. In this chapter and the following three chapters, we will define and explore the various plan-design features. The emphasis is on the qualification rules that apply to qualified plans and the ways in which plan design can be used to meet your client's objectives. The last part of the chapter reviews the different rules that apply to other tax-sheltered plans. Let's start, however, with a brief overview of the plan-design process.

THE PLAN-DESIGN PROCESS

The first step toward effective plan design has already been taken. The fact finder that you set up to choose the best retirement plan can also be used to help you properly design the plan. However, the plan design is dictated not only by the client's objectives but also by the laws and regulations regarding plan qualification. In other words, picking the specific provisions that will constitute the client's plan consists of weighing what the Internal Revenue Code permits against the client's objectives and pocketbook. Take, as an example, the first design feature we consider—which employees should be eligible for the plan. The coverage rules are quite complex. In this case, complexity allows a great deal of freedom in plan design, but it also requires intimate knowledge of the boundaries of the law.

The plan-design process is simplified for insurance agents and other financial services professionals by the use of master and prototype plan documents. With these documents, most of the plan language is standardized and the employer has limited design alternatives, which are contained in a

adoption agreement   document referred to as the *adoption agreement*. The adoption-agreement approach helps the advisor by organizing the design process. The document is relatively simple to follow because it lists the design features and provides several alternatives under each one (for example, the various vesting schedules and the alternative design choices available for early, normal, and deferred retirement). Employers (with your help) then pick from the menu of options that is provided.

The adoption agreement simplifies plan design by directing and limiting available design options, but it also locks out from consideration some important but nonstandard design choices that might meet a unique employer need. Generally, if employers desire this specialized treatment, they should pay the additional fees to have an attorney, consulting firm, or insurance company home office design the plan (called an individually designed plan). On the other hand, employers willing to buy an "off-the-rack" plan probably can save on fees and yet meet their goals and objectives through the use of the standard design options contained in your company's adoption agreement.

You can see that to properly advise the client, the advisor needs to have an in-depth understanding of the rules. Knowing the options in the adoption agreement is not enough. The advisor must know the limits of the law, so the client will be able to decide when it is time to establish a plan that does not fall within the prototype options.

**YOUR FINANCIAL SERVICES PRACTICE:
EFFECTIVE PLAN DESIGN**

As a rule of thumb, any design decision you make in one area of the adoption agreement should be consistent with design decisions you make in other areas of the adoption agreement. In other words, one strategy in designing an effective plan is to ask yourself: Does each design decision consistently support the employer's objectives? For example, if the desire to limit costs attributable to short-service employees motivated the employer to choose the most restrictive age and service requirements offered in the adoption agreement, the same employer objective should also generate a restrictive vesting schedule and a benefit formula that rewards service. This approach to plan design will ensure a design that is correct and complete. However, remember the words of Alfred North Whitehead: "Seek simplicity and distrust it." There may be reasons to stray from design consistency to meet a unique employer objective.

QUALIFIED PLAN COVERAGE REQUIREMENTS

The first major design decision that faces you and your client is to decide which employees to cover under the retirement plan. This decision is directed by extensive and complicated laws and regulations. As a payback for providing valuable tax advantages for tax-advantaged retirement plans (and consequently losing revenue), the legislature requires that retirement plans must cover a broad spectrum of employees and not just a group of highly compensated employees (who are defined by statute).

All qualified plans are governed by the same coverage rules, except that defined-benefit-type plans are subject to an additional coverage requirement. In this section, we review the qualified plan rules. SEPs, SIMPLEs, and 403(b) plans are each subject to separate eligibility requirements, which are discussed at the end of the chapter.

The Definition of a Highly Compensated Employee

Understanding the coverage requirements begins with the identification of the employees who are considered highly compensated employees (HCE). We first encountered the highly compensated group when discussing the 401(k) actual deferral percentage test. As you may recall, highly compensated employees include individuals who are 5-percent owners during the current or previous year and individuals who earned $100,000 (indexed limit for 2006 and 2007) in the preceding year. Under the second category, the employer can elect to limit the group to only those individuals whose earnings put them in the top 20 percent of all employees.

The 410(b) Rule

Sec. 410(b) of the Internal Revenue Code specifies who must be covered under a qualified plan. The rules are meaningful any time the employer decides not to cover all employees under the plan. The employer may want to exclude one class of workers, such as hourly employees, or employees who are part-time or have short service. In other cases, the employer may want to set up two or more plans, each covering a different group of employees. Essentially, a plan can cover any portion of the workforce, as long as it satisfies one of three tests under Sec. 410(b): the percentage test, the ratio test, or the average-benefit test.

When performing any of these tests, note that certain classes of employees can always be excluded from testing. These include collectively bargained employees, employees who have worked less than one year, certain part-time employees (those who work less than 1,000 hours per year), and employees younger than age 21 (discussed in more detail later in this chapter). These employees are referred to as *excludible employees*. Essentially, this means a plan can always exclude those employees defined as excludible, as well as any additional employees as allowed under one of the three coverage tests.

Also, be aware that when testing a 401(k) plan, an individual eligible to make a salary deferral election is considered a participant in the plan, regardless of whether he or she makes the election to make a salary deferral. For other plans, this is not the case. Subject to several exceptions, a participant must actually receive a contribution (or benefit accrual in a defined-benefit plan) in order to be considered a participant for that year.

percentage test

The Percentage Test

A plan will satisfy Sec. 410(b) if it benefits at least 70 percent of employees who are not highly compensated employees. As just described, employees who are not eligible for participation in the plan because they do not meet the age and service requirements or who are covered by a collective-bargaining agreement (discussed later in the chapter) are not counted for purposes of this test.

Example: The law firm of Block, Meyers, and Andrews has 24 employees. Because four of these employees work part-time and have not met the minimum-service requirements for participation in the plan (discussed later in the chapter), the percentage test would apply only to the remaining 20 employees. Of these employees, 12 fall within the statutory definition of highly compensated and eight do not. Six of the eight employees who are not highly compensated belong to the Manhattan office (the one covered by the plan) and two belong to the Teaneck, New Jersey, office (which does not have a plan). Under the percentage test, the plan must benefit at least 70 percent of the eight employees who are not highly compensated (note that employees from both offices are counted). That is, six employees (six out of eight is 75 percent) must be benefited. Because the law firm's Manhattan plan benefits six of the nonhighly compensated employees, the plan passes the percentage test.

---

ratio test

The Ratio Test

The *ratio test* requires a plan to benefit a percentage of nonhighly compensated employees equal to at least 70 percent of the percentage of highly compensated employees benefited under the plan. Again, employees who are not eligible for participation in the plan because they do not meet the age and service requirements or are covered by a collective-bargaining agreement are not counted for purposes of the ratio test.

Example: The Thunder Company has 120 employees on its payroll. Because 20 of these have not yet met the plan's minimum age and service requirements, the ratio test would apply to only 100 employees. Thirty of the remaining employees are highly compensated, and 15 of the 30 highly compensated employees actually participate in the plan (the additional 15 are part of a separate group that does not have a plan). Seventy of the remaining employees are nonhighly compensated, and 40 of the 70 nonhighly compensated employees participate in the plan (the additional 30 are part of the separate group that does not have a plan).

Because 50 percent (15 out of 30) of the highly compensated employees participate in the plan, the ratio test requires that at least 35 percent of the nonhighly compensated employees (70% x 50% = 35%) must benefit under the plan. In other words, at least 25 (35% x 70 = 24.5) nonhighly compensated employees must benefit under the plan. Because Thunder Company has 40 nonhighly compensated employees benefiting under the plan, the plan satisfies the ratio test.

Average-Benefit Test

Another way to satisfy the minimum-coverage requirements is to satisfy the average-benefits test. This is a complex analysis that has three separate parts. Here we will summarize these rules and explain when they are generally applied, but will not get into all of the details.

The first requirement under the average-benefits test is that the plan has to cover employees who represent a *reasonable classification of employees*—which means that the eligibility requirements (specifying who qualifies for participation and who does not) must use some objective means of classification, such as job classification, nature of compensation (salaried or hourly), or geographic location. The second part of the test is a com–plicated percentage test. Suffice it to say that the percentage of nonhighly compensated employees required to be covered under this section is

**average-benefit-
percentage test**

generally quite small. The third part of the test is the *average-benefit-percentage test*. This portion is satisfied if the average-benefit percentage for nonhighly compensated employees is at least 70 percent of the average-benefit percentage of the highly compensated employees. This requirement is different from the others in that it counts benefits earned in any qualified plan sponsored by the employer.

In operation, note that the administrator will test the plan under the less complicated percentage and ratio tests before tackling the more complex average-percentage test. The reason for this test is to provide relief for the larger employer that wants to cover most employees under some qualified plan, but chooses to cover them under two or more separate plans. The employer might want to do this because it has different geographic locations or has workers with very different types of jobs. Although the math is complex, the bottom line is that the employer can generally have such an arrangement as long as, overall, the benefits for nonhighly compensated employees under all of the plans are at least 70 percent of the benefits provided to the highly compensated under all of the plans.

For the small employer sponsoring one plan, the average-benefit test will not result in lower required participation than the ratio test. All of the nonhighly compensated employees who are excluded from the plan are counted as having zero benefits when determining whether the average-percentage test has been satisfied. In other words, the small employer sponsoring one plan will have to satisfy the percentage or ratio test. The average-benefit test will be of no help.

Three Minimum-Coverage Tests

- *Percentage test*—the plan covers at least 70 percent of nonhighly compensated employees
- *Ratio test*— the percentage of nonhighly compensated employees covered is at least 70 percent of the percentage of HCEs covered under the plan
- *Average-benefit test*—the group covered represents a reasonable classification, a complex minimum percentage test is satisfied, and the benefits of nonhighly compensated employees average at least 70 percent of the benefits provided to HCEs, looking at all of the sponsor's retirement plans

---

**separate lines of
business**

Separate Lines of Business

If an employer has *separate lines of business,* the 410(b) tests may be applied separately in each line of business. In order to qualify for this favorable treatment, the separate lines of business must be operated for bona fide business reasons and must have at least 50 employees. The IRS has issued complex regulations for determining whether a separate line of business exists. Because of the difficulty of demonstrating compliance, most employers will look to the separate-lines-of-business rules only as a last resort—when trying to ensure that each plan meets the coverage requirements.

Coverage of Employees in Comparable Plans

For various reasons an employer may want to establish two or more plans for separate groups of employees. The sponsor may have different business locations, or have acquired the retirement plan of a subsidiary. If one or more of the plans cannot satisfy the coverage rules on their own, Sec. 410(b) allows the plans to be aggregated and tested together, as long as their total combined benefits do not discriminate in favor of the highly compensated. Chapter 8 clarifies the nondiscrimination requirements.

The 401(a)(26) Minimum-Participation Rule

401(a)(26) minimum-participation rule

Defined-benefit plans must satisfy a second coverage requirement under Code Sec. 401(a)(26), referred to as the *minimum-participation rule*. Under this rule, an employer's plan is not qualified unless it covers (1) 50 employees or (2) 40 percent of the employer's employees, *whichever is lesser*. However, a special rule applies when there are two employees; in this case, both employees must be covered.

This rule does not count employees who are not eligible because of the age and service requirements or who are part of a group covered by a collective-bargaining agreement. The effect of this rule is that employers with more than 125 employees cannot maintain a plan covering fewer than 50 participants, and if the employer has fewer than 125 employees, then the 40 percent limit applies. The result is that smaller employers are limited to a maximum of two separate plans (in order to meet the 40-percent rule).

Apparently, the justification to have an additional eligibility requirement for defined-benefit plans is because Congress is concerned that small employers would establish defined-benefit plans that only covered the companies' owners and would cover other employees under a separate defined-contribution plan with less value. The minimum-participation requirement eliminates this possibility.

Planning Opportunities under the Coverage Rules

As we have seen, the qualified plan coverage rules provide a significant amount of flexibility. This allows the employer to meet a range of objectives. Some employers will see the value of covering all employees, while some will want to save costs by excluding certain employees. Others will want to provide a different level of benefits for different classes of employees. And some small employers will simply want to maximize retirement benefits for owners and key employees and limit the expense of providing benefits for the rank-and-file employees. Here, we will discuss some of the tools that can be used to satisfy these objectives.

Advantages of Covering Employees

Covering employees does have an associated cost, and an employer may be tempted to limit coverage as much as possible. Before taking this action, the employer should appreciate that there can be real value to covering employees. This is not an idealistic plea for the underdog or merely an opportunity to increase commissions for the financial advisor—there are sound business reasons to cover employees.

First, an employee who is not covered by the plan resents being excluded and will eventually seek employment elsewhere. Even if the employer spent only 40 work-hours training that individual, 80 work-hours have been lost because the training process must be repeated with the replacement. The cycle is also apt to repeat itself several times. What's more, the most important asset a small business can have is experienced rank-and-file employees. There is little room for inexperienced, unproductive, or counterproductive people in any organization, and—especially in small businesses—retirement plans go a long way toward coaxing employees to remain long enough to become experienced, productive workers.

The second reason to cover the rank-and-file in a small business is to encourage loyalty and team spirit. For small businesses, it is crucial that their employees be not only experienced but also committed to the welfare of the business. The result is that the principal reasons to encourage a retirement umbrella that covers all employees is that the business is best served by this arrangement and that it *is* cost-effective to include nonkey employees.

Excluding Employees

If the employer does want to limit coverage, the rules allow the employer to exclude a portion of the workforce. As discussed in this chapter, the rules allow the employer to exclude the following employees:

- All employees who have not satisfied minimum age and service requirements or who are subject to a collective bargaining agreement (often referred to as *excludibles*) can be excluded without issue.
- If the plan covers all of the highly compensated employees, up to 30 percent of the (nonexcludible) nonhighly compensated employees can also be excluded.
- Any HCE can be excluded from coverage.
- If the plan excludes some of the highly compensated employees, even more than 30 percent of the nonhighly compensated employees can be excluded.

Also note that if the employer excludes all highly compensated employees, the plan can cover any group of nonhighly compensated employees without regard to either coverage rule. This strategy will not work for many small employers, but occasionally the employer may be satisfied to provide executive benefits through a nonqualified plan. This approach can make sense if the employer wants to cover a very small percentage of the rank-and-file employees.

More typically, at least some highly compensated are covered. But as you can see in the example below, the coverage tests (specifically the ratio test) allow the exclusion of a significant number of rank-and-file employees when some of the highly compensated employees are excluded from the plan. This rule can be effective for small businesses when some highly compensated employees are not interested in participating in the plan because they are very young, very old, or not interested for other reasons.

Example: Loophole, Inc., has 10 employees (who are not excludibles). Two are highly compensated and eight are not. If the employer establishes a defined-contribution plan that covers one highly compensated employee, only 35 percent, or three, of the nonhighly compensated employees have to be covered. This is because, under the ratio test, 70 percent of the percentage of highly compensated employees covered (50 percent) equals 35 percent.

One important limitation applies to the rules as described. The Age Discrimination in Employment Act (ADEA) prohibits discrimination against individuals aged 40 and older. To avoid problems under this act (and possibly other state laws), a plan provision excluding a group of employees from a qualified plan should be based on a reasonable (and real) job classification. For example, the plan may exclude hourly employees, secretaries, associate attorneys, or other job classifications. It is a good idea to seek the advice of a labor or employment lawyer when addressing this specific issue. Also, remember that defined-benefit plans have to satisfy the minimum participation rule.

Other Planning Strategies

When the employer wants to limit costs for rank-and-file employees, there are a number of other strategies, which include the following:

- *Delay participation.* As described below, the rules allow the employer to defer participation up to 6 months after attaining the eligibility requirements. Taking advantage of these rules eliminates the costs of covering some short-term employees.
- *Minimize the benefit.* In the next chapter, we discuss another way to limit costs—to cover many employees but limit the benefit for rank-and-file employees. This can be accomplished by using a defined-benefit plan, target-benefit plan, or cross-tested profit-sharing plan when the owners are older than the rank-and-file employees.
- *Divide into separate employers.* One strategy that generally will not work is to establish a plan for the key employees, and then create a separate business entity for the rank-and-file employees. As discussed below, in most cases these separate entities will be treated as a single employer, and this creates a problem under the aggregation rules

WHEN SHOULD PARTICIPATION BEGIN?

Once you and your client have decided on the employees who should and must be covered, the next step is to decide when an employee's participation should begin. In general, participation can be delayed for certain employees on the basis of their ages and their years of service with the company.

There are several reasons to delay participation as long as legally possible. For one thing, employees do not start earning benefits until they become plan participants (except in defined-benefit plans, which may count service with the employer prior to the participation date for benefit purposes). Also, by delaying participation, the client's organization can save retirement dollars attributable to turnover. A second cost-saving feature of delayed participation involves the administrative and record-keeping duties associated with tracking employees who leave. Because turnover is highest for employees in their first few years of employment and for younger employees, it makes sense from an administrative standpoint to delay their participation in the plan. Besides, if the retirement plan is funded with individual insurance policies, the employer loses out on funds that provide death benefits and the commissions paid for benefits for employees who leave (the front-end load).

There are, on the other hand, some good reasons to begin participation immediately. These include the maximization of contributions for employees by not delaying coverage and attracting specialized employees by making the plan highly competitive. These specialized employees (such as a computer professional or a high-powered salesperson) usually possess desired skills or profit-making ability, and any delay in participation may make the plan's benefit package less appealing to them.

If your client's circumstances warrant immediate participation, then the plan should be designed appropriately. But even under such circumstances, the client must still adhere to the statutory participation rules. In general, any employee who is not excluded from the plan based upon employment classification must become a participant no later than the first entry date after the employee meets the plan's age and service requirements. The maximum age and service requirements are age 21 and one year of service (commonly referred to as the *21-and-one rule*). After an employee becomes 21 and has completed one year of service, he or she is entitled to join the plan on the next plan entry date.

21-and-one rule

The 2-Year/100 Percent Rule

2-year/100 percent rule

There is one exception that applies to the general 21-and-one rule, and that is a special provision that allows up to a 2-year service requirement if the employee is immediately 100 percent vested upon becoming a participant (called the *2-year/100 percent rule*). This method is desirable if the company's vesting schedules are already as liberal as the 2-year/100 percent schedule and your client desires to delay participation as long as possible. If your client wants both a more restrictive vesting schedule and to delay participation, however, you will have to determine which carries more weight—the maximum-service requirement or the restrictive vesting schedules.

Entry Date

The last component associated with plan participation is the selection of an entry date for employees to become participants in the plan. An employee who meets the plan's minimum age and service requirements, and who is otherwise eligible to participate in the plan, must be allowed to participate no later than the earlier of (1) the first day of the first plan year beginning after the date the employee met the age and service requirements, or (2) the date 6 months after these conditions are met. In other words, entry dates can delay participation up to 6 months after the 21-and-one or 2-year/100 percent hurdles are jumped. For clients who want to delay participation as long as possible, semiannual entry dates should be set up, typically January 1 and July 1. This way, the employer can maximize the pre-participation period. Other typical entry dates include the plan's anniversary date (this can be used only if the age requirement is not more than 20 1/2 and the service requirement is 6 months or less), quarterly entry dates, monthly entry dates, and daily entry dates.

Determining Service

The term *year of service* has a special meaning for purposes of meeting the one-year-of-service or 2-years-of-service eligibility requirements. An employee who works 1,000 hours during the initial 12-month period after being employed will earn a year of service. For example, Larry is hired on October 5, 2001. If Larry has worked at least 1,000 hours or more by October 4, 2002, he has acquired a year of service. Note that Larry does not receive a year of service after he worked his 1,000th hour, but rather on his first anniversary of employment.

The phrase *an hour of service* also has a special meaning; it includes not only the hours an employee works, but also any hours for which an employee is entitled to be paid, such as for vacations, holidays, and sick time. One way to compute the hours for purposes of the 1,000-hour requirement is to count each hour an employee works for which he or she is entitled to be paid (the standard-hours counting method).

Because the standard-hours counting method can be administratively cumbersome, the IRC permits alternative counting methods—called *equivalencies*—to be used. However, in choosing an equivalency, the employer pays a premium of extra hours for using this administratively convenient system. Therefore, another aspect of plan design is to help your client choose the best alternative. Equivalencies include the following:

- The elapsed-time method, which does not look at hours of service worked because service is measured from date of employment to date of severance. For example, if Barbara starts working on January 18, she would have one year of service on the following January 18, regardless of how many hours she actually worked.
- The hours-worked-including-overtime method, which looks at the actual hours worked including overtime but excluding nonworked hours such as vacations, holidays, and sick time. If this test is used, an employee needs to work only 870 hours to earn a year of service.

YOUR FINANCIAL SERVICES PRACTICE:
THE ELIGIBILITY AND PARTICIPATION RULES IN A SAMPLE ADOPTION AGREEMENT

The following sample illustrates how the rules might appear in a typical adoption agreement (note that terms with the first letter capitalized are defined in the plan):

Section B: Eligibility (refers to Section 2 of the plan)

(1)   The Age and Service requirements for participation in the Plan are

    (a)   attainment of age ___ (not to exceed 21)

    (b)   completion of ___ year(s) of service (not to exceed one year, unless the Plan provides full and immediate vesting (Section G). (If the Plan provides for full and immediate vesting, it is not to exceed 2 years.)

(2)   The Plan's entry date will be (check one)

    ( )   daily
    ( )   the Friday in any calendar week
    ( )   the first day of any calendar month
    ( )   quarterly (Jan. 1, April 1, July 1, Oct. 1)
    ( )   semiannually (Jan. 1, July 1)
    ( )   annually (Jan. 1) (Note: If the entry date is annually then the age requirement in Section B(1)(a) cannot exceed 20 1/2 and the service requirement in Section B(1)(b) cannot be more than 6 months.)

(3)   Hours of service shall be determined on the basis of the method selected below. The method selected shall be applied to all employees covered under the Plan. (Check one)

    ( )   On the basis of actual hours for which an employee is paid or entitled to payment
    ( )   On the basis of days worked. An employee shall be credited with 10 hours of service if, under Section 19 of the Plan, such employee would be credited with at least one hour of service during the day.
    ( )   On the basis of weeks worked. An employee shall be credited with 45 hours of service if, under Section 19 of the Plan, such employee would be credited with at least one hour of service during the week.
    ( )   On the basis of semimonthly payroll periods. An employee shall be credited with 95 hours of service if, under Section 19 of the Plan, such employee would be credited with at least one hour of service during the semimonthly payroll period.
    ( )   On the basis of months worked. An employee shall be credited with 190 hours of service if, under Section 19 of the Plan, such employee would be credited with at least one hour of service during the month.

- The hours-worked-excluding-overtime method, which looks at the actual hours worked, excluding overtime, vacations, holidays, and sick time. If this test is used, an employee needs only 750 hours for a year of service.
- The time-period or pay-period method, which looks at the days, weeks, semimonthly pay periods, months, or shifts actually worked by the employee and applies the following equivalencies:
  - a credit of 10 hours of service per day if the employee worked one hour in any day
  - a credit of 45 hours of service per week if the employee worked one hour in any week
  - a credit of 95 hours of service per semimonthly pay period if the employee worked one hour in any pay period
  - a credit of 190 hours per month if the employee worked one hour in any month
  - a credit of the number of hours per shift if the employee worked one hour in any shift
- The equivalencies-based-on-earnings method, which calculates the hours worked on the basis of the employee's earnings. For example, if the employee is paid hourly, the equivalency can be determined by dividing the employee's total earnings by the hourly wage. (If the hourly wage changed over a period, the employer should look at the actual hourly wage, the lowest hourly wage during the period, or the lowest hourly wage paid to employees in the same or similar job classification during that period.) If the employee's earnings are not based on hourly rates, the hourly rate is calculated by translating the employee's salary into an hourly rate—for example, by dividing annual salary by a 40-hour week or 8-hour day.

The choice of an equivalency boils down to two disparate considerations. The first is administrative convenience. By coordinating the hours of service with payroll's records, the employer may be able to use an existing computer or accounting system and eliminate duplication of work efforts. The second and more important concern when choosing an hour-of-service definition is to permanently exclude part-time employees from the plan. This can result in substantial savings for your client. Furthermore, it will not prejudice your client when the coverage rules are applied because part-time employees (with less than 1,000 hours of service) are generally not counted for purposes of the 401(a)(4), 410(b)(1), or 401(a)(26) tests. If your client wants to exclude part-time employees, as is usually the case, then it is likely that the standard-hours counting method should be used in lieu of any equivalency (note that all equivalency methods generously define the hours used). To make sure part-time employees do not slip in under these rules—

and complicate administration of the plan—the employer may want to establish a policy that limits the number of hours part-time employees can work.

Case Study: The Matthew Matt Manufacturing Company

The Matthew Matt Manufacturing Company, makers of wrestling mats, employs 75 full-time employees and 15 part-time employees. Owner Matthew Matt is establishing a qualified plan and is trying to determine the appropriate eligibility and participation provisions. He desires to minimize costs, encourage rank-and-file employees to stay (experienced mat makers are hard to find), and exclude part-time employees from the plan. In addition, Matthew tells you that a competitive wrestling mat company is forming in the area. The relevant questions the financial services professional must address are these:

- Should participation be delayed and, if so, for how long?
- What definition of hour of service should be used?
- What entry date should be used?

In answer to the first question, Matthew Matt should delay participation as a cost-saving measure. When a plan is installed in an existing business, however, the employer must take into account the service already acquired (preplan service) for eligibility purposes. In this case, to placate employees who might jump to the competitor, the plan will count preplan service.

How long Matthew delays participation—which could be for one or 2 years, the statutory maximums—would depend on his decision about vesting and his perception of the competitive threat.

Because Matthew wants to exclude part-time employees to the fullest possible extent, the company will choose the most restrictive method for determining whether the 1,000-hours-of-service requirement has been met. This is generally the standard-hours counting method. However, if Matthew uses his part-time employees seasonally (for 2 months during wrestling season) and needs them for overtime during that period, then the most restrictive method might be the hours-worked-excluding-overtime method. This method looks at the actual hours worked and excludes overtime, the Christmas holidays (which fall in wrestling season), sick time, and the like.

When choosing an entry date, considerations such as administrative convenience and employee morale also come into play. Because employee morale is most important in light of the threat of competition, it will probably be desirable to choose a less restrictive entry date that matches administrative pay practices—monthly, for example.

AGGREGATION RULES

To avoid the coverage requirements, some employers try to segregate their management employees from the rank-and-file employees by creating a related or subsidiary corporation. To close this loophole, the Code contains what are referred to as the *controlled-group rules* that require aggregation of employers that have a sufficient amount of common ownership, and the *affiliated service groups rules* for other situations in which related businesses work together to provide goods or services to the public. When either aggregation rule applies, the employers are treated as one employer for virtually all of the qualified plan rules. Both rules apply to corporations and "trades and businesses," including partnerships, proprietorships, estates, and trusts. Note that the affiliation rules also apply to SEPs, SIMPLEs, and 403(b) plans. Regulations provide guidance for determining ownership interests in these kinds of entities.

A third type of affiliation relates to situations in which individuals are "leased" on a long-term, full-time basis. In some cases, such individuals are treated as working for the recipient for purposes of the coverage requirements. Each of these rules is covered more fully below.

Controlled-Group Rules

controlled groups

There are three types of *controlled groups:* parent-subsidiary, brother-sister, and combined groups. A parent-subsidiary controlled group exists whenever one entity (referred to as the *parent company*) owns at least 80 percent of one (or more) of the other entities. Additional entities may be brought into the group if a chain of common ownership exists. Other entities included in the chain must be at least 80 percent owned by one or more (in combination) of the other entities within the chain.

Example: Corporation A owns 80 percent of Corporations B and C, and Corporations B and C each own 40 percent of Corporation D. Because Corporation D is 80 percent owned by entities within the group, Corporation D is part of the parent-subsidiary controlled group that includes all four corporations.

A brother-sister controlled group exists whenever the same five (or fewer) owners of two or more entities own 80 percent or more of each entity, and more than 50 percent of each entity when counting only *identical ownership*. Identical ownership is tested by counting each person's ownership to the extent that it is identical in each entity. For example, if an individual owns 10 percent of Corporation A and 20 percent of Corporation B, he or she has a 10 percent identical ownership interest with respect to each corporation. The identical ownership interests of each of the five (or fewer) individuals is added together to determine whether the 50-percent test has been satisfied, as shown in table 7-1 for these shareholders.

TABLE 7-1
Identical Ownership

Shareholder	Corporation X	Corporation Y	Identical Ownership
Joe	20%	12%	12%
Sally	60%	14%	14%
Ralph	20%	74%	20%
Total	100%	100%	46%

Under these assumed facts, the 80 percent ownership test has been met, because three individuals who have ownership in each entity own 100 percent of both businesses. However, the 50-percent-identical-ownership-interest test has not been satisfied (only 46 percent identical ownership). Therefore, this group does not constitute a controlled group.

When determining an individual's ownership interest under the brother-sister controlled-group rules, attribution rules require that stock owned by spouses (with one narrow exception) and children under age 21 must be treated as owned by the individual. When a person owns more than 50 percent of an entity, he or she is deemed to own any interest owned in that entity by his or her adult children, grandchildren, parents, and grandparents as well.

The last type of controlled group is the combined group under common control. A combined group exists if an entity is both a common parent in a

Types of Controlled Groups

- Parent-subsidiary
- Brother-sister
- Combined

parent-subsidiary group and a member of a brother-sister group. If this is the case, the two related controlled groups are treated as one controlled group.

Affiliated Service Group Rules

affiliated service group

In 1980, Congress enacted the first *affiliated service group* rules. Small business corporations had managed to divide management and the rank-and-file into separate entities and avoid the controlled-group rules. The rules have been expanded several times over the years to address new avoidance schemes. Today, the law is quite complex, and the details are beyond the scope of this book. However, when working with clients, there are several threshold issues that help advisors to identify when affiliation problems might be present. Except for management services affiliation (discussed below), affiliated groups exist only when all three of the following elements are present:

- when two or more business entities work together to provide one service or product to the public
- when at least one of the entities is a service organization, which is an organization for which capital is not a material income-producing factor. Organizations in the fields of health, law, engineering, actuarial science, consulting, and insurance are automatically deemed service organizations.
- when at least some common ownership exists between the two entities

The affiliation rules come into play regularly in the medical world, where there are partnerships between doctors and hospitals that provide services in outpatient clinics, MRI testing centers, and other cooperative medical centers. In these cases, there must be a careful analysis to see if the MRI testing center, for example, is affiliated with the doctor's medical practice or with the hospital.

Management services affiliation is defined by a much broader rule, which essentially prohibits an executive of any size company from separating him- or herself from the company for the purpose of establishing his or her own retirement plan.

The Leasing of Employees

Instead of hiring employees directly, a business may lease employees from a third party for a number of legitimate reasons. Unfortunately, at one time, leasing of employees was also used as a way to circumvent the minimum-coverage requirements. The employer would lease rank-and-file employees and then exclude them from plan eligibility. Code Sec. 414(n) was enacted to eliminate such practices by requiring that individuals leased on a full-time, ongoing basis would be treated as employees for purposes of the coverage requirements.

leased employee   A *leased employee* is a person who provides services to the recipient and meets all three of the following requirements:

- The services are provided pursuant to an agreement between the recipient and a leasing organization.
- The services are provided on a substantially full-time basis for a period of at least one year.
- The individual's services are performed under the primary direction or control of the service recipient.

**YOUR FINANCIAL SERVICES PRACTICE:
AVOIDING HIDDEN AGGREGATION PROBLEMS**

One common problem the financial services professional faces when setting up a retirement plan is finding out important information at the last minute or after the fact. For example, an employer who is interested in setting up a plan for the ABC Company may also own the XYZ Company, but fails to mention this important information. Because it is possible that the employees of both ABC and XYZ must be considered for the purposes of the coverage requirements, it is important to question the employer about additional holdings, other key employees' additional holdings, and the corporation's additional holdings. (See question 8 in Step 7 in the fact finder in chapter 3.) In the small-company context, the minimum-coverage rules are unforgiving, and an employer who misses a controlled-group issue may very well end up with one or more disqualified plans. The problem is even worse with a SEP or SIMPLE where the coverage rules have no flexibility at all. This is a complex area of the law, and the role of the pension advisor should be to identify affiliation issues and then encourage the client to pursue a final determination from a qualified tax attorney.

Under the regulations, an individual need not be an employee of a leasing organization. The leasing relationship can exist directly with the leased employee, which means that a self-employed individual can be treated as a leased employee. Services are deemed to be substantially full time for a year if the individual is credited with 1,500 or more hours of service (this number is reduced if employees generally work fewer than 40 hours per week). Legislative history indicates that the "primary direction or control" test is determined when considering whether the recipient of the leased employee's services has control of where, when, and how services are performed; the order in which they are performed; who performs them; and whether the leased employee is directly supervised. This same legislative history indicates that clerical workers are generally considered within primary direction and control, while self-employed professionals such as attorneys, accountants, computer programmers, and the like are not.

Even if an individual is a leased employee under the above conditions, he or she will not be treated as an employee of the recipient if leased employees constitute no more than 20 percent of the recipient's nonhighly compensated workforce and the leasing entity maintains a safe harbor plan. A safe harbor plan must be a money-purchase plan with a nonintegrated contribution rate of at least 10 percent of compensation and must provide for immediate eligibility and 100 percent immediate vesting.

The objective of the leased employee rule is to ensure that a company cannot avoid covering a large number of employees by leasing them versus hiring them directly. On the other hand, if the employer leases only a few individuals, the minimum-coverage rules have enough latitude to allow the leased employees to be excluded from the qualified plan—or, in the alternative, the leased individuals can be ignored if the leasing organization maintains a safe harbor qualified plan. In this way, the leased employee rules work fairly well to eliminate abusive situations without penalizing the average employer. In general, the most annoying requirement for employers is that businesses that receive nonemployee services are required to keep records to demonstrate whether individuals are technically considered leased employees. An employer may be exempted from the record-keeping requirement, but only if all three of the following conditions are satisfied:

- All of the recipient's qualified plans must specifically state that leased employees are not eligible to participate.
- No qualified plan of the recipient can be top-heavy.
- The number of leased persons who provide services to the recipient during the plan year must be less than 5 percent of the number of employees (excluding leased persons and HCEs) covered by the recipient's qualified plans.

A final note: The controlled-group rules, affiliated service rules, and leased employee rules were written to eliminate most situations in which entities were artificially separated so a qualified plan would cover only some of the employees. Be careful when looking at any arrangement that "smells bad." The rules are fairly comprehensive—most such schemes are prohibited. This is one area of the law where if it looks too good to be true, it probably is!

OTHER TAX-SHELTERED RETIREMENT PLANS

While the eligibility and participation requirements for qualified plans are quite flexible, this is not the case for SEPs and SIMPLEs. The rules here are rather rigid. The same eligibility requirements that apply to qualified plans apply to 403(b) plans, as well as an additional requirement that applies to salary deferral elections. Also note that the aggregation rules discussed in this chapter apply when performing the coverage tests for 403(b) plans, SEPs, and SIMPLEs.

SEPs

As described in chapter 6, any individual (not subject to a collective bargaining agreement) who is aged 21 and has earned $500 (2007 indexed amount) in 3 of the 5 previous plan years must be a participant as of the first day of the following plan year. Take, for example, an individual who meets the compensation requirement in 2003, 2004, and 2005, and works for a company that maintains a SEP on a calendar-year basis. That person must have become a participant as of January 1, 2006.

Under these inflexible requirements, all long-term employees—even part-timers—must be covered under the plan. This causes problems for larger employers that may want to establish separate plans for different groups of employees and employers with a significant number of part-time employees. Finally, note that nothing in the SEP rules stops an employer from establishing less restrictive eligibility requirements.

SIMPLEs

Similar to SEPs, SIMPLEs have totally inflexible coverage requirements. The rules, however, are different from both the qualified plan and the SEP requirements. The SIMPLE must cover any employee (including those under age 21) who earned $5,000 in two previous calendar years and is reasonably expected to earn $5,000 again in the current year. Employees subject to a collectively bargained agreement can be excluded. SIMPLEs can be maintained only on a calendar-year basis. All employees become eligible to participate as of the January 1 after they have earned $5,000 in two prior years. Essentially, SEPs have a 3-year waiting period, while SIMPLEs have a 2-year waiting period.

403(b) Plans

If a 403(b) plan includes employer contributions (that are not related to a salary reduction agreement), the plan must satisfy the 410(b) requirement discussed earlier in this chapter. An additional coverage rule applies to 403(b) plan salary deferral elections. Essentially, any employee who can contribute $200 or more must be given the option to make a salary deferral election. Exceptions are made for employees who normally work fewer than 20 hours per week and employees eligible to make salary deferral elections to other types of plans, including 401(k) and 457 plans.

CHAPTER REVIEW

Key Terms

adoption agreement [7-1]
percentage test [7-2]
ratio test [7-2]
average-benefit-percentage test [7-2]
separate lines of business [7-2]
401(a) (26) minimum-participation
   rule [7-2]

21-and-one rule [7-4]
2-year/100 percent rule [7-4]
controlled groups [7-5]
affiliated service group [7-5]
leased employee [7-5]

Review Questions

Review questions are based on the learning objectives in this chapter. Thus, a [7-3] at the end of a question means that the question is based on learning objective 7-3. If there are multiple objectives, they are all listed.

1. List two planning tools that can be used in the plan-design process. [7-1]

2. Which of the following employees of the Off the Books Company (a business accounting computer software firm) are considered highly compensated employees in 2007, assuming the company makes the election to limit highly compensated to those in the top 20 percent group? [7-2]

	2006 Salary
Al Abernathy (96% stock owner/president)	$200,000
Becky Brooks (4% stock owner/vice president)	150,000
Charlie Carr (secretary)	125,000
Dick Dawson (treasurer)	60,000
Ellen Elko	30,000
Fran Forcey	25,000
Greg Gillespie	25,000
Hanna Hill	20,000
Isabel Ingram	20,000
James Jordan	20,000

3. Describe the three ways to satisfy the minimum-coverage requirements of IRC Sec. 410(b). [7-2]

4. What do the separate-line-of-business rules allow an employer to do, and what are the basic requirements necessary to satisfy the separate-line-of-business rules? [7-2]

5. Explain the 401(a)(26) nondiscrimination rule and the types of plans subject to this rule. [7-2]

6. Dr. Ebenezer Smith would like to cover the minimum amount of employees in his office's qualified plan. What factors should be brought to his attention regarding the effects of avoiding coverage of rank-and-file employees? [7-3]

7. Discuss the opportunities available for limiting participation under a qualified plan. (7-3)

8. The B&W architectural firm is thinking of amending its qualified plan. [7-4]
    a. List the pros and cons of delaying participation in the plan for as long as possible.
    b. If the B&W firm chooses to have an entry date that occurs only once annually (January 1), what maximum age and service requirements can be used?

9. a. What are the various methods that can be used to count hours of service in a qualified plan? [7-4]
    b. What are the design considerations underlying the selection of an hour-of-service provision?

10. What happens when two companies are treated as one under the controlled group or affiliated service group rules? [7-5]

11. Does an individual who is considered a leased employee have to be covered by the recipient company's retirement plan? [7-5]

12. In addition to their involvement in the Off the Books Company, Al Abernathy and Becky Brooks (see question 7-2) are 50 percent co-owners and the only employees of By the Numbers, Inc., a consulting firm that advises companies about their accounting systems. Answer the following questions about the treatment of these businesses under the nondiscrimination rules:
    a. Will Off the Books and By the Numbers be aggregated for purposes of the nondiscrimination tests?
    b. Assuming that Off the Books has a defined-benefit plan that covers all of its 10 employees and that By the Numbers has no plan, will the Off the Books plan pass the 410(b) nondiscrimination requirements?
    c. Assuming that By the Numbers has a defined-benefit plan that covers its two employees and Off the Books does not have a plan, will the By the Numbers plan pass the 410(b) nondiscrimination requirements?
    d. What effect does the separate-line-of-business exception have on the answer in part (c) above?

13. Describe the coverage rules that apply to SEPs, SIMPLEs, and 403(b) plans. [7-5]

8

Designing Benefit Formulas and Employee Contributions

Learning Objectives

An understanding of the material in this chapter should enable you to

8-1. Identify the rules that relate to the service and compensation that can be considered in a plan's benefit formula.

8-2. Explain the strategies for satisfying the nondiscrimination rules for defined-contribution plans.

8-3. Explain the strategies for satisfying the nondiscrimination rules for defined-benefit plans.

8-4. Discuss the past and current role of voluntary employee after-tax contributions and describe the nondiscrimination rules that apply to these types of contributions.

Chapter Outline

Nondiscrimination Requirements for Employee Contributions and
Employer Matching Contributions   8.22
CHAPTER REVIEW   8.23

NONDISCRIMINATION BENEFITS

When designing the benefit structure in a qualified plan or 403(b) plan, the rules provide for a substantial degree of discretion. The primary limitation is Code Sec. 401(a)(4), which provides that benefits cannot discriminate in favor of highly compensated employees. In this context, the definition of highly compensated is the same as described in previous chapters. In this chapter, we will review the nondiscrimination rules and explore their boundaries.

First, we will give an overview of the nondiscrimination rules. Next, we will review some concepts relevant to a discussion of nondiscrimination, and then discuss the specific impact on defined-contribution and defined-benefit plans. Finally, we will compare these rules to the allocation rules that apply to SEPs and SIMPLEs.

Nondiscrimination Rules

Sec. 401(a)(4) nondiscrimination rule

Qualified plans (and 403(b) plans that include employer nonelective contributions) must be designed to satisfy the *Sec. 401(a)(4) nondiscrimination rule* that a plan cannot discriminate in favor of highly compensated employees (HCEs) with regard to benefits or contributions. The only exception applies to employee contributions and employer matching contributions. As discussed in chapter 5, pre-tax salary deferral contributions are subject to a special nondiscrimination rule referred to as the ADP test. Employee after-tax and matching contributions are subject to the ACP nondiscrimination test.

The requirements of 401(a)(4) are satisfied if either the contributions or the benefits are nondiscriminatory. Under the statutory language, a plan will be deemed nondiscriminatory if contributions or benefits bear a uniform relationship to compensation. For instance, if in a defined-contribution plan contributions are allocated so all participants receive 3 percent of the current year's total compensation, the plan is not discriminatory. If the plan is a defined-benefit plan and each participant earns an accrued benefit of 2 percent of compensation for the current year of service, the plan is also deemed nondiscriminatory.

The more interesting question is to what extent the plan can deviate from the uniform percentage-of-compensation rule without being considered discriminatory. Since the enactment of ERISA, one form of discrimination has been allowed: the plan can have benefits that integrate with Social Security. Essentially, this allows a plan to discriminate in favor of the highly compensated employees to make up for the fact that the Social Security system discriminates against them. However, for many years it was unclear what else could be done, because no regulations clarified the general statutory language. Due to the lack of guidance, designing any other type of formula was risky. Since 1993, when the IRS issued almost 200 pages of final regulations, the situation has changed drastically. The regulations are quite helpful, because they

- establish objective criteria for determining whether a plan violates the nondiscrimination requirement
- clarify that a plan can demonstrate it is not discriminatory by showing that its contributions or benefits are not discriminatory
- establish several safe harbor methods for determining whether the plan satisfies the nondiscrimination standards
- create general tests for testing a plan that chooses not to adopt one of the design safe harbors

With regulations that contain clear, objective rules, a plan can determine at any time whether or not it is in compliance with the nondiscrimination standards, and if the employer is willing to do some testing, the plan design can be quite creative.

After reviewing some preliminary issues, we will more fully discuss exactly what these regulations allow defined-contribution and defined-benefit plans to do.

Accrued Benefits

One key concept under the nondiscrimination rules is that discrimination is tested based on the benefit provided for that year, not the overall benefit provided under the plan. When discussing the total benefit that a participant has earned under a plan up to the present time, this amount is referred to as the participant's *accrued benefit*. This is in contrast to describing the benefit that is expected to be paid out if the participant continues in employment until normal retirement age, which is referred to as the *projected benefit*. The amount earned for the current year is simply referred to as the accrued benefit for the year.

accrued benefit

projected benefit

In a defined-contribution plan, the participant's accrued benefit at any point is his or her present account balance. The accrual for the specific year is the amount contributed to the plan on the employee's behalf for that year.

In a defined-benefit plan, the concept is the same. The accrued benefit is the benefit earned to date, using current salary and years of service. The accrued benefit earned for the year is the additional benefit that has been earned based upon the current year's salary and service.

A number of complex rules apply to the way benefits accrue under a plan. This is due to the fact that before ERISA was enacted, a participant would often be entitled to no benefit until he or she hit normal retirement age after, say, 30 years of employment. In this case, the entire benefit was essentially earned in the final year. This was called backloading the benefit. ERISA imposed rules to prohibit backloading. For example, under the rules, a plan's benefit formula could not be written to say that an individual earns a benefit of one percent of final-average compensation times years of service for the first 10 years of service and 2 percent of final-average compensation for service in excess of 10 years. This would be a prohibited backloading.

Permissible methods of determining a participant's accrued benefit are complex and are well-understood by pension actuaries who work with defined-benefit plans. However, we will simply discuss the most predominant method of accruing benefits today. If you were to see a different benefit accrual method, you might want to discuss the issue with the plan's actuary.

As discussed in chapter 4, the most common benefit formula in a defined-benefit plan is the unit-benefit formula. In most cases, under this formula, the accrued benefit is determined by applying the formula based on current salary and service.

Example: The Average Corporation has a retirement benefit formula of 1.5 percent of final-average compensation times years of service. Normal retirement age is 65. Joe started employment at age 30. At age 40, after 10 years of service, Joe's accrued benefit is 15 percent of his final-average compensation, based on his salary history to date. He has accrued a benefit of 1.5 percent of final-average compensation for the current year. His projected retirement benefit is 45 percent of final-average compensation because he will have earned 30 years of service if he continues working until normal retirement age.

Calculating Service

In chapter 4, we began to discuss the implications of the definition of service for purposes of determining the participant's benefit in a defined-benefit plan. There is one additional concern that is important to consider. Similar to the eligibility and vesting rules, there are minimum service requirements for determining whether the participant is entitled to earn a year of service under the plan. In a defined-benefit plan, a participant is not typically credited with a year of service if he or she has 1,000 hours of service (as is the requirement with the eligibility and vesting rules). In a defined-benefit plan, a year of service can be defined for benefit purposes in a variety of ways, as long as the definition of a year of service

- is applied on a reasonable and consistent basis
- does not require more hours of service than are customarily rendered during a work year in the industry involved
- accrues benefits for less than full-time service on at least a pro rata basis
- gives participants with 1,000 hours at least a partial year of service. (For certain industries that customarily work for seasonal or nontraditional years, 1,000 hours must constitute a full year of service.)

This last requirement means that, unlike the rules that apply to eligibility and vesting, the plan can actually require up to 2,000 hours of service before a full benefit is accrued.

In a defined-contribution plan, contributions must be made for participants who earn 1,000 hours of service for the year. This means an individual can become eligible to participate, receive an allocation for one year, and, if he or she then goes part-time, may not be eligible for contributions in subsequent years. There is an exception. Participants who terminate employment before the last day of the year can be excluded from receiving a contribution for the year, even if they have earned 1,000 hours of service. However, if such persons are excluded, they are also not considered participants under the minimum-coverage requirements. Therefore, having a last-day requirement means the employer could have trouble passing the coverage tests if a significant number of employees terminate employment before the end of the year.

In either a defined-contribution or a defined-benefit plan, hours of service may be determined by using the standard-hours counting method (each hour actually worked is counted, plus hours for which the employee is entitled to be paid, such as vacations and holidays) or by using one of the equivalency methods discussed earlier. The definition of hour of service for contribution or benefit purposes can be different from the definitions used for eligibility or vesting purposes.

Compensation for Benefit-Formula Purposes

When looking at the plan's benefit or contribution formula, benefits are based, in part, on how the plan defines compensation. The definition of compensation can include or exclude overtime, bonuses, and other nonrecurring compensation. In the small-plan market, the plan should be designed with a liberal definition of compensation in order to maximize the amount of contributions or benefits (tax shelter) that can be made. In larger, nonintegrated plans, employers typically ask you to use the definition of compensation that best suits the company's goals. If a restrictive definition is chosen, the definition will have to satisfy IRS nondiscrimination regulations. For example, if executives are the only employees who receive bonuses and rank-and-file employees are the only ones who work overtime, a definition of compensation that includes bonuses but not overtime will be considered discriminatory. Many plans choose an inclusive definition of compensation to avoid the nondiscrimination issue.

A second rule that relates to compensation is that the annual compensation considered in the benefit or contribution formula is limited to the compensation cap, which is indexed for inflation. In 2007, compensation is capped at $225,000.

Example:	George Yungle earns $400,000 in 2007. He notices that the company is contributing 10 percent of compensation for all participants in 2007 to the company's profit-sharing plan. When he looks at his benefit statement, he sees that only $22,000 has been allocated to his account. When he asks the benefit department about this, they inform him that, under the law, compensation cannot exceed the compensation cap of $225,000 (as indexed for 2007).

Amending Benefit Formulas

The process of plan amendment is typically thought of in conjunction with changes mandated by legislative reform and changes necessitated by unforeseen business developments. Some employers may also want to gradually increase benefits for a variety of reasons, including the following:

- A gradual benefit upgrade may satisfy the employer's benefit objective of consistently improving the employee benefits package. Some employers feel that periodic movement in the employee benefits package is necessary in order to retain employees.
- Employers may be skeptical of funding unknown plan costs and may desire to ease into the plan commitment slowly.

- An employer with erratic cash flow may set up a manageable benefit formula that will gradually be increased as cash flow stabilizes, as opposed to adopting a discretionary profit-sharing plan.

The primary legal restriction on plan amendments is the anti-cutback rule. Essentially, the rule provides that benefits that have already accrued cannot be taken away from the participant. Several years ago, the anti-cutback rules were expanded to include other aspects of the participant's benefit, such as the form of benefit payment. Congress considered the form of payment to be an essential part of the benefit promise. For example, if the plan allows benefits to be paid as a life annuity or as a single sum, the plan cannot be amended to take away the single-sum form of payment.

The anti-cutback rules do not, however, prohibit amending the benefit formula on a prospective basis. This applies both to the actual benefit formula and the form of payments.

DEFINED-CONTRIBUTION PLANS

The nondiscrimination rules apply (with the exception of the target-benefit plan) in essentially the same manner for all types of defined-contribution plans. First, we will discuss three major allocation approaches that are currently used: contributions as a level percentage of compensation, integration with Social Security, and cross-testing. Then, we will apply these concepts to specific types of plans.

Level Percentage of Compensation

As mentioned above, the nondiscrimination regulations offer several methods for determining whether the plan satisfies the nondiscrimination rules. One method is to satisfy a safe harbor test that is completely design based. That is, if the plan design fits within the specified safe harbor design, the plan will be deemed to satisfy the nondiscrimination test. To satisfy the basic defined-contribution plan design safe harbor, the plan must

- have a uniform normal retirement age and vesting schedule applicable to all employees, and
- group all employer contributions and forfeitures for the plan year under a single, uniform formula that allocates the same percentage of compensation or the same dollar amount to every participant

This formula is often chosen. In larger companies, a plan that provides the same benefits to everyone is easy to administer and explain. If larger benefits are to be provided to executives, they are provided in a nonqualified environment. Small employers also choose this approach, sometimes for the same reason, although other times simply because this allocation formula is offered as an option in a prototype plan and the owner (and unfortunately sometimes the advisor) does not fully understand other options. In today's qualified plan environment, the small employer should, even in a simple profit-sharing plan, make an informed choice between the level percentage of pay, *integration with Social Security,* and cross-testing methods.

integration with Social Security

Integration with Social Security

Nondiscrimination regulations also provide that the benefit structure can be integrated with Social Security. Under this approach, the employer essentially gets to make larger contributions for those individuals who earn more than the taxable wage base. This is allowed because, under the Social Security system, the employer does not make contributions (pay taxes) on earnings in excess of the wage base. In this way, Social Security actually discriminates against the highly compensated. This disparity can be made up, to a degree, under a qualified plan using the methods described below.

Both money-purchase and profit-sharing plans can use this method, although if an employer sponsors both types of plans, only one plan can have a fully integrated formula. If a defined-contribution plan formula is integrated with Social Security, contributions may be higher (as a percentage of compensation) for those employees who earn more than a specified integration level. If the integration level is set at the current taxable wage base ($97,500 for 2007), HCEs may receive up to 5.7 percent of compensation in excess of the taxable wage base, as long as the employer makes contributions that equal at least 5.7 percent of total compensation.

Example:	Justin, Inc., establishes a money-purchase pension plan that provides for a contribution of 5.7 percent of compensation plus 5.7 percent of compensation in excess of the taxable wage base. Justin, the owner, earns $300,000. The contribution made on his behalf for 2007 is $20,093. This is 5.7 percent of $225,000 (the maximum allowable compensation for 2007, or $12,825) plus 5.7 percent of ($225,000 minus $97,500), which equals $7,268.

If the employer cannot afford to contribute at least 5.7 percent of compensation across the board, the maximum disparity will be reduced. Under the rules, the integrated portion cannot exceed the contribution that is based on total compensation. This means that if 4 percent is contributed based on total salary, an additional 4 percent can be contributed based on compensation in excess of the integration level.

Under the rules, the integration level cannot exceed the taxable wage base. The integration level can be lower, but this generally reduces the maximum disparity allowed. Table 8-1 shows the required reductions. The reason for the reduction is to remove the advantage of setting the integration level just above the compensation level of the highest rank-and-file employee.

Example:	Bakery, Inc.'s rank-and-file workers earn a maximum of $30,000. The owner, Mr. Crueller, earns $225,000. He might want to consider setting the level at $30,000 (instead of the taxable wage base) to maximize the integrated contribution on his own behalf.

TABLE 8-1
Maximum Integration Disparity Using Different Integration Levels

Integration Level	Maximum Disparity Allowed
Taxable Wage Base (TWB)	5.7%
Below the TWB but at least 80% of the TWB	5.4%
Below 80% of the TWB but at least 20% of the TWB.	4.3%
Below 20% of the TWB	5.7%*

* Note that the maximum disparity bounces back to 5.7 percent with a very low integration level. This is because, at very low levels, the rank-and-file employees will also be receiving a contribution based on salary above the integration level.

Even though the required reductions are supposed to remove the advantage of lowering the integration level, it may be worth running the numbers to see what happens in a particular situation. Let's look at our example above. Because $30,000 is between 20 percent and 80 percent of the taxable wage base, the maximum disparity is reduced to 4.3 percent. Comparing the two integration levels, the maximum integrated portion using the $30,000 integration level is $8,385 ($225,000 – $30,000 x 4.3 percent), while the maximum integrated portion using the taxable wage base is $7,268 ($225,000 – $97,500 x 5.7 percent). In this case, there is more than a $1,000 difference, but that is only for this year. If next year the rank-and-file employees' salaries change and the integration level needs to be modified, the amendment process could cost more than the savings involved. In most cases, the "game is not worth the hunt," and the integration level should simply be set at the then-current taxable wage base.

Choosing the Integrated Formula

An integrated formula is an appropriate method for skewing contributions toward highly compensated employees. However, the maximum excess amount that a highly compensated employee can get is only $7,268 (see the Justin, Inc., example above).This means if the business owner wants the maximum allocation allowed under Code Sec. 415(c), other employees would have to get a contribution of almost 17 percent of compensation.

Today, if the business owner's goal is to maximize disparity, he or she should consider the cross-tested allocation formula described below. However, as you will see, these are complex plans that have some extra administrative costs. As an alternative, the integrated plan provides some disparity without much complication. A plan may be adopted by using a standardized prototype plan document. This means that the inexpensive standardized plans sponsored by many insurance companies and other service providers can be adopted at little expense. Also, a plan can be designed to fit within the safe harbor, ensuring ongoing satisfaction of the nondiscrimination regulations without annual testing.

The compensation cap has created another reason for using an integrated formula. Some small-business owners are perfectly happy to establish a plan that allocates the same percentage of compensation for each participant (such as 3, 4, or 5 percent of compensation). However, if the owner earns more than the $225,000 (indexed for 2007) compensation cap, the contribution on behalf of the owner with this type of formula will actually result in a smaller amount (as a percentage of pay) than for other employees.

Example:	Mr. Nice Guy wants to contribute 5 percent of compensation for each employee. If he earns $300,000, because of compensation cap the contribution on his behalf will only be approximately 3.5 percent of compensation!

For this reason, the same business owner might consider the integrated formula simply to make up for the loss associated with the compensation cap.

Cross-testing

If the employer does not want to use a contribution or allocation formula that fits within one of the design safe harbors, virtually any other formula can be adopted as long as, on an annual basis, the plan can demonstrate compliance with the general nondiscrimination test. This can be done in one of two ways: either by testing contributions made to the plan on behalf of each participant or testing benefits that can be provided from contributions and forfeitures made for the year. Testing benefits in a defined-contribution plan is referred to as *cross-testing*. It requires the conversion of allocations into equivalent life annuity benefit amounts by using the methodology described in the regulations. Once these allocations have been converted, the general test is then performed, using benefit accrual rates based on those annuity amounts expressed as a percentage of compensation. This strategy of satisfying the nondiscrimination rules is also referred to as *new comparability*.

In the most practical of terms, the regulations allow discrimination in favor of older workers because it takes a larger contribution to buy a specific benefit for an older worker than it does to buy the same benefit for a younger worker. This is a powerful concept, and the regulations are quite flexible. An employer that decides to go the cross-testing route must understand the following:

- *Mathematical test*—The administrator must perform a test on an annual basis to demonstrate compliance with the nondiscrimination rules.
- *Retroactive compliance*—Even if the test is not satisfied, the plan can be amended, increasing benefits for the nonhighly compensated employees to the extent necessary to satisfy the test.
- *Additional expense*—Plan documents, IRS determination letters, and annual administration are somewhat higher for a cross-tested plan.
- *Minimum contribution*—In most cases, when cross-testing is used, the regulations require a 5 percent minimum contribution for rank-and-file employees.

The simplest method to satisfy the general test is to allocate the contributions and forfeitures in such a way that, after conversion to a monthly benefit accrual at retirement, the rate of accrual is the same for each participant. In this way, the general nondiscrimination test is always satisfied, without further testing. This type of allocation formula is referred to as an *age-weighted formula*. Let's look at an example that demonstrates how age weighting works.

cross-testing

new comparability

age-weighted formula

Example: A plan has three participants. Susan, aged 50, earns $150,000 per year. Her employees, Ralph and Paula, ages 35 and 28, respectively, each earn $30,000 per year. Also, assume the employer wants to contribute $49,000. Use the following steps to determine the appropriate allocation formula that will result in a uniform benefit accrual for each participant:

- First, determine how much would have to be contributed for the year to provide a monthly benefit at age 65 equal to one percent of each participant's compensation. One percent of Susan's $150,000 annual ($12,500 monthly) compensation is $125. One percent of Ralph's and Paula's $30,000 annual ($2,500 monthly) compensation is $25.

- Next, assume it costs $95.38 (see table 8-2) at age 65 to provide a benefit of $1 per month payable for life. Susan would then need $125 x $95.38 = $11,922; Ralph and Paula each would need $25 x $95.38 = $2,384 at age 65 to provide a benefit of one percent of their pay.

- Assuming plan assets earn 8.5 percent, a single contribution of $3,506 today would accumulate after 15 years to the $11,922 Susan would need at age 65 ($11,922 x .2941; see table 8-3). Similarly, a single contribution of $206 today would accumulate after 30 years to the $2,384 Ralph will need at age 65, and a single contribution of $117 today would accumulate after 37 years to the $2,384 Paula will need at age 65.

- Under the age-weighted profit-sharing plan, the actual contribution is discretionary. The contribution will be allocated to participants in proportion to the $3,506, $206, and $117 amounts calculated above. Susan receives 91.57 percent of the total contribution, Ralph receives 5.39 percent of the contribution, and Paula receives the remaining 3.04 percent of the contribution.

- If the employer contributed enough to provide a one-percent benefit accrual for each participant the contribution would be $3,829 ($3,506 + $206 + $117). Since a $49,000 contribution is more than 12 times this amount, the contribution for each employee in this case hypothetically would support a monthly benefit at retirement of 12 percent of compensation.

In this example, age weighting results in a high percentage of the total contribution because the owner is significantly older than the other employees. In many cases, the plan will pass the annual nondiscrimination test because each participant is receiving the same benefit accrual. However, even under this design, nonhighly compensated participants will generally need to receive an allocation of 5 percent of compensation in order to satisfy the regulations.

TABLE 8-2
Annuity Purchase Factors

1984 UP Mortality Table 8.5% Interest

Age	Amount to Purchase $1 Monthly Annuity	Age	Amount to Purchase $1 Monthly Annuity
55	$115.0104	63	$99.7222
56	113.3069	64	97.5720
57	111.5413	65	95.3829
58	109.7158	66	93.1640
59	107.8336	67	90.9263
60	105.8896	68	88.6669
61	103.8869	69	86.3737
62	101.8294	70	84.0346

The age-weighted example is an excellent place to begin the discussion of cross-testing because it illustrates the concept behind the rules. The major problem with the age-weighted formula is that it is contingent upon having the perfect employee census. Even a single older employee can destroy the intended result. In addition, age weighting is hard to explain and might cause employee dissatisfaction. In the example above, Paula might have difficulty understanding why Ralph is entitled to a $2,641 allocation, while she receives only $1,489, because they each earn the same salary.

TABLE 8-3
Discount Factor

8.5% Interest

Years before Retirement Age	Discount Factor	Years before Retirement Age	Discount Factor
1	0.921659	23	0.153150
2	0.849455	24	0.141152
3	0.782908	25	0.130094
4	·0.721574	26	0.119902
5	0.665045	27	0.110509
6	0.612945	28	0.101851
7	0.564926	29	0.093872
8	0.520669	30	0.086518
9	0.479880	31	0.079740
10	0.442285	32	0.073493
11	0.407636	33	0.067736
12	0.375702	34	0.062429
13	0.346269	35	0.057539
14	0.319142	36	0.053031
15	0.294140	37	0.048876
16	0.271097	38	0.045047
17	0.249859	39	0.041518
18	0.230285	40	0.038266
19	0.212244	41	0.035268
20	0.195616	42	0.032505
21	0.180292	43	0.029959
22	0.166167	44	0.027612

TABLE 8-4
Age-Weighted Allocation Method

Name	Age	Monthly Earnings	1% Monthly Annuity	Single Sum at 65	Present Value	Allocation Percentage	Allocation of $49,000
Susan	50	$12,500	$125	$11,922	$3,506	91.57%	$44,869
Ralph	35	2,500	25	2,384	206	5.39	2,641
Paula	28	2,500	25	2,384	117	3.04	1,489

For these reasons, the age-weighted allocation approach is not popular. As the pension industry has grown to understand the general non–discrimination test, the opportunities it provides have become clear. When working with the general nondiscrimination test, the employer can essentially start with any plan allocation formula, which is then tested against the general nondiscrimination test. This design approach is much more satisfying because the employer can first create a design that meets its goals and then analyze whether the design satisfies the test.

For the small employer, one common objective is to allocate the maximum allowed under Code Sec. 415(c) and the minimum required for other employees. The regulations require a 5 percent of compensation allocation to nonhighly compensated employees in most cases in a cross-tested plan. With this objective in mind, the next step is to translate the projected contributions into an accrued benefit for each employee, which is tested under the general nondiscrimination test. If the plan passes, then the design can be adopted. If not, then the contribution level for the nonhighly compensated can be raised, or the contribution for the owners can be lowered, until the test is satisfied.

The actual mechanics of cross-testing are quite complex and are beyond the scope of this book. However, note that the following objectives can generally be accomplished with a cross-tested plan:

- *Skewing contributions*—When the average age of the business owners is 10 years or more older than the nonhighly compensated employees, cross-testing will allow the plan to establish an allocation formula in which the owners receive the maximum Code Sec. 415(c) allocation, while the rank-and-file employees receive substantially less—possibly as low as 5 percent of compensation.
- *Older nonhighly compensated employees*—Unlike age-weighting, cross-testing works even with several older nonhighly compensated employees—as long as the average age of the owners is somewhat greater than the average age of the nonhighly compensated employees.
- *Design flexibility*—One other substantial advantage is the design flexibility allowed under the general test. Often an employer will want to make a larger contribution for a specific group of employees (for example, longer service employees or salespersons). Before these regulations, an employer had little flexibility. Now the opportunities for creative plan designs that meet a number of planning objectives are almost limitless. For example, the employer may decide to contribute 5 percent of pay for new employees, 6 percent for employees with 5 or more years of service, and 7 percent for employees with 10 or more years of service.

Any employer considering a plan with a cross-tested allocation formula must be advised of certain disadvantages. The plan needs to be tested for discrimination on an annual basis. Gathering accurate employee data, especially age information, can be a daunting task. Preliminary testing (at the beginning of the year) and final testing will have to be performed. The plan design may have to change on an annual basis if census data or employee salaries change. For example, the plan may satisfy the rules in year one with a 5 percent allocation for NHCEs, while the next year a 6 percent allocation may be required. A design change must be accompanied by a properly timed plan amendment. Plan document charges, filing for an IRS determination letter, and the ongoing administration costs are typically a bit higher than with other types of defined-contribution plans. The additional costs will typically not stop the employer if the savings under the cross-tested plan (compared to an age-weighted or integrated plan) are substantial.

Types of Plans and Nondiscrimination Approaches

Now that we have looked at the nondiscrimination rules in general, let's examine the types of choices employers commonly make with specific types of plans.

Profit-Sharing Plans

Profit-sharing plans are designed using all three approaches. Today, almost all employers that have been interested in age-weighting or cross-testing have chosen the versatile profit-sharing plan. Discretionary contributions, in-service withdrawals, and the ability to circumvent the qualified joint and survivor annuity rules (see chapter 10) are meaningful qualities for the small-business owner in today's business environment.

401(k) Plans

Remember that 401(k) plans are profit-sharing plans. If the 401(k) plan has a profit-sharing-type contribution, an allocation could be designed that takes advantage of the cross-testing flexibility. Nondiscrimination testing can be confusing in a 401(k) plan because of the different types of contributions allowed and the nondiscrimination rules that apply to different types of contributions. Let's review.

- *Employee salary deferral contributions*—Nondiscrimination is tested solely through the ADP test (see chapter 5). The 401(a)(4) rules do not apply.
- *Employer-matching contributions*—Nondiscrimination is tested solely through the ACP test (which is discussed later in this chapter). The 401(a)(4) rules do not apply.
- *Employee after-tax contributions*—Nondiscrimination is tested solely through the ACP test.

- *Employer profit-sharing contributions*—Only these types of contributions must satisfy the 401(a)(4) nondiscrimination rules discussed in this section.

403(b) Plans

403(b) plans, like 401(k) plans, must be analyzed feature by feature. These plans are subject to the following discrimination requirements:

- *Employee salary deferral contributions*—Unlike in the 401(k) plan, salary deferrals in a 403(b) plan are not subject to any nondiscrimination requirements.
- *Employer-matching contributions*—If the 403(b) plan has a matching contribution, these contributions *do* have to satisfy the ACP test (which is discussed later in this chapter). The 401(a)(4) rules do not apply.
- *Employer nonelective contributions*—If the 403(b) plan has an employer contribution for all eligible employees, these types of contributions must satisfy the 401(a)(4) nondiscrimination rules discussed in this section. Like profit-sharing plans, the 403(b) plan can use either of the design safe harbors: level percentage of compensation or integration with Social Security. The allocation formula also can take advantage of the cross-testing or age-weighted approaches.

Money-Purchase Pension Plans

Even though money-purchase pension plans can take advantage of cross-testing, most employers that choose this allocation approach have chosen profit-sharing plans because contributions are discretionary. Money-purchase plans more typically contain contributions that are a level percentage of compensation or that are integrated with Social Security.

Target-Benefit Pension Plans

The contribution formula established under a target-benefit plan could be tested under the general nondiscrimination test. However, the regulations provide a separate design safe harbor for such plans, and employers that establish such a plan will probably want to take advantage of the design safe harbor.

Several threshold issues determine whether a target plan is suited for a particular employer. First, a target plan, like the age-weighted profit-sharing plan, will not work with even a single older NHCE. Second, because the target plan is a pension plan, the employer must be willing to commit to a timely annual contribution. Third, unlike a defined-benefit plan, the annual contribution is a fixed amount. Finally, the employer must be willing to live with pension plan requirements (including no in-service distributions and the qualified joint and survivor annuity requirements).

Because today an age-weighted profit-sharing plan could be designed to give similar results as in the target-benefit plan, the employer is more likely to choose either the age-weighted or more flexible cross-tested profit-sharing plan. Most employers today are simply not willing to make a commitment to a fixed annual contribution. And for those few who are willing to commit to annual contributions, a defined-benefit plan is often the better choice, due to the flexibility of annual contributions and the ability (in the right circumstances) for the employer to contribute more on the key employees' behalf than in a defined-contribution plan.

SEPs

As you learned in chapter 6, the contribution to a SEP either must be allocated as a level percentage of compensation or integrated with Social Security (in the manner described above). The SEP cannot use a cross-tested or age-weighted allocation formula.

SIMPLEs

Contributions to a SIMPLE are subject to even more rigid rules. If the employer makes a profit-sharing-type contribution, all eligible participants must receive 2 percent of compensation. If, instead, the employer makes a matching contribution, the match is fixed as a dollar-for-dollar match, up to the first 3 percent of compensation deferred.

DEFINED-BENEFIT PLANS

The nondiscrimination rules provide design safe harbors for plans that include level benefits and those that integrate with Social Security. Again, if the employer wants to establish a plan that does not fit within the safe harbor, the formula can be defined in any way, as long as the plan can demonstrate nondiscrimination on an annual basis. Each of these three alternatives is discussed below.

Uniform Percentage of Compensation

There are actually three design-based safe harbors under the regulations. For all three, the plan must have the same benefit formula (and form of payment) for all participants and a uniform retirement age. Most important, the benefit formula must provide, at the normal retirement age—for all participants with the same years of service—either the same dollar benefit or the same percentage of average annual compensation. Also, the plan cannot require mandatory employee contributions.

All of the following designs can satisfy the safe harbors:

- *Unit credit plans*—As long as the above requirements are met, the plan can use a standard unit credit plan that accrues the benefit each year based on the plan's benefit formula.
- *Fractional accruals*—A unit-benefit formula or a flat percentage of pay (with a 25-years-of-service requirement) that accrues benefits using the fractional accrual method can also satisfy the design safe harbor.
- *Fully insured plans*—As long as the above requirements are met and the plan satisfies the definition of a fully insured plan under Code Sec. 412(i), the plan satisfies the nondiscrimination requirements.

In addition, any of these approaches will still satisfy the design safe harbor if the plan is integrated with Social Security as described below.

Integration with Social Security

Similar to the defined-contribution plan, the defined-benefit formula can be designed to provide a greater percentage of benefits for highly paid employees than for rank-and-file employees. Even though the rules are conceptually similar to defined-contribution plans, the integration-level approach for defined-benefit plans applies somewhat differently.

The rules also allow for an integration approach in which a benefit is described and then a portion of an individual's Social Security benefit is subtracted from the total (referred to as *offset integration*). At one time, this was the most common integration approach in defined-benefit plans. However, because under current law this approach rarely works as well as the integration-level approach and is, therefore, not used very often, it will not be discussed here.

Defined-benefit plans that use the integration-level approach are called *excess plans* (or *stepped-up plans*). Here's how an excess plan works:

- The plan has a specified integration level, which is tied to compensation.
- The benefit formula can provide the participant an additional benefit for compensation earned above the integration level.
- The additional or "excess" benefit cannot exceed either of the following limits:

- The excess benefit percentage cannot be more than 0.75 percent of compensation for each year of service and an excess benefit can only be provided on a maximum of 35 years of service, meaning that the maximum excess benefit can not exceed 26.25 percent of compensation.
- In no case can the additional benefit provided, based on compensation in excess of the integration level, exceed the benefit provided based on total compensation.

**covered
compensation**

The integration level in a defined-benefit plan is almost always *covered compensation,* which is the average of the taxable wages for the individual participant using the 35-year period ending with the year that the employee reaches his or her Social Security retirement age. Table 8-5 provides a portion of a covered compensation table for 2007. The concept of covered compensation is confusing for two reasons. First, as you can see in the table, covered compensation is different for participants of different ages, because the average of taxable wage bases depends on the years worked. Older workers will have lower covered compensation levels than younger workers, because the taxable wage bases over their final 35 years of work are lower than those for younger workers using more current years. Second, every year the table for covered compensation changes as cost-of-living increases apply. This means that the covered compensation amount keeps increasing as an individual gets older. To satisfy the integration rules, the plan must define final-average compensation as at least the 3 highest years of compensation.

**TABLE 8-5
2007 Covered Compensation**

Calendar Year of Birth	Calendar Year of Social Security Retirement Age	2007 Covered Compensation
1941	2007	$51,348
1942	2008	53,820
1943	2009	56,232
1944	2010	58,608
1945	2011	60,960
1946	2012	63,276
1947	2013	65,556
1948	2014	67,680
1949	2015	69,732
1950	2016	71,664
1951	2017	73,524
1952	2018	75,300
1953	2019	77,004
1954	2020	78,660

Example: The ABC Corporation has a defined-benefit plan with an integrated benefit formula. The formula provides participants with an annual benefit of one percent of final-average compensation (defined as the average of the highest 3 years of compensation) plus an additional .5 percent of compensation earned in excess of an individual's covered compensation, multiplied by years of service. The additional integrated portion of the benefit is capped at 35 years of service. This benefit formula complies with the integration rules. The excess benefit does not exceed .75 percent per year of service and the excess is only provided on the first 35 years of benefit service. Let's calculate a benefit for Joe who retires at age 65 in 2007 with 30 years of benefit service and a final-average salary of $60,000. Joe's covered compensation is $51,348. Joe's annual benefit is ($60,000 x .30) + ($8,652 x .15) = $19,297.

Other Plan-Design Alternatives

If the employer with a defined-benefit plan wants to establish a benefit formula that does not satisfy any of the safe harbor designs, the plan will have to satisfy the general nondiscrimination tests. Two types of plans are likely to have plan designs that do not satisfy the safe harbors. The first group includes plans that historically have had nonconforming benefit formulas. In other words, the sponsor adopted a formula in the past that today does not satisfy the nondiscrimination safe harbors. If the plan is still meeting the objectives of both employer and employees, the sponsor may choose not to bring the formula into compliance, but instead to go through the testing process.

The second group will be employers that choose to provide different benefit levels for different groups of employees in one plan. The employer might, for example, want to provide different benefit levels for employees of certain classes, in different geographic locations, or in different subsidiaries. The employer here has two choices: either establish one plan with different benefit levels and go through annual nondiscrimination testing, or establish separate plans for each group, with each plan having its own benefit structure. Separate plans may be easier if each plan will be able to satisfy the minimum-coverage requirements of Code Sec. 410(b) as well as the minimum-participation test.

VOLUNTARY EMPLOYEE CONTRIBUTIONS

voluntary after-tax employee contribution

Today, in most cases, qualified plan benefits are funded by employer contributions, with the exception of pretax elective salary deferral contributions that participants make to 401(k) plans, 403(b) plans, and SIMPLEs. However, qualified plans are technically allowed to provide for another type of contribution, the *voluntary after-tax employee contribution*.

Prior to 1987, this feature was quite common in qualified plans because up to 10 percent of compensation could be contributed by any employee without having to consider any of the other contribution limits and without regard to which employees elected to make contributions. This feature was often used primarily by the business owner and other highly compensated employees.

Beginning in 1987, however, many of these provisions were eliminated due to new nondiscrimination requirements and a new rule requiring that all such contributions count against the Code Sec. 415(c) annual addition limit. Because of this, most plans eliminated contributions after 1986; however, many plans still have contributions that were made prior to this date. This is important to note when dealing with a client who is receiving a pension distribution. The principal amount of employee contributions is treated as basis, and is not subject to income tax. Earnings are subject to the same taxation rules that apply to other pension distributions.

The only place where after-tax contributions are still found is in 401(k) plans, where employees are sometimes given the opportunity to make contributions on a pretax or after-tax basis. Some employees prefer after-tax contributions because they can be withdrawn more easily than pretax contributions, which are subject to the special withdrawal requirements discussed in chapter 5.

Nondiscrimination Requirements for Employee Contributions and Employer Matching Contributions

Plans that provide for voluntary employee after-tax contributions must satisfy a nondiscrimination test that is similar to the actual deferral percentage (ADP) test called the *actual contribution percentage* (ACP) test. This test considers after-tax contributions along with matching employer contributions. Under the ACP test, instead of comparing the salary deferrals as a percentage of compensation, we are comparing the matching and after-tax contributions as a percentage of compensation.

In operation, the test is virtually the same as the ADP test. In order to pass the ACP nondiscrimination test for employer matching contributions and employee contributions, one of two requirements must be satisfied:

1. *The 1.25 requirement.* Under this requirement, the contribution percentage for all highly compensated employees for the current year cannot be more than 125 percent of the contribution percentage for nonhighly compensated employees for the previous year.

2. *The 200 percent/2 percent difference requirement.* Under this requirement, the contribution percentage for highly compensated employees for the current year cannot be more than 200 percent of the contribution percentage (in the previous year) for nonhighly compensated employees, and the difference between the two groups must be 2 percent or less.

(Note: For purposes of the nondiscrimination tests, the term *highly compensated employee* is defined as described under the ADP test in chapter 5.)

Table 5-2 (see chapter 5) can be used to determine the maximum contribution percentage limits for highly compensated employees. For example, if the contribution percentage is 6 percent of compensation for nonhighly compensated employees, then the highly compensated employees can have an 8 percent contribution percentage.)

CHAPTER REVIEW

Key Terms

Sec. 401(a)(4) nondiscrimination rule [8-1]
accrued benefit [8-1]
projected benefit [8-1]
integration with Social Security [8-2]
cross-testing [8-2]

new comparability [8-2]
age-weighted formula [8-2]
covered compensation [8-3]
voluntary after-tax employee contribution [8-4]

Review Questions

Review questions are based on the learning objectives in this chapter. Thus, an [8-3] at the end of a question means that the question is based on learning objective 8-3. If there are multiple objectives, they are all listed.

1. Does allocating 3 percent of compensation to each participant in a profit-sharing plan satisfy the 401(a)(4) nondiscrimination requirements? [8-1]

2. Answer the following questions regarding accrued benefits: [8-1]

a. What does the term *accrued benefit* mean in a defined-contribution plan?
b. What does the term *accrued benefit* mean in a defined-benefit plan?
c. What does the term *projected benefit* mean in a defined-benefit plan?

3. In a defined-benefit plan, what are the maximum number of hours of service an employer can require in order to credit a participant with a full year of service for benefit purposes? If the maximum number of hours is required, what happens if the participant earns only 1,000 hours of service? [8-1]

4. Describe the compensation cap and its effect on the benefits of highly compensated employees. [8-1]

5. Answer the following questions regarding Social Security integration in defined-contribution plans:
a. If the employer contributes 8 percent of total compensation for each participant, how much more can be contributed for employees who earn more than the taxable wage base (assuming this is the integration level)?
b. If the employer contributes 3 percent of total compensation for each participant, how much more can be contributed for employees who earn more than the taxable wage base (assuming this is the integration level)?
c. If the employer contributes 8 percent of total compensation for each participant, how much more can be contributed for employees who earn more than $80,000 (assuming this is the integration level)? [8-2]

6. Describe what cross-testing is and how it can be used to channel a larger percentage of the employer's contribution to the older, highly compensated employees. [8-2]

7. What is the major limitation with an age-weighted contribution formula? [8-2]

8. What are the strengths and limitations of the cross-tested formula? [8-2]

9. What type of defined-contribution plan is most often used with the age-weighted or cross-tested contribution formula? [8-2]

10. Describe the nondiscrimination requirements that apply to 401(k) plans. [8-2]

11. Describe the types of allocation formulas that can be contained in a SEP. [8-2]

12. Weese has a final-average salary of $100,000 and has worked for his employer for 20 years. Weese's covered compensation is $51,348, and the plan's benefit formula provides for one percent of final-average compensation plus .75 percent of final-average salary in excess of covered compensation multiplied by years of service (limited to 35 years of service). Does the plan satisfy the integration rules, and what is Weese's benefit under the plan? [8-3]

13. Explain the nondiscrimination requirements for employer matching contributions and employee contributions. [8-4]

9

Helping Clients Choose the Best Loan, Vesting, and Retirement-Age Provisions

---

Learning Objectives

An understanding of the material in this chapter should enable you to

9-1. Describe the reasons for including participant loans in a client's plan and the legal requirements that apply.

9-2. Explain the vesting requirements applicable to qualified retirement plans.

9-3. Identify the design considerations associated with choosing normal, early, and deferred retirement provisions.

Chapter Outline

Three of the most important decisions in designing a plan are:

- deciding whether the plan should permit loans
- choosing the plan's vesting schedules
- choosing the plan's retirement-age provisions

Decisions in these areas significantly affect the makeup of the plan's participants, the makeup of the employer's work force, and the employer's costs.

PLAN LOANS

Most types of retirement plans may allow participants the opportunity to borrow from the plan. Loans provide access to funds without tax consequences. However, loans also add administrative expense and may undermine retirement planning objectives. The decision whether or not to have a loan provision depends upon the type of plan, plan objectives, and the legal restrictions upon plan loans. An informed decision must address the following two important concerns:

- Are plan loans appropriate?
- What legal restrictions will apply?

Are Plan Loans Appropriate for Your Clients?

The Advantages and Disadvantages of Plan Loans

The primary reason to include a loan provision in the plan is so employees (including executives and business owners, to the extent legally permitted) can enjoy the current beneficial use of their retirement savings. In other words, a loan provision in a qualified plan provides the best of both worlds—tax shelter for plan contributions and access to sheltered funds when the need arises without causing a taxable distribution.

There is another side to the story, however. Several good reasons for *not* allowing plan loans also exist. First, a loan provision in the plan may be inconsistent with the employer's objective of providing retirement security. Funds used to repay plan loans are often taken from funds that would have been retirement savings. This might create an unwanted dependence on the employer's plan as the sole source of retirement funds, especially when loans are taken by employees who are close to retirement. Second, loan provisions are labor intensive and costly to administer. They are especially troublesome from an administrative point of view in dealing with the default of a loan. Employers do not relish being put in the untenable position of being a credit agency or hounding their employees for payment. Furthermore, if a loan is defaulted, serious consequences abound, such as the following:

- There is an immediate tax liability to the participant, because the defaulted loan is treated as a current distribution.
- The participant may incur a 10 percent penalty if the distribution occurs prior to age 59½.

Despite their pitfalls, loan provisions are very popular for the following reasons:

- Business owners are eligible for plan loans to the same extent as other employees.
- Administrative problems with plan loans can be minimized by using a program that would only permit loans under a stipulated number of circumstances, such as for college education payments, purchase of a home, or demonstrated financial hardship.
- Administrative problems can also be mitigated by placing a $1,000 minimum on the amount of any loan, thus eliminating pesky small loans.
- Problems with loan defaults can be eliminated if the employer requires both payroll deduction for loan repayments and complete repayment upon termination of employment. If the participant defaults, benefits payable are reduced by the outstanding balance (resulting in a taxable distribution of the amount of default).

Types of Plans

The degree to which a loan provision is considered desirable depends in part on the type of plan involved. Clients who have a 401(k) plan or 403(b) plan should strongly consider a loan provision. In these plans, it can be difficult to get the enrollment necessary to pass the actual deferral percentage test, if participants are concerned that elective deferrals will be locked up until retirement. However, by "unlocking" plan funds through a loan provision, an employer may be able to entice the required participation to satisfy the applicable tests.

Sometimes loan provisions are considered for pension plans of the defined-contribution type. Because pension plans are prohibited from making in-service withdrawals—that is, distributing funds prior to death, disability, termination of employment, or retirement—a loan provision allows "use" of plan assets during employment. However, defined-benefit pension plans seldom contain a loan provision. First, calculating the maximum loan amount requires an actuarial calculation, which increases administrative expenses.

Second, a loan provision undermines the concern for retirement security—usually the number one reason for adopting the plan.

For profit-sharing plans, the consideration is somewhat different. Because a profit-sharing plan may be designed to allow in-service withdrawals, a loan provision is not necessary to provide employees access to plan benefits during employment. However, loans do provide for the use of funds on a tax-free basis.

Employee stock ownership plans (ESOPs) generally do not have loan provisions because plan assets are required to be "primarily invested in employer securities," meaning the plan will not have sufficient cash investments to support a loan provision. For the same reason, stock bonus plans that are heavily invested in employer securities should not have a loan provision.

Finally, note that plan loans are prohibited in SEPs, SIMPLEs, and IRAs. Table 9-1 summarizes the applicable rules.

Legal Parameters for Plan Loans

Plans designed to permit loans must adhere to certain requirements that govern the availability, amount, duration, interest, security, and repayment of the loan.

Loan Availability

As was previously stated, your client can choose to include the option for plan loans or to exclude the option altogether. If plan loans are made available, however, they must be available to all participants on a reasonably equivalent basis and must not be available to highly compensated employees in an amount greater than the amount made available to other employees. In addition, loans must

- be adequately secured
- be made in accordance with specific plan provisions
- bear a reasonable (market) rate of interest

Almost all plans use the participant's accrued benefit as security. Other security can be appropriate, but most plans will want to avoid this because of the administrative complexities. If the participant defaults on the loan, the benefit will be reduced in the amount of the outstanding principal

TABLE 9-1
Desirability of Plan Loans

Plan	Consideration
401(k) plan	A loan provision entices participation so the actual deferral percentage test can be passed.
403(b) plan	A loan provision entices participation so the 401(m) test can be passed.
Contributory plan	A loan provision entices participation so the 401(m) test and 410(b) nondiscrimination tests can be passed.
Pension plans (money-purchase, target-benefit and cash-balance)	A loan provision can get around the restriction against in-service withdrawals.
Pension plans (defined benefit)	Loan provisions are not frequently available because calculating the maximum loan amount requires an actuarial calculation.
Profit-sharing plan	A loan provision is less crucial, because in-service withdrawals are allowed. However, the loan does provide for tax-free access.
Defined-benefit plan	Although a loan provision can be useful (see pension plan), it is often forsaken because of administrative problems.
ESOP	A loan provision is seldom used because of the requirement that the plan be invested primarily in employer stock and because the plan often lacks the cash to loan to participants.
Stock bonus plan	A loan provision is a problem if the plan lacks cash to support the program.
SEP	No loans are permitted.
SIMPLE	No loans are permitted.
IRA	No loans are permitted.

(and accrued interest). If this happens, the participant has a taxable distribution subject to ordinary income tax and the 10 percent early distribution excise tax, if he or she has not attained age 59½ (see chapter 24).

YOUR FINANCIAL SERVICES PRACTICE: PLAN LOANS

Some financial service professionals use loan provisions to overcome the employer's common objection about locking up retirement funds. In some cases, this may eliminate the final hurdle to a sale. On the other hand, some financial service professionals are not fond of plan loans because loans take potential investment funds away from the asset pool. The decision is up to the plan sponsor, who will probably not be as concerned with depleting the asset pool.

Another issue that arises with loans is that, in plans subject to the qualified joint and survivor annuity requirements (see chapter 10), both spouses must sign off on the loan. This is because a loan default can reduce the participant's benefit, which affects the spousal rights to that benefit as well.

Restrictions on Amounts and Repayments

In addition to rules on loan availability, there are limits on the amount each participant can borrow. The limit is $50,000 or one-half of the vested account balance, whichever is less. Under the tax rules, a participant may borrow up to $10,000, even if this amount is more than one-half of the vested benefit. For example, a person with a vested benefit of $13,000 could still borrow up to $10,000. However, in practice, employers typically do not allow loans in excess of the 50 percent limit, because DOL regulations allow only one half of the vested account balance to be used as collateral. Allowing loans in excess of that amount would require additional security—which complicates plan administration.

A participant's loan must be repayable by its terms within 5 years. The one exception to the 5-year rule is if a loan is used to acquire a participant's principal residence. In this case, a reasonable repayment schedule (presumably over the life of any mortgage involved) will suffice. Another important factor concerning the 5-year rule is that "sham" repayments are not allowed. Before 1987, the 5-year rule was subject to frequent abuse. Participants would repay the loan on the last possible date and take out the loan again immediately after repayment. For this reason, the rules were designed so the $50,000 limit is reduced by the highest outstanding loan balance during the one-year period ending the day before the loan date. The rules were also changed to add a restriction that requires level amortization of loan repayments of principal and interest being made at least quarterly.

Example: Bill Smith borrows $50,000 from his qualified plan and pays off the loan on a level amortization basis over 5 years. At the end of 5 years, when the loan is repaid, Bill wants to take out another loan. The maximum amount available for this second loan is limited by the highest outstanding principal balance in the last year of the first loan.

Interest on a plan loan is treated as consumer interest that is not deductible by the employee as an itemized deduction unless the loan is secured by a principal residence. Because plans generally do not want to make loans on this basis, the tax deduction is rarely available. Note that even if a plan wanted to allow loans that would have tax-deductible interest payments, deductions are not allowed (even if secured with a mortgage) if the loan is (1) made to a key employee, as defined by the Code's rules for top-heavy plans (see chapter 10) or (2) made to any participant in a 401(k) or 403(b) plan.

VESTING

Another important design decision is choosing a plan's vesting schedule. The vesting schedule can have some impact on plan costs, but more importantly it should be consistent with the plan's objectives.

Understanding the Vesting System

The vesting concept is perhaps best understood in light of its history. Before the passage of the Employee Retirement Income Security Act (ERISA) in 1974, it was accepted practice in some companies to offer retirement benefits only to employees who retired from the company after completing long periods of service (for example, 30 years). The result was a system that ignored the retirement needs of many, bound others in an unwanted fashion to their company, and shortchanged employees whose service was long but not long enough. Partly as a result of a television documentary and subsequent congressional hearings that publicized horror stories of long-service employees left penniless during retirement, Congress recognized the injustices of this situation and enacted ERISA, which ensured that employees would receive some retirement benefits if they terminated employment prior to reaching normal retirement age. ERISA established rules for determining how much service is required before benefits become

vesting schedules nonforfeitable. These rules were called *vesting schedules*. Subsequent to ERISA, the rules have been changed several times, with each law mandating less and less required service before full vesting occurs. Today the vesting schedules allowed for defined-contribution and defined-benefit plans are somewhat different.

Vesting Schedules for Defined-Benefit Plans

In a defined-benefit plan an employer is required to choose a vesting schedule that is at least as favorable as one of two statutory schedules: the 5-year cliff vesting or the 3-through-7-year graded vesting. The 5-year cliff vesting is a schedule under which an employee who terminates employment prior to the completion of 5 years of service will be entitled to no benefit (zero percent vested). After 5 years of service, the employee becomes fully entitled to (100 percent vested in) the benefit that has accrued on his or her behalf. Five-year cliff vesting is easy to remember if you visualize an employee climbing a cliff for 5 years and finally becoming entitled to the benefits upon reaching the top. The cliff vesting schedule is as follows:

5-Year Cliff Vesting

Years of Service	Percentage Vested
0–4	0
5 or more	100

The other statutory vesting schedule, known as the 3-through-7-year graded schedule, requires no vesting until the third year of service has been completed; at that point, the vested portion of the accrued benefit increases 20 percent for each year served.

3-through-7-Year Graded Vesting

Years of Service	Percentage Vested
0–2	0
3	20
4	40
5	60
6	80
7 or more	100

An employer is allowed to choose a more liberal vesting schedule than either of the statutory vesting schedules. For example, an employer could establish a 2-year cliff vesting schedule or a 4-year graded schedule, where the participant earned an additional 25 percent vesting for each year of service. Also note that top-heavy defined-benefit plans (described further in chapter 10) will be subject to more accelerated vesting schedules that apply to defined-contribution plans. This is often the case for small businesses.

Vesting Schedules for Defined-Contribution Plans

In order to facilitate portability of benefits in defined-contribution plans, the Pension Protection Act of 2006 required more accelerated vesting schedules for defined-contribution plans. Defined-contribution plans are required to choose a vesting schedule that is at least as favorable as 3-year cliff vesting or 2-through-6-year graded vesting. With 3-year cliff vesting an employee who terminates employment prior to the completion of 3 years of service will be entitled to no benefit. After 3 years of service, the employee becomes fully entitled to the benefit that has accrued on his or her behalf.

3-Year Cliff Vesting

Years of Service	Percentage Vested
0–2	0
3 or more	100

The 2-through-6-year graded schedule requires no vesting until the second year of service has been completed; at that point, the vested portion of the accrued benefit increases 20 percent for each year served. After 6 years the participant is fully vested.

2-through-6-Year Graded Vesting

Years of Service	Percentage Vested
0–1	0
2	20
3	40
4	60
5	80
6 or more	100

General Vesting Considerations

The vesting schedules just described apply when a participant terminates employment on a voluntary or involuntary basis. If the participant continues working until the plan's normal retirement age, he must be fully vested regardless of the years of service earned. Plans may also choose to fully vest at attainment of an early retirement age, upon disability, or at death. Also remember that the participant's benefit attributable to employee after-tax contributions or employee pretax salary deferral elections in a 401(k) plan must be 100-percent vested at all times.

In today's pension environment, there are numerous other situations in which benefits must be fully vested at all times. All of them are summarized below. As you can see, Congress keeps whittling away at the vesting restrictions. This is probably because anything less than full and immediate vesting limits benefit "portability"—an important concern to a mobile workforce that changes jobs frequently.

- *SEPs and SIMPLEs*—Contributions to a SEP or SIMPLE must be fully vested at all times (chapter 6).
- *Plan termination*—Benefits must become fully vested upon a full or partial plan termination (chapter 14).
- *Safe harbor 401(k) plans*—Contributions to a 401(k) SIMPLE and contributions made to satisfy the 401(k) safe harbor provisions must be fully vested (chapter 5).
- *Two-year eligibility rule*—In exchange for the ability to exclude employees for 2 years (instead of one), contributions must be fully vested (chapter 7).

Choosing the Most Appropriate Vesting Schedule

The various vesting schedule choices and their exceptions obviously have design implications you must consider in helping your clients make the best choice. To the employer, the major advantage of choosing a restrictive vesting schedule is that it may be able to cut costs attributable to employee turnover. When employees terminate employment prior to being fully vested,

forfeiture

the nonvested portion of the accrued benefit (referred to as a *forfeiture*) can be used to reduce future employer contributions. For example, if five employees terminate employment with the National Furniture Company, each with a $4,000 forfeited benefit, National's contribution for next year is reduced by $20,000. The employer also has the choice in any defined-contribution plan to use forfeitures as an additional contribution for

reallocated forfeiture

remaining employees (in pension parlance, this is referred to as *reallocated forfeitures*). Reallocated forfeitures do not result in a direct cost savings, but they do allow the employer to provide bigger benefits for long-term highly compensated employees at no extra cost.

Forfeitures that are reallocated to employees are added to other contributions, and the aggregate amount cannot exceed the Code Sec. 415 maximum contribution limit. If the plan's benefit formula is already designed to reach this limit, then forfeitures should not be reallocated.

Another advantage of choosing a restrictive vesting schedule is that it helps retain employees. Many employees are convinced that it is economically desirable to delay a job change until they become fully vested (this may not always be the case in reality) and, consequently, stick it out at a company until the vesting requirements are fulfilled. When employers have spent time training employees and having them become acclimated, a restrictive vesting schedule that encourages employees to stay around after they have reached a productive level may pay back the organization for the time it invested.

In contrast to these reasons for adopting a restrictive schedule, there are some good reasons to adopt a more liberal schedule or to have immediate and full vesting:

- to foster employee morale
- to remain competitive in attracting employees
- to meet the design needs of the small employer who desires few encumbrances to participation for the "employee family"

Additional Vesting Rules

The choice of a vesting schedule is only the first in a series of vesting-design choices. The vesting schedule raises several questions that need to be answered through plan design:

- What years of service must be counted for vesting-schedule purposes?
- What happens if an employee leaves employment and then returns?

Vesting-Service Considerations

When determining vesting service, an employee must be credited with a year of service if he or she earns 1,000 or more hours of service in a 12-month period. For vesting purposes, the 12-month period can be measured from the date of hire or based on some other 12-month period. Many employers choose the plan year as the measuring period to simplify administration. Hours of service can be determined by using the standard-hours counting method (each hour actually worked is counted, plus hours for which an employee is entitled to be paid, such as vacations and holidays) or by using any one of the equivalency methods discussed in chapter 7.

In addition to designing these definitions, you can design the plan to exclude certain years of service.

- Years of service earned prior to age 18 can be excluded. (Generally, it is a good idea to exclude vesting service prior to age 18, because turnover is higher among younger employees, and the employer could save on future expenditures because of forfeitures.)
- Years of service before the plan went into effect can be excluded.
- Certain years of service prior to a break in service can be excluded (discussed below).

There are, however, circumstances where the plan cannot be designed to cut service for vesting purposes.

- Service prior to eligibility (past age 18) will be counted even if the employee was not a participant in the plan.
- Service for a different component of the employer, even though the employee was not covered by the plan, must be counted. For example, Sally Jerkins is a 15-year member of the Oakland office, which does not have a pension plan. Her company transfers her to the San Diego office, which does have one. Sally will be 100 percent vested when she transfers to San Diego under the plan's cliff vesting schedule because of her 15 years of service.
- Service with any member of a controlled group of corporations, with a commonly controlled business, or with an affiliated service group must be counted for vesting purposes. For example, George Gray is a 15-year employee of Modern Kitchens, which is under a controlled group with Total Home Concepts. Modern Kitchens has no plan; Total Home has one. When George is hired by Total Home, his years of service from Modern Kitchens will apply for vesting purposes.
- Service with a predecessor employer if the successor employer maintains the predecessor's plan must be counted. In other words, if an employee's company changes hands and the new owners maintain the same plan, service with the old owner counts for vesting purposes.

Breaks in Service

In some limited circumstances, the rules allow a plan to disregard certain years of vesting service during which a participant has had sporadic employment. The employer establishing the plan can take advantage of these rules or choose to disregard them.

break in service

For any of the rules to apply, the participant must first incur a break in service. A *break in service* is a year (using the same measuring period used for determining vesting) in which the individual does not complete more than 500 hours of service. If there is a break in service, there are three rules that may be applicable. Under the first rule, prebreak service may be disregarded until an individual is reemployed and completes a full year of service. For administrative purposes, this is probably a good idea, in case the reemployment does not last.

The second and most useful rule applies only to defined-contribution plans. Under this rule, if an individual has five consecutive breaks in service, the nonvested portion of the benefit earned prior to the break can be permanently forfeited.

Example:	Ralph terminates employment with a $2,000 account balance. He is 50 percent vested and so he is eligible to receive a benefit of $1,000. He returns to the same employer 7 years later. Regardless of how much postbreak service he earns, Ralph cannot earn back the $1,000 benefit that he forfeited.

Most defined-contribution plans should consider adopting this provision. Otherwise, it is possible to have to make up contributions (or hold the forfeitures in a separate account) virtually forever.

**YOUR FINANCIAL SERVICES PRACTICE:
WHEN TO REALLOCATE FORFEITURES**

If a defined-contribution plan is drafted to reallocate forfeitures to the remaining employees, a decision has to be made as to when the forfeitures will occur. One option is to wait until the participant has been gone for 5 years (five one-year breaks in service). This option ensures that the contributions are still available if a terminated employee returns to service and earns the right to such amounts. When the plan does not allow the distribution of benefits before the normal retirement date, the employer should always elect this option. However, if the employer allows immediate payment at termination of employment, the employer may wish to allocate forfeitures on the valuation date immediately following termination. This eliminates both the administrative expense and the confusion involved in maintaining many small accounts for terminated employees. This option makes sense if terminated employees generally do not return to service. If this option is elected, the employer must understand that additional contributions might have to be made if terminees return to service within 5 years.

Under the third rule, prebreak and postbreak service do not have to be aggregated for an individual who is zero percent vested and who then incurs five consecutive one-year breaks in service. This rule is not adopted as regularly as the others because it adds administrative complexity and rarely applies. The employer who has a revolving workforce might want to consider adopting this vesting requirement.

RETIREMENT AGES

The choice of the plan's retirement age should be motivated primarily by business reasons, not tax or plan cost considerations. The employer should carefully consider at what age it wants to encourage employees to retire. The employer has to be concerned about the orderly retirement of older, highly compensated employees, while it does not want to inadvertently encourage its older, more experienced employees to leave and go to competitors. Such issues determine the success or failure of an organization and are much more important than plan cost or tax considerations.

Effective plan design concerning retirement age boils down to the following four questions:

- What should the normal retirement age be?
- Should there be early retirement, and if so, when should it start?
- Should early retirement be subsidized?
- What provisions should be made for deferred retirement?

Normal Retirement Age

normal retirement age

When you are designing the retirement plan, you typically define a *normal retirement age*—that is, the age specified in the plan at which the employee has the right to retire. The term *right to retire* means the employee can retire without the employer's consent and will receive his or her full benefit under the plan. In general, an employer and his or her advisor can choose any age up to 65 as the normal retirement age. Age 62 is another common choice for normal retirement because that is the earliest age at which a retiring worker can receive reduced Social Security benefits. In addition, some retirement ages are set by industry standards. For example, a relatively young age can be chosen if it is the age at which employees customarily retire, such as in professional sports. Finally, some government plans do not link normal retirement to any particular age but take into account only years of service. For example, a plan can be structured to have the normal retirement age after 25 years of service.

Under certain circumstances, the normal retirement age can be greater than 65. This usually occurs in new defined-benefit plans that have a number of older employees, which makes the start-up funding cost prohibitive, or in existing plans that frequently hire people 55 or older. In these cases, the employer should take advantage of an exception to the general rule: For an employee who commences participation in the plan within 5 years of the plan's normal retirement age, the plan can delay actual retirement until the employee's fifth anniversary. For example, a 62-year-old hiree can have a normal retirement age of 67, not 65 as do other employees in the plan.

Early Retirement

An employer can provide retirement benefits earlier than normal retirement age. As with the choice of normal retirement age, the pension tail should not wag the business dog when the employer makes this decision. Typical early retirement ages are 55, 60, and 62. Effective design of a plan that offers early retirement should take into account the practices of the employer's competitors.

Age is not the only determinant of early retirement (especially in defined-benefit plans); both age and service can dictate the early retirement age. One typical early-retirement provision requires age 55 and 10 years of service (in pension parlance, this is known as 55 and 10). The service requirement is valuable for employers who want to ensure enough time to fund the benefit (for example, when life insurance is used to fund the plan). Hence, if cash flow is a problem, a years-of-service requirement is desirable.

If the employer's industry is prone to superannuated employees or if the industry requires physical skills that employees may lack later in their careers, an early-retirement option is a good idea. In addition, an early-retirement option allows for a graceful change in management and the attraction of key employees who consider early retirement a valuable lifestyle choice. However, if the employer fears that certain key employees will take jobs with competitors in order to acquire a second pension check, or if a majority of the organization's business skills and knowledge are centered in a few key people whose loss would devastate the organization, early retirement is probably not a good idea.

The early-retirement benefit can be either subsidized or nonsubsidized. If it is subsidized, the actuarial reductions for early retirement (that is, the percentage reductions taken from the normal-retirement-age benefit to reflect the longer payout period) do not reflect the true cost of providing the benefit, and the difference represents an increased employer cost. For small plans whose owner-employees are looking for tax savings, a subsidized early-retirement program will garner bigger deductions and should be strongly considered as a planning alternative. For medium-sized and large plans, some subsidy may be called for—if, for example, the employer desires to eliminate older employees—but a substantial subsidy can be prohibitively expensive.

Employers who want to offer early retirement (say for competitive reasons), but are not delighted with the prospect of losing experienced employees, should consider nonsubsidized early retirement. If early retirement is not subsidized, the actuarial reduction will reflect as closely as possible the true experience of the early-retirement costs.

Deferred Retirement

A plan should always be designed to accommodate the possibility of deferred retirement—retirement after the normal retirement age. Note that the Federal Age Discrimination in Employment Act prohibits involuntary retirement (except for some executives and employees in high policymaking positions). Also, it is desirable from a business standpoint to make provisions that allow, or even encourage, productive employees to remain on the team. Under the age discrimination law, the employer must continue to make contributions in a defined-contribution plan if a deferred retirement is chosen. In a defined-benefit plan, benefits cannot stop accruing at a specified age; however, the plan can contain a maximum number of years of service for determining benefits under the plan. For example, the benefit formula could be stated as two percent of final-average compensation times years of service, with service limited to 30 years.

**YOUR FINANCIAL SERVICES PRACTICE:
THE RETIREMENT-AGE RULES IN A SAMPLE
ADOPTION AGREEMENT**

Regardless of what the employer chooses with regard to early, normal, and deferred retirement, these decisions are reflected in the plan's definition section, which contains detailed descriptions of the terms *early retirement, normal retirement,* and *deferred retirement,* and it often spells out the actuarial reductions attributable to early retirement. In addition to containing choices with regard to the plan's definition section, the adoption agreement also includes sections for choosing early, normal, and deferred retirement provisions.

The following sample illustrates how the early retirement age sections might appear in a typical adoption agreement:

Section T: Early Retirement Age (refers to Section 20 of the Plan)

(1) Retirement Prior to Normal Retirement Age (Section S) (check one)

    ( ) will not be permitted
    ( ) will be permitted upon attaining age ___ and completing ___ years
of
      ( ) service
      ( ) participation

CHAPTER REVIEW

Key Terms

vesting schedules [9-2]
forfeiture [9-2]
reallocated forfeiture [9-2]

break in service [9-2]
normal retirement age [9-3]

Review Questions

Review questions are based on the learning objectives in this chapter. Thus, a [9-3] at the end of a question means that the question is based on learning objective 9-3. If there are multiple objectives, they are all listed.

1. What are the advantages and disadvantages of designing a plan to include a loan provision? [9-1]

2. To what extent does the type of plan involved affect planning for a loan provision in [9-1]
   a. 401(k) plans
   b. 403(b) plans
   c. contributory plans
   d. defined-contribution pension plans
   e. profit-sharing plans
   f. defined-benefit plans
   g. stock plans
   h. SEPs and SIMPLEs

3. How can a loan provision help a financial services professional to overcome the client's objection that plan funds are being "locked up"? [9-1]

4. The New City Heating Supply Company (an S corporation) has a qualified money-purchase plan that allows employees to take loans up to the maximum legal limit. What is the maximum loan that can be taken by the following employees? [9-1]

Employee	Vested Account Balance	Percentage of Corporate Ownership
a. Mary Woods	$ 17,000	0
b. Peter Muhlenberg	$160,000	0
c. Donna Dickenson	$200,000	50

5. Which of the following sets of vesting schedules can be used in a defined-benefit plan? [9-2]

a. | Years of service | Percentage vested |
|---|---|
| 09–10 | 0% |
| 10 | 100 |

b. | Years of service | Percentage vested |
|---|---|
| 1 | 50% |
| 2 | 60 |
| 3 | 70 |
| 4 | 80 |
| 5 | 90 |
| 6 | 100 |

c. | Years of service | Percentage vested |
|---|---|
| 0–4 | 0% |
| 5 | 50 |
| 6 | 100 |

6. What is the difference between defined-benefit and a defined-contribution plans under the vesting rules? [9-2]

7. a. Under what conditions should an employer choose a restrictive vesting schedule for the plan? [9-2]
   b. Under what conditions should the employer choose a liberal vesting schedule for the plan?

8. Identify the following periods of service that must be included and those that can be excluded for vesting purposes: [9-2]
   a. service prior to eligibility earned by a 20-year-old participant
   b. service earned by a 16-year-old employee
   c. service for a subsidiary of the employer, even though the subsidiary did not have a qualified plan
   d. years of service before the effective date of the plan

9. Identify the three break-in-service rules that may allow the employer to disregard prior service for vesting purposes. [9-2]

10. When should a post-65 normal retirement age be considered? [9-3]

11. What are the advantages and disadvantages of [9-3]
    a. including an early retirement provision in a plan
    b. subsidizing an early retirement benefit

12. Can an employer stop making contributions in a defined-contribution plan once the participant attains age 65, which is the plan's normal retirement age? [9-3]

13. In a defined benefit plan, how can the employer effectively limit the benefits for older, long-service employees without violating age discrimination law? [9-3]

10

Death and Disability Benefits; Top-Heavy Rules

Learning Objectives

An understanding of the material in this chapter should enable you to

10-1.   Explain the death-benefit requirements that apply to qualified plans.

10-2.   Understand how the incidental death-benefit requirements limit the amount of life insurance in a qualified plan.

10-3.   Describe why pre-retirement death benefits are typically provided outside of the qualified retirement plan.

10-4.   Describe common disability provisions found in qualified retirement plans.

10-5.   Determine when a plan is top-heavy, and describe the additional restrictions that apply to a top-heavy plan.

Chapter Outline

The primary purpose of a qualified retirement plan is to provide retirement benefits to employees. The retirement plan, however, can be used to meet the insurance needs of participants by providing both death and disability coverage in the preretirement period.

DEATH BENEFITS

Qualified retirement plans have a number of alternatives regarding the provision of preretirement death benefits. There is a minimum required benefit for certain married participants and a maximum benefit when the plan wants to provide a large benefit through the purchase of life insurance. There is a wide range of options in between. The design of the plan's death benefits will depend on the company's objective, as well as on the other benefit programs that provide for preretirement death benefits.

Mandatory Death Benefits: QPSA and QJSA

There are two mandatory death benefits. For a participant that dies prior to retirement, the plan must provide a spousal benefit called a qualified preretirement survivor annuity (QPSA). For participants receiving retirement benefits, the normal form of distribution from the retirement plan for a married participant must be a qualified joint and survivor annuity (QJSA). The legislative motive behind both of these rules is to protect the spouse's right to a piece of the participant's retirement income.

qualified pre-retirement survivor annuity (QPSA)

The *qualified preretirement survivor annuity (QPSA)* (pronounced "quip-sa") is defined differently for defined-benefit and defined-contribution plans. In both cases, however, the QPSA is required to be provided only for married participants who were married for one year before the participant's death (plans sometimes waive the one-year requirement for administrative convenience). For a defined-benefit plan, the amount of the survivor annuity is basically equal to the amount that would have been paid under the qualified joint and survivor annuity (below). To determine this amount, the plan administrator assumes that the participant retired the day before death, or if the participant was not yet able to retire, left the company the day prior to death, survived until the plan's earliest retirement age, and then retired with an immediate joint and survivor annuity. For a defined-contribution plan, the qualified preretirement survivor annuity is an annuity for the life of the surviving spouse that is at least actuarially equivalent to 50 percent of the vested account balance of the participant as of the date of death.

The QPSA need not be an employer-sponsored benefit; the employer has the choice of requiring employee contributions to fund this benefit or, conversely, reducing the normal benefit actuarially. If the second choice is made, the employee generally has the option of electing out of the QPSA benefit any time after age 35. A written confirmation of the spouse's consent to the election out is required. Many employers choose to pay for the cost of providing the QPSA in order to avoid the administrative and legal problems that could result from the administration of the spousal consent forms.

qualified joint and survivor annuity (QJSA)

The *qualified joint and survivor annuity (QJSA)* must be the normal form of benefit distribution offered to a married participant at retirement. A QJSA is an annuity for the life of the participant, with a survivor annuity for the life of the spouse which is not less than 50 percent (and not more than 100 percent) of the amount of the annuity payable during the joint lives of the participant and his or her spouse. The participant and his or her spouse may waive the right to a QJSA and QPSA provided certain requirements are satisfied. In general, these conditions include providing the participant with a written explanation of the terms and conditions of the survivor annuity, the right to make, and the effect of, a waiver of the annuity, the right of the spouse to waive the survivor annuity, and the right of the participant to revoke the waiver. In addition, the spouse must provide written consent to the waiver, witnessed by a plan representative or a notary public, which acknowledges the effect of the waiver.

The Pension Protection Act of 2006 has amended the QJSA rules somewhat. Effective beginning in 2008, participants will also have to be given the option to elect a qualified optional survivor annuity. A qualified optional survivor annuity is an annuity for the life of the participant with a survivor annuity for the life of the spouse which is equal to 75 percent (if the survivor portion under the QJSA is less than 75 percent) or 50 percent (if the survival portion under the QJSA is greater than or equal to 75 percent) of the survival portion under the QJSA.

YOUR FINANCIAL SERVICES PRACTICE:
PROVIDING MINIMUM DEATH BENEFITS IN QUALIFIED PLANS

Especially in larger defined-benefit plans, the employer will typically provide death benefits outside of the pension plan, and if given a choice will not provide death benefits in the plan. However, by law the employer must provide the QPSA benefit for eligible married participants. In this case, it is not uncommon for the plan to provide the QPSA for married participants and no death benefit for unmarried participants—a situation that the unmarried participants may feel is unfair.

The same strategy could be used in defined-contribution plans, but because individual accounts have accrued for each participant, most employers choose to pay out the entire account balance as a preretirement death benefit for both married and unmarried participants.

These rules apply to all qualified plans; however, plans in the profit-sharing category (including stock bonus plans, ESOPs, and 401(k) plans) are exempt from the QJSA requirement if certain criteria are met. Most advisors encourage employers to take advantage of this exception in order to simplify plan administration. In order to qualify, the plan must not allow any life annuity options and must not accept direct transfers of plan benefits from other plans subject to the QJSA requirements. Finally, the plan must provide that if a married participant dies prior to retirement, the spouse must be entitled to receive 100 percent of the participant's plan benefit, unless the spouse elects to waive the benefit.

Incidental Rules for Death Benefits

Death benefits under a retirement plan must be *incidental* because Uncle Sam is providing tax advantages to the qualified plan for retirement needs, not insurance needs. The word *incidental,* however, may be somewhat of a misnomer, since a fairly substantial incidental death benefit can be provided through the use of life insurance in a qualified plan.

The rules described below apply to qualified plans and 403(b) plans, which are allowed to invest in life insurance. The rules do not apply to SEPs and SIMPLEs because these types of plans cannot have life insurance.

Preretirement Death Benefits

For defined-contribution plans, the basic limit is that the aggregate premiums paid over the entire life of the plan must either be

- less than 50 percent of aggregate employer contributions for permanent insurance or
- no greater than 25 percent of aggregate employer contributions for other types of insurance.

Example: Tim Rivers has an account that includes $100,000 of employer contributions. If he uses variable, universal, or term insurance, the aggregate premiums that can be used to pay for Tim's life insurance total a maximum of $25,000. If he has a whole life policy, the aggregate premiums that can be used to pay for his life insurance total a maximum of $50,000.

The IRS has defined permanent life insurance as insurance on which the premium does not increase and the death benefit does not decrease. Ordinary life insurance and whole life insurance are examples of permanent insurance. Term insurance clearly is not permanent insurance and is subject to the 25-percent limit. The IRS has also indicated that universal life insurance and variable life insurance are subject to the lower 25-percent limit.

In a defined-benefit plan, the plan can meet the incidental benefits requirement using the 25 percent/50 percent test or the 100-to-1 ratio test. Under this test, the death benefit is limited to a maximum of 100 times the expected monthly benefit or, if greater, the reserve for the pension benefit. For example, if the expected monthly benefit is $1,500, then the total death benefit could be $150,000 or the reserve (at the date of death) if greater.

Exceptions

In several situations, death benefits are not subject to the incidental benefit requirements. The incidental limitations do not apply to life insurance bought with nondeductible employee contributions.

A more important exception that can be quite useful is that the incidental limitations do not apply to profit-sharing plans under certain conditions. If the profit-sharing plan permits in-service withdrawals (for example, after 2 years) and if life insurance is purchased with funds that could be withdrawn, there is no incidental limit on the amount of these funds that can be used to purchase life insurance. In other words, the incidental limitation applies only to funds in a profit-sharing plan that have not accumulated under the plan long enough to be distributed. If the profit-sharing plan does not permit withdrawals, however, the incidental rules will apply to all funds.

Incidental Rule for Postretirement Death Benefits

We have been looking at limitations on the amount of death benefits that can be provided if a participant dies *prior* to retirement. However, there are also limitations on the amount of death benefits that can be provided *after* retirement. These rules have become part of the required minimum distribution rules discussed in chapter 25. Conceptually, the rules require that the amount of benefits paid to beneficiaries is incidental to the retirement benefits paid to participants. To do this, the rules impose very specific minimum payout requirements during the participant's lifetime.

Tax Implications of Life Insurance

Table 2001

As discussed in chapter 1, employees are generally not taxed on the benefits promised from, or the contributions made to, a qualified plan. Taxation occurs at the time benefits are received. The one exception is when life insurance is purchased in a plan to provide death benefits. In this case, the current cost of the "pure insurance" protection is subject to taxation. The cost attributable to this pure life protection will be the lower of the actual cost as provided by the carrier or the rates supplied by the IRS table found in Notice 2001-10 referred to as *Table 2001* (see table 10-1). Prior to Table 2001, the PS 58 table was used and the cost of insurance that is included in income is still referred to by many as PS 58 costs.

TABLE 10-1
One-Year Term Premiums for $1,000 of Life Insurance Protection

Age	Premium	Age	Premium	Age	Premium
15	$ .38	37	$ 1.04	59	$ 6.06
16	.52	38	1.06	60	6.51
17	.57	39	1.07	61	7.11
18	.59	40	1.10	62	7.96
19	.61	41	1.13	63	9.08
20	62	42	1.20	64	10.41
21	62	43	1.29	65	11.90
22	.64	44	1.40	66	13.51
23	.66	45	1.53	67	15.20
24	.68	46	1.67	68	16.92
25	.71	47	1.83	69	18.70
26	.73	48	1.98	70	20.62
27	.76	49	2.13	71	22.72
28	.80	50	2.30	72	25.07
29	.83	51	2.52	73	27.57
30	.87	52	2.81	74	30.18
31	.90	53	3.20	75	33.05
32	.93	54	3.65	76	36.33
33	.96	55	4.15	77	40.17
34	.98	56	4.68	78	44.33
35	.99	57	5.20	79	49.23
36	1.01	58	5.66	80	54.56
				81	60.51

Any amounts currently taxed to the participant according to this rule (along with any employee after-tax contributions or employer contributions on which the employee has paid tax) are considered part of an employee's cost basis. When the employee takes retirement distributions from the plan, he or she will not be required to pay taxes on the portion of the distribution attributable to cost basis. In other words, the pure life insurance protection will not be taxed twice.

For a self-employed person with a Keogh plan or a 5 percent owner in an S corporation, the rules are applied differently. The portion of employer contribution that is allocable to the cost of pure insurance protection for the self-employed individual is treated as a nondeductible contribution. Also, at the time of payment, the taxable insurance costs are not recovered tax free by the business owner.

Death Benefit Plan Design

There are innumerable reasons to include life insurance in an employee benefits package, including competitiveness, attraction and retention of employees, and other advantages for the business owner. By including life insurance protection in a benefit package, business owners are able to (1) receive favorable group rates for themselves and their employees, (2) shift a nondeductible personal expense to the company, and (3) if necessary, gain favorable underwriting for ratable or uninsurable individuals (which potentially means life insurance protection without physical exams or medical questions).

Essentially, the most important question facing the financial services professional is not whether death benefits should be provided, but rather what vehicle should provide them. Is it in the employer's best interest to provide the majority of death benefits in a group insurance plan or in a retirement plan? What system will provide the lowest employee and employer cost for the desired benefit level?

Many employers choose to provide the death benefits outside of the qualified plan. One reason is that the benefit structure, especially in defined-benefit plans, does not provide an appropriate amount of insurance. In defined-benefit plans, the death benefit is tied to the participant's benefit (for example, 100 times the monthly retirement benefit). This means the death benefit would be quite small in the early years, when the participant may need the insurance protection the most. Insurance in a defined-contribution plan poses a different problem. Premiums are taken from the participant's account and can have the effect of reducing the ultimate retirement benefits provided. There are also tax reasons that motivate employers to choose to provide death benefits outside the qualified plan. Sec. 79 provides a $50,000 exemption (the premiums paid for the first $50,000 of term insurance covering an employee are not taxable), which further eases the tax bite. Also, the tax treatment of insurance proceeds is more favorable outside of the plan, where in most cases the entire death benefit is not taxable.

For these reasons, most mid-size and large organizations provide death benefits outside of the qualified plan. For small organizations, however, providing the death benefit in the qualified plan may be more administratively convenient, be better serviced by the life agent, and do double duty for the retirement dollar by offering a tax-favored way of providing permanent life insurance. Small business owners also sometimes use qualified plan assets to purchase life insurance for estate planning purposes. If the individual has a life insurance need, the most available assets to pay the premiums may well be in the qualified plan. One popular planning device is to purchase a second-to-die life insurance policy in a profit-sharing plan (pension plans cannot hold second-to-die policies). However, this is a very complicated subject which is outside the scope of this text (it is even somewhat unclear what the IRS's position is on this matter).

DISABILITY BENEFITS

Similar to the issue of death benefits, many employers provide disability benefits, although the question is how to provide the benefits. Most large companies that maintain separate short-term and long-term disability plans do not provide disability income benefits in their retirement programs. If there is an existing disability income program, the financial services professional needs to be concerned primarily with the coordination of the retirement plan and the disability income plan.

Most plans do have some provisions for disability. The most common provision is to fully vest participants if they have to terminate due to a disability. It is also fairly common, especially in a defined-contribution plan, to allow payouts at the time of the disability.

Less common, and much more expensive, is to continue accruing benefit service while the participant is out on disability. Because most company-provided long-term disability benefits will stop at age 65, this is a way to continue building an adequate retirement benefit for the disabled person.

Example: The Northeast Corp. has a defined-benefit plan that provides a monthly life annuity at age 65 in the amount of 2 percent of final average compensation multiplied by years of service. The company also provides a long-term disability program that pays a disability benefit to a disabled worker until age 65. To ensure that the disabled worker has an adequate retirement benefit, the plan counts service (until age 65) for those individuals out on disability.

No matter what form the disability benefit takes, there are two additional decisions about plan design that must be considered. First, the plan must contain a definition of *disability*. One simple, but restrictive, option is to define disability as eligibility for Social Security disability benefits. If the company also has a disability insurance program, another option is to define disability as eligibility for benefits under that plan. Both of these options simplify administration by putting the task of determination and verification on an outside organization.

Second, consider whether or not the retirement plan's disability benefit should have age and service requirements. Reasons to include these requirements are to permit enough time to properly fund the benefit and to limit the benefit to long-service employees. In addition, if there are age and service provisions, the question of whether the disability was attributable to a preexisting condition is also sidestepped. The main reason for *not* having age and service requirements for disability is the negative impression it can create among employees.

TOP-HEAVY RULES

In chapter 1, it was implied that retirement plans were a tug-of-war. On one side of the rope are the government regulations regarding eligibility, coverage, and vesting. On the other side, pulling equally hard, are financial services professionals looking to gain tax shelter and retirement protection for their business owner clients without overspending for the rank and file. The government's intervention stems from a spread-the-wealth philosophy and the desire to get the most for its money when it comes to allowing tax advantages for retirement plans.

The anchor of the government's tug-of-war team is the top-heavy rules, aimed specifically at small employers such as professional corporations and closely held businesses. The rationale for the strict scrutiny of small organizations is that employers and owners of these organizations are more prone to the temptation to shape the organization's retirement plan primarily to shelter taxes for themselves and key employees. As financial services professionals would be the first to attest, the government's suspicion is well-founded. (Clients that fall into the small-plan category are almost invariably interested in tax shelter first and retirement needs second.)

When Is a Plan Top-Heavy?

A defined-contribution plan is top-heavy if more than 60 percent of the account balances of all employees are allocated to key employees. A defined-benefit plan is top-heavy if more than 60 percent of the present value of the accrued benefits for all participants is accrued for key employees.

key employee

An individual is a *key employee* if at any time during the prior year he or she has been any of the following:

- an officer receiving annual compensation in excess of $145,000 (as indexed for 2007). If there are 30 or fewer employees, no more than three officers are treated as key employees. If there are 31 to 500 employees, no more than 10 percent of the employees are treated as officers. And, if there are more than 500 employees, no more than 50 officers are key employees
- a person who owns more than 5 percent of the company
- a person who is more than a 1-percent owner with annual compensation of more than $150,000

The top-heavy test is applied once a year on the determination date. Except for the first year of the plan, the determination date is the last day of the preceding plan year. In the calculation, distributions made within one year of the determination date are counted when determining account balances. However, the accounts of former employees who have not performed any services for the employer during the one-year period ending on the determination date are excluded from the calculation.

Separate plans of the same or related employers are generally aggregated for purposes of top-heavy testing. There is required aggregation of every plan that covers a key employee or that allows a key-employee plan to meet the applicable nondiscrimination and minimum-participation standards. Other plans that are not required to be aggregated may be added on a permissive basis. All these complicating factors demonstrate that the top-heavy determination should be made with the help of a qualified plan administrator.

Top-Heavy Provisions

Plan documents must contain top-heavy language. The plan document must specify that if the plan is or ever becomes top-heavy, certain special rules will become effective. The plan must satisfy the following top-heavy requirements:

- special vesting rules
- minimum benefits for nonkey employees

- a special limit for situations where both a defined-benefit and a defined-contribution plan are present

If these rules are satisfied, a top-heavy plan will continue to remain qualified.

Special Top-Heavy Vesting Schedules

Today the vesting rules that apply to defined-contribution plans and the special top-heavy vesting provisions are the same. This means that the top-heavy vesting requirements only apply to top-heavy defined-benefit plans. A defined-benefit plan that is top-heavy must use a vesting schedule just as favorable as one of the two schedules in the tables below.

3-Year Cliff Vesting

Years of Service	Percentage Vested
0–2	0
3 or more	100

6-Year Graded Schedule

Years of Service	Percentage Vested
0–1	0
2	20
3	40
4	60
5	80
6	100

Minimum Benefits and Contributions for Nonkey Employees

A top-heavy plan must provide minimum benefits or contributions for nonkey employees. For defined-benefit plans, the benefit for each nonkey employee must be at least 2 percent of compensation multiplied by the number of the employee's years of service in which the plan is top-heavy up to a maximum of 10 years (maximum 20 percent benefit accrual). This 2 percent minimum annual accrual is typically larger than the typical plan benefit for nonkey employees, especially if a plan is integrated with Social Security benefits. This means that the top-heavy requirements can result in additional costs for the employer in a defined benefit plan.

For a defined-contribution plan, the minimum employer contribution is generally 3 percent of compensation for nonkey employees. If the plan provides less than a 3 percent contribution for any key employee, then the highest contribution percentage for any key employee is substituted. For example, if an employer with a profit-sharing plan made no contribution for any key employee, then no top-heavy contribution is required for nonkey employees. If the employer contributed 1 percent of compensation for a key employee, then the required minimum contribution for nonkey employees is 1 percent.

In a defined-contribution plan that allocates contributions as a level percentage of compensation, the top-heavy minimum contribution requirements have no effect on plan design or cost. However, if the contribution formula is integrated with Social Security or with any other design that results in larger contributions (as a percentage of compensation) for key employees, the top-heavy minimum will affect plan design. For example, in an integrated profit-sharing plan, the plan typically allocates the first 3 percent of compensation on a pro rata basis, to ensure that the top-heavy minimum is satisfied. Only after 3 percent is allocated does the formula address Social Security integration.

If a sponsor maintains more than one plan, regulations provide that the top-heavy minimum contribution can be made to one, but not both, of the plans. Employers adopting multiple plans need to address this issue in the plan design process, to make sure that both plans do not require minimum contributions.

Planning Considerations

Although larger plans (covering over 100 employees) are rarely top-heavy, top-heavy contingency language must be included in the plan's boilerplate language. Most plans of small businesses (covering 25 or fewer employees) become top-heavy within a few years of formation. For plans that are likely to be top-heavy, instead of providing the top-heavy language as a contingency, these plans are typically designed to satisfy the top-heavy provisions.

The top-heavy rules can cause special difficulty for the small 401(k) plan. The problem is that elective salary deferral contributions count toward determining top-heavy status, which means that even a plan that only contains salary deferral contributions can become top-heavy. Also, because salary deferral contributions are treated as employer contributions, if any key employee defers 3 percent of compensation, the sponsor has to make a top-heavy contribution of 3 percent for nonkey employees. It is important to communicate this possibility to employers so they are not surprised by this information at the end of the year. Remember, this would not happen in a traditional profit-sharing plan because a contribution of zero for the key employees means no required contribution for the nonkey employees.

The problem can even occur if the company makes matching contributions. Matching contributions do count toward satisfying the top-heavy minimum, but there could still be an additional required contribution for those nonkey employees who are not eligible for the matching contributions. A way to solve the top-heavy problem in a 401(k) plan is to make a safe harbor contribution (see chapter 5). If either the matching or nonelective safe harbor contribution is made to the plan, the plan is exempt from the top-heavy rules.

Sometimes, small employers that establish SEPs have very little administrative help. They may not be aware that the top-heavy rules apply to SEPs. Top-heavy status is a problem with a SEP mainly if the plan has a contribution formula integrated with Social Security. SIMPLE IRAs are not required to satisfy the top-heavy rules.

MINI-CASES

In each of the following, fact patterns design the benefit structure, eligibility, vesting, and benefit provisions of the plan in a way that satisfies the employer's objectives.

Case One—Facts

Fast Fun, Inc., is a growing company that manufactures go-carts. The company has decided to adopt a 401(k) plan as its only qualified plan. Fast Fun has 150 employees, and the turnover in the shop is significant. A large number of employees have relatively low wages, and making salary-deferral contributions will be somewhat of a hardship for them. Because this is the company's only plan, the sponsor is prepared to contribute a minimum of 3 percent of compensation each year and possibly, in a good year, a lot more.

Case Two—Facts

Professional Corp. is a group of three owner-physicians and six other support staff. The doctors have decided to establish a profit-sharing plan. They want a plan that has flexible contributions and skews contributions as much toward the doctors as possible. Review plan design options for these doctors.

Case Three—Facts

New Nonprofit, Inc., has been in existence for 4 years. The company has 12 employees and has decided to set up its first pension plan. Because New Nonprofit wants a plan that allows employees to make pretax contributions and creates a retirement savings partnership between the employee and employer, the company considered the 403(b) plan, the 401(k) plan, and the SIMPLE. It chose the SIMPLE because it had the lowest cost and administrative burden, and it met the company's benefit budget (3 percent of payroll). New Nonprofit wants its plan to satisfy its current employees and to keep the company competitive when hiring new employees.

CHAPTER REVIEW

Key Terms

qualified preretirement survivor
   annuity (QPSA) [10-1]
qualified joint and survivor annuity
   (QJSA) [10-1]

Table 2001 [10-2]
key employee [10-5]

Review Questions

Review questions are based on the learning objectives in this chapter. Thus, a [10-3] at the end of a question means that the question is based on learning objective 10-3. If there are multiple objectives, they are all listed.

1. Answer these typical questions about mandatory death benefits that would be asked by prospective plan sponsors. [10-1]
   a. We would prefer not to provide a preretirement death benefit in our defined-benefit plan because we have a life insurance program for employees outside of the plan. What death benefits are we obliged to provide in the plan?
   b. Does the provision of the QJSA have any cost for the sponsor?
   c. We are setting up a profit-sharing plan and want to simplify administration of the plan. What do you suggest with regard to benefit payment options?

2. The owner of Dance Corp. wants to purchase a large amount of universal life insurance with her own profit-sharing account. Is there any way to solve the incidental death benefit problem? [10-2]

3. An employee (aged 50) in a profit-sharing plan has chosen to invest a portion of his account balance to purchase life insurance. If the participant purchases $100,000 of whole life insurance, what is the cost of insurance that has to be included into income if the company's one-year term cost for this coverage is $490? [10-2]

4. What are the different considerations applicable to providing preretirement death benefits in the small-plan market as opposed to the medium- and large-plan market? [10-3]

5. Your client, a small professional corporation, is unsure whether to include death benefits in its employee benefits package. What are the reasons for and against providing death benefits through a qualified retirement plan? [10-3]

6. What types of plan provisions are appropriate for addressing the situation in which a participant becomes disabled? [10-4]

7. Describe the considerations necessary for choosing a definition of disability in a qualified plan. [10-4]

8. a. What is the purpose of the top-heavy rules?

    b. What size organizations do these rules affect the most? [10-5]

9. At the end of the prior year, the Trophy Shop money-purchase plan had the following participants:

Employee	Percentage of Stock Owned	Salary	Account Balance
Allen (president)	95%	$ 85,000	$100,000
McFadden (VP/treasurer)	3	170,000	60,000
McGill	2	50,000	40,000
Melone	0	45,000	12,000
Rosenbloom	0	35,000	8,000

    a. Identify the employees who would be considered key employees for top-heavy testing purposes.
    b. Is the Trophy Shop plan top-heavy? Explain. [10-5]

10. Which of the following vesting provisions would satisfy the top-heavy [10-5]
    a. The participant becomes fully vested after 4 years of service.
    b. The participant becomes fully vested after 2 years of service.
    c. The participant becomes 50 percent vested after 3 years and 100 percent vested after 6 years.

11. What is the minimum required top-heavy contribution if an employer has a top-heavy profit-sharing plan and no contributions are made for any key employees for the year? [10-5]

12. What is the minimum required top-heavy contribution if an employer has a top-heavy 401(k) plan that only contains employee salary deferrals and at least one key employee makes a 5 percent salary deferral to the plan? [10-5]

11

Plan Funding and Investing—Part I

Learning Objectives

An understanding of the material in this chapter should enable you to

11-1. Describe the funding requirements that apply to a qualified plan.

11-2. Identify the various funding instruments, and describe in detail how a trust operates.

11-3. Identify the affirmative duties of plan fiduciaries involved in the investment of plan assets.

11-4. Explain the individual account plan exception that limits fiduciary liability when participants make investment decisions.

11-5. Identify what the prohibited transaction rules are intended to accomplish and how they work.

Chapter Outline

This chapter and the next provide an overview of the issues surrounding plan funding and investing. In this chapter, three important issues are addressed. First is a review of the plan funding requirements. For defined-benefit plans, this topic is involved, while for other types of plans, the issue is straightforward. The next topic is a review of the various funding vehicles that are used in conjunction with tax-advantaged retirement plans. This discussion will familiarize you with what parties are responsible for plan investing. The third topic addresses the legal constraints surrounding the investment of plan assets. Here we will talk about who is legally responsible for making investment decisions, what investment limitations apply, and liability for failing to meet fiduciary standards.

The following chapter focuses entirely on plan investing. There we discuss choosing an appropriate investment policy; then, we look at various investment options. The materials first cover typical investment classes and their role in the investment mix, and then go into specialized insurance products that have been developed to meet specific needs.

PLAN FUNDING REQUIREMENTS

The financial services professional needs to be acquainted with the plan funding requirements, much as the home buyer needs to be familiar with the plumbing and heating systems of a potential purchase. In other words, a passing knowledge of some of the buzzwords and the general implications can help you avoid an unpleasant experience. And although a detailed understanding of the complex requirements and their underlying actuarial voodoo is unnecessary, you should understand enough to be able to school your client in the basics and to deal effectively with a consulting actuary.

Once a tax-advantaged retirement plan is in place, the employer must fund it in order to meet the benefit obligations promised under the plan. At one time, it was possible for the employer to wait until the employee retired and monthly retirement obligations became due before providing for the employee's benefit.

terminal funding approach

This pay-as-you-go system (also called a *terminal funding approach*) is no longer possible. Instead, retirement benefits must be prefunded according to the minimum funding standards that were set out in ERISA.

Under the minimum funding standards, employers are required to (1) set aside funds irrevocably (meaning the pension money is beyond the reach of the employer or the employer's creditors), (2) place the funds with a trustee, custodian, or insurance company, and (3) fund their retirement obligations in advance. Advance funding basically means the employer must pay the retirement liability according to specific rules.

Funding Defined-Benefit Plans

This section explores the legal requirements of defined-benefit plan funding by answering three questions: (1) What is the minimum amount of funding necessary for plan qualification? (2) What role does the plan's actuary play? (3) What is the maximum amount of funding permitted in a defined-benefit plan?

Minimum Funding Standards

Under defined-benefit plans, an organization's annual liability (normal cost) is determined by an actuarial valuation. The rules regarding actuarial valuations—which are complex to start with—become even more complicated if the plan provides benefits based on past service. The intent of the minimum funding standards is to protect against situations in which participants are left empty-handed because promised retirement benefits have not been delivered. To be fair, however, the rules do allow the sponsor the opportunity to spread the cost over a number of years. This means that a plan—especially a newer plan with past service liability—can satisfy the minimum funding rules but not have sufficient assets to pay promised benefits at any one time. This possibility is the reason for the Pension Benefit Guaranty Corporation (PBGC) insurance program.

There are several actuarial cost methods that can be used to determine the normal cost and, if applicable, the past-service liability. These methods are basically a pension subspecialty handled by actuaries and are beyond the scope of this text. However, we will discuss the implications that these tools of actuarial valuation, as controlled by the plan's actuary, have for your client.

The Role of the Plan Actuary

As you might imagine, the most important decision on which the plan actuary advises is what cost method to use for a defined-benefit plan (how to determine the annual employer contribution for a given set of plan benefits and a given group of employees). The right cost method should provide the plan sponsor with flexibility in funding and also meet the employer's tax objectives. It ideally allows large contributions (tax write-offs) in prosperous years and minimum liability in lean years or years when there is a cash-flow crunch.

As a rule of thumb, the actuary can generally recommend a cost method that will provide for relatively level costs from year to year (figure 11-1, chart 1, the projected-benefit cost method) or a method that will provide for lower liability at first but will increase until the plan reaches maturity (chart 2, the accrued-benefit cost method). If there is an attempt to fund for past service, these payments can be used either to round up the projected-benefit cost method (chart 3) or level off the accrued-benefit cost method (chart 4). If the funding for past service is treated as a separate liability, then

FIGURE 11-1
Comparison of Cost Methods[a]

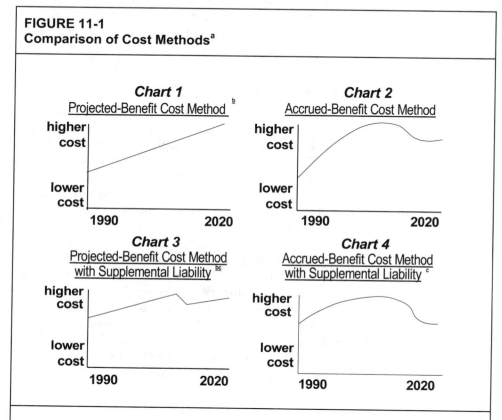

a   Each chart assumes an open group (one in which normal turnover occurs); if the groups are closed (just include a certain group of employees), each chart will have a sharper incline.

b   Level funding means level as a percentage of payroll; the payroll, however, will typically increase over a given period to accommodate inflation.

c   The drop-off for charts 3 and 4 occurs at the end of 30 years, when the past-service liability has been fully amortized. Actually, the plan sponsor can choose to amortize past service in as few as 10 years (for larger write-offs; this is generally chosen by small plans looking for tax shelter) or as many as 30 years.

the past service cost is referred to as a supplemental liability. If it enhances the existing cost method, the plan is said to be without supplemental liability. The graphs in figure 11-1 can be compared with the projected cash-flow needs of the employer and will illustrate to the employer what system is best.

Neither the plan actuary nor the choice of an actuarial cost method bears any relationship to the plan's ultimate cost. The ultimate cost cannot be known until the last benefit is paid and the plan is over. In other words, your client generally will never know his or her ultimate liability when adopting the plan. What the actuary does through the use of a cost method, however, is to set up a situation in which there is flexibility in funding the annual liability for which your client is responsible. For example, the actuary can help to maximize flexibility by setting up a past-service liability rather than amortizing past-service and future-service costs together.

In addition to choosing the cost method, the actuary is responsible for making certain assumptions with regard to several variables; the plan's annual costs vary depending on the assumptions used. These assumptions include the following:

- the number of employees who will be eligible to receive benefits (the higher the number of employees, the higher the annual cost)
- the final-average salary that all the employees will have, if benefits are based on final-average salary (the higher the assumption, the higher the annual cost)
- the mortality rate—the rate at which active employees and already-retired workers will die (the higher the mortality assumption, the lower the annual cost)
- the disability rate—primarily for nonretired participants (the higher the disability assumption, the higher the annual cost)
- the turnover rate, including the rate of new employee replacements (the higher the turnover assumption, the lower the annual cost)
- the retirement ages, if early retirement is an option and is subsidized (the higher the early-retirement assumption, the higher the annual cost)
- the length of the benefit period for retired employees (the longer the life expectancy, the higher the annual cost)
- the investment return—the investment income earned on the plan's accumulated assets (the higher the investment assumption, the lower the estimated annual cost)

funding standard account

No matter what cost methods or assumptions the actuary chooses, he or she must satisfy the *funding standard account,* an accounting tool (required by IRS regulations) that shows whether the plan is "adequately funded." Like an income statement, the funding standard account (which is used for accounting purposes only) is annually debited with plan costs and other amounts necessary to meet the minimum funding standard. It is also credited with the employer's contribution and such other things as decreases in plan liabilities and interest gains (interest gains occur when actual interest earnings exceed expected interest earnings). The cost methods the actuary works with are basically different approaches to funding this account, with different rules for defining the permissible limits of the actual account itself.

(*Planning Note:* If there is a deficiency in the funding standard account, there is a 10 percent excise tax on the amount of the accumulated funding deficiency. If the funding deficiency is not corrected within the permitted time, an excise tax of 100 percent applies to the accumulated funding deficiency.)

What should be obvious by now is that the actuary has a certain leeway in setting the plan's annual cost. Note, however, that this leeway is not unlimited, because the actuary is restricted to reasonable assumptions and IRS-approved funding methods. But the bottom line is that the actuary is able to meet the cash-flow and tax needs of your client, within limits.

The Fully Insured Life Insurance Option

In a defined-benefit plan, the required employer contributions vary over time due to changes in the performance of plan assets. Some employers would prefer fixed costs and can sleep better knowing their liabilities. There is relief for these employers if the plan is fully funded with life insurance policies or annuity contracts. Under a plan that is funded by individual insurance contracts, it is the insurance company's actuary who selects the assumptions and the actuarial cost method. The premium based on that actuary's assumptions is the actual contribution due. Additionally, *fully insured* plans (plans funded in their entirety by level-premium annuities or retirement-income contracts) are exempt from the minimum funding standards (and their corresponding administrative costs, such as actuarial fees) if (1) the insurance contract provides for level premiums from participation until retirement, (2) the benefits under the plan are equal to the benefits provided under the contract, (3) the benefits are guaranteed by a licensed insurance company, (4) premiums are paid on time, (5) there are no rights under the contract subject to a security interest, and (6) there are no policy loans. Because fully insured plans are described in Code Sec. 412(i), they are sometimes referred to as 412(i) plans.

fully insured

Maximum Deductible Contributions

The minimum funding standards helped to eliminate the problem of employers who underfunded their retirement plans and eventually disappointed employees who expected to receive a retirement benefit. However, for some employers, such as small, closely held corporations and professional corporations, the opposite problem exists. Small-business owners generally prefer to make excessive deductible contributions to a pension fund for purposes of accelerating tax deductions and increasing the tax-shelter potential of the qualified plan. To prevent such excessive contributions, there are rules that specify the maximum deductible amount that can be made annually.

Under the current rules, there is often no or little difference between the minimum required contribution and the maximum allowable deductible contribution. From the tax side this means more tax revenue, but it also does not allow employers to make larger contributions in years of economic prosperity. This issue has been addressed by the Pension Protection Act of 2006, discussed below.

Still, for the small-business owner looking to save a large sum over a short period of time, the defined-benefit plan is definitely worth considering. It is the only plan that allows contributions in excess of the Code Sec. 415(c) annual allocation limit (on behalf of each participant) and, for the older owner, a larger benefit can accrue over a relatively short period of time. The cost of covering other employees will depend upon the census. If the other employees are younger than the owners, the cost can be quite reasonable. If the other employees are older, the cost may be more prohibitive. However, using the general nondiscrimination test, the costs can be controlled somewhat. The example below demonstrates how a defined-benefit plan can generate large deductible contributions to fund benefits for the owners, while limiting the cost of the nonhighly compensated employees.

On the other hand, defined-benefit plans also have a significant amount of uncertainty that is difficult for the business owner to understand. Before the business owner establishes a defined-benefit plan, he or she needs to understand the following:

- The maximum lump sum that can be paid out to the owner is tied to an external interest rate that changes over time. If the rate goes up, the benefit that can be paid out goes down. This can be extremely disconcerting for the owner who expects to receive a larger benefit.
- On the opposite side, if the prescribed interest rate goes down, the amount that is paid out will increase. If there are other employees, this means the cost of providing those benefits increases.
- Investment losses are amortized over a relatively short period of time for an older owner, and there can be relatively drastic changes in the required contribution when the value of the plan's assets decreases (such as in a down market).

TABLE 11-1
Defined-Benefit Plan Example

Employee-(Age)	Compensation	Defined Benefit Cost	% of Comp.
HCE-(55)	$210,000	$131,880	62.80%
HCE-(50)	210,000	74,680	35.56%
HHCE-(40)	50,000	9,810	19.62%
NHCE-(33)	35,000	4,150	11.86%
NHCE-(35)	30,000	4,080	13.60%
NHCE-(34)	20,000	2,540	12.70%
NHCE-(31)	20,000	2,070	10.35%
NHCE-(29)	19,000	1,720	9.05%
	$594,000	**$230,930**	

Cost Benefit Analysis

			% of Total
HCE Total		$206,560	89.45%
NHCE Total		$24,370	10.55%
		$230,930	100.00%

Notes:
Normal retirement benefit: 7.62% per year of plan participation.
Maximum 13 years.
Normal retirement age: 65
Actuarial Assumptions: 6%, 1994 GAR-Unisex Mortality

Pension Protection Act of 2006

The Pension Protection Act (PPA) made sweeping changes to the funding requirements for defined-benefit plans. Most of the provisions, however, do not take effect until 2008, and practitioners are just beginning to understand some of the impact of the new law. The PPA completely revises the funding rules for single-employer plans. The new rules eliminate both the mechanism for calculating minimum funding and the deficit-reduction contribution rules. When the new rules are fully implemented (they are phased in over several years) plans will be required to meet a funding target of 100 percent of liability, and funding shortfalls will have to be made up over 7 years. In addition the new law

- increases the maximum deductible contribution limit to allow plan sponsors to contribute more than the minimum required

- prohibits sponsors of certain underfunded plans (referred to as *at-risk plans*) from increasing benefits, paying lump sums or other accelerated forms of benefit, or, in some situations, permitting additional benefit accruals
- limits the funding of executive-compensation programs when a defined benefit plan is severely underfunded
- changes the interest rates used for calculating lump-sum distributions (which in many cases will result in lower lump sums than under the current rules)
- creates new funding-reporting requirements

The PPA also includes a series of provisions designed to improve the financial condition of the Pension Benefit Guaranty Corporation's (PBGC) single-employer program. The process of protecting the PBGC actually started with the Deficit Reduction Act (DRA) of 2005 that increased the flat-rate premium to $30 per participant. The PPA adds an inflation factor to this number, and premiums rise to $31 in 2007. The variable-rate premium charged for underfunded plans does not change, but the change in interest-rate assumptions and the elimination of certain special exemptions could result in higher variable premiums for some underfunded plans.

Funding Requirements for Other Types of Plans

Minimum Required Contribution

Although the minimum funding requirements are most complex for the defined-benefit plan, it is important to note that the requirements do apply to other pension plans as well. This includes the two types of defined-contribution plans that are also pension plans—target-benefit and money-purchase pension plans. The minimum required contribution is the amount required under the plan's contribution formula each year. Failure to meet the required contribution subjects the plan to the 10 percent excise tax on funding deficiencies that applies to defined-benefit plans.

The minimum funding requirements do not apply to profit-sharing plans, stock bonus plans, ESOPs, SEPs, SIMPLEs, or 403(b) plans. Technically, this means that the 10 percent excise tax will not apply for failure to make contributions. However, if the plan document calls for a required annual contribution in one of these types of plans, the employer will have to make the contribution. Otherwise, the plan will face disqualification because the employer failed to follow the terms of the plan.

Maximum Deductible Contribution

When a plan has a specified contribution, this amount essentially constitutes the minimum and maximum allowable contributions. For discretionary profit-sharing plans, stock bonus plans, employee stock ownership plans, or SEPs, the maximum contribution is subject to the limitations discussed previously. That is, no individual can receive an annual allocation in excess of the Code Sec. 415(c) limit and the total employer contribution cannot exceed 25 percent of compensation of all participating employees.

To more fully understand the maximum contribution rules, let's examine a number of examples. The first illustrates the maximum contribution limits when the plan only covers the owner of the company. The example illustrates the interaction between the 25-percent-deduction rule and the Code Sec. 415(c) maximum allocation rule.

Example:	Sylvia is incorporated, she has no other employees, and for 2007 she has $100,000 of compensation. The maximum contribution on her behalf to her profit-sharing plan for 2007 is $25,000 (25 percent of $100,000). Now let's assume that her compensation is $200,000. The maximum contribution would then be $45,000, the Code Sec. 415(c) maximum allocation limit for 2007.

As you can see with a single participant, the maximum deductible contribution limit of 25 percent of compensation can be the prevailing limit. However, note that this deduction limit is an aggregate limit, and when there are a number of employees, the amount allocated to specific individuals can exceed 25 percent of compensation.

Example:	Sally works part-time and earns $20,000 a year. Because Sally and her husband together have adequate income, Sally would like to make a significant salary deferral contribution to her company's 401(k) plan. Assume that Sally makes a salary deferral contribution of $12,000 and the company matches 3 percent of compensation ($600). The total contribution on Sally's behalf is $12,600, substantially more than 25 percent of compensation. This is allowable as long as the plan allows a salary

deferral of this size and, in total, contributions for all employees do not exceed the 25 percent of compensation limit. In a 410(k) plan, it is hard to exceed the 25 percent limit because salary deferral contributions are not counted in the calculation.

For the sole proprietor, there is one way to exceed the 25 percent deduction limit. Salary deferral contributions to a 401(k) plan are not counted toward the 25 percent limit. This means that an owner, without employees, can establish a one-person 401(k) plan and can contribute both 25 percent as a profit-sharing contribution plus make salary deferral contributions.

Example:	Esther, who is incorporated, has compensation of $100,000. If she establishes a 401(k) plan, she can contribute $25,000 (25 percent of compensation) as a profit-sharing contribution as well as $15,500 under the salary deferral feature (for 2007).

If Esther, in this example, is age 50 or older, she can make an additional catch-up election of $5,000 in 2007. This additional contribution is allowed, even if the total allocation exceeds the Code Sec. 415(c) annual allocation limit, because catch-up elections are not counted as allocations under the 415(c) limit.

The one-person 401(k) plan is a method for making larger contributions for the individual with a modest level of compensation. For many individuals in this situation, the profit-sharing plan or SEP will work just as well, especially if they are not in the financial position to contribute more than 25 percent of compensation (20 percent if the entity is unincorporated).

FUNDING VEHICLES

funding instrument

A qualified plan must use a *funding instrument* that must be a trust, custodial account, or group insurance contract. This section discusses these various funding instruments and how they work, as well as the typical parties involved in the investment of plan assets. The rules are different for the other tax-advantaged retirement plans.

As discussed in chapter 6, SEPs and SIMPLEs must use individual retirement accounts and annuities, while 403(b) plans must use annuity contracts or mutual fund custodial accounts.

Trusts

Trusts are the most popular funding vehicles for qualified plans. The trust approach allows for tremendous flexibility in both investments and benefit design.

A trust used for a qualified plan is based on the same principles of trust law as trusts used for other purposes. This means the grantor of the trust is the plan's sponsor; the grantor transfers the *res* (the plan assets) to trustees of the trust; and the trust makes payments as specified to the beneficiaries of the trust (the plan participants and their beneficiaries).

Like all trusts, a trust used for a qualified plan contains a trust agreement, which is set up primarily to control the receipt, investment, and disbursement of funds. A typical trust agreement spells out the following particulars:

- the irrevocability of trust assets
- the trustee's investment powers (the investment discretion of a trustee varies from plan to plan; in some cases, the employer wants to maintain full control; in others, the trustee or investment manager has almost unchecked discretion)
- the allocation of fiduciary responsibility to a named fiduciary (who is responsible for the plan and becomes the target of legal action when required)
- the payments of benefits and plan expenses
- the rights and duties in case of plan termination

If the plan is large enough, the trustees may also keep records of employer and employee contributions, each participant's salary and service, and account and benefit information. In smaller plans, this function is handled outside the trust agreement by the employer, third-party plan administrator, or consulting company.

An essential part of the trusteed plan is the plan trustees, who may be corporate (banks and trust companies) and/or individuals related to the business.

Functions of Plan Trustees

- Accept and invest employer contributions
- Pay benefits to plan participants
- Provide periodic accounting to the employer of investments, receipts, disbursements, and other transactions that involve plan assets
- Maintain administrative records, if appropriate

It is important to remember that, when carrying out these duties, trustees have a fiduciary relationship to plan participants. As discussed further in the next section, the fiduciaries must act in the best interest of the plan participants. Thus, a business owner who is also a plan trustee cannot act in his or her own self-interest. Also, the trustee must act prudently, as compared to other plan trustees, meaning that a business executive should think carefully before choosing to become a plan trustee.

In large plans, sometimes the trustee acts primarily as custodian of plan assets, while the fund is invested by several investment managers. Investment managers will also be plan fiduciaries, subject to essentially the same standard of care in handling plan investments. Similarly, in smaller plans, the executives will act as trustees, while one or more corporate investment managers is responsible for investing. Regardless of the arrangement, in all cases, those responsible for investing plan assets are responsible to act in accordance with the plan documents and in accordance with the funding and investment policies (discussed further in the next chapter), which are established by the employer or a committee made up of executives of the employer.

In lieu of a trust agreement, the funding vehicle can also be a custodial account with a bank (or other person as authorized by IRS regulations under Code Sec. 401(f)) as custodian. With the custodial-account approach, the custodian is the record keeper, with others actually investing plan assets.

Common Trust Funds

common trust fund

Generally, the assets of one trust cannot be commingled or pooled with the assets of other trusts; a separate accounting and segregation of trust assets is usually required. However, an exception to this rule applies to common trust funds. *Common trust funds,* which are sponsored and operated by banks and trust companies, permit the pooling of funds from all participating trusts (typically many small-plan sponsors). The trust buys units of a common fund, which either increase or decrease in value depending on investment return. The common trust fund was developed because relatively small trust fund plans could not adequately diversify their investment portfolios on their own. In addition to eliminating the diversification problem, common trust funds also provide the potential for higher return (because of their size, they can attract expert investment advice), lower brokerage fees, and liquidity of funds to meet cash requirements.

Split-Funded Plans

split-funded plan

A *split-funded plan* refers to a plan that uses a trust fund arrangement, but chooses to invest a portion of plan assets in insurance and annuity contracts. Insurance products can include individual insurance and annuity contracts or any of the group funding products discussed in the next chapter. This approach can be used to take advantage of the flexibility of the trust approach while also taking advantage of the guarantees of insurance products, the ability to provide significant death benefits through the plan, or simply the yields available in a group product.

Annuity Plans

A pension plan under which retirement benefits are provided completely by annuity or insurance contracts does not have to maintain a trust fund. This applies to both individual and group products. However, to avoid the trust requirement, the terms of the plan must be incorporated in the policy. This is not practical with individual policies and, therefore, individual policies are generally issued under a trust fund agreement, with the trustee as owner of the policies. With a group policy, it is more common for the master contract to be the sole investment vehicle.

As we saw in the discussion of trusteed plans, split-funded plans, and annuity plans, the pension plan can be funded with any combination of trust fund and insurance product investments. What will distinguish the insurance product is not the type of documentation, but the strength of the investment contracts. This subject is discussed more fully in the following chapter.

LEGISLATIVE ENVIRONMENT FOR PLAN INVESTING

The legislative scheme for making sure plan assets are invested appropriately focuses on controlling the behavior of those individuals (and business entities) most responsible for the investment of plan assets. These individuals, referred to as fiduciaries, are required to make investment decisions in accordance with certain standards and to avoid certain prohibited transactions. Below is an overview of who is considered a fiduciary, affirmative obligations, prohibited transactions, and penalties these parties may face for failing to meet appropriate standards of care.

Before beginning this discussion, it is important to note that the rules discussed in this section apply to plans that are covered by title I of ERISA. This generally includes qualified plans, SEPs and SIMPLEs, and, in some cases, 403(b) plans. As discussed in chapter 6, certain 403(b) programs that allow only for employee salary deferrals (and no other employer contributions) are not be subject to the ERISA rules discussed below.

In addition to the ERISA limitations, there are several other special investment limitations. First, plans funded with IRAs (SEPs and SIMPLEs) cannot invest in life insurance or collectibles (see chapter 6). Second, 403(b) plans have even more investment limitations, as assets can be invested only in annuity contracts, mutual funds, and life insurance. On the other hand, there are no specific prohibited investment classes for qualified plans.

Individuals Considered Fiduciaries under ERISA

fiduciaries

Individuals who are considered *fiduciaries* for their role in the investment of plan assets include persons who have discretionary authority over the disposition of plan assets and individuals who render investment advice for a fee (or other direct or indirect compensation). Practically speaking, this includes the sponsoring company, plan trustees, investment managers (including insurance companies), and officers of the company who participate in the selection of trustees and/or investment managers.

Service providers, such as accountants, lawyers, and administrative firms, are generally not considered fiduciaries unless they have control over plan assets. Even individuals who sell investments to the plan are generally not considered fiduciaries. According to Department of Labor (DOL) regulations, rendering investment advice for a fee means

- the exercise of discretionary control over the purchase or sale of securities or
- the provision of investment advice regularly on the purchase and sale of assets, with such advice being the primary basis for the investment of plan assets

This definition is rather limited and excludes most individuals who sell insurance or other investment products. However, determining whether someone is a fiduciary is based on the facts and circumstances (regardless of whether the individual is specifically identified as a fiduciary), and even commissioned insurance agents have been determined to have been fiduciaries when the agent's advice has been determined to be the primary basis for the investment of plan assets.

Affirmative Fiduciary Obligations

Fiduciaries involved in the investment of plan assets are required to make decisions within the framework of four rules:

- the exclusive-benefit rule
- the prudent-fiduciary rule
- the diversification requirement
- the requirement that investment decisions conform with plan and trust documents

Each of these rules is described in more detail below.

Exclusive-Benefit Rule

exclusive-benefit rule

Fiduciaries are required to discharge their duties solely in the interest of the plan's participants and beneficiaries for the exclusive purpose of providing benefits and defraying reasonable expenses. This *exclusive-benefit rule* means the fiduciary must act first and foremost in the plan participant's interest. However, if the investment is good for the employees, it is not necessarily illegal to have a collateral benefit for the employer. Nevertheless, investment decisions that involve any consideration other than the financial interest of plan participants can be quite tricky. The DOL, in Bulletin 94-1, has indicated that a fiduciary can consider benefits to the employees (such as job security) as long as the investment return is commensurate with alternative investments with similar risks. This opinion is considered somewhat controversial and could be changed in later opinions or by legislation. If a fiduciary sees the possibility of a conflict of loyalty between the plan participants and another party (employer), according to the DOL,[1] he or she should seek the advice of a competent, independent advisor, and possibly elect not to participate in the decision.

Prudence

prudent-fiduciary rule

According to the *prudent-fiduciary rule*, fiduciaries must act with the care, skill, prudence, and diligence (under prevailing circumstances) that a prudent person acting in a like capacity and familiar with such matters would use in the conduct of an enterprise of a like character and with like aims. Note that this standard compares, for example, plan trustees with other experienced plan trustees. With regard to the choice of prudent investments, DOL regulations[2] refer to six factors that should be considered:

1. the role of the investment as part of the plan's overall portfolio
2. whether the investment is reasonably designed as part of the portfolio
3. the risk of loss and opportunity for gain
4. the diversification of the portfolio
5. the liquidity and current return relative to the anticipated cash flow requirements of the plan
6. the projected return of the portfolio relative to the funding objectives of the plan

ETHICS
MUTUAL FUND SCANDAL OF 2004

In 2003 and 2004 the mutual fund industry underwent scrutiny for late trading and market-timing abuses. Here are excerpts from a statement by Assistant Secretary of the Employee Benefits Security Administration Ann L. Combs from February 17, 2004 discussing the duties of retirement plans fiduciaries with regard to the scandal.

"As significant investors in mutual funds, plan fiduciaries, understandably, are concerned about the impact of reported late trading and market-timing abuses on their pension plans and the steps that should be taken to protect the interests of their plans' participants and beneficiaries. Although investors generally could not anticipate the late trading and market-timing problems identified by Federal and state regulators, plan fiduciaries nonetheless are now faced with the difficult task of assessing the impact of these problems on their plans' investments and on investment options made available to the plans' participants and beneficiaries.

As fiduciaries conduct their review, it is important to remember that ERISA requires that fiduciaries discharge their duties prudently. The exercise of prudence in this context requires a deliberative process. In this regard, fiduciaries, deciding whether to make any changes in mutual fund investments or investment options, must make decisions that are as well informed as possible under the circumstances.

In cases where specific funds have been identified as under investigation by government agencies, fiduciaries should consider the nature of the alleged abuses, the potential economic impact of those abuses on the plan's investments, the steps taken by the fund to limit the potential for such abuses in the future, and any remedial action taken or contemplated to make investors whole. To the extent that such information has not been provided or is not otherwise available, a plan fiduciary should consider contacting the fund directly in an effort to obtain specific information. Fiduciaries of plans invested in such funds may ultimately have to decide whether to participate in settlements or lawsuits. In doing so, they will need to weigh the costs to the plan against the likelihood and amount of potential recoveries.

The appropriate course of action will depend on the particular facts and circumstances relating to a plan's investment in a fund. Plan fiduciaries should follow prudent plan procedures relating to investment decisions and document their decisions. The guiding principle for fiduciaries should be to ensure that appropriate efforts are being made to act reasonably, prudently, and solely in the interests of participants and beneficiaries."

One court[3] indicated that proper fiduciary procedures included

- employing proper methods to investigate, evaluate, and structure the investment, including the retention of a professional advisor if the fiduciary lacks sufficient expertise
- acting in a manner consistent with others who have a similar capacity and familiarity with such matters
- exercising independent judgment when making investment decisions

Being prudent does not mean fiduciaries have to avoid risky investments. DOL Interpretive Bulletin 95-1 clarifies that an investment that has substantial risk is not in itself a problem, as long as the expected return is commensurate with the risk, and the risk is weighed against the anticipated return in the context of the plan's investment portfolio and of its funding, liquidity, and diversification needs.

Diversification of Investments

diversification requirement

The *diversification requirement* means that trustees have the duty to diversify the plan's investments to minimize the risk of large losses, unless it is clearly prudent not to do so under the plan. According to the legislative history of ERISA,[4] "clearly prudent" language was intended to mean that if a fiduciary were sued for failing to diversify investments, once the plaintiff demonstrated that assets were not diversified, the defendant fiduciary would have the burden of proof to demonstrate why his or her actions were appropriate. Apparently, the diversification referred to here means both diversification among asset classes and diversification within a single asset class.

Conformance with Documents

Finally, fiduciaries are required to operate the plan in accordance with the document and instruments that govern the plan. Trust instruments spell out the types of investments that are allowed, whether any types of investments are prohibited, and who is responsible for making the decisions. Problems in this area do arise when trustees and others make investment decisions without carefully consulting relevant documents. If the plan has a funding policy, an investment policy, or both (discussed further below), these documents must be carefully followed as well.

**YOUR FINANCIAL SERVICES PRACTICE:
EDUCATING FIDUCIARIES**

At the DOL Employee Benefits Security Administration website (www.dol.gov/ebsa) there are a number of interesting items about fiduciaries of small retirement plans. In 2002 a DOL working group on fiduciary education and training discussed the lack of sophistication among small-plan fiduciaries and the serious need for education of nonprofessional fiduciaries. In the small-plan market the primary educator is the financial services professional. This is a valuable and important role. Fulfilling it well can mean satisfied clients and a competitive edge in the market. The DOL website does contain some documents that your clients may want to read—most notably the booklet entitled, "Meeting Your Responsibilities."

Limitations: The Individual Account Plan Exception

Because qualified plans of the defined-contribution type allocate dollars to the separate accounts of participants, the sponsoring employer has the option either to direct the trustees to invest plan assets or to give participants some choice over the investment of individual accounts. Because SEPs and SIMPLEs are funded with individual IRAs, participants almost always have investment options. Similarly, 403(b) plans almost always give participants investment choices.

ERISA Sec. 404(c) (individual account plan exception)

If a defined-contribution plan, SEP, SIMPLE, or 403(b) plan gives individual participants options with regard to the investment of their own plan benefits, it makes sense that the fiduciaries should not be responsible for the participant's investment decisions. *ERISA Sec. 404(c) (individual account plan exception)* grants such fiduciary relief by providing that in the case of a participant exercising independent investment direction over his or her own account, no fiduciary will be liable for losses that arise from such participant direction.

General Requirements

In order to qualify for this relief, the plan must conform to strict DOL requirements. The DOL's general rule is that the plan must provide an opportunity for a participant or beneficiary to exercise control over the assets in his or her account and offer the individual an opportunity to choose from a broad range of investment alternatives.

More specifically, the rules require the following:

- *Number of investment options*—Participants must have the opportunity to choose from at least three investment alternatives, each with materially different risk and return characteristics. Also, in the aggregate, the options must offer a balanced mix appropriate for a participant and, when combined with the other investments, have the effect of minimizing risks.
- *Employer stock*—Securities of the plan sponsor can also be an investment option; however, this cannot be one of the three core options.
- *Diversification*—To meet diversification requirements, the investment options generally must be look-through investments, such as mutual funds, pooled separate accounts, or guaranteed-investment contracts.
- *Election frequency*—The opportunity to change investment elections with respect to each investment alternative must be appropriate in light of market volatility. At a minimum, the three core investment alternatives must offer the opportunity to change investment choice at least quarterly.
- *Exercise of control*—The participant must be given a reasonable opportunity to forward investment instructions to the fiduciary either in writing or otherwise (as long as the participant can request a written confirmation).
- *Adequate information*—The participant must also be provided with specific information regarding the investment options. The central item is a description of the investment alternatives and a general description of the risk and return characteristics of each alternative. Participants must also be informed about procedures for making elections, any expenses involved, and to whom to go for additional information. Also note that participants must be notified that the plan is seeking to qualify for the fiduciary limitations under ERISA Sec. 404(c).
- *Information upon request*—Upon request, the participant has the right to receive additional information about each investment alternative, including copies of the prospectus, description of operating expenses (as a percentage of net assets), and other detailed financial information about each option.

Participants Failing to Exercise Control

A fiduciary generally is not eligible for ERISA 404(c) relief unless the participant actually exercises control over the investment of his or her account. In some cases, especially with plans that provide for automatic enrollment, some participants fail to provide investment instructions. To encourage plans to provide for automatic enrollment, the Pension Protection Act of 2006 created an exception to protect fiduciaries in such cases. Under the exception, a participant failing to provide investment direction will be deemed to have exercised control over assets in his or her account (allowing the fiduciaries protection under 404(c)) if the plan invests in a qualified default investment alternative. In addition, participants must be notified about

- the circumstances under which assets will be invested in a qualified default investment alternative
- the investment objectives of the default investment alternative
- the right to direct investments out of the default investment alternative

Proposed regulations issued subsequent to the PPA have offered a complex description of a qualified default investment alternative; The regulations attempt to provide specific guidance while giving the fiduciaries a range of possible investment alternatives. The regulations generally prohibit employer securities as a choice, but allow employer stock in, for example, a mutual fund, if it meets the investment objectives of the fund. The default investment must be diversified and managed by either a professional investment manager or an investment company registered under the Investment Company Act of 1940.

Limitations on Relief

Note that a plan offering individual investment options is not required to satisfy the requirements of ERISA 404(c). If the rules are not satisfied, then the fiduciary could still be liable if the participant makes an imprudent investment choice. Meeting the requirements is the best way to protect the plan fiduciaries. However, if a plan sponsor decides that meeting the requirements in the DOL regulations is impractical, yet still wants to give participants investment choices, the next best line of protection is adequate fiduciary insurance and employer indemnification. Also, in this case, employee investment education and communication can also serve to minimize risk.

If all the rules are satisfied, then ERISA Sec. 404(c) indicates that the fiduciary will not be liable for a breach of duty because of the participants' exercise of control over investment decisions. In other words, the fiduciary is not responsible for the results of the participant's asset allocation decision.

Example:　　　Emily, aged 60, decides to invest all of her 401(k) account in an aggressive growth stock mutual fund, shunning the four other, less risky alternatives. In the following year, the value of her account drops by 20 percent. Under Sec. 404(c), the fiduciary should not be liable for Emily's loss because it was her decision.

Still, Sec. 404(c) does not get the fiduciary completely off the hook. Fiduciaries are obligated to ensure that participant investment choices do not constitute *prohibited* transactions. Further, investment choices must conform to other fiduciary obligations, such as compliance with plan documents. Most important, fiduciaries are never granted relief from the obligation to prudently select the available options. In the example above, if the aggressive growth fund available to Emily has had inferior performance—as compared to similar aggressive growth funds—then the fiduciary may have a liability problem.

prohibited transactions

Prohibited Transactions

parties in interest

A large number of transactions are prohibited because they are deemed by their nature to be contrary to the interest of plan participants. Their common denominator is that they include transactions involving the plan and those parties close to the plan or employer (referred to as *parties in interest*). More specifically, these individuals are defined as any individuals in the following eight categories:

1. all plan fiduciaries, as well as plan counsel to, and employees of, the plan
2. plan service providers
3. sponsoring employers
4. employee organizations (for example, unions) whose members are covered
5. 50-percent owners of an employer or an employee organization described in paragraphs (3) or (4)
6. relatives of individuals described in paragraphs (1), (2), (3), or (5)
7. organizations (including corporations, partnerships, and trusts) that are owned by persons described in paragraphs (1), (2), (3), (4), or (5)
8. employees, officers, directors, and 10-percent owners of the sponsoring employer or others described in paragraph (2), (3), (4), (5), and (7)

There are several different categories of prohibited transactions. The first category prohibits a fiduciary from causing the plan to engage in a transaction if the fiduciary knows or should know that such transaction constitutes a direct or indirect

- sale, exchange, or leasing of any property between the plan and a party in interest;
- lending of money or other extension of credit between the plan and a party in interest;
- furnishing of goods, services, or facilities between the plan and a party in interest;
- transfer to, or use by or for the benefit of, a party in interest of any plan assets; or
- acquisition, on behalf of the plan, of any employer security or employer real property in violation of ERISA Sec. 407(a).

Another category of prohibited transactions involves the investment in the sponsoring employer's stock or real property. First, a plan can only hold *qualifying employer securities,* (defined as stock or marketable obligations), and *qualifying employer real property* (property leased from the plan to the employer). Second, a plan may not acquire any qualifying employer security or qualifying employer real property if, immediately after such acquisition, the aggregate fair market value of employer securities and employer real property held by the plan exceeds 10 percent of the fair market value of the plan's assets. However, the 10 percent limitation does not apply to profit-sharing-type plans (including profit-sharing, stock bonus, 401(k), and employee stock ownership plans) as long as the plan provides that more than 10 percent of its assets can be invested in qualifying employer real property or qualifying employer securities.

A third category of prohibited transactions involves self-dealing. Here, the fiduciary is required to avoid using plan assets for his or her own interest or account. This prohibition includes receiving compensation from any party in connection with a transaction that involves the plan's assets.

Prohibited-Transaction Exemptions

prohibited-transaction exemptions

As you can see, the prohibited-transaction rules are extremely broad. Without *prohibited-transaction exemptions,* even common, everyday events—such as service providers receiving payment from the plan—would be prohibited. Because of the breadth of the prohibited-transaction rules, many exemptions are provided. Exemptions come in several different forms: statutory, administrative, and individual.

Statutory Exemptions

The most commonly used statutory exemptions under ERISA include

- payment of reasonable compensation to parties in interest for services rendered necessary for the plan's operation
- loans to parties in interest who are participants or beneficiaries of the plan if certain conditions are met. (This exception was described in chapter 9.)
- loans to employee stock ownership plans if specific conditions are met
- relief for plans for bank employees and insurance companies that want to invest in the sponsor's investment vehicles, as provided by several statutory exemptions
- certain pooled fund transactions involving banks, trust companies, and insurance companies
- distribution of assets in accordance with the terms of the plan

In addition to these exemptions, ERISA Sec. 408(c) clarifies that the prohibited-transaction rules do not prohibit any fiduciary from receiving benefits as a participant from a plan, receiving reasonable compensation for services rendered to the plan (full-time employees of the plan sponsor may not be paid), receiving reimbursement for expenses incurred, or serving as fiduciary in addition to being an officer, employee, agent, or other representative of a party in interest.

Also, a plan may acquire or sell qualifying securities from any party without violating the prohibited-transaction rules, as long as adequate security is paid, no commission is charged for the transaction, and the plan does not violate the 10 percent limitation.

Eligible Investment Advice

To ensure that participants in 401(k) plans and other plans that have individual investment direction get adequate investment advice, Congress recently enacted a prohibited-transaction exemption allowing for the provision of investment advice through an "eligible investment advice arrangement." If the requirements under the provision are met, then the provision of investment advice, any transactions pursuant to the advice, and the receipt of compensation by the advisor are exempt from prohibited-transaction treatment.

An eligible investment-advice arrangement has to provide that fees will not vary depending on the investment option selected, or that a computer model under an investment-advice program will be used. With defined-contribution plans the arrangement must be expressly authorized by a plan fiduciary. Also, the exemption does not preclude the use of plan assets to pay for investment advice.

If a computer model is used as the basis of any investment advice, it must apply generally accepted investment theories and use relevant information about the participant or beneficiary. An eligible investment expert must certify that the model meets these requirements. In addition, if a computer model is used, the only investment advice that may be provided under the arrangement is the advice generated by the computer model.

Defined-contribution plans must be audited annually by an independent auditor. The auditor must issue a report of the audit results to the fiduciary that authorized the arrangement. Also, before the program begins the fiduciary adviser must provide participants with written notice containing information about the terms of the arrangement, past investment performance, and any fees that will be charged. Participants also have to be notified of the adviser's status as a fiduciary of the plan.

The *fiduciary adviser* is defined as a provider of investment advice to a plan participant or beneficiary. To qualify, the fiduciary has to be registered as an investment adviser, registered as a broker or dealer, or an employee of a bank trust department or insurance company. Fiduciaries avoid ERISA violation by complying with the terms of the investment agreement. ERISA assigns to employers responsibility for the prudent selection and periodic review of a fiduciary adviser.

Administrative Exemptions

ERISA Sec. 408(a) allows the Secretary of Labor to grant certain administrative exemptions from the prohibited-transaction rules. These exemptions can be individual in nature, or they may be *class exemptions,* which can be relied on by the general public. Class exemptions have almost the same effect as statutory exemptions. The DOL has granted a large number of class exemptions that can be relied upon by the employer.

Individual Exemptions

If neither a statutory nor a class exemption applies, then an employer can request an individual exemption from the DOL. To grant such an individual exemption, the DOL must find that the transaction is

- administratively feasible
- in the interest of the plan and its participants and beneficiaries
- protective of the rights of the plan's participants and beneficiaries

Common Problems

Examples of common types of transactions that would be forbidden by the prohibited-transaction rules include

- loans to the company, company owners, and relatives
- contributions other than cash, in most cases
- purchasing plan assets from the company or other party in interest
- property owned by the plan that is used by the business owner (such as art or other collectibles)
- property that is owned by the plan (such as real estate) that is used by the company or other prohibited party

Especially in the small-plan market, the prohibited-transaction rules pose real problems. It may not be evident to the small-business owner what is wrong with the transactions described above. There are two principal reasons for this. First, the small-business owner with an entrepreneurial spirit may incorrectly look at the money in the plan as capital that should be used to build the business. As the owner often sees it, what is good for the business is good for the plan participants. Second, when a significant portion of the plan assets are for the benefit of the business owner, he or she may have a hard time distinguishing plan assets from personal assets.

Fiduciary Liability

Being a plan fiduciary is a serious matter. Remember that fiduciaries are required both to satisfy the affirmative duties and to ensure that no prohibited transactions occur. Plan fiduciaries under ERISA are personally liable to the plan to make good any losses that result from the fiduciary's breach of duty. In addition, a fiduciary is required to restore to the plan any profits realized by the fiduciary through the use of plan assets. A court can subject the fiduciary to other equitable or remedial relief as the court deems appropriate. In some egregious cases, the fiduciary can even be criminally liable.

As well as being personally liable for his or her own breaches, a fiduciary is generally liable for the acts of cofiduciaries. A fiduciary will be liable for the breach of a cofiduciary if

- the fiduciary participates knowingly in, or knowingly undertakes to conceal, an act or omission of such other fiduciary, knowing such act or omission is a breach
- by the fiduciary's failure to comply with ERISA, he or she enables the other fiduciary to commit a breach

- the fiduciary has knowledge of a breach by the cofiduciary, unless the fiduciary makes reasonable efforts under the circumstances to remedy the breach

Essentially, this means that if one fiduciary knows of a breach of duty by another fiduciary, he or she must take steps to correct that situation. In many cases, this can mean suing the other fiduciary.

Segregation of Plan Assets

When a tax-advantaged retirement plan such as a 401(k) plan, SIMPLE, or 403(b) plan contains employee salary deferrals, the DOL has prescribed how quickly those salary deferrals must be contributed to the plan. Under the DOL regulations, salary deferrals have to be segregated from the employer's general assets (contributed to the plan) as soon as is administratively feasible but never later than the 15th day of the month following the month of the salary deferral. For example, deferral elections for all pay periods ending in June must be contributed by July 15. This is true regardless of whether employees are paid weekly, biweekly, or monthly.

CHAPTER REVIEW

Key Terms

terminal funding approach [11-1]
funding standard account [11-1]
fully insured [11-1]
funding instrument [11-2]
common trust fund [11-2]
split-funded plan [11-2]
fiduciaries [11-3]
exclusive-benefit rule [11-3]

prudent-fiduciary rule [11-3]
diversification requirement [11-3]
ERISA Sec. 404(c) (individual
 account plan exception) [11-4]
prohibited transactions [11-5]
parties in interest [11-5]
prohibited-transaction
 exemptions [11-5]

Review Questions

Review questions are based on the learning objectives in this chapter. Thus, an [11-3] at the end of a question means that the question is based on learning objective 11-3. If there are multiple objectives, they are all listed.

1. Briefly describe the objective of the current minimum funding requirements that apply to qualified plans. [11-1]

2. Discuss the role that the plan actuary plays with regard to recommending cost methods and making actuarial assumptions. [11-1]

3. Describe a trusteed plan. [11-2]

4. Describe the other funding vehicles available to the qualified plan. [11-2]

5. a. What parties are generally considered fiduciaries for their involvement in investing plan assets? [11-3]
   b. What parties close to this process are not fiduciaries?

6. Name the four affirmative duties that fiduciaries are required to satisfy. [11-3]

7. What are the primary requirements for fiduciaries to be eligible for ERISA 404(c) relief? [11-4]

8. If ERISA 404(c) relief is given, what decisions are still the responsibility of the fiduciaries? [11-4]

9. Explain whether each of the following is a prohibited transaction: [11-5]
   a. the sale of real estate owned by the ABC plan to the wife of the treasurer of the ABC Company
   b. loaning money from the plan to an officer of the corporation (the plan contains a loan provision that permits loans on a nondiscriminatory basis)
   c. the acquisition of 25 percent of employer stock by a defined-benefit plan
   d. the acquisition of real estate from the plan for less than its market value by the plan's trustee for her personal use

10. Your client is a business owner who acts as the trustee of her company's pension plan. The plan owns real estate that the expanding company would like to buy at market value. What, if anything, can your client do to avoid the consequences of the prohibited-transaction rules? [11-5]

NOTES

1. DOL Adv. Op. Lty. No. 84-09A and DOL reg. 2550.408b-2(e).
2. Reg. 29 CFR 2550.404a-1(b).
3. *Lanka v. O'Higgins*, 810 F. Supp 379 (N.D.N.Y. 1992).
4. Conference Committee Report to ERISA, H.R. Rep. No. 93-1280.

12

Plan Funding
and Investing—Part II

Learning Objectives

An understanding of the material in this chapter should enable you to

12-1. Discuss the importance of investment guidelines.

12-2. Describe investment characteristics that are relevant in pension investing.

12-3. Describe the various group pension contracts and identify the circumstances under which a plan sponsor should use a separate-investment-accounts contract, a guaranteed-investment contract, and an investment-guarantee contract.

12-4. Explain how life insurance and annuities are commonly used as plan investments.

Chapter Outline

ESTABLISHING INVESTMENT GUIDELINES

Why Establish Investment Guidelines?

Now that you are familiar with ERISA's fiduciary requirements, you can see that the rules are relatively complex and that fiduciaries have a strong incentive to meet their obligations. The first, and probably most important, tool for ensuring compliance is clearly written plan investment guidelines. Essentially, *investment guidelines* are written instructions that provide structure for those involved in investing plan assets. These are crucial for the following reasons:

investment guidelines

- *to satisfy fiduciary obligations*—Investment guidelines help to establish procedures. They clarify who is responsible for what, when various tasks need to be completed, and how performance will be evaluated. They encourage a disciplined approach to fiduciary management and help to establish a paper trail.
- *to be the first line of defense*—If the Department of Labor (DOL) or plan participants question the investment performance, courts will look for a rationale for the investments chosen. The investment guidelines should be the fiduciary's most powerful shield.
- *to avoid investing in a vacuum*—An investment decision simply cannot be made or properly evaluated in a vacuum. A Treasury bill is a great investment when the main concern is protecting principal, but a terrible investment for long-term capital growth. Appropriate investment decisions must follow clear objectives.

For all of these reasons, it is extremely important to establish clear investment guidelines that tie the investment policy into the plan's objectives, clarify who is responsible for the various decisions surrounding the investment of plan assets, specify investment guidelines and goals, and establish procedures for reviewing both the investment performance and the plan's investment guidelines.

Who Establishes Investment Guidelines?

ERISA requires every plan to have a named fiduciary and a plan administrator that are responsible for the operation of the plan. Many companies appoint a benefits committee to fulfill both roles. In a very small company the committee may consist of simply the owner or owners. In larger organizations it may include the chief financial officer, the human resources director, and others. A crucial part of the benefits committee's work is making decisions about plan assets. In large companies the benefits committee will sometimes delegate this responsibility to a separate investment committee.

Regardless of who is making the investment decisions, it is important to understand that ERISA holds all fiduciaries, regardless to the size of the firm or the individual's background, to a professional standard. So the decision makers need to act professionally in all situations. This means meeting regularly, deliberating, and write down conclusions. The responsibilities include:

- writing an investment policy statement
- selecting, evaluating, and removing any investment managers
- monitoring the activities of all service providers to the plan
- reviewing investment management fees paid by the plan
- ensuring that proper financial reporting occurs

Funding Policy and Plan Objectives

funding policy

Every plan is required to establish a *funding policy*—procedures for establishing and carrying out a funding program consistent with the plan's objectives and ERISA requirements. .A funding policy addresses the level and timing of contributions necessary to fund benefit obligations throughout the life of a retirement plan.

In a defined-benefit plan, the policy should address the minimum funding requirements, provide a process for reviewing the policy periodically, and most important, require documentation of actions taken and reasons for those actions.

The funding policy and the investment guidelines are driven by the plan's objectives. In a defined-benefit plan, the primary objective is to provide sufficient funds to pay both current and future benefit obligations. In addition, there is the goal of minimizing long-term total required contributions. And, in most cases, there will be concern about the variability in annual contributions. The second and third objectives are generally at odds with one another, because minimizing costs over the long haul requires taking some risks. With risk usually comes volatility in the investment return, and, thus, a degree of variability in the required contributions. How important this is to a particular plan depends, in part, on how well-funded the plan is—the more well-funded plan has a higher tolerance for volatility. Also, the tolerance for volatility depends upon whether the sponsoring entity is cyclical in nature.

In a defined-contribution plan, the funding policy is simpler. If the plan calls for a specified contribution, the policy simply addresses the timing of contributions. With discretionary contributions in a profit-sharing plan, the employer establishes a policy for determining how and when contributions are to be made. Also, in a defined-contribution plan, there should be less conflict with the plan's objectives because the employer's contribution is not tied to the plan's investment performance. The employer does not have to be concerned about the long-term cost of funding the plan or short-term variability. The only objective is to provide for the retirement needs of the participants.

However, because participants will be of different ages and have different needs and risk profiles, many defined-contribution plans pass the investment decisions on to the participants. In such plans, the objective at the trust level is somewhat different. Here the goal is to offer participants a number of sufficiently diverse investment vehicles—each with different risk and return characteristics—so each participant will be able to assemble a portfolio that will meet his or her individual investment needs. Also, to assist participants in the formation of appropriate investment objectives, the trustees will have to provide them with suitable education.

Investment Responsibilities

Investment guidelines should identify all of the parties involved in the investment of plan assets and should address each individual's specific responsibilities. To do this requires, first, a review of the plan and trust documents. These documents offer more detail on accountability issues than most people realize. Commonly, the document provides that either the employer or an investment committee is responsible for establishing and periodically reviewing the investment policy. The employer often retains the responsibility of choosing and monitoring the trustee and any investment managers. Trustees are responsible for investing plan assets in accordance with the stated investment goals and reporting to the employer or investment committee, unless some or all of this responsibility is passed on to one or more investment managers. The trustees will always account for, and report on the status of, plan assets. In some cases, there may also be consultants who help with the selection and monitoring of investment managers.

Investment Policy

investment policy

The plan's *investment policy* should identify the appropriate degree of risk and yield for the trust and the importance of yield in relation to safety of principal and the plan's cash-flow needs. These decisions must be made in relation to the plan's objectives and the investment objectives. When trying to determine the plan's objectives, it is helpful to ask the following questions:

- Are there other resources available to pay benefits if investment performance is bad in the short run?
- What is the appropriate investment horizon?
- What is an acceptable level of risk?
- What is the minimum level of investment return necessary to accomplish the goals?

These questions are relevant to the plan trustees when they are responsible for investment decisions, as well as to plan participants in cases where they have investment control.

Investment Goals

The next step is to establish concrete performance objectives for monitoring investment performance. It is almost always more sensible to evaluate investments based on appropriate benchmarks as opposed to specific rates of return. If more than one investment manager is involved, a specific set of investment guidelines should be established for each manager and cover the following:

- permissible categories of investments
- asset allocation ranges among different investment classes
- appropriate investments within categories (such as specified bond quality)
- diversification concerns, such as maximum holding in specific investments, limits on small capitalization stocks, and limits on any particular sector
- policies regarding proxy voting
- limitations based on fiduciary rules, prohibited transactions, and so on

Monitoring Investment Management

Another part of the investment policy includes procedures for periodically checking performance against benchmarks. The safest course of action is to track performance on a continual basis, and to meet with investment managers on a quarterly, semiannual, or annual basis. Investment performance should be evaluated over relatively long periods, although significant deviation in short-term performance can be a warning sign. Performance can be evaluated against peer groups as well as against benchmarks.

Reviewing Investment Guidelines

The final part of the investment procedure should be a plan for an annual review of the investment guidelines to ensure that they are still appropriate. Again, it is important to keep accurate records of any meetings that discuss, reconfirm, or change the guidelines.

INVESTMENT CONSIDERATIONS

Almost every investment option available to an individual investor is available to a pension plan sponsor. In fact, pension funds can be invested in such a large number of products that it is impossible to cover them all fully in this text. Instead, in the rest of this chapter, we will concentrate on several objectives: identifying certain basic investment characteristics, clarifying the role of major asset classes in the asset mix, and finally, reviewing several of the products that the insurance industry typically markets to pension funds.

Investment Considerations Specific to Pension Investing

Let's start by looking at several aspects that need to be considered before selecting investments. One factor is the investment's tax treatment. Because qualified plans and other tax-advantaged plans are tax exempt (at the trust level), investments that also have special tax advantages are generally not appropriate for the plan. This is because the investor pays a premium for the tax advantage. For example, tax-free municipal bonds have a lower investment return than comparable taxable bonds. Because the trust does not benefit from the special tax treatment, these types of investments should generally be avoided.

Another concern is investment liquidity. This refers to the ability to convert the investment to cash in a short period of time. An adequate portion of the pension assets needs to be sufficiently liquid so benefit payments can be made without the need to sell long-term investments at a bad price.

A third consideration is the investment's stability. A stable investment has little fluctuation in value. For example, money market accounts and Treasury bills have almost no variability. As mentioned above, stability of the investments can affect the short-term variability of plan contributions to a defined-benefit plan. The downside of investments with little variability is that they also have low rates of return.

Unrelated Business Income Tax

When considering plan investments, qualified plans must be concerned about the unrelated business income tax (UBIT). If a qualified plan is deemed to operate an unrelated trade or business, any earnings (reduced by deductions allowed in connection with such business) will be taxable income to the trust, which reduces the return on the investment by the amount of the tax. If there is UBIT, the trust must also file a tax return and the UBIT is reported on the annual Form 5500.

For a qualified plan, operating any trade or business on a regular basis, either directly or as a partner in a partnership, will be considered operating an unrelated business. This broad language means that a plan participating in any limited partnership has to carefully evaluate whether the investment could generate UBIT.

The primary objective of this rule is to eliminate a source of unfair competition for taxable enterprises. A distinction must be made between operating a business (which would result in unfair competition) and a passive investment (which would not). A "trade or business" generally includes any activity carried on for the production of income from the sale of goods or performance of services.

From a practical perspective, this issue is most likely to arise when a pension trust is considering an investment in a limited partnership. In this case, it would be appropriate for the investment to provide a legal opinion about the UBIT issue in the prospectus. If the issue is not addressed, the plan should seek legal counsel to determine whether the investment could result in UBIT.

In addition to the UBIT determined above, a percentage of the plan's unrelated debt-financed income is also to be taxed as UBIT. Such income is taxed to the extent that the plan acquires income-producing assets by means of debt financing. There are exceptions; an important one is that debt-financed property does not include property whose use is substantially related to the trust's exempt purpose. This exception generally exempts ESOP debt-financed purchases from the tax. Again, this is a complicated area that requires careful investigation if the plan is considering a debt-financed investment.

Diversification Requirements for Defined-Contribution Plans

As required by the Pension Protection Act of 2006, defined-contribution plans holding publicly-traded employer securities plans must permit participants the option to diversify investments. The right to choose alternative investments applies at all times to employee contributions invested in employer securities. With employer contributions, participants who have earned 3 years of service (as measured under the plan's vesting rules) must be permitted to direct such amounts to alternative investments.

The diversification requirements do not apply to an ESOP as long as it is a separate plan and does not have salary deferral or a matching contribution account. The requirements also do not apply to a one-participant retirement plan (defined in chapter 13). A transition rule allows for the rules to be phased in over 3 years (beginning in 2007) for employer securities acquired before 2007. However, the transition rule does not apply to plan participants who have 3 years of service and have attained age 55 by the end of 2006.

A plan subject to the diversification requirements is required to give participants a choice of at least three additional investment options. Each investment alternative must have materially different risk and return characteristics. Plan sponsors must allow diversification elections at least quarterly (on the same basis as the opportunity to make other investment changes, except as provided in regulations or securities laws).

Investment Classes

Cash Equivalents

cash equivalents

To satisfy the need to make other investment transactions and to have readily accessible money to pay benefits, plans generally invest some of a plan's assets in instruments that are known as *cash equivalents*. Typically, cash equivalents have either no specified maturity date or one that is one year or less in the future.

A number of different investments are considered cash equivalents. The investment with the least risk of default is the U.S. Treasury bill (T-bill). These obligations of the U.S. government have maturity dates of 90 days, 180 days, or one year when issued, and are backed by the full taxing authority of the government. They can be readily sold and converted to cash at a modest cost. Other federal government agencies also issue short-term marketable obligations. These are available with a range of maturity dates, and generally pay a slightly higher interest rate than T-bills.

Another category, bank deposits, includes savings accounts and certificates of deposit (CDs) at banks, savings and loans, and credit unions. Savings accounts face minimal risk and are subject to few restrictions on withdrawals. CDs, which are deposits for a specified period of time (such as 3, 6, or 12 months), generally impose a loss of a portion of the interest earnings as a penalty for a withdrawal before maturity, although some banks have eliminated this penalty or reduced it to a minimal amount. Banks also sell negotiable CDs. with a minimum denomination of $100,000. However, trades in negotiable CDs have a minimum denomination of $1 million. Several New York–based CD dealers handle most secondary market trading. The first $100,000 in principal of a negotiable CD is covered by FDIC insurance. Unfortunately, this means that most of the principal of high-denomination CDs ($1 million or more) is uninsured. Despite the lack of FDIC insurance guarantee, negotiable CDs are considered essentially as safe as commercial paper. Hence, the yields on these two instruments are nearly identical.

Money market deposit accounts (MMDAs) and money market mutual funds (MMMFs) are other popular cash equivalents. Both MMDAs and MMMFs hold portfolios of short-term obligations of the federal government and its agencies, of state and local governments, and of businesses. The securities are, in most cases, completely liquid without penalty. Money market instruments pay a yield slightly lower than the underlying investments (to account for management fees), but also allow greater diversification, protecting the plan from default risk.

Other investments that have the characteristics of cash equivalents include short-term obligations of state and local governments and of businesses and the long-term debt obligations of governments, businesses, and nonprofit institutions that are to mature within one year.

Bonds

Bond owners are creditors of the issuing institution, whether it is a government, business, or nonprofit organization. This status grants the investors the legal right to enforce their claims to interest income and principal repayment as contained in the agreement that specifies the terms and conditions of the debt issue. In the case of business debt instruments, debt claims have priority over any claims of its owners.

Bond issues of state and local governments (both of which are referred to as *municipals*) and of businesses typically are quality rated by Standard and Poor's Corporation (S&P) and/or Moody's Investors Service. These ratings express the likelihood that the issuer will default on the timely payment of interest or principal. Based on a financial analysis of the issuer, a letter grade is assigned to each bond issue. Bonds rated at the top of the B grade (BBB for S&P, Baa for Moody's) or higher are considered to be *investment quality*. Lower ratings are assigned for bonds assessed as *speculative*. The lower the quality rating, the greater the risk of default and the higher the interest rate (return) that the investor can expect to earn.

Government Bonds. Governmental debt includes securities of the federal, state, and local governments. Some federal bonds are backed by the full faith and credit of the U.S. government. For example, all U.S. Treasury obligations have such backing. Other U.S. government bonds issued by federal agencies or organizations, such as the Tennessee Valley Authority or the U.S. Postal Service, are not direct obligations of the U.S. Treasury. These bonds, known collectively as agency bonds, provide investors with a return greater than that available on U.S. Treasury bonds. A few of these agency bonds have guarantees that effectively place the full faith and credit of the U.S. Treasury behind the bonds.

Some state and local government bonds, known as *general obligations,* are backed by the taxing power of the state or local government. Others, usually issued by agencies of a state or local government, are known as *revenue bonds.* They are backed by the revenues earned from such ventures as turnpikes, airports, and sewer and water systems. Without the taxing authority behind them, these revenue bonds are viewed as riskier and pay investors a somewhat higher interest rate than do general obligation bonds.

Maturities of governmental debt instruments vary from more than one year to 30 years. Bonds with maturities of 10 years or less are often referred to as being of intermediate-term duration and have somewhat less risk than longer-term bonds. If such a risk difference does exist, intermediate-term obligations would pay a slightly lower rate than would longer duration bonds.

Corporate Bonds. Businesses are major contributors to the supply of debt securities available in the marketplace. These securities, either notes if intermediate term or bonds if long term, have various characteristics, which are detailed in the indenture. Some of the more frequently encountered characteristics include the following:

- *secured*—a promise backed by specific assets as further protection to the bondholder should the corporation default on payment of interest or principal
- *debenture*—an unsecured promise, based only on the issuer's general credit status, to pay interest and principal
- *callable*—an option exercisable at the issuer's discretion to redeem the bond prior to its maturity date at a specified price
- *convertible*—an option exercisable by the bondholder to exchange the bond for a predetermined number of common or preferred shares

For bonds of the same quality rating, these features affect the interest rate available to the investor. If the feature provides a benefit to the bondholder, such as being secured or convertible, a lower interest rate is paid. If the feature provides a benefit to the issuer, such as the flexibility of not having specific assets pledged as collateral (debenture) or the presence of a call feature, the interest rate is higher.

When plan assets are invested by the trustee, bonds are often used to ensure that the plan will have sufficient cash to pay expected benefits as they arise. For example, if a defined-benefit plan expects to pay out monthly benefits to current beneficiaries in the amount of $50,000 a month, bonds are purchased in the amount necessary to generate a stream of interest payments in this amount. Also, bonds are used simply because they provide more stable returns than equities and higher returns than the cash equivalents mentioned above.

Equity Securities

Equity investments represent an ownership position in a business. As such, they represent a higher short-term risk for the investor than do debt investments, but they also offer higher potential long-term return. Because most retirement plans have long-term investment goals, equity investments play a significant role in the asset mix.

Example:	The 2001 *Pension & Investments* survey of the 1,000 largest employee benefit funds showed that defined-benefit plans held 63.7 percent of their assets in equities, while defined-contribution plans held 61.7 percent of assets in equities.

By far, the most popular equity investment for pension trusts is in common stock of publicly traded corporations. Investors in common stock have the ultimate ownership rights in the corporation. They elect the board of directors that oversees the management of the firm. Each common share receives an equal portion of the dividends distributed, as well as any liquidation proceeds. If the firm is unsuccessful, losses will occur that can lead to cessation of any dividend payments and, if losses continue, to eradication of the common equity ownership and eventual bankruptcy.

Current income distributed as dividends to shareholders is at the sole discretion of the board of directors. The board is under no legal obligation to make dividend payments and may instead retain the profits within the business. Only by threatening to elect, or actually electing, a new board can common shareholders force a dividend payment, regardless of the profitability of the business.

The owners of common stock also vote on major issues, such as mergers, name changes, sale of a major part of the business, or liquidation. Finally, common stockholders sometimes have a *preemptive right,* which is the right to maintain their relative voting power by purchasing shares of any new issues of common stock of the corporation.

Mutual Funds

An open-end investment company, popularly called a *mutual fund,* continually sells and redeems its shares at net asset value, that is, the value of the fund's assets divided by the number of outstanding shares. Mutual funds acquire a portfolio of securities in which each of the fund's shares represents a proportionate interest in the total portfolio. As sales and redemptions of the fund's shares take place, the size of the fund's total portfolio changes, increasing when additional shares are sold and decreasing when shares are redeemed.

Mutual funds can be differentiated on the basis of their portfolio objectives. These major categories include

- *money market mutual funds*—These funds own a portfolio of short-term interest-bearing securities. As mentioned earlier, investors use them as an alternative to cash.
- *bond funds*—These companies own a portfolio of bonds. Subcategories include some that invest only in U.S. government issues, municipal issues, corporate issues, or low-quality (junk) bonds. Further subcategories can be short-term (up to 4 or 5 years), intermediate-term (5 to 10 years), or long-term (10 or more years in duration) bond funds.
- *common stock companies*—These companies hold a portfolio of common stocks and perhaps a small number of preferred stocks. Subcategories include those that invest primarily in conservative (defensive) stocks, growth stocks, aggressive growth stocks, or foreign stocks.
- *mixed portfolio companies*—These companies own a portfolio of bonds, stocks, and other investment instruments. Subcategories include balanced companies and income companies.

Another way to distinguish funds is to look at whether they are actively managed (securities chosen individually by management) or passively managed. A common passive strategy includes those funds referred to as *index funds*. An index fund owns a portfolio that replicates a major market index, such as the S&P 500. Passive strategies generally result in lower management fees.

In addition to the fees charged by the management of the fund, funds have various acquisition fees. In many cases, fees that would apply to individual investors are waived for the pension fund. If fees exist, they must be carefully evaluated.

Mutual funds are more and more frequently used in pension plans. With small plans, assets may be too small to be handled by an investment manager. Like the common trust fund (described in the previous chapter), mutual funds provide an easy way to achieve diversification. Mutual funds also provide liquidity and ease of entry and exit. As mutual fund return data is published and studied, it simplifies evaluation of investment performance.

When participants in defined-contribution plans are given investment choices, mutual funds (and other look-through investments such as common trust funds and insurance contracts) are becoming the primary form of investment. These types of investments allow participants to build individualized portfolios while still taking advantage of professional management and asset diversification. In addition, these look-through investments are required in order to take advantage of the fiduciary liability relief described in the previous chapter.

GROUP PENSION PRODUCTS

allocated

Historically, group pension departments of insurance companies offered a distinct contrast to plans invested directly in the types of assets discussed above under a trust agreement. Early group pension products were generally *allocated,* meaning assets were committed to provide benefits for specific employees, while trust funds were unallocated. Another distinction was that the group pension products were replete with guarantees (everything from guaranteed interest rates to annuity purchase guarantees), and trust funds offered no guarantees. While the guarantees constituted something of an advantage, they also made the early group pension products less competitive because providing long-term guarantees required conservative actuarial projections for investment return. A third difference was that group pension contracts were inflexible in the timing of contributions and restrictive regarding the types of benefit formulas for which they were suitable. As you might expect, group pension products were less than competitive in attracting pension funds.

As time wore on, new group pension products were designed to provide the employer with more flexibility in both plan design and timing of contributions. In addition, the weighty long-term guarantees that fettered companies and kept them from offering competitive investment returns were removed and replaced with guarantees on a floor rate for investment return. Also, companies began to segregate their pension assets from the insurance companies' general accounts, which permitted separate account investing that was tailored to diverse pension needs.

One final hurdle that insurance companies had to overcome was the commingling of contributions for the current and all prior years. In times of rising interest rates, the insurance contracts appeared to be noncompetitive because they were selling a portfolio rate of interest that was weighed down by the lower rates of prior years. To counteract this, the new-money method (also known as investment-year method) was developed. Under the new-money method, each deposit made by an employer is credited with the rate of interest that the funds actually earned in that year. Thus, in times of rising interest rates, the rates are not based on a company-based time-weighted portfolio, but on a series of annual competitive rates (as with a trust fund plan).

The net result of all this change has placed group pension products on a par with trust funds. Distinctions between them remain, but that does not keep them from being competitive; in fact, the distinctive features of group pension products make them more advantageous under some circumstances.

Traditional Group Pension Products

Three group pension products that have been in existence for some time and are still used today (although some insurance companies have discontinued underwriting them) are the group deposit-administration contract (DA), the immediate-participation-guarantee contract (IPG), and the pension-funding contract (PF).

group deposit-administration contract
unallocated group pension contract

The *group deposit-administration contract* was the first *unallocated group pension contract* (meaning assets were not allocated to individual participants). The DA is funded by a series of employer contributions made throughout the year. Contributions are accounted for under two different systems—one that reflects investment guarantees that are given (the active-life fund) and one that reflects the actual investment experience. At retirement, the active-life fund is debited with the amount taken out, which is enough to purchase an immediate annuity for the participant in the amount provided by the plan. The annuity purchase rates are also guaranteed in the contract. Under a DA contract, the investment experience is rated annually and dividends are paid to the contract holder if the experience fund exceeds the reserve necessary for future benefits and expenses. The group deposit-administration contract is able to offer interest and annuity rate guarantees because it accumulates a contingency reserve, and because it has control (through dividend computations) over the rate at which actuarial gains pertaining to guaranteed items are created.

immediate-participation-guarantee contract

Because some employers object to the reserves and other insurance company controls and, instead, seek an immediate reflection of actual investment and mortality experience, a second (and more popular) product is available—the *immediate-participation-guarantee contract*. An IPG is an unallocated funding instrument that holds benefit amounts in a commingled fund. At retirement, one of two things happens: (1) either the fund is charged directly with benefit payments or (2) the fund is charged with a single annuity premium. The IPG contract contains no interest guarantees, but, as the name indicates, it allows a plan sponsor to have an immediate reflection of the actual investment and mortality experience under the plan (which is the major selling point of a trust fund plan).

The IPG contract typically contains conservative guarantees of annuity rates for retired lives. They were, however, the first group pension contract that did not provide annuities as a matter of course. In other words, even though annuity rates are guaranteed, annuities are not automatically purchased at retirement.

pension-funding contract

A product that evolved from the IPG contract but spurned the use of any annuity guarantees was the *pension-funding contract* (PF). The only significant difference between a PF contract and an IPG contract is that, under a PF contract, there are no guarantees whatsoever for retirees, no annuity purchases are made, and no funds are earmarked for retired employees.

The Current Generation of Group Pension Products

Three newer group pension products are today's big sellers. In general, these products are giving trust fund plans stiff competition and are yielding big rewards for many insurance companies. These products include

- separate-investment accounts contracts
- guaranteed-investment contracts (GICs)
- investment-guarantee contracts (IGs)

Take note that different companies tag these products with different names and/or have special variations of the generic product, so it is important to check for the product name and any variation from the generic.

Separate-Investment Accounts Contracts

separate-investment accounts contract

The most basic of the third-generation contracts is the *separate-investment accounts contract*. Under this contract, the plan fund manager can either invest in one of the separate accounts offered by the insurance company or split investments among the various accounts offered. A separate-investment account is similar in concept to a mutual fund. Like a mutual fund, a separate-investment account is generally pooled (takes allocations from a variety of plan sponsors instead of from individual investors) and is always participating (that is, accounts are maintained at market value, and the actual investment experience is reflected directly in the fund's value). A second similarity to mutual funds is that the separate-investment account has preestablished types of investments—for example, a bond or equity fund can be chosen. A third similarity to mutual funds is that each fund has a directed-investment philosophy and certain investment goals. (For example, an equity separate-investment account might have a directed philosophy of investing in dividend-producing equities.) And a fourth similarity to mutual funds is that the sales appeal of any separate-investment account is based on its competitive market history.

Separate-investment accounts contracts generally require a minimum deposit. The plan sponsor can allocate these funds to one or all of the different funds available and can usually transfer funds among the accounts whenever desired. This allows the plan sponsor to play the market by changing investment strategies to meet market trends.

Unlike assets held in an insurance company's general account, assets in separate accounts are not subject to the claims of the insurance company's creditors. This makes separate-investment accounts especially popular in an environment of low interest rates. In such periods, institutional investors become quite concerned about the risk of loss that could result due to the failure of the insurance company. Insulation from this risk through the use of separate accounts can be an important selling point.

However, the chief selling point of a separate-investment-accounts contract is the competitiveness of the investment's rate of return. Unlike that of most pension products, this competitive posture is generally well-advertised in trade magazines, such as *Pensions and Investment Age;* therefore, selling should be coordinated with the home office's advertising strategy. Another unique feature of these contracts is that there is a wealth of literature (from general philosophy reports to detailed quarterly investment reports) that can be used as a sales tool.

Guaranteed-Investment Contracts (GICs)

guaranteed-investment contract (GIC)

One of the most popular types of pension-funding products issued through group pension departments of insurance companies is the *guaranteed-investment contract (GIC).* As the name implies, a guaranteed-investment contract guarantees the pension plan's investment (both principal and interest). The insurance company receives plan assets at a specified date or dates, guarantees them at a stipulated rate of interest, and returns the principal and interest at a specified time or times. In fact, a GIC is analogous to a certificate of deposit for pension plans because, like a CD, it offers a predetermined rate of return. The GIC guaranteed rate is spot-rated—that is, it is based on the insurance company's ability to immediately purchase an underlying investment vehicle (for example, a zero coupon or deep discount bond).

A second similarity to a certificate of deposit is that a GIC guarantees the principal. Another similarity is that GICs permit withdrawals only on specified dates, sometimes only on the contract ending date. Some withdrawal flexibility is available, however, because GICs can be structured to pay out interest annually or to distribute the principal investment piecemeal (this is known as a strip feature). This flexibility is important for plan sponsors who must meet plan cash-flow needs, such as plan expenses and benefit payouts to retirees. In addition, although the length of a GIC is usually somewhere between 3 and 7 years (typically 5 years), investment flexibility can be achieved by the purchase of a short-term GIC for as little as one year.

When a GIC is offered as one of several investment options in a participant-directed defined-contribution plan, an exception is made to the withdrawal limitations that normally apply to a GIC. In this case, there is almost never a penalty for the participant who elects to move assets within the family of available investment choices.

The withdrawal limitation for the trustee-invested plan is a real consideration for the investor. However, in exchange for leaving money with the insurance company, the pension plan is assured of guaranteed interest rates that often extend for the length of the contract. These projected investment returns provide a safety net for the pension fund manager by effectively minimizing any downside risk and by allowing plan actuaries and accountants to make accurate predictions about the GIC-invested portion of the pension portfolio. On the other hand, GICs will not gain from an upside swing in the market. For this reason, they are more appropriate when interest rates are high and expected to fall or when interest rates are expected to remain stable.

Varieties of GICs. There are two basic types of GICs. The simpler of the two, the *bullet GIC*, contains a guarantee-of-interest-and-principal feature and can vary from 3 to 7 years in length. The bullet GIC is an investment vehicle structured to take a single-sum deposit for a specified period of time. Both the amount of deposit and the lock-in period are a product of the pension fund manager's investment strategy.

The bullet GIC can work well in a defined-benefit plan, but the inflexible timing of contributions led to the establishment of the *window GIC*. The window GIC helps to meet the need for periodic contributions inherent in some defined-contribution plans, which credit an employee's account balance with the plan contribution when monthly or semimonthly salaries are paid. When a window GIC is used, the interest guarantees are locked in at the contract inauguration, but the timing of contributions is usually left open for up to a year. In return for this option, the guaranteed rate is lower than the rate for a corresponding bullet GIC.

A second way the window GIC is different from the bullet GIC is that the precise contribution amount is not known; the third difference is that in a window GIC, the withdrawal amounts are not known. Window GICs are marketed for defined-contribution plans because, under these plans, the exact yearly dollar contribution is not known when the contract is signed, but only at the end of the year, after all contributions have been made. Window GICs also are popular as a guaranteed-investment option in a participant-directed defined-contribution plan.

One common twist to the window GIC is to guarantee the first-year rate but leave the years 2-through-5 rate open during that first year. Pension fund managers can then lock in a rate later that year. For example, if they gamble that rates will rise and they win, they can lock in the higher rate that comes up late in the first contract year as their 2-through-5 guarantee. If they gamble that rates will rise and they do not, the insurance company can lock in the lower rate as a guarantee for years 2 through 5. Because this involves risk for the insurance company, guarantees are generally lower.

Sales Appeal. The major selling point of a GIC is that it provides a competitive guaranteed rate of return. A second selling point is that the risk associated with GIC investments is limited. Credit risks (the inability of the carrier to pay principal and interest at maturity) are greatly minimized when one is dealing with a company that has an established investment track record.

And market risk (the possibility that rates may shift during the lock-in period) can be minimized by choosing the window GIC option of floating the guarantee for a year. The third selling point of GICs is that they fit nicely in most pension portfolios by providing a conservative investment foundation on which investments that carry more risk can be placed. A fourth selling point is that assets held in GICs can be valued at book value, while assets held in bonds, for example, have to be valued at market value. In defined-benefit plans, where variability in asset valuation can cause big fluctuations in required contributions, GICs have a clear advantage over bonds. A final selling point of GICs is their pension orientation. GICs uniquely meet the primary investment concerns of pension managers because they maximize long-term rates of return and generate cash flow to match required benefit payments while preserving the safety of principal.

YOUR FINANCIAL SERVICES PRACTICE: GIC SALES

The bullet GIC market is extremely sensitive to interest rates. When interest rates are high, you will be able to do a lot of bullet GIC business; when interest rates are low, however, you will have problems selling. The window GIC, on the other hand, has a fairly steady market because defined-contribution plans that have a guaranteed-interest-account option under their plan have to place their money somewhere each year, regardless of interest rates.

Investment-Guarantee Contracts (IGs)

investment-guarantee contract (IG)

A third type of no-service group pension product is the *investment-guarantee contract (IG)*. The IG contract is similar to a GIC in many ways. Both GICs and IGs are often structured to receive predetermined contributions (based on the plan's contribution or benefit formula), pay a guaranteed rate of interest; receive contributions during a window period (like a window GIC); and typically last 5 years. However, the IG's major difference is that contributions are received for the 5-year period rather than for the one-year window or one-shot bullet payment. Also, the guarantees given to the plan sponsor for years 2 through 5 are only a floor amount. Under an IG contract, the funds may receive a higher interest rate than projected if the actual investment experience of an investment account exceeds the guarantees.

Because the insurance company is taking on more risk the farther out in time it projects guarantees, the IG interest guarantees are typically on a declining scale. The guarantee for year 3 is lower than the guarantee for year 2, and these declining guarantees are attributable to the market and investment-placement risks that insurance companies take. The plan sponsor, however, is more concerned with both the initial year's guarantee and the offering company's competitive posture. As with any participating contract, the offering company's

TABLE 12-1
Comparison of Group Insurance Products

Type of Contract	Amount of Contribution	Timing of Contribution	Investment Guarantees	When to Sell
Separate-Investment Accounts Contract	Typically $100,000 or more	Ongoing	None; competitive history of the offering company is important	Generally, at any time; sales are easier when coordinated with home-office advertising, and/or the reporting of favorable returns
Bullet GIC	Precisely known, typically $100,000 or more	One-time, within 3 days of sale	Guaranteed at the outset for the length of the contract	When interest rates are high and expected to drop
Window GIC	Based on the plan's benefit formula, typically a percentage of annual contributions of $100,000 or more	Over a window period of up to one year	Guaranteed at the outset for the length of the contract	At all times, if the client offers a guaranteed account to employees
IG Contracts	Based on the plan's benefit formula, typically $50,000 a year or $250,000 over 5 years	Over the length of the contract	Guaranteed at the beginning of each contract year and the outset of the contract	When interest rates are low and expected to rise, or if the market is unstable and the client wants to keep options open

investment history is a key selling point because the investor is hoping that the actual results will exceed the floor guarantees.

Sales Appeal. The major selling point of an IG contract is that it allows plan funds to receive the experience account or the guarantee, whichever is better. Thus, the pension fund manager knows that downside risk is eliminated (by the guarantee) but not at the risk of locking in a static rate for an extended period. To put it another way, fund managers can sleep at night because of the guarantee, and the sky is the limit if the investment environment takes a sharp upswing. A second selling point is that the risks associated with IG investments are limited. As with GICs, credit risks are minimized when the offering company has a history of good performance. For IGs, unlike GICs, the market risk of an upturn during the investment period is eliminated because the fund's actual experience will be credited. A final selling point for IGs is their pension orientation. Like GICs, IGs uniquely meet the investment concern of pension managers because they maximize long-term rates of return and generate cash flows to match the required benefit payments while preserving safety of principal.

LIFE INSURANCE PRODUCTS AS A FUNDING VEHICLE

Life Insurance

As was the case with group pension products, life insurance in qualified plans has undergone an evolution of sorts. Over the years, the use of life insurance in a qualified plan has shifted from emphasis on the fully insured plan to a split-funded, life-and-side-fund approach.

In time, fully insured plans were replaced with a split-funded approach, which combined an ordinary life contract with a side fund. The ordinary life contract generates the lowest scale of cash values, so a significant amount of funding can be provided through the side fund. This approach offers the best of both worlds—the preretirement death-benefit coverage of a fully funded plan and the investment discretion and contributions-timing discretion that is built into the side fund.

If life insurance is used in a defined-benefit plan, the trustee purchases separate contracts on the life of each participant. In defined-contribution plans, life insurance is typically offered as a participant-directed option. If the participant elects life insurance coverage, premiums are paid out of the participant's account balance. In either case, the trustee applies for the insurance, pays the premiums when due, is custodian of the individual contracts, and—even though the insured individual applies for the contract—has legal ownership of the insurance contract.

The insurability of individuals is seldom a serious problem under a life-insurance-funded plan because (1) evidence of insurability is sometimes waived, (2) substandard rates can be used, and (3) graded or graduated death benefits can be used. Also, like group term life insurance plans, some individual policy plans establish nonmedical amounts using a formula based on the amount of volume under the particular plan. The plan's disability benefit can be provided either through a waiver-of-premium clause or a rider or by fully vesting the cash value. If an employee leaves before retirement, disability, or death, his or her vested interest can be taken care of in several ways: (1) the contract can be transferred to the participant; (2) a paid-up policy in the amount that is currently funded can be transferred; (3) the trustee can borrow the unvested portion and assign the contract; or (4) the policies can be cashed in for their surrender value.

Annuities as a Funding Vehicle

Annuities are traditionally thought of as a common method of distributing retirement funds to retirees. However, they can play another role when it comes to funding the retirement plan. Like the use of life insurance, the use of annuities to fund retirement plans has changed. The original retirement annuity products offered a noncompetitive investment return and lacked contribution flexibility—two drawbacks that led to their downfall. Under these contracts, the objective was to fund the retirement benefit by funding an annuity that built sufficient cash values at retirement to pay out benefits.

Annuity contracts used to fund retirement plans are typically deferred annuities, with the plan sponsor agreeing to fund (over the employee's career) an annuity that will begin spinning out payments at retirement. These annuities can be either fixed (where the monthly return is predetermined and guaranteed) or variable (where the underlying annuity investments, such as stocks, bonds, and money markets, let the annuities' return float with market conditions). The variable annuity tends to be the more popular of the two because it gives the plan sponsor more investment discretion—within limits. This is particularly important when the plan sponsor is a small-business owner who wants some investment control over his or her own retirement. Most plan-funding annuities are sold in this small, closely held business/professional-corporation market.

Annuities are sometimes used to fund plans in situations in which life insurance is not available because of underwriting considerations. Although life insurance underwriting requirements are not typically stringent in the retirement arena, there are times when a prospect is uninsurable and the "guaranteed issue" or graded death benefit amount is not sufficient. In these cases, annuities are suitable substitutes for life insurance in filling the funding need. A second reason annuities are used to fund plans is the guaranteed payout rates they sometimes offer. If this is the case, the same annuity that is used for funding purposes is also used for payout purposes.

CHAPTER REVIEW

Key Terms

investment guidelines [12-1]
funding policy [12-1]
investment policy [12-1]
cash equivalents [12-2]

allocated [12-2]
group deposit-administration
　contract [12-3]

unallocated group pension
   contract [12-3]
immediate-participation-
   guarantee contract [12-3]
pension-funding contract [12-3]
separate-investment accounts
   contract [12-3]

guaranteed-investment
   contract (GIC) [12-3]
investment-guarantee
   contract (IG) [12-3]

Review Questions

Review questions are based on the learning objectives in this chapter. Thus, a [12-3] at the end of a question means that the question is based on learning objective 12-3. If there are multiple objectives, they are all listed.

1. Why is it so important to establish investment guidelines? [12-1]

2. Name the common objectives of a defined-benefit plan. [12-1]

3. Name the common objectives of a defined-contribution plan. [12-1]

4. What is the primary objective that the trustees must satisfy when plan participants have investment options? [12-1]

5. What questions are helpful to ask when determining the plan's investment policy? [12-1]

6. Name the specific areas that should be addressed when identifying investment goals. [12-1]

7. What types of investments must a pension plan look at carefully in order to be sure that they do not result in unrelated business taxable income? [12-2]

8. Explain the role that cash equivalencies, bonds, and stocks have in the pension portfolio. [12-2]

9. Describe how the diversification requirements that apply to defined contribution plans apply differently to employee and employer contributions. [12-2]

10. Describe the major characteristics of the immediate-participation guarantee contract. [12-3]

11. A separate-investment-accounts contract can be compared to a mutual fund. Explain some of the similarities. [12-3]

12. Why does the separate-account contract reduce the risk to the investor? [12-3]

13. A guaranteed-investment contract (GIC) is similar to a certificate of deposit. Explain some of the similarities and differences. [12-3]

14. Plan sponsor Gillman owns a lacrosse equipment manufacturing company. Gillman's investment objectives for his defined-benefit plan include (1) receiving a guaranteed rate of return, (2) maintaining principal, and (3) protecting against downside risk. [12-3]

    a. Why is a GIC desirable for Gillman?
    b. What investment strategy should the Gillman Company take if it wants to avoid placing interest-rate bets?
    c. Which GIC variety should Gillman choose if he suspects interest rates are high and are expected to drop?

15. What are the major advantages of an investment-guarantee contract, and when should it be used? [12-3]

16. Explain what type of pension contract is most appropriate under each of the following circumstances: [12-3]

    a. The plan sponsor is small ($50,000 in annual contributions) and expects the current low interest rates are going to increase.
    b. The plan sponsor has a defined-contribution plan (annual contributions of $200,000) and expects interest rates to drop.
    c. The plan sponsor intends to maintain certain investment discretion, wants to make ongoing contributions, and does not require guarantees to be made.
    d. The plan sponsor has a defined-benefit plan, has annual contributions of $200,000, and expects interest rates to drop.

17. Why are annuities typically used as investments in retirement plans? [12-4]

13

Plan Installation and Administration

Learning Objectives

An understanding of the material in this chapter should enable you to

---

13-1.   Describe the steps that must be taken to install a corporate plan.

13-2.   Identify the key ongoing responsibilities of plan administration.

13-3.   Describe how divorce and compliance problems can complicate plan administration.

Chapter Outline

Once the plan has been selected and designed according to employer specifications and the funding approach has been decided upon, the tasks of plan installation and plan administration begin. The role of the financial services professional in these processes varies from case to case. Some clients want you to provide ongoing consulting, while others allow you to take a more passive posture. Most financial services professionals will want to choose the latter role and delegate the responsibilities associated with plan installation and administration to a third-party administrator. This will enable you to use your time more efficiently, freeing you up for sales and design consulting. There are, however, occasions that call for client hand-holding and troubleshooting on your part. For these times, you need a general understanding of the installation and administration processes and the documents that are an integral part of these processes. The objective of this chapter is to provide you with this understanding through an overview of plan installation and plan administration. If a more detailed review of the plan-installation and plan-administration process is needed, the loose-leaf services described in chapter 2 should be consulted. These services provide a wealth of information about filing requirements, as well as supplying copies of current forms and instructions.

Also, a variety of software packages are available that aid in the process of plan installation and administration. Software packages are widely available in the following areas:

- actual deferral percentage test calculation (monitors whether 401(k) plans meet the ADP test)
- actuarial valuations (a must for firms with defined-benefit plans)
- claims processing (typically used in conjunction with welfare benefit plans)
- document preparation (both plan and summary plan description)
- employee benefit statement preparation (typically used in conjunction with welfare benefit plans)
- nondiscrimination testing (monitors whether plans meet 410(b) and 401(a)(26) tests)
- top-heavy analysis (monitors top-heavy status of plan)
- 5500 forms preparation (very popular method for simplifying government filings)
- pension check processing (processes benefit payments)
- loan processing (useful for processing loans and tracking plan loan repayments)

SETTING UP A CORPORATE PLAN

The first step in the plan-installation process is for the employer to legally adopt the plan. This can be done through a resolution of the corporate board of directors, which can either adopt a particular plan document or simply adopt the major provisions of the plan. The corporate resolution should be adopted before the end of the tax year, if the employer wants the plan to be effective in that year. If the company's securities are offered in the open market, the plan is also generally submitted for stockholder approval (although it is not legally necessary). Notice of the establishment of the plan and details about the plan should be presented to stockholders in a proxy statement.

At the same time that the plan is approved, the corporate board of directors should also approve the trust instrument (if any) that will be used. Recall that a trust provides for the irrevocable deposit of plan assets. In other words, once assets, such as individual life insurance policies or cash, are transferred to the trust, the employer or the employer's creditors cannot recapture these assets. (The employer may, however, recapture assets that exceed promised benefits at the termination of the plan.) Under some state laws, a nominal contribution to the trust may be necessary in order to establish its existence.

If a group pension contract is used instead of a trust, the board will review a specimen contract. If the board wishes to adopt the contract, it will authorize the submission of a letter of application with premium. Note that the group pension contract must be submitted for approval to the state insurance department in the state where the corporation is domiciled. The state insurance department reviews the contract to see if the insurer has sufficient reserves to pay benefits and if the contract meets other state specifications.

Another step that must be completed before the end of the first tax year is notifying the participants of the new plan. This can be an oral explanation at an employee meeting or a written letter that is either mailed or posted at work—for example: "It is our pleasure to announce the ABC Company is adopting a qualified 401(k) plan. The details of the plan are as follows. . . ." Alternatively, the summary plan description (see below) can be used to satisfy this requirement.

For a plan funded with employer contributions, the employer typically adopts the plan at the end of the tax year in which it wants to receive a tax-deductible contribution. The reason is that the employer may not know until the end of the year whether it has funds available to contribute to a plan. In this case, the plan is made effective retroactive to the first day of the year, and a tax-deductible contribution can be made for the whole year. For example, if the employer is on a calendar tax year, the plan may be adopted on December 31, effective as of the previous January 1. However, if the plan is a contributory plan (a 401(k) or 403(b) plan), it should be adopted prior to the beginning of the first year of the plan's operation. This is necessary to allow time to enroll participants in the program. For such a plan, application is best accomplished through one or more enrollment meetings.

enrollment meeting

If the plan is contributory or if salary reductions are required under a 403(b) plan or a 401(k) plan, an additional step must be taken. When this is the case, the employees are asked to attend an *enrollment meeting*. The enrollment of an adequate number of employees in the plan is crucial for purposes of meeting the nondiscrimination rules and passing the actual deferral percentage test (401(k) plans only). Employers usually request the financial services professional to attend the enrollment meeting and use his or her selling skills to persuade the rank-and-file employees to make the necessary contributions or salary reductions.

**YOUR FINANCIAL SERVICES PRACTICE:
401(k) PLANS AND THE NEGATIVE ELECTION**

The IRS has approved a strategy that can increase enrollment in 401(k) plans. A plan can require that all participants start off with a default contribution of a specified amount (typically 3 percent) into a default investment account. Participants have to make an affirmative election to choose not to participate. This "negative election" approach can help to include those individuals who fail to participate because they never get around to filling in the form.

The enrollment meeting begins with the financial services professional describing the plan and spelling out the benefits and trade-offs of plan participation for the employees. The meeting typically contains a question-and-answer period during which the employees can voice their concerns and receive clarification on important issues. (*Planning Note:* Many financial services professionals present a slide show or movie that addresses the most typical questions. This often heads off the common problem of having one or two employees cause trouble by harping on the plan's negative aspects.) The meeting typically concludes with the completion and signing of enrollment forms and salary reduction agreements or authorization to withhold mandatory contributions from an employee's pay.

The enrollment meeting (or if an enrollment meeting is not required, a separate meeting) can be used to secure the information to apply for individual life insurance contracts if they are being used wholly or in part to fund the plan. In addition, medical examinations can also be conducted at this time, if required by underwriting.

Regardless of whether a trust or group pension contract is used, the entire first year's contribution should be made prior to filing the employer's tax return for the year in which the plan is adopted. (For a corporate employer using a calendar year, the date for filing the tax return for a given year is generally March 15 of the following year, but this can be extended to September 15.) As long as this requirement is met and the plan is in final form, the employer will be able to deduct contributions if the plan qualifies. (*Planning Note:* The plan should be adopted subject to the right to be rescinded if it does not qualify, and the trust or group pension contract should allow contributions to be returned if the plan does not qualify.)

advance-determination letter

In order to determine whether the plan qualifies, the employer should file an application for an *advance-determination letter* with the IRS. The employer is not required to receive IRS approval, but instead can wait for an IRS audit to determine whether the plan is qualified. However, this is not recommended because of the risk of disqualification (which means a retroactive loss of the tax deduction). The forms and documents used to file for an advance-determination letter include the following:

- IRS Form 5300 (Application for Determination for Employee Benefit Plan) or IRS Form 5307 (Short Form Application for Determination for Employee Benefit Plan—this form is used for master or prototype plans and volume submitter plans)
- IRS Form 8717 (User Fee for Employee Plan Determination Request)
- Schedule Q (Nondiscrimination Requirements)
- IRS Form 2848 (Power of Attorney and Declaration of Representative)
- copies of the plan and the trust or group pension contract

Make sure the determination letter is applied for before the tax return filing date (plus extensions). If the request for an advance-determination letter is submitted before the tax return is due, the IRS will extend the time limit for amending the plan. A retroactive amendment will then be possible, enabling the employer to receive a deduction for the current year. If the filing deadline is missed, it is highly unlikely that the IRS will allow the plan to be amended retroactively or that a deduction will be allowed for the initial contribution. Retroactive amendment is common if the IRS objects to some provisions of the proposed plan. (*Planning Note:* A determination letter is typically issued within 6 months after the application is filed. Although the IRS has a maximum of 270 days to make a ruling, no determination letter will be received before 60 days to give interested parties a chance to comment.)

**YOUR FINANCIAL SERVICES PRACTICE:
SMALL EMPLOYER TAX INCENTIVES**

The Economic Growth and Tax Relief Reconciliation Act of 2001 provided for several incentives to encourage small employers (100 or fewer employees) to establish a plan. The law provides up to a $500 income tax credit for administrative and retirement-education expenses for any small business that adopts a new qualified plan, SIMPLE or SEP. The credit is available for each of the first 3 years of the plan's existence.

In addition, a small employer that sponsors a qualified plan is not required to pay a user fee for a determination letter request in the first 5 years of the plan's existence. To be eligible for both rules, the plan must cover at least one nonhighly-compensated employee, meaning that a plan covering just a sole-proprietor will not be eligible.

---

notice to interested parties

Immediately preceding the filing of the request for an advance-determination letter, the employer should issue the *notice to interested parties* of the intent to install a qualified plan. The IRS will not issue an advance-determination letter unless interested parties have been notified that an application for one has been filed. The notice to interested parties goes to all employees eligible to be in the plan and to ineligible employees if they work at the same location as the eligible employees. The notice should indicate that qualification is being sought and that the employees have the right to submit comments on the plan to the IRS and the Department of Labor.

summary plan description (SPD)

The final and most important step in the employee communications process is the issuing of the *summary plan description (SPD)*. A summary plan description is an easy-to-read booklet that explains the plan to the participants. The SPD may be prepared by the financial services professional, the insurer, or the employer. In any case, employers are required to give SPDs to participants within 120 days after the plan is adopted by the board of directors. (*Planning Note:* In addition to being used with retirement plans, SPDs are also required for most welfare benefit plans. For this reason, it may be wise to suggest that your client combine all the SPDs (and other information) in an employee handbook.)

An SPD bridges the gap between the legalese of the pension plan and the understanding of the average participant by effectively communicating how a plan works, what benefits are available, and how to obtain these benefits. The SPD must strike a balance between clarity and depth. To this end, the Department of Labor suggests the frequent use of examples, the elimination of technical jargon and long complex sentences, the inclusion of a table of contents, and the use of clear cross-references. Other good ideas include the following:

- cross-referencing only to materials already discussed, not to materials that have yet to be discussed
- using short paragraphs (three or four sentences)
- using short sentences (20 words or less) and familiar words with few syllables

An SPD must be fair and evenhanded. It cannot be used to persuade employees to join the plan, but must merely explain the plan. The regulations specifically state that an SPD cannot downplay the negative consequences of involvement—for example, it cannot gloss over plan terms that may cause a participant to lose benefits or fail to qualify for them.

At the same time, the SPD must be accurate. Employees have sued and won cases where the SPD promised something that was not contained in the document. The best way for the employer to protect itself is to include a disclaimer stating that if there is a conflict between the plan and the SPD, the plan provisions will be determinative.

The SPD regulations dictate what kind of language to use, what kind of information to have, and what group of people must get the information. The regulations also require that every 5 years, participants whose plans have been modified must receive an updated SPD, and every 10 years—regardless of whether the plan has been modified—a new SPD must be issued. The following is a list of items that the SPD must contain:

- a provision identifying the plan—for example: "This is the ABC Company profit-sharing plan"
- the names and addresses of people responsible for the plan
- the employer identification number
- the plan administrator's name, address, and telephone number
- the name and address of the person designated for service of legal process
- the name, title, and business address of each trustee
- a statement to the effect if the plan is collectively bargained
- an explanation of the plan's eligibility requirements for participation and benefits and normal retirement age
- an explanation of any joint and survivor benefits
- an explanation of any terms that could result in a participant's losing benefits
- a PBGC insurance provision, if applicable
- a description and explanation of the plan provisions for determining years of service for eligibility to participate, vesting, breaks of service, and benefit accrual
- a list of the sources of plan contributions
- the name of the funding agency
- the plan year's ending date
- the procedures for presenting claims for benefits under the plan and remedies for benefits denied under the plan
- a statement of ERISA rights (this statement is standard text promulgated by the Department of Labor)

Table 13-1 summarizes all of the steps required to establish a qualified retirement plan.

TABLE 13-1
Summary of Steps in Setting Up a Corporate Plan

Steps	Timetable
1. Secure a corporate resolution adopting the plan.	Before the end of the tax year
2. Secure a corporate resolution approving the trust document or group pension contract.	Before the end of the tax year
3. Notify participants of the plan's adoption and its major terms.	Before the end of the tax year
4. Conduct an enrollment meeting if necessary.	For 401(k) and 403(b) plans, shortly after plan adoption
5. Give notice of the filing for advance determination to interested parties.	Before the date for filing the employer's tax return
6. File for an advance-determination letter.	Before the date for filing the employer's tax return
7. Make the first year's contribution.	Before the date for filing the employer's tax return
8. Supply a summary plan description to employees.	Within 120 days after the plan is adopted

ANNUAL ADMINISTRATION OF A CORPORATE PLAN

Every qualified plan has a plan administrator who is responsible for the administration of the plan. Typically, the plan administrator is the employer (in larger plans, the employer's director of human resources) or an individual or committee designated by the employer. The plan administrator receives help from a variety of sources. If the plan has a trust, the trustee may assist the plan administrator with administrative matters, but more frequently the trustee restricts his or her activities to investing the plan's assets. With insured plans, the insurer will generally provide a great number of administrative services, from computer support to producing manuals, which guide the plan administrator through the administrative process. In addition to the trustee or insurance company, the plan administrator can also look to a variety of third-party administrators (TPAs) who perform everything from turnkey services to only one specific service, such as administering the actual deferral percentage test. As a financial services professional, you will sometimes be asked to suggest or secure a TPA.

Annual Report

One of the plan administrator's principal duties is to comply with ERISA's reporting and disclosure requirements. All qualified plans are subject to these reporting and disclosure requirements (except some church and state plans). The most important reporting and disclosure requirement is filing the annual return/report with the IRS. (*Planning Note:* Financial services professionals are sometimes asked to advise plan administrators on how to comply with the reporting and disclosure requirements and may be called on to help in the filing of forms.)

Form 5500

Today, almost all filers are required to file Form 5500, which is a short main form with basic identifying information. There are also 13 schedule attachments focused on particular subjects and/or filing requirements—five pension schedules, seven financial schedules, and one fringe benefit schedule. Filers will have to complete only those schedules applicable to the specific type of plan. The schedules most commonly filed by pension plans include:

- Schedule A of Form 5500 (Insurance Information). This form is filed if any benefits are provided by an insurance company.
- Schedule B of Form 5500 (Actuarial Information). This form is used for most defined-benefit plans.
- Schedule P of Form 5500 (Annual Return of Fiduciary of Employee Benefit Trust). This form starts the 3-year statute of limitations running on the filing of the form.
- Schedules H and I (Financial Information). These forms (H for large plans and I for small plans) report financial information about the plan.
- Schedule R (Retirement Plan Information). This form includes information on pension plan distributions and funding requirements, as well as information on the coverage requirements for tax-qualified plans.
- Schedule SSA of Form 5500 (Annual Registration—Statement Identifying Separated Participants with Deferred Vested Benefits). This form is filed if a covered participant separates from service and the participant is entitled to a deferred vested benefit.

Audit Requirement

Federal law generally requires employee benefit plans with 100 or more participants to have an audit as part of their obligation to file an annual return/report (Form 5500). The auditor must be licensed or certified as a public accountant and individual auditors should not have any financial interests in the plan or the plan sponsor that would affect their ability to render an objective, unbiased opinion about the financial condition of the plan. The scope of the audit is more limited when plan assets are held by banks or insurance companies and written certifications are provided by the institutions holding those assets.

A quality audit will help protect the assets and the financial integrity of the plan, as well as ensure that the fiduciaries carry out their responsibility to file a complete and accurate annual return/report. The IRS has indicated that the most common reason for deficient accountants' reports is the failure of the auditor to have experience with employee benefit plan audits. So it is important for the administrator to choose an auditor with the appropriate level of experience.

One-Participant Plans

Qualified plans referred to as *one-participant plans* are allowed to file Form 5500-EZ instead of Form 5500. A plan is considered to be a one-participant plan if it only covers (a) the business owner and his or her spouse (if the business is wholly owned by the owner and spouse) or (b) partners in a business partnership, or the partners and their spouses. In addition, to qualify as a one-participant plan, the plan must meet the minimum-coverage requirements on its own, and the plan cannot cover a business that is a member of an affiliated service group, a controlled group of corporations, or a group of businesses under common control.

A plan that satisfies all of the above one-participant requirements does not have to file Form 5500-EZ if its assets total $250,000 or less at the end of the current year and every previous plan year. The same exception applies for an employer that has two or more one-participant plans that together had total plan assets of $250,000 or less at the end of every plan year. However, note that all one-participant plans *must* file Form 5500-EZ for their final plan year even if the total plan assets have *always* been less than $250,000. The final plan year is the year in which distribution of all plan assets is completed. The Pension Protection Act of 2006 increased the dollar amount from $100,000 to $250,000 for plan years beginning in 2007. The Act also called for simplified reporting for plans with fewer than 25 participants.

When Form 5500 or Form 5500-EZ is required, it must be filed annually by the last day of the seventh month after the plan year ends. An extension of up to 2½ months may be granted if Form 5558 is filed.

In addition to filing the 5500 family of forms with the IRS, administrators of defined-benefit plans must also supply the Pension Benefit Guaranty Corporation with annual premiums and filings (Form PBGC-1). Form PBGC-1 is due no later than 7 months after the close of the plan year (July 31 for a calendar-year plan).

Participant Communications

summary of material modification (SMM)

Plan administrators are required not only to file forms with appropriate federal agencies, but also to keep plan participants informed. New participants must be furnished with a summary plan description within 90 days. If the plan is amended in any significant way participants must be notified of the changes. The summary plan description could be modified or the sponsor can explain the changes in a written *summary of material modification (SMM)*. Material modifications do not include every plan change, but only the major changes shown in table 13-2.

TABLE 13-2
Material Modifications

- Name and address of sponsor/employer
- Name and address of plan administrator
- Structure of plan
- Name of plan
- Type of plan
- Agent for service of process
- Persons performing functions for the plan
- Sources and method of determining contributions
- Method of asset accumulation
- Procedure for presenting claims
- Eligibility requirements
- Vesting provisions
- Features of portability or reciprocity
- Length of service to determine participation, vesting, and benefit accrual
- Break-in-service rules
- Requirements for pension benefits
- Basis for computing retirement benefits
- Circumstances causing loss of pension benefits
- Joint and survivor annuity rules
- Disposition of employee's contributions
- Requirements for welfare benefits
- Circumstances causing loss of welfare benefits
- Fiduciaries' names and addresses

summary annual report (SAR)

To notify participants of the funding status of the plan, the plan administrator must automatically provide participants with a summary of the annual report within 2 months after the due date of the annual report (by the end of the 9th month after the end of the plan year unless an extension applies). The summary annual report must state whether contributions were made to keep the plan funded in accordance with minimum funding requirements, or whether contributions were not made, and the amount of the deficit. The current value of plan assets is also required to be disclosed. In addition, a participant must be provided with a copy of the full annual report on written request. Beginning in 2008, the Pension Protection Act replaces the SAR for defined-benefit plans with a new, detailed funding notice. The SAR still must be distributed for defined-contribution plans.

Furnishing plan participants with a personal benefit statement is another important aspect of plan administration. The Pension Protection Act of 2006 substantially revised these rules. Previously, benefit statements were only required upon the request of a participant or beneficiary. The rules now require regular distribution of statements and provide more guidance as to what has to be included in a benefit statement. A benefit statement must be written to be understood by the average plan participant, and must indicate the current value of accrued benefits and the extent to which benefits are vested. If the benefit structure is integrated with Social Security, the statement must explain how this works.

The rules contain significant differences between the requirements for defined-contribution and defined-benefit plans. With defined-contribution plans, the sponsor must provide benefit statements at least:

- quarterly for participants who self-direct investments
- annually for all other participants
- upon written request (limited to one request per year)

The benefit statements for defined-contribution plans must also include a statement about any restrictions that apply to investment direction, the value of the participant's investments, an explanation of the importance of diversification, and direction to the DOL's website for investment and diversification information.

The administrator of a defined-benefit plan generally has to furnish a pension benefit statement at least once every 3 years to participants currently employed. As an alternative the administrator can annually distribute statements notifying participants of the availability of the pension benefit statement.

Failure to provide the required benefit statement may result in penalties of up to $100 per day per participant. Regardless of the legal requirements, benefit statements are an important communication tool. Regular statements

---

**YOUR FINANCIAL SERVICES PRACTICE:
BENEFIT STATEMENTS**

Beginning in 2007, defined-contribution plans that provide for participant investment direction must provide quarterly benefit statements. The law change was a response to the Enron and WorldCom bankruptcies, and may provide a valuable protection for participants. As there is no exemption for small plans (except for plans that only cover business owners) this provision can also be burdensome on small retirement plans. Compliance will add additional administrative expense, and noncompliance can result in a $100-per-day-per-participant penalty. The cost for the statements could be passed on to the plan participants, but this is not a very satisfactory result, and hopefully the DOL will provide some relief for small plans. The financial services community will need to change practices to help satisfy these requirements. One mitigating factor is that the law allows distribution of statements by email. Also the DOL is required to create a model benefit statement before September 2007.

---

help ensure employee awareness of benefits and enable the employer to meet the organizational objectives of retaining and motivating employees.

Another aspect of plan administration is counseling participants about plan choices—especially about participant contributions and investment alternatives (assuming that the participants have them). Periodic notices of the plan's terms, enrollment meetings, investment alternative education, and even more general retirement planning education has become commonplace in the American workforce today. As described in chapter 11, plans are now allowed to offer an "eligible investment advice arrangement" so that participants in plans that allow for participant-directed investment can receive appropriate advice.

The distribution of benefits from qualified plans has become an extremely complicated and time-consuming process. The distribution process typically includes the following:

- distribution information—the process typically begins when the participant requests a distribution from the plan
- election forms—participants will be given forms identifying the optional forms of distribution. These forms will be supported with written materials (and sometimes personal meetings) explaining the value of each option and the impact of electing one option over another.
- qualified joint and survivor annuity—if the distribution is to a married participant and the qualified joint and survivor annuity rules apply, the participant and spouse will have to sign off on any optional form of distribution
- direct rollover—virtually all participants receiving a distribution from a qualified plan must be given an election form that allows them to elect to roll the benefit directly to an IRA

- income tax treatment—in most cases, participants must be given general information about tax implications of a pension distribution
- 1099-R forms—tax forms distributed to participants (and filed with the IRS) identifying the amount of the distribution and whether any portion is considered basis (not subject to income tax)

Another facet of plan administration involves amending plan documents. This may be required because the sponsor wants to make a design change or plan enhancement, or because the law has changed requiring plan amendments for the plan to remain "qualified." When a plan is amended, in general, the sponsor needs to consider whether or not to resubmit the plan for an IRS determination letter. As with the initial qualification letter, submitting the plan is generally the safer approach. In some cases, the submission process is simpler because the IRS only reviews the amendment, not the entire plan.

Summary of Plan-Administration Responsibilities

- Filing annual return or report (5500 or 5500-EZ)
- Filing annual premiums with PBGC (Form PBGC-1)
- Holding employee meetings
- Distributing SPDs to new participants
- Distributing summary annual report (SAR)
- Distributing SMM (if plan is amended)
- Furnishing personal benefit statements
- Counseling participants on participant options
- Handling benefit distributions
- Amending the plan when necessary

Special Issues Applicable to Keogh Plans

The rules for setting up and administering a qualified plan for a sole proprietor or partnership (still referred to as Keogh plans) are essentially the same as for a corporation. There are a few differences, however.

- A Keogh plan that satisfies the one-participant rule either files Form 5500-EZ or has no filing requirements if assets total $100,000 or less (see former discussion).
- A plan that covers only owners (and their spouses) may not be subject to ERISA, meaning that no summary plan description is required.

- The deductible contribution is calculated differently due to the "net income" calculation discussed in chapter 3.
- A letter or some other document should be used by a sole proprietorship or partnership to formally adopt the plan. This is the corollary to the corporate resolution that adopts the plan.

The following are some other considerations that are important when installing a Keogh plan:

- The role of the financial services professional takes on greater significance when the client establishes a Keogh plan because such clients typically do not have an administrative arm to carry out the multiple functions associated with plan installation and administration.
- Like corporate plans, a qualified plan must be established by December 31 (with a calendar year tax year) in order for a deduction to be taken for the year. Plan contributions, however, can be made up until the tax return deadline plus extensions. If the year has ended, it may still be possible to adopt a SEP (simplified employee pension), which can be established up to April 15 (or later if the taxpayer files an income tax extension).
- A business owner can shift documents from one master plan to a different one without incurring penalties. (*Planning Note:* If your client is currently under another organization's master Keogh plan, the possibility for a painless switch exists.)

ADDITIONAL ADMINISTRATIVE ISSUES

In the life of a tax-advantaged retirement plan, there are a number of other administrative issues that periodically need to be addressed. Here are several key items that come up on a regular basis.

Divorce

Retirement plans subject to ERISA must satisfy an anti-alienation rule, which generally prohibits a participant from assigning a pension plan asset to another individual. However, an exception to the anti-alienation rule exists in cases of divorce or legal separation. In this case, a plan is allowed to pay out benefits to an alternate payee (spouse, former spouse, child, or other dependent), but only subject to a court order, and only if the court order meets certain qualification requirements. These orders are referred to as *qualified domestic relations orders (QDROs).*

YOUR FINANCIAL SERVICES PRACTICE:
QUALIFIED DOMESTIC RELATIONS ORDERS

There are two ways in which a settlement of pension rights can be made under a qualified domestic relations order (QDRO):

- an immediate cash settlement (which is often made from nonpension sources)
- a settlement under which payments to the nonparticipant spouse are deferred until payments are due to the participant spouse

In both cases, valuation is fundamental. Before the parties can agree on how to divide the pension, its value must be determined. If the plan is a defined-contribution plan, valuation is relatively easy—the participant has an individual account and the plan sponsor must provide its value to the participant at least annually. However, if participation in the plan has extended over a period longer than the marriage, this amount must be reduced by a "coverture fraction" that is based on the relation between the length of the marriage and the duration of the plan coverage. This can be a simple mathematical ratio, or it can reflect rates of contribution and interest over time.

If the plan is a defined-benefit plan, the parties will probably need an actuary's assistance in determining the present dollar value of pension benefits. For a participant in a defined-benefit plan, the benefit at any time before retirement is expressed as an amount of expected pension at retirement age that the participant has accrued up to that point. For example, if the participant is aged 45, the plan might express his accrued benefit as "$10,000 per month beginning at age 65." In order to determine current worth, at age 45, an actuarial calculation must be made. In this calculation, the interest rate and mortality assumptions are critical. The assumptions do not necessarily have to be the same as those used by the plan for funding purposes. There is no federal standard for actuarial assumptions in this area, although PBGC interest rates for valuing plans on termination are sometimes used as guidelines. The total amount determined must also be multiplied by a coverture fraction, as for the defined-contribution plan where the participant was not married to the current (imminently departing) spouse during the entire time of his or her plan coverage.

Many open and controversial issues exist in these determinations. For example, should the valuation take taxes into account? What about inflation? Or possible future increases in the participant's salary? These are issues of state law that may vary and may not have been considered or decided by the state's courts. The use of an expert actuary is advisable, particularly in disputed cases, so that the actuarial assumptions and other valuation assumptions can be supported in court proceedings if necessary.

It is the plan administrator's duty to review court orders and determine whether they qualify as a QDRO. The plan administrator is required to establish procedures for reviewing a court order, and must notify all affected parties of the procedures when the plan receives a court order. If the order fails, as long as the parties made a good-faith effort to draft the order, the administrator should explain the deficiencies and work toward an order that satisfies the rules.

For a domestic relations order to be a QDRO, it must contain certain information, including:

- the name and address of the participant and each alternate payee
- the name of each plan affected by the order
- the amount of the benefit to be paid, which can be stated as a specific dollar amount or as a percentage of the total benefit, or use of some other methodology which allows the administrator to determine the amount to be paid out
- the number of payments to be made or the time period involved

Practically speaking, it is in everyone's best interest to ensure that court orders satisfy the QDRO requirements. The plan administrator's procedures should help the process and plans can (but are not required to) provide model language to the parties involved. The Department of Labor has drafted model QDRO documents that may be used. The DOL has very useful explanatory information at its Employee Benefit Security Administration website at www.dol.gov/ebsa.

Compliance Problems

No matter how well intentioned the sponsor and plan administrator, it is easy to fail to satisfy one of the many requirements that apply to qualified plans and other tax-sheltered vehicles. The types of problems that commonly occur include the following:

- The plan fails to include an employee who is an eligible participant under the terms of the plan.
- The plan fails to cover the number of employees required by the minimum coverage requirements.
- The plan fails to satisfy established loan procedures.
- The contribution or allocation formula does not satisfy the nondiscrimination requirements of Code Sec. 401(a)(4).
- The plan is not amended in a timely fashion when the law changes.
- The plan administrator does not follow the plan's terms.
- Plan assets are not contributed efficiently.
- The plan fails to file Form 5500 punctually.
- The plan engages in a prohibited transaction.

Over the last several years, both the IRS and the DOL have established voluntary compliance programs that reward plans for voluntarily correcting compliance problems. Today this means that when a compliance problem arises, the administrator should in most cases take the following steps:

- Determine how to correct the deficiency.
- Determine which rules have been violated and the penalties involved.
- Determine which IRS or DOL voluntary correction program prescribes how to successfully bring the plan back into compliance with the rules.
- Determine the voluntary compliance procedure, correct the problem, make any required government submissions, and pay any required fines.

As described below, the IRS and DOL compliance programs have now become extremely comprehensive and address almost every compliance problem that could arise. In this environment, the plan administrator should always consider entering into these programs, instead of waiting until the problem is discovered by an IRS or DOL plan audit.

Plan sponsors should also consider periodic audits of their plans by an objective third party. An independent review of the plan and its operation may turn up not only hidden problems in everyday operation but opportunities to improve benefits for participants or reduce plan administration costs.

Employee Plans Compliance Resolution System (EPCRS)

The IRS has a comprehensive system of correction programs for sponsors of retirement plans that have failed to meet the qualification requirements for a period of time. This system, the Employee Plans Compliance Resolution System (EPCRS), permits plan sponsors to correct these failures and thereby continue to provide their employees with retirement benefits on a tax-favored basis. In other words, the correction and sanctions are an alternative to disqualifying the plan. A plan sponsor that has compliance problems needs to review the program carefully to see the appropriate steps involved.

Because this program continues to evolve, it is best here to talk about the program more generally than specifically. First, it's helpful to understand that the IRS established EPCRS based on the following general principles:

- Sponsors and administrators should be encouraged to establish administrative practices and procedures that ensure that these plans are operated properly.

- Sponsors and administrators should satisfy the applicable plan document requirements of the Code.
- Plan sponsors and administrators should make voluntary and timely correction of any plan failures, whether involving discrimination in favor of highly compensated employees, plan operations, the terms of the plan document, or adoption of a plan by an ineligible employer. Timely and efficient correction protects participating employees by providing them with their expected retirement benefits, including favorable tax treatment.
- Voluntary compliance is promoted by providing for limited fees for voluntary corrections approved by the Service, thereby reducing employers' uncertainty regarding their potential tax liability and participants' potential tax liability.
- Fees and sanctions should be graduated in a series of steps so that there is always an incentive to correct promptly.
- Sanctions for plan failures identified on audit should be reasonable in light of the nature, extent, and severity of the violation.
- Administration of EPCRS should be consistent and uniform.
- Plan sponsors should be able to rely on the availability of EPCRS in taking corrective actions to maintain the tax-favored status of their plans.

EPCRS includes three different programs: the Self-Correction Program (SCP), the Voluntary Correction Program (VCP), and the Audit Closing Agreement Program (Audit CAP).

- *Self-correction (SCP).* A plan sponsor that has established compliance practices and procedures may, at any time, correct insignificant operational failures without paying any fee or sanction. In addition, in the case of a qualified plan that is the subject of a favorable determination letter or in the case of a 403(b) plan, the plan sponsor generally may correct even significant operational failures without payment of any fee or sanction. In most cases to qualify for self-correction the plan must have adopted practices and procedures to ensure compliance.
- *Voluntary correction with service approval (VCP).* With more serious types of compliance problems, a plan sponsor, at any time before audit, may pay a limited fee and receive the Service's approval for correction of the problem.
- *Correction on audit (Audit CAP).* If a failure is identified on audit, the plan sponsor may correct the failure and pay a sanction. The sanction imposed will bear a reasonable relationship to the nature,

extent, and severity of the failure, taking into account the extent to which correction occurred before audit.

Voluntary Fiduciary Correction Program (VFCP)

The DOL also sponsors a voluntary compliance program called the voluntary fiduciary correction program (VFCP). The VFCP is a voluntary enforcement program that encourages the correction of possible violations of Title I of ERISA. The program allows plan officials to identify and fully correct certain transactions, such as prohibited purchases, sales and exchanges, improper loans, delinquent participant contributions, and improper plan expenses. The program includes 18 specific transactions and their acceptable means of correction, eligibility requirements, and application procedures. If an eligible party documents the acceptable correction of a specified transaction, the U.S. Department of Labor will issue a no-action letter.

Delinquent Filers Voluntary Compliance Program (DVCP)

The VFCP does not address, however, penalties resulting from the late filing of Form 5500. For these type of violations, the DOL has established the Delinquent Filers Voluntary Compliance Program (DVCP). The program provides plan administrators with the opportunity to pay reduced civil penalties for voluntarily complying with the annual reporting requirements. For plans eligible for the program, compliance with the DVCP also results in the elimination of any penalties that the IRS is also allowed to impose for late filing of Form 5500. The program only applies to plans subject to Title I of ERISA, which means that most plans that only cover the owner and are required to file Form 5500-EZ are not eligible for the program.

CHAPTER REVIEW

Key Terms

enrollment meeting [13-1]
advance-determination letter [13-1]
notice to interested parties [13-1]
summary plan description (SPD)
    [13-1]

summary annual report (SAR)
    [13-2]
summary of material modification
    (SMM) [13-2]

Review Questions

Review questions are based on the learning objectives in this chapter. Thus, a [13-3] at the end of a question means that the question is based on learning objective 13-3. If there are multiple objectives, they are all listed.

1. What role does the financial services professional play in the plan-installation and plan-administration processes? [13-1]

2. What are the steps involved in adopting a corporate plan? [13-1]

3. Why is the summary plan description (SPD) frequently used as a means of fulfilling the employer's obligation to explain the plan to participants? [13-1]

4. Discuss the makeup of an SPD with regard to [13-1]
    a. the limitations on using the SPD as a marketing piece
    b. the plan provisions that it must explain

5. a. Who is typically appointed to be the plan administrator? [13-2]
    b. What individuals and organizations help the plan administrator manage the plan?

6. Identify each of the following: [13-2]
    a. Form 5500
    b. Schedule A of Form 5500
    c. Schedule SSA of Form 5500
    d. Form 5500-EZ
    e. Form PBGC-1

7. Describe the responsibility of the plan administrator with regard to [13-2]
    a. distributing the summary annual report
    b. issuing personal benefit statements
    c. counseling participants concerning plan options
    d. amending the plan document

8. How does the process of installation and administration of a Keogh plan differ from the installation and administration of a corporate plan? [13-2]

9. Describe the administrator's role when he or she is presented with a domestic relations order from a court ordering the division of a pension benefit. [13-3]

Plan Termination

Learning Objectives

An understanding of the material in this chapter should enable you to

14-1. Identify reasons for, alternatives to, and limitations on terminating a qualified retirement plan.

14-2. Describe the steps for terminating a defined-contribution plan.

14-3. Describe the steps for terminating a defined-benefit plan.

14-4. Identify the impact of reverting assets to the employer in a defined-benefit plan.

14-5. Explain what is unique about the distribution of plan assets at the time of plan termination.

14-6. Review the circumstances in which a plan may be terminated by operation of law.

Chapter Outline

Business owners who are contemplating the establishment of a retirement plan need to know that qualified plans must be permanent, rather than temporary, programs. The IRS seeks assurance that the plan is intended to meet the retirement needs of present and future employees rather than function as a tax shelter for key employees. This does not mean, however, that the business owner must be saddled with a plan indefinitely. If business conditions change substantially, the plan can still be terminated, as long as the plan has been drafted to reserve the employer's right to terminate it.

The term *plan termination* used herein means the complete dissolution of the plan: participants receive no additional plan benefits, contributions cease (after meeting remaining obligations), plan assets are liquidated, and benefits are distributed. The employer who is considering the termination of a plan may not be fully aware of the consequences and administrative burdens of such a decision. This chapter explores the procedures and ramifications of plan termination and reviews less drastic alternatives.

TO TERMINATE OR NOT TO TERMINATE

Why Plan Termination?

The employer may wish to terminate a plan for any number of business reasons, such as the following common ones:

- The employer is no longer in a financial position to make further plan contributions.
- The plan benefits are not meaningful amounts, and participants are limited in their ability to make deductible IRA contributions.
- The employer may want to switch plan designs (for example, switching from a defined-benefit to a defined-contribution approach) to lower plan costs and ease administrative complexity.
- The company may want to switch to an employee stock ownership plan (ESOP) to purchase the stock of a retiring owner.
- The employer may want to accommodate a substantial change in business operations, such as the sale or merger of the business.

Chapter 14   Plan Termination   **14.3**

Alternatives to Plan Termination

Plan termination is much more than simply ceasing additional employer contributions. It also means notifying proper governmental agencies, liquidating assets, and distributing funds to participants—all of which generate a great deal of paperwork and administrative expense. Before deciding to terminate a plan, the employer should consider other alternatives.

Ceasing Further Benefit Accruals

A defined-benefit or defined-contribution plan can be amended to cease further benefit accruals—as long as benefits already earned are not reduced. With defined-contribution plans, this strategy can be used to cease employer contributions. This approach may make sense to the employer who expects to resume making contributions later or who is concerned about participants squandering retirement benefits if they receive them now. Ceasing accruals in a defined-benefit plan does not always result in a complete cessation of contributions, depending upon the plan's funding status. Ceasing accruals will, however, limit the plan sponsor's future funding obligations.

Regardless of the type of plan involved, one issue that must always be considered is whether additional benefit accruals must be awarded for the current year. Under ERISA, benefit accruals cannot cease until 15 days after plan participants have been notified of the amendment. Therefore, the effective date of the amendment that ceases accruals must be a minimum of 15 days after notice is given. Once the effective date is established, a determination is made whether participants are entitled to another year of benefit accrual. The rule is that participants are entitled to an accrual if they meet all service eligibility requirements *prior to* the effective date of the amendment.

| *Example:* | Alpha Corporation maintains a money-purchase pension plan with a calendar plan year. The plan is amended to cease accruals effective September 1 (and participants are given notice of the amendment by the preceding August 15). If the plan awards a benefit accrual to participants who have completed 1,000 hours of service, full-time employees will have met the 1,000-hour requirement by September 1 and will be entitled to an accrual for the current plan year. |

An amendment ceasing accruals for current participants usually should include a provision prohibiting other employees from becoming new plan participants. Because new participants will not be eligible for any benefits, adding them simply compounds the administrative burden. Under the law, a plan that is not currently providing benefit accruals does not have to satisfy any minimum-coverage requirements, so prohibiting new members does not cause any coverage problems.

Effect on Defined-Benefit Plans. Ceasing further benefit accruals in a defined-benefit plan does not change the plan's essential nature—the plan is still required to pay promised benefits as they become due, employees continue to vest under the same vesting schedule,[1] and the employer is still required to meet the minimum funding obligations. If assets are not sufficient to meet the projected payouts, the actuary may determine that additional contributions are still necessary. Plans subject to the PBGC insurance program must continue paying insurance premiums. The rising costs of these premiums over the last few years could weigh in favor of terminating the plan versus discontinuing further benefit accruals.

Effect on Defined-Contribution Plans. In a money-purchase plan, or any other plan with required contributions, the only additional contributions necessary when accruals cease are those to fund the prior or current year's obligation.

Whether the same vesting provisions can continue to apply or whether full vesting occurs depends upon the type of plan involved. Any defined-contribution plan that is a pension plan (money-purchase and target-benefit plans) should be able to continue using the same vesting schedule. On the other hand, in profit-sharing plans, participants become fully vested when employer contributions are completely discontinued. (See below for a more complete discussion.)

Amending the Plan into Another Type

In some circumstances, the employer has the choice to amend the plan into another type of plan, rather than terminate the plan and start up a new one. This is a tricky area and legal consultation should be sought. However, some general guidelines can be provided. A defined-contribution plan of one type usually can be amended into another type of defined-contribution plan. For example, a money-purchase plan can be amended into a profit-sharing plan. The amendment must be carefully drafted to ensure that subtle differences between the types of plans are addressed.

Likewise, a defined-benefit plan of one type can be amended into another type of defined-benefit plan. In the large plan market, this sometimes happens when a traditional defined-benefit plan is amended into a cash-balance-type plan. One type of amendment is clearly prohibited: defined-benefit plans cannot be amended into defined-contribution plans, and defined-contribution plans cannot be amended into defined-benefit plans.

Limitations on Plan Termination

Several issues may discourage or prohibit the plan sponsor from terminating the plan. These issues are addressed below.

Temporary Tax Shelters

As a general rule, retirement plans may not be set up as a subterfuge to tax-shelter funds for the benefit of key employees. If they have been, plan termination can result in retroactive disqualification. For plans terminated within a few years after establishment, the IRS presumes the employer did not intend for the plan to be permanent. To rebut this assumption, the employer must provide a reason of "business necessity beyond the employer's control." Acceptable reasons for an early termination appear to be change in ownership by merger, liquidation or dissolution of the business, a change in ownership by sale or transfer, adverse business conditions, a significant change in the pension law, or a change in the company's retirement plan strategy, resulting in the adoption of a replacement plan. Practically speaking, the permanency issue is not a concern when the plan has been maintained for at least 10 years.

Insufficient Plan Assets

In defined-contribution plans, plan benefits are based upon the individual accounts, which represent all the assets held by the plan. This means that additional employer contributions are generally not required when a plan is terminated. However, for any plan that requires specified employer contributions, promised contributions that have not been made at the time of termination must still be made.

Defined-benefit plans, on the other hand, are a totally different story. In defined-benefit plans, assets never equal the present value of promised benefits. The plan will either have more than enough or not enough assets to pay promised benefits. When assets are insufficient to pay benefits, plans subject to the Pension Benefit Guaranty Corporation (PBGC) insurance program may not be able to be terminated at all. The PBGC has a financial interest at this point, and strict rules (described below) apply. If the plan cannot be terminated, the employer generally will want to amend the plan to cease all further benefit accruals to limit its future liability. If a plan with insufficient assets is not subject to the PBGC program, the plan may be terminated and strict rules on how plan assets are allocated to the participants apply. (The rules that apply to plans with excess assets are discussed more fully below.)

Plan Problems

Plan termination is a time when the IRS scrutinizes the operation of the plan. The plan sponsor should correct any compliance problems prior to considering plan termination. The IRS currently maintains a voluntary compliance program, which allows sponsors who are willing to correct compliance problems to do so with a minimum of penalties.

TERMINATING A DEFINED-CONTRIBUTION PLAN

Compared with the termination of a defined-benefit plan covered by the PBGC insurance program, termination of a defined-contribution plan is relatively easy. However, each of the following steps must be taken:

- A corporate resolution terminating the plan must be adopted, and the plan and trust must be amended to terminate further accruals. As discussed above, the issue of whether participants have accrued a benefit for the current year has to be carefully considered.
- The plan termination date must be scheduled at least 15 days after participants are notified. Because the termination effectively ceases benefit accruals, the ERISA rule requiring that participants be notified 15 days before the amendment becomes effective applies.
- The employer must make any remaining required contributions for the previous year or for this year's benefit accruals.
- Sometimes when the laws regarding qualified plans change, plan sponsors are allowed an extended period in which to incorporate amendments that reflect the new law. If this is the case at the time of a plan termination, conforming amendments should be added to the plan.
- Plan assets must be liquidated in preparation for distribution. Note that assets can be distributed in kind as long as the highly compensated employees are not given special treatment.
- Benefit distribution paperwork (described below) must be prepared.
- In the year that benefits are distributed, when the annual IRS Form 5500 is filed, it is marked as the "final form."

Submitting the Plan to the IRS

At the time of plan termination, the sponsor of a qualified plan can voluntarily request an IRS approval letter. If granted, the IRS letter states that the plan termination does not adversely affect the qualified status of the plan. Although the submission is voluntary, in recent history, the IRS has audited plans that terminate without the request of such a determination letter.

The determination letter gives the sponsor and plan participants the assurance that distributed benefits will be eligible for the special tax treatment afforded to qualified plans. Unfortunately, the IRS determination letter is not a guarantee that the plan will not be audited later. However, the auditing process should go more smoothly if the determination letter had been requested. For these reasons, it is generally a good idea for the plan sponsor to request the IRS determination letter.

To request a determination letter, the plan sponsor must complete and submit Form 5310. Also, all plan participants and beneficiaries must be given notice of the submission. In addition to announcing the submission, the notice should inform participants that they are allowed to send comments to the IRS or Department of Labor (DOL). Strict rules apply to who must receive the notice as well as how and when it is to be distributed.

TERMINATING A DEFINED-BENEFIT PLAN

An extremely complex termination procedure applies for defined-benefit plans covered under the PBGC insurance program. For plans that are not covered, the procedures are similar to those described above.

Plans Covered under the PBGC Insurance Program

Overview

The Pension Benefit Guaranty Corporation (PBGC) is a federal agency that insures participants against the loss of benefits that arise from complete or partial termination of a defined-benefit plan. When this agency was discussed in chapter 2, we mentioned that the PBGC

- covers all qualified defined-benefit plans (except for plans of professional-service employers with 25 or fewer active participants)
- collects compulsory premiums
- guarantees benefits (up to a maximum of approximately $4,000) in case of employer default

- oversees plan terminations initiated by the employer
- initiates terminations if a plan is financially strained
- taps up to 30 percent of the net worth of employers whose plans have terminated and left the PBGC liable for payments

Here, we will explore the PBGC's practices and requirements for plan terminations initiated voluntarily by the employer. However, note that the PBGC also has the right to terminate a plan in financial difficulty (as discussed further at the end of the chapter).

Voluntary Plan Termination

When an employer wishes to terminate a defined-benefit plan covered under the PBGC program, the employer faces three issues:

- Can the plan be voluntarily terminated?
- When can the plan be terminated?
- How can the plan be terminated?

The Single Employer Pension Plan Amendments Act (SEPPAA) addresses and provides answers to each of these questions. SEPPAA introduced a major change to the plan termination process. Now a plan can be terminated only if it meets specific conditions; if it does not, the plan must continue until the conditions are satisfied. Technically speaking, a termination is allowed only if the plan satisfies conditions for a standard or a distress termination.

standard
termination

Standard Termination. The employer can initiate a *standard termination* only if the plan has sufficient assets to pay all plan benefits. If the plan does not currently have sufficient assets, the plan may still qualify for a standard termination if the employer agrees to make up the difference with a single payment, or if a 50-percent owner of the company agrees to waive benefits due under the plan.

distress termination

Distress Termination. If the plan does not have sufficient assets to pay promised benefits, the plan may qualify—in extreme circumstances—for a *distress termination*. To qualify, the employer must fall within one of the following categories:

- It faces liquidation in bankruptcy or insolvency proceedings.
- It faces reorganization in bankruptcy or insolvency proceedings.
- It can demonstrate to the PBGC that it will be unable to pay its debts when due and will be unable to continue the business.

- It can prove that the cost of providing coverage has become unreasonably burdensome as a result of a decline in the workforce.

Setting the Termination Date. Assuming an employer is able to terminate the plan under SEPPAA, the next consideration is the termination date. This date has great importance because it establishes the limits on the employer's liability. The date is contingent upon notification of participants of the upcoming termination. The actual termination date must be from 60 to 90 days after the notification.

Steps in a Plan Termination. Once the date is established, in order to keep the termination date, all of the following PBGC-required procedures must be completed in a timely manner:

- the issuance of a notice of intent to terminate to participants and beneficiaries at least 60 days, and no more than 90 days, before the proposed termination date
- the filing of a notice of the termination on Form 500 (including an actuaries certificate that assets are sufficient to pay promised benefits) with the PBGC on or before the 180th day after the proposed termination date
- the distribution of assets to satisfy plan obligations within 180 days after the PBGC 60-day review period

In addition to the requirements established by the PBGC, the plan also must take each of the steps required for terminating a defined-contribution plan. To summarize, these include

- the adoption of a corporate resolution to terminate the plan and amendment of the plan and trust to terminate further accruals
- the making of any remaining required contributions
- the adoption of plan amendments to conform with law changes
- a decision as to whether to voluntarily request IRS approval on Form 5310 and notification of participants
- the liquidation of plan assets in preparation for distribution
- the preparation of benefit distribution paperwork (described below)
- the filing of the final 5500 annual return/report

Plans Not Covered under the PBGC Insurance Program

When a plan is not subject to PBGC regulation, it need not conform to the PBGC's rigid termination procedures. Because of this, a non-PBGC plan can be terminated even if it does not have sufficient assets to pay all of the plan benefits. When this is the case, the law prescribes a specific method for dividing the plan assets among the participants. In many cases, to avoid bad feelings (and potential lawsuits), the owners will decide to have all of the deficiency taken from their own benefits.

The administrative burden is not as great with the non-PBGC plan because the PBGC filing requirements do not have to be satisfied. However, the sponsor does have to take all of the steps required for terminating a defined-contribution plan, as described above.

Reversion of Excess Plan Assets

As stated earlier, a defined-benefit plan may, at any point in time, have more assets than necessary to pay benefits promised under the plan. This generally occurs when plan assets outperform the actuaries' assumptions. Before the mid-1980s, an employer could terminate a plan and receive an asset reversion from an overfunded terminated defined-benefit plan without penalty (although the amount was and still is treated as taxable income to the employer).

However, beginning in the mid-1980s, the law began to make the practice of terminating plans to recover surplus assets less desirable by adding penalty taxes to the amount of excess assets returned to the employer. Congress took its strongest action to date in promoting these goals when it passed the Revenue Reconciliation Act of 1990. The Act (Code Subsection 4980) created a 50 percent excise tax on all reversions except when the employer shares the reversion with employees, in which case the excise tax is only 20 percent.

To qualify for the 20 percent tax rate, the employer must either (1) establish a qualified replacement plan to which it transfers assets equal to 25 percent of the reversion or (2) provide pro rata increases in benefits of qualified participants in connection with the plan termination equal to at least 20 percent of the reversion.

Note that in order to revert plan assets to the employer, the plan must specifically state that excess assets will revert at the time of plan termination. Under a recent law change, a plan that does not have such a provision may not be amended to do so at the time of the termination.

When a plan has excess assets, the employer is not under any obligation to revert the excess. The assets may be, and often are, allocated among plan participants. The law provides some discretion in the allocation method, and the actuary should provide several alternatives. In the small-plan setting, the actuary generally looks for a method that allocates the lion's share of the excess to the business owner. This can work quite well, unless the owner's benefit is already approaching the maximum benefit limitations. If the owner can get a significant piece of the excess, the reallocation method has clear tax advantages—benefits can be rolled into an IRA and tax deferral can continue. On the other hand, if the owner's share of the excess is limited, he or she may prefer the reversion approach.

DISTRIBUTIONS FROM A TERMINATING PLAN

In one significant way, the process of distributing plan benefits at the time of plan termination is different than in other situations. If the plan is to pay single-sum benefits, then the paperwork involved is the same as for normal benefit payouts. On the other hand, if participants are to receive deferred annuity payments at retirement, the plan purchases deferred annuities and much of the normal distribution paperwork will be completed at the time the annuity begins.

The form of benefit payout at plan termination depends solely upon the terms of the plan. If the plan does not offer a lump-sum option, the employer purchases a single-premium annuity contract (SPAC) from an insurance company, and all benefit payouts are made through that contract. If the plan does offer a lump-sum option, participants must be given a choice to receive a single sum or the deferred annuity. At the employer's election, a single-sum option can be added at the time of termination; however, such an option may not be removed. In most cases, when a plan has a lump-sum option, participants elect this option.

The employer who is considering the addition of a lump-sum option in a defined-benefit plan should do so carefully. Under the law, single-sum benefits are calculated by using the lower of the plan's specified interest rate or a rate specified by the PBGC. When interest rates in the market are low, the PBGC rate can also be quite low. Therefore, in many cases, the provision of benefits in the form of a lump sum can prove to be more expensive than the purchase of a deferred annuity.

Single-Premium Annuity Contracts (SPACs)

single-premium annuity contract

Employers who wish to purchase paid-up annuities to satisfy the distribution obligation from a terminating plan purchase a *single-premium annuity contract*. SPACs are issued through group pension departments of insurance companies and sold to plans that are terminating. In return for the single premium, the insurance company assumes the transferred plan liabilities and issues annuity certificates that ensure participants receive their benefits.

At the time that participants retire, they choose a distribution option from among the various ones available. The law requires that the SPAC distribution options match the original plan distribution options. At the time of payout, the insurer provides election forms, qualified joint and survivor notices, and so on.

SPACs are typically difficult for an insurer to price (that is, to determine how much money is required from the employer to pay the benefit obligations under the plan). The insurer must first assess the liabilities under the plan, a process complicated by discrepancies in terminology from plan to plan and the presence of any atypical design features. The second step, finding the present value of future obligations, can be even trickier. At this stage, the insurer must apply assumptions with regard to interest return, mortality, early retirement (which is particularly important if the early-retirement benefit is subsidized), and other variables. A third difficult aspect of pricing a SPAC lies with the one-time expense charge. Theoretically, the employer could be making benefit payments 50 years or more in the future. Determining expenses for that length of time can be almost impossible. All of these pricing difficulties affect the insurance company because (1) the single premium required can vary significantly from company to company, (2) a SPAC that is priced too high will not be competitive and, (3) a SPAC that is priced too low will lose money.

With the failure of several insurance companies, note that the DOL is quite concerned about the choice of carriers when a SPAC is purchased. The employer and other plan fiduciaries may be held personally liable if the insurer cannot pay up—if it is determined that the fiduciaries did not use reasonable care when choosing the carrier. On a practical level, this means the fiduciaries should

- obtain several SPAC quotes
- document how and why the particular choice was made
- review the company's insurance ratings by using a number of rating services
- be especially careful when they choose a lower quote, if that insurer is also rated lower than the competition
- consider hiring independent consultants to further analyze the company's financial condition

Remember that fiduciaries are not liable simply if the insurer fails—only if they behaved in an imprudent manner.

Distribution Paperwork

If the plan does not allow lump-sum payments and a SPAC is being purchased, participants do not make a distribution election at the time of the termination. The actual benefit election is made at retirement. However, if participants have the option to receive a lump sum, then the paperwork is similar to any other plan distribution (discussed in detail in the previous chapter). The following summarizes the various items that must be given to and completed by participants:

- benefit election form
- notice and election forms for applicable qualified joint and survivor annuity rules
- notice and election forms for the right to have benefits transferred directly to an IRA or other qualified plan
- IRS Form 1099-R for lump-sum distributions

TERMINATIONS BY OPERATION OF LAW

In the preceding part of this chapter, we discussed plan terminations initiated by the employer. Here, we discuss a quite different topic: plan terminations that occur due to the operation of law. This may occur in three separate situations:

- a partial termination of any qualified plan, resulting from a sudden reduction in the number of plan participants or a reduction in plan benefits
- the termination of a profit-sharing plan as a result of a complete discontinuance of contributions
- the involuntary termination of a defined-benefit plan by the PBGC

Finally, we will discuss one other situation that arises periodically, abandoned plans. These typically are defined-contribution plans of employers that go out of business or otherwise terminate, so that there is essentially no employer entity to terminate the plan. The Department of Labor has established a procedure to liquidate plans for such financial services firms.

Partial Terminations

partial plan termination

As mentioned previously, when a plan is terminated, the Tax Code requires that plan benefits become fully vested. This rule also applies to those participants who are affected by a *partial plan termination*. Unfortunately, this term is not defined in the Code. Under the regulations, the decision whether a partial termination exists is based on a review of all the facts and circumstances. The factors in this determination are

- whether the number of plan participants has been substantially reduced, *and*
- whether plan amendments have adversely affected the rights of employees to vest in benefits under the plan.

When there is a reduction in the number of participants, there is no specified number or percentage drop that triggers a partial termination. Each case is decided by the facts and circumstances. However, any time plan participation drops by more than 20 percent, corporate counsel should look into the issue. Drop-offs in participation may occur due to layoff, an amendment excluding previously eligible participants, or (in rare occurrences) voluntary termination of employment. Under the various cases and rulings, a partial termination is certainly more likely if the reduction is within the employer's control; however, the IRS has indicated that a partial termination may exist even when participants terminated employment voluntarily. The result of a determination that a partial termination exits is that all participants eliminated from the plan become fully vested.

Reduction in the number of participants is the most likely scenario in which the partial termination issue will arise. However, amendments that adversely affect participants' rights to vest can result in a partial termination. A partial termination can also occur in a defined-benefit plan if the reduction (or cessation) of benefit accruals results in—or increases the possibility of—a reversion to the employer.

Profit-Sharing Plans

The same Code section that governs partial terminations states that in profit-sharing-type plans (which include 401(k) plans and ESOPs), participants become fully vested at the time of a complete "discontinuance of contributions." Again, the determination is based on a facts-and-circumstances test. In making the determination, the IRS considers whether contributions have been recurring and substantial, and whether there is any reasonable probability that the lack of contributions will continue indefinitely. This vague standard makes it difficult for the sponsor to determine whether the rule applies in a particular case. As a practical matter, the issue should be reviewed if no substantial contributions are made to a plan for 2 years or more.

The IRS—especially at the time a plan terminates—will definitely review the complete discontinuance issue. In many situations, plans are terminated well after the date that contributions have ceased. In this scenario, the IRS is likely to determine that benefits became fully vested at the time contributions stopped, not when the plan was actually terminated. Such a determination can cause major headaches when forfeited benefits have already been reallocated to other participants.

Involuntary Terminations of Defined-Benefit Plans

In the case of a defined-benefit plan covered by the PBGC insurance program, the PBGC has the right to involuntarily terminate a plan in very limited circumstances. The reason it does so is to protect itself from mounting liabilities under a plan that shows no promise of meeting its obligations. The PBGC can institute termination proceedings if it determines that the interests of the plan participants would be better served by the termination, and if any one of the following occurs:

- Minimum funding standards have not been satisfied.
- Benefits cannot be paid when they are due.
- A substantial lump-sum payment has been made to a substantial owner who is a plan participant.
- The long-run liability of the company to the PBGC is expected to increase unreasonably.

Abandoned Plan Program

Significant business events such as bankruptcies, mergers, acquisitions, and other similar transactions affecting the status of an employer can result in employers, particularly small employers, abandoning their individual-account retirement plans such as 401(k) plans. When this happens, custodians such as banks, insurers, and mutual fund companies are left holding the assets of the abandoned plans without the authority to terminate and distribute benefits. In these situations, participants and beneficiaries have great difficulty accessing the benefits they have earned.

In response, the Labor Department's Employee Benefits Security Administration (EBSA) has issued regulations (1) establishing standards for determining when a plan is abandoned, (2) identifying simplified procedures for winding up the plan and distributing benefits to participants and beneficiaries, and (3) providing guidance on who may initiate and carry out the winding-up process. Information about the program is available under the Abandoned Plan Program section of EBSA's web site at www.dol.gov/ebsa.

Abandoned Plans

A plan generally will be considered abandoned if no contributions or distributions from the plan have been made for a period of at least 12 consecutive months and it is determined that the sponsor no longer exists, cannot be located, or is unable to maintain the plan. Only a qualified termination administrator (QTA) may determine whether a plan is abandoned under the regulations. To be a QTA, an entity must hold the plan's assets and be eligible as a trustee or issuer of an individual retirement plan under the Internal Revenue Code. An eligible entity could be a bank, trust company, mutual fund family, or insurance company.

Termination and Winding-Up Process

The regulations establish specific procedures that QTAs must follow, including:

- Notifying EBSA prior to, and after, terminating a plan.
- Locating and updating plan records.
- Calculating benefits payable to participants and beneficiaries.
- Notifying participants and beneficiaries of the termination, their rights and options.
- Distributing benefits to participants and beneficiaries.
- Filing a summary terminal report.

A QTA is not required to amend a plan to accommodate the termination. The regulations include model notices that the QTA may use.

Fiduciary Liability

The regulations establish a fiduciary safe harbor for distributions from terminating individual account plans (whether or not abandoned) on behalf of missing participants. In most cases, the account of a missing participant will be transferred directly to an individual retirement plan. QTAs that follow the regulations will be considered to have satisfied the prudence requirements of ERISA with respect to winding-up activities. Also, a QTA does not have an obligation to conduct an inquiry or review to determine whether or what breaches of fiduciary responsibility may have occurred with respect to a plan prior to becoming the QTA. A QTA is not required to collect delinquent contributions on behalf of the plan, provided that the QTA informs EBSA of known delinquencies.

Accompanying the regulations is a class exemption that provides relief from ERISA's prohibited transaction restrictions. The exemption covers transactions where the QTA selects and pays itself

- for services rendered prior to becoming a QTA
- to provide services in connection with terminating and winding up an abandoned plan

- for distributions from abandoned plans to IRAs or other accounts maintained by the QTA resulting from a participant's failure to provide direction

Annual Reporting Relief

The regulations provide annual reporting relief, under which QTAs are not responsible for filing a Form-5500 Annual Report on behalf of an abandoned plan, either in the terminating year or any previous plan years. However, the QTA must complete and file a summary terminal report at the end of the winding-up process.

CHAPTER REVIEW

Key Terms

standard termination [14-3]   partial plan termination [14-6]
distress termination [14-3]   involuntary terminations [14-6]
single-premium annuity contract
   (SPAC) [14-5]

Review Questions

Review questions are based on the learning objectives in this chapter. Thus, a [14-3] at the end of a question means that the question is based on learning objective 14-3. If there are multiple objectives, they are all listed.

1. Explain the reasons employers typically terminate a qualified plan. [14-1]

2. Identify alternatives to plan termination. [14-1]

3. What problems can get in the way of a plan termination? [14-1]

4. Describe the steps required for terminating a defined-contribution plan. [14-2]

5. Explain why the employer should consider submitting the plan for IRS approval upon plan termination. [14-2]

6. What is the major difference between terminating defined-benefit plans covered by the PBGC and terminating those that are not covered? [14-3]

7. What does the employer have to do to qualify for the lower 20 percent reversion excise tax? [14-4]

8. Describe a single-premium annuity contract (SPAC). [14-5]

9. Identify the three situations in which a termination by operation of law can occur. [14-6]

NOTE

1. Participants may have to become fully vested in accordance with the rule discussed in the section on partial plan terminations. Under this rule, full and immediate vesting is only an issue if the plan has excess assets at the time the amendment is adopted.

Nonqualified Retirement Plans: An Overview

Learning Objectives

An understanding of the material in this chapter should enable you to

---

15-1. Compare nonqualified plans with qualified plans.

15-2. Discuss the tax implications of a nonqualified plan.

15-3. Choose the appropriate nonqualified plan for the employer.

15-4. Identify the key design considerations when establishing a nonqualified plan.

15-5. Review the funding requirements and the advantages of funding with life insurance.

15-6. Describe how a plan can be designed to better protect the interests of the participants.

15-7. Discuss the installation and administration concerns for nonqualified plans.

15-8. Explain when Code Sec. 457 applies to a deferred-compensation arrangement.

15-9. Describe an executive-bonus life insurance plan.

Chapter Outline

Up to this point, the emphasis has been on the use of a tax-sheltered retirement plan to meet the needs of the small business and the small-business owner. However, a second lucrative market is open to financial services professionals who are servicing the retirement needs of the business and the business owner. This market is the nonqualified plan market, which includes nonqualified deferred-compensation plans and executive-bonus plans. These plans help the business owner and selected employees save for retirement without being subject to the requirements that apply to qualified plans. As a trade-off for allowing the employer complete discretion in plan design and in choosing the employees who will be covered by the plan, the employer loses the central advantage of a qualified plan—that is, the ability to make a before-tax contribution on the employee's behalf that is simultaneously deductible to the business. Instead, the employer is entitled to an immediate deduction only if the employee is currently taxed, or conversely, the employee may defer tax only if the employer's deduction is deferred.

This chapter will also review many of the issues involved in the implementation of nonqualified plans. The questions that must be addressed include the following:

- Is it more advantageous for a cost-conscious client to use a qualified or a nonqualified plan?
- What tax considerations underlie the use, design, and funding of a nonqualified plan?
- Should a plan be funded, unfunded, or informally funded?
- Should a rabbi trust be used, and if so, how can it be designed in a state-of-the-art manner?
- Should a secular trust or a surety bond be used to secure payments under a nonqualified plan?
- What are the ERISA implications of using nonqualified plans?
- How are nonqualified plans installed and administered?
- Should life insurance products be used to pay for nonqualified plan benefits?

It is only after understanding these issues that we can accurately serve our clients' needs.

**YOUR FINANCIAL SERVICES PRACTICE:
THE ALLURE OF THE NONQUALIFIED MARKET**

Several factors prompt financial services professionals to become involved in the nonqualified market. Some get involved because nonqualified deferred-compensation and executive-bonus plans help them to provide comprehensive services to their clients. A combination of life insurance, individual annuities, qualified plans, and nonqualified plans allows the financial services professional to provide a comprehensive umbrella of retirement coverage. Others prefer the nonqualified market because it means contact with an upscale clientele, and this, in turn, provides networking opportunities. A third reason to be involved is that life insurance is often the most appropriate funding vehicle.

Nonqualified deferred-compensation plans are sometimes referred to as salary continuation plans, deferred-compensation plans, or nonqualified plans. These aliases, however, can be misleading because they all have other meanings. For example, the term *salary continuation plan* is sometimes used to refer to sick days and disability benefits. Likewise, *deferred compensation* sometimes refers to qualified pension and profit-sharing plans. The term *nonqualified plans* can refer to a myriad of plans that fail to meet various qualification standards. Because we will discuss only nonqualified deferred-compensation plans in chapter 15, we will call them nonqualified plans for short. In the marketplace, however, it is wise to make sure everybody is on the same wavelength and is not tripped up by the confusing nomenclature.

NONQUALIFIED VERSUS QUALIFIED PLANS

As we have seen, qualified pension and profit-sharing plans are retirement plans that meet standards set out in the Employee Retirement Income Security Act (ERISA) and Internal Revenue Code. The major requirements for qualification have been identified and discussed in earlier chapters. As a payback for adhering to these burdensome rules, plan contributions are immediately deductible by the employer, earnings on plan funds are tax deferred, and, when qualified plan funds are distributed to employees, tax-saving strategies such as forward averaging and rollovers may be available. The "White Collar" example in chapter 1 illustrates the vast economic gain available through this tax-saving "interest-free loan."

TABLE 15-1
Qualified and Nonqualified Plans Compared

Characteristic	Qualified Plan	Nonqualified Plan
Tax deferred to employee	Yes—always	Yes (unless considered funded)
Tax consequences to employer	Immediate deduction	Deduction deferred (unless considered funded)
Earnings accumulate tax free	Yes—always	No (unless tax shelter used)
Special tax treatment at retirement for employee	Yes (rollovers and forward averaging)	No
Ability to lower costs by only covering selected employees	No (must meet nondiscrimination rules)	Yes—always
Plan administration requirements	Burdensome and expensive	Minimal and inexpensive
Reporting and disclosure requirements	Burdensome and expensive	Minimal and inexpensive
Ability to attract, retain, and motivate employees	Effective	More effective

In contrast, a nonqualified plan cannot simultaneously give the employer the benefit of an immediate tax deduction and give the employee the benefit of a tax deferral. Most nonqualified plans are structured to defer the taxation of retirement benefits for executives. Unlike qualified plans, however, nonqualified deferred-compensation plans postpone the employer's deduction until the benefit has been paid to the executive and has been included in his or her income. In addition, earnings on money put aside to fund the plan will be taxed in the year it is earned unless a tax shelter, such as life insurance, is used. Finally, distributions from nonqualified plans cannot be rolled over to delay taxation (see table 15-1).

Despite the dismal tax comparison, nonqualified plans are favored over qualified plans in many cases for a variety of reasons, including

- design flexibility (see below)
- lower administrative costs
- cost-saving discriminatory coverage

This last reason is perhaps the chief motivation for an employer to install a nonqualified plan. Business owners claim they can save significant sums of money by excluding rank-and-file employees from the plan. In the minds of many employers, the tax savings garnered under a qualified plan are overshadowed by the ability to avoid paying benefit costs for the majority of their employees. A short case study helps to illustrate this point (see also table 15-1).

Case Study: The Smallco Company

Smallco is a company of 10 people and is owned by two sisters. The sisters earn a salary of $100,000 each; the payroll for the additional employees is $240,000 (average salary, $30,000). If Smallco were to install a profit-sharing plan that provides a benefit of 25 percent of salary to all employees, the qualified plan would cost $110,000 plus administrative expenses ($110,000 equals 25 percent of the total payroll of $440,000). If Smallco were to provide a 25 percent nonqualified plan for the two owners and no benefits for the other employees, however, then the cost to the plan would be reduced to $50,000 plus the cost of deferring the deduction.

Determining the Cost of Deferring the Deduction

Smallco is in the 34 percent marginal tax bracket. The deferral of the deduction would thus immediately cost Smallco 34 cents on every dollar put

---

YOUR FINANCIAL SERVICES PRACTICE:
EFFECTIVE COMPENSATION PLANNING

Clients often mistakenly believe that implementing a qualified plan will increase costs because the benefits are an additional compensation—sort of a windfall—for rank-and-file employees. This commonly held opinion is correct only if benefits are an increase to the overall compensation package. If benefits are a piece of what is already being paid to an employee, however, employer costs are not increased. In other words, the employer should focus on how employees are paid, not on how much he or she pays them. Effective compensation planning dictates that employers give employees (and themselves) the opportunity to save for retirement with the tax advantages that are only available through a qualified plan. Unfortunately, for many employers it is the perception that counts, not the reality.

One way to satisfy stubborn prospects is to *gradually* shift current compensation to deferred compensation. This can be accomplished by lowering future salary increases by a small percentage, which will be used to fund a deferred-compensation plan.

---

into the plan. Because $50,000 is being contributed, Smallco would thus "lose" $17,000 in tax savings (34 percent tax rate multiplied by the $50,000 contribution). In addition, Smallco loses the amount it could have gained by investing the $17,000. This, of course, will be offset by the amount that will be deducted when the benefits are paid. There is no way to accurately predict the employer's cost for deferring the deduction because of the interest and time assumptions that must be used (not to mention potential shifts in tax rates). But even assuming that it costs Smallco $1.40 (a conservatively high figure) to provide $1 in benefits, the total plan cost in real dollars will only be $70,000. This amount is $40,000 less than what the qualified plan would cost. In addition, Smallco's administrative costs will be significantly lower.

TAX CONSIDERATIONS

With nonqualified plans, the employer receives a deduction at the time that the participant has taxable income. In almost all cases, the plan is designed to defer income tax to the participants until distributions are made. Tax can generally be deferred as long as the deferred compensation is subject to a substantial risk of forfeiture.

A substantial risk of forfeiture is a significant limitation or duty that requires the fulfillment of a meaningful effort by the executive, and there must be a definite possibility that the event that will cause the forfeiture could occur. A traditional vesting provision is clearly a substantial risk of forfeiture. Requiring that an executive continue to provide consulting services to a company after retirement may or may not be a substantial risk of forfeiture, depending upon the specific facts and circumstances.

Economic Benefit Doctrine

If the benefit is not subject to a risk of forfeiture, taxes can still be deferred as long as the distribution does not run afoul of the economic benefit doctrine generally codified in Code Sec. 83 or the constructive receipt doctrine now codified in Code Sec. 409A. Under the economic-benefit doctrine, an *economic* (or financial) *benefit* conferred on an executive as compensation should be included in the person's income to the extent that the benefit has an ascertainable fair market value. In other words, if a compensation arrangement provides a current economic benefit to an executive, that person must report the value of the benefit even if he or she has no current right to receive the benefit.

The economic benefit doctrine means that if a contribution is made to an irrevocable trust for a participant and the benefit is nonforfeitable, the amount will be subject to income tax. This is one reason that nonqualified plan benefits are not as secure as those under a qualified plan. To avoid current income tax, any assets held to pay benefits must remain the property of the sponsor, or be placed in a trust that can be accessed to satisfy the claims of the sponsor's creditors (typically called a rabbi trust).

Code Sec. 409A

Another doctrine that may affect the deferral of the taxable event is the constructive receipt doctrine. Code Sec. 409A has codified the constructive receipt rules. Technically, the Code provision states that deferred amounts that are not subject to a substantial risk of forfeiture are currently includible in gross income and are subject to an additional 20 percent penalty tax unless they meet certain distribution, acceleration of distribution, and deferral election rules. These requirements must be contained in the plan document governing the nonqualified plan.

Distribution Rule

Under a nonqualified plan, distributions may not be made earlier than one of the following events:

- Separation from service. Moreover, if the employee is a "key employee" of a publicly traded company, as defined under the top-heavy rules of Code Sec. 416(i), a distribution upon separation from service may not begin until 6 months after separation.

- Disability. Disability is defined as either the strict Social Security definition of total and permanent disability, or disability under an accident and health plan covering employees of the employer, under certain conditions.
- Death of the employee.
- A time specified under the plan.
- A change in ownership or control, which proposed regulations indicate occurs on the date that a person or several individuals acting as a group acquires enough additional stock to own more than 50 percent of the total fair market value or total voting power of the corporation's stock.
- Occurrence of an unforeseeable emergency.

Proposed regulations state that an occurrence of an unforeseeable emergency includes a severe financial hardship to the participant, a spouse, a dependant, and in some cases a primary beneficiary resulting from an illness or accident, and loss of the participant's property due to casualty or other similar extraordinary and unforeseeable circumstances that are beyond the participant's control. For example, the imminent foreclosure of the participant's primary residence may constitute an unforeseeable emergency. In addition, the need to pay for medical expenses, including nonrefundable deductibles, as well as for the costs of prescription drug medication, may constitute an unforeseeable emergency. Finally, the need to pay for the funeral expenses of a spouse or a dependent may also constitute an unforeseeable emergency. However, the purchase of a home and the payment of college tuition are generally not unforeseeable emergencies.

The amount cannot exceed the amount necessary for the emergency plus taxes on the distribution, and distributions are not allowed to the extent that the hardship may be relieved through reimbursement or by liquidation of the participant's assets.

Acceleration of Distributions

Sec. 409A does not permit any acceleration of the time payments under the nonqualified plan, except as allowed by regulatory guidance. The IRS has created a number of exceptions, including:

- Payments made to meet the requirements of a domestic relations order.
- Payments that are necessary to satisfy the conflict of interest divestiture requirements.

- A *de minimis* cashout rule allowing the cashing out of the remaining interest in a plan as long the amount does not exceed $10,000. The cashout must be made before the later of 2½ months after termination of employment or December 31 of the year of termination of employment.
- Payments for FICA taxes.

Employees' Elections to Defer

An election to defer compensation for a particular year must generally be made not later than the close of the preceding taxable year. For the first year of eligibility, the election may be made with respect to services to be performed beginning within 30 days after eligibility for participation. For performance-based compensation based on services performed over a period of at least 12 months, the election may be made no later than 6 months before the end of the period.

These election rules require that the time and form of distributions must be specified at the time of initial deferral. The plan can either specify the form and timing or give participants a choice. A limited exception allows a participant to further delay payment of an existing benefit as long as the election is made at least 12 months before it becomes effective.

Code Sec. 83

In the typical nonqualified plan where the employee simply has a contractual right to receive money in the future and even if the plan uses informal funding, as discussed below, Sec. 83 is not a consideration. However, if a nonqualified plan becomes funded, Sec. 83 will control the tax consequences of the plan.

Sec. 83 of the Code taxes the transfer of property in connection with the performance of services. If, in connection with the performance of services, property is transferred to a person other than the person for whom the services are performed, the excess of (i) the property's fair market value at the first time the rights of the person having the beneficial interest in the property are transferable or are not subject to a substantial risk of forfeiture, whichever occurs first, over (ii) the amount, if any, paid for the property becomes taxable income to the person providing the services. For this purpose, property is defined to include real and personal property, other than money or an unfunded and unsecured promise to pay money in the future. Property also includes a beneficial interest in assets (including money) which are transferred or set aside from the claims of the transferor's creditors—for example, in a trust or escrow account.

Code Sec. 3121(v)(2)

Code Sec. 3121(v)(2) provides a special timing rule for determining when amounts deferred under a nonqualified plan must be designated as wages for purposes of the employment taxes imposed by the Federal Insurance Contributions Act (FICA) (unlike the regular income tax provisions, which generally require income recognition when deferred amounts are actually or constructively received). The special timing rule states that an amount deferred under a nonqualified plan must be considered wages for employment tax purposes as of the later of the date the services are performed, or when there is no substantial risk of forfeiture of the rights to such amount—even if the deferred amount is not subject to income taxes at that time. There is also a nonduplication rule which generally provides that once a deferred amount is taken into account for employment tax purposes, neither that amount nor income attributable to it will be treated as FICA wages in the future.

Once it is determined that benefits are being provided under a nonqualified plan, the determination of the deferred amount that will be subject to employment taxes depends on whether the amounts are held in an account balance plan or a nonaccount balance plan. An account balance plan is one in which

- principal amounts are credited to an individual account for an employee.
- the income attributable to the principal amounts is credited (or debited) to the individual account.
- the benefits payable to the employee are based solely on the balance credited to the individual account.

Under an account-balance plan, the amount taken into account as wages is the principal amount that is credited to the executive's account, increased (or decreased) by income (or loss) attributable to that amount through the date the amount is required to be taken into account as FICA wages.

Example: Under Woodsworth Company's nonqualified plan for employee Frank Myers, 10 percent of his annual compensation is credited on his behalf on December 31 of each year. In addition, a reasonable rate of interest is credited quarterly on the balance credited to Frank as of the last day of the preceding quarter. All amounts credited under the plan are 100% percent vested after Frank completes 5 years of service. The benefits payable to Frank are based solely on the balance credited to his account under the plan. Frank was hired on March 1, 2003, and began participation in the plan on January 1, 2004. When Frank becomes vested in 2008, his account under the plan has a balance of $88,456 as of December 31, 2007. The company must treat the $88,456 account balance as wages for employment tax purposes for 2008.

A nonaccount balance plan, such as a defined-benefit plan, does not meet the requirements for an account-balance plan. In a nonaccount balance plan, the amount taken into account is the present value of the future payments to which the executive has obtained a legally binding right (that is, he or she has met the vesting requirement). The income attributable to the amount taken into account is defined as the increase, due to the passage of time, in the present value of any future payments to which the executive has a legally binding right. Employers may use any reasonable actuarial assumptions and methods in determining present value. Moreover, an employer can elect not to take into account any amount, even if vested, unless the value is "reasonably ascertainable." An amount is "reasonably ascertainable" when there are no actuarial or other assumptions needed to determine the amount deferred other than interest, mortality, or cost-of-living assumptions.

Example: Software Development, Inc., has a fully vested nonqualified plan that gives Bill Vista, now aged 45, the right to a $500,000 lump sum benefit at age 65. The amount deferred is reasonably ascertainable because only interest and mortality assumptions are needed to determine it. If the $500,000 is instead payable to Bill at the later of age 55 or his termination of employment, the amount deferred will no longer be reasonably ascertainable because the present value of the benefit is contingent on when Bill terminates his employment.

Due to the potential mismatch of income and employment taxes, employment taxes should not be an afterthought in planning for deferred compensation. Tax planning that considers income tax consequences but neglects employment taxes is inadequate. The combined employment tax rate for employers and employees is 15.3% percent on wages up to the taxable wage base, but it falls to 2.9 percent on wages over the taxable wage base. Thus, timing is an important factor in planning for the avoidance of employment taxes. To the extent possible, deferred amounts should be treated as wages under Sec. 3121(v)(2) after an executive has earned more than the taxable wage base for the year.

Finally, nonprofit organizations and governments have different tax considerations than do their taxable counterparts. These considerations are discussed below as part of the material on Sec. 457 plans.

CHOOSING A NONQUALIFIED PLAN

Choosing the right nonqualified plan requires that the advisor considers the employer's objectives and understands the various options available.

Determining the Company's Needs

The nonqualified market is a very important part of a financial services practice in the retirement field because it allows financial services professionals to deal successfully with client situations that are otherwise unsolvable, such as the following:

- The client wants to provide a second tier of executive retirement benefits in addition to the qualified plan in order to attract and retain strong executives.
- The client wants to limit coverage to certain executives.
- The client wants a plan that is less of an administrative burden than a qualified plan.
- The client wants to give executives the opportunity to save more of their current income. Sometimes the program dovetails with a 401(k) plan, and only salary deferrals above the 401(k) plan go into the nonqualified program.
- The client is an owner of a closely held business who is looking to temporarily save taxes and may want to have income retained in the company. This makes sense when the corporate tax rate is lower than the individual tax rate. Note, however, that the IRS may challenge a plan that allows a controlling (50 percent) shareholder to defer compensation.[1]
- The client is the owner of a closely held business that is just starting up and the company lacks the cash to pay owner-employees their full salaries. Making the promise to pay the executive compensation later establishes the obligation to pay additional income and helps avoid problems with the IRS about "reasonable compensation" in later years when the owners are receiving large payouts.

- The client wants to meet the organization's objectives of attracting executives, retaining executives, and providing for a graceful transition in company leadership. Although qualified plans can achieve similar objectives, nonqualified plans can be more effective because they are subject to fewer design restrictions.

NONQUALIFIED PLAN FACT FINDER

Client Name: _____

Step 1: Identify concerns

Listed below are some typical concerns that organizations have when instituting a nonqualified plan. Grade each of these concerns by scoring 1 for very valuable, 2 for valuable, 3 for moderately valuable, and 4 for least valuable.

1. Avoid the nondiscrimination requirements of a qualified plan. [1][2][3][4]
2. Allow executives to defer current income for their own tax-shelter purposes. [1][2][3][4]
3. Exceed the 415 maximum benefit and contribution limits of a qualified plan. [1][2][3][4]
4. Supplement qualified-plan benefits that are not stretched to the maximum limits. [1][2][3][4]
5. Recruit talented executives from outside the company. [1][2][3][4]
6. Retain executives by inducing them to stay with the company. [1][2][3][4]
7. Induce executives to take early retirement. [1][2][3][4]
8. Induce executives to provide consulting services after retirement. [1][2][3][4]
9. Keep executives from competing with the company. [1][2][3][4]
10. Adjust executive retirement benefits to include not only the compensation considered under the qualified plan but all compensation. [1][2][3][4]

Step 2: List in order the primary reasons for establishing a nonqualified plan.

1.
2.
3.

Once your client has indicated that one or more of the above situations is applicable, your next step is to focus the client on the important issues involved in selecting and designing a nonqualified plan. In addition, you need to discern the organization's needs and objectives. A nonqualified plan fact finder can accomplish these steps.

The fact finder above will

- provide a working framework for soliciting the client's goals
- serve as a due-diligence checklist, which will ensure that important discussions have not been omitted
- operate as a training tool for those who have little or no experience with nonqualified plans
- educate the client about the various needs, objectives, and considerations that are relevant to plan selection and design

Choosing the Right Type of Plan

When you have a full understanding of the client's objectives, you can choose the proper nonqualified plan. There are many varieties of nonqualified plans, but our focus will be primarily on deferred-compensation plans. Several terms commonly used in this field that are helpful to understand include

golden handshakes

golden handcuffs

golden parachutes

- *golden handshakes*—additional benefits that are intended to induce early retirement
- *golden handcuffs*—additional benefits that are intended to induce an executive to remain employed, rather than leaving prematurely
- *golden parachutes*—substantial payments made to executives who are terminated upon change of ownership or corporate control
- *incentive pay*—bonuses given for accomplishing short-term goals that can be used by the executive for retirement purposes

There are two major types of nonqualified plan designs: the salary reduction plan and the supplemental executive-retirement plan. Each approach is discussed below.

Salary Reduction Plans

salary reduction plans

If the employer wants to permit executives to defer current income (in essence, to allow a nonqualified 401(k) look-alike arrangement), a so-called salary reduction plan can be used. *Salary reduction plans* typically give participants the option to defer regular compensation, bonuses, or commissions. These plans are appropriate when executives in the highest marginal income tax bracket anticipate being in a lower tax bracket after retirement. It can also be appropriate simply as a means of income leveling for highly compensated employees whose income would otherwise drop sharply after retirement. What makes the nonqualified salary reduction plan more flexible than the 401(k) plan is that it has no maximum deferral limits. It should also be designed to exclude rank-and-file employees.

A salary reduction plan either can be initiated at the executive's individual option during contract negotiations or offered as a package of perks to selected managers or highly compensated employees. In either circumstance (consistent with the requirements of Sec. 409A), the agreement of deferral should be entered into prior to the date on which the services are actually performed to avoid unwanted tax consequences.

Candidates for a salary reduction plan include

- employers who want to provide a low-cost benefit for highly compensated and management employees (the only employer cost is the cost of the deferral of the tax deduction and the tax on the earnings from the deferred amounts)
- small closely held businesses whose owners' individual tax rate is higher than the corporate tax rate
- organizations that wish to set conditions on a certain amount of executives' salaries or bonuses to induce desired results

Example: Before the beginning of each year, the Baltimore Company offers its top executives the opportunity to defer up to $50,000 of their following year's compensation. Deferred amounts grow at some specified interest rate and the accumulated amount will be paid out over a 15-year period, beginning at the later occurrence of either age 55 or termination of employment.

Supplemental Executive Retirement Plans

supplemental executive retirement plan (SERP)

A *supplemental executive retirement plan (SERP)* satisfies the employer's objective of complementing an existing qualified plan that is not already stretched to the maximum limits by bringing executive retirement benefits (or contributions) up to desired levels. Unlike salary reduction plans, SERPs are additional employer-provided benefits.

SERPs can complement the underlying qualified plan in one of two ways. They can be designed to provide the "missing piece" of retirement benefit (or contribution) that the employer wants the executive to have. For example, if the employer wants to provide a replacement of 60 percent of an executive's final-average salary and the underlying qualified plan only provides for a 40-percent replacement, the SERP can be designed to provide a benefit equal to 20 percent of the final-average salary. However, in cases where the exact benefit (or contribution) is unknown, such as when an integrated unit-benefit formula is used, SERPs can be designed a second way: to provide for the total benefit or contribution desired (for example, all 60 percent), taking into account or offsetting the benefits provided by the qualified plan. This type of SERP is called an offset SERP.

Candidates for SERPs include employers who want to

- cut back benefits under their qualified plans due to increased costs
- provide a higher income replacement ratio for executives than they can afford (or want) to provide for rank-and-file employees
- defeat the $225,000 cap (as indexed for 2007) on compensation that can be considered in determining benefits
- provide a benefit based on total compensation for executives while continuing to provide a benefit based on base pay for rank-and-file employees
- provide a COLA benefit for executives without having to provide a similar benefit to rank-and-file employees

---

Nonqualified Plan Objectives

- Alternative to qualified plan
- Second tier of benefits
- Cover a select group of highly paid employees
- Salary deferral for executives
- Instant benefit program for executives of a new company
- Meet a wide range of compensation goals
- Satisfy special needs of specific highly compensated employees

---

DESIGN CONSIDERATIONS

Even though they are designed to avoid the rules of ERISA (which, as discussed later, most plans are), salary reduction plans and SERPs still have tremendous design flexibility. Without legislative and regulatory constraints, plan design is an interesting and challenging assignment. Let's look at the most common design features used in these plans.

Forfeiture Provisions

A forfeiture provision in a nonqualified plan sets forth certain conditions under which an employee forfeits the benefits he or she would normally get under the plan. Salary reduction plans do not typically contain forfeiture provisions because they represent an employee election to reduce the employee's own salary, which he or she had an absolute right to receive. However, forfeiture provisions are very common in SERPs because they help to achieve a multitude of employer objectives. Let's look at some client problems and see how forfeiture provisions can help solve them.

Successful Transition of Company Leadership

Some businesses are dependent on the special contributions of a few key executives. The retirement of these executives may prove devastating to the organization's profit-making ability. To prevent a drop in revenue and to ensure a smooth transition, a nonqualified deferred-compensation plan can contain a provision that requires the executive to provide consulting services after retirement or else forfeit any benefit under the plan.

Retention of Executives

If your client is concerned about inducing an executive to stay on board instead of leaving prematurely, a so-called golden-handcuffs provision should be incorporated into the plan. There are several ways to design this provision. The employer who is not concerned about recruiting executives will probably prefer a provision that requires the executive to forfeit *all* rights under the plan if he or she terminates employment prior to normal retirement age. If executive recruiting is a strong concern, the forfeiture of benefits can be designed to include liberal vesting requirements. For example, the plan may provide *no* vesting to an employee who works less than 5 years, 50 percent vesting to an employee who terminates with between 5 and 10 years' service, and 100 percent vesting to an employee who terminates after 10 or more years. If recruiting is a concern but not a priority, a more conservative vesting schedule can be used.

Competition from Former Employees

A major problem for employers in service industries is an employee who goes to work for a competitor or sets up a competing business. A covenant-not-to-compete provision can deter this behavior. A covenant-not-to-compete provision calls for the forfeiture of nonqualified benefits that have not yet been paid if the employee enters into competition with the employer by opening a competing business. To avoid legal problems, the covenant-not-to-compete provision must be carefully drafted. The provision should be reasonable in terms of the geographical area and the time period it covers. For example, a covenant that says a former employee cannot compete in the Northeast for 10 years after the employee leaves employment is probably a violation of public policy and not valid. If the employee is restricted from working for 2 years in the same county, however, the provision is probably valid. The facts and circumstances will be determinative. Because the rules for noncompetition clauses vary from state to state, your client should consult an attorney before designing such a provision.

Protecting the Executive

Up to this point, the assumption has been that your client is a taxable business entity. However, your financial services practice may also include solving problems for executives who are negotiating a nonqualified arrangement with their employer. If this is the case, keep the following points in mind:

- A SERP can be set up to protect selected executives against involuntary termination if the company changes hands by structuring the plan to pay out or increase benefits under this contingency (a so-called takeover trigger—the executive's alternative if a golden parachute does not exist).
- Nonqualified plans can be designed to protect your client against involuntary termination because of a change in the control of the business by providing for immediate vesting and/or immediate payouts at the time of the change in control. The challenge, however, is to design the nonqualified plan so the existence of the accelerated payout does not result in immediate taxation and so the payout is not so large as to deter potential buyers. To avoid immediate taxation, the plan has to satisfy the requirements of Code Sec. 409A (discussed above). Under Sec. 409A, a payment upon a change of control is allowed only if the new owners control enough additional stock to own more than 50 percent of the total fair market value or total voting power of the corporation's stock.
- Consistent with the requirements of Sec. 409A, nonqualified plans can be designed to allow withdrawals prior to termination in cases of an unforeseeable emergency. As required by Section 409A, the plan should spell out the circumstances that constitute an allowable distribution, or it should provide for an independent third party to make the determination.
- Your client should ask for a binding-arbitration clause in case of a dispute. This will save on litigation costs.

Other Features in Plan Design

In addition to forfeiture provisions, there are several other important design features to be considered in nonqualified plans. In fact, in the limited circumstance where a plan is not required to meet ERISA standards, the only real constraints on plan design are the market forces at work and the designer's imagination. In general, however, the design features of a nonqualified plan are similar to those of a qualified plan except that they are not inhibited by IRS restrictions. The following is an overview of some of those standard design features.

Benefit or Contribution Structure

Nonqualified plans can be designed as either defined-benefit or defined-contribution plans. Salary reduction plans are usually designed as defined-contribution plans because they allow executives to *contribute* a deferred amount of salary each year. SERPs can also be set up as defined-contribution plans, but are more frequently set up as defined-benefit plans. When SERPs are set up as defined-benefit plans, the benefit formula should jibe with the employer's objectives. This may mean supplementing the employer's qualified plan or avoiding duplication in benefits by the coordination of all benefits received under the employer's qualified and other benefit plans, retirement benefits earned with other employers, and Social Security benefits. Meeting employer objectives may also mean indexing benefits, weighing benefits for length of service (such as in a unit-benefit formula), or both.

Eligibility

Participation in nonqualified plans is typically restricted to company executives. In fact, it is almost always necessary to restrict participation to management and highly compensated employees in order for the plan to be exempt from ERISA requirements. Under what is referred to as the "top-hat exemption" of ERISA, the plan *must,* by definition, be unfunded and maintained "primarily" for a select group of management or highly compensated employees.

In a salary reduction plan or a SERP, the executive's title or position typically dictates inclusion in, or exclusion from, the plan. (For example, all executives above the level of first vice president might be included.) A second way to determine eligibility is by salary. When salary determines eligibility, the chosen dollar amount should be indexed. By taking this precaution, the employer does not risk substantial cost increases caused by the inclusion of executives who are not at the top level but whose salaries have inflated over time. A third common way to determine eligibility is to appoint a compensation committee. When this is done, the members of the committee, usually retain absolute control over plan membership.

Disability Provisions

Nonqualified plans frequently contain disability provisions. The employer can stipulate whether disability will be treated like any other termination of employment or whether special provisions will apply. However, care should be taken to coordinate any plan disability benefit with any insured disability benefit that may also cover the employee Most disability insurance policies reduce the insured benefit by any disability benefits paid by the employer. In addition, the employer must choose whether service will continue to accrue if a disability occurs—in which case the plan should contain a definition of disability.

Retirement Age

Another key plan design issue is retirement age. In general, the normal retirement age of the nonqualified plan is the age at which benefits become payable without forfeiture. The employer's personnel objectives determine whether a "young" retirement age (50–62) or an "old" retirement age (65–70) is chosen. If the employer wants to control salary costs by keeping a young work force, then a young retirement age should be chosen (typically, this is coordinated with a young normal retirement age in the qualified plan). If the executives involved have knowledge or experience that is crucial to the employer, however, a later retirement age should be selected.

Key Plan Design Considerations

- Salary deferral or supplemental benefit
- Benefit structure
- Eligibility
- Disability and death benefits
- Forfeiture provisions
- Hardship withdrawals
- Change in control and insolvency triggers

Death Benefits

Nonqualified plans can provide death benefits, which can cover the preretirement period, the postretirement period, or both. The death benefit chosen depends in part on what type of life insurance is used to fund the plan (if any) and what type of annuity is used for distribution from the plan. The choice of a death benefit should, therefore, be closely coordinated with the life insurance product used in the plan.

PLAN FUNDING

Nonqualified plans can be funded, unfunded, or informally funded. As you have probably concluded by now, plan funding for tax purposes and "storing" assets to pay future nonqualified promises are two different things from a tax standpoint. Let's take a closer look.

Funded Plans

A nonqualified deferred-compensation plan is considered funded for tax purposes when, in order to meet its promise of providing benefits under the plan, the company contributes specific assets to an escrow or trust account in which the executive has a current beneficial interest. In other words, to pay benefits, the company sets aside funds that are beyond the reach of the company's general creditors. In addition, a nonqualified plan is funded if the obligation to the executive is backed by a letter of credit from the employer or by a surety bond obtained by the employer. If a nonqualified plan is considered funded, the executive is subject to taxation upon the later to occur of either when contributions are made to the plan or when the employee becomes vested in the benefit (under the economic-benefit doctrine codified in Sec. 83). As discussed later, ERISA rules concerning participation, funding, vesting, fiduciary enforcement, and reporting and disclosure also apply to a funded plan. Because this generally defeats the purpose of the plan, most nonqualified plans are designed to be unfunded for both tax and ERISA purposes. One exception, discussed later, is the secular trust, which is typically utilized when benefit security is determined to outweigh the need for income tax deferral.

Unfunded Plans

A nonqualified deferred-compensation plan is considered unfunded for tax purposes if there is no reserve set aside to pay the promised benefit under the plan. Rev. Rul. 60-31 states that a mere promise to pay that is not represented by notes or secured in any way is not regarded as a receipt of income. Therefore, as long as the requirements of Section 409A are satisfied, an unfunded, unsecured promise by an employer to pay compensation at some future date does not constitute current taxable income to an executive.

Informally Funded Plans

Unfunded plans that do not make contingencies for storing funds to pay nonqualified promises pose a major problem for the executive because benefit payments hinge on the employer's fiscal health at the time benefits become payable. In addition, many executives wonder if their own status will be different by the time they collect. Management change, business buyouts (through hostile takeover or otherwise), or a demotion due to performance problems or "office politics" may put the executive in an untenable position when he or she approaches the time to collect benefits. The executive is relying mainly on the corporation's unsecured (albeit contractual) promise to pay. Thus, executives are caught on the horns of a dilemma. On one hand, if the plan is funded, executives will be taxed immediately. On the other hand, executives do not want to risk their retirement on an unsecured promise to pay. Because executives want the best of both worlds—as much security as possible without triggering immediate taxation—many plans are informally funded. A plan is informally funded when a reserve is set up to pay the nonqualified benefit, but the assets of the reserve are retained as assets of the company, subject to the claims of the company's creditors. In other words, as long as the executive does not have a current beneficial interest, the plan is considered unfunded for tax purposes. When a plan is informally funded, it is important to consider the other side of the equation—the company's deduction.

Income Tax Effects on the Employer

Under the cash method of accounting, a taxpayer is not entitled to a deduction until benefits have been paid to executives. Some employers are subject to the accrual method of accounting. However, under this method, a taxpayer is entitled to a deduction in the year during which all events have occurred that give rise to the liability, if the amount of such liability can be determined with reasonable accuracy. However, the timing of deductions for the payment of nonqualified deferred compensation comes under special IRS regulations. Unlike the usual tax accounting rules applicable to other deductions, Reg. 1.404(b)-1T allows a deduction for nonqualified deferred compensation only in the year in which the payment is includible in the executive's gross income. Although unfunded deferred-compensation arrangements often qualify as deductible expenses under the usual accrual requirements, Reg. 1.404(b)-1T takes precedence and delays the deduction for the employer until the income is taxable to the executive.

"Funding" Nonqualified Plans with Life Insurance

Corporate-owned life insurance (COLI) is a popular way for most publicly held and almost all closely held businesses to set up a reserve against future obligations under a nonqualified plan. No single type of contract is best. Most employers, however, prefer policies with premium and investment flexibility and low mortality and expense costs. In addition, because the policy values are generally used to finance retirement benefits, permanent rather than term coverage is indicated.

Advantages of COLI

The use of COLI is attractive for many reasons:

- The tax-free inside buildup that occurs in a life insurance policy is important to a nonqualified plan because, unlike those of a qualified plan, earnings on nonqualified plan assets are not tax deferred.
- Life insurance proceeds received by the employer can protect the employer against an executive's premature death. This works two ways. If the executive is not fully vested in his or her promised benefit at death, or if no death benefit is provided, the excess death benefit received by the employer can be used to cushion the employer against anticipated losses owing to the executive's death. If the executive is fully vested in a substantial death benefit and dies shortly after entering the plan, the life insurance policy will be able to pay the promised benefit in full, whereas the other reserves would have been inadequate.
- Life insurance proceeds received by the employer upon the death of the executive are generally tax free.
- Policies can be borrowed against to help pay the cost of future premiums. If cash flow is a problem, knowing that the funding of his or her benefit will not suffer should give the executive an added sense of security.
- Life insurance funding provides the employer with flexibility. The employer can either use the policy's cash values to pay nonqualified benefits, or use other assets and keep the policy in force until death. If the latter course is taken, the employer can often receive more from the insurance company as death proceeds than it pays out under the plan.
- Life insurance policies can be used to provide a supplemental disability benefit. The waiver-of-premium clause in a life policy will enable the executive to get the full nonqualified benefit even if he or she becomes disabled.
- If life insurance purchased on the executive's life is owned by the employer, premiums are paid by the employer, and the employer is the sole beneficiary, then constructive-receipt, economic-benefit, and Sec. 83 problems are avoided.
- If the nonqualified plan requires the plan to pay a life income to the executive, by electing a life-income option, the employer can transfer

to the insurance company the risk that the executive will live beyond his or her normal life expectancy.

Disadvantages of COLI

Two major disadvantages of using life insurance to fund a nonqualified plan concern the limitation on a corporate deduction for interest paid on policy loans (previously discussed) and the alternative minimum tax on corporate assets. The alternative minimum tax (AMT) offers some impediment to the use of life insurance to fund a nonqualified plan because the life insurance that is payable to the employer, although not subject to regular taxes, may be subject to the AMT. If so, employer costs are increased. Employers should be advised that they may need to purchase additional insurance so they can pay any AMT as well as their obligations under the plan. Although the AMT is usually about 15 percent of the death benefit (and in many cases far less), some experts suggest that the employer obtain slightly over 15 percent more life insurance than the amount needed to fund the plan. In any case, the employer's tax advisor should be consulted to determine whether the AMT will apply.

In addition, the Pension Protection Act of 2006 (PPA) has added another disadvantage to the use of life insurance to fund a nonqualified plan. Under the PPA a portion of the proceeds from COLI policies issued after August 17, 2006 on the lives of certain employees will become taxable to the employer. The provision of the Code allowing life insurance proceeds to be received tax-free has been amended by the PPA to provide that death benefits exceeding premiums and other amounts paid for the COLI contract will be taxable to the employer, unless the insured is notified of and consents to the coverage and one of the following exceptions applies:

- the insured is a director or a highly-compensated employee when the COLI is purchased;
- the insured was an employee within 12 months before death; or
- the death benefits are paid to the insured's heirs or used to purchase an equity interest in the employer from the insured's heirs.

In addition, the employer must file an annual information return which reports certain information regarding the COLI and must keep whatever records are necessary to establish that the requirements for income exclusion have been met.

This new provision is aimed primarily at COLI policies covering a broad-based employee group which are in effect an investment vehicle for the employer. As long as the employee notice and consent requirements are satisfied, the death benefits of the typical COLI policies on key employees will remain non-taxable to the employer because one of the statutory exceptions will be satisfied. The key element, though, is that the notice and consent requirements be met for all COLI policies issued after August 17, 2006.

BENEFIT SECURITY

Because of the income tax and ERISA issues involved in nonqualified plans, it is quite difficult to make benefits as secure for the participants as they are with qualified plans. To solve the security issue, there are three possible solutions: the rabbi trust, the secular trust, and the surety bond. (Unfortunately, no solution is totally satisfactory.)

Rabbi Trust

rabbi trust

With the *rabbi trust* (first conceived in 1981 to provide benefit security for a rabbi), contributions are made to a separate trust. Under the terms of the trust, assets generally cannot revert to the company—meaning that plan assets will be available to pay plan benefits, even if new hostile management takes over the company. However, to avoid current taxation to the participants, the trust's assets remain subject to the claims of the employer's creditors.

For many years, a sponsor wanting the IRS to rule on the validity of the rabbi trust agreement had to request a private letter ruling. In Rev. Proc. 92-64, the IRS made the use of the rabbi trust more secure by providing a model trust agreement. In order to have IRS approval of a deferred compensation agreement today, the sponsor in almost all cases must use the IRS's model rabbi trust form.

The model trust generally conforms to IRS guidelines already well known from prior IRS private letter rulings. Optional paragraphs are provided to allow some degree of customization. The model contains some relatively favorable provisions. For example, it allows the use of "springing" irrevocability. Springing irrevocability is a provision under which, if there is a change in employer ownership, the trust becomes irrevocable. Similarly, at the change in control, the employer can be required to make an irrevocable contribution of all remaining deferred compensation. Also, the model permits the rabbi trust to own employer stock. However, the model does not allow "insolvency triggers" that hasten payments to executives when the employer's net worth falls below a certain point. (The IRS fears that accelerating benefit payments when the employer's financial position deteriorates may result in all benefits being paid before any creditors have a chance to attach the trust's assets.) Other requirements, either contained in the model trust or in prior rulings, include the following:

- The assets in a rabbi trust must be available to all general creditors of the company if the company files for bankruptcy or becomes insolvent.
- The participants must not have greater rights than unsecured creditors.
- The plan must provide clear rules describing when benefits will be paid.
- The company must notify the trustee of any bankruptcy or financial hardship that the company is undergoing. When a bankruptcy or financial hardship occurs, the trustee should suspend payment to the trust beneficiary and hold assets for the employer's general creditors.

Example: Another way to protect the participants in the event of a hostile takeover is to give the trustee control over the investment of plan assets upon the change in control. This prevents the "bad guys" from making investments in illiquid employer-leased real estate or an employer-related venture.

Consistent with the requirements of Sec. 409A, participants can elect the form of distribution from the rabbi trust when contributions to the trust are made without triggering constructive receipt. In addition, a change in the form of business organization by the employee's company (from a partnership to an S corporation, for example) will not adversely affect the rabbi trust.

Finally, consistent with the requirements of Sec. 409A, executives can take a hardship withdrawal from a rabbi trust without triggering constructive receipt. The withdrawal is limited to an amount reasonably needed to meet the emergency. In addition, the emergency must be unforeseeable—that is, pose a severe financial hardship to the participant or result from a loss of property due to casualty or other similar extraordinary and unforeseeable circumstances beyond the participant's control.

Although rabbi trusts accomplish the dual objectives of deferring taxation and providing a measure of retirement security to executives, they have one important disadvantage: they provide no benefit security for executives should the employer go bankrupt. In other words, the executive must stand in line with other general creditors if the employer files for bankruptcy. Rabbi trusts, therefore, are very effective in providing retirement security if the employer is unwilling to pay promised benefits, but they do not provide security if the employer becomes insolvent.

Secular Trusts

In situations where the employer's ability to pay promised benefits comes into question, some professionals recommend a secular trust in lieu of a rabbi trust. Like a rabbi trust, a *secular trust* calls for an irrevocable contribution on the employer's part to finance promises under a nonqualified plan. Unlike a rabbi trust, however, funds held in a secular trust cannot be reached by the employer's creditors. This means that executives can expect to receive promised benefits even if the employer goes bankrupt (giving the participants a similar level of security that qualified plans have). However, there is a significant price for this security. Contributions to the trust are taxable at the later of the date when contributions are made or benefits become nonforfeitable. (See the earlier discussion of Sec. 83.)

secular trust

TABLE 15-2 **Comparison of Funding Approaches**				
Type of Plan	Funds Set Aside Prior to Retirement	Secured against Unwillingness to Pay	Secured against Employer Insolvency	Delayed Taxation for Executives
Unfunded pay-as-you-go plan	No	No	No	Yes
Rabbi trust	Yes	Yes	No	Yes
Secular trust	Yes	Yes	Yes	No

Unfortunately, several IRS private letter rulings have also indicated that in some circumstances, trust earnings would be subject to double taxation: once when earned at the trust level and again when actually paid out to the employee. Because of the tax issues and because individual tax rates (for executives) are generally higher than the corporate rate, secular trusts are not commonly used today.

Surety Bonds

For the executive who feels uncomfortable with the possibility of benefits going unpaid from a rabbi trust because of an employer bankruptcy but who wants to avoid the use of a secular trust because of the tax consequences, an alternative may be available. A *surety bond* provides for a

surety bond

bonding company to pay promised benefits if the employer defaults on the promise to pay nonqualified benefits—thus providing the executive with an indirect means of securing the employer's unsecured promise.

In order to prevent the purchase of a surety bond from triggering a constructive-receipt, economic-benefit, or Sec. 83 problem, certain precautions must be taken. The executive must bear the cost of the surety bond, and the employer should not have an involvement with the bonding company. If these precautions are taken, the executive can have the security of continued protection for nonqualified retirement payments.

The downside is that surety bonds for nonqualified plans can be expensive and difficult to obtain. Premiums are typically one to 3 percent of the annual amount deferred, plus earnings. The employer must also have a strong balance sheet to qualify for the coverage. In addition, very few insurance companies provide this type of coverage. Finally, renewal of the bond can be difficult if the employer experiences an economic downturn. Surety bonds are issued for a range of from 3 to 5 years and may not be renewed if bankruptcy is on the horizon. Ironically, this is when they are most needed!

THE INSTALLATION OF NONQUALIFIED PLANS

ERISA Considerations

top-hat exemption

When designing a nonqualified plan, in almost all cases, the employer will want to avoid coverage under ERISA by satisfying the *top-hat exemption* of ERISA. This requires that the plan be unfunded and maintained by an employer, primarily for the purpose of providing deferred compensation for a select group of management and/or highly compensated employees. The "unfunded" requirement is generally not problematic, as the employer can still utilize one of the informal funding approaches discussed above. The more difficult task is determining which employees can be covered as highly compensated employees. Unfortunately, the DOL has not provided any clear guidance on this issue. It is clear, however, that the Code's definition of highly compensated is not determinative here. From a practical perspective, a plan that covers only a few highly paid executives will probably comply. As the group gets bigger, however, there is less certainty. To safeguard the plan, the plan documents should specify that the employer has the right to amend the plan to limit the group of covered employees, conforming to any future DOL guidance on this issue.

An unfunded top-hat plan is exempt from ERISA's participation, vesting, benefit, accrual, funding, and fiduciary provisions. It is still subject to ERISA's reporting, disclosure, administration, and enforcement provisions. However, the reporting provisions can be satisfied simply by filing a statement with the DOL (at the time the plan is established) that includes the following information: the employer's name and address, the employer's identification number, a declaration that the employer maintains the plan primarily to provide deferred compensation to a select group of management or highly paid employees, the number of such plans maintained by the employer, and the number of employees in each plan.

A second type of nonqualified plan that is exempt from ERISA coverage is an excess-benefit plan. This type of plan is not as prevalent as the top-hat plan, but it nevertheless can be useful in the appropriate circumstances. An excess-benefit plan is a plan maintained by an employer solely for the purpose of providing benefits for certain employees in excess of the limitations on contributions and benefits imposed by Section 415 of the Code on plans to which that section applies, without regard to whether the plan is funded. Unfunded excess-benefit plans are totally exempt from ERISA; those which are funded are partially exempt.

Example: An employer's profit sharing plan provides for a contribution of 25 percent of compensation. For an employee who is earning compensation equal to the Section 401(a)(17) cap ($225,000 in 2007), Section 415 limits the contribution on the employee's behalf to $45,000. Without Section 415, the employee would be entitled to a contribution of $56,250. The employer can adopt an excess-benefit plan to enable the employee to receive an additional annual contribution of $11,250.

The advantage of using an excess-benefit plan as compared to a top-hat plan is that an excess-benefit plan can cover any employee, not just a member of a select group of management and highly-compensated employees. The disadvantage of an excess-benefit plan is that only a small number of employers provide a qualified retirement plan that by design provides the maximum contributions or benefits allowable under Section 415. In addition, the Section 415 limitations are not the only provisions which can operate to reduce a participant's benefits or contributions. The following are rules that also impose restrictions which could have a similar impact: Section 401(a)(17) (imposing a cap on COLA-adjusted compensation), Section 401(a)(30) (limitation on elective deferrals), and the Section 401(k) ADP and ACP nondiscrimination tests. However, for those plans that can qualify, an excess-benefit plan is very easy to design and implement.

Installation Process

The final issue we will consider in connection with your client's nonqualified plans is their installation and administration. In order to install a nonqualified plan, the employer should adopt a corporate resolution authorizing the purchase of life insurance to indemnify the business for the expenses it is likely to incur. A second resolution should authorize the production of either a contract or plan document that will spell out both the employer's and the executives' benefits and obligations. In addition, a rabbi trust document or a secular trust document should be created. Finally, the ERISA statement referred to above should be completed and sent to the Department of Labor.

SEC. 457 PLANS

Up to this point, nonqualified plans have been examined in the context of the for-profit business where the business owner and selected employees want to save for retirement without being subject to the requirements that apply to qualified plans. In that context, the employer is entitled to an immediate deduction only if the employee is currently taxed, or conversely, the employee may defer tax only if the employer's deduction is deferred.

The tax tension that exists between employers and employees of for-profit companies is absent for employers that are tax-exempt entities. Because a tax deduction is meaningless for a tax-exempt employer, the tax-exempt employer is more inclined to allow an employee to defer compensation than is its for-profit counterpart. Recognizing this difference between for-profit and tax-exempt employers, Congress established a separate tax regime applicable to deferred compensation for employees and independent contractors employed by state and local governments and tax-exempt organizations. These tax rules are found in Code Sec. 457.

Sec. 457 deferred-compensation plans

There are two types of *Sec. 457 deferred compensation plans*: 457(b) eligible plans and 457(f) ineligible plans. The former are similar to qualified retirement plans and are intended to ensure that tax-favored savings are used primarily for retirement purposes. The deferred compensation in an eligible plan is taxed when it is paid or made available to the employee. A participant in a 457(f) ineligible plan will be taxed on deferred compensation if his right to receive those amounts is not subject to a substantial risk of forfeiture.

457(b) Eligible Plan

The five principal requirements applicable to a 457(b) eligible plan are the following:

- Participation limited to service providers—Only employees and independent contractors who perform services for the employer may participate.
- Maximum annual deferral amount—The plan must provide that the maximum amount of compensation which may be deferred under the plan for the taxable year may not exceed the lesser of $15,500 (the applicable dollar amount for 2007) or 100 percent of the participant's includible compensation. The term includible compensation means compensation for services performed for the employer which is currently includible in gross income (after taking into account the deductions allowed under Section 457 and other similar income tax provisions.) Prior to 2002, amounts excluded from income under Section 403(b) and Section 401(k) plans were required to reduce the maximum allowable Section 457(b) deferral. This was a major deterrent to the use of 457(b) eligible plans. However, since 2002 this is no longer the case, and it has provided a significant impetus to the adoption of 457(b) eligible plans as supplemental plans in recent years.
- Timing of deferral election—The plan must provide that compensation will be deferred for a calendar month only if an agreement providing for such deferral has been entered into before the beginning of the month. However, with respect to a new employee, a plan may provide that compensation is to be deferred for the calendar month during which the participant first becomes an employee if an agreement providing for such deferral is entered into on or before the first day on which the participant becomes an employee.
- Timing of distributions—Amounts cannot be made available under the plan to participants or beneficiaries earlier than (i) the calendar year in which the participant attains age 70½, (ii) when the participant has a severance from employment with the employer, or (iii) when the participant is faced with an unforeseeable emergency. In addition, the plan must comply with the minimum distribution requirements of Code Section 409(a)(9). Finally, a plan may permit a distribution of benefits pursuant to a qualified domestic relations order. If an amount becomes available pursuant to one of the distribution events described in (i), (ii) or (iii), above, a participant can elect, but only once, to defer commencement of distributions, provided that payments have not yet begun. Participants in a nongovernmental 457(b) eligible plan cannot avoid taxation by rolling over a distribution into an IRA or another plan.
- Property rights—All amounts of compensation deferred under the plan, all property and rights purchased with such amounts, and all

income attributable to such amounts must remain solely the property of the employer, subject to the claims of the employer's general creditors, until the deferred compensation is made available to the participants and beneficiaries.

Example: Smithtown Health System (SHS) maintains a Sec. 403(b) plan for its employees. Under this plan, employees can contribute the maximum allowable deferrals. SHS matches 50 percent of these deferrals up to 6 percent of compensation. SHS also makes a nonelective contribution equal to 5 percent of compensation. SHS can adopt a 457(b) eligible plan, which will allow the employees to supplement their 403(b) elective deferrals by making additional elective deferrals up to the $15,500 limit.

Similar to 401(k) and 403(b) plans, 457(b) eligible plans may allow additional salary deferrals to employees who attain age 50 prior to the end of the plan year. For 2007, this catch-up amount is $5,000. For employees nearing normal retirement, a 457(b) eligible plan may allow them to make a special catch-up contribution. However, this special catch-up contribution is limited: For one or more of the participant's last 3 taxable years ending before he or she attains normal retirement age under the plan, the applicable dollar amount under the 457(b) eligible plan for the taxable year shall not exceed the lesser of

- twice the applicable dollar amount in effect, or
- the sum of (i) the maximum deferral amount for the taxable year and (ii) the amount of the maximum deferral for any taxable years before the taxable year that has not previously been used under either the maximum deferral amount or the special 457 catch-up provision.

The special 457(b) eligible plan catch-up contribution may only be utilized once by a participant.

Coordination with ERISA

A 457(b) eligible plan can cover any group of employees or independent contractors. However, as a practical matter, in order to avoid ERISA coverage, a 457(b) eligible plan must limit its coverage to those employees who will allow the plan to qualify as an ERISA top-hat plan. A 457(b) eligible plan must avoid ERISA coverage because if the plan becomes subject to ERISA it would have to satisfy the ERISA funding requirements, which in turn would result in the plan no longer satisfying one of the requirements for being a 457(b) eligible plan; in other words, the plan must be unfunded. Consequently, tax-exempt employers generally structure their 457(b) eligible plans to cover a select group of management and highly-compensated employees. On the other hand, a 457(b) eligible plan established by a state or local government is exempt from ERISA and consequently, does not have to satisfy the top-hat plan exemption.

457(f) Ineligible Plan

If a plan does not meet the requirements of Sec. 457(b), then the deferred compensation is included in the compensation of the participant when there is no longer a substantial risk of forfeiture. These noncomplying plans are referred to as 457(f) ineligible plans. Because employees do not want to pay tax on compensation they have not yet received, almost all 457(f) ineligible plans provide for distributions when the deferred compensation vests. A 457(f) ineligible plan is broadly defined to include any agreement or arrangement.

Example:	John Donovan is an executive of a non-profit corporation. John has earned a bonus of $100,000, payable in 3 years together with interest, provided that John remains employed for the entire 3-year period. The $100,000 amount exceeds the limit under Section 457(b), so this is a 457(f) ineligible plan. Because John must work for 3 years in order to receive the bonus, it is subject to a substantial risk of forfeiture and will not be taxable until the end of the 3-year period. At that time the bonus will be paid.

Although 457(b) eligible plans are exempt from Sec. 409A, 457(f) ineligible plans are not. Accordingly, 457(f) ineligible plans must satisfy the Sec. 409A restrictions on the timing of distributions, acceleration of deferrals, and deferral elections. However, unlike taxable employers, the penalty for failing to meet the Section 409A requirements is not so much the acceleration of taxation, since employees of tax exempts are already subject to tax when the substantial risk of forfeiture lapses. Rather, the real penalty is the 20-percent additional tax imposed on an employee who has violated the requirements of Sec. 409A.

EXECUTIVE-BONUS LIFE INSURANCE PLANS

Sec. 162 plan

An alternative that can be used in combination with, or in lieu of, the previously discussed nonqualified plans is an executive-bonus life insurance plan (also known as a *Sec. 162 plan*). Like a nonqualified plan, an executive-bonus life insurance plan can be provided on a discriminatory basis to help business owners and select executives save for retirement. The executive-bonus life insurance plan, however, does not provide for the deferral of income. Under an executive-bonus life insurance plan, the corporation pays a bonus to the executive for the purpose of purchasing cash-value life insurance. The executive is the policy owner, the insured, and the person who designates the beneficiary. The corporation's only connection (albeit a major one) is to fund premium payments and, in a few cases, to secure the application for insurance. Bonuses can be paid out by the corporation in either of two ways. The corporation can pay the premiums directly to the insurer or pay the bonus to the executive, who in turn pays the policy premiums. In either case, the corporation deducts the contribution at the time it is made (this is in direct contrast to most deferred-compensation plans) and includes the amount of the payment in the executive's W-2 (taxable) income.

**YOUR FINANCIAL SERVICES PRACTICE:
NONRETIREMENT APPLICATIONS FOR EXECUTIVE-BONUS PLANS**

In addition to being a retirement planning tool, executive-bonus life insurance plans can be used in several other ways to serve your clients. Some planners use them in lieu of superimposed group term life insurance (life insurance over the tax-sheltered $50,000 limit). Another use of Sec. 162 plans is to help the executive to purchase an insurance policy to fund a cross-purchase buy-sell agreement. Without these agreements, partners may not have the assets to continue the business when one of them retires or dies. A third use of executive-bonus life insurance plans is to provide the executive's estate with a source of liquid funds to pay estate taxes. Restrictions on the amount of insurance that may be used under group term life plans and qualified retirement plans make the liquidity issue an important executive concern.

Because payments made under executive-bonus life insurance plans are W-2 income, bonuses are subject to federal, state, and local withholding requirements and to Social Security taxes (unless the wage base has already been exceeded) and Medicare taxes.

Implementation of Sec. 162 Plans

Executive-bonus plans are fairly easily implemented. First, as with all forms of nonqualified compensation, a corporate resolution that authorizes the business expenditure should be obtained. Second, those in charge should select the executives to be included in the plan and the amount of benefits they will receive. Third, either the executive or the corporation should secure the application for insurance. And finally, the executive should apply for the policy as the owner and designate the policy's beneficiary.

Double-Bonus Plans

Concern over the receipt of additional taxable income from executive-bonus life insurance plans has caused many employers to provide a second bonus to alleviate any tax that the business owner or executive may pay. (These plans are typically called double-bonus plans.) There will be a tax on the second bonus, so the work sheet below helps to calculate the total amount needed for both bonuses

double-bonus plans

TABLE 15-3
Double-Bonus Work Sheet

Step 1: State the target premiums (the amount of the first bonus).   _____

Step 2: Specify the applicable tax rate (including federal state, local, and all other applicable taxes).   _____

Step 3: Subtract the step 2 amount from 1.00.   _____

Step 4: Divide the step 1 amount by the step 3 amount to find the amount of both bonuses.   _____

Example: JANCO wants to provide executive Kathy Beamer with a $10,000 nontaxable bonus to pay the premium under her cash-value life policy. JANCO will have to provide Kathy with $16,666.67, determined as follows:

Step 1: State the target premiums. $10,000.00

Step 2: State the individual's tax rate   .40

Step 3: Subtract the step 2 amount from 1.00.   .60

Step 4: Divide the step 1 amount by the step 3 amount to find the amount of both bonuses. $16,666.67

Note that the 40 percent tax rate used in the example includes a 31 percent federal tax rate, a 4 percent state tax rate, city taxes of 3.55 percent and Medicare taxes of 1.45 percent. In lieu of the work sheet, the following formula can be used:

$$\frac{\text{Amount of first bonus}}{1 - \text{tax rate}} = \text{Amount of both bonuses}$$

CHAPTER REVIEW

Key Terms

golden handshakes [15-3]
golden handcuffs [15-3]
golden parachutes [15-3]
salary reduction plans [15-3]
supplemental executive retirement
    plan (SERP) [15-3]

Sec. 457 deferred compensation
    plans [15-8]
Sec. 162 plan [15-9]
double-bonus plans [15-9]

Review Questions

Review questions are based on the learning objectives in this chapter. Thus, a [15-3] at the end of a question means that the question is based on learning objective 15-3. If there are multiple objectives, they are all listed.

1. What are the advantages for a financial services professional of becoming involved in the nonqualified deferred-compensation market? [15-1]

2. Discuss the differences between a qualified and a nonqualified plan. [15-1]

3. Will a post-retirement consulting agreement always be considered a substantial risk of forfeiture? [15-2]

4. An executive has just become fully vested in a $20,000 account balance held in an irrevocable trust. The benefit cannot be paid out for 5 more years. Under what theory is this distribution subject to current income tax? [15-2]

5. Code Sec. 409A would allow distributions in a nonqualified plan in which of the following circumstances? [15-2]
   a. Upon the death of the participant
   b. Payable to the participant 10 years from now
   c. As a financial hardship to pay for a family member's college tuition
   d. As a financial hardship for a spouse's funeral expenses

6. What is the general rule that determines when deferred compensation is considered wages for employment tax purposes? [15-2]

7. Identify the planning situations in which a nonqualified deferred-compensation plan should be used. [15-3]

8. Rhonda Rolodex is the owner of The Mainline Office Supply Company. In order to "keep her top people happy," Rhonda would like to set up a nonqualified plan for the top 20 executives in her 200-employee company. Rhonda has asked her financial services professional how she can best accomplish this objective. How should the planner advise Rhonda? [15-3]

9. Briefly describe the following: [15-3]
    a. golden handshakes
    b. golden handcuffs
    c. golden parachutes
    d. incentive pay

10. Describe a salary reduction plan. [15-3]

11. Describe a supplemental executive retirement plan (SERP). [15-3]

12. Jersey Technical Electronics (JTE) has been a very successful business, thanks to the personal contacts Sue Edison has throughout the industry. The owners of JTE fear that Sue, now 60, will retire shortly and the business will suffer. How can a nonqualified plan with a consulting clause help? [15-4]

13. Explain how a nonqualified plan can be designed to help in the following situations: [15-4]
    a. Rayco, Inc., is concerned about its key executives leaving prior to retirement age.
    b. Lawyer Prudence Juris is concerned that one of her junior partners will leave, taking some of the firm's clients with her.

14. Howard Hayes, an executive at a local manufacturing firm, has asked his insurance agent what provisions he should ask the firm's owners to put into his nonqualified plan. What provisions should the agent suggest? [15-4]

15. Briefly describe how nonqualified plans can be designed with regard to their [15-4]
    a. benefit structure
    b. eligibility provisions
    c. disability provisions
    d. retirement age provisions
    e. death benefit provisions

16. List the reasons why life insurance is frequently used to fund nonqualified deferred compensation plans. [15-5]

17. How does a rabbi trust work? [15-5]

18. How does a secular trust work? [15-6]

19. What is the top-hat exemption from ERISA? [15-7]

20. Discuss the procedures for installing and administering a nonqualified plan. [15-7]

21. Describe a 457 plan. [15-8]

22. Describe an executive-bonus life insurance plan. Also, calculate the correct bonus amount if the insurance premium is $5,000 and the executive's tax rate is 40 percent. [15-9]

16

Equity-Based Compensation Plans: An Overview

Learning Objectives

An understanding of the material in this chapter should enable you to

16-1. Identify the reasons for using equity-based compensation.

16-2. Identify the factors in assessing whether one or more forms of equity-based compensation are appropriate for a particular closely held corporation.

16-3. Describe common features of a nonqualified stock option program and the tax consequences of such a program.

16-4. Compare incentive stock options with nonqualified options.

16-5. Identify uses of employee stock purchase plans and the advantages of such programs.

16-6. Explain the tax treatment of restricted stock, phantom stock and stock appreciation rights programs.

Chapter Outline

Up to this point, the emphasis has been on the use of a tax-sheltered retirement plan or a nonqualified deferred-compensation plan to meet the needs of the small business and the small-business owner. However, another lucrative market is open to financial services professionals who are servicing the retirement and capital accumulation needs of businesses and their owners. This market involves the various methods and arrangements by which employees are compensated through the transfer of stock or equity of the employer to its executives and managers. These equity-related compensation techniques are generally referred to as equity-based compensation,

REASONS FOR USING EQUITY-BASED COMPENSATION

Equity-based compensation is a popular component of a company's total compensation package for at least three reasons. First, because stock is a capital asset under current tax law, it has the potential to offer the employee who receives it capital gain treatment for any increase in its value. Second, it serves as an incentive for employees who receive it. Once an employee owns stock in the employer, he or she can share directly in the consequences of his or her efforts through increases in the stock's value. Third, in the appropriate circumstances it may be a less costly form of compensation than cash or other forms of property to the employer and its controlling shareholders. However, as will be discussed later in this chapter, in the private company context this potential advantage has to be examined very closely.

Whether an employer is a public company or a closely held corporation, there is a positive cachet associated with receiving an award of stock in the employer. The receipt of stock is generally perceived as an acknowledgement that the recipient is such a valued employee that he or she is worthy of receiving a "piece of the action." Moreover, in large public companies stock compensation also aligns the interests of the executives with those of the shareholders. In this context, incentives are structured so that the executives will perform in a manner that will cause the value of the stock to increase.

In "start-up" companies, stock compensation is often used because cash is in short supply and stock is the best way to attract and retain qualified executives. The executive expects that a substantial gain will be realized if the employer is successful and is subsequently sold or eventually goes public. Conversely, stock compensation is not as popular with closely held corporations where there is little possibility of the company going public and where the stock has less value to the executive because there is no public market for it. Nevertheless, there are ways to overcome these disadvantages and to utilize stock compensation to reward and motivate the executives of smaller companies.

Equity-based compensation plans help the business owner and selected employees accumulate wealth for retirement and for other financial needs without being subject to the requirements that apply to qualified retirement and savings plans. Moreover, they have the potential of turning what otherwise might have been ordinary income into the more favorable capital gains. However, similar to nonqualified deferred-compensation arrangements, there is a trade-off for allowing the employer complete discretion in plan design and in choosing the employees who will be covered by an equity-based compensation plan—that is, the employer loses the ability to make a before-tax contribution on the employee's behalf that is simultaneously deductible to the business. Instead, the employer is entitled to an immediate deduction only if the employee is currently taxed, or conversely, the employee may defer tax only if the employer's deduction is deferred.

Current tax law generally provides favorable tax treatment to equity-based compensation for both the employer and the employee. As will be seen when each form of equity-based compensation is analyzed individually, the thrust of the applicable tax provisions is to ensure that, from the employee's perspective, the transfer of a stock award is properly analyzed so that it can be divided into the proper amounts of compensation income and capital gain and that the timing of the income realization is properly determined. Similarly, from the employer's perspective, the tax law seeks to limit the employer's deduction to the amount of the employee's ordinary income and to correlate the timing of the deduction with the occurrence of the employee's taxable event.

ASSESSING THE CLOSELY HELD BUSINESS

As a financial services professional, the primary market for the design of and the planning for equity-based compensation is the closely held corporation and its owner-employees. In assessing whether one or more forms of equity-based compensation are appropriate for a particular closely held corporation, the following seven considerations should be evaluated and discussed with the client.

Valuation

By definition, equity-based compensation arrangements relate in one way or another to the value of the employer's stock. Such valuation can be important in at least four points in time: when the program is established, when a stock award is received by an employee, when the stock award becomes vested, and when the employee decides to sell or otherwise dispose of the stock award. These valuation issues are particularly acute when there is no public market for the employer's stock. Under these circumstances, the employer must decide on an appropriate valuation formula for the stock awarded under its program. As will be discussed in greater detail later in this chapter, a proper valuation formula is also important for tax purposes. If the valuation formula produces a value that the IRS determines to be less than fair market value, a stock award may be treated as deferred compensation and may become subject to the requirements of Code Sec. 409A.

There is no single approach to determining the best valuation formula. Any number of factors, such as book value, earnings per share, or net revenue, can be taken into account under the valuation formula. However, no matter how the stock's value is measured or determined, the valuation should be sensitive to those aspects of the corporation's financial performance that the corporation wants the recipients of the stock awards to be motivated to improve. In addition, the same valuation formula should be used for all purposes under the program. In other words, it should be applied even handedly so that stock awarded under the program is valued no differently than the stock that is being repurchased by the corporation.

Mechanism for Repurchasing Stock

If an equity-based compensation program is to be successful in retaining and motivating employees, the award recipients must have a market within which the employee can sell or otherwise realize an economic benefit from his or her equity interest. This is fairly simple when the employer's stock is publicly traded and there is an institutional market for the shares. However, in the case of a closely held corporation, the "market" typically takes the form of a contractual obligation of either the corporation or the other shareholders to repurchase the employee's equity interest at a formula price, whenever the employee decides to sell or when the employee's relationship with the employer is terminated. Consequently, in this context, both employer and employee have a strong interest in entering into some form of shareholders' agreement, which will prevent shares from being sold to third parties or from being retained by a person who is no longer an employee.

When an employer provides the market for the stock awarded to employees under an equity-based compensation program, the program becomes hard to differentiate from a typical deferred-compensation arrangement. For example, if an employee exercises an option in order to obtain stock having a value of $1,000 and the stock's value increases at the rate of 10 percent per year, this is no different than the employee deferring $1,000 from his or her income and receiving a 10 percent return on that deferral. In either event, at the end of 15 years, the employee is entitled to a payment of almost $4,200. A significant difference between these two arrangements arises in connection with how the $4,200 is treated for tax purposes. Under the stock program, the employer makes the $4,200 payment with after-tax dollars—that is, the payment represents a capital transaction, and the employee recognizes a capital gain of $3,200 ($4,200 less the $1,000 purchase price). Under the deferred-compensation arrangement, the employer is entitled to a tax deduction for its $4,200 payment, as additional compensation, and the employee is taxed on $4,200 of ordinary income. The after-tax result of the stock award favors the employee while the after-tax result of the deferred-compensation arrangement favors the employer. Consequently, in determining whether to adopt an equity-based compensation plan, the employer must factor into its decision the additional tax cost associated with having to repurchase the shares awarded under the program.

Performance Criteria

Equity-based compensation plans can differ in the degree to which they reward both the overall success of the employer and the performance of particular employees. Some equity-based compensation plans allow employees to benefit from the change in the employer's overall worth. For employees whose responsibilities can directly affect such net worth, this may be an appropriate measure of their performance. On the other hand, for employees whose responsibilities don't directly affect the "bottom line," it may be more appropriate to have their equity compensation determined by matters which are within their control. Thus, their equity compensation might relate to growth in the sales of one or more product lines or to improvements in the efficiency with which various products are produced. The choice of whether to use explicit performance criteria and, if such criteria are appropriate, which ones should be utilized, should be left to the employer to determine, based on the purpose for the equity-based compensation plan.

Extent of Employee's Economic Risk

Another factor that provides a basis for distinguishing among various forms of equity-based compensation is the extent to which the employee is economically put at risk as a consequence of entering into the equity compensation arrangement. For example, a direct purchase of stock by an employee generally results in economic risk to the employee to the extent of the purchase price. In other words, if the stock falls in value, the employee will suffer an economic loss. On the other hand, in the case of some equity-based compensation programs, the employee suffers no out-of-pocket cost and in turn will not suffer a loss if the stock does not appreciate in value. For example, an employer may sell shares of stock to an employee for $100 a share. In conjunction with the sale, the employee agrees that upon termination of his or her employment, he or she will sell the stock back to the employer for the greater of its fair market value or the amount paid for the shares. In this case, the employee, as a practical matter, has not incurred any economic risk. In designing an equity-based compensation program, the employer must determine the extent to which its employees will incur an economic risk as a consequence of receiving a stock award.

Federal Tax Consequences

The federal tax consequences of a particular equity-based compensation program are an important consideration from both the employee's and employer's perspectives. The employee's objective is to maximize the after-tax benefit of any stock award. Under current tax law, the maximum tax rate applicable to compensation income is 35 percent, while the lowest federal tax rate on long-term capital gains is 15 percent. Thus, there is a significant tax advantage to the employee arising from the adoption of an equity-based compensation program that results in the recognition of long-term capital gains income.

Moreover, almost without exception, the most frequently used forms of equity-based compensation involve a trade-off between the employer and employee as to the timing of the taxable event. In general, the employer cannot claim a tax deduction with respect to an equity-based compensation award until the employee is taxed on the income realized in connection with the receipt of the award. As a result, the employer generally prefers forms of equity-based compensation that permit it to claim a tax deduction as soon, and in as large an amount, as possible. The employee, on the other hand, can be expected to favor a stock award that defers the imposition of tax or that enables the employee to realize capital gain, rather than compensation income.

In the context of private companies, one of the major planning issues faced by the financial services professional is how to maximize the tax benefits of a stock award program for both the employer and its employees. In many circumstances, the interests of the employer and its employees may very well be contradictory. For example, under Sec. 83, if an employee can reduce the ordinary income consequence of a property transfer and increase its capital gain potential, he or she is better off. But the employer, on the other hand, has given up a deduction to the extent that ordinary income has been changed to capital gain.

Given the structure of the tax law, in many cases the employer nevertheless utilizes compensation techniques that tend to favor the employees' interests. There is nothing wrong with this approach, as long as it is undertaken with a clear understanding of what the costs, including lost tax benefits, are to the employer. Consequently, good planning should not focus solely upon the tax results to the employee, but should consider the total effect of any proposed program on both employer and employee. This concept will be looked at more closely in the context of choosing between the issuance of nonqualified stock options and incentive stock options.

Corporate Structure

Up to this point, it has been assumed that a closely held corporation that is considering the adoption of an equity-based compensation arrangement is treated as a C corporation for federal tax purposes. However, given the increased use of pass-through entities by business owners, the employer may have elected to be taxed under Subchapter S of the Code (an "S corporation") or that the employer is a limited liability company (LLC) that has elected to be taxed as a partnership. In both of these circumstances, there are additional considerations to be evaluated before adopting an equity-based compensation arrangement.

S Corporation

With respect to an S corporation, an individual who owns more than 2 percent of the corporation's outstanding stock is treated as a partner in a partnership for purposes of the provisions of the Code which relate to employee fringe benefits. For this purpose, employee fringe benefits include, among other things, group term life insurance and medical plans. Thus, an employee who receives more than a 2 percent interest in an S corporation's stock may find that his life insurance coverage and medical benefits are no longer excludible from income. This reduction in the employee's tax benefits should be understood and accepted by the employee before any stock awards are made.

LLC

Even though a business owner who operates his or her business in the form of an LLC may perceive the business as being no different than a regular corporation, the award of equity-based compensation to an employee of the LLC has tax consequences that differ in several material respects from those of a grant of equity compensation by a corporation to an employee. First, an LLC can provide an unrestricted equity award in one of two forms, a profits interest or a capital interest. A profits interest is an unrestricted interest in the LLC's future profits. However, a profits interest does not entitle the holder to receive a share of the proceeds from the sale of the LLC's assets in connection with its liquidation. On the other hand, a capital interest typically includes a profits interest as well as the right to receive a share of the sales proceeds if the LLC's assets are sold in connection with its liquidation.

If an employee of an LLC is awarded a profits interest in exchange for providing services, he or she is generally not subject to taxation at the time of receipt. However, future allocations or distributions to the recipient with respect to the profits interest will be taxable. If an employee receives a capital interest in exchange for services, the recipient of the capital interest is immediately subject to taxation on ordinary income equal to the fair market value of the capital interest (reduced by any amount paid for the interest), and the LLC becomes entitled to a deduction equal to the amount of income recognized (the deduction is allocated to the member or members of the LLC whose capital has been transferred to the recipient). There also may be other tax consequences to the LLC and its members associated with the transfer of the capital interest.

Following the transfer of either a profits interest or a capital interest, the recipient must be treated as a member of the LLC. This means that in most circumstances the recipient no longer can be treated as an employee for tax purposes. Similar to what happens to a 2 percent S corporation shareholder, the new LLC member will lose the tax benefits associated with those welfare and fringe benefits that are only available to employees, such as group term life insurance and medical plans. Given the complexity of the possible tax consequences to the LLC and its members, an LLC should not undertake the adoption of an equity-based compensation program without the advice of a tax attorney, an accountant, or another qualified tax advisor.

Other Legal and Accounting Considerations

Apart from the design and operational considerations addressed above, there are a number of legal and accounting factors that must be considered in assessing whether an employer is a candidate for implementing an equity-based compensation program.

- The employer must evaluate whether the accounting treatment of a particular form of equity-based compensation is acceptable from a financial reporting standpoint.
- State or federal law may require that certain forms of equity-based compensation receive stockholder approval before they become effective.
- As discussed in chapter 15, to avoid the requirements of Title I of ERISA, equity-based compensation arrangements should be designed to satisfy the requirements for being a "top hat" plan—that is, an unfunded plan that is maintained primarily for the purpose of providing deferred compensation for a select group of management or highly compensated employees.

Another consideration for a closely held corporation that is related to the ERISA issue is whether stock awards made under a particular equity-based compensation arrangement will be considered a public offering, which requires filing a registration statement with respect to those awards under the Securities Act of 1933 (1933 Act) or comparable state securities laws. Generally, a stock plan that issues stock or options to a limited number of key executives who are familiar with the employer's overall operations and affairs can be considered a private offering that will not require registration under the 1933 Act. Conversely, if the plan covers a broad group of employees, some or all of whom are not familiar with the employer's operations, then the awards may constitute a public offering that requires a registration statement to be filed under the 1933 Act or under the state securities laws. Because all closely held corporations want to avoid this result, it is important to include the employer's corporate attorney and accountant in the planning process.

OTHER PRELIMINARY CONCERNS

Creating a Plan or Program

Two common approaches are used to grant equity-based compensation awards. Under the more favored approach, the awards are granted pursuant to a plan maintained by the employer issuing the stock. The plan establishes the general terms of any awards to be granted, and permits the employer's compensation committee or other designated group to exercise discretion in granting individual awards to employees or other recipients and in establishing the individual terms and conditions applicable to the awards, consistent with the plan's general limitations or restrictions. Under the second approach, each award is granted on an ad hoc basis by the board of directors or other granting authority without any governing document. Under this approach, the only limitations on the terms of the award are found in applicable law, stock exchange requirements, and the employer's own by-laws or other governing corporate documents. This chapter will generally address equity-based compensation awards that are granted pursuant to some form of plan or other governing document or agreement.

One of the more practical reasons that plans are the preferred approach to awarding equity-based compensation is that several forms of equity-based compensation require shareholder approval; the use of a plan document greatly simplifies the process of obtaining the required approval. For example, as will be discussed later in this chapter, shareholder approval is required for the issuance of incentive stock options and for the adoption of an employee stock purchase plan. In addition, shareholder approval is required to exempt certain stock awards from the $1 million cap on deductible compensation paid to top officers of public companies and (under some stock exchange rules) to use authorized and unissued shares to satisfy awards made to officers and directors.

For public companies, use of a plan is also important to maintain favorable shareholder relations. Due to the potential dilution associated with equity-based compensation, institutional shareholders often have a negative view of such awards unless they are made pursuant to a plan that identifies the type of awards that can be made as well as the total value of the equity-based compensation to be delivered and that has been submitted to shareholders for approval. Similarly, stock plans may have a positive effect on employee relations. Stock awards will be more effective in motivating executives if the executives are satisfied that the stock awards will not be made on an arbitrary basis.

Accounting Considerations

For public companies, at one time the use of equity-based compensation received favorable treatment for financial accounting purposes on the books of the company. This is no longer the case. Under generally accepted accounting principles (as articulated in FAS 123(R), Share-Based Payment), all stock awards now have some accounting expense associated with them. FAS 123(R) generally requires companies to measure compensation costs based on the award's grant date fair value. For example, the grant date value of stock options must be estimated using option pricing models that take into account the option's exercise price, the expected option term, the current price of the underlying stock and that price's expected volatility, expected dividends, and the risk-free interest rates for the option's expected term. Acceptable pricing models include the binomial option-pricing model (a lattice model) and the Black-Scholes-Merton option-pricing formula.

The resulting compensation cost must be recognized over the period during which the employee is required to provide service in exchange for the award—that is, the vesting period. However, the total amount of the compensation cost recognized for an award of stock options is based solely on the number of options that eventually vest. The compensation cost attributable to nonvested options (the options for which the requisite service is not rendered) is never recorded. FAS 123(R) also requires that if a stock award is modified, an incremental compensation cost must be recognized in an amount equal to the excess of the fair value of the modified award over the fair value of the original award before its modification.

Finally, FAS 123(R) requires expense recognition of employee stock purchase plan (ESSP) options if certain criteria are not met. Under such criteria, any purchase discount may not exceed the per share amount of share issuance costs that would have been incurred to raise a significant amount of capital by a public offering. The safe harbor discount for this purpose is 5 percent or less. Accordingly, if the purchase discount under the ESSP is more than 5 percent (a discount of up to 15 percent is allowed under Code Sec. 423), an expense recognition will be required with respect to options issued under the ESSP.

Public Corporations

If you counsel a public company or represent employees of one or more public companies, there are special limitations that affect stock awards granted to employees of public companies. Financial services professionals must be familiar with these limitations when working with such clients.

$1 Million Cap on Compensation

Sec. 162(m) of the Code limits to $1 million per covered individual the amount that a public company may deduct as "employee remuneration." This limitation applies to any publicly held company whose chief executive officer and certain other officers are required to have their compensation reported in the employer's proxy statement. Not all compensation is taken into account for purposes of the Sec. 162(m) deduction cap. Sec. 162(m) defines "applicable employee remuneration" by what it is not, providing that the limit takes into consideration all remuneration, other than commissions, qualified plan and fringe benefit contributions, and performance-based compensation. The latter form of compensation is the primary exception to the Sec. 162(m) limitation.

Generally, performance-based compensation is paid only if certain preestablished objective performance formulas or goals are met. Moreover, the performance goals must be established by a compensation committee consisting of two or more outside directors of the corporation. However, because stock rises and falls in value based on the employer's stock price which in turn reflects corporate performance, stock options and stock appreciation rights (SARs) are automatically considered to have satisfied the requirements for performance-based compensation as long as certain other conditions are satisfied. These conditions include that the option exercise price equal fair market value on the date of grant and that the shareholders approve the terms of the option plan. Once a stock option or SAR qualifies as performance-based compensation, the amounts realized in connection with the exercise of those forms of compensation are no longer subject to the $1 million cap on compensation. Thus, for executives whose compensation can be limited by Sec. 162(m), the goal is to maximize the amount of performance-based compensation that they receive.

Insider Trading Restrictions

Rule 16b-3, referred to as the short swing profit recovery rule, is issued by the SEC under the authority of Sec. 16 of the Securities Exchange Act of 1934. Under this section, insiders (a corporation's officers, directors, and greater than 10 percent shareholders), must disgorge profits from purchases and sales within 6 months of each other. A purchase for purposes of this restriction includes the grant of an option. However, Rule 16b-3 does provide an exemption for securities issued under a employee benefit plan if certain requirements are satisfied. Chief among these requirements is that the shareholders approve the plan. Thus, if the requirements of Rule 16b-3 are met, the grant of an option will not be characterized as a purchase under the short swing profit recovery rule.

Proxy Disclosure Requirements

The SEC requires that a public company disclose in its proxy statement the compensation paid to its senior executives and directors. However, for proxy statements issued after December 15, 2006, the SEC substantially revised and enlarged the scope and form of disclosure of a public company's reportable compensation practices and arrangements. In addition to salary, bonuses, and other forms of compensation, the new disclosure rules require that options and any other forms of equity awards granted to senior executives and directors during the applicable year must be disclosed in a table, using the award's compensation cost as recognized by the corporation for financial accounting purposes under FAS 123(R). Thus, for a corporation's senior executives and directors, there is more transparency as to the value of the compensatory equity awards that they receive.

STOCK OPTION PLANS

Up until the recent changes in accounting rules that affect how stock options are treated for financial statement reporting purposes, stock option programs had been one of the most popular forms of equity-based compensation, both from the employer's and the participants' perspectives. And despite the accounting treatment changes, stock options are still a popular form of equity-based compensation, particularly from the employee's perspective. In this section, we will review the three types of stock option plans, design considerations, and planning for the participant. Even if a financial services professional does not work with employers to design stock option programs, he or she must be familiar with the tax considerations when working with employees who have been awarded one or more of the various forms of stock options.

What Is an Option?

An option affords its holder the right to acquire the property subject to the option privilege by paying the exercise price within the period set forth in the option agreement. Typically, an option is only exercised when it is "in the money,"—that is, the value of the underlying property exceeds the exercise price. At the time of grant, a stock option's value includes the following three components:

- the intrinsic value of the option. This element refers to the excess, if any, of the stock's value over the exercise price. In most cases involving compensatory stock options, this element does not have any value because those options typically have an exercise price equal to the fair market value of the stock on the date of grant.

- the leverage value of the option. This element refers to the fact that an option allows an employee to hold onto it without risking capital or having to pay taxes until the option is exercised. This value is equivalent to the return that the holder could earn on funds that do not otherwise have to be committed to paying the exercise price. This leverage value is similar to an interest-free loan. However, the leverage value decreases as the period to the expiration of the option draws nearer.

- the option's price protection. This element refers to the fact that an option holder suffers no economic loss if the value of the underlying stock falls below the exercise price. This price protection value is particularly relevant for more volatile stocks where the probability of an option finishing out of the money is higher.

Nonqualified Stock Options (NQSOs)

nonqualified stock options (NQSOs)

Nonqualified stock options (NQSOs) are options to purchase shares of company stock at a stated price over a given period of time (frequently 10 years). The option price normally equals 100 percent of the stock's fair market value on the date the option is granted, but if adverse tax consequences are to be avoided, it is no longer possible, as a practical matter, to set the option price below this level. (This issue will be discussed in greater detail below.) Typically, the employee may exercise the options by paying cash equal to the exercise price or by tendering previously owned shares of stock.

At the time the NQSO is exercised, the excess of the fair market value of the stock over the option price is taxed as ordinary income and is also subject to FICA tax and income tax withholding. The company receives a tax deduction in the amount of the executive's income recognized from the exercise of the option in the year of such recognition, as long as the withholding requirements are met. The executive's tax basis in the shares received upon exercise of the option is equal to the sum of the exercise price and the amount that the executive recognized as income.

Example: The employer grants to Ellie Executive the right to purchase 500 shares of common stock at the market price ($20/share at the time of issuance) at any time over the next 10 years. After 3 years, the market price has risen to $60/share. Ellie purchases all 500 shares at $20/share ($10,000). She now has $20,000 ($40 x 500) of ordinary income, which is the

> difference between the purchase price ($10,000) and the current market value ($30,000). Ellie's basis in her 500 shares is $30,000, the sum of the $10,000 exercise price and her $20,000 of ordinary income.

Clearly NQSOs will be valuable to the employee only if the price of the underlying stock has risen since the date the option was issued. However, there is a possibility of a large gain if the price increases substantially. The employee generally may choose to exercise the options at any time during a specified period (typically 10 years) without limitation.

Many NQSOs are not exercisable for a period of time after the options are granted. Sometimes all options granted at a specific time become vested at once (referred to as *cliff vesting*) after a specified number of years. For example, the company grants 500 options that become exercisable 3 years from the date of the grant as long as the participant is still employed on that date. Another approach is to vest a portion of the options each year (referred to as *graded vesting*). For example, one third of the options is vested after one year and two thirds after 2 years, with full vesting after 3 years. It is also possible to have accelerated vesting upon the occurrence of a change in control of the company or upon the participant's death or disability. Also, be aware that the vesting provisions within a single company can be different for options granted at different times or to different individuals. Unless the terms of the stock option plan provide otherwise, there are no nondiscrimination or uniformity requirements applicable to stock option grants.

Several newer vesting approaches are being used today. In some cases, vesting is subject to the company (or employee) satisfying certain performance goals. Another approach offered in some pre-IPO (prior to the initial public offering) companies is referred to as early exercise. Under this arrangement, the participant is allowed to immediately exercise options when they are granted, but the stock remains restricted (forfeitable if the employee does not complete a specified period of service or does not remain employed until the IPO is completed). Because the employee could forfeit the stock, there is generally no income tax treatment until the vesting restrictions lapse. As an alternative, the employee can make a Sec. 83(b) election (discussed below) and pay tax at the time of the early exercise. Once exercised, the program is really a restricted stock plan (discussed below).

The duration of the exercise period for an NQSO is most often 10 years, but termination of employment prior to the end of that period can shorten the duration. It is common for a terminating employee to have the options lapse between 60 and 180 days after termination of employment, and even possible for the options to lapse at termination of employment if the participant is terminated for cause or violates a *noncompete clause.*

noncompete clause

To exercise the options, the employee needs cash to pay the option price for the stock. Although this often requires borrowing, once the options are exercised, the employee may sell a sufficient number of the shares to repay the loan. If the employer is the source of the employee's loan, care must be taken in how the loan is structured. If the employer provides a nonrecourse loan (that is, the employee does not have any personal liability) that is only secured by the stock obtained through the exercise of an option, this form of loan will cause the exercise of the stock option to be ignored for tax purposes pursuant to Code Sec. 83. This is the case because the employee has not taken any personal risk that the stock's value will decline. Accordingly, even though the option has been exercised, there has been no transfer of stock for tax purposes. The employee does not recognize any income as a consequence of the exercise of the option and will not have a taxable event until the loan has been repaid and the stock no longer secures the loan. At that time, the employee will recognize income equal to the excess of the then value of the stock over the exercise price.

For example, an employee has an option to purchase 1,000 shares of Company X stock with an exercise price of $50. When the value of Company X stock has reached $100 a share, the employee decides to exercise the option by obtaining a nonrecourse loan from Company X in the amount of $50,000, which must be repaid one year from the date of the loan. The employee will not have a taxable event when the option is exercised. Rather, the taxable event will occur one year later when the employee repays the loan. For tax purposes, a transfer of property is considered to have occurred at that time. When the loan repayment is made, if Company X stock has a value of $125 a share, the employee will be required to report $75,000 of compensation income, the difference between the exercise price and the fair market value of the stock on the date the stock is transferred for tax purposes. The $25 of additional stock value that accrued between the time that the option was exercised and the time that the loan was repaid must be treated as ordinary income and not capital gain. This tax result is the same whether the loan proceeds are used to exercise an option or to purchase the stock directly from the employer. In either event, no transfer of property occurs until the loan is repaid and the employee's income recognition is deferred until a transfer of property has taken place. However, if the loan is obtained from an unrelated third party, the usual taxation rules apply. The special rule described above only applies where the loan is from the employer. Accordingly, if loans are to be used to exercise options or purchase stock, then, if possible, the employer should negotiate with its bank to provide the loans to the employees so that they do not have to come from the employer.

Many stock option programs adopted by public companies today offer cashless exercise transactions pursuant to Regulation T issued by the Federal Reserve Board. Under Regulation T a stockbroker is permitted to extend credit to an employer on behalf of an employee for the purpose of exercising an option. In other words, the options are exercised with broker financing and the broker simultaneously sells some or all of the stock received in connection with the option exercise in order to repay the broker's loan. What the employee receives are shares, cash, or both having a value equal to the gain realized upon the exercise of the option (the spread), net of any brokerage commissions and any required tax withholding. Although this transaction is substantially similar to a stock appreciation right that is payable in cash (discussed below), the employer avoids having to make any cash payment.

If the employee prefers to hold option shares for their potential future appreciation, devising a method to raise the cash necessary to purchase shares becomes an important part of retirement planning. In addition, if employer stock constitutes a disproportionate share of a retiring employee's investment portfolio, planning for the systematic repositioning of the portfolio is another consideration for the practitioner.

Impact of Sec. 409A

Prior to the addition of Code Sec. 409A, the grant of an NQSO with an exercise price of less than fair market value was generally a non-event for tax purposes. There may have been adverse accounting treatment at the time of grant, but the taxable event continued to arise only when the option was exercised. Section 409A has added a new consideration to this scenario.

As discussed in the last chapter, Sec. 409A was added to the Code for the purpose of regulating deferred compensation. Although stock options had never previously been characterized as deferred compensation for tax purposes, under Sec. 409A discounted stock options are nevertheless treated as deferred compensation and must satisfy the 409A requirements. The most relevant of these requirements to stock options is that deferred compensation may not be distributed earlier than separation from service, disability, death, a specified time, or pursuant to a fixed schedule. For an option, this means that the exercise of the option can only take place upon the occurrence of one of those events, which is not how the typical stock option is written.

If a discounted stock option runs afoul of Sec. 409A, the holder of the option will be subject to income tax at the time that the option becomes exercisable, that is, vested, rather than the date on which the option is exercised. The amount subject to tax is the spread between the exercise price and the fair market value of the underlying stock on the vesting date. In addition, the option holder will incur a 20 percent penalty on the amount of income that is treated as additional compensation under Sec. 409A. Moreover, the employer has an employment tax and withholding obligation with respect to the amount required to be included in the employee's income.

Example:	The employer grants to Paula President an option to purchase 500 shares of common stock. At the time of this grant, the stock has a fair market value of $20 per share. However, the exercise price of the option is $10 per share. The option can be exercised at any time after the third anniversary of the date of grant. After 3 years, the value of the stock has increased to $60 per share. On the third anniversary of the grant date, Paula must recognize income equal to $25,000
	(500 x $50). In addition, Paula is also subject to a penalty of $5,000 ($25,000 x .2).

The application of Sec. 409A to discounted stock options is of particular importance to closely held corporations that grant stock options. This is because closely held corporations may inadvertently grant discounted stock options due to a faulty evaluation. Although there has yet to be any experience with how Sec. 409A will be applied, it is very possible that the IRS may apply a strict interpretation of Sec. 409A with respect to the valuation of a closely held corporation's stock in determining whether options presumed to be granted "at the money" should instead be treated as discounted stock options. The same issue can arise in connection with the issuance of incentive stock options (discussed below), which are required to be granted at fair market value, but on closer examination it may be determined that the exercise price was not fair market value. Accordingly, closely held corporations should give serious consideration to having an independent appraisal of their stock prepared prior to the grant of any stock options in order to confirm that the exercise price of each stock option is not less than the stock's fair market value.

The proposed regulations under Sec. 409A provide guidance on three acceptable methods of determining fair market value, one of which is an independent appraisal. Once these regulations are finalized, it will be advantageous to use one of the methods set forth in the regulations. It will shift the burden to the IRS to establish that both (i) the option's exercise price is below fair market value and (ii) the company's method of valuation was unreasonable.

Finally, the option grants that are now subject to Sec. 409A are grants made after October 3, 2004 and options issued before October 3, 2004 that are either (i) amended after October 3, 2004, or (ii) not fully vested as of December 31, 2004. On the other hand, it is not impossible to structure an option so that it complies with Sec. 409A. It primarily requires that stricter rules regarding the timing of exercise have to be built into the option grant.

For example, a closely-held corporation that expects to be acquired for its current fair market value may determine that a discounted option that is exercisable solely upon a change in control is a better compensation device than is a regular option that is exercisable at any time.

Incentive Stock Options (ISOs)

incentive stock option (ISO)

An *incentive stock option (ISO)* is an option to purchase shares of the company stock at 100 percent or more of the stock's fair market value on the date the option is granted, for a period of up to 10 years. The option plan itself may not have a duration of more than 10 years and must be approved by shareholders within one year of the plan's adoption. ISOs are taxed more favorably to the employee than NQSOs, but are less flexible. The stock's aggregate fair market value (determined at the date of grant) subject to ISOs which become exercisable for the first time by an employee in any calendar year cannot exceed $100,000. This means that if an employer grants 20,000 ISOs to an employee and the value of the underlying stock is $10 per share, then no more than 50 percent of the ISOs (10,000 x $10 = $100,000) may become vested in any calendar year. An ISO is exercisable only by an employee and cannot be transferred to anyone, except in the event of death. The favorable tax treatment is also conditioned on satisfying certain holding period requirements before sale of the option shares. In addition, any option granted to a shareholder of 10 percent or more of a company's voting stock must be priced at 110 percent or more of the stock's fair market value, with an option term of no more than 5 years. As in the case of NQSOs, the options may be exercised by paying cash or by tendering previously owned shares of stock.

When the employee exercises the ISO, there is no regular income tax owed. However, the excess of the stock's fair market value at the time of exercise over the option exercise price—that is, the *spread*—is a tax-preference item that may trigger an alternative minimum tax obligation (discussed below). If the shares are held for at least 2 years from the date the option was granted and at least one year from the date of exercise, the tax on the gain realized upon the sale of the option stock is payable at a long-term capital-gains rate. This gain is equal to the increase in the stock's value from the date the ISO is granted to the date the stock is sold.

Example: Alex, an executive of Private Company, receives an ISO for 1,000 shares of company stock. The exercise price of the options and the stock's fair market value on the date of grant is $10. One year later, Alex exercises his ISOs and receives 1,000 shares of stock. Alex holds these shares for another 2 years and then sells them for $15 per share. At that time Alex has a long-term capital gain of $5,000 (1,000 x $5).

If the holding period requirements are not met, the gain to the extent of the spread at the time of exercise is taxed as ordinary income; the remainder is taxed as capital gain. Such an early sale is referred to as a disqualifying disposition. In the event of a disqualifying disposition, the employer becomes entitled to a deduction in the taxable year of such disposition equal in amount to the employee's income.

Example: Same facts as the preceding example except that Alex exercises his ISOs 6 months after the date of grant when the value of the stock is $12 per share. Alex then sells his shares a year later for $15 a share. This is a disqualifying disposition. As a result, Alex recognizes ordinary income in the year of the disqualifying disposition in the amount of $2,000 (1,000 x $2). In addition, because Alex held his shares for a year, he will also report a long-term capital gain of $3,000 (1,000 x $3).

Because the capital-gains rate can be significantly lower than ordinary income tax rates, satisfying the holding period requirements is quite important. In addition to the lower rate, capital gains on the sale of stocks acquired through incentive stock options can be used to offset capital losses from the sale of other securities. Still, the employee needs to consider the alternative minimum tax implications of holding stock after exercise.

As with NQSOs, ISOs provide the employee with the possibility of large gains. Within limits, the employee can choose the timing of exercise of the ISOs to maximize gains. Also, as with NQSOs, the participant needs to have a full appreciation of the terms of the program, including the vesting and duration provisions, before any liquidation strategy can be conceived.

Finally, one of the tax consequences associated with the exercise of ISOs is that the spread upon exercise of an ISO is treated as a preference item for purposes of the alternative minimum tax (AMT). This means that an employee may be surprised to learn that he or she has an income tax liability as a result of exercising an ISO even though the general rule is that the exercise of an ISO is not a taxable event. Looking back at the first example above, if at the time of exercise the stock has a value of $12 a share, Alex will have a tax preference amount equal to $2,000 when the ISOs are exercised (1,000 x $2). This AMT preference item may or may not affect Alex's actual income tax liability, depending on his overall tax situation. However, if an employee does pay AMT in connection with the exercise of an ISO, that AMT amount is available to offset any capital gains tax due on the sale of the option shares.

It is important that the financial services professional pay attention to the danger of the AMT. If an employee exercises a large number of ISOs at a time when the value of the underlying stock has increased substantially in value, the employee may incur an AMT liability. However, with proper planning the employee can minimize the effect of an ISO exercise on AMT liability. Some strategies that can be used to minimize the AMT include the following:

- Limit the number of ISOs exercised in any year. Calculate the number of ISOs to exercise in a year so that the regular tax will equal the AMT.
- Plan ahead by estimating how many ISOs can be exercised in each future year without triggering AMT.
- Exercise ISOs as early in the year as possible and then monitor the stock price throughout the year. If the stock price decreases and the employee believes that the decline will continue, then he or she should consider selling the stock. This technique eliminates the tax preference item and avoids the risk of paying AMT on phantom income. If the stock price increases and the employee believes that the appreciation will continue, then he or she should hold the stock. In that event the increasing value of the stock will hopefully result in any AMT payment being recouped when the stock is eventually sold.

Tax Withholding and Employment Taxes

In order to engage in cash flow planning, it is important for an employee to understand the income tax withholding and employment tax obligations that apply to stock options. With respect to ISOs, there is no federal income tax withholding requirement, even when the employee has a disqualifying disposition. Similarly, no employment taxes are payable in connection with the exercise of an ISO. This is another advantage that ISOs have over NQSOs.

With respect to NQSOs, income tax withholding is required, as is the payment of FICA and FUTA taxes. These withholding and tax obligations arise at the time that the NQSO is exercised, assuming that the option stock is nonforfeitable.

Choosing and Designing a Plan

Similar to deferred-compensation plans, stock option programs can be used to attract, motivate, and retain the services of an employee. Unlike compensation programs, stock programs can transform the executive's interest in the company from that of an employee to a part-owner. A stock option program also does not involve the outlay of any cash by the employer, either at the time of issuance or at the time the participant exercises the option.

However, this does not mean there is no cost associated with the establishment of a stock option program. If the value of the company's stock increases a great deal, there is the lost opportunity of selling the stock to a third party at the market price. A company should not consider a stock option program unless it has first carefully evaluated the potential costs and has a clear understanding of the objectives it is trying to accomplish.

When choosing between the two types of stock option programs, remember that the tax impact on the employer is quite different. With an ISO, the employer gets no tax deduction, while with the nonqualified program, the employer receives a deduction in the amount the participant declares as income at the time of exercise. This makes the cost of providing benefits with an ISO more expensive than with a nonqualified program. In addition, the nonqualified program is more flexible.

In the review of NQSOs and ISOs, we discussed the major plan design alternatives that the employer has with each type of option plan. As you can see, as with nonqualified deferred compensation, there is a great deal of flexibility in choosing the proper plan design. The issues are similar to the design considerations discussed in chapter 15.

What may be a little different about designing an option program is that the employer and employees do not have the same interest in which type of option program is adopted. Due the favorable capital gains treatment, employees generally favor ISOs. Because employers do not obtain any deduction from the exercise of an ISO, they tend to favor NQSOs. However, this tension is not irreconcilable. Due to the flexibility of NQSOs, a program can be designed where the employer obtains a full tax deduction for the options granted and the employee is effectively taxed at a capital gains rate on the income recognized when the options are exercised.

Example: Widget Corporation adopts an NQSO program for its employees. The program provides for the grant of NQSOs and for the company to pay a bonus to employees who exercise their options equal to the sum of (i) the additional federal taxes payable by the employees by reason of using an NQSO and (ii) an amount equal to the federal taxes payable on the amount determined in (i). If Frank has a marginal tax rate of 30 percent and has annual earnings in excess of the taxable wage base, it would take a payment of $16.45 by the company to make-up for the excess income and Medicare taxes that Frank would have to pay on each $100 of gain. The tax gross-up amount determined under (ii) is $7.55. This makes the total amount payable to Frank for each $100 of gain equal to $24. Consequently, after Frank pays his federal income and Medicare taxes on each $100 of gain and the bonus amount attributable to that gain, he is left with $85 ($124 x (100% − 31.45%)), which is equivalent to being taxed at a 15 percent capital gains rate.

In the example above, from Widget Corporation's perspective, if its marginal tax rate is 35 percent, it receives a tax benefit of $35 from each $100 of Frank's gain. Because each $100 of Frank's gain is a non-cash expense for the company, the $35 tax benefit represents a true economic gain. The company also realizes a tax benefit from the bonus paid to Frank as well as the additional Medicare taxes paid on the sum of the $100 gain and the bonus amount. This additional tax benefit is $9 (($1.45 + $24.35) x 35%). This results in a net tax savings to the company of $18.20 ($44 − $25.80) per $100 of gain. If Frank's state and local taxes are factored in (assuming that they impose a more favorable tax rate on capital gains, which is not always the case), the net tax savings will be reduced somewhat, but the company will still be better off than if it had issued ISOs.

Exercising NQSOs and ISOs

Employees who participate in an NQSO or ISO program have a difficult time choosing the optimal timing strategy for exercising their stock options. There are no rules of thumb that apply to every situation. Because there is a risk to every alternative, in some ways making the right choice is more of an art than a science. Also, remember that the most serious mistakes employees make are often the simplest ones—for example, letting valuable options lapse because of a misunderstanding or a failure to monitor the options.

A employee's decision making can be facilitated by having a clear structure to the process. The following provides a logical process to follow. The first step is to identify clear financial goals. Knowing for what the proceeds will be used, such as buying a home in 2 years or retiring in 10 years, will go a long way to bringing the right decision into focus.

The next step is to get a complete understanding of the option program. The types of questions to ask include:

- Are the options nonqualified or ISOs?
- When do options become vested and does vesting occur at once (cliff vesting) or over time (graded vesting)?
- Will the options become vested earlier if the participant dies, becomes disabled, or if there is a change in ownership?
- Are the options exercisable before they become vested?
- What is the duration of the option period?
- How long are options exercisable after termination of employment due to (a) death, (b) disability, (c) retirement, (d) voluntary termination, or (e) involuntary termination of employment?
- Do options lapse if the participant goes to work for a competitor?
- Does the company intend to grant additional options in the future?
- Where the employer is a closely held corporation, what are the terms that control the repurchase of option shares by the employer?

Knowing the rules also means understanding the tax implications. Once the type (nonqualified or ISO) is determined, the client needs to have a full appreciation of the tax timing issues. A participant does not really know the value of the options until he or she knows the value after the exercise price and after all taxes have been paid. As discussed above, the alternative minimum tax is a real issue for those holders of ISOs who choose to retain the stock to take advantage of the lower capital-gains rate.

The development of an option exercise and a stock liquidation strategy is generally best suited to employees who hold stock in, or options issued by, a public company. Once the employee of a public company understands the plan and has a general idea of what the funds will be used for, the next step is to develop a long-term liquidation plan. This can be facilitated by asking questions such as

- How many additional options are likely to be granted?
- How much wealth should be tied into the employer's stock?
- How long will employment with the company continue?

Because many employees of public companies acquire sizable blocks of stock in their company through various incentive plans, one important planning consideration is often the systematic liquidation of this stock and the purchase of other securities to better diversify the employee's investment portfolio at his or her retirement. The plan should include a strategy for which stock to liquidate first.

The plan should also have an action strategy. For example, who is going to notify heirs if the participant dies and still has stock options? What steps are in place to ensure that valuable options do not lapse? How often will the plan be reevaluated and adjusted for changing conditions?

The financial advisor can be a very important part of the process because the advisor is typically better suited than the employee to help model asset allocation, long-term projections, and tax analysis.

When devising a long-term plan, in addition to taking the above steps, the employee may want to consider some of the following strategies.

- Because stock prices historically rise over time, holding the options until the end of the exercise period is a good place to start when formulating a strategy.
- Countervailing considerations, such as diversifying the portfolio, exercising the options to meet a specific financial goal, or a realistic assessment that the stock price is unlikely to continue to increase, can be good reasons to sell sooner.
- Arguably, because options are a bonus, liquidating the position (selling the stock) at the time the options are exercised ensures a positive cash position—and does not tie up the employee's assets.
- Alternatively, if stock appreciation is relatively certain, an employee in a high tax bracket (who can afford to take some risk) should exercise early and hold the stock to change the tax treatment from ordinary income (up to 35 percent tax rate) to long-term capital gains (15 percent tax rate). However, this strategy requires cash to purchase the stock and the possibility that the gain will be lost.
- When choosing which options to exercise, first consider exercising the oldest options, even if they are not the lowest priced.
- Pay attention to the price behavior of the company's stock.
- Consider exercising the options and selling the stock (cashless transactions) over a period of time instead of all at once. This allows the price to be averaged and reduces the risk of receiving a low price for all the options, and it allows the employee to invest the proceeds into new investments over time, also reducing risk.

Gifting Opportunities

NQSOs are assets with a strong potential for growth. Accordingly, they are attractive candidates for gifts so that the anticipated appreciation can be removed from the donor's estate. The most important feature of a stock option for gift tax purposes is that it can be transferred. As discussed below, incentive stock options are required to be nontransferable in order to obtain favorable tax treatment. Thus, incentive stock options are not available for making gifts.

On the other hand, NQSOs are a more favorable vehicle for estate planning. NQSOs do not have to be nontransferable to obtain favorable tax consequences and there is no other non-tax reason why NQSOs have to be nontransferable. Moreover, in 1998 the IRS approved the transfer of NQSOs as an acceptable estate planning technique and confirmed the income and gift tax consequences of such transfers.

The favorable estate planning results that can be obtained from the transfer of NQSOs are dependent upon the making of a completed gift. A gift is complete when the donor has parted with all dominion and control over the property so that the donor no longer has the power to change its disposition. If a donor makes an incomplete gift, the gift tax consequences are deferred until the gift is completed, at which time the property may have appreciated in value.

The income and gift tax consequences of the transfer of an NQSO are determined by the regulations under Sec. 83 that address the disposition of a stock option. If the disposition of non-vested property is made in an arm's length transaction, compensation is realized by the employee to the extent that the amount realized from the disposition exceeds the amount, if any, paid for the property. In that event, the property is no longer subject to Sec. 83. If the disposition of non-vested property occurs in a non-arm's length transaction, like a gift, the employee realizes compensation income equal to the amount of money or the value of property, if any, received by the employee in connection with the disposition. In addition, Sec. 83 continues to apply to the transferred property, except that the amount previously included in income when the property was transferred is treated as an amount paid for the property.

Applying these principles to gifts of NQSOs, the IRS has determined that when an NQSO is transferred to a family member as a gift, there is no income tax consequence at that time. However, when the option is subsequently exercised by the donee, the donee receives the option shares, but the income tax consequences of the exercise are imposed on the donor as if the transfer had not occurred. In other words, the donor reports the difference between the exercise price and the fair market value of the stock on the date of exercise as income. This income continues to be wages for purposes of federal income tax withholding and employment taxes. The good news for the donor is that the shares and the income tax paid in connection with the exercise of the option have been removed from his estate. The latter payment can also be characterized as a further gift to the donee without any gift tax liability. The donee, on the other hand, has obtained the shares for a bargain price and has a basis in those shares equal to their fair market value.

Example: The employer grants to Dan Donor a vested option to purchase 500 shares of common stock at the market price ($20/share at the time of issuance) at any time over the next 10 years. After 3 years, the market price has risen to $60/share. Dan then gives the option to his son, Peter. After 5 more years, the stock price has increased to $120/share. At that time, Peter purchases all 500 shares at $20/share ($10,000). Dan now must report $50,000 ($100 x 500) of ordinary income, which is the difference between the purchase price ($10,000) and the current market value ($60,000). Peter's basis in his 500 shares is $60,000, the sum of the $10,000 exercise price and the $50,000 of ordinary income recognized by Dan.

Looking at the gift tax side of the transfer, the IRS takes the position that the transfer of nonvested NQSOs is not a completed gift. The rationale for this position is that, until the employee has completed all of the services required in order for the options to become vested, he or she does not possess an enforceable property right, which can be transferred for federal gift tax purposes. Thus, only vested NQSOs can be the subject of a completed gift. When a gift of vested NQSOs is made, the NQSOs must be valued for gift tax purposes. The IRS provides Rev. Proc. 98-34 for the purpose of establishing a safe harbor method of valuing nonpublicly traded stock options on publicly traded stock for gift and estate tax purposes. Under this revenue procedure, the taxpayer can use a generally recognized option pricing model, such as the Black-Scholes model or an accepted version of the binomial model, as long as certain conditions are met. The trade-off for using this safe harbor valuation method is that the options may be overvalued. The safe harbor approach does not allow any discount to be applied to the valuation produced by the option pricing model. For example, no discount can be taken for lack of transferability or due to the termination of the option following a termination of employment.

NQSOs are very attractive for gift-giving to family members and can also be used to make charitable gifts. In addition, NQSOs can play an important role in facilitating estate planning in any number of ways. As an example, consider this hypothetical plan of a husband and wife who own an incorporated family business. As part of his estate planning, the husband sells to each of his four children for fair market value (FMV) an option to purchase the shares of the business on a pro rata basis. The options are exercisable on the death of the last survivor of the husband and the wife and the exercise price is the FMV of the shares at the time the options become exercisable. By their terms, the options may be exercised by tendering cash or an installment note payable in no more than 15 years, or a combination of both.

At the same time, the family established a private foundation. The husband, wife, and the four children are members of the foundation's board and participate in its gift-giving program. The husband's will bequeaths the stock of the business to a marital trust for the wife's benefit. On the wife's death, or on the husband's death if the wife predeceases him, the shares pass to the foundation. This avoids estate tax due to the estate tax charitable deduction.

Under this plan, the children are required to pay the foundation the FMV of the shares of the business that it holds. The purchase price can be paid over a 15-year period, thus allowing payment to be made from the cash flow of the business.

Employee Stock Purchase Plans

A third form of stock option program which can be an addition to, or a substitute for, an ISO or NQSO program is the employee stock purchase plan. These plans are designed to satisfy and take advantage of the special tax rules contained in Code Sec. 423. Since participation in a Sec. 423 stock purchase plan must be broad based, resulting in widespread employee ownership of the employer's stock, such plans are usually only adopted by employers who want to promote that goal. Moreover, due to the valuation, accounting, securities law, and recordkeeping requirements that apply to a program covering large groups of employees, Sec 423 stock purchase plans are typically adopted by large, publicly held companies.

Sec. 423 stock purchase plan

Under a *Sec. 423 stock purchase plan*, the employer is allowed to discount the price of the stock up to 15 percent of the market value. However, this discount can actually be much larger under the look-back rules. A plan can offer the employees the option to purchase the stock over a specified period of time. During this option period, the option price can be the lesser of 85 percent of the fair market value of the stock at the time such option is granted, or 85 percent of the fair market value of the stock at the time such option is exercised. When the plan gives employees the option of the lower of the two prices, the maximum exercise period is 27 months.

Example: Breen, Inc., gives eligible employees the right to purchase stock over the next 12 months at 85 percent of the current market price, or if lesser, 85 percent of the stock price at the time the option is exercised. If the stock price is $10 at the beginning of the purchase period and goes up to $20 at the time the stock is purchased, the purchase price is just $8.50. If the price goes down to $5, the price of the purchase is $4.25.

Tax Consequences

At the time stock is purchased under a Sec. 423 plan, there are no tax consequences. Taxes are paid only at the time of the sale of the stock, and the tax consequences depend upon whether a holding period requirement has been satisfied. The requirement is that the stock is not sold within 2 years after the date that the option is granted nor within one year after the shares are purchased. When the holding period is satisfied and there is a gain from the sale, the gain is ordinary income up to the amount by which the stock's fair market value, when the option was granted, exceeded the option price. Any excess gain is capital gain. If there is a loss from the sale, it is a capital loss, and there is no ordinary income. The employer gets no deduction when the holding period requirements have been satisfied.

Example:	Y Corporation grants an option under its employee stock purchase plan to buy 100 shares of stock of Y Corporation for $20 a share at a time when the stock had a value of $22 a share. Eighteen months later, when the value of the stock is $23 a share, Rachel exercises the option to purchase 100 shares, and 14 months after that she sells the stock for $30 a share. In the year of sale, Rachel must report as wages the difference between the option price ($20) and the value at the time the option was granted ($22). The rest of the gain ($8) is capital gain, figured as follows:

Selling price ($30 x 100 shares)	$3,000
Purchase price (option price) ($20 x 100 shares)	– 2,000
Gain	$1,000
Amount reported as wages [($22 x 100 shares) – $2,000]	– 200
Amount reported as capital gain	$ 800

If the employee does not meet the holding period requirement, the ordinary income is the amount by which the stock's fair market value exceeded the option price at the time of exercise. This ordinary income is *not* limited to the gain from the sale of the stock. The basis in the stock then becomes the market value for determining future capital gains or losses. The employer receives a deduction in this case in the amount of ordinary income included by employees.

Example: The facts are the same as in the previous example, except that Rachel sold the stock only 6 months after she exercised the option. Because she did not hold the stock long enough, she must report $300 as wages and $700 as capital gain, figured as follows:

Selling price ($30 x 100 shares)	$3,000
Purchase price (option price) ($20 x 100 shares)	– 2,000
Gain	$1,000
Amount reported as wages [($23 x 100 shares) – $2,000]	– 300
Amount reported as capital gain	$ 700

Qualification Requirements

For the employer that is considering an employee stock purchase plan, be aware that to qualify, the plan must meet the following requirements:

- The plan provides that options to purchase stock are granted only to employees.
- The plan is approved by the stockholders within 12 months before or after the date such plan is adopted.
- No employee can be granted an option if such employee, immediately after the option is granted, owns stock possessing 5 percent or more of the total combined voting power or value of all classes of stock.
- The plan must cover all employees except those with less than 2 years of employment, employees whose customary employment is 20 hours or less per week, employees whose customary employment is for not more than 5 months in any calendar year, and highly compensated employees.
- All employees granted such options shall have the same rights and privileges, except that the amount of stock which may be purchased by any employee under such option may bear a uniform relationship

to the total compensation, or the basic or regular rate of compensation, of employees, and the plan may provide that no employee may purchase more than a maximum amount of stock fixed under the plan.

- The employer cannot permit an employee to buy more than $25,000 of stock in any one year, for each calendar year from grant date through the date on which the option is exercised. This limit is based upon the stock's fair market value when the option is granted. This limit, however, is cumulative. For example, if the stock's fair market value on the date of grant in 2006 is $200 per share and no shares are purchased in 2006, 250 shares may be purchased in 2007.

Planning

If the employer sponsors an ESSP, employees can earn a significant return on their investment. If the plan does not use the look-back rule, but simply provides a 15 percent discount off the current market price, the employees immediately earn a return of 17.6 percent when they purchase stock. For example, if the stock is selling at $10 and the employee purchases the stock at $8.50 (a 15 percent discount), the participant has earned $1.50. On an investment of $8.50, the return is 17.6 percent ($1.50/$8.50). Of course, if the participant holds the stock to satisfy the holding period requirements, the stock's value could possibly decline.

When the plan has a look-back purchase price, the potential gain is much higher. If, for example, the stock can be purchased at a 15 percent discount off the price at the time the period begins and the stock price rises from $10 at the beginning of the period to $20 at the time the stock is purchased, the participant has a return of 135 percent ($11.50/$8.50).

From the employer's perspective, establishing an ESSP is a much bigger commitment than that made under the other forms of stock option programs. Stock option programs are generally limited to certain executives while ESSPs must cover most full-time employees. The employer must be committed to the concept (and the cost) of encouraging employee stock ownership through a discount program.

OTHER FORMS OF EQUITY-BASED COMPENSATION

Phantom Stock

phantom stock

Phantom stock is the name given to what is essentially a bookkeeping entry on behalf of the executive as if he or she had been given stock in the company. Units analogous to company shares are granted to executives pursuant to a contractual undertaking, and the value of the units generally equals the market value of the stock underlying the units at the time of grant. Phantom units mature at a fixed date, typically at retirement or 5 to 15 years after the grant of the phantom stock. On the maturation date, the company may pay the executive (in cash or stock) the difference between the initial value of the units and the current value of the units based on the stock's current market price. In some plans, dividend equivalents may be credited to the units just as dividends would be paid to the underlying stock.

Example: Employer grants Executive A 100 shares of phantom stock valued at $5,000 ($50 per share). The phantom stock matures after 5 years and at maturity its value has increased to $7,500 ($75 per share). At that time, the employer pays the employee $2,500, the difference between the value at the time of the grant and the value at the time of maturity.

On the payment date, the appreciation in the value of the units is taxed to the executive as ordinary income and is subject to withholding and employment taxes. The company takes a tax deduction in the amount of the executive's taxable income from the units.

As with other incentive plans, the executive has the possibility of large gains. Although one advantage of phantom stock over stock options is that the executive avoids the financing cost associated with exercise of the options, in some cases gains may be capped by company-imposed maximums designed to limit the company's potential payment. Because payment is typically triggered by retirement, the executive generally has no flexibility in choosing when to value the award. In cases where the issuer is a public company and the executive can control the form or timing of the unit's valuation or settlement, trading restrictions similar to those applicable to stock options also apply to insiders holding phantom stock.

Restricted Stock

restricted stock plan

In a *restricted stock plan,* the executive is given (usually at no cost) shares of company stock. The shares are actually stamped with specific restrictions, which require that the executive give the shares back to the company upon a specified event. Most commonly, the restriction is that if the executive stops working prior to some specified date, he or she will have to forfeit some or all of the shares. Another common restriction is a clause that requires forfeiture if the executive terminates employment and goes to work with a competitor (commonly called a noncompete clause). Dividends on the stock are usually paid to the executive during the entire period in which he or she holds the restricted stock.

From a tax perspective, the shares of restricted stock are generally not taxed until the substantial limitations on the stock lapse. At that time, the value of the stock will be treated as ordinary income to the executive and will be deductible as compensation expense to the employer. Any dividends paid to the executive will also be treated as compensation income—both includible as income to the executive and deductible as compensation by the employer.

Example:	Company grants to Billy Bigshot 200 shares of stock worth $20,000. The stock is restricted and will be forfeited unless Billy works until age 65, at which time the stock becomes nonforfeitable and freely transferable by Billy. At age 65, Billy retires and decides to hold the stock, which is now valued at $80,000. For the year in which Billy attains age 65, he must report $80,000 of ordinary income and the company is entitled to an $80,000 deduction.

In the preceding example, Billy could have chosen to report income in the year that the restricted stock was transferred to him. This decision to accelerate the reporting of income is referred to as a "Sec. 83(b) election," taking its name from the section of the Code that authorizes the election. When a Sec. 83(b) election is made, the amount of ordinary income that is recognized is based on the stock's fair market value on the date of grant. The employer is also entitled to a corresponding deduction. Subsequently, when the stock vests and is sold, there is a capital gain, assuming that the stock has appreciated in value. The capital gain is long-term or short-term, depending on the holding period which is measured from the date of grant, rather than the date on which ownership of the stock vests in the employee.

Example:	If in the preceding example Billy had decided to make a Sec. 83(b) election, in the year of transfer he would have recognized $20,000 of ordinary income. Then at his retirement he would not have had to report any additional income. Later, if Billy sold the stock for $100,000, he would have had a long-term capital gain of $80,000, assuming the holding period requirements had been met.

While a Sec. 83(b) election can often result in considerable tax savings, it is not a decision that should be taken lightly. A Sec. 83(b) election involves no small amount of risk. For example, if Billy had left the company before becoming vested in his stock, he would have reported $20,000 of income that he never received. However, the tax law would not permit Billy to take a tax deduction of any kind for the taxes paid in connection with his Sec. 83(b) election. Moreover, if the stock goes down in value after the Sec. 83(b) election is made and the stock is eventually sold at a loss, the loss must be taken as a capital loss on the employee's tax return even though the income from the Sec. 83(b) election was previously taxed at ordinary income rates. Nevertheless, an executive who (1) does not expect to lose the stock, (2) has the money to pay taxes at the time of the grant, and (3) expects the stock to greatly appreciate in value may want to consider the election.

In order to make a Sec. 83(b) election, certain procedures must be followed. These procedures include the following:

- The election must be made within 30 days of the stock transfer.
- The election must be sent to the IRS within that 30-day period.
- The election must be attached to the executive's tax return for the year in which the election is made.
- A copy of the election must be provided to the employer.

For all intents and purposes, a Sec. 83(b) election should be considered irrevocable. It is only under the most highly unusual circumstances that the IRS will consider allowing a taxpayer to revoke a Sec. 83(b) election.

For the employer, restricted stock plans are another way to tie the employee to the company (through the vesting provision) and to tie the benefit to the performance of the company stock. From the employee's perspective, this type of deferred compensation is relatively secure because the stock is titled in the executive's name, meaning that the company's creditors cannot get to this asset if the company performs badly. (However, if the company performs badly, the stock may not be worth very much in any event.) Another advantage is that the employee does not have to pay anything in order to get stock ownership, unlike stock option plans. The biggest limitation, from the employee's perspective, is the possibility of forfeiture.

Stock Appreciation Right

stock appreciation right (SAR)

A *stock appreciation right (SAR)* is an arrangement under which an executive has the right to receive the amount of the increase in the value of employer stock during a specified period. The executive receives the increase in value by cashing out or exercising the SAR, similar to a stock option.

Example: Wanda Wunderkind receives SARs with respect to 1,000 shares of employer stock when the stock is valued at $100 a share and the SARs may be exercisable for 3 years. For a period of 3 years, Wanda has the right at any time to receive cash in the amount of the increase in value of up to 1,000 shares of stock since the time that the SARs were granted. If after year 1 the stock value has increased to $110 a share, Wanda can exercise 100 of her SARs and receive a cash payment of $1,000. Similarly, if after year 2 the stock value increases to $200 a share, Wanda can exercise her remaining 900 SARs and receive a cash payment of $90,000.

The grant of an SAR does not result in taxation because the executive only has the right to receive income in the future. However, due to the fact that an employee has the unfettered right to receive the current increase in the value of the underlying stock upon request, an SAR does raise an issue of constructive receipt. However, based on a consistent line of revenue rulings (issued before the enactment of Sec. 409A), the IRS has taken the position that a substantial limitation on the executive's ability to receive the current increase in stock value results from the fact that the executive loses the right to future appreciation in the stock once she exercises the SAR. In other words, the executive must surrender a valuable right in order to exercise the SAR. However, care must be taken at the end of the SAR term. Because there will be no more future appreciation to be lost, any value in the SAR at that time may be constructively received by the holder if the SAR has not been exercised.

Once an SAR has been exercised, the amount received by the executive is taxable as ordinary income. The employer generally receives a deduction for the same amount. The ordinary income recognized by the executive is subject to income tax withholding and is considered wages subject to employment taxes.

CHAPTER REVIEW

Key Terms

nonqualified stock options (NQSOs) [16-3]

noncompete clause [16-3]
incentive stock option (ISO) [16-4]

Sec. 423 stock purchase plan [16-5]   restricted stock plan [16-6]
phantom stock [16-6]   stock appreciation right [16-6]

Review Questions

Review questions are based on the learning objectives in this chapter. Thus, a [16-3] at the end of a question means that the question is based on learning objective 16-3. If there are multiple objectives, they are all listed.

1. What are three key reasons that equity-based compensation is a popular compensation component? [16-1]

2. What are the points in time that valuation of the stock is important in the lifespan of an equity-based program? [16-2]

3. Describe what is meant by the concept of the employee's "economic risk." [16-2]

4. What legal considerations must be used in evaluating an equity-based compensation program? [16-2]

5. What are the advantages of granting awards under a clearly defined plan or program? [16-2]

6. What is the intrinsic value of a stock option? [16-3]

7. What are the tax consequences of nonqualified stock options? [16-3]

8. What are the tax consequences of incentive stock options? [16-4]

9. What are the tax consequences of the sale of 100 shares of stock, assuming the stock was purchased under a Sec. 423 stock purchase plan and the participant satisfied both the 2-year and one-year holding requirements? [16-5]

Stock price at beginning of option period ($5 x 100)	$500
Purchase price ($4.25 x 100)	$425
Stock price at the time of purchase ($10 x 100)	$1,000
Stock price at the time of sale ($15 x 100)	$1,500

10. What is the objective of a phantom stock plan? [16-6]

11. Explain the tax-timing strategies available to an executive covered by a restricted stock plan. [16-6]

12. Explain how an SAR rewards the executive. [16-6]

Individual Retirement Plans—Part I

Learning Objectives

An understanding of the material in this chapter should enable you to

---

17-1.   Identify the different types of individual retirement arrangements.

17-2.   Describe the contribution limits that apply to IRAs and Roth IRAs.

17-3.   Determine who is eligible to make deductible and nondeductible IRA contributions.

17-4.   Determine who is eligible to make a Roth IRA contribution.

17-5.   Describe a Roth IRA conversion and when this transaction is allowed.

Chapter Outline

OVERVIEW

    Individual retirement plans are a vital part of the financial planning business. They are important both to the financial security of clients and to the business efforts of financial services professionals. Even though the best opportunities are for lower- and middle-class workers, wealthy individuals often have plans with large sums that have been rolled over from employer-sponsored tax-advantaged retirement plans.

    Over the years, Congress has changed the IRA rules numerous times. The changes in the last few years have all been favorable. The Taxpayer Relief Act of 1997 added the Roth IRA and made the deductible IRA available to more taxpayers. The Economic Growth and Tax Relief Reconciliation Act of 2001 increased the maximum allowable contribution limits and added a catch-up contribution for older participants. The Pension Protection Act of 2006 made the increased contribution limits permanent and added a cost-of-living adjustment to the various IRA and Roth IRA income phaseout limits. As a result, proper use of traditional IRAs, the newer Roth IRAs, and rollover IRAs can go a long way toward providing retirement security. The financial services professional can help clients achieve their goals by explaining the IRA rules, encouraging saving for retirement, and marketing IRA investments.

IRA

Roth IRA

    With the introduction of the Roth IRA, there are now two types of savings vehicles that are called IRAs (individual retirement accounts). The traditional plan is still referred to as an *IRA*; the newer plan is referred to as a Roth IRA. Traditional IRAs are similar to employer-sponsored tax-sheltered retirement plans in many ways. Both are tax-favored savings plans that encourage the accumulation of savings for retirement because they allow contributions to be made with pretax dollars and earnings to be tax deferred until retirement. With *Roth IRAs*, contributions are made on an after-tax basis, but earnings are not taxed and qualifying distributions are tax free. Because the tax benefits of both types of plans result in a significant loss of revenue to the federal government, the stringent rules encourage retirement savings but at the same time try and minimize revenue loss.

    The funding vehicles and types of allowable investments are the same for both traditional IRAs and the Roth IRA. As will be discussed in chapter 18, both types of IRAs can have as funding instruments a trust or custodial account (individual retirement account) or an annuity contract (individual retirement annuity). With either type of funding vehicle, a wide array of traditional investment strategies can be used.

CONTRIBUTION LIMITS

The maximum allowable contribution to an IRA or Roth IRA for 2007 is the lesser of $4,000 or 100 percent of compensation. The $4,000 limit applies to all traditional IRAs and Roth IRAs to which a taxpayer contributes for the year. For example, if the taxpayer makes a $4,000 contribution to a traditional IRA, no contributions can be made to a Roth IRA for the year. The maximum contribution limit is scheduled to become $5,000 in 2008 and be indexed for inflation in years thereafter.

Example:	Dana is a college student and earns $2,500 for the year from a part-time job. The maximum contribution she can make to an IRA or Roth IRA is $2,500 because her earnings are less than the maximum contribution.

Compensation is earnings from wages, salaries, tips, professional fees, bonuses, and any other amount a taxpayer receives for providing personal services. In addition, alimony and separate-maintenance payments are also considered compensation for IRA purposes. Compensation does not include earnings and profits from property, such as rental and dividend income, or amounts received as a pension or annuity. As a general rule, if it is income the taxpayer worked for in a given year, the contribution can be made; if it is derived from investments or retirement income, it is not eligible.

For self-employeds, compensation includes earned income from personal services, reduced by any contributions to a qualified plan on behalf of the individual. Self-employeds with a net loss from self-employment cannot make IRA contributions unless they also have salary or wage income. In this case, they do not have to reduce the amount of salary income by the net loss from self-employment. If there are both salary or wage income and net income from self-employment, the two amounts are combined to determine the amount that can be contributed.

Example:	In his first year in business, Don, a self-employed creator of computer software, had a net loss of $17,000, largely due to start-up costs. However, he received $4,000 from part-time teaching. Don may contribute up to $4,000 to an IRA because his salary will not be reduced by his self-employment loss.

Spousal IRAs

If a married person does not work or has limited compensation, his or her spouse can contribute up to $4,000 to a *spousal IRA* (which can be either a traditional or a Roth IRA) as long as the following conditions are satisfied:

- The taxpayer is married at the end of the year and files a joint tax return.
- The spouse earns less than the taxpayer.
- The couple has compensation that equals or exceeds contributions to the IRAs of both persons ($8,000 if $4,000 is contributed for each).

Spousal IRAs can be set up even if the taxpayer does not contribute to his or her own account, or contributions can be made for both spouses, or the taxpayer can make contributions just to the taxpayer's IRA even though a spousal IRA already exists. However, no more than $4,000 can be placed in either IRA for the year (unless the individual is eligible for the catch-up contribution discussed below).

Catch-up Election

An individual who has attained age 50 before the end of the taxable year can contribute an additional $1,000 (the limit for 2007–2008). For example, in 2007, a 55-year-old individual could contribution up to $5,000 to an IRA or Roth IRA (assuming he or she was otherwise eligible under the phaseout limits discussed below).

Example:	In 2007, John and Sarah are married, file jointly, and have an AGI of $120,000. They are each eligible to make Roth IRA contributions. Because they are both over 50 years old, the maximum contribution for each is $5,000, or $10,000 in total.

Timing of Contributions

Contributions to an IRA or Roth IRA can be made at any time during the tax year for which the contribution relates or up to April 15 of the following year. Contributions for the year can be made at once or over time.

Excess Contributions

excess contribution

An *excess contribution* is any amount contributed to an IRA or Roth IRA that exceeds the maximum contribution limit. Excess contributions will result in an excise tax of 6 percent on the excess. The penalty tax can be avoided by withdrawing the excess amount (plus earnings) by the tax deadline for the year. The taxpayer does have to include the excess amount in his or her gross income and may be subject to the 10 percent Section 72(t) premature distribution tax on the earnings withdrawn. With traditional IRAs, excess contributions are relatively rare because most taxpayers can contribute $4,000—even though only a portion of that may be deductible. However, excess contributions may be more common in the Roth IRA because the maximum allowable contribution is reduced when the taxpayer's adjusted gross income (AGI) exceeds a specified amount.

Recharacterization

recharacterization

A taxpayer may be able to treat a contribution made to one type of IRA as made to another type of IRA. This transaction is called a *recharacterization* and it requires that the contribution be transferred from the trustee of the first IRA (the one that the contribution was made to) to the trustee of the second IRA by the due date, plus extensions, of the individual's tax return for the year that the contribution was made. Taxpayers may make this change simply because they change their minds or to solve a tax problem. Take the person who contributes $4,000 to a Roth IRA during the year, and then discovers after the year's end that he or she earned too much and was not eligible to make the contribution. If that person was eligible for either a nondeductible or deductible contribution to a traditional IRA, the Roth IRA contribution could be recharacterized as a traditional IRA contribution to resolve the problem of the excess contribution to the Roth IRA. A recharacterization also requires the following steps:

- Include in the transfer any net income attributable to the contribution. If there was a net loss, the contribution transferred is reduced by the amount of the loss.
- Report the recharacterization on your tax return for the year during which the contribution was made.
- Treat the contribution as having been made to the second IRA on the date that it was actually made to the first IRA.

TRADITIONAL IRAS

Any person under age 70½ who earns compensation can make a contribution to an IRA. For some, the contribution will not be deductible, but earnings will be tax deferred until benefits are distributed. However, most individuals making traditional IRA contributions do so in order to receive an income tax deduction. Not all taxpayers are eligible.

Eligibility for Deductible Contributions

IRA contributions will always be deductible if neither the taxpayer nor the taxpayer's spouse is an active participant in an employer-maintained retirement plan. If the taxpayer is an active participant, then the contribution is deductible only if his or her adjusted gross income falls below prescribed limits (designed to approximate a middle-class income). If an individual is not an active participant, but his or her spouse is, then the contribution is deductible (for the nonparticipant) if the couple's income is less than a different higher income threshold.

Example: Brendan, who is single and has an AGI of $180,000 for 2007, is self-employed and is not an active participant in a retirement plan. Because he has more than $4,000 of income from employment and is not an active participant in an employer-sponsored plan, he can make a deductible contribution of $4,000 to an IRA. This example illustrates that when a single person is not an active participant, he or she can always make a deductible IRA contribution, regardless of the income level.

Active Participant Status

active participant

An individual is an *active participant* if he or she is a participant in an employer-maintained retirement plan. Employer plans include every type of qualified plan—defined-benefit pension plans, money-purchase plans, target-benefit plans, profit-sharing plans, and stock plans. They also include 403(b) tax-sheltered annuity plans, SEPs, and SIMPLEs. Federal, state, or local government plans are also taken into account. An employee who is covered only by a nonqualified plan is not considered an active participant and can, therefore, make deductible IRA contributions.

The term *active participant* has a special meaning that depends on the type of plan involved.

Defined-Benefit Plans.   An individual who is eligible to participate in a defined-benefit plan is considered an active participant in the plan. This is true even if he or she declines to participate or does not earn a benefit accrual for the year. One exception is that if the defined-benefit plan is frozen—meaning that no additional benefits are accruing for any participant—than participants will not be considered active participants in the plan.

Defined-Contribution Plans.   A person is an active participant in a defined contribution plan if the plan specifies that employer contributions must be allocated to the individual's account (as in a money-purchase pension plan). For defined-contribution plans with discretionary contributions, such as profit-sharing plans and 401(k) plans, the participant must actually receive a contribution to be considered an active participant. Any type of contribution will count, including elective salary deferral contributions and even reallocated forfeitures from a terminated participant's account. SEPs, SIMPLEs, and 403(b) plans are treated as defined-contribution plans under these rules.

A special rule applies when contributions are completely discretionary under the plan and are not made until after the end of the plan year (ending with or within the employee's tax year in question). In this case, to recognize that a plan participant may not know whether he or she is an active participant by the time the IRA contribution deadline arrives, the employer's contribution is attributable to the following year.

Example:	Sally first becomes eligible for XYZ Corporation's profit-sharing plan for the plan year ending December 31, 2006. The company is on a calendar fiscal year and does not decide to make a contribution for the 2006 plan year until June 1, 2007. Sally is not considered an active participant in the plan for the 2006 plan year. However, due to the 2007 contribution, she is an active participant for the 2007 plan year.

When the plan year of the employer's plan (regardless of whether the plan is a defined-benefit or defined-contribution plan) is not the calendar year, an individual's active-participant status is dependent upon whether he or she is an active participant for the plan year ending with or within the particular calendar year in question.

Example:	Susan first becomes eligible for the ABC Corporation's money-purchase pension plan for the plan year June 1, 2006, to May 30, 2007. Susan is an active participant for 2007 (but not 2006) because the plan year ended "with or within" calendar year 2007.

Finally, note that in determining active-participant status, participation for any part of the plan year counts as participation for the whole plan year, and that whether or not the participant is vested in his or her benefit has no bearing on the determination.

Example:	Jeffery makes salary deferral contributions to the GHI Corporation's 401(k) plan in January. The plan has a calendar plan year. On February 1, he terminates employment and does not participate in another retirement plan for the rest of the year. Jeffrey was not entitled to the employer-matching contribution or any other employer contribution for the year. However, Jeffery is still an active participant because salary deferral contributions count as an allocation to his account, and he was in the plan for a portion of the plan year.

Income Level

If an individual is an active participant, fully deductible contributions are allowed only if the taxpayer has adjusted gross income (AGI) below a specified level. The deduction is then phased out over a range, with no deduction allowed if a specified threshold is exceeded. The phaseout ranges as shown in table 17-1 depend upon the participant's income tax filing status.

When applying the phaseout limits, calculation of the AGI is somewhat modified. AGI is determined without regard to the exclusion for foreign earned income, but Social Security benefits includible in gross income and losses or gains on passive investments are taken into account. Also, contributions to an IRA or Roth IRA are not deducted.

TABLE 17-1
2007 Limits for Deductible IRA Contributions

Filing Status	Full IRA Deduction	Reduced IRA Deduction	No IRA Deduction
Individual (or head of household)	$52,000 or less	$52,000.01– $61999.99	$62,000 or more
Married filing jointly	$83,000 or less	$83,000.01– $102,999.99	$103,000 or more
Married filing separately	$0	$.01–$9,999.99	$10,000 or more

For taxpayers whose AGI falls between the no-deduction level and the full-deduction level, the deduction is reduced pro rata. To compute the reduction, use the following formula:

$$\text{Deductible amount} = \text{max. contribution} - \left(\text{max. contribution} \times \frac{\text{AGI} - \text{filing status floor}}{\text{phaseout range}} \right)$$

Two operational rules apply to taxpayers who fall into the reduced IRA category. First, the IRS allows the adjusted limitation to be rounded up to the next $10 increment. For example, if the formula for Kay shows her eligible to make a deductible contribution of $758.43, her deductible contribution is rounded up to $760. The second rule that applies to the reduction formula mandates a $200 floor. In other words, even if Ed's deductible IRA contribution works out to $57, Ed is still entitled to make a $200 deductible contribution.

Example: Bob and Rita Dufus (a married couple under age 50 filing jointly) are both working, are both active participants, and have a combined adjusted gross income of $93,000 for 2007. Bob and Rita can each make the full IRA contribution of $4,000 (total $8,000). However, only a portion of each contribution is deductible. Because their AGI is $10,000 more than the lower limit for married couples ($83,000) they each lose one half (totally phased out over $20,000) of the deductible contribution. Each can deduct $2,000 (total $4,000). Using the formula,

$$\$4,000 - \left(\$4,000 \times \frac{\$93,000 - \$83,000}{\$20,000} \right)$$

Married Taxpayers with Spouses Who Are Active Participants

If a married taxpayer and his or her spouse are both active participants, then the deduction rules just described apply to both IRAs. However, the rules are different when only one spouse is an active participant. In this case, a $4,000 deductible IRA contribution is allowed for the nonactive participant spouse as long as the couple's AGI does not exceed $156,000. The deduction is phased out if the couple's joint AGI exceeds $156,000 and will be gone entirely if their AGI is $166,000 or more (as indexed for 2007). These phaseout rules apply in the same way as the other deductible IRA phaseout rules. A deductible contribution is not available for the nonactive participant spouse if the couple files separate tax returns.

Example: Joe and Jane Morgan, each aged 43, ask you whether they are allowed to make deductible contributions for 2007. They file a joint tax return. Only Joe works outside of the home, and their expected adjusted AGI for 2007 is $110,000. Only Joe is an active participant in an employer-sponsored retirement plan. Joe cannot make a deductible IRA contribution on his own behalf because their adjusted AGI will exceed $103,000 (the phaseout amount in 2007). However, the couple can make a $4,000 deductible IRA contribution to Jane's spousal IRA because their AGI is less than $156,000.

Rollover Contributions

In addition to annual contributions, an IRA is allowed to accept certain rollover contributions. The IRA rollover permits the financial services professional to manage and service large asset accumulations. This opportunity continues to grow as more company pension plans today give participants a lump-sum option and workers continue to accumulate large sums in their company's 401(k) plan.

There are several types of rollovers that involve individual retirement arrangements. This subject is discussed further in chapter 24, but here is a brief overview:

rollover

- *Rollover* from one individual retirement arrangement to another individual retirement arrangement. Taxpayers can withdraw all or part of the balance in an IRA and reinvest it within 60 days in another IRA. The reasons for doing this include changing trusts or custodial accounts (because of dissatisfaction with investment performance or service) or even the temporary use of the IRA asset. This type of rollover can only occur once each year.

trustee-to-trustee transfer

- *Trustee-to-trustee transfer.* An IRA owner who wants to change service providers can transfer the account directly from one trustee (or custodian) to another. Trustee-to-trustee transfers ensure that the participant does not violate the 60-day rule.

- *Rollover from a qualified plan or 403(b) plan to an IRA.* Under the rules applicable today, most distributions made from a qualified plan, 403(b) plan, or 457 plan sponsored by the government can be rolled over (in full or in part) into a new or existing IRA. The rollover is not allowed when the distribution is part of a series of periodic payments over the participant's life expectancy or over a period of 10 years or more, or if the distribution is a hardship withdrawal from 401(k) plan. The problem with this type of rollover is that distributions from the qualified plan, 403(b) annuity, or 457 plan will be subject to a 20 percent income tax withholding.

direct rollover

- *Direct rollover.* To avoid the 20 percent withholding, a participant in a qualified plan, 403(b) annuity, or 457 plan should elect instead what is referred to as a *direct rollover* from the plan to the IRA. These plans are required to give participants a form in which they elect the direct payment to the IRA trustee. When the direct rollover is elected, the normal 20 percent income tax withholding requirements on the distribution do not apply.

Tax Treatment of Distributions

Taxpayers can generally withdraw all or part of their IRAs at any time. Unless the participant has made nondeductible contributions, distributions from IRAs are treated as ordinary income and are subject to federal income tax. Nondeductible contributions are withdrawn tax free on a pro rata basis. If the participant dies, payments to beneficiaries are still subject to income tax. However, the income is treated as "income in respect to a decedent," which means that income taxes are reduced by the amount of estate taxes paid as a result of the IRA.

If distributions are made prior to age 59½, the Sec 72(t) excise tax imposes an additional 10 percent tax unless an exception applies. Exceptions are made for payments on account of death, disability, or for the payment of certain medical expenses. Another exception allows substantially equal periodic payments over the remaining life of the participant and a chosen beneficiary. Another allows payments for qualified higher education expenses for education furnished to the taxpayer, the taxpayer's spouse, or any child or grandchild of the taxpayer or taxpayer's spouse at an eligible educational institution. A final exception is for distributions to pay for acquisition costs of a first home for the participant, spouse, or any child, grandchild, or ancestor of the participant or spouse. However, this exception has a $10,000 lifetime limit per IRA participant.

IRAs are also subject to rules that control the maximum length of the tax-deferral period. These are minimum-distribution rules that generally require distributions to begin when the participant attains age 70½ and also require specified payments at the participant's death. Each of these tax subjects are covered in greater depth in chapter 24.

ROTH IRAS

Determining whether an individual is eligible to make a contribution to a Roth IRA is simpler than with a traditional IRA. Eligibility is entirely dependent upon an individual's adjusted AGI and tax filing status. An individual's active participant status is not relevant. Also, unlike traditional IRAs, contributions can even be made after attainment of age 70½.

A single taxpayer with AGI of $99,000 or less (as indexed for 2007) can make the maximum allowable Roth IRA contribution (as long as he or she has compensation from employment and has not made contributions to other IRAs or Roth IRAs). The ability to contribute to a Roth IRA is phased out for single taxpayers with an adjusted AGI between $99,000 and $114,000 (pro rata reduction over $15,000 income spread). For married couples filing jointly, each spouse can make the maximum contribution as long as the couple's adjusted AGI is $156,000 or less (as indexed for 2007). The ability to contribute to a Roth IRA is phased out for joint filers with an AGI between $156,000 and $166,000 (pro rata reduction over $10,000 income spread). For married taxpayers filing separately, the phaseout range is $0 to $10,000. For purposes of this calculation, the AGI is adjusted in the same way as for traditional IRAs.

Example: Joe and Jane Morgan, the same couple who asked about deductible IRA contributions, also want to know about their Roth options for 2007. Remember that they are each aged 43, they file a joint tax return, and their expected adjusted AGI for 2007 is $110,000. Only Joe is an active participant in an employer-sponsored retirement plan. Assuming that they don't make any contributions to other traditional IRAs or Roth IRAs, a $4,000 contribution to a Roth IRA could be made for both Joe and Jane Morgan because their income does not exceed $156,000. Now that they know their options, the couple decides to make a $4,000 deductible IRA contribution for Jane and a Roth IRA contribution for John.

Rollovers and Conversions

Distributions from one Roth IRA can be rolled over tax free to another Roth IRA. As with traditional IRAs, the rollover has to occur within 60 days and can only occur once a year. The transaction can also be made as a trustee-to-trustee transfer.

Also, amounts in a traditional IRA can be rolled over to a Roth IRA if certain eligibility requirements are satisfied. Such transactions are referred to as *Roth IRA conversions*. The conversion can be accomplished with a distribution from a traditional IRA, which is contributed (rolled over) to a Roth IRA within 60-days. Or the conversion can be accomplished with a direct transfer of assets to a Roth IRA, either with a new trustee or with the same trustee. A conversion can also occur if the IRA is a SEP-IRA or a SIMPLE-IRA, except that SIMPLEs cannot be converted in the first 2 years. Before 2008, amounts cannot be converted directly from a qualified plan or 403(b) annuity to a Roth IRA. The amount would have to be rolled into a traditional IRA and then converted into a Roth IRA. The Pension Protection Act of 2006 simplified these rules: beginning 2008 the conversion can occur directly from the qualified plan, 403(b) plan, or even a government-sponsored 457 plan.

An individual is eligible to convert from a traditional IRA to a Roth IRA for years prior to 2010 if his or her AGI for the tax year does not exceed $100,000. The dollar limit is the same for both single individuals and married couples filing jointly—married couples filing separately are not eligible for a conversion.

When an amount is rolled over from a traditional IRA, the distribution (valued at the time of the distribution from the IRA) is subject to income tax (taxed as ordinary income), but is not subject to the 10 percent early distribution excise tax. However, because this could result in the avoidance of the 10 percent early distribution tax, individuals who withdraw converted amounts from a Roth IRA within 5 tax years of the conversion are subject to the 10 percent Sec. 72(t) penalty tax on early withdrawals (unless one of the exceptions to that tax applies).

Example: Candy Street converted a $100,000 IRA last year when she was age 44. The following year Candy decides to start a business and withdraws $60,000. Since she paid income tax on the $100,000 at the time of the conversion, she can withdraw the $60,000 without paying ordinary income tax. However, since the withdrawal is within 5 years of the conversion Candy will have to pay a $6,000 Sec. 72(t) early withdrawal penalty tax. The tax can still be avoided if one of the exceptions to the penalty tax applies, for example if Candy was taking the withdrawal to pay for qualified higher-education expenses.

The rules require that the conversion occur before the end of the year for which the conversion is being made. Technically, this means that if an individual wants to convert an IRA in 2006, the amount must be distributed from the traditional IRA by December 31, 2006. However, it can still be rolled over within 60 days of the end of the year.

Example: Brendan Bartels is single and wants to convert his $80,000 IRA to a Roth IRA in 2006. He withdraws the $80,000 from the traditional IRA on December 31, 2006. On February 15, 2007, he rolls the benefit into a Roth IRA. This transaction is treated as a 2006 transaction, and Brendan is taxed on the value at the time the amount was distributed from the IRA.

Because a conversion has to occur before the end of the year, it is quite possible that the individual's AGI is not yet known at the time of the conversion. For example, Sally, who is single, expects to have an AGI of $95,000. On December 1, 2006, she converts a $10,000 IRA. After the year ends and she calculates her taxes, it turns out that she had an AGI of $102,000 for 2006. The law allows an undoing of the Roth IRA conversion without penalty as long as the amount is transferred back to a traditional IRA by the due date of the tax return (plus extensions) for the year, and that any earnings on the account are also returned. In IRS Publication 590, the IRS indicates that even if the taxpayer has filed his or her tax return, the recharacterization can occur up until October 15, as long as an amended return is filed. Recharacterizations can only occur once for each tax year.

YOUR FINANCIAL SERVICES PRACTICE:
ROTH IRA CONVERSIONS IN A DOWN MARKET

When an IRA is converted into a Roth IRA, the participant pays taxes on the value of the converted amount on the date of conversion. This means that when the market is down and IRA values are low, it is a good time to convert an IRA into a Roth. If the value of the converted Roth IRA continues to decline, the individual still has a safety net. The account can be recharacterized as a traditional IRA, generally up until the October 15 of the following year.

Beginning in 2010, an important change will occur for Roth IRA conversions. The income cap will be eliminated, giving high-income taxpayers the opportunity to convert a traditional IRA into a Roth IRA. For conversions in 2010, taxpayers will also have the option to recognize all taxable income from the conversion in 2010, or to spread the income over the next two tax period (2011 and 2012). With the value of the Roth IRA some taxpayers may want to prepare for this opportunity by maximizing contributions to tax-advantaged plans and IRAs. Since there are no income limits on nondeductible contributions, one way to plan for this opportunity is to maximize contributions to nondeductible IRAs.

Tax Treatment of Roth IRA Distributions

Any "qualified distribution" from a Roth IRA is free from federal income taxes. Qualified distributions must satisfy two requirements. First, the distribution must be made after the 5-tax-year period beginning with the first tax year for which a contribution was made to any Roth IRA established for the individual. Second, the distribution has to be (1) made on or after the date on which the owner attains age 59½, (2) made to a beneficiary or the owner's estate on or after the date of the owner's death, (3) attributable to the owner's disability, or (4) made to pay for up to $10,000 of qualified first-time homebuyer expenses.

If these requirements are not satisfied, the distribution is referred to as a nonqualifying distribution. Generally, an individual can withdraw his or her Roth IRA contributions (or converted contributions) without income tax consequences. Once all contributions have been withdrawn, amounts representing earnings are subject to both income tax and the 10 percent

Sec. 72(t) excise tax. The tax treatment of Roth IRAs is discussed further in chapter 24.

CHAPTER REVIEW

Key Terms

IRA [17-1]	active participant [17-3]
Roth IRA [17-1]	rollover [17-3]
spousal IRA [17-2]	trustee-to-trustee transfer [17-3]
excess contribution [17-2]	direct rollover [17-3]
recharacterization [17-2]	

Review Questions

Review questions are based on the learning objectives in this chapter. Thus, a [17-3] at the end of a question means that the question is based on learning objective 17-3. If there are multiple objectives, they are all listed.

1. How are traditional IRAs similar to qualified plans? [17-1]

2. How is a Roth IRA different from a traditional IRA? [17-1]

3. Answer these common client questions about contributions to IRAs and Roth IRAs for 2007. [17-2]
    a. If I make the maximum contribution to a traditional IRA, can I make additional contributions to a Roth IRA?
    b. I'm a college student and I'm not planning to work in 2007. Can my parents make a Roth IRA contribution for me?
    c. When is the last date I can make a contribution for 2007?
    d. I made a Roth IRA contribution of $4,000, expecting that my income would be under the allowable threshold. I ended up earning too much and now am ineligible to make the contribution. What do I do now?

4. What do you think are the governmental policies that are fostered with the IRA deduction rules that consider active participant status and income phaseouts? [17-3]

5. Which of the following employees is considered an active participant? [17-3]
    a. John has a target-benefit Keogh plan to which he contributes annually.
    b. Barb works for an employer who maintains a defined-benefit plan, but Barb is not eligible to participate in the plan.
    c. Patty is a member of a 401(k) plan and makes a 5 percent salary reduction that is not matched.

d.   Bob is a member of his employer's profit-sharing plan; the employer has announced that no contribution will be made for the year.

e.   Tim's employer does not have any form of retirement plan. Tim's wife works for an employer who contributes an amount equal to 10 percent of her salary each year to a money-purchase plan.

6.   For taxpayers who are active participants in an employer-sponsored retirement plan, what are the adjusted AGI phaseout ranges for deductible IRA contributions in 2007 for [17-3]
a.   a single taxpayer
b.   a married taxpayer who is filing jointly

7.   George and Mary Barke (marrieds filing jointly) have a combined adjusted AGI of $89,634 in 2007. Each is aged 45. George is an active participant in an employer-maintained plan but Mary is not. What is the amount of the deductible IRA contribution that George and Mary can make for 2007, assuming that both earn more than $4,000? [17-3]

8.   John is changing jobs at age 35. He is entitled to a distribution of $47,000 from his former company's 401(k) plan. This amount is about the same amount that a terrific car that John wants to buy costs. He's asked you for your advice. What would you say to John? [17-3]

9.   Answer the following common Roth IRA client questions. [17-4]
a.   How do I know if I'm eligible to make a Roth IRA contribution?
b.   I'm 72 years old. Can I make a contribution to a Roth IRA?
c.   I'd like to start a Roth IRA, but I'm concerned about needing some of the money in the case of emergencies. Could you explain the tax consequences?

10.   In 2007, Joe, age 52, converts a $100,000 IRA to a Roth IRA. [17-5]
a.   What are tax consequences of this transaction?
b.   Assuming that the conversion was Joe's first Roth IRA, what are the tax consequences of a withdrawal of $15,000 2 years later to pay for a new car?

11.   Given the following facts, what are Edward and Alice's IRA and Roth IRA options for 2007? [17-5]

Names: Edward and Alice Sillyman
Ages: Edward 53, Alice 48
Adjusted AGI: $ 110,000
Employment status: Alice is employed and earns $105,000 and Edward is not employed.
Marital status: Married
Tax filing status: Joint tax return
Active participant status: Alice is an active participant, Edward is not.

18

Individual Retirement Plans—Part II

Learning Objectives

An understanding of the material in this chapter should enable you to

18-1. Describe the two types of funding vehicles that can be used with IRAs.

18-2. Identify appropriate as well as prohibited investments in an IRA.

18-3. Discuss appropriate uses of IRAs and Roth IRAs.

Chapter Outline

In addition to the legal and tax implications concerning IRAs, there are also several financial implications. Note that both traditional IRAs and Roth IRAs are subject to the same investment rules. Let's take a closer look.

FUNDING VEHICLES

Individual retirement plans can be established with one of two different funding vehicles:

- individual retirement accounts
- individual retirement annuities

Individual Retirement Accounts (IRAs)

Individual retirement accounts (IRAs) are the most popular type of individual retirement arrangement. The IRA document itself is a written trust or a custodial account whose trustee or custodian must be a bank, a federally insured credit union, a savings and loan association, or a person or organization that receives IRS permission to act as the trustee or custodian (for example, an insurance company). No one receives IRS permission to be the trustee of his or her own IRA because the IRS mandates arm's-length dealing between the beneficiary of the IRA trust and those in charge of enforcing IRA rules.

The IRA trust or custodial account must be established for the exclusive benefit of the participant and his or her beneficiaries, and benefits must be nonforfeitable. The document must limit contributions to the maximum allowable deductible or nondeductible contribution allowed each year. The document must also state that distributions will satisfy the required minimum distribution provisions. IRA funds may not be commingled with other assets except in a common trust fund or common investment fund.

Individual Retirement Annuities (IRA Annuities)

An *individual retirement annuity (IRA annuity)* is an annuity contract typically issued by insurance companies. IRA annuities are similar to IRAs except that the following additional rules apply because of their annuity investment feature:

- The IRA annuity is nontransferable. In other words, unlike the proceeds from other annuities, the IRA annuity proceeds must be received by either the taxpayer or a beneficiary. Individuals cannot set up an IRA annuity and then pledge the annuity to another party or put the annuity up as a security for a loan. For example, if loans were made under an automatic premium-loan provision, the plan would be disqualified.
- The premium cannot exceed the current year's maximum contribution amount. Any refund of premiums must be applied before

the close of the calendar year following the year of the refund toward payment of future premiums or the purchase of additional benefits.

The primary reason for choosing one IRA funding vehicle over another is the investor's desired return balanced against the amount of risk he or she is willing to accept. There are, however, secondary reasons that make IRA annuities worth considering when the return/risk factors are comparable with other investments. If a deferred annuity is chosen, features like a guaranteed death benefit, waiver-of-premium coverage in case of disability, and a guaranteed rate of return can have value to certain individuals. Immediate annuities provide guaranteed payments for a specified period.

TYPES OF INVESTMENTS

self-directed IRAs

IRAs can be invested in a multitude of vehicles, running the gamut from mutual funds to limited partnerships, from investments with minimal risk and modest returns to speculative investments with promises of greater return. IRAs are typically invested in certificates of deposit, money market funds, mutual funds, limited partnerships, income bond funds, corporate bond funds, and common stocks and other equities. *Self-directed IRAs* (IRAs in which the taxpayer is able to shift investments between general investment vehicles offered by the trustee) are also popular because they give the investor investment flexibility and the ability to anticipate or react to interest-rate directions and market trends.

Clearly, investment decisions need to follow from the client's retirement goals. The job of a financial services professional is to induce the client to generate a retirement strategy first and an investment strategy second. The financial strategy needs to consider the client's lifestyle, other financial resources, and the client's degree of risk aversion.

When forming an investment strategy, another consideration is the tax-advantaged nature of IRAs. Investment earnings are not subject to income tax while held in the plan. This means that it is generally not appropriate to invest in tax-sheltered vehicles, such as municipal bonds—which generally offer a lower rate of return than taxable investments.

Investment Restrictions

Investment of IRAs is generally open to all of the investment vehicles available outside IRAs. There are, however, a few exceptions:

- investment in life insurance
- investment in collectibles
- prohibited transactions

Life Insurance

Investment in life insurance is not allowed for an IRA even though defined-benefit and defined-contribution retirement plans allow an "incidental" amount of life insurance. IRAs, however, are not subject to the same rules (or underlying logic) and are considered to be strictly for retirement purposes. Therefore, no incidental insurance is available.

Collectibles

If IRA funds are invested in collectibles, the amount invested is considered a distribution, subject to income tax and possibly the 10 percent excise tax on distributions made prior to age 59 1/2. Collectibles include works of art, Oriental rugs, antiques, rare coins, stamps, rare wines, and certain other tangible property.

There is an exception for certain coins and precious metals. IRA funds can be invested in one, one-half, one-quarter, or one-tenth ounce U.S. gold coins, or one-ounce silver coins minted by the Treasury Department. Funds can also be invested in certain platinum coins and certain gold, silver, palladium, and platinum bullion. However, investments in bullion are allowed only when the IRA trustee has physical possession of the bullion.

Prohibited Transactions

Generally, a prohibited transaction is the improper use of an IRA by the participant, a beneficiary, or any disqualified person. Disqualified persons include fiduciaries and members of the IRA participant's family (spouse, ancestor, lineal descendant, and any spouse of a lineal descendant). These are the same prohibited transaction rules that apply to qualified plans (and are discussed in chapter 11).

The following are examples of prohibited transactions with a traditional IRA.

- Borrowing money from it.
- Selling property to it.
- Receiving unreasonable compensation for managing it.
- Using it as security for a loan.
- Buying property for personal use (present or future) with IRA funds.

In many cases, an IRA will not have an outside fiduciary, but it may in some cases. Just as with employer-sponsored retirement plans, a fiduciary includes anyone who does any of the following:

- Exercises any discretionary authority or discretionary control in managing an IRA or exercises any authority or control in managing or disposing of its assets.
- Provides investment advice for an IRA for a fee, or has any authority or responsibility to do so.
- Has any discretionary authority or discretionary responsibility in administering an IRA.

Penalties

Failure to satisfy the investment restrictions can be severe. If the participant borrows any money from an annuity the entire value of the annuity contract (not just the amount borrowed) is included in the owner's income. Similarly, if a loan is taken from an IRA account, the account is disqualified. If the participant pledges the account as collateral for a loan, then the amount pledged is treated as a distribution.

If the participant or a beneficiary engages in a prohibited transaction in connection with an IRA at any time during the year, the account stops being an IRA as of the first day of that year, and all its assets are treated as a distribution, subject to income tax. If someone other than the owner or beneficiary of a traditional IRA engages in a prohibited transaction, that person may be liable for certain taxes. In general, there is a 15-percent tax on the amount of the prohibited transaction and a 100-percent additional tax if the transaction is not corrected.

Investment in a prohibited collectible has a somewhat less severe penalty. Here the result is that the value of the collectible purchased is deemed to be distributed and will be subject to tax. Since investments in life insurance are prohibited by the terms of the investment vehicle, a life insurance investment would disqualify the IRA.

In addition to these penalties, deemed distributions to a participant under age 59½ will also be subject to the 10-percent Sec. 72(t) early withdrawal penalty tax.

Clearly, clients and their advisors need to be very careful not to violate the investment restrictions in order to avoid penalties.

IRAS USED WITH SEPs AND SIMPLEs

IRAs are also used as the funding vehicle for two types of employer-sponsored retirement plans, SEPs and SIMPLEs. Obviously, the contribution limits are different, but in most other ways the IRAs operate under the same rules that apply to IRAs established by individuals. This means that the investment restrictions are the same, benefits must be fully vested at all times, distributions are taxed the same, and in most instances benefits can be rolled from one IRA to another. (Note that the IRA rules prohibit loans to participants. This prohibition means that SEPs and SIMPLEs cannot include participant loan programs.)

When an employer establishes a SEP, SEP IRA accounts are established for each participant. When an employer establishes a SIMPLE, a SIMPLE IRA is adopted for each participant. SIMPLE IRAs are subject to several special rules. If a distribution is made from a SIMPLE IRA in the first 2 years of participation and the participant is under age 59½, the penalty tax under Code Sec. 72(t) becomes a 25 percent excise tax (the tax is usually 10 percent). Because of this tax, there is a prohibition on transfers from a SIMPLE IRA to a regular IRA in the first 2 years of participation. Otherwise, participants could circumvent the 25 percent tax. SIMPLE IRAs may not accept rollovers from any vehicle other than another SIMPLE IRA account.

IRAs AND THE FINANCIAL SERVICES PROFESSIONAL

For the financial services professional, understanding IRAs requires more than just knowing the various rules, restraints, and tax implications associated with them. The financial services professional must also analyze whether a current client's interests are best served by making IRA contributions and must identify potential clients who need IRA assistance. Many financial services professionals must even ask themselves whether selling IRAs is appropriate for them.

Should Your Client Make an IRA or Roth IRA Contribution?

The first step in determining whether a client should use IRAs is to determine their eligibility for the various options. Tables 18-1 and 18-2 summarize the available options for both single and married (filing jointly) taxpayers in 2007.

The last several years have seen important favorable changes for IRAs. Even though IRA planning has become considerably more complicated, it has also opened up opportunities for your clients. Looking at IRAs under the current playing field, here are some general observations for your clients.

TABLE 18-1
IRA Options for Singles in 2007

Type of Contribution	Tax Benefit	Availability
Nondeductible	–After-tax contributions with tax deferral on earnings –Distributions of earnings taxed as ordinary income	Individuals who have not yet attained age 70 1/2 with compensation from personal services (does not include investment income)
Deductible	–Tax deduction on contributions with tax deferral on earnings –All distributions taxed as ordinary income	–Individuals who have not yet attained age 70 1/2 with compensation who are not active participants in an employer sponsored retirement plan –Deduction phased out for individuals who are active participants with AGI between $52,000 and $62,000
Roth	–After-tax contributions –No tax on qualifying distributions	–Individuals of any age with compensation –Ability to make contribution phased out with AGI between $99,000 and $114,000
Converting an IRA to a Roth IRA	Income tax paid at the time the IRA is converted to the Roth IRA	Cannot make conversion if AGI exceeds $100,000 for the year

- The maximum contribution to IRAs is rising. For 2007, the limit is $4,000 and will increase to $5,000 in 2008. Those aged 50 or older can make an additional contribution of $1,000.
- The special spousal rule provides that for married couples filing jointly with AGI less than $150,000 and only one spouse covered in an employer-sponsored retirement plan, the other spouse can contribute the maximum amount on a deductible basis to a traditional IRA.

TABLE 18-2
IRA Options for Marrieds Filing Jointly in 2007

Type of Contribution	Tax Benefit	Availability
Nondeductible	–After-tax contributions with tax deferral on earnings –Distributions of earnings taxed as ordinary income	Individuals* who have not yet attained age 70 1/2, with compensation from personal services (does not include investment income)
Deductible	–Tax deduction on contributions with tax deferral on earnings –All distributions taxed as ordinary income	–Individuals* who have not yet attained age 70 1/2 with compensation who are not active participants in an employer-sponsored retirement plan –If one spouse is an active participant, then the deduction is phased out (for the spouse who is not an active participant) for AGI between $156,000 and $166,000 –Deduction phased out for individuals who are active participants with AGI between $83,000 and $103,000
Roth IRA	–After-tax contributions –No tax on qualifying distributions	–Individuals* of any age with compensation –Ability to make contribution phased out with AGI between $156,000 and $166,000
Converting an IRA to a Roth IRA	–Income tax paid at the time the IRA is converted to the Roth IRA	Cannot make conversion if AGI exceeds $100,000 for the year

*For a married couple, a spousal IRA can be established if one spouse does not have compensation from employment.

- The Roth IRA offers a significant tax benefit that is available to many taxpayers who cannot make deductible IRA contributions. For example, an individual earning $70,000 and who is a 401(k) plan participant cannot make a deductible IRA contribution, but can make a $4,000 contribution to a Roth IRA.
- Choosing between a Roth IRA and a deductible IRA (or other pre-tax savings vehicle like a 401(k) plan) can be difficult (see below). However, both are great ways to save for retirement.

- Many taxpayers will resist converting traditional IRAs to Roth IRAs. Doing so creates a current tax liability. However, conversions can accomplish a number of objectives and can be the appropriate economic choice for many individuals—that is, as long as the law does not change again.
- The IRA rules offer little for taxpayers with high-end income. However, older, more affluent individuals can provide encouragement—and funds—to their children and grandchildren to take advantage of these opportunities. Also, some advisors are so enthusiastic about the advantages of the Roth IRA conversion that they may be encouraging clients to manipulate their income to get below the $100,000 AGI threshold.
- The IRA rules offer little to those at the lower end of the earnings scale. These individuals are least likely to have sufficient income to afford a contribution, and will be most likely to need emergency withdrawals that will not qualify for special tax treatment.

Let's look at several of these points in greater depth.

Easier Access to IRA funds

Sometimes it is difficult to convince your clients of the importance of saving for retirement. With younger clients, it can be helpful to point out that by making just nine $4,000 contributions from age 18 to age 26—and no contributions thereafter—an IRA at age 65 will be larger than an IRA funded with a $4,000 contribution each year from age 27 to age 65 (see table 18-3). For clients who think their company-sponsored retirement plan is sufficient, point out to them that if postretirement inflation is 4 percent per year, a $1 loaf of bread at age 65 will cost $2.19 at age 85.

Another concern of clients is the effect of the 10 percent premature excise tax. If money is withdrawn too soon, the tax will reduce the client's savings. For some, this is good news because it acts as an incentive to keep their money in the plan. However, it would also be irresponsible to advise a client to make IRA contributions if he or she could not leave the money in the plan for a significant period of time. Still, there is a point at which it pays a taxpayer to make IRA contributions, even when a premature withdrawal is the taxpayer's intention. The break-even or get-ahead date depends on the tax bracket of the employee when contributions are made, the interest

TABLE 18-3
IRA Funding Plans[1]

Plan One			Plan Two		
Age start		18	Age start		27
Age end		26	Age end		65
Amount per year		$4,000	Amount per year		$4,000
Rate of return		8%	Rate of return		8%
Value at age 65		$1,004,764	Value at age 65		$951,765
Total amount contributed		$36,000	Total amount contributed		$152,000
Age	**Amount**	**Value**	**Age**	**Amount**	**Value**
18	$4,000	$ 4,320	18	0	0
19	4,000	8,985	19	0	0
20	4,000	14,024	20	0	0
21	4,000	19,466	21	0	0
22	4,000	25,344	22	0	0
23	4,000	31,691	23	0	0
24	4,000	38,546	24	0	0
25	4,000	45,950	25	0	0
26	4,000	53,946	26	0	0
27	0	58,262	27	$4,000	$ 4,320
28	0	62,923	28	4,000	8,986
29	0	67,957	29	4,000	14,024
30	0	73,393	30	4,000	19,466
.	.	.	.	.	.
.	.	.	.	.	.
.	.	.	.	.	.
.	.	.	.	.	.
60	0	683,825	60	4,000	630,507
61	0	738,531	61	4,000	685,267
62	0	797,614	62	4,000	744,408
63	0	861,423	63	4,000	808,281
64	0	930,337	64	4,000	877264
65	0	1,004,764	65	4,000	951,764

[1]This comparison is hypothetical; no guarantees are implied for specific investments. The interest rate is assumed to remain unchanged for the entire period.

earned under the IRA, the tax bracket of the person when distributions are withdrawn, and the ratio of nondeductible contributions to the total IRA balance at the time of withdrawal. If the taxpayer's tax bracket is lower at the time of withdrawal, the break-even point will be shorter. (The converse is also true: a higher tax bracket at distribution time will mean a longer break-even point.)

Another answer to a client's concerns about the premature excise tax is that withdrawals can be made to pay for educational expenses and up to $10,000 of first homebuying expenses. These exceptions mean that young persons who are also concerned about saving for homeownership and for their children's college education can withdraw funds for these purposes without penalty.

Choosing the Roth IRA over the Nondeductible IRA

Many taxpayers who do not have the option to make deductible IRA contributions will, however, have the opportunity to make Roth IRA contributions. The ability to contribute to Roth IRAs is phased out for single taxpayers with AGI between $99,000 and $114,000 and married couples filing jointly with AGI between $156,000 and $166,000 (as indexed for 2007). Individuals who have the choice between nondeductible IRA contributions and Roth IRA contributions should almost always choose the Roth IRA. Tax-free distributions are clearly better than tax deferral.

In fact, it's difficult to argue for nondeductible contributions at all today because the price of tax deferral is turning investment gain into ordinary income. Arguably, investing directly in securities (outside of the IRA context) may be more attractive, since capital gains can be deferred until the sale and qualifying sales will be taxed at a maximum 15 percent tax rate. Also, securities left to heirs avoid income taxes on the growth over the participant's life.

In contrast, the tax advantages of the Roth IRA are clear. As long as distributions satisfy the eligibility requirements, the entire distribution avoids income tax—even distributions to death beneficiaries. The Roth IRA can even be used to save (up to $10,000) as a down payment for a first home. Like other IRAs, Roth IRA funds can be invested in stocks, bonds, or other investment vehicles. Even the Roth IRA participant who needs early withdrawals is taxed favorably. The participant can withdraw contributions without any income tax consequences, and because the penalty tax applies in the same manner as to traditional IRAs, additional amounts (subject to income tax) can be withdrawn (for example, for educational expenses) without having to pay the 10 percent penalty tax.

A good candidate for the Roth IRA would be a 401(k) participant who has maximized his or her contribution to the 401(k) plan, is not eligible for a deductible IRA contribution, and still wants to save more for retirement. In this case, the next place to save is definitely the Roth IRA. The harder question to answer would be, "Should the 401(k) participant who has been putting away 6 percent of compensation each year and who wants to save more contribute more to the 401(k) plan or contribute to a Roth IRA?" This individual is now choosing between the deductible savings and the tax-free saving alternatives. The issues involved in this decision are discussed below.

Choosing the Roth IRA over the Deductible IRA

Some taxpayers will be in the position to choose between a deductible IRA contribution or the Roth IRA. Similarly, many employees may be choosing between making additional contributions to a 401(k) plan or the Roth IRA. In the 401(k) setting, if the employer is going to match the contribution, the advantage usually goes to the 401(k) plan, because the employer match is like an instant return on the participant's contribution. However, if the contribution is not matched, then the 401(k)-to-Roth IRA comparison is essentially the same as the deductible IRA-to-Roth IRA comparison.

Comparing the financial effect of the two options is difficult, partially because it involves assumptions about rates of return in the future, tax rates in the future, and the timing of withdrawals. Numerous computer software programs are available to help with this comparison, and they can be quite valuable in helping to make choices.

Even though individual analysis is best, here are some general considerations. It is clearest that when the individual expects to be in a higher tax bracket in retirement than at the time of the contribution, the Roth IRA is the more appropriate vehicle. For example, take the young person in the 17 percent (15 percent federal and 2 percent state) bracket today who expects to be in a 42 percent bracket at the time of distribution. Table 18-4 gives an example of such an individual, who has $2,000 to contribute at

TABLE 18-4
Comparing Deductible IRAs to Roth IRA Accumulations

Age	30%/17%		30%/30%*		17%/42%*		30%/42%*	
	Roth	Deductible	Roth	Deductible	Roth	Deductible	Roth	Deductible
25	$1,400	$2,000	$ 1,400	$2,000	$ 1,660	$ 2,000	$ 1,400	$ 2,000
70	$44,688	$52,987	$44,688	$44,688**	$52,967	$37,027**	$44,688	$37,027**

*   The first number represents the combined federal and state income tax rate at the time of contribution and the second number represents the tax rate at the time of distribution.

** Assumes that the entire accumulation is distributed and taxed at age 70.
Assumes growth at 8%.

age 25 and withdraws this amount at age 70. If $2,000 is contributed to the traditional IRA, after taxes are paid at age 70, she will have $37,027. However, if $1,660 is contributed to a Roth IRA ($2,000 less taxes) at age 70, she will have $52,967. This is a significant difference.

If an individual expects his or her tax rate to go down in retirement, the opposite is true—the deductible IRA shows a greater accumulation ($52,987 for the deductible IRA versus $44,688 for the Roth IRA). However, for many taxpayers this is a relatively unlikely scenario.

If the tax rates are the same at the time of contribution and at the time of withdrawal, the accumulations shown in table 18-4 for the Roth IRA and the deductible contribution are the same (each $44,688). However, if the tax rates remain the same, there are still advantages to the Roth IRA. In our example, the participant withdraws all of the Roth IRA at age 70, but one of the Roth IRA's powerful features is that distributions are not required during the participant's lifetime. If the beneficiary is the spouse, distributions can be delayed even further to the death of the spouse. After that, distributions can be made over the expected lifetime of the beneficiary or beneficiaries. This tax deferral can be quite powerful, and makes the Roth IRA a good way to pass on wealth to the next generation.

Also, there is another strength to the Roth IRA. The tax-free source of income gives the participant more flexibility in how and when to liquidate other taxable assets in retirement. The tax-free funds in a Roth IRA can be used in retirement to

- minimize taxable withdrawals from traditional IRAs or qualified plans
- minimize taxable income to stay in a lower tax bracket
- provide for a source of income that will not increase the portion of Social Security benefits that are taxed
- fund life insurance premiums for estate planning purposes
- provide liquidity for estate taxes
- minimize liquidation of other taxable investments such as stocks and mutual funds—which receive a step-up if left intact to heirs

Because of the Roth IRA's many strengths, the following types of clients should consider the Roth IRA over the deductible IRA:

- individuals in the 15 percent federal income tax bracket
- individuals in the 25 and 28 percent federal income tax brackets who expect to be in a higher bracket at retirement
- individuals who have already accumulated significant assets for retirement on a tax-deferred basis and who may want to use the Roth IRA as a way to create a more balanced (from a tax perspective) portfolio
- individuals who are more concerned about estate planning than retirement planning

IRA-to-Roth IRA Conversions

The Roth IRA conversion is an important strategy for certain taxpayers. Unfortunately, many individuals who would be most interested—singles and couples earning more than $100,000—will not be eligible to do it. Others simply will not be willing to pay the taxes before they have to. However, in a significant number of cases, it appears that the Roth IRA conversion can really result in greater after-tax accumulations. It is a good idea to run computer simulations for real clients to see for yourself the effect of a conversion. Consider the following when making the conversion decision:

- Conversions work for young persons because there will be a long accumulation period over which the Roth IRA is growing tax free.
- Individuals who have most of their retirement savings in IRAs and Roth IRAs should consider converting at least some of those amounts to Roth IRAs. As discussed above, a nontaxable source of income in retirement can be used for a number of retirement or estate planning purposes.
- If taxes are paid out of the IRA when it is converted to a Roth IRA, the 10 percent premature excise tax may apply. This detracts from the value of the conversion. If possible, other sources should be used for paying the taxes.

Even though it may appear at first glance that older persons should not convert, conversion can have significant estate-planning implications. Remember that if the taxpayer does not need to make withdrawals for living expenses, the law does not require any withdrawals until after the participant's death. If the spouse is the beneficiary, no withdrawals are required over his or her life either. This means that the tax-free accumulation period for even an older person can be quite long. In addition, after death, the Roth IRA can be distributed over the beneficiary's entire lifetime. Even if the older participant were to die shortly after the conversion, the income taxes paid at the conversion reduce the value of the estate, offsetting the Roth IRA accumulation period.

Because of the value of the Roth IRA conversion, planners are beginning to consider the impact of the elimination of the income cap in 2010 (described in detail in chapter 17). Some taxpayers may want to prepare for this opportunity by maximizing contributions to tax-advantaged plans and IRAs. Since there are no income limits on nondeductible contributions, one way to plan for this opportunity is to maximize contributions to nondeductible IRAs.

THE IRA MARKET—POTENTIAL CLIENTS

As you have seen, just about every taxpayer is a candidate for an IRA. In fact, because of their broad-based appeal and general attractiveness to the public, IRAs make a great door opener. Also, mass marketing of IRAs is possible—and this paves the way to an increased client base. Once the door is open, you can easily explain IRAs, which will lead naturally into a discussion of an overall retirement and financial plan.

deemed IRAs

For financial services professionals who work primarily with employers, note that qualified plans, 403(b) annuities, and even government 457 plans may be written to allow participants to make voluntary IRA or Roth IRA contributions directly to the plan. These accounts are referred to as *deemed IRAs*. If a plan so provides, the document must require separate accounting for the IRA or Roth IRA contributions, and the contributions would have to meet the requirements applicable to either traditional IRAs or Roth IRAs.

Having a deemed IRA account does not affect the qualification and contribution limits that otherwise apply to the qualified plan or 403(b) plan. For example, in a 401(k) plan, a participant could make both the maximum salary deferral and the IRA or Roth IRA contribution to the plan (as long as he or she is eligible under the IRA rules to make the contribution). The deemed IRA is also not subject to the ERISA reporting and disclosure, participation, vesting, funding, and enforcement requirements that are otherwise applicable to the plan.

If you are considering whether to advise your employer-client to institute a deemed IRA, your client must consider the following factors:

- Because these accounts are treated as IRAs and Roth IRAs, the normal rules concerning eligibility to make a contribution or deduct it still apply.
- There may be an advantage to the individual to have an IRA account within a company plan because the IRA contributions are subject to ERISA's exclusive benefit and fiduciary rules. This may mean that the accounts will be eligible for more protection from attachment by a taxpayer's creditors than traditional or Roth IRAs.
- The downside for the employer is that there will be increased administrative effort and expense to maintain the additional accounts. The plan also becomes more complicated and difficult to explain to participants.

Whether you are involved with IRAs in the individual market or through the employee benefit market, it is important to be aware that selling IRAs has its drawbacks. First, IRA commissions are generally not generous. (They are typically lower than on most insurance products.) Second, because of the wide variety of investments and the fluctuating returns offered, clients tend to shift investment vehicles, which translates into administrative and financial headaches. However, many planners believe that IRAs represent an ideal supplemental sale despite these drawbacks and that involvement with the IRA products leads to financial success for themselves and their clients.

CHAPTER REVIEW

Key Terms

self-directed IRAs [18-2]   deemed IRAs [18-3]

Review Questions

Review questions are based on the learning objectives in this chapter. Thus, an [18-3] at the end of a question means that the question is based on learning objective 18-3. If there are multiple objectives, they are all listed.

1. a. What is an individual retirement account (IRA)? [18-1]
    b. What is an individual retirement annuity, and what special rules apply to the annuity contract?

2. What are some of the advantages of investing in an individual retirement annuity? [18-2]

2. Which of the following items is/are permissible IRA investments? [18-2]
    a. investment in life insurance
    b. investment in antiques
    c. investment in gold bullion
    d. investment in real estate that is owned by the client

4. Why are IRAs associated with SIMPLE plans referred to as SIMPLE IRAs? [18-3]

5. Explain the IRA and Roth IRA options for the following individuals in 2007: [18-3]
    a. Carlos, a single 35-year-old taxpayer, has an adjusted gross income (AGI) of $80,000 and is not an active participant in an employer-sponsored retirement plan in 2007.
    b. Anthony, a single 45-year-old taxpayer, has an AGI of $120,000 and is an active participant in a qualified retirement plan.

c.   Sam and Sally, each under age 50, are married and file a joint tax return. Sam has an AGI of $120,000 and is an active participant in an employer-sponsored retirement plan. Sally does not work outside of the home.

d.   Della and George, aged 40, are married and file a joint tax return. Della earns $90,000 and George earns $85,000 (joint AGI is $175,000). They are both active participants in employer-sponsored retirement plans.

6.   Why may the nondeductible IRA be an inappropriate retirement investment vehicle in today's tax environment? [18-3]

7.   When is the Roth IRA potentially more advantageous than the deductible IRA contribution? [18-3]

8.   Describe the deemed IRA account. [18-3]

Social Security

Learning Objectives

An understanding of the material in this chapter should enable you to

19-1.   Identify workers who are and those who are not covered by the Social Security system.

19-2.   Understand the breadth of coverage that Social Security provides concerning the retirement security of Americans.

19-3.   Describe how Social Security is funded.

19-4.   Explain the eligibility requirements for retirement benefits, survivors benefits, and disability benefits.

19-5.   List and explain the types of benefits clients receive from the Social Security system.

19-6.   Describe how to calculate benefits.

19-7.   Identify the impact of taking benefits early or late and what happens if an individual works after benefits begin.

19-8.   Explain how to request information about and apply for benefits.

19-9.   Calculate the portion of Social Security benefits that is subject to tax.

19-10. Determine when it is appropriate to begin benefits prior to full retirement age.

Chapter Outline

BACKGROUND/HISTORY

Social Security

Social Security is arguably the most important retirement plan in the United States. Social Security is much more than retirement, however. Technically, *Social Security* is the old-age, survivors, disability, and health insurance (OASDHI) program of the federal government. In addition to retirement benefits, the Social Security system also provides benefits to disabled workers and to families of workers who have died, retired, or become disabled. Currently, approximately 52 million Americans—one out of every six—receive retirement, survivors, and disability benefits from Social Security. In addition, the hospital insurance (HI) program provides health care coverage through Medicare to retirees, the disabled, and their families.

Historically, Social Security has been a work in progress. The system has been changed a number of times to meet the ever-changing needs of the people it serves. Currently further changes are being debated in Washington. When these changes are sorted out, they will represent another chapter in a long and storied history for the Social Security system. For an overview of the history of Social Security, see the timeline in table 19-1.

Planners need to be familiar with the entire Social Security system. This chapter focuses on OASDI benefits, which include old-age retirement benefits, disability benefits, and survivor benefits. Medicare, along with other retiree health care issues, will be discussed in a later chapter.

EXTENT OF COVERAGE

Close to 90 percent of the workers in the United States are in covered employment under the Social Security program. This means that these workers have wages (if they are employees) or self-employment income (if they are self-employed) on which Social Security taxes must be paid. For this reason, it is important for the planner to understand potential clients who are not covered under the Social Security program. The following are the major categories of workers who may not receive benefits under the program:

TABLE 19-1
History of Social Security

1935	FDR signs the Social Security Act providing for old-age insurance
1939	Survivors benefits are added
1940	First benefits are paid out
1950	Truman extends coverage to many farm and domestic workers, state and municipal employees, and some professionals
1956	Disability coverage added by Eisenhower; women become eligible for some benefits at 62 rather than 65
1965	Johnson adds Medicare
1972	Benefit increases pegged to the cost of living
1983	Social Security Reform Act
2006	Medicare Part D drug benefits added

- people with less than 40 quarters of coverage (discussed later)
- civilian employees of the federal government who were employed by the government prior to 1984 and who are covered primarily under the Civil Service Retirement System. Coverage for new civilian federal employees under the entire program was one of the most significant changes resulting from the 1983 amendments to the Social Security Act. It should be noted, however, that all federal employees have been covered under Social Security for purposes of Medicare since 1983.
- railroad workers. Under the Railroad Retirement Act (RRA), employees of railroads have their own benefit system that is similar to OASDI. However, they are covered under Social Security for purposes of Medicare.
- employees of state and local governments unless the state has entered into a voluntary agreement with the Social Security Administration. However, this exemption applies only to those employees who are covered under their employer's retirement plan. Under an agreement

with the Social Security Administration, the state may either require that employees of local governments also be covered or allow local governments to decide whether to include their employees.

- American citizens working abroad for foreign affiliates of U.S. employers, unless the employer owns at least a 10 percent interest in the foreign affiliate and has made arrangements with the Secretary of the Treasury for the payment of Social Security taxes. However, Americans working abroad are covered under Social Security if they are working directly for U.S. employers rather than for their foreign subsidiaries.

- ministers who elect out of coverage because of conscience or religious principles

- workers in certain jobs, such as student nurses, newspaper carriers under age 18, and students working for the school at which they are regularly enrolled or doing domestic work for a local college club, fraternity, or sorority

- certain family employment. This includes the employment of a child under age 18 by a parent. This exclusion, however, does not apply if the employment is for a corporation owned by a family member.

- certain workers who must satisfy special earnings requirements. For example, self-employed persons are not covered unless they have net annual earnings of $400 or more.

One last point concerning the extent of coverage—many of the groups not covered (for example, federal workers in the civil service retirement system and railroad workers covered by the RRA) have significant pensions that account for the lack of Social Security coverage. In addition, nonworking spouses (those with less than 40 quarters of coverage) may be entitled to a spousal benefit under the system. In other words, many of those excluded from coverage are "taken care of" in other ways.

BREADTH OF COVERAGE

According to the Social Security Administration, Social Security replaces about 40 percent of the average worker's preretirement earnings. For more affluent clients, this percentage will be lower, however, because of the way benefits are structured to favor lower-paid workers over higher-paid workers. America's reliance on Social Security, particularly for middle- and lower-income Americans, is staggering. Consider this:

- Only about 10 percent of American senior citizens live in poverty; without Social Security, it would be nearly 50 percent.

- For nearly two-thirds of seniors (65 percent), Social Security is their major source of income. In other words, it is more than one-half of what they have to live on in retirement.
- Social Security is the only source of income for nearly one-third of seniors.

One can conclude from these statistics that the breadth and importance of the Social Security system is divided along (for lack of a better term) "class"

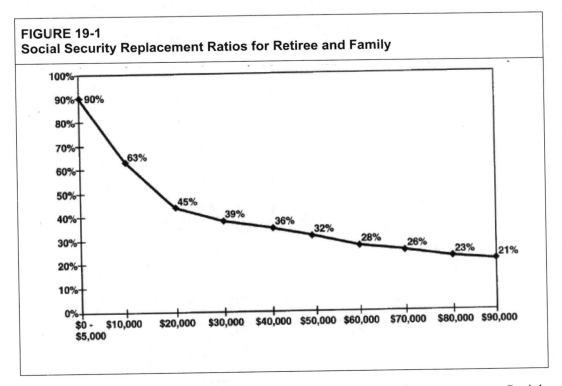

FIGURE 19-1
Social Security Replacement Ratios for Retiree and Family

lines. For people in the upper-middle- and upper-income groups, Social Security, while important, is not vital. For people below those levels, however, Social Security is crucial to financial well being.

FUNDING

All benefits of the OASDI program are financed through a system of payroll and self-employment taxes paid by all persons covered under the program. Employers of covered persons are also taxed.

TABLE 19-2
Changes in Tax Rate and Wage Base under Social Security

Year	Wage Base	Tax Rate	Maximum Employee Tax
1950	$ 3,000	1.50%	$ 45.00
1955	4,200	2.00	84.00
1960	4,800	3.00	144.00
1965	4,800	3.65	174.00
1970	7,800	4.80	374.40
1975	14,100	5.85	824.85
1980	25,900	6.13	1,587.67
1985	39,600	7.05	2,791.80
1986	42,000	7.15	3,003.00
1987	43,800	7.15	3,131.70
1988	45,000	7.51	3,379.50
1989	48,000	7.51	3,604.80
1990	51,300	7.65	3,924.45
1991	first 53,400	7.65	
	next 71,600	1.45	5,123.30
1992	first 55,500	7.65	
	next 74,700	1.45	5,328.90
1993	first 57,600	7.65	
	next 77,400	1.45	5,528.70
1994	first 60,600	7.65	
	additional wages	1.45	*
1995	first 61,200	7.65	
	additional wages	1.45	*
1996	first $62,700	7.65	
	additional wages	1.45	*
1997	first $65,400	7.65	
	additional wages	1.45	*
1998	first $68,400	7.65	
	additional wages	1.45	*
1999	first $72,600	7.65	
	additional wages	1.45	*
2000	first $76,200	7.65	
	additional wages	1.45	*
2001	first 80,400	7.65	
	additional wages	1.45	*
2002	first $84,900	7.65	
	additional wages	1.45	*
2003	first $87,000	7.65	
	additional wages	1.45	*
2004	first $87,900	7.65	
	additional wages	1.45	*
2005	first $90,000	7.65	
	additional wages	1.45	*
2006	first $94,000	7.65	
	additional wages	1.45	*
2007	first $97,500	7.65	*
	additional wages	1.45	*

* No determinable maximum because of unlimited wage base for Medicare tax

---

> **FIGURE 19-2**
> **Social Security Trust Funds**
>
> - Disability
> - Old-age and survivors
> - Medicare Part A
> - Medicare Part B
>
> *Out of every dollar paid in Social Security taxes, 69 cents goes to the old-age and survivors trust fund, 19 cents goes to the Medicare trust fund, and 12 cents goes to the disability trust fund.

taxable wage base

FICA tax

SECA tax

Currently, an employee and his or her employer pay a tax of 7.65 percent each on the first $97,500 (2007) of the employee's wages. This is called the *taxable wage base*. Of this tax rate, 6.2 percent is for OASDI and 1.45 percent is for Medicare. (This is also called the *FICA tax*—Federal Insurance Contributions Act.) The 1.45 percent Medicare tax rate is also levied on all wages in excess of $97,500. The tax rates are currently scheduled to remain the same after 2007. However, the wage bases are adjusted annually for changes in the national level of wages. The tax rate for the self-employed is 15.3 percent on the first $97,500 of self-employment income and 2.9 percent on the balance of any self-employment income. (This is also known as the *SECA tax*—Self-Employment Contributions Act.) The SECA tax is equal to the combined employee and employer rates. An individual must continue paying FICA (or SECA) taxes as along as he or she continues employments, even if Social Security benefits have already begun.

Over the years, both the tax rate and the wage base have been dramatically increased to finance increased benefit levels under Social Security as well as new benefits that have been added to the program. Table 19-2 shows the magnitude of these increases for selected years.

The Social Security program is essentially based on a system of pay-as-you-go financing with limited trust funds. This means that current payroll taxes and other contributions the program receives are used to pay the current benefits of persons who are no longer paying Social Security taxes because of death, old age, or disability. This is in direct contrast to private insurance or retirement plans, which are based on advance funding, whereby assets are accumulated from current contributions to pay the future benefits of those making the contributions.

All payroll taxes and other sources of funds for Social Security (such as income tax on Social Security benefits and interest earned by the current surplus) are deposited into four trust funds: an old-age and survivors fund, a disability fund, and two Medicare funds. Benefits and administrative expenses are paid out of the appropriate trust fund from contributions to that fund and any interest earnings on excess contributions.

In the early 1980s, considerable concern arose over the potential inability of payroll taxes to pay promised benefits in the future. Through a series of changes, the most significant being the 1983 amendments to the Social Security Act, these problems were addressed for the OASDI portion of the program—at least in the short run. The changes approached the problem from two directions. On the one hand, payroll tax rates were increased; on the other hand, some benefits were eliminated and future increases in other benefits were scaled back.

The trust fund for old-age and survivors benefits will continue to grow and will be very large by the time the current baby boomers retire. At that time (2017), the fund will begin to decrease as the percentage of retirees grows rapidly. (Currently there are 76 million baby boomers. When they begin to retire, 50,000 will reach retirement age every day.) Projections indicate that the fund will be adequate only to the year 2040 (see figure 19-3).

ELIGIBILITY FOR BENEFITS

To be eligible for benefits under OASDI, an individual must have credit for a minimum amount of work under Social Security. This credit is based on

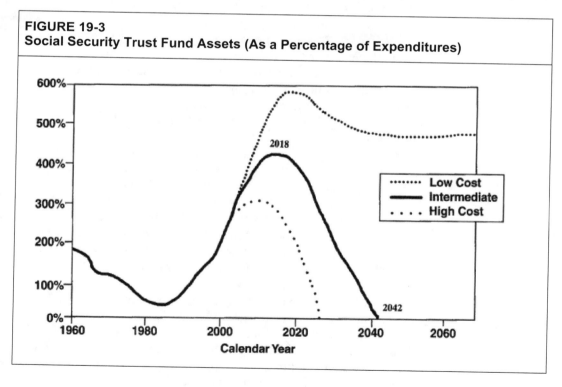

FIGURE 19-3
Social Security Trust Fund Assets (As a Percentage of Expenditures)

quarters of coverage. For 2007 a worker receives credit for one quarter of coverage for each $1,000 in annual earnings on which Social Security taxes are paid. However, credit for no more than 4 quarters of coverage may be earned in any one calendar year. Consequently a worker paying Social Security taxes on as little as $4,000 (that is, $1,000 x 4) during the year will receive credit for the maximum 4 quarters. As in the case of the wage base, the amount of earnings necessary for a quarter of coverage is adjusted annually for changes in the national level of wages. Prior to 1978, a worker could receive credit for only one quarter of coverage in any given calendar quarter. Therefore it was necessary to be earning wages throughout the year in order to receive the maximum number of credits. Now a worker with the appropriate level of wages can receive credit for the maximum number of quarters even if all wages are earned within one calendar quarter.

quarters of coverage

fully insured

Quarters of coverage are the basis for establishing an insured status under OASDI. The three types of insured status are fully insured, currently insured, and disability insured. A person is *fully insured* if he or she has 40 quarters of coverage. Once a client acquires 40 quarters of credit, he or she is fully insured for life even if covered employment under Social Security ceases. (Please note: There are some exceptions to the 40 quarter rule for people born before 1930.)

Currently Insured

currently insured

If a worker is fully insured under OASDI, there is no additional significance to being *currently insured*. However, if a worker is not fully insured, certain survivors' benefits are still available if a currently insured status exists. To be currently insured, it is only necessary that a worker have credit for at least 6 quarters of coverage out of the 13-quarter period ending with the quarter in which death occurs.

Disability Insured

disability insured

In order to receive disability benefits under OASDI, it is necessary to be *disability insured*. At the minimum, a disability-insured status requires that a worker (1) be fully insured and (2) have a minimum amount of work under Social Security within a recent time period. In connection with the latter requirement, workers aged 31 or older must have credit for at least 20 of the last 40 quarters ending with the quarter in which disability occurs; workers between the ages of 24 and 30, inclusively, must have credit for at least half the quarters of coverage from the time they turned 21 and the quarter in which disability begins; and workers under age 24 must have credit for 6 out of the last 12 quarters, ending with the quarter in which disability begins.

A special rule for the blind states that they are exempt from the recent-work rules and are considered disability insured as long as they are fully insured.

TYPES OF BENEFITS CLIENTS RECEIVE

As its name implies, the OASDI portion of Social Security provides three principal types of benefits:

- retirement (old-age) benefits
- survivors benefits
- disability benefits

Retirement Benefits

full retirement age

A worker who is fully insured under OASDI is eligible to receive monthly retirement benefits as early as age 62. However, the election to receive benefits prior to attainment of *full retirement age* results in a permanently reduced benefit. In 2007, the full retirement age (sometimes called normal retirement age) is age 65 years and 10 months. Planners should note that this represents a change from the long-standing practice of full benefits being paid at age 65. Table 19-3 indicates a client's full retirement age, depending on their year of birth. In addition, the following dependents of persons receiving retirement benefits are eligible for monthly benefits:

TABLE 19-3
Social Security Normal Retirement Age

Year of Birth	Retirement Age
1937 and earlier	65 years
1938	65 and 2 months
1939	65 and 4 months
1940	65 and 6 months
1941	65 and 8 months
1942	65 and 10 months
1943–54	66 years
1955	66 and 2 months
1956	66 and 4 months
1957	66 and 6 months
1958	66 and 8 months
1959	66 and 10 months
1960 and after	67 years

- a spouse aged 62 or older. However, benefits are permanently reduced if this benefit is elected prior to the spouse's reaching full retirement age. Planners should be aware that this benefit is also available to an unmarried divorced spouse if the marriage lasted at least 10 years. However, the benefit is not payable to a divorced spouse who has remarried unless the marriage is to a person receiving Social Security benefits as a widow, widower, parent, or disabled child.

- a spouse of any age if the spouse is caring for at least one child of the retired worker, and the child is (1) under age 16 or (2) disabled and entitled to a child's benefit as described below. This benefit is commonly referred to as a mother's or father's benefit.
- dependent, unmarried children under 18. This child's benefit will continue until age 19 as long as a child is a full-time student in elementary or secondary school. In addition, disabled children of any age are eligible for benefits as long as they were disabled before reaching age 22.

It is important to note that retirement benefits, as well as all other benefits under Social Security, are not automatically paid upon eligibility but must be applied for.

Survivors Benefits

All categories of survivors benefits are payable if a worker is fully insured at the time of death. However, three types of benefits are also payable if a worker is only currently insured. The first is a lump-sum death benefit of $255, payable to a surviving spouse living with a deceased worker at the time of death or, if there is no such spouse, to children eligible for monthly benefits. If neither category exists, the benefit is not paid.

There are two categories of persons who are eligible for income benefits as survivors if a deceased worker was either fully or currently insured at the time of death:

- dependent, unmarried children under the same conditions as previously described for retirement benefits
- a spouse (including a divorced spouse) caring for a child or children under the same conditions as previously described for retirement benefits

The following categories of persons are also eligible for benefits, but only if the deceased worker was fully insured:

- a widow or widower at age 60. However, benefits are reduced if taken prior to age 65. This benefit is also payable to a divorced spouse if the marriage lasted at least 10 years. In addition, the widow's or widower's benefit is payable to a disabled spouse at age 50 as long as the disability commenced no more than 7 years after (1) the worker's death or (2) the end of the year in which entitlement to a mother's or father's benefit ceased.

- a parent aged 62 or over who was dependent on the deceased worker at the time of death

Disability Benefits

A disabled worker under the full retirement age is eligible to receive benefits under OASDI as long as he or she is disability insured and meets the definition of disability under the law. The definition of disability is very rigid and requires a mental or physical impairment that prevents the worker from engaging in any substantial gainful employment. The disability must also have lasted (or be expected to last) at least 12 months or be expected to result in death. A more liberal definition of disability applies to blind workers who are aged 55 or older. They are considered disabled if they are unable to perform work that requires skills or abilities comparable to those required by the work they regularly performed before reaching age 55 or becoming blind, if later.

Disability benefits are subject to a waiting period and are payable beginning with the sixth full calendar month of disability. Besides the benefit paid to the worker, other categories of benefits—the same as those described under retirement benefits—are available to the spouse and dependents of the worker.

As previously mentioned, certain family members not otherwise eligible for OASDI benefits may be eligible if they are disabled. Disabled children are subject to the same definition of disability as workers. However, disabled widows or widowers must be unable to engage in any gainful (rather than substantial gainful) employment.

Eligibility for Dual Benefits

In many cases, a person is eligible for more than one type of OASDI benefit. Probably the most common situation occurs when a person is eligible for both a spouse's benefit and a worker's retirement benefit based on his or her own Social Security record. In this case and in any other case when a person is eligible for dual benefits, only an amount equal to the highest benefit is paid.

Termination of Benefits

Monthly benefits to any Social Security recipient cease upon death. When a retired or disabled worker dies, the family members' benefits that are based on the worker's retirement or disability benefits also cease, but the family members are then eligible for survivors benefits. When a married worker dies, if his or her spouse was receiving a spousal benefit of 50 percent, the surviving spouse will be bumped up to the full amount that the deceased worker was receiving.

Disability benefits for a worker technically terminate at the full retirement age for that worker, but are then replaced by comparable retirement benefits. In addition, any benefits payable because of disability cease if the definition of disability is no longer satisfied. However, the disability benefits continue during a readjustment period that consists of the month of recovery and 2 additional months.

As long as children are not disabled, benefits will usually terminate at age 18, but may continue until age 19 if the child is a full-time student in elementary or secondary school.

The benefit of a surviving spouse terminates upon remarriage unless remarriage takes place at age 60 or later.

AMOUNT OF BENEFITS CLIENTS CAN EXPECT

PIA
AIME

With the exception of the $255 lump-sum death benefit, the amount of all OASDI benefits is based on a worker's primary insurance amount (PIA). The *PIA,* in turn, is a function of the worker's average indexed monthly earnings *(AIME),* on which Social Security taxes have been paid.

Calculation of AIME

Even though calculation of the AIME is rather complex and somewhat unnecessary (the Social Security Administration will do it for the client or the client can use the Social Security Web site [www.ssa.gov] to do it for himself or herself), planners should still be aware how the system works. A rough understanding of how to calculate the AIME will enable an advisor to maximize planning opportunities. The list below sketches how the process works, as well as pointing out planning issues.

- First, list the earnings on which Social Security taxes were paid for each year up to and including the year of death or the year prior to disability or retirement. This list includes all applicable years even if there were no wages subject to Social Security tax, in which case zero is used for covered wages. Also note that in any given year someone earning in excess of the taxable wage base for the year will be credited only up to the taxable wage base that year and not his or her actual salary. *Planning Note:* "Zero years" can really hurt a client's benefit. This is one reason that women who took time off to have children often have lower benefits than their male counterparts.

- Second, index these earnings by multiplying them by an indexing factor that reflects changing wage levels. The only years that are indexed are those prior to the indexing year, which is the year a worker turned 60 for retirement purposes or 2 years preceding the year of death or disability for purposes of survivors or disability benefits. Therefore, the indexing factor for the indexing year and subsequent years is one. For years prior to the indexing year, the indexing factor for each year is equal to the average annual covered wages in the indexing year divided by the average annual covered wages in the year in which earnings are to be indexed. Average annual covered wages are the average wages on which Social Security taxes were paid. Each year the government makes the figure for the previous year available. *Planning Note:* Earnings after age 61 (which are not indexed) can be substituted for earnings in earlier years if they result in a higher benefit.

- Third, determine the number of years to be included in the calculation. For retirement and survivors benefits, the number of years is typically 35 (5 less than the minimum number of quarters necessary to be fully insured). Disability benefits, too, may be calculated by subtracting a certain number from the minimum number of quarters necessary for fully insured status. This number is five for workers aged 47 or over, four for workers aged 42 through 46, three for workers aged 37 through 41, two for workers aged 32 through 36, one for workers aged 27 through 31, and zero for workers under age 27. However, for survivors or disability benefits, at least 2 years must remain for purposes of calculating benefits. (Note: Up to 3 additional years may be dropped from the calculation if the worker had no income during the year and had a child under the age of 3 living in his or her household during the entire year.) *Planning Note:* Because only 35 years are used, a client who has earned the taxable wage figure or more for 35 years will typically get the maximum benefit. Consequently, working longer will typically not help the client to optimize his or her benefit because it is already at the maximum.

- Fourth, determine the years to be excluded from the calculation. These will be the years with the lowest indexed earnings. Of course, the number of years determined in the previous step must remain. *Planning Note:* Typically the lowest 5 years are dropped, including years with zeros.

- Fifth, add the indexed earnings for the years to be included in the AIME calculation and divide the result by the number of months in these years.

As mentioned earlier, the calculation of the AIME for retirement or disability benefits excludes the year in which retirement or disability takes place. However, the indexed earning for that year can be substituted for the lowest year in the calculation if the result will be a larger AIME.

Determination of PIA and Monthly Benefits

Once a worker's AIME has been calculated, his or her PIA is determined by applying a formula to the AIME. The 2007 formula is as follows:

- 90 percent of the first $680 of AIME
- plus 32 percent of the AIME in excess of $680 and less than $4,100
- plus 15 percent of the AIME in excess of $4,100

The dollar figures in this formula are adjusted annually for changes in the national level of wages.

The formula used to determine a worker's retirement benefit is the formula for the year in which the worker turned age 62. Therefore, a worker retiring at age 65 and 10 months in 2007 would use the 2005 formula rather than the 2007 formula. The formula used to determine survivors and disability benefits is the formula in existence for the year in which death or disability occurs, even if application for benefits is made in a later year.

The PIA is the amount a worker will receive if he or she retires at normal retirement age or becomes disabled, and it is the amount on which benefits for family members are based.

In 2007, a worker who has had average earnings during his or her lifetime can expect an average monthly retirement benefit of $1,044 ($12,528 per year). A worker who has continually earned the maximum income subject to Social Security taxes can expect a benefit of about $2,116 a month ($25,392 annually) for retirement purposes and a lower benefit for purposes of disability and survivors benefits. If a worker is retired or disabled, the following benefits are paid to family members:

Category	Percentage of Worker's PIA
Spouse at full retirement age	50%
Spouse caring for disabled child or child under 16	50%
Child under 18 or disabled	50% each

If the worker dies, survivors benefits are as follows:

Category	Percentage of Worker's PIA
Spouse at full retirement age	100%
Spouse caring for disabled child or child under 16	75%
Child under 18 or disabled	75% each
Dependent parent	82.5% for one, 75% each for two

family maximum

However, the full benefits described above may not be payable because of a limitation imposed on the total benefits that may be paid to a family. This *family maximum* will usually be reached if three or more family members (including a retired or disabled worker) are eligible for benefits. The family maximum for purposes of retirement and survivors benefits can be determined for 2005 from the following formula, which, like the PIA formula, is adjusted annually based on changing wage levels:

150 percent of the first $869 of PIA
plus 272 percent of the PIA in excess of $869 through $1,255
plus 134 percent of the PIA in excess of $1,255 through $1,636
plus 175 percent of the PIA in excess of $1,636

The family maximum for purposes of disability benefits is limited to 85 percent of the worker's AIME or 150 percent of the worker's PIA, whichever is lower. However, in no case can the maximum be reduced below the worker's PIA.

If the total amount of benefits payable to family members exceeds the family maximum, the worker's benefit (in the case of retirement and disability) is not affected, but the benefits of other family members are reduced proportionately.

When the first child loses benefits at age 18, the other family members will each have benefits increased. When a second family member loses eligibility, the remaining two family members will each receive the full benefit because the total benefits received by the family will now be less than the family maximum.

Other Factors Affecting Benefits

Benefits Taken Early

Persons can retire as early as age 62, but the monthly benefit is permanently reduced. The reduction is 5/9 of 1 percent for each of the first

36 months of entitlement immediately preceding the age at which 100 percent of PIA is payable (scheduled to increase to age 67 by the year 2022), plus 5/12 of 1 percent for each of up to 24 earlier months.

For example, a person aged 62 in 2007 (born in 1945) has a full retirement age of 66. If she retires in 2007 and it is 48 months prior to her full retirement age, she would multiply 36 months by 5/9 of 1 percent (a 20 percent reduction) and 12 months by 5/12 of 1 percent (a 5 percent reduction) and would therefore receive a 25 percent reduction of their full retirement benefit.

A spouse who elects retirement benefits prior to a full retirement age of 65 will have benefits reduced by 25/36 of one percent per month, and a widow or widower will have benefits reduced by 19/40 of one percent per month.

Delayed Retirement

Workers who delay applying for retirement benefits until after attainment of normal retirement age are eligible for an increased benefit. For persons born between 1917 and 1924, the increase is 3 percent for each year of delay up to age 70. The increase is 3.5 percent per year for persons born in 1925 or 1926 and 4 percent for persons born in 1927 or 1928. To encourage delayed retirement, the percentage will gradually increase to 8 percent for those born in 1943 or later. (See table 19-4 for a summary of the early and delayed retirement percentages.)

Earnings Test

earnings test

Benefits are reduced for Social Security beneficiaries under the full retirement age if their work wages exceed a specified level. The rationale behind having a reduction tied to wages, referred to as an *earnings test*, is that Social Security benefits are intended to replace lost wages but not other income such as dividends or interest. In 2007, Social Security beneficiaries under full retirement age (65 years and 10 months) are allowed earnings of $12,960 ($1,080/month). This figure is adjusted annually on the basis of national wage levels. If a beneficiary earns in excess of the allowable amount, his or her Social Security benefit is reduced. For persons under age 65 years and 10 months, the reduction is $1 for every $2 of excess earnings. A different formula applies for the calendar year in which an individual attains the full retirement age. For that year, the reduction is only $1 for every $3 of excess earnings and counts only earnings before the month the individual reaches full retirement age. Also, for that year the threshold is higher: $34,440 ($2,870/month) in 2007. Once an individual attains the full retirement age, he or she can earn any amount of wages without a reduction of benefits.

The reduction in a retired worker's benefits resulting from excess earnings is applied to all benefits paid to the family. If large enough, this

TABLE 19-4
Social Security Retirement Ages—Reductions and Delayed Retirement Credit

Birth Year	Year Age 62	Delayed Retirement Credit	Normal Retirement Age	Earliest Eligibility Age	For Commencement at Age				
					62	65	66	67	70
1933	1995	5.5%	65	62	−20	0	5 1/2	11	27 1/2
1934	1996	5.5%	65	62	−20	0	5 1/2	11	27 1/2
1935	1997	6%	65	62	−20	0	6	12	30
1936	1998	6%	65	62	−20	0	6	12	30
1937	1999	6.5%	65	62	−20	0	6 1/2	13	32 1/2
1938	**2000**	6.5%	65 2/12	62	−20 5/6	−1 1/9	5 2/5	12	31 2/5
1939	2001	7%	65 4/12	62	−21 2/3	−2 2/9	4 2/3	11 2/3	32 2/3
1940	2002	7%	65 6/12	62	−22 1/2	−3 1/3	3 1/2	10 1/2	31 1/2
1941	2003	7.5%	65 8/12	62	−23 1/3	−4 4/9	2 1/2	10	32 1/2
1942	2004	7.5%	65 10/12	62	−24 1/6	−5 5/9	1 1/4	8 3/4	31 1/4
1943–1954	**2005–2016**	**8%**	**66**	**62**	−25	−6 2/3	0	8	32
1955	2017	8%	66 2/12	62	−25 5/6	−7 7/9	−1 1/9	6 2/3	30 2/3
1956	2018	8%	66 4/12	62	−26 2/3	−8 8/9	−2 2/9	5 1/3	29 1/3
1957	2019	8%	66 6/12	62	−27 1/2	−10	−3 1/3	4	28
1958	2020	8%	66 8/12	62	−28 1/3	−11 1/9	−4 4/9	2 2/3	26 2/3
1959	2021	8%	66 10/12	62	−29 1/6	−12 2/9	−5 5/9	1 1/3	25 1/3
1960 & later	2022 & later	8%	67	62	−30	−13 1/3	−6 2/3	0	24

reduction may totally eliminate all benefits otherwise payable to the worker and family members. In contrast, excess earnings of family members are charged against their individual benefits only. For example, a widowed mother who holds a job outside the home may lose her mother's benefit, but any benefits received by her children will be unaffected.

Cost-of-Living Adjustments

COLA

OASDI benefits are increased automatically each January as long as there has been an increase in the CPI for the one-year period ending in the third quarter of the prior year. This is known as a cost-of-living adjustment or *COLA*. The increase is typically the same as the increase in the CPI since the last COLA, rounded to the nearest 0.1 percent.

Social Security COLAs			
1999	1.3%	2002	2.6%
2000	2.4%	2003	1.4%
2001	3.5%	2004	2.1%
		2005	2.7%
		2006	4.1%
		2007	3.3%

Offset for Other Benefits

Disabled workers under full retirement age who are also receiving workers' compensation benefits or disability benefits from certain other federal, state, or local disability programs will have their OASDI benefits reduced to the extent that the total benefits received (including family benefits) exceed 80 percent of their average current earnings at the time of disability. In addition, the monthly benefit of a spouse or surviving spouse is reduced by two-thirds of any federal, state, or local government pension that is based on earnings not covered under OASDI.

REQUESTING INFORMATION AND FILING FOR BENEFITS

Earnings and Benefit Estimate Statement

Beginning in 1999, the Social Security Administration began to send an annual *Earnings and Benefit Estimate Statement* to each worker who is not currently receiving benefits and who is over age 25. The statements are mailed automatically to clients 3 months prior to their birthday. In addition, clients seeking a revised version or more detail can use the primary insurance amount calculators on the Social Security website (www.socialsecurity.gov).

When clients receive their statements, they should be instructed to check if the earnings history is correct. If the Social Security Administration has underestimated your clients' yearly earnings, they will get less Society Security than they are entitled to. Have clients' W-2s or tax returns available for the affected years. What's more, you can try to have the return corrected even if you don't have old tax returns.

The statements also contain important information for both planner and client, including:

YOUR FINANCIAL SERVICES PRACTICE:
THE EARNINGS TEST IN THE YEAR OF RETIREMENT

As we have seen, the earnings test can have a significant impact on a client because Social Security benefits are reduced by $1 for every $2 over the threshold level ($12,960 in 2007). Many clients who retire in mid-year may have already earned more than the yearly earnings limit. Under a special rule, a client can receive a full Social Security check for any whole month he or she is retired regardless of yearly earnings. In 2007, a person is considered "retired" if he or she earns under $1,080 per month (1/12 of $12,960) and thus will not be subject to the harsh treatment of the earnings test.

Example: John Smith retires at age 63 on August 30, 2007. He will make $45,000 through August. In September, he takes a part-time job earning $500 per month. Although his earnings for the year exceed the 2007 limit ($12,000), he gets his regular Social Security benefit from September through December because his earnings in those months are under $1,000. If John earns over $1,000 for any of those months (September to December), he will not receive a benefit for the month(s) he goes over the limit. In 2008, only the yearly limits apply to John.

One final point: Clients who are about to retire will often be able to negotiate their consulting pay, severance pay, and final months' salary all in one package. The planner should make the client aware of the earnings test and recommend negotiated solutions that avoid exceeding applicable thresholds in the year of retirement and in subsequent years.

Example: Suzanne Walsh, aged 62, will retire this year from her job as a professor at the university. She will, however, continue to teach part-time for several years. If she negotiates her final salary to be somewhat higher than the norm and her adjunct teaching salaries to be somewhat lower than the norm—and under the applicable earnings test threshold—she can restructure her affairs to avoid earnings test implications even though she is paid the same amount.

- the estimated Social Security retirement benefit the client will receive— the Social Security Administration calculates its estimated benefits by assuming that the client will make about the same as his or her latest earnings. If your client's earnings are likely to increase or decrease from present levels, then the benefit will change accordingly. *Planning Note:* Your client can request a statement with his or her own assumptions being used (online at www.ssa.gov or use Form SSA-7004).

  The Social Security benefit estimates given are in current dollars. Let the client know that each subsequent year's statement will be adjusted for cost of living increases. What's more, depending on the accumulation model (calculation of client needs) that you use, you may have to estimate adjustments to the projected benefit in "retirement time" dollars.

- the estimated disability and survivors benefits that your client will get from Social Security

- the full retirement age of the client—according to the Retirement Confidence Survey, 59 percent of workers in the nation expect to reach full eligibility sooner than they actually are scheduled to reach it.

Obtaining additional information about the Social Security system generally or getting specific information about benefits is easy—simply a telephone call away. The Social Security Administration can be reached at (800) 772-1213. Forms, brochures, and even applications for benefits can be obtained by calling this number; in fact, applications can even be made by phone or online at www.socialsecurity.gov.

OASDI benefits will not begin until an application for benefits is made. Most applications can be taken by phone at the number mentioned above or on the Internet. To ensure timely commencement, clients should be encouraged to apply for benefits 3 months in advance. However, benefit claims can technically be filed up to 6 months after benefits are due to commence because benefits can be paid retroactively for 6 months (longer in the case of a disability). If a client believes that he or she is entitled to a benefit, encourage him or her to file an application. A simple information request will not be given the same attention as a benefit application. Another important reason for filing an application is that if benefits are erroneously denied, they will be paid retroactively as of the application date once the snafu is straightened out. Also if, after benefits begin, an individual becomes aware that he or she is eligible for a second, larger benefit (for example, a spousal benefit), he or she must file an application in order to ensure receipt of the correct benefit.

TAXATION OF SOCIAL SECURITY BENEFITS

Until 1984, all Social Security benefits were received free of federal income taxation. Since that time, however, the rules have required individuals with substantial additional income to pay tax on a portion of their benefits. Until 1994, the maximum amount of Social Security benefits subject to tax was 50 percent. However, in 1994 the maximum percentage increased to 85 percent for certain taxpayers.

provisional income

The portion of the OASDI benefit that is subject to tax is based on what is referred to as the individual's *provisional income.* Provisional income is the sum of the following:

- the taxpayer's adjusted gross income
- the taxpayer's tax-exempt interest for the year
- half of the taxpayer's Social Security benefits for the year

If the provisional income is less than what is referred to as the *base amount*—$25,000 for a single taxpayer and $32,000 or less for a married taxpayer filing jointly—Social Security benefits are not taxable. If the provisional income is between the base amount and $34,000 ($44,000 for a married taxpayer filing jointly), up to 50 percent of the Social Security benefit will be includible in taxable income. If the provisional amount exceeds $34,000 ($44,000 for a married taxpayer filing jointly), up to 85 percent of the Social Security benefit will be includible in taxable income. To summarize, table 19-5 identifies the various cutoff points.

TABLE 19-5 **Portion of OASDI Benefits Subject to Federal Income Tax**		
Taxpayer Filing Status	Provisional Income Threshold	Amount of Benefits Subject to Federal Income Tax
Single Single Single	under $25,000 $25,000–$33,999 $34,000 or more	0 percent up to 50 percent up to 85 percent
Married filing jointly Married filing jointly Married filing jointly	under $32,000 $32,000–$43,999 $44,000 or more	0 percent up to 50 percent up to 85 percent
Married filing separately (and living in the same household)	$0	up to 85 percent

The general description of how much is included and the various cutoffs is often sufficient for planning purposes. However, the planner may have occasion to actually calculate the specific amount of benefits that are includible as taxable income. The following explanation and example can be used to make this determination.

Step 1: Calculate provisional income.

Step 2: Determine appropriate thresholds based on the individual's tax filing status.

Step 3: The amount of Social Security benefits included as taxable income is the smallest number obtained from performing the following three calculations:

   (a) 50 percent of any provisional income that exceeds the base threshold plus 35 percent of any amount in excess of the second threshold

   (b) 85 percent of the benefits

(c) 50 percent of the benefits, plus 85 percent of any amount in excess of the second threshold

---

Example:

Peggy and Larry Novenstern are married and file jointly. They have an adjusted gross income of $40,000 (not considering Social Security benefits) plus $5,000 of tax-free bond interest, and are entitled to a $15,000 Social Security benefit.

Step 1: Provisional income equals:

preliminary adjusted gross income	$40,000
tax-free bond interest	5,000
50 percent of Social Security benefits	7,500
provisional income	$52,500

Step 2: Determine income in excess of the applicable thresholds.

Excess over base threshold:
($52,500 – $32,000) $20,500
Excess over second threshold:
($52,500 – $44,000) $8,500

Step 3: Amount includible in taxable income is the lowest of the following three amounts:

(a) 50 percent of excess over base threshold plus 35 percent of excess over second threshold (.5 x $20,500 + 35 x 8,500) = $13,225
(b) 85 percent of $15,000 = $12,750
(c) 50 percent of $15,000 + 85 percent of 8,500 = $14,725

In this case, the $12,750 (85 percent of the benefit) is included as adjusted gross income.

WHEN TO TAKE EARLY RETIREMENT BENEFITS

One of the questions most frequently asked by clients considering early retirement is whether they should begin taking Social Security retirement benefits prior to the date that full benefits are payable. In 2007, a worker may retire at age 65 years and 10 months and receive full benefits or begin receiving reduced benefits as early as age 62. (Note that currently nearly 50 percent of males and 60 percent of females begin benefits at this age.)

After the client looks at some threshold issues, the decision often rests on the economic issue: Are the additional benefits received in the years before full retirement age sufficient to offset the benefits that will be forfeited after full retirement age if retirement benefits begin early?

Threshold Issues

The decision of whether an individual should elect to receive benefits early comes up in different contexts. For the retiring worker, it generally arises in three situations: as part of the decision regarding at what age to retire, as an issue of need for the individual who has been involuntarily terminated, and as an economic issue for the individual who has other potential sources of income in the early years of retirement. For this third category, the primary issue is an economic one, which is discussed in depth below. However, even for this group, one threshold issue must be addressed: Is the individual considering returning to work at any time prior to full retirement age? If so, then he or she may lose benefits due to the substantial employment rules.

Although the early retirement reduction factor may affect the decision to elect early retirement, more central to this decision is whether the individual will have sufficient pension benefits and/or personal savings to meet retirement needs. When advising these clients, be aware that they (1) generally are not fully aware of the financial effects of having a longer retirement period, (2) do not fully understand the impact on their pension benefits when they choose to retire early, and (3) do not understand that early commencement may (or may not) substantially lower Social Security benefits (due to factors other than the early retirement reduction factor).

Social Security benefits will be most affected when the individual has a short working history or has recently seen a drastic upswing in wages. In order to determine whether early retirement will have a substantial effect on benefits, an individual can request benefit information from the Social Security Administration. Two separate information requests should be made, one indicating that early retirement will occur, and the other indicating that benefits will begin at full retirement age. Assuming—after considering all relevant information—that an individual can afford to retire, then he or she will still have to decide whether taking early Social Security benefits makes economic sense.

When to Elect Early Benefits: The Economic Issue

As mentioned in the previous section, the primary factor in determining whether to elect reduced early benefits will be an economic one. Clients will be better off receiving early retirement benefits if the present value of the additional benefits received before full retirement age exceeds the present value of the higher benefits that are forgone after full retirement age and worse off if the opposite is true. Clearly if a person does not survive to full retirement age, electing to receive early retirement benefits is the better choice. But in most situations, a person will live past full retirement age, and a break-even life expectancy can be used as a guideline when deciding whether to elect early retirement benefits. Table 19-6 presents break-even life expectancies.

TABLE 19-6
Break-even Life Expectancy for Early Social Security Benefits[1]

Benefit Class	Age Early Benefits Begin	Real (Inflation-Adjusted) Discount Rate[2]			
		0%	1%	2%	3%
Retiring Worker	62	77.00	78.00	79.02	80.08
	63	78.00	79.01	80.05	82.01
	64	79.00	80.02	81.07	83.05
Spouse	62	74.00	74.07	75.03	76.00
	63	75.00	75.08	76.05	77.03
	64	76.00	76.09	77.07	78.07
Healthy Surviving Spouse	60	77.07	78.09	80.03	82.03
	61	78.07	79.10	81.06	83.09
	62	79.07	81.00	82.09	85.02
	63	80.07	82.01	84.00	86.08
	64	81.07	83.02	85.03	88.02
Disabled Surviving Spouse	50	102.08	117.00	167.02	N/A
	55	90.01	95.07	105.03	132.02
	60	77.07	78.09	80.03	82.03

1. The break-even life expectancies are expressed in a format of years and months. For example, 79.02 is age 79 years 2 months. An age 65 full retirement age is assumed.
2. The real (inflation-adjusted) discount rate is derived by the following formula: real discount rate = (nominal discount rate − inflation rate)/(1 + inflation rate). For planning purposes, subtracting the assumed growth rate of Social Security benefits from the nominal discount rate is sufficient.

TABLE 19-6 (continued)
Break-even Life Expectancy for Early Social Security Benefits[1]

		Real (Inflation-Adjusted) Discount Rate				
4%	5%	6%	7%	8%	9%	10%
82.08	85.05	89.09	99.01	N/A[3]	N/A	N/A
84.03	87.06	92.11	107.01	N/A	N/A	N/A
85.11	89.08	96.05	122.10	N/A	N/A	N/A
77.00	78.01	79.07	81.07	84.07	90.01	117.01
78.04	70.09	81.06	84.01	88.02	97.09	N/A
79.09	81.04	83.06	86.09	92.07	118.05	N/A
85.00	89.03	97.05	N/A	N/A	N/A	N/A
86.10	91.10	102.08	N/A	N/A	N/A	N/A
88.08	94.07	109.08	N/A	N/A	N/A	N/A
90.08	97.98	120.00	N/A	N/A	N/A	N/A
92.08	100.12	149.03	N/A	N/A	N/A	N/A
N/A	N/A	N/A	N/A	N/A	N/A	N/A
N/A	N/A	N/A	N/A	N/A	N/A	N/A
85.00	89.03	97.05	N/A	N/A	N/A	N/A

3. N/A means the break-even life expectancy for the given assumed real discount rate is infinite. Electing to receive reduced early benefits at this discount rate is always optimal.

Conclusion

Whether to take reduced early Social Security retirement benefits is a critical decision for many retirees. Once certain threshold issues are considered, the decision is often an economic one. Will I receive more benefits (over the long run) if I begin benefits now or wait until normal retirement age? The essential factors involved in this decision are a person's life expectancy, the assumed real (inflation-adjusted) discount rate, and the number of months before normal retirement age at which the benefits will begin. Table 19-6 presents guideline break-even life expectancies based on these essential factors to assist planners in advising their clients when and when not to take reduced early retirement benefits.

CHAPTER REVIEW

Key Terms

Social Security [19-1]
taxable wage base [19-3]
FICA tax [19-3]
SECA tax [19-3]
quarters of coverage [19-4]
fully insured [19-4]
currently insured [19-4]
disability insured [19-4]
full retirement age [19-4]

AIME [19-6]
PIA [19-6]
family maximum [19-6]
earnings test [19-7]
COLA [19-7]
Earnings and Benefit Estimate
   Statement [19-9]
provisional income [19-9]

Review Questions

Review questions are based on the learning objectives in this chapter. Thus, a [19-3] at the end of a question means that the question is based on learning objective 19-3. If there are multiple objectives, they are all listed.

1. Which workers are not covered under Social Security? [19-1]

2. What percentage of seniors have Social Security as their only source of income? [19-2]

3. What is the Social Security tax rate for employees, employers, and self-employed individuals? [19-3]

4. In 2007, Sally earns $5,000 for employment subject to Social Security taxes between January 1 and April 1. She does not work for the remainder of the year. How many quarters of coverage does she earn? [19-4]

5. What is the earliest age at which a retired worker and his or her spouse are entitled to receive Social Security benefits? [19-5]

6. How long must a couple be married before a divorced spouse is eligible for a spousal retirement benefit? [19-5]

7. Describe the survivor and disability benefits available under the Social Security system. [19-5]

8. Discuss the general rule that applies when a client is eligible for dual benefits under the Social Security system. [19-5]

9. How many years of income are generally used to calculate the average indexed monthly earnings (AIME) for an individual eligible for retirement benefits? [19-6]

10. Calculate the primary insurance amount (PIA) for an individual retiring at age 62 in 2007 with an AIME of $4,000. [19-6]

11. Patty, born in 1964, is planning on taking Social Security benefits at age 62. Her PIA will be decreased by what percentage? [19-7]

12. George, born in 1950, is planning to retire and begin receiving Social Security benefits at age 68. His PIA will be increased by what percentage in order to reflect his late retirement?[19-7]

13. How does the earnings test work? [19-7]

14. Describe the information contained in the statement mailed to Social Security participants who are aged 25 and older. [19-8]

15. What steps must be followed to ensure timely payment of all Social Security benefits to which a client is entitled? [19-9]

16. From an economic perspective, when will clients be better off electing Social Security benefits? [19-10]

20

Introduction to Individual Retirement Planning

Learning Objectives

An understanding of the material in this chapter should enable you to

20-1. List the skills that a pension student has learned regarding individual retirement planning.

20-2. Identify the role of the retirement planner and the steps in the retirement planning process.

20-3. Describe the following critical issues that affect retirement planning:

- availability of private pensions
- women and retirement
- need for education and planners
- changing face of retirement
- baby boomers and retirement
- roadblocks to retirement savings
- retirement objectives

20-4. Discuss the retirement ladder.

Chapter Outline

In addition to servicing the pension needs of a business and a business owner, identifying the Roth and regular IRA opportunities for individual clients, and understanding how the Social Security system applies to a client's situation (chapters 1 through 19), practitioners must also attend to the individual financial goals that clients have for their retirement. The following chapters, therefore, examine the remaining issues financial services professionals face when helping a client plan for retirement.

In essence, you have come to the logical conclusion concerning your study of planning for retirement needs. You started with an analysis of the pension system as codified in ERISA and the Internal Revenue Code. At that time, your client was the small business owner. You focused on the qualified plan needs of the business and then turned to the nonqualified plan needs for executives and business owners. Once again you served two masters—both the business and the business owner. You then turned your attention to the needs of the individual client and the individual retirement plan system (Roth and regular IRAs). Finally, you explored the workings of the Social Security system. Now, in this last part of the text, you continue to focus on the individual as your client and take a comprehensive look at planning for his or her successful retirement.

THE ROLE OF THE RETIREMENT PLANNER

It may surprise you to know that retirement planning is a relatively young discipline. Consider this: In 1930, only one in 10 workers was covered by a pension program and Social Security did not exist! For Americans who lived early in the 20th century, "retirement" meant moving from fieldwork to household chores. In the middle of the century, retirement was thought of as a short and sedentary experience. Consequently the need for a retirement planner did not exist until recently.

Today, however, retirement is no longer synonymous with rocking chairs. Instead retirement is thought of as a vibrant and significant time of

---

**YOUR FINANCIAL SERVICES PRACTICE:
PENSION KNOWLEDGE HELPS WITH
RETIREMENT PLANNING EXPERTISE**

The previous chapters will benefit you greatly in your individual retirement planning practice. When you were studying ERISA, IRAs, and Social Security, you were also learning a great deal about individual retirement planning. For example, you are now proficient in the following skills that an individual retirement planner must have. These include:

- understanding the type(s) of retirement plan(s) being provided to your clients including the plans benefit or contribution formula
- analyzing the key provisions of your clients' retirement plan including their vesting schedules, hardship withdrawal and loan rules, and matching contribution and elective deferral options
- identifying and using documents like the summary plan description and the personal benefit statement
- appreciating the importance of before-tax and/or tax-free savings vehicles as a method to maximize retirement savings
- diagnosing the ramifications of starting Social Security benefits prior to full retirement age
- choosing an appropriate Keogh plan for a self-employed person with Schedule C income
- recognizing the specifications for and importance of the ESOP diversification rules
- determining the IRA options that best fit your clients' needs
- interpreting the tax rules applicable to Social Security benefits and nonqualified stock plans
- explaining how Social Security and pension benefits are calculated and how your client can optimize their benefits under each system
- cataloging the fiduciary protection, QDRO assurance, and PBGC refuge and bankruptcy shield afforded your clients under law

As you can see a significant foundation has already been laid for our study of individual retirement planning.

---

life, which may last 30 years or longer. If Norman Rockwell, the renowned American illustrator, were alive today, he might put a face on today's retirement by portraying active seniors engaged in a variety of recreational activities. Gone are the days of the frail seniors sitting in rocking chairs. They have been replaced with active and involved people who need help in planning for a dynamic time of life.

Does the Retirement Planner Have an Impossible Task?

Retirement planning is a multidimensional field that requires the planner to be schooled in the nuances of many financial planning specialties as well as other nonfinancial areas. Unfortunately, some so-called planners approach retirement planning from only one point of view (for example, investments). The perspective offered by limited specialization, however, is inadequate for dealing with the diversified needs of the would-be retiree. A client is better served by a team of planners who have complementary specialized backgrounds or by a single planner who is experienced in a variety of important retirement topics.

Whether the retirement team or the multi-area individual is the vehicle, the holistic approach to retirement planning is the most professional method by which a client's needs can be fully and adequately met. Holistic retirement planning requires the planner to communicate with clients concerning the following topics:

- the effect of financial well-being on the quality of life
- employer-provided retirement plan options
- Social Security considerations
- personal savings and investments
- IRAs and Roth IRAs
- income tax issues
- tax planning for distributions and other distribution issues
- Medicare choices
- health insurance planning including medigap insurance and long-term care insurance
- wealth accumulation for retirement
- asset allocation and risk
- long-term care options (living options)
- retirement communities
- relocation possibilities and reverse mortgages
- wellness, nutrition, lifestyle choices, and other gerontological issues
- assessment of current savings needed to achieve retirement goals
- financial gerontology
- estate planning

A word of caution is in order at this point. Understanding how to plan for a client's retirement is much more art than science. There is no one-size-fits-all approach to retirement planning. For example, an attempt to describe the average retiree is like trying to describe the average book—even if it could be done, the information would not be very useful. Retirees are wealthy and poor, male and female, old and not-so-old. They are single, married, and widowed; they have children and they do not have children. They are healthy and unhealthy, happy and unhappy, active and sedentary, sophisticated and naive.

A further complication is that planning does not always begin early enough in the financial life cycle. While the axiom "it's never too early or too late to plan for retirement" is true, it requires a completely different approach to plan for a client's retirement when it is too late to influence the client's ability to retire with financial security. Conversely, planning at a relatively young age opens up a multitude of opportunities for clients and presents different planning challenges.

Because client circumstances and objectives are like snowflakes—there are no two alike—planners must be able to meet a variety of situations creatively and cannot rely on a "formula approach" to solve their clients' problems.

Your Financial Services Practice: Additional Responsibilities

In addition to being a "Jack of all trades," retirement planners now must undertake several responsibilities that may not have been a part of their traditional financial practice. These aspects of a retirement planning practice include

- incorporating retirement planning as a segment of comprehensive financial planning
- dealing with other professionals who advise the client
- dealing with clients from every age group (Retirement planning is for young clients as well as clients who are near or at retirement or who have retired already.)
- conducting retirement planning seminars

Retirement Resources

In order to measure up to the Herculean task of retirement planning, retirement planners must familiarize themselves with the various resources available in this field. Organizations such as the Society of Financial Service Professionals, the Financial Planning Association, the National Council on Aging, and the American Society on Aging offer a forum that provides newsletters, conferences, and a chance for interaction with other planners. In addition, planners should make their clients aware of the American Association of Retired Persons, an organization that provides information on services for the elderly including a valuable resource for retirement information. Planners may also want to check the numerous retirement planning websites.

1. *www.ssa.gov*—This site allows individuals to project the benefits they will receive from Social Security; it also provides a great deal of information regarding Social Security.
2. *www.EBRI.org*—The home page of the Employee Benefit Research Institute presents updates, databases, and surveys that have been recently issued.
3. *www.ASEC.org*—The American Savings Education Council provides the ballpark estimate calculator that enables people to calculate their savings need for retirement. It also contains links to different financial calculators.
4. *www.irs.gov*—The IRS website provides useful publications on many retirement issues.
5. *www.benefitscheckup.org*—This is a new service that allows seniors, their families, and caregivers to quickly and easily identify what programs and services they may qualify for and how to access them.

Steps in the Retirement Planning Process

The process for retirement planning is similar to the process for financial planning.

Step 1: Establish Client-Planner Relationships

It is essential to establish a working relationship with the client. This involves the identification and explanation of issues, concepts, and products related to the retirement process. The planner should describe the services he or she provides, the steps involved in the process, and the documentation (such as the summary plan description) required.

Step 2: Determine Goals and Expectations and Gather Client Data

This step begins by listening to the client's goals and hopes for retirement. Listening skills are important because it is easy for a planner to impose his or her concept of retirement on the client or to assume that he or she believes is important is also important to the client. However, clients have a variety of objectives that range from never working again to working full time during retirement. Clearly, planners have their work cut out for them as they deal with a plethora of client expectations and, in some cases, help frame those expectations through the education process.

In addition to sorting through the various lifestyle options for retirement, planners must also focus at this stage on conducting a financial inventory of retirement assets and an assessment of the strategies available to a client. For example, planners must account for all resources allocated to retirement and all opportunities a client has, such as the ability to contribute to a Roth IRA or the availability of a 401(k) plan at work.

YOUR FINANCIAL SERVICES PRACTICE:
IMPORTANT FACT-FINDING TOOLS

In addition to the typical information concerning assets and liabilities, securities holdings, and annual income, retirement planners need to look at the following:

- wills and trusts
- long-term care policies
- Social Security statements
- employer health benefit policies
- employer summary plan descriptions
- employer benefit statements

Step 3: Analyze and Evaluate the Client's Financial Status

In this step, the planner looks at the client's current situation as well as his or her future goals in order to determine the appropriate strategies for that particular client. This includes conducting a retirement needs analysis as well as an analysis of the client's risk tolerance, risk management strategies, and risk exposures. For example, do clients have adequate disability insurance and long-term care insurance? Do their current investment allocations adequately achieve their financial goals? Are they currently saving enough for retirement? What tax planning and distribution strategies are available and do they make sense for the client's situation? Planners need to evaluate and analyze current retirement plan exposures (for example, premature distribution tax), current retirement plans, current retirement strategies, and Social Security benefits.

Step 4: Develop and Present the Retirement Plan

The planner should develop and prepare a retirement plan tailored to meet the client's goals and objectives and commensurate with the client's values, objectives, temperament, and risk tolerance. In addition to the client's current financial position, the plan should include the client's projected retirement status under the status quo as well as projected statements if the planner's recommendations are followed. The planner should also provide a current asset allocation statement along with strategy recommendations and a statement that assumes that recommendations will be followed. Investments should be summarized, and the planner should propose an investment policy statement and additional policy recommendations. The plan should also include an assessment of distribution options and tax strategies for retirement. Finally, the plan should include a list of prioritized action items and engage issues such as housing and health care.

After developing and preparing the plan, the planner should present it to the client for review. The planner should collaborate with the client to ensure that the plan meets the stated goals and objectives; then the planner should revise it as appropriate.

Step 5: Implement the Retirement Plan

The planner should assist the client in implementing the recommendations. Often this requires coordinating with other professionals, such as human resource professionals, accountants, attorneys, real estate agents, investment advisors, stock brokers, and insurance agents.

Step 6: Monitor the Retirement Plan

After the plan is implemented, the planner should periodically monitor the plan, evaluate the soundness of recommendations, and review its progress with the client. The planner should discuss and evaluate changes in the client's personal circumstances such as family births or deaths, illness, divorce, or change in job status. Any relevant changes in tax laws, benefit and pension options, and the economic environment should be reviewed and evaluated before the planner makes recommendations to accommodate new or changing circumstances.

CRITICAL ISSUES THAT AFFECT RETIREMENT PLANNING

To better understand the retirement planning discipline, let's look at the different issues affecting the world of retirement today. By laying this foundation, the planner should be able to understand the rules and strategies discussed later in the book in the context of the retirement planning environment as it currently exists.

Issue One: Private Pension Availability

Clients who work for medium- and large-sized employers typically have an advantage over their counterparts in small firms when it comes to retirement planning. One fact of life in retirement planning is that as the size of the organization increases, the chance of having a pension program increases. For example:

- Eighty-five percent of workers for employers with 100 or more employees have an employment-based plan available to them.

- Fifty percent of workers for employers with 25 to 99 employees have an employment-based plan available to them.
- Twenty percent of workers for employers with less than 25 employees have an employment-based plan available to them.
- The Employee Benefits Research Institute says over 25 million employees working for small businesses are not covered by company retirement plans.

Issue Two: Women and Retirement

Women have unique problems that make it difficult to achieve a financially successful retirement. For one thing, women are less likely than men to have a pension at work because they historically work in industries that ignore pensions. Second, they have lower earnings, which obviously makes it harder to save for retirement. Third, they experience higher turnover than men, so they are more adversely affected by plan vesting schedules. Fourth, they outlive men so, all else being equal, women need to save more than men. Fifth, they are more likely to be caregivers than men, and thus often forgo income to care for a loved one. Sixth, they are more likely to be single or widowed and the responsibility of retirement in these instances is not shared. And finally, according to studies, they invest pension assets too conservatively and thus self-inflict an additional savings burden. Table 20-1 gives some indication of just how much women feel they are behind their male counterparts in being financially prepared for retirement.

TABLE 20-1
Gender Comparisons Among Workers

RETIREMENT CONFIDENCE

Overall confidence in having enough money to live comfortably throughout retirement

Males:	29 percent very confident 47 percent somewhat confident 24 percent not confident	Females:	17 percent very confident 48 percent somewhat confident 35 percent not confident

Confidence in doing a good job of preparing financially for retirement

Males:	28 percent very confident 49 percent somewhat confident 23 percent not confident	Females:	18 percent very confident 49 percent somewhat confident 32 percent not confident

Confidence levels about having enough money to take care of long-term care expenses in retirement

Males:	16 percent very confident 39 percent somewhat confident 44 percent not confident	Females:	10 percent very confident 33 percent somewhat confident 56 percent not confident

RETIREMENT PREPARATIONS	
Have saved for retirement	
Males: 69 percent in 2002 68 percent in 2001 79 percent in 2000 71 percent in 1999 69 percent in 1998 70 percent in 1997	Females: 64 percent in 2002 62 percent in 2001 72 percent in 2000 70 percent in 1999 57 percent in 1998 68 percent in 1997
Have done a retirement savings needs calculation	
Males: 37 percent in 2002 44 percent in 2001 58 percent in 2000 54 percent in 1999 49 percent in 1998 39 percent in 1997	Females: 27 percent in 2002 35 percent in 2001 49 percent in 2000 44 percent in 1999 40 percent in 1998 32 percent in 1997
Retirement planning and saving status	

Males: 6 percent ahead of schedule
39 percent on track
26 percent a little behind
    schedule
28 percent a lot behind schedule
	Females: 4 percent ahead of schedule
	30 percent on track
	25 percent a little behind
	    schedule
	37 percent a lot behind schedule

Source: 2002 Retirement Confidence Survey, Employee Benefit Research Institute, American Savings Education Council, Mathew Greenwald & Assts. Reprinted by permission.	

Issue Three: The Need for Education and Planners

In a recent study, more than 90 percent of human resource and financial managers believed that employees are ill-prepared to make their own retirement decisions. In the same study, 86 percent of human resource and financial managers felt their employees needed financial advice regarding retirement assets above and beyond the current educational information they were receiving. This represents a huge opportunity and challenge for financial services professionals. Professionals who can meet this need can provide a necessary service to business clients and also increase their individual client base. Consider the following factors that indicate the importance of a planner:

- Seminar presentations are an invaluable mechanism that financial services professionals can provide; 401(k) participation jumps 17 percent when seminars are offered. Contribution rates are also up.
- According to one study, 65-year-olds without a written financial plan are twice as likely to find retirement a time of financial worry as their counterparts who have a plan, according to one study.

- According to another survey, 57 percent concede they have not calculated nor do they know how much they need to save each year to reach their retirement goal.
- In the most recent year for which statistics were available, 6 in 10 job changers cashed out their retirement savings instead of rolling them into another type of plan.

Based on the above insights, it is apparent that clients will need education and active involvement from financial service professionals.

Issue Four: The Changing Face of Retirement

It is very important for planners to realize that retirement planning is a dynamic environment. Not only do products, services, and tax laws seem to change on a regular basis, but the very nature of retirement also is in flux. Some interesting studies show differences for those planning to retire in the future. For example, surveys show that current workers *expect* to work longer than current retirees actually worked before retiring. Surveys also show that many baby boomers say they plan to work after they retire because they enjoy working and want to stay involved. (See table 20-2.)

TABLE 20-2 Major Reasons for Working in Retirement Cited by Workers and Retirees		
	Workers	**Retirees**
• Enjoy working and want to stay involved	65%	56%
• Keep health insurance or other benefits	45	24
• Want money to buy extras	33	22
• Want money to make ends meet	33	11
• Help support children or other household members	15	4
• Try a different career	13	18
Source: 2002 Retirement Confidence Survey, Employee Benefit Research Institute, American Savings Education Council, Mathew Greenwald & Assts. Reprinted by permission.		

Another responsibility changing the nature of retirement is that of a caregiver. The retirees of today and tomorrow are increasingly responsible for caring for parents, children, and grandchildren. Caregiving by retirees of aging parents is well-documented. Apparently, however, a parent's job never ends! According to the U.S. Census Bureau, about 5.5 million children (or 7.7 percent of all children in the United States) were living in homes with a grandparent. Three-quarters of the time, the grandparent maintains the home. (Remember that Norman Rockwell retirement picture? Now picture a grandmother having a catch with her granddaughter as the mother gets into a car to go to work.)

Issue Five: Baby Boomers and Retirement

baby-boom
generation

Retirement planning is important for *every* generation—a person is never too old or too young to plan for retirement. Special attention must be paid, however, to the needs of those born from 1946 to 1964, the so-called *baby-boom generation.* This generation represents roughly one-third of the population and, as it has progressed through the life cycles, it has greatly impacted everything from crowding in grammar schools to the housing market. The question remains: What will the implications of this demographic tidal wave have on retirement?

YOUR FINANCIAL SERVICES PRACTICE:
THE GRAYING OF AMERICA

Considering that the number of people over age 60 will triple by 2030 to 1.4 billion (16 percent of the world's population), the need for retirement planners and practitioners familiar with eldercare issues is certain to intensify as the baby-boom generation matures. In fact, the closer a person gets to retirement, the more he or she realizes the great need for products and services provided by the financial services industry. Ironically, retirement planning is not just about older people. Planners are well-aware that the process should begin at the early stages of a client's life cycle. However, over the next 10 years, the fledgling field of retirement planning should mature along with the baby-boom generation. For this reason, the timing of practitioners currently entering this field is perfect because the opportunities to serve both clients and themselves in a rewarding career are great

---

Issue Six: Roadblocks to Retirement Saving

No matter what the generation, the question remains: Why don't more Americans plan for retirement? The answer lies in the many distractions that hinder retirement savings.

Perhaps the biggest roadblock to retirement planning is the tendency of many working people to use their full after-tax income to support their current standard of living. Whatever the reason for their lack of retirement savings, clients must follow a budget that allows them to live within their means and that also provides for retirement savings. Make your clients aware that a 90/10 spending ratio is generally desired. Under a 90/10 spending ratio, 90 percent of your clients' earnings is directed toward their current standard of living, and at least 10 percent is directed toward other long-term financial objectives, such as their own retirement.

A second impediment to retirement saving is unexpected expenses including uninsured medical bills; repairs to a home, auto, or major appliance; and periods of unemployment. The client should set up an emergency fund to handle these inevitable problems. Approximately 3 to 6 months' income is usually set aside for this objective.

Inadequate insurance coverage is a third impediment to retirement saving. Regardless of whether it is life, disability, health, home, or auto, many individuals continue to remain uninsured or underinsured. Because the client cannot always recover economically from such losses, one important element of retirement planning is protection against catastrophic financial loss that would make future saving impossible. Agents should conduct a thorough review of their clients' insurance needs to make sure they are adequately covered. Two areas that are often overlooked are disability insurance and liability insurance for the professional. Make sure your client is adequately protected in both of them.

Whatever distractions face your clients, it is important to educate them about the need to plan for retirement. Clients must realize that saving is possible only for a limited time during their lives, but consumption occurs throughout their lives and can increase at any time because of illness or inflation. This imbalance makes it essential for clients to save sufficient assets during their working years to ensure attainment of retirement goals.

Issue Seven: Retirement Objectives

A client's retirement objectives vary significantly depending on many factors including health, age, marital status, number and ages of children, differences in the ages of husband and wife, and personal preferences. Also, a client's objectives vary depending on his or her personal definition of retirement. For some, retirement is the last day they *have* to work; for others it is the last day they *want* to work; and for still others it is the last day they *can* work. Table 20-3 contains a ranking of some typical retirement objectives. (The ranking identifies how a surveyed group of CLUs, ChFCs, and members of the Registry of Financial Planning Practitioners feel their clients would generally rate their retirement objectives.)

TABLE 20-3
Ranking of Retirement Objectives in Order of Priority

1. maintaining preretirement standard of living
2. maintaining economic self-sufficiency
3. minimizing taxes
4. retiring early
5. adapting to noneconomic aspects of retirement
6. passing on wealth to others
7. improving lifestyle in retirement
8. caring for dependents

THE RETIREMENT LADDER

For years, traditional thinking indicated that financial needs during retirement are met from three primary sources often referred to as the legs of the three-legged stool. The sources include Social Security benefits (chapter 19), employer-sponsored pension plan benefits (chapters 1–16), and personal savings (chapters 17–18). There is no doubt that these sources remain an integral part of retirement security. However, the three-legged stool analogy does not do justice to the myriad sources of income needed for financial independence in retirement. For this reason, let us now think of the stool being replaced by the retirement ladder (figure 20-1).

The federal Social Security system provides retirement benefits to a large portion of retired workers. Two statistics clearly demonstrate the importance of Social Security benefits: (1) around 90 percent of all individuals aged 65 and older report Social Security benefits as a source of income, and (2) Social Security represents more than 40 percent of total income for this group. Company-sponsored retirement plans also remain an important foundation for a secure retirement. Nearly 95 million Americans are covered by a company-sponsored retirement plan. However, only slightly more than 30 percent of the population aged 65 and older have pension income and, to the surprise of many, pension income for current retirees represents only about 20 percent of total retirement income. Personal savings also remain important. However, just from watching the news most of us are aware of the low savings rate for Americans today. It should be noted, however, that over 50 percent of people aged 65 and older have interest income, and approximately 25 percent have dividend income.

In addition to the big three sources, one of the key rungs on the ladder of retirement success is proper planning. As we discussed a few pages ago, this represents a huge opportunity and challenge for financial services professionals.

Another key resource for retirement security is sufficient insurance protection in all forms of insurance. In all phases of life, an insurance checkup is needed to ensure financial security. From renter's insurance to long-term care, seniors often find themselves lacking the protection they need. Clients who have medigap coverage, long-term care insurance, and other protections will not only *be* more financially secure but they will *feel* more secure than clients who do not have these protections.

fiscal welfare

For clients of limited means, one of the keys to financial security in retirement concerns fiscal welfare and social assistance. *Fiscal welfare* is an indirect payment made to individuals through the tax system. An example is the retirement savings contribution credit. The retirement savings contributions credit is a tax credit of up to $1,000 ($2,000 if married filing

FIGURE 20-1
The Ladder of Retirement Security

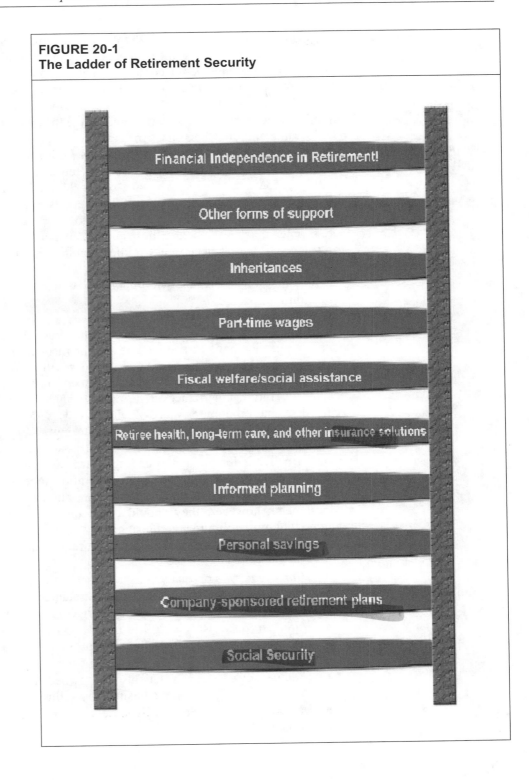

jointly) that is given as an incentive for lower income clients to save for their future. It is available to the client if he or she makes an "eligible contribution" that includes a contribution to a traditional or Roth IRA; a 401(k), 403(b), or 457 plan; a SIMPLE; or a salary reduction SEP (SARSEP). *Social assistance* is a type of social benefit that contains eligibility criteria designed in part to encourage the able-bodied poor to work by providing minimal benefits. An example of social assistance would be supplemental security income. *Supplemental Security Income (SSI)* is a benefit program administered by the Social Security Administration that pays monthly income to clients who are 65 or older, blind, or disabled. An individual client who qualifies for the full benefit can receive close to $600 per month and a couple can receive close to $900 per month. In addition, state supplements may increase these amounts depending on the client's state of residence. Planners need to assist clients in understanding these important social programs.

social assistance

Supplemental Security Income (SSI)

Part-time wages are another important rung on the retirement ladder. Over 2 million people or 23 percent of the 65–69 cohort remain in the labor force. Also, according to a recent AARP survey, 66 percent of older workers plan to work well into their retirement years. For all people aged 65 and older, 16.3 percent have earned income and the median income is $15,000.

For some clients, inheritances will add to their financial security in retirement. According to AARP, only 15 percent of baby boomers expect to receive any future inheritances. The median value of inheritances already received by baby boomers was $47,900, and less than 2 percent received over $100,000. It is important to know that the bulk of wealth is concentrated in the hands of the wealthiest 10 percent. It is also important to know that parents are living longer and spending down accumulated assets or have annuitized their wealth so that second generation inheritances are unlikely. This does not mean that clients will not get an inheritance from their parents. It does mean, however, they should count on inheritances as a financial planning tool only in limited circumstances.

There are a variety of other sources of retirement income including:

- *Home equity.* For many, this represents the largest asset they will have in the later retirement years. Strategies such as downsizing to free up cash or using a reverse mortgage may be considered.
- *Life insurance.* Receiving life insurance from a deceased spouse or cashing out a whole life policy may provide retirement protection for some.
- *Family business assets.* Clients who owned their own business may be able to capitalize on the business by selling it at retirement.
- *Rental property.* Some clients may receive rental income from property they own.

Tomorrow's retirement will be funded from sources beyond the traditional three-legged stool. The time has come for planners and clients to adjust projections for how much they will need in retirement to account for additional streams of income. Planning based on a stool can get clients only so high. Planning based on a ladder will bring them to greater heights.

CHAPTER REVIEW

Key Terms

baby-boom generation [20-3]
fiscal welfare [20-3]
social assistance [20-3]

Supplemental Security Income (SSI) [20-3]

Review Questions

Review questions are based on the learning objectives in this chapter. Thus, a [20-3] at the end of a question means that the question is based on learning objective 20-3. If there are multiple objectives, they are all listed.

1. Gina Neuman is an insurance agent who would like to conduct individual retirement planning for her clients. What topics does she already have expertise from her ERISA training that will allow her to serve her clients? [20-2]

2. List the topics that comprise the field of holistic retirement planning. [20-2]

3. List some organizations that can supply retirement planners with information and strategies for their clients. [20-3]

4. Identify and discuss the six steps in the retirement planning process. [20-3]

5. What are the problems specific to the retirement security needs of women? [20-3]

6. What are some characteristics of the changing face of retirement? [20-3]

7. List some of the roadblocks to successful retirement. [20-3]

8. List and explain the rungs of the retirement ladder. [20-4]

Retirement Needs Analysis: The Assumptions

Learning Objectives

An understanding of the material in this chapter should enable you to

21-1. Discuss the factors that should be considered when choosing a retirement age and a life expectancy assumption.

21-2. Describe the replacement-ratio approach for determining the income needed in the first year of retirement, considering the

   a. estimated replacement ratio
   b. decrease in taxation for retirees
   c. factors that reduce living expenses for retirees
   d. factors that increase living expenses for retirees

21-3. Describe the expense-method approach for determining the income needed in the first year of retirement.

21-4. Describe the impact inflation has on funds needed for retirement.

21-5. Discuss the total return on investment assumption and some of the common retirement investing strategies that help to shape it.

Chapter Outline

One major question that is encountered when planning for retirement is whether sufficient savings exist to provide enough income for the retirement years. More specifically, clients want to know how much they have to squirrel away each year so that they can maintain their current standard of living after they retire. There is no precise method that specifies exactly how much is enough. However, the planner can take several steps to create a workable retirement plan and calculate a funding target for the client. This chapter and chapter 22 explore these steps by

- addressing the crucial assumptions needed to help calculate the postretirement monetary need (current chapter)
- providing a method for computing and funding the client's retirement need (chapter 22)

ASSUMPTION ONE: RETIREMENT AGE

The existence of the Social Security and Medicare programs has created an expectation that Americans would retire when both Social Security and Medicare benefits were available. Until recently, most retirement planning tended to support this perception by anticipating retirement to occur at age 65. Thus, workers and advisors almost invariably planned, economically and psychologically, for retirement at this age. However, for a variety of reasons that will be discussed later, age 65 is no longer a magic number for retirement.

What, then, is retirement age? As a practical matter, the average retirement age (which is slightly over age 62) is irrelevant to the retirement planner. What is important is the unique retirement-age goal for each individual client.

Major factors that help to frame that goal include government and employer programs and policies. For example, not only the key Social Security and Medicare ages (age 62 for early (albeit reduced) Social Security benefits, age 65 for Medicare coverage, and depending on the year of birth, anywhere between age 65 and 67 for full (unreduced) Social Security benefits) but also the early, normal and deferred retirement ages in the client's qualified plan. Also important are the client's lifestyle goals, family responsibilities, and individual financial circumstances, as well as his or her willingness to incur the risks of portfolio performance, inflation, and adverse changes in government and employer policies. Let's take a closer look at some other things that should be considered when your client selects a retirement age.

Factors Affecting the Choice of a Retirement Age

1. Early Social Security benefits available at age 62. (These benefits are reduced).
2. Medicare eligibility at age 65.
3. Full retirement age for Social Security. (Anywhere from 65 to 67 depending on the year of birth)
4. Early retirement age as defined in the employer plan.
5. Normal retirement age as defined in the employer plan.
6. Lifestyle goals.
7. Family responsibilities.
8. Specific financial conditions applicable when the decision is being made.
9. Perspective on investment performance, inflation and changes in government programs that may impact financial resources.

Reasons Clients Choose Early Retirement (Or Have It Thrust Upon Them)

Several factors encourage younger retirement ages. Some workers have succeeded in saving and investing and are able to retire before 65 in comfort, even with reduced Social Security and retirement benefits. Other people simply want to retire earlier and will accept a lower standard of living if necessary.

A trend in recent years is for corporations to trim expenses by offering incentives for older, higher-paid employees to retire early. These so-called *golden handshakes* are dangled in front of employees in the forms of extra lump-sum payouts (typically based on years of service—for example, two weeks pay for each year of service), extra retiree medical coverage (for example, the employer promising to pick up COBRA payments) and increases in accrual rates (for defined-benefit plans). Golden handshakes provide tempting offers even in cases where they are not a wise financial decision. What's more, in some cases corporations cut back by eliminating the older employees without offering any incentives. Because older people can have trouble finding new positions, an employer cutback often amounts to the end of a worker's career—a forced retirement that is early and permanent.

Another reason people choose to retire early centers on health. Some clients' personal heath situation makes continuation of work difficult or impossible. For others, the need to care for a spouse or parent with health problems (even though they are in good health themselves) forces an early retirement. Fear of bad health in the future becomes an impetus for some workers to retire now while they have the health to enjoy it.

List 1: Summary of Reasons for Early Retirement

1. financial goals have been met. The client can continue his or her standard of living throughout retirement.
2. financial goals have been compromised. The client has a personal desire to trade a lower standard of living for freedom from employment.
3. corporate downsizing with incentives (golden handshakes). These incentives often encourage an early retirement.
4. corporate downsizing without incentives. When a business contracts in size, some people who are near retirement age are forced into early retirement.
5. actual health issues. Clients may retire early because they have health concerns and work compounds their problems.
6. caregiving health issues. Some clients retire early because they have caregiving responsibilities for a parent or spouse.
7. perceived health issues. Clients in good health may want to retire early while they can enjoy life. They fear poor health later will limit their activity and do not want to ruin the opportunity of an active retirement.
8. health and pension incentives. The structure of the employer's health and pension plan may encourage early retirement. For example, a client with retiree health coverage at age 62 and a pension that provides 60 percent of salary may perceive that he or she is working for 40 cents on a dollar.
9. nonfinancial factors. In some instances, the death of a spouse can encourage early retirement. In others, such as in the two-wage-earner family, there may be a desire to retire together even though one spouse is younger than the other (the younger spouse would take early retirement).
10. problems in the workplace. Some people retire because their jobs have grown intolerable. For example, a recent change makes the job environment a difficult one. These changes range from, "I cannot work in this changed environment" to "I feel they just do not care about quality any more and I cannot work that way."

Yet another reason people choose early retirement is the availability of company-paid health benefits and a good pension system at their place of employment. Many corporations offer medical insurance at reduced rates to early retirees to bridge the gap until eligibility for Medicare. Others continue to pay for retirement benefits throughout the retirement period. Some clients with defined-benefit plans feel they are working for only part of their salary. In other words, some argue that if their pension will be $50,000 and their salary is $100,000, then it makes no sense to keep working.

Other reasons early retirement occurs include:

- spouse's death
- spouse's retirement
- problems and/or changes in the workplace

A recent Retirement Confidence Survey, sponsored by the Employee Benefit Research Institute and the Principal Financial Group, revealed that *45 percent of current retirees retired earlier than they had planned*! Reasons most frequently cited for earlier-than-planned retirement include health problems or disability (40 percent), downsizing or closure (14 percent), family reasons (14 percent), other work-related reasons (12 percent), and miscellaneous (20 percent). Because these reasons typically arise unexpectedly, few of these retirees had enough time to prepare adequately. They simply did not know when they would retire.

Reasons Clients Should View Early Retirement Skeptically

From the planner's perspective, there are many reasons to advise a client against early retirement. First, as noted in chapter 19, the Social Security full retirement age is being increased from 65 to 67. Clients affected by this change should be aware that the early retirement benefit paid at age 62 will also be reduced. For an individual born in 1937 or earlier, it is 80 percent of the individual's primary insurance amount (discussed in detail in chapter 19). For those with a full retirement age of 67, the benefit will drop to 70 percent of the client's primary insurance amount.

Early retirement also affects the client's pension benefits. In a defined-benefit plan, the final-average salary and years-of-service components of the client's benefit formula will be lower than they otherwise would be if the client remained employed. In addition, there is typically an actuarial reduction in the pension annuity to account for a larger payout period. In a defined-contribution plan, a client's account balance will be smaller than it otherwise would be if the client remained employed. The client loses the opportunity to make (or have his or her employer make) contributions based on a percentage of peak (end-of-career) salary and, where applicable, may lose the matching contributions attributable to those contributions.

Other ways in which early retirement can affect financial security include the following:

- increased exposure to inflation (because of the longer retirement period)
- lack of health insurance prior to Medicare. Some employers either do not offer retiree coverage or reserve the right to cancel it. An accounting rule known as *FASB 106* discourages health plans for retirees by requiring firms to lower current reported earnings in anticipation of future health care costs. Since its implementation, some corporations have reneged on what retirees thought was a pledge of future coverage.
- an adverse effect on the calculation of Social Security benefits (the 35 years used in the PIA calculation may have to include years with reduced or no earnings)

Planning Note: If you err on the conservative side and plan for a retirement date that occurs prior to your client's actual retirement date, you will overestimate the retirement need and, consequently, the client will have more funds than necessary. Conversely, a planned retirement date that occurs after the actual retirement starting date will underestimate the retirement income need and leave the client with less funds than necessary.

Other Considerations

Be aware that some clients are planning to work past age 65. At one time, turning 65 meant mandatory retirement. Now federal law (the Age Discrimination in Employment Act) specifies that many mandatory retirement policies represent age discrimination and are illegal. What's more, pension benefits that continue to increase after age 65, lack of success in personal investing, and longer life expectancies are among the factors that encourage older retirement ages. Also, many people choose to retire long after 65 because they enjoy their work and /or they derive a large part of their personal identity from work.

Another consideration when determining a "later" target retirement date is the client's fixed long-term liabilities, such as educational expenses incurred for children. In some cases, the client has very little discretion over the retirement date until these liabilities have been paid.

For most clients, specification of a retirement age is based on nonfinancial criteria. If the client indicates the desire to retire at age 64, the planner's responsibility is to help determine whether that is a financially viable goal. At the same time, the planner must advise the client of negative aspects of the chosen age. Often the planner provides the client with a variety of scenarios (for example, if x age is targeted, y level of savings is needed per year); in some circumstances, this information may cause the client to postpone retirement so that a proper amount of income can be saved.

ASSUMPTION TWO: LIFE EXPECTANCY

Clients are living longer than prior generations and, in many cases, living longer than expected. According to the U.S. Census Bureau, there are over 68,000 centenarians. This is double that of the 1990 census! Furthermore, by the year 2050, it is projected that there will be over 1.1 million centenarians.

Many clients mistakenly rely on life expectancy at birth to set their expectations. However, life expectancy at age 65 is much different (89.5 versus 85.1 for females) and a more accurate measure for retirement. Even if clients were to use accurate life expectancy tables, remember that many clients will outlive the tables. Earlier-than-expected retirement (issue one) in combination, with increased longevity (issue two) can be a disastrous one-two punch for knocking out retirement security and sending clients into financial trouble.

To establish the proper life expectancy, planners must take a close look at clients' personal and family health history. For example, an obese, alcoholic smoker with diabetes, a heart condition, a family history of cancer, and multiple reckless driving citations is unlikely to reach the life expectancy. A cautious, healthy, and health-conscious individual with a good family medical history and an enthusiasm for life is likely to live beyond the expected span.

How long will retirement last? To estimate the expected retirement period, take the following steps:

- Look up statistical life expectancy data by using the retirement ages of the client and his or her spouse. (See Appendices 3 and 4)
- Adjust the estimate up or down for factors such as health, lifestyle, and family history.
- Use consumer Web sites or proprietary software that projects longevity based on family and personal health history.

Even after this analysis, remember it is only an estimate. Financial conservatism dictates that planner and client should assume a longer-than-expected retirement period and add a few years to the estimate. Alternatively, the planner can set aside a separate class of assets that will only be consumed if the client outlives his or her planned life expectancy (otherwise these assets can be used for estate planning). Consider that it is the anxiety of possibly outliving one's money that causes clients to select life annuities or interest-only payout provisions at retirement. Such clients implicitly assume a longer-than-average life span. For any reasonable life span estimate, there is some probability that the typical client will outlive his or her assets. Although this statement is mathematically obvious, it often serves as a wake-up call, further emphasizing the importance of accumulating a substantial retirement fund that the client will not outlive.

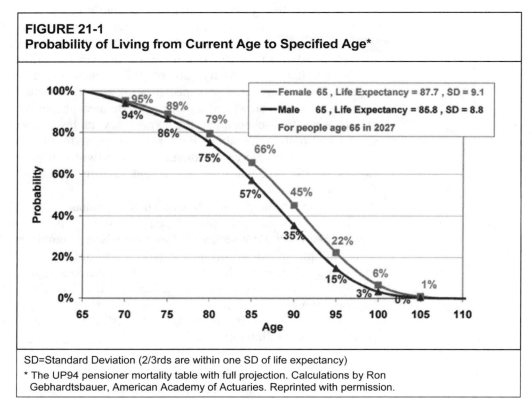

FIGURE 21-1
Probability of Living from Current Age to Specified Age*

SD=Standard Deviation (2/3rds are within one SD of life expectancy)

* The UP94 pensioner mortality table with full projection. Calculations by Ron Gebhardtsbauer, American Academy of Actuaries. Reprinted with permission.

ASSUMPTION THREE: EXPECTED STANDARD OF LIVING DURING RETIREMENT

The standard of living enjoyed during the years just prior to retirement largely influences the client's expectations for his or her postretirement standard of living. For this reason, the planner encounters different situations depending on how close the client is to his or her retirement date. With this in mind, let's examine the differences that exist between clients of various age groups.

Late-Career Clients

For almost all clients, the years immediately prior to retirement represent their peak earning years and their highest standard of living. Clients who are near the end of their careers are concerned about maintaining their current standard of living. As a group, these clients are the most interested in retirement planning and are the most willing to make adjustments to their preretirement lifestyle to compensate for inadequate retirement savings.

Mid-Career Clients

The client who is in the middle of his or her career has a different perspective on his or her postretirement standard of living. Employment has permitted this client to establish a comfortable standard of living, but he or she envisions still further increases in income and in lifestyle. For these clients, the desired standard of living during retirement will be based on their expectations of success in their career and the attendant increases in their standard of living. In other words, these clients will prefer to enjoy an unknown and yet-to-be-realized standard of living during their retirement years. Planners must first make the best estimate possible based on the client's educational background, job experiences, personal ambitions, and career plan. The estimated retirement standard of living can be computed by applying a growth factor to the client's current salary and approximating the client's final-average salary.

Early-Career Clients

These clients typically have too little experience to estimate what their retirement needs will be and probably have not thought about the standard of living they will expect at that time. For this reason, estimating a retirement standard of living at this stage is too tentative. The planner should instead concentrate efforts on encouraging these clients to use regular IRAs or Roth IRAs, or to make contributions to the employer 401(k) plan. Note also that early-career clients as well as mid-career clients are less likely than late-career clients to adjust their current lifestyle for retirement planning purposes. Younger clients are more likely to be distracted by other priorities and will tend to ignore the future because current problems take precedence. In this situation, the retirement planner must try to make saving for retirement a priority in spite of these distractions. One way to accomplish this is to talk about retirement planning in terms of financial independence planning. The change in terminology focuses clients on the goal of being able to control their own financial future, which is desirable even to younger clients.

In addition to understanding the standard of living the client expects during retirement, planners must also be prepared to estimate the income stream a client will need during retirement. One of the essential parts of this process is estimating the income a client will need in the first year of retirement. Let's examine the two generally accepted methods for determining this, the replacement-ratio method and the expense method.

The Replacement-Ratio Method

replacement-ratio method

One way to estimate how much a client will need in the first year of retirement is to apply the replacement-ratio method. The *replacement-ratio method* assumes that the standard of living enjoyed during the years just prior to retirement will be the determinant of the standard of living needed in the first year of retirement. Under the replacement-ratio method, the planner can estimate the amount needed in the first year of retirement, regardless of the client's age, by using a replacement ratio that is geared to continue the same standard of living (for late-career clients) or the estimated standard of living (for mid-career clients). In general, a 60 to 80 percent replacement ratio is used. In other words, the amount of income needed to be financially independent in the first year of retirement without drastically altering the client's standard of living varies between 60 and 80 percent of the average gross annual income of the average of the last 3 years of employment. For example, if a client with an income in the years prior to retirement of $95,000, $100,000, and $105,000, respectively, has an 80 percent target rate, then the client should target a replacement ratio of about $80,000 (80 percent of the $100,000 average). Support for this range rests upon the elimination of some employment-related taxes and some expected changes in spending patterns that reduce the retiree's need for income (such as expenditures that will either decrease or disappear in the retirement years).

Reductions in Taxation. In many circumstances, retirees can count on a lower percentage of their income going to pay taxes in the retirement years. Some taxes are reduced or eliminated, and in other cases retirees may enjoy special favorable tax treatment. Let's take a closer look at the potential reductions in taxation that are granted to retirees.

Social Security Taxes. FICA contributions (old-age, survivors, disability, and hospital insurance) are levied solely on income from employment. Distributions from pensions, IRAs, retirement annuities, and other similar devices are not considered income subject to FICA or SECA (self-employment FICA) taxes. Hence, for the retiree who stops working entirely, Social Security taxes are no longer an expenditure.

Increased Standard Deduction. For a taxpayer aged 65 or over, an additional amount is added to the standard deduction. If the taxpayer is married and his or her spouse is also 65 or older, both spouses receive the additional standard deduction.

Social Security Benefits Exclusion. As we discussed in chapter 19, some or all of a client's Social Security benefits will be received tax free. To reiterate, table 21-1 below identifies the various cutoff points.

TABLE 21-1
Portion of OASDI Benefits Subject to Federal Income Tax

Taxpayer Filing Status	Provisional Income Threshold	Amount of Benefits Subject to Federal Income Tax
Single	under $25,000	0 percent
Single	$25,000–$33,999	up to 50 percent
Single	$34,000 or more	up to 85 percent
Married filing jointly	under $32,000	0 percent
Married filing jointly	$32,000–$43,999	up to 50 percent
Married filing jointly	$44,000 or more	up to 85 percent
Married filing separately (and living in the same household)	$0	up to 85 percent

State and Local Income Taxation. In some states, Social Security benefits are fully exempt from state income taxation; in others, some taxation of these benefits might occur if the state's income tax is assessed on the taxpayer's taxable income as reported for federal income tax purposes. In addition, some states grant extra income tax relief for seniors by providing increased personal exemptions, credits, sliding scale rebates of property or other taxes (the amount or percent of which might be dependent on income), or additional tax breaks.

Deductible Medical Expenses. For taxpayers who itemize deductions, it might be easier to exceed the 7.5 percent threshold for deductibility of qualifying medical expenses (including costs for long-term care insurance) owing to the reduced retirement income level and often increased medical expenses.

Work-Related Expenses. The costs of proper clothing for work, commuting, parking, and meals purchased during work hours are eliminated when a person retires. In addition, other expenses, such as membership dues in some professional or social clubs, may be reduced because of retired status or may be eliminated if no longer necessary.

Home Ownership Expenses. By the time of retirement, many homeowners have "burned the mortgage" and no longer have this debt-reduction expenditure.

Absence of Dependent Children. The expense of supporting dependent children is usually completed by the time a client enters retirement. Be cautious, however, because retirees, especially those who married later in life, occasionally have children who are not self-supporting and will require continued financial support during some of the clients' retirement years.

Senior Discounts. Special reductions in price are given to seniors. Some reductions, such as certain AARP discounts, are available at age 50. Many businesses, however, require proof of age 65 (usually by having a Medicare card) to qualify for discounts on prescriptions, clothing, and restaurant meals. Discounts typically range from 5 to 15 percent of an item's cost.

No Longer Saving for Retirement. For many retirees, retirement is not a time to continue to save for retirement. Payments to contributory pension plans, lack of eligibility for IRA or Keogh plan contributions, or just the psychological fact of being retired help to weaken retirees' motivation to save for the future. Note that a retired worker's income can fall by the amount being saved with no concurrent reduction in standard of living. Therefore, a retired worker who has been saving 10 percent of income needs only to maintain an inflation-protected 90 percent (before tax) of income to enjoy the same purchasing power.

Fewer Automobiles. Retirees often consciously decide to reduce their automobile expenditures, either by owning fewer automobiles or by purchasing a replacement less frequently. In either case, the dollar cost for automobile insurance and the cash flow for financing automobiles tend to decline during the retirement years.

Age-Related Reductions. As a client grows older in retirement, he or she often cuts back on expenses and adopts a more sedentary lifestyle. For example, at some age driving becomes impossible or restricted and, at that point, car and other expenses decline. Some practitioners argue that these declines are mitigated by increased costs for medical care. Data from the Bureau of Labor Statistics, however, indicates that even though health care expenses increase over retirement, the increase does not significantly mitigate the decrease in other expenses.

Living Expenses in the Early Years of Retirement

Some retirement planners are uncomfortable with recommending a planned reduction in income in the first year of retirement. These planners believe that certain factors suggest that during the first year of retirement, at

---

ILLUSTRATION 21-1
Justification of a 60 to 80 Percent Replacement Ratio

Joe Jones, aged 64, has a fixed salary of $100,000 and would like to maintain his current purchasing power when he retires next year. If Joe has no increased retirement-related expenses, he can do this by having a retirement income of 70 percent of his final salary (as illustrated below). If Joe has increased retirement-related expenses, a somewhat higher figure should be used. (Note that postretirement inflation will be accounted for later.)

Working salary		$100,000
less retirement savings		15,000.00
less FICA taxes		7,030.00
less reduction in federal taxes	(extra $1,250deduction for being 65)	350.00
	(no tax on portion of Social Security received)	1,138.00
less annual commuting expenses to work		450.00
less mortgage expenses	(mortgage expires on retirement date)	6032.00
Reductions subtotal		30,000
Total purchasing power needed at 65		$ 70,000
Percentage of final salary needed		70%

---

least as much, if not more, income will be required to maintain the preretirement standard of living. Let's take a closer look at these factors.

Medical Expenses. Without question, medical expenses will increase over time for virtually all clients. The mere act of aging and the associated health problems generate additional demands for medical services. Even if advancing age does not create an increase in an individual's demands for medical services, inflation in these costs will. Furthermore, increases in inflation are not evenly distributed in the various medical care disciplines, and those services that will potentially affect retirees have been hit hardest. Although retirees are often covered by Medicare and other health insurance, the trend in these coverages has been toward cost containment—defined by the government and the insurance companies as shifting more of the medical cost to the insured via larger deductibles and coinsurance payments. These higher medical expenses would be in addition to the increased premiums for the insurance.

**YOUR FINANCIAL SERVICES PRACTICE:
WARNING YOUR CLIENTS ABOUT THE RISKS**

Whether or not your clients accept a 60 to 80 percent replacement ratio or feel that something more is necessary, there is no definitive answer to absolutely determine if the postretirement income should be less than, equal to, or greater than that of the preretirement years.

Estimating financial needs during the first year of retirement is like trying to hit a moving target when you are blindfolded: Your aim is obscured by many unknown variables and it is hard to draw a bead on the target. For example, the planner and client must establish what standard of living is desired during retirement, when retirement will begin, what inflation assumptions should be made before and after retirement, and what interest can be earned on invested funds. In addition, for clients who are forced by economic necessity to liquidate their retirement nest egg, the client and planner must estimate the life expectancy over which liquidations will occur. Many of these variables can dramatically change overnight and without warning—for example:

- The client may be planning to retire at age 65 when health considerations, or perhaps a plant shutdown, force retirement at age 62.
- A younger client may be planning on a relatively moderate retirement lifestyle, but business success mandates that a more lucrative retirement lifestyle be planned.

Travel, Vacations, and Other Lifestyle Changes. Many clients expect to devote considerably more time to travel and vacations upon retirement than they did during their working years. Increased leisure time, once a scarce commodity, now provides the opportunity to travel. Unfortunately, vacationing can be an expensive activity. Indeed, an increase in vacation activities represents a rise in the standard of living and will require additional income.

Dependents. As previously stated, parents usually need less income during the first year of retirement because they no longer financially support their children, who typically become self-supporting prior to parental retirement. However, many retirees still have dependents to support. Many parents have children with mental or physical problems who will require long-term custodial and financial care throughout the retirement years. Other retirees, because medical care, surgical techniques, and drugs are helping to prolong life, may have to provide for their aged parents who no longer possess the wherewithal to do so themselves.

ILLUSTRATION 21-2
Understanding the Expense Method

Your clients, Bob and Betty Smith, both aged 64, would like to maintain their current purchasing power when they retire next year. They can do this by having an annual income of $40,860 as illustrated below. Note that the figures are estimates of their expenses during retirement (some are higher than their current expenses and some are lower than their current expenses). Also note that postretirement inflation will be accounted for later.

Estimated retirement living expenses and required capital (in current dollars)

	Per Month x 12 =	Per Year
1. Food	$ 500	$ 6,000
2. Housing		
a. Rent/mortgage payment	400	4,800
b. Insurance (if separate payment)	25	300
c. Property taxes (if separate payment)	150	1,800
d. Utilities	180	2,160
e. Maintenance (if owned)	100	1,200
3. Clothing and Personal Care		
a. Wife	75	900
b. Husband	75	900
4. Medical Expenses		
a. Doctor (HMO)	75	900
b. Dentist	20	240
c. Medicines	75	900
5. Transportation		
a. Car payments	130	1,560
b. Gas	50	600
c. Insurance	50	600
d. Car maintenance (tires and repairs)	30	360
6. Miscellaneous Expenses		
a. Entertainment	150	1,800
b. Travel	200	2,400
c. Hobbies	50	600
d. Other	100	1,200
e. Club fees and dues	20	240
7. Insurance	100	1,200
8. Gifts and contributions	50	600
9. State, local, and federal taxes (if any)	800	9,600
10. Total expenses (current dollars)	$3,405	$40,860*

*Note: An adjustment should be made for future years to reflect a more sedentary lifestyle and reduced spending on the part of the client.

The Expense Method

A second way planners can estimate their client's retirement needs is by using the expense-method approach. The expense method of retirement planning focuses on the projected expenses that the retiree will have in the first year of retirement. As with the replacement-ratio method, it is much easier to define the potential expenses for those clients who are at or near retirement. For example, if the 64-year-old near-retiree expects to have $3,000 in monthly bills ($36,000 annually), then the retirement income for that retiree should maintain $36,000 worth of purchasing power in today's dollars. If, however, a younger client is involved, more speculative estimates of retirement expenses must be made (and periodically revised).

A list of expenses that should be considered includes expenses that may be unique to the particular client, as well as other, more general expenses.

Some expenses that tend to increase for retirees include the following:

- utilities and telephone
- medical/dental/drugs/health insurance
- house upkeep/repairs/maintenance/property insurance (until a move occurs)
- recreation/entertainment/travel/dining (during the early years of retirement)

Conversely, some expenses tend to decrease for the retiree. These include the following:

- mortgage payments
- food
- clothing
- income taxes
- property taxes
- transportation costs (car maintenance/insurance/other)
- debt repayment (charge accounts, personal loans)
- child support/alimony
- household furnishings

ASSUMPTION FOUR: EXPECTED INFLATION BEFORE AND DURING RETIREMENT

Another assumption that greatly affects the postretirement monetary need is the amount of expected inflation before and after retirement. The importance of inflation's effect on retirement cannot be overstated. Inflation erodes the client's purchasing power over time, making it difficult to maintain economic self sufficiency. Consider that if a client needed $2,000 in 1980, he or she will need around $5,000 today (2007) to maintain the same purchasing power. Planners can use the inflation calculators at www.bls.gov to demonstrate the long-term deleterious effects of inflation to their clients. Also, inflation's importance can be illustrated by showing the changes in retirement savings needed when the assumption in a computer model or worksheet is changed. For example, changing from 4 percent inflation to 6 percent inflation in one retirement needs calculator increased the amount of savings needed by 20 percent! (*Planning Note:* If you err on the conservative side and assume a higher inflation rate than the actual inflation rate, you will overestimate the retirement need and, consequently, the client will have more funds than necessary. Conversely, an estimate that assumes a lower inflation rate than the actual inflation rate will underestimate the retirement need and leave the client with less funds than necessary.)

Forecasting inflation is not an easy task. Lacking a crystal ball, a proxy for the expected inflation rate is needed. Because retirement income planning can encompass a long time span, one school of thought is to recommend taking historical averages of inflation over 40 years or more.

A second school of thought suggests that the structure of the economy and prices have changed too drastically to use 40 years or more. This group would argue that the figures from the last 15 years are a more appropriate measure of inflation. Note that in both cases long-term inflation is used instead of focusing on the yearly consumer price index reports.

In addition to considering long-term historical rates (no matter what the period), the planner must be aware of the forces that are likely to operate in the future and the following factors:

- Personal buying habits affect a clients actual inflation experience (keep in mind that services, which tend to be used more often by retirees, inflate at a higher rate than goods).
- Inflation varies by region.
- Medical inflation is twice the national average.
- The CPI may not be an accurate gauge of inflation for seniors because it relies heavily on housing.
- Planning for a younger worker can be troublesome because inflation over 60 years needs to be considered.

Because there is no exact method of predicting the inflation rate, you must use your best judgment as to future economic prospects and your clients' risk-aversion tendencies. A risk-averse client will probably want a more conservative figure projected, whereas a risk taker may feel comfortable with an optimistically low-inflation assumption. For someone in the middle, a 4 percent assumption could prove to be a viable rate to use during both the accumulation period and the retirement period. However, both you and your client must recognize that if long-term inflation does not match the expected rate, revisions in planning must be made.

ILLUSTRATING THE EFFECT OF INCREASES IN INFLATION AND STANDARD OF LIVING

In general, the higher the inflation rate and standard-of-living increases that a client experiences, the greater the amount of retirement income that will be needed. The compound interest formula can be used to make the necessary projection for the purpose of illustrating this. This formula is

$$FV = PV\,(1 + r)^n$$

where FV = the target dollar expenditure at retirement
PV = the dollar expenditures for the current standard of living
r = a rate of growth in the dollar expenditures for the standard of living
n = the number of years from time of planning until target retirement date

The rate of growth, or r, can stand for (1) the rate of increase in the level of the standard of living, (2) the rate of inflation that requires more dollars being spent to maintain the current standard of living, or (3) a combination of both. For example, if no inflation is expected, but the client anticipates a 20 percent increase in his or her standard of living between now and retirement 10 years hence, the result is an average annual 1.84 percent compound increase in the standard of living and r equals .0184 in the formula. If no growth in the standard of living is anticipated before retirement, but inflation is expected to average 4 percent annually over the 10 years to retirement, then r equals .04 in the above formula.

When the standard of living is expected to rise during the planning period and inflation is expected to continue, then r, the growth rate, can be *approximated* by adding the rates of growth in both the standard of living and inflation to estimate the needed income at or during retirement. For example, if the standard of living is expected to rise at 1.84 percent annually and inflation at 4 percent annually, then the combined result is a needed 5.84 percent increase in income. In this case, r equals 5.84. (For technical accuracy, these rates should be multiplied together [1.0184 x 1.04 = 1.059] rather than added, but because of the many necessary assumptions about the future, the inaccuracy from approximating is acceptable.)

ASSUMPTION FIVE: TOTAL RETURN ON INVESTMENTS

The traditional way to estimate a client's total return on investments is to determine his or her risk tolerance, select an appropriate portfolio based on it, and then use historical averages to predict future returns. In other words, if a client currently has an asset allocation model in place, the historical averages of that portfolio should be used as a proxy for future returns. Planners should be mindful of the after-tax rate of return, which will depend in part on the ability to invest in qualified plans and other tax shelter vehicles. Planners should also be aware of a client's ability to increase savings based on future salary increases (called a step-up rate). In other words a step-up rate represents the amounts savings will be increased each year.

A thorough discussion about total return on investments would require another textbook to do it justice. In the remaining part of this chapter, however, we would like to propose some commonly accepted strategies about retirement investing that will help to frame the total return on investment assumption.

Retirement Investment Strategies

There are a variety of investment strategies and planning opportunities available to clients who are in the process of accumulating a nest egg for retirement. It is appropriate at this point to sketch out some of the thinking on which the financial planning community generally agrees in order to better understand the assumptions used for total return on investments. Below you will find a brief overview of these commonly accepted retirement investment strategies.

risk tolerance

A good place to start might be to discuss the relationship between risk tolerance and retirement investing. One of the first obligations of a financial planner is to assess a client's risk tolerance. *Risk tolerance* identifies the point at which a client falls on a spectrum that ranges from risk averse (that is, risk intolerant or conservative) to aggressive. Once a risk tolerance level has been identified, the planner can make suitable investment recommendations. The first strategy deals with the fact that whatever the clients' risk tolerances, they should be encouraged to be aggressive—particularly in the earlier years—when it comes to building their retirement portfolio. This so-called concept of "time diversification" recommends that investors with long-term investment objectives should be willing to invest in what are considered higher risk, higher return investments than they would tolerate for short-term objectives. Although there is academic debate over the validity of this concept, experts agree that when clients have many years of employment before they retire, they can alter their savings habits should substantial investment losses occur in the early years of saving for retirement. Hence, they are in a position to accept additional risk. In order to facilitate long-term aggressive investing (relatively speaking), it may be a good idea to educate clients about financial risks (because unknown risks naturally loom larger than known risks) and to suggest they reduce the frequency with which they review their portfolios (because constant scrutiny leads to second-guessing and excessive concern about risk). (*Planning Note:* The retirement planner must exercise caution when recommending investment vehicles. The portfolio must fall within the client's "zone of acceptance." Otherwise the client may reject the full set of recommendations and either do nothing, which would be detrimental to the client, or, worse yet from the planner's standpoint, look to someone else to do his or her retirement planning.)

A second retirement investment strategy centers on the integration of buy-and-hold philosophy, dollar cost averaging, and asset allocation modeling. Most planners agree that retirement investing should not be influenced by attempts at market timing. Long-term goals are likely to be achieved by a buy-and-hold strategy that includes periodic monitoring and selective repositioning. For this reason, the second strategy is to use dollar cost averaging with individual stocks (diversifying by adding new stocks over time) and to hold those stocks for a long period of time. Individual stocks should be utilized instead of mutual funds in portfolios that should grow to be sizable and where regular cash additions are expected. This is because, over time, individual holdings allow more opportunities for tax-efficient investing and they avoid the fees associated with funds. In portfolios that are not expected to be large or where the menu is restricted to mutual funds, mutual funds are fine. However, care should be exercised to acquire funds with negligible or no loads, no 12b(1) charges, low expense ratios, and low portfolio turnover ratios. (*Planning Note: Dollar cost averaging* (DCA), an approach in which a fixed dollar amount is invested in a security in each period, is consistent with a buy-and-hold strategy. Clients who use this approach will purchase more units of a security when its price is low and fewer units of a security when its price is high. Over a long period of time, the investor ends up with a lower average cost for the security than was the average acquisition price for each transaction. For example, dollar cost averaging occurs when an individual makes monthly contributions to a specific mutual fund in a 401(k) plan.)

dollar cost averaging

Another idea concerns the risk of investing for retirement using the stock of one's employer. Investments in company stock may be desirable in some instances (for example, when a discounted stock purchase plan is offered or when a 401(k) match in employer stock is offered), but such investments must be limited. The third strategy therefore is to limit an employee's investment in company stock. The primary problem of over-investment in employer stock is the double whammy of the company's performance declining and the employee simultaneously being laid off. At this point, not only have the securities of the company declined in value, but also the employee/investor takes on the extra burden of being unemployed. Hence, there could be concurrent substantial declines in both his or her current standard of living and his or her financial position. A second troublesome reason for over-investment in employer stock centers on diversification requirements. Even investing in other companies in the same industry presents a similar problem.

The next idea involves tax efficiency in retirement investing. Because there is no taxation of earnings of investments in tax-qualified plans as the assets accumulate prior to distribution, a commonly suggested rule of thumb (and a fourth strategy) is to hold fixed income investments in tax-deferred accounts and equity investments in taxable private savings accounts. The reasoning for this rule of thumb is simple. Fixed-income investments pay interest, which is taxed as ordinary income anyway. Holding these investments in a tax-deferred account, therefore, does not change the fact that this income will still be taxed as ordinary income and still has the benefit of delaying taxation. With Roth IRA or Roth 401(k) accounts, an investor can even avoid taxation on what is otherwise taxable as ordinary income.

Equity investments pay dividends and provide capital gains (assuming the investor is fortunate enough to own stocks that go up in value). Under current tax laws, most dividend income and all capital gains are taxed at lower marginal rates. Furthermore, capital gains are not taxed until the investments are sold. By placing equities in tax-deferred accounts (except for Roth IRAs and Roth 401(k)s), the dividend income and capital gains are eventually taxed as ordinary income (that is, a withdrawal from a tax-deferred account) and do not retain their special tax status. The exception to this rule is that the current allocation of investment dollars between tax-deferred accounts and taxable private savings accounts should not determine the equity-bond allocation decision. In some cases, a client must compromise between the most tax-efficient form of investing and the desired asset allocation mix.

Another strategy focuses more on savings than investing. It is important that clients make the most of their IRA and 401(k) opportunities. In 2007, the amount a client can save each year in an IRA and 401(k) is $4,000 and $15,500, respectively. The contribution limit is $1,000 more for an IRA and $5,000 more for a 401(k) if the client is 50 or older because of catch-up provisions written into the law. One way to accumulate the additional savings is to encourage the client to bank either a percentage or the whole amount of any raise he or she expects. What they never receive, they won't miss! As they grow closer to retirement, banking the raises tends to set a more manageable standard of living for which they can plan. In other words, they will be better able to reach their retirement expectations because they chose to bank their raises in the final years of employment.

Finally, it is important to involve both spouses in retirement investing decisions. All too frequently only one spouse manages the family's finances. If this spouse is the first to die or has any type of dementia, the surviving spouse faces a significant financial crisis because of his or her lack of financial awareness. Many financial advisors insist that the financially unaware spouse be involved with all retirement financial decisions and also become involved in the day-to-day finances.

TABLE 21-2
Summary of Accumulation Strategies

1. Clients should be encouraged to invest at the aggressive limit of their risk tolerance.
2. Use dollar cost averaging to invest in individual stocks over time and use a buy-and-hold approach to these stocks.
3. Investment in employer stock should be limited because of diversification concerns (both stock diversification and human capital diversification).
4. Hold fixed income investments in tax-deferred accounts (such as 401(k) plans) and equity investments in taxable private savings accounts.
5. Make the most of tax deferral opportunities by using future raises as fodder for future savings
6. Include both spouses in the decision making and planning process.

CHAPTER REVIEW

Key Terms

replacement-ratio method [21-2]   dollar cost averaging [21-5]
risk tolerance [21-5]

Review Questions

Review questions are based on the learning objectives in this chapter. Thus, a [21-3] at the end of a question means that the question is based on learning objective 21-3. If there are multiple objectives, they are all listed.

1. List the factors that affect the choice of a retirement age. [21-1]

2. What factors may encourage a client to retire early? [21-1]

3. Why should early retirement be viewed skeptically from a financial planning perspective? [21-1]

4. What factors should be considered when estimating life expectancy. [21-1]

5. What ranges of replacement ratios are generally chosen by retirement planners in order to maintain a client's preretirement standard of living during the first year of retirement? [21-2]

6. Why can retirees, in some cases, count on less of their income going to pay taxes during their retirement years? [21-2]

7. Explain the expense-method approach to retirement planning. [21-3]

8. a. What factors tend to increase a client's living expenses after retirement? [21-2]
   b. What factors tend to reduce a client's living expenses after retirement?

9. What inflation assumption is considered appropriate for a client who is willing to accept a moderate risk? [21-4]

10. List and briefly define some investing strategies for accumulating retirement assets. [21-5]

Determining Postretirement Monetary Needs: Case Study

Learning Objectives

An understanding of the material in this chapter should enable you to

22-1. Explain the steps used when determining the amount of the postretirement monetary need.

22-2. Discuss the methods that can be used for establishing a savings schedule.

22-3. Determine a client's retirement need using a work sheet.

Chapter Outline

In this chapter, we turn our attention from the various pieces of the retirement-planning puzzle to a method for actually solving the puzzle of putting together a retirement plan. Putting together a retirement plan for a client is basically a three-step process. In the first step, the planner conducts fact finding to become familiar with the client's feelings, goals, and factual circumstances. In the second step, the planner must calculate the amount of the client's retirement need. This process is complicated by the mathematical equations that are involved, because planners must account for the time value of money and inflation. The third and final step in putting together a retirement plan is to establish a savings schedule and investment portfolio for the client so he or she can fund the amount of the needed savings.

Because the best way to understand these steps is to examine how they apply in a particular situation, this chapter presents a case study that examines the retirement needs of Joe and Betty Brown.

FACT FINDING

Your clients, Joe and Betty Brown, have provided the following information:

- Joe is married and his wife, Betty, is a homemaker.
- Both Joe and Betty are currently 55 years old.
- Joe expects to retire at age 65.
- Joe earns $54,000 a year.
- Joe is in the 28-percent (federal, state, and local) marginal tax bracket.
- Joe's company has a defined-benefit pension plan. If Joe continues employment until age 65, he can expect to receive a $20,000-a-year pension. (That figure is in today's dollars; his actual pension at retirement will be larger.) Joe's pension will be payable in the form of a 50 percent joint and survivor annuity. Joe's pension will not be offset by Social Security payments.

- Joe owns $150,000 in common stock, which pays $6,000 per year in dividends. Joe has reinvested all after-tax income from the portfolio every year except one, when he and Betty spent the money on a trip to Europe.
- Joe owns some non-income-producing assets, such as a home (current market value $250,000) and personal effects (worth about $100,000). The mortgage on the home will be paid off in 2 years.
- Both Joe and Betty have a fairly sophisticated understanding of investments.
- Joe and Betty have been married for 30 years, and the marriage is very stable.
- Both Joe and Betty are in good health.
- Both Joe and Betty feel they have average, or better than average, life expectancies.

FINANCING THE DESIRED RETIREMENT LIFESTYLE

Several steps must be taken to determine the finances necessary for providing Joe and Betty with a continuation of their current lifestyle throughout retirement. These steps include

(1) adding up the existing sources of retirement income
(2) finding the amount of income needed to achieve the desired retirement lifestyle
(3) estimating the retirement-income status (RIS)
(4) determining what resources need inflation protection
(5) calculating the target amount

Step 1: Adding Up the Existing Sources of Retirement Income

Joe indicates that he will have the following sources of income:

- *Social Security*—The Social Security Administration has informed Joe that he will receive $1,407 monthly ($938 for Joe and $469 for Betty) in Social Security benefits (current dollars) at age 65. This translates into a $16,884 annual income in current dollars.
- *Pension*—Joe's pension is $20,000 a year in current dollars.
- *Private Savings*—Joe does not intend to liquidate his $150,000 equity portfolio. Joe will, however, use the $6,000 in dividends for living expenses during retirement. Because he has no desire either to take the equity out of his home or sell any personal effects, these assets will not be used to produce a stream of income for retirement.

Step 2: Finding the Amount of Income Needed to Achieve the Desired Retirement Lifestyle

To find the amount of income needed to achieve the desired retirement lifestyle, you can either apply the desired replacement ratio to your client's salary or use the expense-method approach.

Replacement-Ratio Method

If the client expects an increase in his or her standard of living, a growth factor must be incorporated to determine Joe's final salary. Joe, however, would like his retirement income to provide a standard of living comparable to his existing standard of living and does not need to apply a growth factor to his current lifestyle. Because he will no longer be saving for retirement, paying Social Security taxes, or incurring work-related expenses, Joe estimates that 80 percent of his preretirement income from employment will be sufficient. In other words, in today's dollars Joe wants to have $43,200 (80 percent of his current salary of $54,000) when he retires. In tomorrow's dollars, Joe is looking to have this amount keep pace with inflation. (For example, if inflation rose 4 percent per year for 10 years, Joe would need $63,947 to have his current purchasing power during the first year of his retirement.)

Example: Suppose, instead, that Joe had anticipated that his standard of living would increase 2 percent per year until retirement. (In other words, his salary would increase 2 percent more than inflation, and Joe would use the commensurate increase in real income to improve his lifestyle.) If this is the case, a growth factor of 2 percent should be applied to Joe's current $54,000 salary using the future value formula discussed in chapter 21:

$$PV = PV(1 + r)^n$$

where n = number of years before target retirement date

r = inflation rate

In this case, however, instead of inflation the r would stand for the desired growth rate that the client expects (2 percent). Under these circumstances, the salary considered would be

$$V = \$54,000(1+r)^n \quad 10$$
$$= \$54,000(1+.02)$$
$$= \$65,826$$

> Keystrokes for HP 10BII:
> 54000 [+/-][PV]
> 2[I/YR]
> 10 [N]
> [FV] = 65,826

Because Joe only needs 80 percent of this salary in current dollars, Joe would want $52,660 in today's dollars when he retires in order to maintain his anticipated purchasing power. In tomorrow's dollars, Joe would want this amount to keep pace with inflation.

Because Joe had not anticipated any real growth or inflation factor in retirement, we can use the $43,200 target achieved by applying an 80 percent replacement ratio to his current salary when estimating Joe's retirement income need.

Expense-Method Approach

If Joe were to use the expense-method approach to determine the amount of income he would need during retirement, he and Betty would sit down with the planner to estimate their expenses in their first year of retirement. Let's assume that Joe will have annual expenses of $43,200 (the same as the replacement-ratio method). Note, however, that the expense-method approach and the replacement-ratio method will seldom provide the same number.

Step 3: Estimating the Retirement-Income Status (RIS)

To determine the amount of additional savings he will need to accumulate, Joe must subtract his annual target for retirement income from his estimated amount of annual retirement income (table 22-1).

The retirement-income status (RIS) can be either a positive or negative number. A positive RIS indicates a surplus because current sources exceed the target amount. A negative RIS indicates a deficit and suggests the need for additional savings. When the RIS is negative, it will be labeled RID (retirement-income deficit) and used with a positive sign to avoid dealing with negative numbers.

In current dollars, Joe appears to be in the enviable position of having nearly adequate retirement income to meet his desired retirement standard of living (a RID of only $316). However, this may be misleading because these values ignore the effects of inflation before and after retirement.

TABLE 22-1		
Calculation of Annual Retirement-Income Status (in Today's Dollars)		
Estimated annual retirement income		
Social Security	$16,884	
Pension	20,000	
Private savings	6,000	$42,884
(dividends)		
Annual target retirement income		$43,200
Annual retirement-income status (RIS)		$ – 316

4: Determining What Resources Need Inflation Protection

Up to this point, we have determined that Joe will have a $316 gap between what his Social Security, pension, and private savings will provide and what his desired annual income during retirement will be. At this point, we have a partial picture of the retirement need for Joe and Betty. To calculate the true retirement need, however, we must provide inflation protection, both before and after retirement, for all Joe's retirement resources. In chapter 21, when the effect of inflation was explored, it was determined that a 4 percent rate of inflation could be used as an estimate. Using that estimate, let's take a closer look at each of the retirement resources.

Social Security

To a certain extent, Social Security is inflation protected because it is geared toward increases in the consumer price index (CPI). This assumes, however, that the law will remain unchanged and that the CPI accurately reflects inflation as it affects Joe. For Joe's purposes, we can assume that the law will not change and that the indexation of Social Security is a reasonable reflection of inflation increases.

Pension

We can assume that Joe's pension is inflation protected until retirement because it is a defined-benefit plan based on final-average salary. We cannot, however, assume any inflation protection after retirement. For this reason, in addition to funding the retirement-income deficit (RID), Joe will need to fund an amount that can be used to bolster his non-inflation-proof pension benefits (that is, to keep pension purchasing power constant). This amount is called the decline in purchasing power (DIPP).

Dividends

Dividend income from a stock portfolio is generally considered to be inflation protected if the principal is left intact. For Joe's purposes, we can assume his dividend income will be inflation protected both in the preretirement and postretirement periods. The fact that Joe is not liquidating his principal provides a hedge against inflation because he can annuitize the principal if he needs additional retirement income.

Retirement-Income Deficit (RID)

Joe must account for the effect of preretirement and postretirement inflation on the purchasing power of the income from the monies that he will accumulate to fund the RID. For example, when a 4 percent rate of inflation is added to the RID ($316 in today's dollars), the RID grows to $468 by the time Joe reaches age 65.

Keystrokes for HP 10BII:
316 [+/-][PV]
4 [I/YR]
10 [N]
[FV] = 468

Table 22-2 summarizes the impact of inflation on Joe's resources.

TABLE 22-2
Inflation's Impact on Joe's Resources

Source of Income	Inflation Protected
Social Security benefits	Yes
Pension	Not after retirement
Dividends	Yes
Retirement-income deficit	No

Step 5: Calculating the Target Amount

The next step is to examine how much Joe will need to accumulate to fund the RID and the pension DIPP. This sum is the target amount of funds that Joe needs in addition to his current stock portfolio to achieve his desired standard of living during retirement. To accomplish this, the planner must make many assumptions about the future. In addition to estimating inflation at, for example, 4 percent, assumptions must be made about the amount of investment return that Joe will earn on accumulated funds and about the method Joe will use to liquidate his saved funds.

Investment Return

In addition to the information on investment assumptions provided in the previous chapter, we should consider some other issues.

Generally, a higher rate of return means a greater variability of the return and, hence, a greater risk. Thus, if your client seeks a higher return on invested monies, there will be a commensurate increase in the likelihood that the targeted amount of retirement funds will not be accumulated. A general guideline for this risk-return tradeoff is that the more important the financial objective is to the client, the less the risk that should be assumed. Some planners believe that accumulating funds for retirement is the most important reason for investing and would recommend investment vehicles that have relatively low risk. They argue that because Joe's retirement date is only 10 years away, he will have little opportunity to make up any investment losses that might occur during this relatively short period. For this reason, a conservative investment strategy might be best. Others argue that because Joe and Betty are likely to live many years in retirement, it is not the time to change strategies because the holding period will still be significant. In the end, it is the clients' decision to make after both schools of thought have been explained to them.

An additional consideration is whether Joe can use a tax-deferred investment vehicle, such as a traditional IRA, or can make a nondeductible voluntary contribution to his pension plan during the accumulation period. If so, earnings on monies set aside would accumulate free of current income taxation. With such a vehicle, 8 percent could be earned on relatively low-risk investments. If currently taxable investments of the same risk characteristic were employed, then the return (r) times one minus the client's marginal tax rate (t), or $r(1-t)$, would be earned after tax. In other words, because Joe is in the 28 percent marginal tax bracket, he may only have an after-tax yield of 5.76 percent on an investment that yields 8 percent interest before tax [$.08(1-.28)$].

Liquidation of Funds

Several paths can be followed when using the funds accumulated to meet Joe's retirement-income deficit and to meet the decline in purchasing power of Joe's pension. One such option is to not liquidate the assets at all. Under this option, Joe will need to accumulate a fund that would earn sufficient income each year without reducing the accumulated capital. A second alternative would involve accumulating a fund that could be systematically liquidated over a specified number of years. At the end of the specified time, the capital would be depleted. (*Planning Note:* The longer the liquidation period that is assumed for depleting assets, the greater the amount of funds that will be needed for the retirement target.)

YOUR FINANCIAL SERVICES PRACTICE:
PROTECTING CLIENTS FROM OUTLIVING INCOME

A planner should exercise caution when liquidating a client's assets over a specified period of time. Many planners mistakenly rely on the figures given in mortality tables to determine the liquidation period. The problem with this approach is that one-half of the population lives beyond the tabular life expectancy. For this reason, many planners underestimate the client's life expectancy when determining the liquidation period. Even when extending the liquidation period beyond the tabular life expectancies, planners can encounter trouble. Statistics show that 20 percent of the people who reach age 65 will live to age 95.

One way for a planner to be cautious is by recommending that a client purchase a life annuity with his or her accumulated savings. A life annuity permits clients to continue to receive payments until they die, regardless of how long they live. In those cases when clients live beyond the life expectancy on which the annuity was based, the client experiences what is known as mortality gain. The insurance company does not necessarily lose money when it pays mortality gain, however, because theoretically an equal number of people die before the life expectancy on which the annuity was calculated and experience mortality loss.

The Mathematics

Once the planner has made assumptions about the investment return and the liquidation period, these assumptions, as well as the client's retirement-income deficit (RID) and decline in purchasing power (DIPP), are applied in mathematical equations to calculate the target accumulation. To simplify the process, we'll do separate calculations for the RID fund and for the DIPP.

Amount Needed to Fund the Retirement-Income-Deficit (RID) Fund. Assume that Joe wants the inflation-protected income stream to last for a specified period, such as 25 years from the date of his retirement, at which point the fund would be exhausted. In this case, you need to calculate the stream of payments that Joe would like to receive from an inflation-protected retirement-income deficit and discount the payments to the value at retirement age, assuming the principal will be paid out along with the interest. Equation 22-1 is the appropriate equation.

Assuming that inflation stays constant at 4 percent, that Joe retires at age 65 (recall that Joe's retirement-income deficit had risen from $316 to $468 at age 65), that he expects to liquidate the fund over 25 years, and that he earns an aggressive 8 percent interest after tax, he will need $7,717 at retirement:

$$\text{Funds needed (RID fund)} = \$468 \times (1 + .08) \times \left[\frac{1 - \left(\frac{1.04}{1.08} \right)^{25}}{.08 - .04} \right]$$

$$= \$7,717$$

Keystrokes for HP 10BII:	
1 [Orange][P/YR]	(to set payments/year to 1)
[Orange] [BEG/END]	(to set calculator to BEGIN)
1.08 ÷ 1.04 – 1 x 100 = [I/YR	(to adjust investment return for inflation)
25 [N]	
468 [+/-] [PMT]	
[PV] = 7,717	

If Joe's desired liquidation period were 35 years with the same inflation and interest rates, using equation 22-1, $9,264 would be needed at retirement.

EQUATION 22-1
Funds Needed at the Client's Retirement Date for Total RID—Liquidating Principal*

$$\text{Funds needed (RID funds)} = \text{Retirement date RID} \times (1 + int) \times \left[\frac{1 - \left(\frac{1 + inf}{1 + int} \right)^n}{int - inf} \right]$$

where n = liquidation period expressed in years
int = interest rate
inf = inflation rate

* This equation calculates the funds needed to provide an income stream that is inflation protected but will be completely liquidated after a given number of years.

Keystrokes for HP 10BII for funds needed (RID funds):

1 [Orange][P/YR]	(to set payments/year to 1)
[Orange] [BEG/END]	(to set calculator to BEGIN)
(1+int%) ÷(1+infl%) – 1 x 100 = [I/YR]	(to adjust investment return for inflation)

Number of years in retirement [N]
(Retirement Date RID) [+/-] [PMT]
[PV] = ?

If Joe wants generate income without reducing principal, he must use a different equation. Equation 22-2 calculates the stream of payments Joe would receive from an inflation-protected retirement income deficit fund and discounts the payments to the value at retirement age, assuming the principal will not be liquidated and only interest will be paid out.

EQUATION 22-2
**Funds Needed at the Client's Retirement Date for Total
RID—Not Liquidating Principal***

$$\text{Funds needed (RID fund)} = \text{RID} + \frac{\text{RID} (1 + \text{inf})}{\text{int} - \text{inf}}$$

where int = interest rate
inf = inflation rate

---

* This equation calculates the funds needed for an inflation-protected income stream that will continue forever (no liquidation of principal). The payments will increase each year by the estimated rate of inflation.

Because this is a perpetual stream, the number of payments, N, is equal to infinity. With no N to input in the financial calculator, the funding need is solved by using the formula above and not by using the time value of money functions on the financial calculator.

With the same interest and inflation assumptions, this equation becomes

$$\text{Funds needed (RID fund)} = \$468 + \frac{\$468 (1.04)}{.08 - .04}$$

$$= \$12,636$$

Table 22-3 summarizes Joe's situation for determining the RID fund.

TABLE 22-3 Retirement-Income-Deficit Fund	
Liquidation Method	Sum Needed At Age 65
25-year liquidation	$ 7,717
35-year liquidation	$ 9,264
Income only	$12,636

Amount Needed to Fund the Decline in Purchasing Power (DIPP). In addition to funding the retirement-income deficit, Joe must set aside additional funds to maintain the purchasing power of his pension. In this case, first calculate the present value of the stream of payments that Joe should be receiving from an inflation-proof pension and then determine the present value of a stream of level payments for the same period. The difference between these present values represents the supplemental funds Joe needs to make his pension benefits inflation proof. Use equation 22-3 to solve this problem. (The income to be protected in this case is only the pension income.)

EQUATION 22-3
Funds Needed at the Client's Retirement Date for Total DIPP—Liquidating Principal*

$$\text{DIPP} = \begin{matrix} \text{income} \\ \text{needing} \\ \text{inflation} \\ \text{protection} \end{matrix} \times (1 + \text{int}) \times \left[\frac{1 - \left(\dfrac{1 + \text{inf}}{1 + \text{int}} \right)^n}{\text{int} - \text{inf}} \right] -$$

$$\begin{matrix} \text{income} \\ \text{needing} \\ \text{inflation} \\ \text{protection} \end{matrix} \times (1 + \text{int}) \times \left[\frac{1 - \left(\dfrac{1}{1 + \text{int}} \right)^n}{\text{int}} \right]$$

where n = liquidation period expressed in years
int = interest rate
inf = inflation rate

---

* This equation calculates the funds needed to provide an inflation-protected supplement to a level or fixed-income stream for a given number of years. This provides increasing payments to supplement the fixed-payment stream.

Keystrokes for HP 10BII:

1 [Orange][P/YR]	(to set payments/year to 1)
[Orange] [BEG/END]	(tto set calculator to BEGIN)
(1+int%) ÷ (1+infl%) – 1 x 100 = [I/YR]	(to adjust investment return for inflation)
Number of years in retirement [N]	
DIPP [+/-] [PMT]	
[PV] = ?	Note: This is the present value (at retirement) of N years worth of inflation-adjusted pension payments.
8[I/YR]	(changes the interest rate to 8 percent with no inflation adjustment)
[PV] = 341,309	Note: This is the present value (at retirement) of N years worth of pension payments.

The difference between the two present values is the present value of the inflation adjustment at retirement.

EQUATION 22-4
Funds Needed at the Client's Retirement Date for Total DIPP—Not Liquidating Principal*

$$\text{DIPP} = \begin{matrix} \text{income} \\ \text{needing} \\ \text{inflation} \\ \text{protection} \end{matrix} \times \left[1 + \left(\frac{1 + \text{inf}}{\text{int} - \text{inf}} \right) \right] -$$

$$\begin{matrix} \text{income} \\ \text{needing} \\ \text{inflation} \\ \text{protection} \end{matrix} \times (1 + \text{int}) \left(\frac{1}{\text{int}} \right)$$

where int = interest rate
      inf = inflation rate

* This equation calculates the funds needed to provide an inflation-protected supplement to a level or fixed-income stream for an unlimited number of years. This provides increasing payments to supplement the fixed-payment stream.

Note that it is projected that Joe's pension at age 65 will have grown from $20,000 (at age 55) to $29,605, assuming a 4 percent inflation rate. Therefore, Joe will need $146,877 at retirement determined as follows:

$$DIPP = \$29{,}605\,(1.08) \left[\frac{1 - \left(\frac{1.04}{1.08}\right)^{25}}{.08 - .04} \right] - \$29{,}605\,(1.08) \left[\frac{1 - \left(\frac{1}{1.08}\right)^{25}}{.08} \right]$$

$$= \$29{,}605\,(1.08)\,(15.26850409) - \$29{,}605\,(1.08)\,(10.67477619)$$

$$= \$488{,}186 - \$341{,}309$$

$$= \$146{,}877$$

<u>Keystrokes for HP 10BII:</u>

1 [Orange][P/YR]	(to set payments/year to 1)
[Orange] [BEG/END]	(to set calculator to BEGIN)
1.08 ÷ 1.04 – 1 x 100 = [I/YR]	(to adjust investment return for inflation)
25 [N]	
29605 [+/-] [PMT]	
[PV] = 488,186	Note: This is the present value (at age 65) of 25 years worth of inflation-adjusted pension payments.
8[I/YR]	(changes the interest rate to 8 percent with no inflation adjustment)
[PV] = 341,309	Note: This is the present value (at age 65) of 25 years worth of pension payments.

The difference between the two present values is the present value of the inflation adjustment at age 65: 488,186 – 341,309 = 146,877

Using the same formula for a 35-year liquidation, the amount needed will be $213,363[1]. However, if Joe desires to have income growing but not have the principal reduced, he must use Equation 22-4[2].

Using the same interest and inflation rate assumptions, Joe would need

$$DIPP = \$29{,}605 \times \left[1 + \frac{1.04}{.04} \right] - \$29{,}605 \times 1.08 \times \frac{1}{.08}$$

$$= \$29{,}605 \times 27 - \$29{,}605 \times 13.5$$

$$= \$399{,}667$$

Table 22-4 summarizes Joe's situation for determining the decline in the purchasing power fund.

TABLE 22-4 Decline in Purchasing Power Fund	
Liquidation Method	Sum Needed at Age 65
25-year liquidation 35-year liquidation Income only	$146,877 $213,363 $399,667

Adding Up the Total Funds Needed. To determine exactly how much he will need at retirement, Joe must add together the amount necessary to fund the RID and the amount necessary to fund the DIPP. Note that Joe could choose different liquidation methods for the retirement-income-deficit fund and the decline in the purchasing-power fund. For example, he could use a 25-year liquidation for the RID fund and a 35-year liquidation for the DIPP. This method would be most appropriate if he wanted to hedge on his and Betty's life expectancy. Assuming Joe chooses the same liquidation for both, which is the more common choice, table 22-5 indicates the target amount that Joe will need to accumulate in addition to other retirement resources.

TABLE 22-5 Target Accumulation						
Liquidation Method	Retirement Income-Deficit Fund	+	Decline in Purchasing-Power Fund	=	Total Target Fund
25-year 35-year Income only	$ 7,717 $ 9,264 $ 12,636		$146,877 $213,363 $399,667		$154,594 $222,627 $412,303

YOUR FINANCIAL SERVICES PRACTICE: CALCULATING YOUR CLIENT'S TARGET

When calculating your client's target, you should keep the following in mind:

- Equations 22-1 and 22-2 are applicable to the retirement-income deficit and calculate an annuity due (payments start immediately). Equations 22-3 and 22-4 are applicable to the decline in purchasing power and calculate an immediate annuity that delays the start of payments for one period (in this case one year).
- The decline in purchasing power (DIPP) is not just for pensions. The DIPP calculation also applies to any other sources of income that will not be adjusted for inflation after retirement. For example, a cash value life insurance policy that will be converted to level annuity payments at retirement to use as a retirement resource is not inflation protected after retirement and will be added to the pension income to get the income needing inflation protection in equations 22-3 and 22-4.

IMPLEMENTING A SAVINGS SCHEDULE TO FUND THE TARGET AMOUNT

Once a target has been calculated, the planner's focus turns toward using this data to set up a savings schedule. Joe could use a variety of techniques to fund his retirement target, including making a lump-sum payment from gain realized on the sale of his home and/or the liquidation of his stock portfolio. (If the portfolio is liquidated, a new target must be calculated because the old target included dividends from the portfolio as a source of retirement income.) In addition to making a lump-sum payment, Joe could fund the payments in the remaining years until retirement. The two most popular methods of doing this are (1) funding the payments on a level basis until retirement or (2) using the annual-funding method that increases payments annually to coordinate payments with increasing income (the stepped-up method).

Level Annual Funding

If Joe wanted to use level annual funding until retirement at age 65, equation 22-5 should be used. This equation essentially calculates the amount of annual payments (based on the fact that the payments made are earning compound interest) so a level amount is saved annually.

EQUATION 22-5
Level Annual Funding*

$$\text{Annual funding} = \frac{\text{Target amount (from table 22-5)}}{\left[\dfrac{(1 + int)^n - 1}{int}\right] \times (1 + int)}$$

where int = interest rate

n = number of years in accumulation period

* This equation provides a way to calculate the level investment (savings) payment necessary to accumulate the target amount over a given number of years (n) if those funds earn interest at the assumed interest rate throughout the n-year accumulation period. (If the funds are producing taxable income, the interest rate should be an after-tax rate.) Any target amount can be used, and it should represent the dollar amount desired at the end of the n-year period.

Keystrokes for HP 10BII, Level Annual Funding:	
1 [Orange][P/YR]	(to set payments/year to 1)
[Orange] [BEG/END]	(to set calculator to BEGIN)
Number of year to target date [N]	
Int% [I/YR]	
Target [FV]	
[PMT] = ?	

For example, if Joe wanted to have a 25-year liquidation (target amount $154,594), he would need to make $9,881 payments at the beginning of each year until retirement, determined as follows:

$$\text{Annual funding} = \frac{\$154,594}{\left[\dfrac{(1 + .08)^{10} - 1}{.08}\right] \times (1 + .08)}$$

$$= \$9,881$$

Keystrokes for HP 10BII:	
1 [Orange][P/YR]	(to set payments/year to 1)
[Orange] [BEG/END]	(to set calculator to BEGIN)
10 [N]	
8 [I/YR]	
154594[FV]	
[PMT] = -9,881[3]	

Using this same formula, the level annual amount needed to fund for a 35-year liquidation target ($222,627) would be $14,229 and to fund the income-only target ($412,303) would be $26,353. Table 22-6 summarizes the level annual payments needed.[4]

TABLE 22-6 Level Annual Funding	
Liquidation Method	Level Annual Payment
25-year liquidation 35-year liquidation Income only	$ 9,881 $14,229 $26,353

Stepped-Up Annual Funding

If Joe wants to use stepped-up annual funding, use equation 22-6. This equation calculates an increasing scale of payments that Joe would need to fund the target amount. Equation 22-6 only shows the first year's annual payment.

EQUATION 22-6
Stepped-Up Annual Funding*

$$\text{First-year funding} = \frac{\text{Target amount} \times (\text{int} - \text{inf})}{\left[1 - \left(\frac{1 + \text{inf}}{1 + \text{int}}\right)^n\right] \times \left[(1 + \text{int})^{(n+1)}\right]}$$

where int = interest rate

inf = inflation rate

n = number of years in accumulation period

*This equation calculates the level of first-year investment (saving) contribution to an accumulation fund that will accumulate a target amount by the end of a given period of years (n) if the fund earns the assumed interest rate throughout the n-year period and contributions to the fund increase at the assumed inflation rate. Note that inflation rate is really the growth rate of the funding contribution each year. It could be any rate the client is capable of contributing to the accumulation fund.

To determine payments in subsequent years, multiply the prior year's payment by one plus the inflation rate.

If Joe wants a stepped-up annual funding method to coordinate savings increases with salary increases and have a 25-year liquidation (target amount $154,594), he must make a first payment of $8,437, determined as follows:

$$\text{Annual funding} = \frac{\$154,594 \times (.08 - .04)}{1 - \left[\frac{1.04}{1.08}\right]^{10} \times (1.08)^{11}}$$

$$= \$8,437$$

Keystrokes for HP 10BII:	
1 [Orange][P/YR]	(to set payments/year to 1)
[Orange] [BEG/END]	(to set calculator to BEGIN)
154594[FV]	
8[I/YR]	
10[N]	
[PV] = -71,607	Note: we find the PV of $154,594 discounting 10 years at 8 percent so we can solve for PMT. Adjusted interest rates (below) don't work for future values, only present values, so we need to convert the FV to a PV.
0 [FV]	(clears FV register)
1.08 ÷ 1.04 – 1 x 100 = [I/YR]	(to adjust investment return for inflation)
[PMT] = 8,437	

Joe's second-year payment would be $8,774.48 ($8,437 x 1.04), and his third-year payment would be $9,125.46 ($8,774 x 1.04). Table 22-7 shows all ten of Joe's payments.

TABLE 22-7
25-Year Liquidation Target/Stepped-Up Payments

Age	Year	Payment
55	1	$ 8,437
56	2	8,775
57	3	9,125
58	4	9,490
59	5	9,870
60	6	10,265
61	7	10,675
62	8	11,103
63	9	11,547
64	10	12,008

	Keystrokes for HP 10BII:	
1 [Orange][P/YR]	(to set payments/year to 1)	
[Orange] [BEG/END]	(to set calculator to BEGIN)	
222627[FV]		
8[I/YR]		
10[N]		
[PV] = -103,119	Note: we find the PV of $222,627 discounting 10 years at 8 percent so we can solve for PMT. Adjusted interest rates (below) don't work for future values, only present values, so we need to convert the FV to a PV.	
0 [FV]	(clears FV register)	
1.08 ÷ 1.04 – 1 x 100 = [I/YR]	(to adjust investment return for inflation)	
[PMT] = 12,149		

For the 35-year target ($222,627), an initial payment of $12,149 is required. Table 22-8 illustrates payments under this system.

TABLE 22-8
35-Year Liquidation Target/Stepped-Up Payments

Age	Year	Payment
55	1	$12,149
56	2	12,635
57	3	13,140
58	4	13,666
59	5	14,213
60	6	14,781
61	7	15,372
62	8	15,987
63	9	16,627
64	10	17,291

	Keystrokes for HP 10BII:	
1 [Orange][P/YR]	(to set payments/year to 1)	
[Orange] [BEG/END]	(to set calculator to BEGIN)	
412303[FV]		
8[I/YR]		
10[N]		
[PV] = -190,976	Note: we find the PV of $412,303 discounting 10 years at 8 percent so we can solve for PMT. Adjusted interest rates (below) don't work for future values, only present values, so we need to convert the FV to a PV.	
0 [FV]	(clears FV register)	
1.08 ÷ 1.04 – 1 x 100 = [I/YR]	(to adjust investment return for inflation)	
[PMT] = 22,500		

For the income-only target ($412,303), an initial payment of $22,500 is necessary. Table 22-9 illustrates the payments under this system.

TABLE 22-9
Retirement-Income-Only Target/Stepped-Up Payments

Age	Year	Payment
55	1	$22,500
56	2	23,400
57	3	24,336
58	4	25,309
59	5	26,322
60	6	27,375
61	7	28,470
62	8	29,608
63	9	30,793
64	10	32,025

Sources of Funding

Joe will probably decide to use savings from his current income to meet whatever payment schedule he chooses. If Joe can manage to save 22.5 percent of his salary (note that this becomes increasingly feasible after mortgage payments cease), he can meet the 35-year stepped-up annual funding schedule (table 22-8). This strategy is illustrated in table 22-10.

TABLE 22-10
Joe's Savings Strategy

Age	Salary	22.5 Percent Savings	35-year Liquidation (from table 22-8)
55	$54,000	$12,150	$12,149
56	56,160	12,636	12,635
57	58,406	13,141	13,140
58	60,743	13,667	13,666
59	63,172	14,214	14,213
60	65,699	14,782	14,781
61	68,327	15,374	15,372
62	71,060	15,989	15,987
63	73,903	16,628	16,627
64	76,859	17,293	17,291

In addition to a 22.5 percent savings from Joe's current salary, Betty could become employed in an effort to earn additional savings. (Note that if this is the case, a recalculation might be necessary to account for an increased Social Security benefit as a retirement resource.) Another option is for Joe to delay retirement until beyond age 65, thereby increasing the amount of time to save and decreasing the target amount.

YOUR FINANCIAL SERVICES PRACTICE: ETHICAL CONSIDERATIONS

When a planner completes a retirement needs analysis for a client, it is important for ethical reasons to communicate the following:

- The numbers are only good-faith estimates and should be periodically recalculated for better accuracy.
- The fluid (speculative) nature involved in placing numbers on expected future needs .
- The existence of different methodologies may result in different estimates. (Financial planners may feel comfortable sending their clients a "ballpark estimate," which is a retirement calculator linked to the Department of Labor and Internal Revenue Service Web pages. The ballpark estimate can be found at www.asec.org as well.)

Planners should carefully choose software and assumptions that will serve the client's needs and not unduly call for excess savings or underestimate the expected need. *It is unconscionable and probably legally actionable for a planner to consciously overestimate the amount needed in order to garner more assets under management.*

Regardless of the method Joe and Betty choose, they will be faced with making additional investments of the funds being used to provide for the targeted amount. Planners should give advice concerning these investments and should make investment-return assumptions that are consistent with expected investment results.

DETERMINING RETIREMENT NEEDS USING A WORK SHEET

We now have the methodology; let's apply it to two work sheets.

Consumer Work Sheet

Table 22-11 can be used to illustrate the percentage of salary a person needs to save each year. Conceptually, this work sheet makes most of the assumptions for you—for example, an 80 percent replacement ratio (step 2) and a 25-year life expectancy (see line 8 explanation). While this simplicity can be a limitation for a planner (as discussed earlier), it can be a blessing for the weary client. For this reason, planners may want to use this type of work sheet as an informational piece in a client mailer (with strong comments about its limitations).

Example: The financial information for Bob and Donna:

- They are 15 years from retirement.
- Their current combined salary is $100,000.
- They have a defined-benefit plan of $2,000 a month ($24,000 annually).
- Their combined Social Security benefits are estimated to be $18,000.
- They have $130,000 in IRAs, 401(k) plans, and mutual funds

Using the work sheet in table 22-11, Bob and Donna can see that they need to save 25 percent of their current salary.

Determining Retirement Needs Using a Planner's Work Sheet

The work sheets in tables 22-12, 22-13, 22-14, and 22-15 allow the planner to focus on tailoring a retirement needs analysis to a particular client. The first step is to list a variety of assumptions (these are discussed with the clients prior to filling out the work sheets). The second step is to list factors generated from time-value-of-money tables. An explanation of how each factor was determined follows the work sheets in the commentary for tables 22-16 through 22-23. The third step is to calculate the amount the clients need to save in the initial year.

Case Study Facts

Ann (aged 44) and Robert Stack (aged 46) are married and have two children. Ann and Robert both plan to retire in 19 years unless their planner counsels otherwise. Robert will be 65 and Ann will be 63 when they retire. Pertinent financial data includes the following:

- Ann earns $35,000 as a schoolteacher.
- Robert earns $140,000 as an engineer.
- Ann has $64,000 in her 403(b) retirement plan.
- Ann will receive a pension of $1,400 a month at age 63.

- Robert has a 401(k) plan with $120,000 in it.
- Robert has no defined-benefit plan at work.
- Robert will receive $1,100 a month from Social Security when he retires at age 65.
- Ann will receive $800 a month from Social Security when she retires at age 63.
- Both Social Security amounts are in today's dollars and, where applicable, reflect early retirement reductions.
- The Stacks have joint savings of $50,000 earmarked for retirement.
- They have sufficient savings to meet their other long-term financial goals, including sending their children to college.

After an initial interview with the planner, it was decided that the following assumptions will be used:

- an inflation rate of 4 percent
- an expected duration of retirement of 25 years. (Note that the Stacks have decided to set aside the potential gain from the sale of their home and vacation home to cover them should they live longer than the 25-year period—if not, this will be part of the legacy they leave their children.)
- an after-tax rate of return of 8 percent prior to retirement
- an after-tax rate of return of 7 percent after retirement
- an 80 percent replacement ratio
- a savings step-up rate of 6 percent. (This means that the annual allocation to savings will increase by 6 percent each year until retirement.)

(Worksheets begin on the following pages.)

TABLE 22-11
Work Sheet: Calculation of Retirement Expenses—Alternative 2[*]

	Your Circumstances	Example
1. Current annual gross salary	$_____	$ 100,000
2. Retirement-income target (multiply line 1 by 0.80 percent target)	$_____	80,000
3. Estimated annual benefit from pension plan, not including IRAs, 401(k)s, 403(b)s, or profit-sharing plans[1]	$_____	24,000
4. Estimated annual Social Security benefits[1]	$_____	18,000
5. Total retirement benefits (add lines 3 and 4)	$_____	42,000
6. Income gap (subtract line 5 from line 2)[2]	$_____	38,000
7. Adjust gap to reflect inflation (multiply line 6 by factor A, below)	$_____	68,400
8. Capital needed to generate additional income and close gap (multiply line 7 by 16.3)[3]	$_____	1,114,920
9. Extra capital needed to offset inflation's impact on pension (multiply line 3 by factor B, below)	$_____	204,000
10. Total capital needed (add lines 8 and 9)	$_____	1,318,920
11. Total current retirement savings (includes balances in IRAs, 401(k)s, profit-sharing plans, mutual funds, CDs)	$_____	130,000
12. Value of savings at retirement (multiply line 11 by factor C, below)	$_____	416,000
13. Net capital gap (subtract line 12 from line 10)	$_____	902,920
14. Annual amount in current dollars to start saving now to cover the gap (divide line 13 by factor D, below)[4]	$_____	25, 578
15. Percentage of salary to be saved each year (divide line 14 by line 1)[5]	_____%	25%

Years to Retirement	Factor A	Factor B	Factor C	Factor D
10	1.5	7.0	2.2	17.5
15	1.8	8.5	3.2	35.3
20	2.2	10.3	4.7	63.3
25	2.7	12.6	6.9	107.0
30	3.2	15.3	10.1	174.0

[1] Lines 3 and 4: Employers can provide annual estimates of your projected retirement pay; estimates of Social Security benefits are available from the Social Security Administration at (800) 937-2000. Both figures will be stated in current dollars, not in the high amounts that you will receive if your wages keep up with inflation. The work sheet takes this into consideration.

[2] Line 6: Even if a large pension lets you avoid an income gap, proceed to line 9 to determine the assets you may need to make up for the erosion of a fixed pension payment by inflation.

(Continued on following page)

TABLE 22-11 (Continued)
Factors for Work Sheet Calculations Assuming 4 Percent Inflation and 8 Percent Rate of Return

[3] Line 8: This calculation includes a determination of how much capital you will need to keep up with inflation after retirement and assumes that you will *deplete the capital over a 25-year period.*

[4] Line 14: Amount includes investments earmarked for retirement and payments by employee and employer to defined-contribution retirement plans such as 401(k)s and 403(b)s. The formula assumes you will increase annual savings at the same rate as inflation.

[5] Line 15: Assuming earnings rise with inflation, you can save a set percentage of gross pay each year, and the actual amount you stash away will increase annually.

* Copyright 1989 *U.S. News & World Report,* L.P. Reprinted with permission.

TABLE 22-12—Planner's Work Sheet
Step 1: List Assumptions

	Assumptions	
A1.	Inflation rate prior to retirement	4%
A2.	Inflation rate after retirement	4%
A3.	Number of years until retirement	19 years
A4.	Expected duration of retirement	25 years
A5.	Rate of return prior to retirement	8%
A6.	Rate of return after retirement	7%
A7.	Savings step-up rate	6%

TABLE 22-13
Planner's Work Sheet—Step 2: Calculate Factors

The following factors were calculated using tables 22-16 through 22-23, which follow your blank work sheet in this book. Each table has a detailed explanation (and example) of how to extract the appropriate factor.

	Factors		Assumptions (from table 5-3)
F1.	Preretirement inflation factor	2.11	Table 22-16; years = A3, rate = A1
F2.	Retirement needs present value factor	17.936	Table 22-17; years = A4, rate = A6 minus A2
F3.	Current assets future value factor	4.32	Table 22-16; years = A3, rate = A5
F4.	Defined-benefit income present value factor	12.469	Table 22-17; years = A4, rate =A6
F5.	Savings rate factor	0.01435	Table 22-21; years = A3, rate = A5; use A7 to find appropriate table

TABLE 22-14
Planners Work Sheet
Step 3: Computation of Retirement Need and Amount to Be Saved

COMPUTATIONS

L1.		Projected annual retirement budget	$140,000	(80% of $175,000)
L2.	−	Social Security benefit	22,800	(Ann & Robert annual total)
L3.	=	Net annual need in current dollars	$117,200	
L4.	X	F1 factor	2.11	
L5.	=	Inflation-adjusted annual need	$247,292	
L6.	X	F2 factor	17.936	
L7.	=	Total resources needed for retirement		$4,435,429
L8.	=	Total in defined-contribution plans	$184,000	
L9.	+	Total private savings ear marked for retirement	50,000	
L10.		Current assets available for retirement	$234,000	
L11.	X	F3 factor	4.32	
L12.	=	Future value of current assets		$1,010,880
L13.		Annual income from defined benefit plan	$16,800	(Ann's annual pension)
L14.	X	F1 factor	2.11	
L15.	=	Inflation-adjusted annual income from defined-benefit plan	$35,448	
L16	X	F4 Factor	12.469	
L17.	=	Lump-sum value of defined-benefit plan		$442,001
L18.		Total resources available for retirement (line 12 and line 17)		$1,452,881
L19.		Addition amount you need to accumulate by retirement		$2,982,548
L20.	X	F5 factor		0.01435
L21.	=	Amount you need to save—first year		$42,800
				(24% of salary)

(Savings in each subsequent year must increase by the savings step-up rate, 6%)

TABLE 22-15
Retirement Planning Work Sheet

ASSUMPTIONS

A1.	Inflation rate prior to retirement	_____
A2.	Inflation rate after retirement	_____
A3.	Number of years until retirement	_____
A4.	Expected duration of retirement	_____
A5.	Rate of return prior to retirement	_____
A6.	Rate of return after retirement	_____
A7.	Savings step-up rate	_____

FACTORS

F1.	Pre-retirement inflation factor	_____
F2.	Retirement needs present value factor	_____
F3.	Current assets future value factor	_____
F4.	Defined-benefit present value factor	_____
F5.	Savings rate factor	_____

COMPUTATIONS

L1.		Projected annual retirement budget	_____	
L2.	–	Social Security benefit	_____	
L3.	=	Net annual need in current dollars	_____	
L4.	X	F1 factor	_____	
L5.	=	Inflation-adjusted annual retirement need	_____	
L6.	X	F2 factor	_____	
L7.	=	Total resources needed for retirement		_____
L8.		Total in defined-contribution plans	_____	
L9.	+	Total private savings earmarked for retirement	_____	
L10.	=	Current assets available for retirement	_____	
L11.	X	F3 factor	_____	
L12.	=	Future value of current assets		_____
L13.		Annual income from defined-benefit plan	_____	
L14.	X	F1 factor	_____	
L15.	=	Inflation-adjusted annual income from defined-benefit plan	_____	
L16.	X	F4 factor	_____	
L17.	=	Lump-sum value of defined-benefit plan		_____
L18.		Total resources available for retirement (line 12 and line 17)		_____
L19.		Additional amount you need to accumulate by retirement		_____
L20.	X	F5 factor		_____
L21.	=	Amount you need to save—first year		_____

THE INFLATION AND FUTURE VALUE FACTORS

Table 22-16 is used to select the appropriate Preretirement Inflation Factor (F1) and Current Assets Future Value Factor (F3) for use in the

TABLE 22-16
Future Value Factors

Yrs	0%	1%	2%	3%	4%	5%	6%
1	1.00	1.01	1.02	1.03	1.04	1.05	1.06
2	1.00	1.02	1.04	1.06	1.08	1.10	1.12
3	1.00	1.03	1.06	1.09	1.12	1.16	1.19
4	1.00	1.04	1.08	1.13	1.17	1.22	1.26
5	1.00	1.05	1.10	1.16	1.22	1.28	1.34
6	1.00	1.06	1.13	1.19	1.27	1.34	1.42
7	1.00	1.07	1.15	1.23	1.32	1.41	1.50
8	1.00	1.08	1.17	1.27	1.37	1.48	1.59
9	1.00	1.09	1.20	1.30	1.42	1.55	1.69
10	1.00	1.10	1.22	1.34	1.48	1.63	1.79
11	1.00	1.12	1.24	1.38	1.54	1.71	1.90
12	1.00	1.13	1.27	1.43	1.60	1.80	2.01
13	1.00	1.14	1.29	1.47	1.67	1.89	2.13
14	1.00	1.15	1.32	1.51	1.73	1.98	2.26
15	1.00	1.16	1.35	1.56	1.80	2.08	2.40
16	1.00	1.17	1.37	1.60	1.87	2.18	2.54
17	1.00	1.18	1.40	1.65	1.95	2.29	2.69
18	1.00	1.20	1.43	1.70	2.03	2.41	2.85
19	1.00	1.21	1.46	1.75	2.11	2.53	3.03
20	1.00	1.22	1.49	1.81	2.19	2.65	3.21
21	1.00	1.23	1.52	1.86	2.28	2.79	3.40
22	1.00	1.24	1.55	1.92	2.37	2.93	3.60
23	1.00	1.26	1.58	1.97	2.46	3.07	3.82
24	1.00	1.27	1.61	2.03	2.56	3.23	4.05
25	1.00	1.28	1.64	2.09	2.67	3.39	4.29
26	1.00	1.30	1.67	2.16	2.77	3.56	4.55
27	1.00	1.31	1.71	2.22	2.88	3.73	4.82
28	1.00	1.32	1.74	2.29	3.00	3.92	5.11
29	1.00	1.33	1.78	2.36	3.12	4.12	5.42
30	1.00	1.35	1.81	2.43	3.24	4.32	5.74
31	1.00	1.36	1.85	2.50	3.37	4.54	6.09
32	1.00	1.37	1.88	2.58	3.51	4.76	6.45
33	1.00	1.39	1.92	2.65	3.65	5.00	6.84
34	1.00	1.40	1.96	2.73	3.79	5.25	7.25
35	1.00	1.42	2.00	2.81	3.95	5.52	7.69
36	1.00	1.43	2.04	2.90	4.10	5.79	8.15
37	1.00	1.45	2.08	2.99	4.27	6.08	8.64
38	1.00	1.46	2.12	3.07	4.44	6.39	9.15
39	1.00	1.47	2.16	3.17	4.62	6.70	9.70
40	1.00	1.49	2.21	3.26	4.80	7.04	10.29
41	1.00	1.50	2.25	3.36	4.99	7.39	10.90
42	1.00	1.52	2.30	3.46	5.19	7.76	11.56
43	1.00	1.53	2.34	3.56	5.40	8.15	12.25
44	1.00	1.55	2.39	3.67	5.62	8.56	12.99
45	1.00	1.56	2.44	3.78	5.84	8.99	13.76

Retirement Planning Work Sheet. An explanation of the use of the table follows.

TABLE 22-16 (Continued)
Future Value Factors

Yrs	\multicolumn{8}{c}{Rate}
	7%	8%	9%	10%	11%	12%	15%	20%
1	1.07	1.08	1.09	1.10	1.11	1.12	1.15	1.20
2	1.14	1.17	1.19	1.21	1.23	1.25	1.32	1.44
3	1.23	1.26	1.30	1.33	1.37	1.40	1.52	1.73
4	1.31	1.36	1.41	1.46	1.52	1.57	1.75	2.07
5	1.40	1.47	1.54	1.61	1.69	1.76	2.01	2.49
6	1.50	1.59	1.68	1.77	1.87	1.97	2.31	2.99
7	1.61	1.71	1.83	1.95	2.08	2.21	2.66	3.58
8	1.72	1.85	1.99	2.14	2.30	2.48	3.06	4.30
9	1.84	2.00	2.17	2.36	2.56	2.77	3.52	5.16
10	1.97	2.16	2.37	2.59	2.84	3.11	4.05	6.19
11	2.10	2.33	2.58	2.85	3.15	3.48	4.65	7.43
12	2.25	2.52	**2.81**	3.14	3.50	3.90	5.35	8.92
13	2.41	2.72	3.07	3.45	3.88	4.36	6.15	10.70
14	2.58	2.94	3.34	3.80	4.31	4.89	7.08	12.84
15	2.76	3.17	3.64	4.18	4.78	5.47	8.14	15.41
16	2.95	3.43	3.97	4.59	5.31	6.13	9.36	18.49
17	3.16	3.70	4.33	5.05	5.90	6.87	10.76	22.19
18	3.38	4.00	4.72	5.56	6.54	7.69	12.38	26.62
19	3.62	4.32	5.14	6.12	7.26	8.61	14.23	31.95
20	3.87	4.66	5.60	6.73	8.06	9.65	16.37	38.34
21	4.14	5.03	6.11	7.40	8.95	10.80	18.82	46.01
22	4.43	5.44	6.66	8.14	9.93	12.10	21.64	55.21
23	4.74	5.87	7.26	8.95	11.03	13.55	24.89	66.25
24	5.07	6.34	7.91	9.85	12.24	15.18	28.63	79.50
25	5.43	6.85	8.62	10.83	13.59	17.00	32.92	95.40
26	5.81	7.40	9.40	11.92	15.08	19.04	37.86	114.48
27	6.21	7.99	10.25	13.11	16.74	21.32	43.54	137.37
28	6.65	8.63	11.17	14.42	18.58	23.88	50.07	164.84
29	7.11	9.32	12.17	15.86	20.62	26.75	57.58	197.81
30	7.61	10.06	13.27	17.45	22.89	29.96	66.21	237.38
31	8.15	10.87	14.46	19.19	25.41	33.56	76.14	284.85
32	8.72	11.74	15.76	21.11	28.21	37.58	87.57	341.82
33	9.33	12.68	17.18	23.23	31.31	42.09	100.70	410.19
34	9.98	13.69	18.73	25.55	34.75	47.14	115.80	492.22
35	10.68	14.79	20.41	28.10	38.57	52.80	133.18	590.67
36	11.42	15.97	22.25	30.91	42.82	59.14	153.15	708.80
37	12.22	17.25	24.25	34.00	47.53	66.23	176.12	850.56
38	13.08	18.63	26.44	37.40	52.76	74.18	202.54	1020.67
39	13.99	20.12	28.82	41.14	58.56	83.08	232.92	1224.81
40	14.97	21.72	31.41	45.26	65.00	93.05	267.86	1469.77
41	16.02	23.46	34.24	49.79	72.15	104.22	308.04	1763.73
42	17.14	25.34	37.32	54.76	80.09	116.72	354.25	2116.47
43	18.34	27.37	40.68	60.24	88.90	130.73	407.39	2539.77
44	19.63	29.56	44.34	66.26	98.68	146.42	468.50	3047.72
45	21.00	31.92	48.33	72.89	109.53	163.99	538.77	3657.26

ANNUITY FACTORS

Table 22-17 is used to select the appropriate Retirement Needs Present Value Factor (F2) and Defined-Benefit Present Value Factor (F4) for use in

TABLE 22-17
Present Value of Annuity Factors

Yrs	0%	1%	2%	3%	4%	5%	6%
				Rate			
1	1.000	1.000	1.000	1.000	1.000	1.000	1.000
2	2.000	1.990	1.980	1.971	1.962	1.952	1.943
3	3.000	2.970	2.942	2.913	2.886	2.859	2.833
4	4.000	3.941	3.884	3.829	3.775	3.723	3.673
5	5.000	4.902	4.808	4.717	4.630	4.546	4.465
6	6.000	5.853	5.713	5.580	5.452	5.329	5.212
7	7.000	6.795	6.601	6.417	6.242	6.076	5.917
8	8.000	7.728	7.472	7.230	7.002	6.786	6.582
9	9.000	8.652	8.325	8.020	7.733	7.463	7.210
10	10.000	9.566	9.162	8.786	8.435	8.108	7.802
11	11.000	10.471	9.983	9.530	9.111	8.722	8.360
12	12.000	11.368	10.787	10.253	9.760	9.306	8.887
13	13.000	12.255	11.575	10.954	10.385	9.863	9.384
14	14.000	13.134	12.348	11.635	10.986	10.394	9.853
15	15.000	14.004	13.106	12.296	11.563	10.899	10.295
16	16.000	14.865	13.849	12.938	12.118	11.380	10.712
17	17.000	15.718	14.578	13.561	12.652	11.838	11.106
18	18.000	16.562	15.292	14.166	13.166	12.274	11.477
19	19.000	17.398	15.992	14.754	13.659	12.690	11.828
20	20.000	18.226	16.678	15.324	14.134	13.085	12.158
21	21.000	19.046	17.351	15.877	14.590	13.462	12.470
22	22.000	19.857	18.011	**16.415**	15.029	13.821	12.764
23	23.000	20.660	18.658	16.937	15.451	14.163	13.042
24	24.000	21.456	19.292	17.444	15.857	14.489	13.303
25	25.000	22.243	19.914	17.936	16.247	14.799	13.550
26	26.000	23.023	20.523	18.413	16.622	15.094	13.783
27	27.000	23.795	21.121	18.877	16.983	15.375	14.003
28	28.000	24.560	21.707	19.327	17.330	15.643	14.211
29	29.000	25.316	22.281	19.764	17.663	15.898	14.406
30	30.000	26.066	22.844	20.188	17.984	16.141	14.591
31	31.000	26.808	23.396	20.600	18.292	16.372	14.765
32	32.000	27.542	23.938	21.000	18.588	16.593	14.929
33	33.000	28.270	24.468	21.389	18.874	16.803	15.084
34	34.000	28.990	24.989	21.766	19.148	17.003	15.230
35	35.000	29.703	25.499	22.132	19.411	17.193	15.368
36	36.000	30.409	25.999	22.487	19.665	17.374	15.498
37	37.000	31.108	26.489	22.832	19.908	17.547	15.621
38	38.000	31.800	26.969	23.167	20.143	17.711	15.737
39	39.000	32.485	27.441	23.492	20.368	17.868	15.846
40	40.000	33.163	27.903	23.808	20.584	18.017	15.949
41	41.000	33.835	28.355	24.115	20.793	18.159	16.046
42	42.000	34.500	28.799	24.412	20.993	18.294	16.138
43	43.000	35.158	29.235	24.701	21.186	18.423	16.225
44	44.000	35.810	29.662	24.982	21.371	18.546	16.306
45	45.000	36.455	30.080	25.254	21.549	18.663	16.383

the Retirement Planning Work Sheet presented. An explanation of the use of the table follows.

TABLE 22-17 (Continued)
Present Value of Annuity Factors

				Rate				
Yrs	7%	8%	9%	10%	11%	12%	15%	20%
1	1.000	1.000	1.000	1.000	1.000	1.000	1.000	1.000
2	1.935	1.926	1.917	1.909	1.901	1.893	1.870	1.833
3	2.808	2.783	2.759	2.736	2.713	2.690	2.626	2.528
4	3.624	3.577	3.531	3.487	3.444	3.402	3.283	3.106
5	4.387	4.312	4.240	4.170	4.102	4.037	3.855	3.589
6	5.100	4.993	4.890	4.791	4.696	4.605	4.352	3.991
7	5.767	5.623	5.486	5.355	5.231	5.111	4.784	4.326
8	6.389	6.206	6.033	5.868	5.712	5.564	5.160	4.605
9	6.971	6.747	6.535	6.335	6.146	5.968	5.487	4.837
10	7.515	7.247	6.995	6.759	6.537	6.328	5.772	5.031
11	8.024	7.710	7.418	7.145	6.889	6.650	6.019	5.192
12	8.499	8.139	7.805	7.495	7.207	6.938	6.234	5.327
13	8.943	8.536	8.161	7.814	7.492	7.194	6.421	5.439
14	9.358	8.904	8.487	8.103	7.750	7.424	6.583	5.533
15	9.745	9.244	8.786	8.367	7.982	7.628	6.724	5.611
16	10.108	9.559	9.061	8.606	8.191	7.811	6.847	5.675
17	10.447	9.851	9.313	8.824	8.379	7.974	6.954	5.730
18	10.763	10.122	9.544	9.022	8.549	8.120	7.047	5.775
19	11.059	10.372	9.756	9.201	8.702	8.250	7.128	5.812
20	11.336	10.604	9.950	9.365	8.839	8.366	7.198	5.843
21	11.594	10.818	10.129	9.514	8.963	8.469	7.259	5.870
22	11.836	11.017	10.292	9.649	9.075	8.562	7.312	5.891
23	12.061	11.201	10.442	9.772	9.176	8.645	7.359	5.909
24	12.272	11.371	10.580	9.883	9.266	8.718	7.399	5.925
25	12.469	11.529	10.707	9.985	9.348	8.784	7.434	5.937
26	**12.654**	11.675	10.823	10.077	9.422	8.843	7.464	5.948
27	12.826	11.810	10.929	10.161	9.488	8.896	7.491	5.956
28	12.987	11.935	11.027	10.237	9.548	8.943	7.514	5.964
29	13.137	12.051	11.116	10.307	9.602	8.984	7.534	5.970
30	13.278	12.158	11.198	10.370	9.650	9.022	7.551	5.975
31	13.409	12.258	11.274	10.427	9.694	9.055	7.566	5.979
32	13.532	12.350	11.343	10.479	9.733	9.085	7.579	5.982
33	13.647	12.435	11.406	10.526	9.769	9.112	7.591	5.985
34	13.754	12.514	11.464	10.569	9.801	9.135	7.600	5.988
35	13.854	12.587	11.518	10.609	9.829	9.157	7.609	5.990
36	13.948	12.655	11.567	10.644	9.855	9.176	7.617	5.992
37	14.035	12.717	11.612	10.677	9.879	9.192	7.623	5.993
38	14.117	12.775	11.653	10.706	9.900	9.208	7.629	5.994
39	14.193	12.829	11.691	10.733	9.919	9.221	7.634	5.995
40	14.265	12.879	11.726	10.757	9.936	9.233	7.638	5.996
41	14.332	12.925	11.757	10.779	9.951	9.244	7.642	5.997
42	14.394	12.967	11.787	10.799	9.965	9.253	7.645	5.997
43	14.452	13.007	11.813	10.817	9.977	9.262	7.648	5.998
44	14.507	13.043	11.838	10.834	9.989	9.270	7.650	5.998
45	14.558	13.077	11.861	10.849	9.999	9.276	7.652	5.998

Selecting the Preretirement Inflation Factor (F1)

The appropriate F1 factor depends on the assumed annual inflation rate prior to retirement (line A1 of the Retirement Planning Work Sheet) and the number of years until retirement (line A3 of the Retirement Planning Work Sheet). The F1 factor is found in table 22-16 by looking in the column with the interest/inflation rate equal to the inflation rate specified in line A1 and the row with the number of years equal to that specified in line A3 of the Retirement Planning Work Sheet. For example, if you assume inflation will average 6 percent per year until retirement (A1) and you expect to retire in 18 years (A3), the appropriate preretirement inflation factor (F1) is 2.85.

Selecting the Current Assets Future Value Factor (F3)

The appropriate F3 factor depends on the assumed rate of return on investment prior to retirement (line A5 of the Retirement Planning Work Sheet) and the number of years until retirement (line A3 of the Retirement Planning Work Sheet). The F3 factor is found in table 22-16 by looking in the column with the interest/inflation rate equal to the rate of return specified in line A5 and the row with the number of years equal to that specified in line A3 of the Retirement Planning Work Sheet. For example, if you assume you can invest at a rate of 9 percent per year until retirement (A5) and you expect to retire in 12 years (A3), the appropriate current assets future value factor (F3) is 2.81.

Selecting the Retirement Needs Present Value Factor (F2)

The appropriate F2 factor depends on the assumed annual inflation rate after retirement, the expected duration of retirement, and the assumed rate of return on investment after retirement (lines A2, A4, and A6, respectively, of the Retirement Planning Work Sheet [table 22-12]). The F2 factor is found using a two-step process. First, you must determine the inflation-adjusted interest rate. This is estimated by subtracting your assumed inflation rate after retirement (A2) from your assumed investment rate of return after retirement (A6).

Specifically,

Value from A6	–	Value from A2	=	Inflation-Adjusted Rate
_____	–	_____	=	_____

Next, you can find the F2 factor in table 22-17 in the column with the inflation-adjusted interest rate equal to that just computed and the row with the number of years equal to that specified in line A4 of the Retirement Planning Work Sheet. For example, if you assume inflation will average 5 percent per year after retirement (A2) and you expect to earn 8 percent on your investments after retirement (A6), your inflation-adjusted interest rate would be

Value from A6	–	Value from A2	=	Inflation-Adjusted Rate
8%	–	5%	=	3%

If your expected duration of retirement is 22 years (A4), the appropriate retirement needs present value factor (F2) is found by looking in the 3 percent column and the 22-year row of table 22-17. In this case, F2 is 16.415.

Selecting the Defined-Benefit Present Value Factor (F4)

The appropriate F4 factor depends on the assumed rate of return on investment after retirement and the expected duration of retirement (lines A6 and A4 of the Retirement Planning Work Sheet, respectively). The F4 factor is found in table 22-17 by looking in the column with the interest rate equal to the rate of return specified in line A6 and the row with the number of years equal to that specified in line A4 of the Retirement Planning Work Sheet. For example, if you assume you can invest at a rate of 7 percent per year after retirement (A6) and you expect your retirement needs to last 26 years (A4), the appropriate defined-benefit present value factor (F4) is 12.654.

THE SAVINGS RATE FACTOR

Tables 22-18 through 22-23 are used to select the appropriate Savings Rate Factor (F5) for use in the Retirement Planning Work Sheet. An explanation of the use of the tables follows.

Selecting the Savings Rate Factor (F5)

The appropriate F5 factor depends on the number of years until you plan to retire, the average annual rate of return you expect to earn on investment until retirement, and your savings step-up rate (lines A3, A5, and A7 of table 22-15, the Retirement Planning Work Sheet, respectively). To find the appropriate F5 factor, you must first select the table corresponding to your savings step-up rate (A7). The tables correspond to step-up rates ranging from 0 percent to 10 percent, with the step-up rate increased by 2 percentage points in each successive table.

The savings step-up rate is the rate at which you plan to increase or step up the amount you save each year. Frequently, the step-up rate is set equal to the rate at which a person expects his or her annual earnings to grow. If the step-up rate is set equal to the earnings growth rate, the amount that must be saved each year remains a fixed proportion of those growing earnings. Therefore, the "burden" of saving for retirement remains the same each year relative to your growing income. For example, if you expect your earnings to grow at an average annual rate of 6 percent per year and want your required savings each year to be constant relative to your earnings, you would use the table showing a 6 percent savings step-up rate.

Once you have selected the table corresponding to your desired step-up rate, you would find your savings rate factor (F5) in the appropriate column and row. For example, if you expect your earnings to grow at an average annual rate of 6 percent per year and want your required savings each year to be constant relative to your earnings, you would use the table showing a 6 percent savings step-up rate corresponding to your assumed investment rate of return prior to retirement (A5) and the number of years until you plan to retire (A3), respectively. For example, if your step-up rate is 6 percent (A7), your assumed rate of return is 8 percent (A5), and you plan to retire in 10 years, your savings rate factor (F5) is 0.05031 (table 22-21).

Remember, line 21 of the Retirement Planning Work Sheet (table 22-15) calculates the amount you need to save the first year. In each subsequent year, you must increase the amount you save by your assumed savings step-up rate if you are to reach your goal. For example, assume your savings step-up rate is 5 percent and the amount calculated in line 21 of the Retirement Planning Work Sheet is $1,000. In the second year, you would have to save $1,050; in the third year, $1,102.50; in the fourth year, $1,157.62; and so on.

The amount you must save each year is calculated by multiplying the prior year's savings amount by (1 + the step-up rate). For example, if your savings step-up rate is 6 percent, you would compute each subsequent year's savings amount by multiplying the previous year's savings amount by 1.06.

If you specify a zero percent savings step-up rate, you will reach your retirement accumulation goal by saving the same level amount each year as determined in line 21 of the Retirement Planning Work Sheet (table 22-15), assuming your actual investment rate of return matches your assumed rate of return.

(Text continues on page 22.48.)

TABLE 22-18
Yearly Savings Rate Factors
0% Savings Step-up Rate (A7)

Yrs	\multicolumn{6}{c}{Assumed Rate of Return (A5)}					
	1%	2%	3%	4%	5%	6%
1	0.99010	0.98039	0.97087	0.96154	0.95238	0.94340
2	0.49259	0.48534	0.47826	0.47134	0.46458	0.45796
3	0.32675	0.32035	0.31411	0.30803	0.30210	0.29633
4	0.24384	0.23787	0.23207	0.22643	0.22096	0.21565
5	0.19410	0.18839	0.18287	0.17753	0.17236	0.16736
6	0.16094	0.15542	0.15009	0.14496	0.14002	0.13525
7	0.13726	0.13187	0.12671	0.12174	0.11697	0.11239
8	0.11950	0.11423	0.10918	0.10435	0.09974	0.09532
9	0.10568	0.10051	0.09557	0.09086	0.08637	0.08210
10	0.09464	0.08954	0.08469	0.08009	0.07572	0.07157
11	0.08560	0.08057	0.07580	0.07130	0.06704	0.06301
12	0.07807	0.07310	0.06841	0.06399	0.05983	0.05592
13	0.07170	0.06678	0.06216	0.05783	0.05377	0.04996
14	0.06624	0.06137	0.05682	0.05257	0.04859	0.04489
15	0.06151	0.05669	0.05220	0.04802	0.04414	0.04053
16	0.05737	0.05260	0.04817	0.04406	0.04026	0.03675
17	0.05372	0.04899	0.04461	0.04058	0.03686	0.03344
18	0.05048	0.04579	0.04146	0.03749	0.03385	0.03053
19	0.04758	0.04292	0.03865	0.03475	0.03119	0.02794
20	0.04497	0.04035	0.03613	0.03229	0.02880	0.02565
21	0.04260	0.03802	0.03386	0.03008	0.02666	0.02359
22	0.04046	0.03591	0.03179	0.02808	0.02473	0.02174
23	0.03850	0.03399	0.02992	0.02626	0.02299	0.02007
24	0.03671	0.03223	0.02820	0.02460	0.02140	0.01857
25	0.03506	0.03061	0.02663	0.02309	0.01995	0.01720
26	0.03353	0.02912	0.02518	0.02170	0.01863	0.01595
27	0.03212	0.02774	0.02385	0.02042	0.01742	0.01481
28	0.03082	0.02646	0.02261	0.01924	0.01631	0.01377
29	0.02960	0.02527	0.02147	0.01815	0.01528	0.01281
30	0.02846	0.02417	0.02041	0.01714	0.01433	0.01193
31	0.02740	0.02313	0.01942	0.01621	0.01346	0.01112
32	0.02641	0.02217	0.01849	0.01534	0.01265	0.01038
33	0.02547	0.02126	0.01763	0.01452	0.01190	0.00969
34	0.02459	0.02041	0.01682	0.01376	0.01120	0.00906
35	0.02377	0.01961	0.01606	0.01306	0.01054	0.00847
36	0.02298	0.01886	0.01534	0.01239	0.00994	0.00792
37	0.02225	0.01814	0.01467	0.01177	0.00937	0.00741
38	0.02155	0.01747	0.01404	0.01118	0.00884	0.00694
39	0.02088	0.01683	0.01344	0.01064	0.00835	0.00650
40	0.02025	0.01623	0.01288	0.01012	0.00788	0.00610
41	0.01965	0.01566	0.01234	0.00963	0.00745	0.00572
42	0.01908	0.01511	0.01184	0.00917	0.00704	0.00536
43	0.01854	0.01460	0.01136	0.00874	0.00666	0.00503
44	0.01802	0.01411	0.01090	0.00833	0.00630	0.00472
45	0.01753	0.01364	0.01047	0.00794	0.00596	0.00443

TABLE 22-18 (Continued)
Yearly Savings Rate Factors
0% Savings Step-up Rate (A7)

Yrs	\multicolumn{8}{c}{Assumed Rate of Return (A5)}
	7%	8%	9%	10%	11%	12%	15%	20%
1	0.93458	0.92593	0.91743	0.90909	0.90090	0.89286	0.86957	0.83333
2	0.45149	0.44516	0.43896	0.43290	0.42697	0.42116	0.40445	0.37879
3	0.29070	0.28522	0.27987	0.27465	0.26956	0.26460	0.25041	0.22894
4	0.21049	0.20548	0.20061	0.19588	0.19129	0.18682	0.17414	0.15524
5	0.16251	0.15783	0.15330	0.14891	0.14466	0.14054	0.12897	0.11198
6	0.13065	0.12622	0.12194	0.11782	0.11385	0.11002	0.09934	0.08392
7	0.10799	0.10377	0.09972	0.09582	0.09209	0.08850	0.07857	0.06452
8	0.09109	0.08705	0.08319	0.07949	0.07596	0.07259	0.06335	0.05051
9	0.07802	0.07415	0.07046	0.06695	0.06361	0.06043	0.05180	0.04007
10	0.06764	0.06392	0.06039	0.05704	0.05388	0.05088	0.04283	0.03210
11	0.05921	0.05563	0.05224	0.04906	0.04605	0.04323	0.03571	0.02592
12	0.05224	0.04879	0.04555	0.04251	0.03966	0.03700	0.02998	0.02105
13	0.04640	0.04308	0.03997	0.03707	0.03437	0.03185	0.02531	0.01718
14	0.04144	0.03824	0.03526	0.03250	0.02994	0.02756	0.02147	0.01408
15	0.03719	0.03410	0.03125	0.02861	0.02618	0.02395	0.01828	0.01157
16	0.03351	0.03053	0.02780	0.02529	0.02299	0.02088	0.01561	0.00953
17	0.03030	0.02743	0.02481	0.02242	0.02024	0.01826	0.01336	0.00787
18	0.02749	0.02472	0.02221	0.01994	0.01788	0.01602	0.01147	0.00650
19	0.02500	0.02234	0.01994	0.01777	0.01582	0.01407	0.00986	0.00539
20	0.02280	0.02023	0.01793	0.01587	0.01403	0.01239	0.00849	0.00446
21	0.02083	0.01836	0.01616	0.01420	0.01247	0.01093	0.00732	0.00370
22	0.01907	0.01670	0.01459	0.01273	0.01109	0.00965	0.00632	0.00307
23	0.01749	0.01521	0.01319	0.01143	0.00988	0.00854	0.00546	0.00255
24	0.01606	0.01387	0.01195	0.01027	0.00882	0.00756	0.00472	0.00212
25	0.01478	0.01267	0.01083	0.00924	0.00787	0.00670	0.00409	0.00177
26	0.01361	0.01158	0.00983	0.00833	0.00704	0.00594	0.00354	0.00147
27	0.01255	0.01060	0.00893	0.00751	0.00630	0.00527	0.00307	0.00122
28	0.01158	0.00971	0.00812	0.00677	0.00564	0.00468	0.00266	0.00102
29	0.01070	0.00891	0.00739	0.00612	0.00505	0.00416	0.00231	0.00085
30	0.00989	0.00817	0.00673	0.00553	0.00453	0.00370	0.00200	0.00071
31	0.00916	0.00751	0.00613	0.00500	0.00406	0.00329	0.00174	0.00059
32	0.00848	0.00690	0.00559	0.00452	0.00364	0.00293	0.00151	0.00049
33	0.00786	0.00634	0.00510	0.00409	0.00327	0.00261	0.00131	0.00041
34	0.00729	0.00584	0.00466	0.00370	0.00294	0.00232	0.00114	0.00034
35	0.00676	0.00537	0.00425	0.00335	0.00264	0.00207	0.00099	0.00028
36	0.00628	0.00495	0.00389	0.00304	0.00237	0.00184	0.00086	0.00024
37	0.00583	0.00456	0.00355	0.00275	0.00213	0.00164	0.00074	0.00020
38	0.00542	0.00420	0.00325	0.00250	0.00191	0.00146	0.00065	0.00016
39	0.00503	0.00388	0.00297	0.00226	0.00172	0.00131	0.00056	0.00014
40	0.00468	0.00357	0.00272	0.00205	0.00155	0.00116	0.00049	0.00011
41	0.00435	0.00330	0.00248	0.00186	0.00139	0.00104	0.00042	0.00009
42	0.00405	0.00304	0.00227	0.00169	0.00125	0.00093	0.00037	0.00008
43	0.00377	0.00281	0.00208	0.00153	0.00113	0.00083	0.00032	0.00007
44	0.00351	0.00259	0.00191	0.00139	0.00101	0.00074	0.00028	0.00005
45	0.00327	0.00240	0.00174	0.00126	0.00091	0.00066	0.00024	0.00005

TABLE 22-19
Yearly Savings Rate Factors
2% Savings Step-up Rate (A7)

Yrs						

Yrs	1%	2%	3%	4%	5%	6%
1	0.99010	0.98039	0.97087	0.96154	0.95238	0.94340
2	0.48773	0.48058	0.47360	0.46677	0.46009	0.45356
3	0.32035	0.31411	0.30803	0.30210	0.29633	0.29071
4	0.23671	0.23096	0.22538	0.21997	0.21470	0.20959
5	0.18656	0.18115	0.17590	0.17083	0.16592	0.16116
6	0.15317	0.14800	0.14301	0.13820	0.13355	0.12907
7	0.12934	0.12437	0.11958	0.11498	0.11056	0.10631
8	0.11149	0.10669	0.10208	0.09766	0.09343	0.08938
9	0.09764	0.09297	0.08852	0.08426	0.08020	0.07633
10	0.08657	0.08203	0.07772	0.07361	0.06970	0.06599
11	0.07753	0.07311	0.06892	0.06495	0.06119	0.05762
12	0.07001	0.06571	0.06164	0.05779	0.05415	0.05072
13	0.06367	0.05946	0.05550	0.05177	0.04826	0.04496
14	0.05824	0.05413	0.05028	0.04665	0.04326	0.04008
15	0.05355	0.04953	0.04577	0.04226	0.03898	0.03592
16	0.04945	0.04553	0.04186	0.03845	0.03527	0.03232
17	0.04585	0.04201	0.03843	0.03511	0.03204	0.02920
18	0.04266	0.03890	0.03541	0.03218	0.02920	0.02646
19	0.03981	0.03613	0.03272	0.02958	0.02670	0.02405
20	0.03726	0.03365	0.03032	0.02727	0.02448	0.02192
21	0.03495	0.03142	0.02817	0.02520	0.02249	0.02003
22	0.03286	0.02940	0.02623	0.02334	0.02071	0.01834
23	0.03097	0.02757	0.02447	0.02166	0.01912	0.01682
24	0.02923	0.02591	0.02288	0.02014	0.01767	0.01546
25	0.02764	0.02438	0.02142	0.01876	0.01637	0.01423
26	0.02618	0.02298	0.02009	0.01750	0.01518	0.01312
27	0.02483	0.02170	0.01887	0.01635	0.01410	0.01211
28	0.02359	0.02051	0.01775	0.01529	0.01311	0.01120
29	0.02243	0.01942	0.01672	0.01432	0.01221	0.01036
30	0.02136	0.01840	0.01576	0.01343	0.01138	0.00960
31	0.02036	0.01746	0.01488	0.01261	0.01062	0.00890
32	0.01943	0.01658	0.01406	0.01185	0.00992	0.00826
33	0.01856	0.01576	0.01330	0.01114	0.00927	0.00767
34	0.01774	0.01500	0.01259	0.01049	0.00868	0.00713
35	0.01697	0.01429	0.01193	0.00988	0.00813	0.00664
36	0.01625	0.01362	0.01131	0.00932	0.00762	0.00618
37	0.01558	0.01299	0.01073	0.00879	0.00714	0.00576
38	0.01494	0.01240	0.01019	0.00830	0.00670	0.00537
39	0.01434	0.01184	0.00969	0.00784	0.00629	0.00501
40	0.01377	0.01132	0.00921	0.00742	0.00591	0.00467
41	0.01323	0.01083	0.00876	0.00702	0.00556	0.00436
42	0.01272	0.01036	0.00834	0.00664	0.00523	0.00408
43	0.01224	0.00992	0.00795	0.00629	0.00492	0.00381
44	0.01178	0.00951	0.00758	0.00596	0.00463	0.00356
45	0.01134	0.00912	0.00723	0.00565	0.00436	0.00333

Assumed Rate of Return (A5)

TABLE 22-19 (Continued)
Yearly Savings Rate Factors
2% Savings Step-up Rate (A7)

	Assumed Rate of Return (A5)							
Yrs	7%	8%	9%	10%	11%	12%	15%	20%
1	0.93458	0.92593	0.91743	0.90909	0.90090	0.89286	0.86957	0.83333
2	0.44717	0.44092	0.43480	0.42882	0.42296	0.41722	0.40072	0.37538
3	0.28522	0.27987	0.27466	0.26957	0.26461	0.25976	0.24592	0.22496
4	0.20463	0.19980	0.19511	0.19055	0.18612	0.18181	0.16959	0.15134
5	0.15656	0.15210	0.14779	0.14361	0.13956	0.13564	0.12460	0.10836
6	0.12475	0.12059	0.11657	0.11269	0.10894	0.10533	0.09524	0.08065
7	0.10223	0.09830	0.09453	0.09091	0.08742	0.08407	0.07480	0.06161
8	0.08550	0.08179	0.07823	0.07483	0.07157	0.06845	0.05989	0.04795
9	0.07263	0.06911	0.06575	0.06254	0.05949	0.05658	0.04867	0.03783
10	0.06246	0.05911	0.05592	0.05290	0.05004	0.04732	0.03999	0.03016
11	0.05424	0.05105	0.04803	0.04518	0.04249	0.03995	0.03316	0.02425
12	0.04749	0.04445	0.04158	0.03889	0.03636	0.03398	0.02769	0.01961
13	0.04186	0.03896	0.03624	0.03369	0.03131	0.02908	0.02326	0.01595
14	0.03711	0.03434	0.03176	0.02935	0.02711	0.02503	0.01964	0.01302
15	0.03307	0.03042	0.02796	0.02569	0.02358	0.02163	0.01665	0.01067
16	0.02959	0.02706	0.02472	0.02257	0.02059	0.01877	0.01416	0.00876
17	0.02657	0.02416	0.02194	0.01990	0.01804	0.01634	0.01208	0.00722
18	0.02394	0.02164	0.01953	0.01760	0.01585	0.01426	0.01033	0.00595
19	0.02164	0.01943	0.01743	0.01561	0.01396	0.01248	0.00885	0.00492
20	0.01960	0.01750	0.01559	0.01388	0.01233	0.01094	0.00760	0.00407
21	0.01780	0.01579	0.01398	0.01236	0.01091	0.00961	0.00653	0.00337
22	0.01620	0.01428	0.01256	0.01103	0.00967	0.00846	0.00562	0.00280
23	0.01477	0.01294	0.01130	0.00986	0.00858	0.00746	0.00485	0.00232
24	0.01349	0.01174	0.01019	0.00882	0.00763	0.00658	0.00418	0.00193
25	0.01234	0.01067	0.00920	0.00791	0.00679	0.00581	0.00361	0.00160
26	0.01130	0.00971	0.00831	0.00710	0.00605	0.00514	0.00312	0.00133
27	0.01037	0.00884	0.00752	0.00638	0.00539	0.00455	0.00270	0.00111
28	0.00952	0.00807	0.00681	0.00574	0.00482	0.00403	0.00234	0.00092
29	0.00875	0.00737	0.00618	0.00516	0.00430	0.00358	0.00203	0.00077
30	0.00806	0.00673	0.00561	0.00465	0.00385	0.00317	0.00176	0.00064
31	0.00742	0.00616	0.00509	0.00419	0.00344	0.00282	0.00152	0.00053
32	0.00684	0.00564	0.00463	0.00378	0.00308	0.00250	0.00132	0.00044
33	0.00631	0.00517	0.00421	0.00341	0.00276	0.00222	0.00114	0.00037
34	0.00583	0.00474	0.00383	0.00308	0.00247	0.00198	0.00099	0.00031
35	0.00539	0.00435	0.00349	0.00279	0.00222	0.00176	0.00086	0.00025
36	0.00498	0.00399	0.00318	0.00252	0.00199	0.00156	0.00075	0.00021
37	0.00461	0.00366	0.00290	0.00228	0.00178	0.00139	0.00065	0.00018
38	0.00426	0.00337	0.00264	0.00206	0.00160	0.00124	0.00056	0.00015
39	0.00395	0.00309	0.00241	0.00187	0.00144	0.00110	0.00049	0.00012
40	0.00366	0.00285	0.00220	0.00169	0.00129	0.00098	0.00043	0.00010
41	0.00339	0.00262	0.00201	0.00153	0.00116	0.00088	0.00037	0.00009
42	0.00315	0.00241	0.00183	0.00139	0.00104	0.00078	0.00032	0.00007
43	0.00292	0.00222	0.00168	0.00126	0.00094	0.00070	0.00028	0.00006
44	0.00271	0.00205	0.00153	0.00114	0.00084	0.00062	0.00024	0.00005
45	0.00252	0.00188	0.00140	0.00103	0.00076	0.00055	0.00021	0.00004

TABLE 22-20
Yearly Savings Rate Factors
4% Savings Step-up Rate (A7)

Yrs	1%	2%	3%	4%	5%	6%
			Assumed Rate of Return (A5)			
1	0.99010	0.98039	0.97087	0.96154	0.95238	0.94340
2	0.48298	0.47592	0.46902	0.46228	0.45568	0.44924
3	0.31411	0.30803	0.30210	0.29633	0.29071	0.28522
4	0.22980	0.22428	0.21891	0.21370	0.20864	0.20372
5	0.17932	0.17418	0.16920	0.16439	0.15972	0.15520
6	0.14575	0.14090	0.13623	0.13172	0.12736	0.12316
7	0.12184	0.11724	0.11282	0.10856	0.10446	0.10052
8	0.10396	0.09958	0.09537	0.09134	0.08747	0.08375
9	0.09011	0.08592	0.08190	0.07807	0.07440	0.07089
10	0.07908	0.07505	0.07122	0.06756	0.06407	0.06075
11	0.07009	0.06622	0.06255	0.05905	0.05573	0.05258
12	0.06264	0.05892	0.05539	0.05205	0.04888	0.04589
13	0.05636	0.05278	0.04940	0.04620	0.04318	0.04033
14	0.05102	0.04757	0.04431	0.04125	0.03836	0.03565
15	0.04641	0.04309	0.03996	0.03702	0.03426	0.03168
16	0.04241	0.03920	0.03619	0.03337	0.03073	0.02827
17	0.03890	0.03580	0.03291	0.03020	0.02768	0.02533
18	0.03580	0.03281	0.03002	0.02742	0.02501	0.02277
19	0.03305	0.03016	0.02748	0.02498	0.02267	0.02054
20	0.03059	0.02781	0.02522	0.02282	0.02061	0.01857
21	0.02839	0.02569	0.02320	0.02090	0.01878	0.01683
22	0.02640	0.02380	0.02139	0.01918	0.01715	0.01529
23	0.02460	0.02209	0.01977	0.01764	0.01569	0.01392
24	0.02296	0.02053	0.01830	0.01626	0.01439	0.01270
25	0.02147	0.01913	0.01697	0.01500	0.01322	0.01160
26	0.02011	0.01784	0.01576	0.01387	0.01216	0.01062
27	0.01886	0.01667	0.01466	0.01285	0.01120	0.00973
28	0.01771	0.01559	0.01366	0.01191	0.01034	0.00893
29	0.01665	0.01460	0.01274	0.01106	0.00955	0.00820
30	0.01567	0.01369	0.01190	0.01028	0.00883	0.00755
31	0.01476	0.01285	0.01112	0.00956	0.00818	0.00695
32	0.01392	0.01208	0.01041	0.00891	0.00758	0.00641
33	0.01314	0.01136	0.00975	0.00831	0.00703	0.00591
34	0.01242	0.01069	0.00914	0.00775	0.00653	0.00546
35	0.01174	0.01007	0.00857	0.00724	0.00607	0.00504
36	0.01111	0.00950	0.00805	0.00677	0.00564	0.00467
37	0.01052	0.00896	0.00757	0.00633	0.00525	0.00432
38	0.00997	0.00846	0.00712	0.00593	0.00489	0.00400
39	0.00945	0.00800	0.00670	0.00555	0.00456	0.00371
40	0.00897	0.00756	0.00631	0.00521	0.00425	0.00344
41	0.00851	0.00715	0.00594	0.00488	0.00397	0.00319
42	0.00808	0.00677	0.00561	0.00459	0.00371	0.00296
43	0.00768	0.00641	0.00529	0.00431	0.00346	0.00275
44	0.00730	0.00608	0.00499	0.00405	0.00324	0.00256
45	0.00695	0.00576	0.00471	0.00380	0.00303	0.00238

TABLE 22-20 (Continued)
Yearly Savings Rate Factors
4% Savings Step-up Rate (A7)

Yrs	\multicolumn{8}{c}{Assumed Rate of Return (A5)}

Yrs	7%	8%	9%	10%	11%	12%	15%	20%
1	0.93458	0.92593	0.91743	0.90909	0.90090	0.89286	0.86957	0.83333
2	0.44293	0.43676	0.43072	0.42481	0.41902	0.41336	0.39706	0.37202
3	0.27987	0.27466	0.26957	0.26461	0.25977	0.25504	0.24154	0.22107
4	0.19893	0.19429	0.18977	0.18538	0.18111	0.17695	0.16516	0.14753
5	0.15082	0.14658	0.14247	0.13849	0.13463	0.13090	0.12036	0.10485
6	0.11910	0.11518	0.11140	0.10775	0.10422	0.10082	0.09129	0.07749
7	0.09673	0.09308	0.08957	0.08620	0.08295	0.07983	0.07117	0.05881
8	0.08019	0.07678	0.07351	0.07038	0.06738	0.06450	0.05658	0.04549
9	0.06754	0.06433	0.06128	0.05836	0.05558	0.05292	0.04567	0.03568
10	0.05758	0.05457	0.05171	0.04899	0.04640	0.04394	0.03729	0.02830
11	0.04959	0.04675	0.04407	0.04152	0.03911	0.03684	0.03073	0.02263
12	0.04306	0.04038	0.03786	0.03548	0.03324	0.03112	0.02551	0.01823
13	0.03765	0.03512	0.03275	0.03052	0.02843	0.02647	0.02131	0.01476
14	0.03311	0.03072	0.02849	0.02640	0.02445	0.02264	0.01790	0.01200
15	0.02926	0.02701	0.02491	0.02295	0.02114	0.01945	0.01510	0.00980
16	0.02598	0.02385	0.02187	0.02004	0.01834	0.01678	0.01278	0.00802
17	0.02315	0.02114	0.01928	0.01756	0.01598	0.01452	0.01085	0.00659
18	0.02071	0.01880	0.01704	0.01543	0.01396	0.01261	0.00924	0.00542
19	0.01857	0.01677	0.01512	0.01361	0.01223	0.01098	0.00789	0.00447
20	0.01670	0.01500	0.01344	0.01202	0.01074	0.00958	0.00675	0.00369
21	0.01506	0.01344	0.01198	0.01065	0.00945	0.00838	0.00578	0.00305
22	0.01361	0.01208	0.01070	0.00945	0.00834	0.00734	0.00496	0.00252
23	0.01232	0.01087	0.00957	0.00841	0.00737	0.00644	0.00427	0.00209
24	0.01117	0.00980	0.00858	0.00749	0.00652	0.00566	0.00367	0.00173
25	0.01015	0.00885	0.00770	0.00668	0.00578	0.00498	0.00316	0.00144
26	0.00924	0.00801	0.00692	0.00596	0.00512	0.00439	0.00273	0.00119
27	0.00842	0.00726	0.00623	0.00533	0.00455	0.00387	0.00235	0.00099
28	0.00768	0.00658	0.00562	0.00478	0.00405	0.00342	0.00203	0.00082
29	0.00702	0.00598	0.00507	0.00428	0.00360	0.00302	0.00176	0.00068
30	0.00642	0.00543	0.00458	0.00384	0.00321	0.00267	0.00152	0.00057
31	0.00588	0.00494	0.00414	0.00345	0.00286	0.00237	0.00131	0.00047
32	0.00538	0.00450	0.00374	0.00310	0.00255	0.00210	0.00114	0.00039
33	0.00494	0.00410	0.00339	0.00279	0.00228	0.00186	0.00099	0.00033
34	0.00453	0.00374	0.00307	0.00251	0.00204	0.00165	0.00085	0.00027
35	0.00417	0.00342	0.00279	0.00226	0.00182	0.00146	0.00074	0.00023
36	0.00383	0.00312	0.00253	0.00203	0.00163	0.00130	0.00064	0.00019
37	0.00352	0.00285	0.00230	0.00183	0.00146	0.00115	0.00056	0.00016
38	0.00324	0.00261	0.00209	0.00165	0.00131	0.00102	0.00048	0.00013
39	0.00299	0.00239	0.00190	0.00149	0.00117	0.00091	0.00042	0.00011
40	0.00276	0.00219	0.00172	0.00135	0.00105	0.00081	0.00036	0.00009
41	0.00254	0.00201	0.00157	0.00122	0.00094	0.00072	0.00032	0.00008
42	0.00235	0.00184	0.00143	0.00110	0.00084	0.00064	0.00027	0.00006
43	0.00217	0.00169	0.00130	0.00099	0.00076	0.00057	0.00024	0.00005
44	0.00200	0.00155	0.00118	0.00090	0.00068	0.00051	0.00021	0.00004
45	0.00185	0.00142	0.00108	0.00081	0.00061	0.00045	0.00018	0.00004

TABLE 22-21
Yearly Savings Rate Factors
6% Savings Step-up Rate (A7)

Yrs	\multicolumn{6}{c}{Assumed Rate of Return (A5)}

Yrs	1%	2%	3%	4%	5%	6%
1	0.99010	0.98039	0.97087	0.96154	0.95238	0.94340
2	0.47831	0.47134	0.46453	0.45788	0.45137	0.44500
3	0.30803	0.30211	0.29633	0.29071	0.28522	0.27987
4	0.22312	0.21781	0.21265	0.20763	0.20276	0.19802
5	0.17236	0.16748	0.16276	0.15818	0.15375	0.14945
6	0.13867	0.13414	0.12976	0.12553	0.12144	0.11749
7	0.11473	0.11048	0.10639	0.10246	0.09866	0.09501
8	0.09688	0.09289	0.08905	0.08536	0.08182	0.07843
9	0.08309	0.07932	0.07571	0.07225	0.06894	0.06577
10	0.07214	0.06858	0.06517	0.06191	0.05881	0.05584
11	0.06325	0.05988	0.05666	0.05359	0.05067	0.04789
12	0.05591	0.05271	0.04967	0.04677	0.04402	0.04141
13	0.04976	0.04672	0.04384	0.04110	0.03851	0.03606
14	0.04454	0.04166	0.03892	0.03634	0.03390	0.03159
15	0.04007	0.03732	0.03473	0.03229	0.02998	0.02782
16	0.03619	0.03359	0.03113	0.02882	0.02664	0.02460
17	0.03282	0.03034	0.02801	0.02582	0.02376	0.02184
18	0.02985	0.02750	0.02529	0.02321	0.02127	0.01946
19	0.02724	0.02500	0.02290	0.02093	0.01910	0.01740
20	0.02492	0.02278	0.02079	0.01893	0.01720	0.01559
21	0.02284	0.02082	0.01892	0.01716	0.01552	0.01401
22	0.02099	0.01906	0.01726	0.01559	0.01404	0.01261
23	0.01932	0.01748	0.01578	0.01419	0.01273	0.01138
24	0.01781	0.01607	0.01445	0.01294	0.01156	0.01029
25	0.01645	0.01479	0.01325	0.01183	0.01052	0.00932
26	0.01521	0.01364	0.01217	0.01082	0.00958	0.00845
27	0.01409	0.01259	0.01120	0.00992	0.00875	0.00768
28	0.01306	0.01163	0.01031	0.00910	0.00799	0.00699
29	0.01212	0.01077	0.00951	0.00836	0.00731	0.00636
30	0.01126	0.00997	0.00878	0.00769	0.00670	0.00580
31	0.01047	0.00925	0.00812	0.00708	0.00614	0.00530
32	0.00975	0.00858	0.00751	0.00653	0.00564	0.00484
33	0.00908	0.00797	0.00695	0.00602	0.00518	0.00443
34	0.00846	0.00741	0.00645	0.00556	0.00477	0.00406
35	0.00790	0.00690	0.00598	0.00514	0.00439	0.00372
36	0.00737	0.00642	0.00555	0.00476	0.00404	0.00341
37	0.00688	0.00598	0.00515	0.00440	0.00373	0.00313
38	0.00643	0.00558	0.00479	0.00408	0.00344	0.00287
39	0.00602	0.00520	0.00446	0.00378	0.00318	0.00264
40	0.00563	0.00485	0.00415	0.00351	0.00293	0.00243
41	0.00527	0.00453	0.00386	0.00325	0.00271	0.00224
42	0.00493	0.00424	0.00360	0.00302	0.00251	0.00206
43	0.00462	0.00396	0.00335	0.00281	0.00232	0.00190
44	0.00433	0.00370	0.00313	0.00261	0.00215	0.00175
45	0.00406	0.00346	0.00292	0.00243	0.00199	0.00161

TABLE 22-21 (Continued)
Yearly Savings Rate Factors
6% Savings Step-up Rate (A7)

Yrs	\multicolumn{8}{c}{Assumed Rate of Return (A5)}							
	7%	8%	9%	10%	11%	12%	15%	20%
1	0.93458	0.92593	0.91743	0.90909	0.90090	0.89286	0.86957	0.83333
2	0.43877	0.43268	0.42671	0.42088	0.41516	0.40957	0.39347	0.36873
3	0.27466	0.26957	0.26461	0.25977	0.25505	0.25044	0.23726	0.21726
4	0.19342	0.18894	0.18459	0.18035	0.17624	0.17223	0.16086	0.14383
5	0.14529	0.14125	0.13734	0.13355	0.12988	0.12631	0.11626	0.10144
6	0.11368	0.11000	0.10644	0.10300	0.09968	0.09647	0.08749	0.07443
7	0.09149	0.08810	0.08484	0.08170	0.07868	0.07577	0.06768	0.05610
8	0.07516	0.07203	0.06903	0.06615	0.06338	0.06073	0.05341	0.04311
9	0.06273	0.05983	0.05705	0.05440	0.05186	0.04944	0.04280	0.03362
10	0.05301	**0.05031**	0.04774	0.04529	0.04296	0.04074	0.03471	0.02651
11	0.04525	0.04273	0.04035	0.03808	0.03594	0.03390	0.02842	0.02109
12	0.03894	0.03660	0.03438	0.03229	0.03031	0.02844	0.02345	0.01690
13	0.03375	0.03156	0.02950	0.02756	0.02573	0.02402	0.01947	0.01362
14	0.02942	0.02738	0.02546	0.02367	0.02198	0.02040	0.01625	0.01103
15	0.02578	0.02388	0.02209	0.02042	0.01886	0.01741	0.01363	0.00897
16	0.02269	0.02091	0.01925	0.01770	0.01626	0.01492	0.01148	0.00732
17	0.02005	0.01839	0.01684	0.01540	0.01407	0.01284	0.00970	0.00598
18	0.01778	0.01622	0.01478	0.01344	0.01221	0.01108	0.00822	0.00491
19	0.01582	0.01435	0.01301	0.01177	0.01063	0.00959	0.00698	0.00403
20	0.01411	0.01274	0.01148	0.01033	0.00928	0.00832	0.00595	0.00332
21	0.01261	0.01133	0.01016	0.00909	0.00812	0.00724	0.00507	0.00274
22	0.01130	0.01010	0.00901	0.00802	0.00712	0.00630	0.00434	0.00226
23	0.01015	0.00903	0.00801	0.00708	0.00625	0.00550	0.00371	0.00187
24	0.00913	0.00808	0.00713	0.00627	0.00550	0.00481	0.00318	0.00155
25	0.00823	0.00724	0.00635	0.00556	0.00485	0.00422	0.00273	0.00128
26	0.00743	0.00650	0.00568	0.00493	0.00428	0.00370	0.00235	0.00106
27	0.00672	0.00585	0.00508	0.00439	0.00378	0.00325	0.00202	0.00088
28	0.00608	0.00527	0.00455	0.00391	0.00334	0.00285	0.00174	0.00073
29	0.00551	0.00475	0.00408	0.00348	0.00296	0.00251	0.00150	0.00061
30	0.00500	0.00429	0.00366	0.00311	0.00263	0.00221	0.00129	0.00050
31	0.00454	0.00387	0.00329	0.00277	0.00233	0.00195	0.00112	0.00042
32	0.00413	0.00350	0.00296	0.00248	0.00207	0.00172	0.00096	0.00035
33	0.00376	0.00317	0.00266	0.00222	0.00184	0.00152	0.00083	0.00029
34	0.00343	0.00288	0.00240	0.00199	0.00164	0.00134	0.00072	0.00024
35	0.00313	0.00261	0.00216	0.00178	0.00146	0.00119	0.00062	0.00020
36	0.00285	0.00237	0.00195	0.00160	0.00130	0.00105	0.00054	0.00017
37	0.00261	0.00215	0.00176	0.00143	0.00116	0.00093	0.00047	0.00014
38	0.00238	0.00196	0.00159	0.00129	0.00103	0.00082	0.00040	0.00012
39	0.00218	0.00178	0.00144	0.00116	0.00092	0.00073	0.00035	0.00010
40	0.00199	0.00162	0.00130	0.00104	0.00082	0.00065	0.00030	0.00008
41	0.00183	0.00147	0.00118	0.00094	0.00074	0.00057	0.00026	0.00007
42	0.00167	0.00134	0.00107	0.00084	0.00066	0.00051	0.00023	0.00006
43	0.00153	0.00123	0.00097	0.00076	0.00059	0.00045	0.00020	0.00005
44	0.00141	0.00112	0.00088	0.00068	0.00053	0.00040	0.00017	0.00004
45	0.00129	0.00102	0.00080	0.00062	0.00047	0.00036	0.00015	0.00003

TABLE 22-22
Yearly Savings Rate Factors
8% Savings Step-up Rate (A7)

Yrs	Assumed Rate of Return (A5)					
	1%	2%	3%	4%	5%	6%
1	0.99010	0.98039	0.97087	0.96154	0.95238	0.94340
2	0.47373	0.46685	0.46013	0.45356	0.44713	0.44084
3	0.30211	0.29633	0.29071	0.28522	0.27987	0.27466
4	0.21666	0.21155	0.20659	0.20176	0.19707	0.19251
5	0.16568	0.16105	0.15657	0.15222	0.14800	0.14392
6	0.13192	0.12768	0.12358	0.11961	0.11578	0.11207
7	0.10801	0.10409	0.10031	0.09666	0.09315	0.08976
8	0.09023	0.08660	0.08310	0.07974	0.07650	0.07339
9	0.07656	0.07317	0.06992	0.06681	0.06382	0.06096
10	0.06574	0.06258	0.05956	0.05667	0.05391	0.05126
11	0.05700	0.05405	0.05124	0.04855	0.04599	0.04354
12	0.04981	0.04706	0.04444	0.04194	0.03956	0.03729
13	0.04382	0.04125	0.03880	0.03647	0.03426	0.03216
14	0.03877	0.03636	0.03408	0.03190	0.02985	0.02790
15	0.03446	0.03221	0.03007	0.02805	0.02613	0.02433
16	0.03076	0.02865	0.02665	0.02477	0.02298	0.02131
17	0.02755	0.02558	0.02371	0.02195	0.02029	0.01873
18	0.02475	0.02291	0.02116	0.01952	0.01798	0.01653
19	0.02230	0.02058	0.01895	0.01741	0.01597	0.01463
20	0.02014	0.01853	0.01700	0.01557	0.01423	0.01298
21	0.01823	0.01672	0.01530	0.01396	0.01271	0.01155
22	0.01653	0.01512	0.01379	0.01254	0.01138	0.01029
23	0.01502	0.01370	0.01245	0.01129	0.01020	0.00920
24	0.01367	0.01243	0.01127	0.01018	0.00917	0.00823
25	0.01245	0.01130	0.01021	0.00920	0.00825	0.00738
26	0.01136	0.01028	0.00926	0.00832	0.00744	0.00663
27	0.01038	0.00937	0.00842	0.00753	0.00672	0.00596
28	0.00949	0.00854	0.00766	0.00683	0.00607	0.00537
29	0.00868	0.00780	0.00697	0.00620	0.00549	0.00484
30	0.00795	0.00713	0.00636	0.00564	0.00498	0.00437
31	0.00729	0.00652	0.00580	0.00513	0.00451	0.00395
32	0.00669	0.00597	0.00530	0.00467	0.00410	0.00357
33	0.00614	0.00547	0.00484	0.00426	0.00372	0.00323
34	0.00564	0.00502	0.00443	0.00389	0.00339	0.00293
35	0.00518	0.00460	0.00405	0.00355	0.00308	0.00266
36	0.00477	0.00422	0.00371	0.00324	0.00281	0.00241
37	0.00439	0.00388	0.00340	0.00296	0.00256	0.00219
38	0.00404	0.00356	0.00312	0.00271	0.00233	0.00199
39	0.00372	0.00328	0.00286	0.00248	0.00213	0.00181
40	0.00342	0.00301	0.00263	0.00227	0.00195	0.00165
41	0.00316	0.00277	0.00241	0.00208	0.00178	0.00150
42	0.00291	0.00255	0.00222	0.00191	0.00163	0.00137
43	0.00268	0.00235	0.00204	0.00175	0.00149	0.00125
44	0.00247	0.00217	0.00188	0.00161	0.00136	0.00114
45	0.00228	0.00200	0.00173	0.00147	0.00125	0.00104

TABLE 22-22 (Continued)
Yearly Savings Rate Factors
8% Savings Step-up Rate (A7)

	Assumed Rate of Return (A5)							
Yrs	7%	8%	9%	10%	11%	12%	15%	20%
1	0.93458	0.92593	0.91743	0.90909	0.90090	0.89286	0.86957	0.83333
2	0.43469	0.42867	0.42278	0.41701	0.41137	0.40584	0.38994	0.36550
3	0.26957	0.26461	0.25977	0.25505	0.25044	0.24594	0.23307	0.21354
4	0.18807	0.18376	0.17956	0.17548	0.17151	0.16765	0.15667	0.14023
5	0.13996	0.13612	0.13239	0.12878	0.12528	0.12189	0.11230	0.09814
6	0.10849	0.10503	0.10168	0.09845	0.09532	0.09230	0.08382	0.07147
7	0.08650	0.08336	0.08033	0.07740	0.07459	0.07188	0.06433	0.05349
8	0.07040	0.06753	0.06478	0.06213	0.05958	0.05714	0.05038	0.04083
9	0.05821	0.05558	0.05306	0.05065	0.04835	0.04614	0.04008	0.03164
10	0.04873	0.04632	0.04401	0.04181	0.03972	0.03772	0.03226	0.02480
11	0.04121	0.03899	0.03688	0.03487	0.03296	0.03114	0.02623	0.01961
12	0.03514	0.03309	0.03115	0.02931	0.02757	0.02592	0.02149	0.01563
13	0.03017	0.02828	0.02650	0.02482	0.02323	0.02173	0.01773	0.01253
14	0.02606	0.02432	0.02268	0.02113	0.01968	0.01832	0.01471	0.01010
15	0.02262	0.02102	0.01951	0.01809	0.01676	0.01552	0.01226	0.00817
16	0.01973	0.01824	0.01685	0.01555	0.01434	0.01321	0.01026	0.00664
17	0.01727	0.01590	0.01462	0.01342	0.01231	0.01128	0.00862	0.00541
18	0.01517	0.01390	0.01272	0.01163	0.01061	0.00967	0.00726	0.00442
19	0.01337	0.01220	0.01111	0.01010	0.00917	0.00831	0.00614	0.00362
20	0.01181	0.01073	0.00972	0.00880	0.00795	0.00716	0.00520	0.00297
21	0.01046	0.00946	0.00853	0.00768	0.00690	0.00619	0.00441	0.00244
22	0.00929	0.00836	0.00751	0.00672	0.00601	0.00536	0.00376	0.00201
23	0.00826	0.00741	0.00662	0.00590	0.00524	0.00465	0.00320	0.00166
24	0.00737	0.00657	0.00584	0.00518	0.00458	0.00404	0.00273	0.00137
25	0.00658	0.00584	0.00517	0.00456	0.00401	0.00352	0.00233	0.00113
26	0.00588	0.00520	0.00458	0.00402	0.00352	0.00307	0.00200	0.00093
27	0.00527	0.00464	0.00406	0.00355	0.00309	0.00268	0.00171	0.00077
28	0.00472	0.00414	0.00361	0.00314	0.00272	0.00234	0.00147	0.00064
29	0.00424	0.00370	0.00321	0.00278	0.00239	0.00205	0.00126	0.00053
30	0.00381	0.00331	0.00286	0.00246	0.00211	0.00179	0.00108	0.00044
31	0.00343	0.00297	0.00255	0.00218	0.00186	0.00157	0.00093	0.00036
32	0.00309	0.00266	0.00228	0.00194	0.00164	0.00138	0.00080	0.00030
33	0.00279	0.00239	0.00204	0.00172	0.00145	0.00121	0.00069	0.00025
34	0.00252	0.00215	0.00182	0.00153	0.00128	0.00107	0.00060	0.00021
35	0.00227	0.00193	0.00163	0.00137	0.00114	0.00094	0.00051	0.00017
36	0.00206	0.00174	0.00146	0.00122	0.00101	0.00083	0.00044	0.00014
37	0.00186	0.00157	0.00131	0.00108	0.00089	0.00073	0.00038	0.00012
38	0.00169	0.00141	0.00117	0.00097	0.00079	0.00064	0.00033	0.00010
39	0.00153	0.00127	0.00105	0.00086	0.00070	0.00057	0.00029	0.00008
40	0.00138	0.00115	0.00095	0.00077	0.00062	0.00050	0.00025	0.00007
41	0.00126	0.00104	0.00085	0.00069	0.00056	0.00044	0.00021	0.00006
42	0.00114	0.00094	0.00077	0.00062	0.00049	0.00039	0.00019	0.00005
43	0.00104	0.00085	0.00069	0.00055	0.00044	0.00035	0.00016	0.00004
44	0.00094	0.00077	0.00062	0.00050	0.00039	0.00031	0.00014	0.00003
45	0.00086	0.00070	0.00056	0.00044	0.00035	0.00027	0.00012	0.00003

TABLE 22-23
Yearly Savings Rate Factors
10% Savings Step-up Rate (A7)

Yrs	\multicolumn{6}{c}{Assumed Rate of Return (A5)}					
	1%	2%	3%	4%	5%	6%
1	0.99010	0.98039	0.97087	0.96154	0.95238	0.94340
2	0.46924	0.46245	0.45581	0.44932	0.44297	0.43676
3	0.29634	0.29071	0.28522	0.27987	0.27466	0.26957
4	0.21041	0.20550	0.20072	0.19607	0.19155	0.18716
5	0.15927	0.15487	0.15061	0.14648	0.14247	0.13859
6	0.12550	0.12152	0.11768	0.11396	0.11037	0.10689
7	0.10165	0.09804	0.09454	0.09117	0.08792	0.08478
8	0.08401	0.08070	0.07751	0.07444	0.07149	0.06864
9	0.07048	0.06745	0.06453	0.06173	0.05904	0.05645
10	0.05984	0.05705	0.05438	0.05181	0.04935	0.04700
11	0.05129	0.04872	0.04627	0.04392	0.04167	0.03952
12	0.04430	0.04194	0.03968	0.03753	0.03547	0.03351
13	0.03851	0.03633	0.03426	0.03228	0.03040	0.02860
14	0.03365	0.03165	0.02974	0.02793	0.02620	0.02456
15	0.02954	0.02770	0.02595	0.02428	0.02269	0.02119
16	0.02604	0.02434	0.02273	0.02119	0.01974	0.01837
17	0.02302	0.02146	0.01998	0.01857	0.01724	0.01598
18	0.02042	0.01898	0.01762	0.01632	0.01510	0.01395
19	0.01816	0.01683	0.01558	0.01439	0.01327	0.01221
20	0.01618	0.01496	0.01381	0.01272	0.01169	0.01072
21	0.01445	0.01333	0.01227	0.01126	0.01032	0.00943
22	0.01292	0.01189	0.01092	0.01000	0.00913	0.00832
23	0.01158	0.01063	0.00974	0.00889	0.00809	0.00735
24	0.01039	0.00952	0.00869	0.00792	0.00719	0.00651
25	0.00933	0.00853	0.00778	0.00706	0.00639	0.00577
26	0.00839	0.00766	0.00696	0.00631	0.00569	0.00512
27	0.00755	0.00688	0.00624	0.00564	0.00508	0.00455
28	0.00680	0.00619	0.00560	0.00505	0.00453	0.00405
29	0.00613	0.00557	0.00503	0.00453	0.00405	0.00361
30	0.00553	0.00502	0.00452	0.00406	0.00363	0.00322
31	0.00500	0.00452	0.00407	0.00365	0.00325	0.00288
32	0.00451	0.00408	0.00367	0.00328	0.00291	0.00257
33	0.00408	0.00368	0.00330	0.00295	0.00261	0.00230
34	0.00369	0.00333	0.00298	0.00265	0.00235	0.00206
35	0.00334	0.00300	0.00269	0.00239	0.00211	0.00185
36	0.00302	0.00272	0.00243	0.00215	0.00190	0.00166
37	0.00274	0.00246	0.00219	0.00194	0.00171	0.00149
38	0.00248	0.00222	0.00198	0.00175	0.00154	0.00134
39	0.00225	0.00201	0.00179	0.00158	0.00138	0.00120
40	0.00204	0.00182	0.00162	0.00143	0.00125	0.00108
41	0.00185	0.00165	0.00146	0.00129	0.00112	0.00097
42	0.00167	0.00149	0.00132	0.00116	0.00101	0.00087
43	0.00152	0.00135	0.00120	0.00105	0.00091	0.00079
44	0.00138	0.00123	0.00109	0.00095	0.00083	0.00071
45	0.00125	0.00111	0.00098	0.00086	0.00075	0.00064

TABLE 22-23 (Continued)
Yearly Savings Rate Factors
10% Savings Step-up Rate (A7)

	Assumed Rate of Return (A5)							
Yrs	7%	8%	9%	10%	11%	12%	15%	20%
1	0.93458	0.92593	0.91743	0.90909	0.90090	0.89286	0.86957	0.83333
2	0.43068	0.42474	0.41892	0.41322	0.40765	0.40219	0.38647	0.36232
3	0.26461	0.25977	0.25505	0.25044	0.24594	0.24155	0.22898	0.20991
4	0.18289	0.17873	0.17469	0.17075	0.16692	0.16320	0.15261	0.13672
5	0.13482	0.13117	0.12762	0.12418	0.12085	0.11761	0.10847	0.09493
6	0.10352	0.10027	0.09712	0.09408	0.09113	0.08829	0.08029	0.06862
7	0.08176	0.07884	0.07602	0.07331	0.07069	0.06817	0.06112	0.05099
8	0.06591	0.06328	0.06075	0.05831	0.05597	0.05373	0.04749	0.03865
9	0.05397	0.05159	0.04931	0.04712	0.04502	0.04302	0.03748	0.02974
10	0.04475	0.04259	0.04053	0.03855	0.03667	0.03487	0.02995	0.02316
11	0.03747	0.03551	0.03364	0.03186	0.03017	0.02855	0.02416	0.01821
12	0.03164	0.02986	0.02816	0.02655	0.02502	0.02357	0.01966	0.01442
13	0.02690	0.02528	0.02374	0.02228	0.02090	0.01960	0.01610	0.01150
14	0.02300	0.02153	0.02013	0.01881	0.01756	0.01639	0.01326	0.00922
15	0.01977	0.01842	0.01716	0.01596	0.01483	0.01378	0.01098	0.00742
16	0.01707	0.01584	0.01469	0.01360	0.01258	0.01163	0.00913	0.00600
17	0.01479	0.01367	0.01262	0.01164	0.01072	0.00986	0.00762	0.00486
18	0.01286	0.01184	0.01089	0.00999	0.00916	0.00838	0.00638	0.00396
19	0.01122	0.01029	0.00942	0.00861	0.00785	0.00715	0.00536	0.00323
20	0.00981	0.00896	0.00817	0.00743	0.00675	0.00612	0.00451	0.00264
21	0.00860	0.00783	0.00710	0.00643	0.00582	0.00525	0.00381	0.00216
22	0.00756	0.00685	0.00619	0.00558	0.00502	0.00451	0.00322	0.00177
23	0.00665	0.00601	0.00541	0.00486	0.00435	0.00388	0.00273	0.00145
24	0.00587	0.00528	0.00473	0.00423	0.00377	0.00335	0.00232	0.00120
25	0.00519	0.00465	0.00415	0.00369	0.00328	0.00290	0.00197	0.00099
26	0.00459	0.00410	0.00364	0.00323	0.00285	0.00251	0.00168	0.00081
27	0.00407	0.00362	0.00320	0.00283	0.00248	0.00217	0.00143	0.00067
28	0.00361	0.00320	0.00282	0.00248	0.00217	0.00189	0.00122	0.00055
29	0.00320	0.00283	0.00249	0.00217	0.00189	0.00164	0.00104	0.00046
30	0.00285	0.00251	0.00219	0.00191	0.00166	0.00143	0.00089	0.00038
31	0.00254	0.00222	0.00194	0.00168	0.00145	0.00124	0.00076	0.00031
32	0.00226	0.00197	0.00171	0.00148	0.00127	0.00108	0.00065	0.00026
33	0.00202	0.00176	0.00152	0.00130	0.00111	0.00095	0.00056	0.00022
34	0.00180	0.00156	0.00135	0.00115	0.00098	0.00083	0.00048	0.00018
35	0.00161	0.00139	0.00119	0.00102	0.00086	0.00072	0.00041	0.00015
36	0.00144	0.00124	0.00106	0.00090	0.00076	0.00063	0.00036	0.00012
37	0.00129	0.00111	0.00094	0.00079	0.00067	0.00055	0.00031	0.00010
38	0.00115	0.00099	0.00084	0.00070	0.00059	0.00049	0.00026	0.00008
39	0.00103	0.00088	0.00074	0.00062	0.00052	0.00043	0.00023	0.00007
40	0.00093	0.00079	0.00066	0.00055	0.00046	0.00037	0.00020	0.00006
41	0.00083	0.00070	0.00059	0.00049	0.00040	0.00033	0.00017	0.00005
42	0.00075	0.00063	0.00053	0.00043	0.00036	0.00029	0.00015	0.00004
43	0.00067	0.00056	0.00047	0.00039	0.00031	0.00025	0.00013	0.00003
44	0.00060	0.00050	0.00042	0.00034	0.00028	0.00022	0.00011	0.00003
45	0.00054	0.00045	0.00037	0.00030	0.00025	0.00020	0.00009	0.00002

CONCLUSION

The planner's work sheet that you have just reviewed, as well as the other material in this chapter, will help you and your client to set goals and to better understand the retirement needs analysis. Properly utilizing the tools provided and properly analyzing the assumptions needed will assist clients immeasurably. We feel it bears repetition, however, that this is an art form, not a science. The numbers are not absolute. Your best judgment should be used in conjunction with what this chapter has given you to achieve the best results for your client.

CHAPTER REVIEW

Review Questions

Review questions are based on the learning objectives in this chapter. Thus, a [22-3] at the end of a question means that the question is based on learning objective 22-3. If there are multiple objectives, they are all listed.

1. Using the replacement-ratio method, find the amount of income needed (in today's dollars) to fund the desired retirement lifestyle for the following clients: [22-1]
    a. Jane is 63 years old, earns $100,000, and anticipates no increase in standard of living between now and retirement at age 65. Jane is comfortable assuming an 80 percent replacement ratio.
    b. Keith is 45 years old, earns $50,000, and anticipates a 2 percent growth rate in lifestyle until retirement at age 65. Keith would be comfortable with a 90 percent replacement ratio.

2. Explain how to determine a client's retirement income status. [22-1]

3. Discuss which of the following retirement resources needs inflation protection from the client: [22-1]
    a. Social Security benefits
    b. pension benefits
    c. dividend income from a stock portfolio
    d. the client's retirement income deficit

4. Tom has a taxable investment that earns 10 percent interest. Tom pays taxes at a marginal rate of 28 percent. What is the after-tax rate of return that Tom will receive? [22-1]

5. Discuss the methods that can be used to liquidate retirement funds. [22-1]

6. What method can be used to help keep clients from outliving their retirement savings? [22-1]

7. What amount of money would it take to have a retirement income that provides $16,000 worth of purchasing power throughout a 35-year retirement period (assuming the fund earns 7 percent interest and the benefits increase by 3 percent each year)? [22-1]

8. How much money does your client have to accumulate by retirement in order to protect against the inflation-related loss of purchasing power on a $33,000 level annual pension (assuming the fund assets earn 6 percent interest, inflation will be 2 percent, and the funds will be payable for 30 years)? [22-1]

9. Your client (aged 48) would like to use level annual funding to accumulate $350,000 at retirement (at age 65). Determine the amount of the level annual contribution assuming contributed funds earn 7 percent interest. [22-2]

10. Your client (aged 60), would like to use stepped-up annual funding to accumulate $150,000 by retirement (at age 65). Assume (1) an 8 percent interest rate and (2) an increase in contributions each year by a 4 percent inflation rate. [22-2]
    a. Determine the amount of the first annual contribution.
    b. Determine the amounts of contributions for the remaining 4 years.

11. Kevin and Julie (both aged 45) are married and have a combined income of $80,000. In addition, they have $300,000 set aside for retirement in Kevin's 401(k) plan, and are expecting no money from a defined-benefit pension from Julie's employment. Both will receive $10,000 (totaling $20,000) from Social Security. They make the following assumptions: [22-3]
    a. inflation rate prior to retirement: 4 percent
    b. inflation rate after retirement: 4 percent
    c. number of years until retirement: 19
    d. expected duration of retirement years: 25
    e. rate of return prior to retirement: 8 percent
    f. rate of return after retirement: 7 percent
    g. savings step-up with rate: 6 percent
    Using the retirement planning worksheet from the text, calculate the amount they need to save next year.

NOTES

1. For keystrokes on the financial calculator, input 35[N] instead of 25[N] in the previous example. $585,999 − $372,636=$213,363.

2. Again, because N is infinite, a financial calculator solution using time value of money inputs isn't possible.

3. The solution is a negative number because the financial calculator requires at least one of the cash flows to be negative. In this case, it makes sense that Joe invests ($9,881) each year to receive $154,594 at age 65.

4. Changing the future value [FV] in the keystrokes shown above will solve for the required annual investments for the 35-year liquidation and the income-only result.

Additional Retirement Planning Issues

Learning Objectives

An understanding of the material in this chapter should enable you to

---

23-1.   Identify what a client needs to know about the home as a financial asset.

23-2.   Describe housing alternatives, including age-restricted housing and life-care communities.

23-3.   List the factors to consider when a client decides to retire out of state.

23-4.   Review ways to use the home as a financial asset.

23-5.   Identify benefits that are included and excluded under Medicare.

23-6.   Identify the solutions to the pre-Medicare/postretirement health care gap.

23-7.   List and explain the characteristics of long-term care insurance policies.

23-8.   Identify the types of documents individuals can use to control their own medical care after they become unable to make decisions for themselves.

Chapter Outline

CHOOSING TO MOVE

Housing issues that face the retiree vary from client to client. Planners need to understand that the disposition of the family homestead and the decision of where to reside during the retirement years are, first and foremost, personal choices with a different meaning for every client. In other words, the psychological attachment to the home in many cases far outweighs the financial and tax wisdom involved with thinking of the home as an asset. It is in this context that financial services professionals must deal with planning for the disposition of a retired client's home. Factors to take into consideration include

- Although one's house remains the same, the character of the neighborhood can change during retirement with the deaths and/or departures of friends.
- The house that was suitable for raising a family may not be suitable for retirement.
- The costs of heating, cooling, cleaning, and maintaining a house with empty rooms and a child-sized yard can be prohibitive.
- Even a mortgage-free house can be a financial drain that robs the retiree of income. Besides the additional costs involved in maintaining a home, the equity that can be gained from its sale can be used to provide needed retirement income.

Tax Implications of Selling a Home

When considering whether or not to move into another living arrangement, clients need to understand the tax implications of selling their home. Today the rules are quite liberal, and in most cases the gain will not be subject to federal income tax (note that some states do not follow the federal scheme). This means that if the client would prefer condo living or a smaller home, replacing the old home with a less expensive one will free up assets.

IRC Sec. 121

Specifically, *IRC Sec. 121* provides that taxpayers of any age who sell their homes can exclude up to $250,000 of their gain ($500,000 for married taxpayers filing jointly). To qualify for the exclusion, the property must have been owned and used by the taxpayer as a principal residence for an aggregate of at least 2 years out of the 5 years ending on the date of sale.

For married taxpayers, both spouses have to meet the 2-year use requirement—otherwise the available exclusion is $250,000 rather than $500,000. However, the couple can qualify for the higher $500,000 amount even if just one spouse owns the home.

The exclusion may generally be used only once every 2 years. If a single taxpayer marries someone who has used the exclusion within the past 2 years, that taxpayer is allowed a maximum exclusion of $250,000 (rather than $500,000) until 2 years have passed since the exclusion was used by either spouse. If the taxpayer fails to meet the ownership and use rules and the sale of the home is due to a change of employment, change of health, or other "unforeseen" circumstance, a reduced exclusion may still be available.

YOUR FINANCIAL SERVICES PRACTICE:
PLANNING FOR A LATER MARRIAGE

Even though the current home sale exclusion rule is quite flexible, it could cause problems for a couple planning to marry if each owns a home that they plan to sell. If the sales occur after the marriage, the 2-year rule could prohibit the use of the exclusion for both homes. In this case, the couple should consider selling one or both homes prior to the marriage.

Planning for a Move

downsize

A common reason for changing residences at retirement is to *downsize*—that is, to purchase a retirement residence that costs less than the one being sold in order to transfer a portion of the gain (enhanced by tax breaks) into cash for retirement. Retirees may also change residences to relocate to an area where their dollars can be stretched further because the living costs are lower. Others move to avail themselves of living circumstances uniquely geared to the retired population. These residences include life-care communities and other senior living arrangements. Still others move because they need current care, such as nursing homes and assisted living arrangements. Let us take a look at these issues, starting with life-care communities.

**YOUR FINANCIAL SERVICES PRACTICE:
RESIDENCE CHOICES LITERATURE**

The Internet offers easy access to a wealth of information about senior housing. Several resources are listed here. See www.seniorresource.com for housing information for seniors. The American Seniors Housing Organization (www.seniorhousing.com) is an organization for those in the senior housing industry. Senior sites (www.seniorsites.com) list housing and services offered through nonprofit organizations. New LifeStyles (www.newlifestyles.com) is a resource for senior residential care housing options. Finally, AARP (www.aarp.org) is an excellent resource for a wide range of information for seniors.

Life-Care Communities

There are many varieties of life-care communities (also called continuing-care retirement communities) throughout the United States. In fact, because of the number of options that exist, it may be best to explain what life-care communities are by explaining what they are not. Life-care communities are not simply retirement villages where people over a specified age reside; nor are they simply nursing homes where senior patients go for custodial and medical care. A *life-care community* is a combination of the two extremes, plus a little bit of everything in between. Although life-care communities are often thought to be only for the wealthy, the truth is that there are substantial variations in price among these communities, and the majority of them are nonprofit organizations.

life-care community

While it is true that facilities, fees, and services vary widely from one life-care community to the next, several common features do exist. Most frequently your clients will pay a one-time up-front fee that can range from $20,000 to $500,000, depending on the quality of the community and the nature of the contract. In some cases, the fee is nonrefundable; in others, the fee is fully refundable if the individual retiree, couple, or surviving spouse leaves. And in still other cases, the fee is refundable based on an agreed-upon schedule. In addition to a one-time up-front fee, residents generally pay a monthly fee that can range from less than $1,000 per month to more than $5,000 per month. In part, the monthly fee depends on the dwelling unit chosen and any services rendered.

The residential accommodation may be a single-family dwelling or an apartment. It can change with the retiree's needs to a skilled-nursing facility or a long-term care facility. Most life-care communities point with pride to the safety of the facility and its accessibility to those who are suffering from one or more diseases associated with aging.

Services may include the following:

- some level of housekeeping, including linen service
- some level of meal preparation (taking one or more meals in a common dining hall)
- facilities for crafts, tennis, golf, and other types of recreation
- transportation to and from area shopping and events
- supervision of exercise and diet
- skilled-nursing care (if needed)
- long-term care, including custodial care (if needed)

One key element to the life-care contract is the guarantee of space in a nursing home or assisted living facility if it becomes necessary. The guarantee of long-term care can be approached in several ways. One approach is to pay in advance for unlimited nursing home care at little or no increase in monthly payments. Another approach is to cover nursing home care up to a specified amount with a per diem rate paid by your client for usage over and above the specified amount.

Retirees need to be careful when choosing a life-care community. With such a large financial commitment, the retiree will want to scrutinize contracts and be sure the selected organization will be able to fulfill its promises.

Other Housing Options

age-restricted housing

There is a wide range of senior housing arrangements between independent living and a life-care community. *Age-restricted housing* options include apartment buildings, retirement hotels, condominiums, subdivisions, and mobile home parks. These housing communities can provide safety, companionship, and special services. It is not uncommon for these communities to have special recreation and leisure facilities, such as golf courses, craft rooms, swimming pools, game rooms, and libraries. Many housing communities also contain amenities to make living almost self-contained—for example, food stores, banks, hairdressers, and other services.

Under the Federal Fair Housing law, a community can restrict age but only if the rules of one of two statutory exemptions are followed. Under the first, a community can restrict residents to age 62 or older. However, if this limitation is imposed, no individuals younger than that age are allowed. This could cause a problem if a retiree moved in and later found that a child or grandchild needed housing. A more flexible exemption allows a community to limit eligibility to age 55. With this exception, some individuals under age 55 can be allowed as long as 80 percent of all residents are 55 or older and at least one resident in each living unit is aged 55 or older. This alternative is often a better option for many retirees.

Of course, age-restricted housing is not for everyone; some find this type of living depressing and prefer being in a broader community with a variety of ages. A client needs to weigh this concern with the services offered by the facility.

Relocation Out of State

The decision to relocate to another state is often motivated by such factors as climate, location of friends and relatives, and affection for the area itself. For clients considering such a move, it is important to weigh the decision carefully because it is not easily reversible. Factors to consider with respect to relocating out of state include

domicile

- If one spouse should die, will the other want to cope with another uprooting?
- What are state income taxes, property taxes, transfer taxes, and death taxes?
- For the client with more than one home, which state would be declared the domicile? (*Domicile* is the client's intended permanent home. Such factors as where the client spends time, is registered to vote, has a driver's license, where his or her planner resides, and where his or her will is executed help to determine what residence is the client's permanent home.)
- Does the state or local government provide specific tax breaks for seniors?

Finally, before any move, the individual should consider looking for a replacement home that is equipped to meet his or her needs. Obviously, changes could later be made to a home, but it would probably be less expensive to purchase a home that already includes such characteristics.

PLANNING FOR CLIENTS REMAINING IN THEIR HOMES

A financial planner may look at a client's large, four-bedroom house and see unnecessary heating and maintenance costs. The client, on the other hand, sees the extra rooms as necessary for returning children and visiting relatives. There are other benefits to remaining in a current home. Starting life over in a new location means developing new routines, finding new merchants and service providers, and losing old friends and neighbors who can be relied on for companionship and favors. The value of the retiree's social network is often crucial to his or her sense of well-being.

Retirees who stay in their homes will probably want to make some changes to make the home safer and to minimize ongoing maintenance. This means taking actions such as adding guard rails in the shower and slip-proofing bathroom and tub floors and other floor surfaces. The outside of the home should be examined for cracked or uneven sidewalks and inadequate lighting. Additional handrails may be appropriate both inside and outside the house. Other changes that might be helpful to reduce ongoing home maintenance are the addition of siding or replacement windows. Appliances such as dishwashers, garbage disposals and compactors, central vacuuming systems, and water filters (versus bottled water) can reduce daily labor.

Retirees who stay in their homes also need to be prepared for the possibility of needing additional services. This requires financial readiness, but also research to see what is available in their area. The types of services that may be needed include

- outdoor home maintenance and gardening
- indoor home maintenance
- cleaning services
- driving services
- home care ranging from meal preparation to help with bathing and dressing
- emergency call/response systems

Creating Income from the Home

Clients who have paid off their mortgages and want to "age in place" may still be able to tap the equity in their homes if they need finances to maintain their current standard of living. There are a number of options for this group, including a sale-leaseback, a home-sharing arrangement, and a reverse mortgage.

sale-leaseback

Under a *sale-leaseback* arrangement, your client sells his or her house to an investor and then rents it back from the investor under a lifetime lease. Thus, your client can garner extra retirement resources, make use of the home sale exclusion, and still remain in his or her home. Often the purchaser is a family member, because the sale of the house removes it from the retiree's estate. The sale-leaseback agreement can specify future rents or stipulate how changes in the rental rate will be determined (for example, a periodic market value appraisal by a neutral third party). The agreement should also clearly spell out that it is the new owner's responsibility to pay property taxes, special assessments, insurance, and major maintenance and repairs.

Another way to use the home as an asset is a home-sharing arrangement. Home sharing helps people stay independent; it can also provide companionship and reduce housing costs. In forging a home-sharing arrangement, the client should carefully consider what he or she is looking for. Is the arrangement more about friendship and companionship or simply a means of lowering expenses? Either motivation can result in a successful relationship, as long as the parties entering into the arrangement are clear. If the arrangement is with a relative or friend, it is important either to enter into a formal agreement or at least to discuss expectations about how the arrangement will work and also to agree on how the arrangement will end.

Reverse Mortgages

reverse mortgage

A *reverse mortgage* is a loan against an individual's home that requires no repayment as long as the individual continues to live in the home. In other words, a reverse mortgage is a strategy that allows a client to live in his or her home and take substantial amounts of money for current needs with no current payments. They are typically available only when all of the owners are aged 62 or older and when the home is the principal residence. Also, the home must either have no debt or only a small debt that can be paid off with part of the reverse mortgage loan.

The federally sponsored Home Equity Conversion Mortgage (HECM) program is the most popular type of reverse mortgage. FHA insures HECM loans to protect lenders against loss if amounts withdrawn exceed equity when the property is sold. Any lender authorized to make HUD-insured loans, such as banks, mortgage companies, and savings and loan associations, can participate in the HECM program. There are also a number of other privately sponsored programs.

The amount of loan payments made to the client depends on the client's age (or clients' joint ages), the amount of equity the home currently has or is expected to have, and the interest rate and fees that are being charged. For example, it has been indicated that based on recent interest rates, a 65-year-old could borrow up to 26 percent of the value of the home while an 85-year-old could borrow up to 56 percent. The amount that can be received also depends on the mortgage program selected. In many cases, the HECM program pays the largest amount; however, in some cases, certain special needs loans offered by a state or local government program may be more favorable. For very expensive homes, a private mortgage program may be the best choice.

Payment options vary depending on the specific program, but generally fall within a number of categories:

- immediate cash advance—a lump-sum payment at closing
- credit line account—the option to take cash advances up to the maximum loan value during the life of the loan. Some credit line

programs have a fixed maximum while others offer a limit that increases with a stated interest rate each year.

- monthly cash advance—a definitive monthly payment that can be stated as a specific number of years, as long as the person lives in the home. Some programs also allow the participant to purchase a life or joint and survivor annuity that will make payments over the individual's entire life.

**YOUR FINANCIAL SERVICES PRACTICE:
FINDING A REVERSE MORTGAGE PROGRAM**

To find out more about the HECM program call (888-466-3487) or visit HUD at www.hud.gov for lists of approved counseling agencies that counsel individuals about the program and of approved lenders. Additional information is available from two nonprofit organizations: the American Association of Retired Persons (AARP) Home Equity Conversion Information Center (202-434-6044) and the National Center for Home Equity Conversion (NCHEC) at 7373 147th St., Room 115, Apple Valley MN 55124. To find out about other types of reverse mortgage programs, visit the National Reverse Mortgage Lenders Assn. at www.reversemortgage.org or call 202-939-1765 for an up-to-date list of lenders that clearly tells you which reverse mortgage products are offered by each listed lender.

The amount of the debt grows based on the amount paid and accumulated interest. Typically, the loan only has to be repaid when the last surviving borrower dies, sells the home, or permanently moves away. Most loans are nonrecourse, meaning the maximum amount that has to be repaid is the value of the home. If property values have eroded, the borrower has received a windfall and the lender ends up with a loss.

Because these programs are truly loans, if the retiree wants or needs to sell the home, any equity that exceeds the loan balance is the property of the retiree. If the property is sold at death, the heirs receive the additional equity. Also, because these are loans, payments received by the retiree as part of the mortgage program are not considered taxable income and interest expense is deductible but only at the time it is paid (when the loan is repaid).

MEDICARE AND RETIREE HEALTH CARE

Any discussion of planning for a retiree's health care should start with an analysis of the Medicare system. Today, discussing Medicare is a fairly complex proposition, because eligible persons can choose from the original system as well as a number of other options.

Medicare Part A

Medicare Part B

The original Medicare program consists of two parts. *Medicare Part A* is the hospital portion. It provides benefits for expenses incurred in hospitals, skilled-nursing facilities, hospices (in limited circumstances), and for home health care for a condition previously treated in a hospital or skilled-nursing facility. *Medicare Part B* is the supplementary medical insurance portion of Medicare. It provides benefits for physicians' and surgeons' fees, diagnostic tests, certain drugs and medical supplies, rental of certain medical equipment, and home health service when prior hospitalization has not occurred. Part C of Medicare is a series of options that beneficiaries can elect in lieu of the original program. Part D is a drug benefit that is available to all Medicare beneficiaries. Let's take a closer look at the entire Medicare system, starting with the question of eligibility.

Eligibility for Medicare

Most of your senior clients will be eligible to receive health benefits under the federal government's Medicare program. Part A is available *at no cost* to most persons aged 65 or older. Among those eligible are

- everyone aged 65 and over who is receiving a monthly Social Security retirement or survivor's benefit
- people aged 65 and over who have deferred receiving Social Security retirement benefits (these people must apply for Medicare; others in "pay status" are automatically enrolled)
- 65-year-old civilian employees of the federal government who did not elect into the Social Security system under the 1983 law
- people who receive or are eligible to receive railroad retirement benefits
- any spouse aged 65 and over of a fully insured worker who is at least aged 62

Any other people (aged 65 or older) who do not meet the requirements to receive Part A at no cost may voluntarily enroll by paying a premium ($410 per month in 2007). Any person enrolled for Part A of Medicare is eligible for Part B. However, a monthly premium must be paid. This annually adjusted premium represents only about 25 percent of the cost of the benefits provided for many clients. Starting in 2007, Medicare Part B enrollees with higher incomes ($80,000 single, $160,000 MFJ) will pay higher premiums based on the extent their income exceeds the threshold. See the chart below.

Medicare: Part B Monthly Premium Changes

Starting in 2007, changes instituted by the Medicare Modernization Act require those with higher incomes to pay a greater percentage of Medicare Part B costs. Before the law change, Part B beneficiaries were responsible for premiums approximately equal to 25 percent of the total cost of the benefit. (The federal government pays the remaining 75 percent.) In order to bolster Medicare's sustainability, beneficiaries with incomes over specified thresholds will pay a monthly premium equal to 35, 50, 65, or 80 percent of the total cost, depending on their income level, by the end of the three-year transition period. The numbers for 2007 are listed below.

	2005 Modified Adjusted Gross Income	**Part B Premium**
Single	$80,000 or less	$93.50
MFJ	$160,000 or less	
Single	Over $80,000 up to $100,000	$105.80
MFJ	Over $160,000 up to $200,000	
Single	Over $100,000 up to $150,000	$124.40
MFJ	Over $200,000 up to $300,000	
Single	Over $150,000 up to $200,000	$142.90
MFJ	Over $300,000 up to $400,000	
Single	Over $200,000	$161.40
MFJ	Over $400,000	

YOUR FINANCIAL SERVICES PRACTICE: MISCONCEPTIONS ABOUT MEDICARE ELIGIBILITY

Clients can have several misconceptions about eligibility for Medicare that should be corrected. It is important to point out the following:

- Those who retire early and elect to start Social Security at age 62 are *not* eligible for Medicare until they reach age 65.
- Spouses who are younger than 65 and are married to a retiree over age 65 are *not* eligible for Medicare until they turn 65.
- Despite the Part B premiums, the system offers a relatively good value. In other words, rejecting Part B coverage to avoid paying premiums is not usually the best choice.

Enrolling in Medicare is quite simple. Those who will have started receiving Social Security at or before age 65 will receive a notice that they will be automatically enrolled at age 65. If a client does not want Part B coverage, he or she must reject it in writing within 2 months of receiving the notice. Others should contact their local Social Security office (see the phone book for the local address and phone number or go online at www.medicare.gov or call 1-800-633-4227) about 3 months before their 65th birthday to sign up for Medicare.

Part A Benefits

benefit period

Part A pays for inpatient hospital services for up to 90 days in each *benefit period* (also referred to as a *spell of illness*). Benefit period is a key concept. A benefit period begins the first time a Medicare recipient is hospitalized and ends only after the recipient has been out of a hospital or skilled-nursing facility for 60 consecutive days. A hospitalization after that 60-day period then begins a new benefit period. There is no limit on the number of benefit periods a person may have during his or her lifetime. In addition to 90 days of hospital coverage within each benefit period, Medicare covers an additional 60 *lifetime reserve days* over an individual's lifetime.

lifetime reserve days

Example: Barbara goes into the hospital for 45 days, goes home for 2 weeks, and returns to the hospital for 80 days. Barbara's 125 days of hospitalization will be considered to be within one benefit period because there was not a gap of 60 days between hospital visits. Barbara is covered for 90 days under the benefit period rule. In addition, Barbara chose to use 35 of her reserve days to cover the full amount of time she spent in the hospital (125 days).

Covered services for Part A hospital benefits include what you would expect, including operating expenses, semi-private room and meals, nursing services, social services, use of hospital equipment, rehabilitation services, and diagnostic testing. In each benefit period, covered hospital expenses are paid in full for 60 days, subject to an initial deductible of $992 per benefit period (2007 figure). A coinsurance charge of $248 (2007 figure) applies to each of the next 30 days (days 61–90), and a coinsurance charge of $496 (2007 figure) applies to lifetime reserve days.

In many cases, a patient may no longer require continuous hospital care but may not be well enough to go home. Consequently, Part A provides benefits for care in a skilled-nursing facility. This coverage can be triggered only if a physician certifies that skilled-nursing care or rehabilitative services are needed for a condition that was treated in a hospital within the last 30 days. The Part A skilled-nursing facility per diem for days 21 through 100 is $124 (2007 figure).

Starting in 1998, Parts A and B of Medicare began to share the costs of providing home health care. If a patient can be treated at home for a medical condition, Part A will pay up to the full cost for up to 100 home visits by a home health agency, but only if the visits occur after a hospital or skilled-nursing facility stay. Home health agencies specialize in providing nursing services and other therapeutic services. Part B covers additional visits or visits that do not occur after a hospital stay. To receive these benefits, a person must be confined at home and treated under a home health plan set up by a physician. The care needed must include skilled-nursing services, physical therapy, or speech therapy.

Hospice benefits are available under Part A of Medicare for terminally ill persons who have a life expectancy of 6 months or less. The election of hospice benefits has an effect on the participant's other eligible benefits under Medicare.

There are some circumstances under which Part A of Medicare will not pay benefits. Luxury services and elective surgeries are not covered and most services provided outside of the United States are not covered. Procedures performed in a federal facility, such as a veterans' hospital, and services covered under workers' compensation are also excluded. In other cases, Medicare is the secondary payer of benefits. This is the case

- when primary coverage under an employer-provided medical expense plan is elected by (1) an employee or spouse aged 65 or older or (2) a disabled beneficiary
- when medical care can be paid under any liability policy, including policies providing automobile no-fault benefits
- in the first 18 months for end-stage renal disease when an employer-provided medical expense plan provides coverage. By law, employer plans cannot specifically exclude this coverage during the 18-month period.

Medicare pays only if complete coverage is not available from these sources, and then only to the extent that benefits are less than would otherwise be payable under Medicare.

Part B Benefits

Part B of Medicare provides primarily for doctors' expenses. These include physicians' fees and surgeons' fees (including anesthesia). It also includes a number of other diagnostic and therapeutic expenses, such as

- diagnostic tests in a hospital or a physician's office
- physical or occupational therapy
- radiation therapy
- medical supplies and devices

- ambulance service
- Pap smears and yearly mammograms
- flu and pneumococcal vaccine and its administration
- emergency room care
- drugs and biologicals that cannot be self-administered

With some exceptions, Part B pays 80 percent of the approved charges for covered medical expenses after the satisfaction of an annual deductible. Out-of-hospital psychiatric services are generally limited to 50-percent reimbursement. Annual maximums may also apply to some services, such as psychiatric services and physical therapy.

Although the preceding list may appear comprehensive, there are numerous medical products and services not covered by Part B, some of which represent significant expenses for senior clients. They include the following:

- custodial care
- routine physical, eye, and hearing examinations and tests that are part of such exams (except some mammograms and Pap smears)
- routine foot care
- immunizations (except flu or pneumococcal vaccinations or immunizations required because of an injury or immediate risk of infection)
- cosmetic surgery, unless it is needed because of an accidental injury or to improve the function of a malformed part of the body
- dental care, unless it involves jaw or facial bone surgery or the setting of fractures
- dentures
- eyeglasses
- hearing aids
- orthopedic shoes

Part D Drug Benefits

The Medicare Prescription Drug, Improvement, and Modernization Act of 2004 (MMA) added a prescription drug benefit to Medicare—Medicare Part D. Part D is a voluntary prescription drug benefit available to all Medicare beneficiaries entitled to Part A and enrolled in Part B. The program is run through private plans and the act provides that most eligible persons will have access to at least two plans. The cost for the premium depends on the chosen plan and can average about $30–$35 per month.

Each plan will develop a list of covered drugs. Although all prescription drugs do not have to be covered, a plan must cover at least two prescription drugs in each therapeutic category and class.

The standard prescription drug program has an annual deductible of $250. After the deductible, the plan will pay 75 percent of the next $2,000 of prescription drug costs covered by the plan. Benefits then cease until a beneficiary's total drug costs (including the deductible) reach $5,100. The plan will then pay 95 percent of covered drug costs in excess of $5,100.

ADDITIONAL COVERAGE FOR THOSE ELIGIBLE FOR MEDICARE

Medigap insurance

For many years, individuals who wanted more coverage than the original Medicare plan could purchase a supplemental plan, generally called *Medigap insurance*, through an insurance company. This is still true, but today those eligible for traditional Medicare can now opt out of it in favor of a managed care plan. These alternatives typically limit the participant's choice of medical service providers in exchange for additional services. Also, some Medicare recipients may be eligible for retiree medical coverage at work. Each of these three options is discussed below.

No matter what the medical program, few if any cover long-term custodial care. For this contingency, many individuals should consider a long-term care policy. This is discussed in a later section of the chapter.

Medicare Supplement (Medigap) Insurance

For retired clients who do not have employer-provided insurance or who have inadequate amounts, there is Medicare supplement (Medigap) insurance. Medigap is a tool that can be used by private insurance planners to supplement the inadequacies of the Medicare program and to relieve seniors of part or all of their cost-sharing burden. In other words, as one expert puts it, Medigap "eliminates the risk of unpredictable and uncontrollable bills by converting them into a predictable and affordable series of insurance payments."

Medigap policies are regulated by both the state and the federal governments. Laws protect consumers and provide for the following:

- notice that no individual needs more than one Medigap policy
- notice that Medicaid-eligible individuals do not need a Medigap policy
- easy comparison among rival policies
- guaranteed renewability
- automatic policy changes whenever Medicare deductibles and coinsurance change

Most important is that the law guarantees that, for 6 months immediately following enrollment in Medicare medical insurance (Part B), a person aged 65 or older cannot be denied Medigap insurance because of health problems. To protect insurance companies, there is the possibility that a preexisting conditions clause will apply during the first 6 months of the policy's life. This clause, however, is the maximum insurer protection against adverse selection allowed under the law.

Under National Association of Insurance Commissioners (NAIC) direction, up until 2006, 10 standard policy forms for Medigap coverage have been available (referred to as Policies A–J). Because of the Part D drug benefits, policies H, I, and J are no longer sold and two new policies, K and L, have been created. The law does not require insurance companies to sell all of the standardized forms. However, policies that are sold must conform to the standards and be identifiable as one of the forms. All policies must provide the following basic benefits:

YOUR FINANCIAL SERVICES PRACTICE:
MEDIGAP 6-MONTH WINDOW

Probably the single most important information to convey to clients about Medigap policies is the 6-month window period after initial Medicare eligibility at age 65. If the client does not purchase a policy at that time, he or she could be denied if he or she has serious health problems.

- coverage for either all of the Medicare Part A inpatient hospital deductible or none of it. Insurers are not permitted to pay only a portion of the deductible.
- coverage for the Part A daily coinsurance amount for the 61st day through the 90th day of hospitalization in each Medicare benefit period
- coverage for the Part A daily coinsurance amount for each of Medicare's 60 nonrenewable, lifetime hospital inpatient reserve days used
- after all Medicare hospital benefits are exhausted, coverage for the hospital charges that otherwise would have been paid by Medicare for a lifetime maximum of 365 days
- reasonable costs of the first three pints of blood
- coverage for the Part B coinsurance amount after the policyowner pays the Part B annual deductible

Policy A (see table 23-1) is the standard for the base policy with the minimum coverage and the lowest premium. All other Medicare supplement standard policy forms must contain everything provided in policy A, plus the additional coverage set forth for the specific standard form being complied with. A significant number of Medicare supplement insurers have decided to restrict their offering to fewer than all of the policy forms. Any insurance company selling more than one variation must sell policy A as one of the available choices.

TABLE 23-1
What the 10 Standard Medigap Policies Offer

√ Policy offers this benefit   μ Policy does not offer this benefit

Policy type	A	B	C	D	E	F	G			
Basic benefits	√	√	√	√	√	√	√			
Part A–hospital deductible	μ	√	√	√	√	√	√			
Part B–doctor deductible	μ	μ	√	μ	μ	√	μ			
20% coinsurance	√	√	√	√	√	√	√			
Part B–% excess doctor bill	μ	μ	μ	μ	μ	100%	80%			
Additional 365 hospital days	√	√	√	√	√	√	√			
Skilled-nursing coinsurance	μ	μ	√	√	√	√	√			
At-home recovery	μ	μ	μ	√	μ	μ	√			
Prescription drugs	μ	μ	μ	μ	μ	μ	μ			
Preventive care	μ	μ	μ	μ	√	μ	μ			
Health care abroad	μ	μ	√	√	√	√	√			

The two new Medicare supplement plans (available beginning in 2006) are designated as plans K and L. These plans provide the basic Medicare supplement benefits plus the Part A hospital deductible and skilled-nursing supplements plans, plans K and L require cost sharing by the insured for certain covered services, subject to an out-of-pocket limit.

Plan K requires the insured to pay 50 percent of the following:

- the Part A deductible
- the daily co-payment for days 21 through 100 of skilled-nursing facility care
- the first 3 pints of blood
- the percentage participation for Part B services

When the insured's out-of-pocket payments for these services plus the Part B deductible equal $4,000, Plan K will pay 100 percent of the self-responsible amounts for Medicare services for the rest of the calendar year.

Plan L is similar to Plan K, except that the percentage that insured must pay is 25 percent rather than 50 percent. In addition, the out-of-pocket limit is $2,000.

Today, insurance companies can also offer Medigap policies that are referred to as Medicare SELECT. A Medicare SELECT policy must meet all the requirements that apply to a Medigap policy, and it must be one of the prescribed benefit packages. The only difference is that a Medicare SELECT policy may require that the recipient use doctors or hospitals within its network in order to receive full benefits. Because of this limitation, a Medicare SELECT policy generally has a lower premium than a regular Medigap policy.

Managed Care Option under Medicare

Under Part C of Medicare, participants may now elect to have their Medicare benefits provided by a managed care plan such as a health maintenance organization (HMO), a preferred-provider organization (PPO), or an insurance company. The participant must still pay the Part B premium for Medicare and may—in some plans, in some regions of the country—have to pay an additional premium to the managed care plan. Managed care plans in many large cities do not charge a separate or additional premium.

Each managed care plan subcontracts for the Department of Health and Human Services to provide benefits at least equal to, and sometimes better than, those available under Medicare. Medicare then reimburses the managed care plan for services it provides to participants electing the managed care coverage. The managed care plans usually provide additional benefits, such as prescription drugs, eyeglasses, hearing aids, and routine physical exams; also, they usually eliminate deductibles and lower copay amounts to very nominal levels. These additional benefits are often similar to what is provided by Medigap policies. Because of this redundancy, the managed care participants tend to drop Medigap policies.

The important factor in managed care plan operations is that services must be provided to participants by qualified providers who are affiliated with, or have contracted with, the plan. The participant is not able to seek covered services from health care providers outside the plan except in emergencies. By electing the managed care option, the participant gives up the right to covered benefits from any licensed provider of his or her choice. The choices are narrowed to those approved by the specific managed care plan. For these reasons, it may not be advisable for people who travel frequently or live part of the year outside the geographic region of the plan to select managed care.

Persons who elect the managed care option may drop the plan coverage and return to the regular Medicare program by notifying both the local Social Security office and the managed care plan. Medicare coverage will usually be restored within a month of the request.

Returning to regular Medicare benefits can present a problem for persons not healthy enough to purchase a new Medigap policy.

**YOUR FINANCIAL SERVICES PRACTICE:
THE MEDICARE WEBSITE**

The Medicare website can be an invaluable tool for you and your clients (www.medicare.gov). It contains search tools that can help you choose the best Medicare plan option and more. Below are search tools offered as links on the site.

Medicare Personal Plan Finder
Helps you to compare health plans in your area

Prescription Drug Assistance Programs

Shows programs that offer discounted or free medications

Participating Physician Directory
Locates Medicare participating physicians in your area

Helpful Contacts
Finds phone numbers and websites

Your Medicare Coverage (coming soon)
Shows your health care coverage in the original Medicare plan

Medicare Health Plan Compare
Compares health plans in your area

Nursing Home Compare
Compares nursing homes in your area

Dialysis Facility Compare
Compares dialysis facilities in your area

Supplier Directory
Locates participating Medicare suppliers in your area

Publications
Views, orders, or downloads Medicare publications

Local Medicare Events
Includes events on Medicare-related topics

Medigap Compare
Locates supplemental insurance policies to cover expenses not paid by Medicare

---

Employer-Provided Health Benefits

In addition to Medicare, some individuals (generally employees of large private and public employers) receive employer-provided health care coverage that continues after retirement. Although coverage has been shrinking in recent years, this type of benefit is still available to a significant number of employees in larger companies.

The types of plans provided by employers vary a great deal—some are quite generous and others pay only a small proportion of the retiree's medical expenses. Also, in most cases, the employer retains the right to amend or terminate benefits into the future.

If the retiring employee has to pay some or all of the premium for the plan, then he or she must decide whether to buy into the program or to pursue an individual Medigap policy. Even if the coverage is provided without cost, both the adviser and the retiree must fully understand the extent of the coverage in order to determine whether additional Medigap coverage is still necessary. Also note that some employers will actually offer retirees regular Medicare-supplement policies similar to those that individuals can buy on their own.

MEDICAL COVERAGE BEFORE ELIGIBLITY FOR MEDICARE

One problem that is not solved by a Medigap policy is the health gap that occurs after early retirement and before age 65 when Medicare (and Medigap) starts. Statistics show that slightly over 50 percent of those who retire early do not have employer-provided health insurance. For those in that group, the effect can be devastating. A financial planning challenge awaits clients and planners alike, especially because poor health may have been the reason for early retirement in the first place. Let's take a closer look at what can be done.

COBRA Coverage

The Consolidated Omnibus Budget Reconciliation Act of 1985 (COBRA) established the option for a retiring employee to buy into the employer's group health plan. COBRA continuation coverage allows an employee to continue health benefits under the employer's plan for 18 months after retirement. The period is extended to 29 months in the case of retirement due to disability and 36 months if the insurance is through a spouse's plan and the spouse dies, the couple divorces, or the spouse becomes eligible for Medicare.

YOUR FINANCIAL SERVICES PRACTICE:
CONVERSION SOLUTION—
THE POST-COBRA AND PRE-MEDICARE GAP

For clients who retire at age 62, COBRA coverage only protects them until age 63½. Because Medicare does not start until age 65, clients are often left scrambling for coverage in the interim. One solution is the automatic conversion privilege associated with many employer-provided group health insurance plans.

What is more, planners will be pleased to know that this privilege still exists when COBRA coverage runs out. (Conversion to an individual policy with no evidence of insurability should be accomplished within 31 days of termination of the group coverage.) The downside may be the prohibitive costs associated with the individual policy. The upside is guaranteed coverage despite poor health or preexisting conditions.

The COBRA requirements apply to all health care plans of employers (except for churches) with 20 or more employees. If the employer has a medical plan but COBRA does not apply, state law may provide for a similar continuation requirement. The continuation period varies; it may be as short as 3 months and as long as 18 months.

Under COBRA, your client will take over the entire premium for coverage. This can equal the full cost of group coverage, and the employer can add an additional 2 percent for administrative charges.

In many cases, the group coverage is a relative bargain, especially in cases of poor health or a preexisting condition, where comparable coverage is not available at any price. If the individual is healthy, he or she may want to compare the price of an individual policy to the COBRA benefits to get the best possible deal.

Other Options

One solution to the pre-Medicare health care gap can be coverage under a spouse's plan. For couples who can keep one spouse in the workforce, this coverage offers the best solution possible. A problem, however, is that one reason for early retirement may be to perform care-giving services for a spouse. In such cases—and in other cases—spousal coverage may not be a viable solution.

A second option is to purchase an individual policy. Surprisingly, this can be a viable solution in some instances. Individual policies may be available through a conversion from an employer provided group plan. If this is not the case, most states have a program to ensure that insurance is available. The problem with individual policies generally will not be their availability; it will be their prohibitive cost.

For clients who are at or near the poverty level, Medicaid may provide the answer. These state-run systems provide health care coverage; however, coverage is available only to the poorest percentage of the population. Finally, many people choose to go uninsured. People in this group postpone health treatment, which ultimately jeopardizes their health and increases Medicare costs.

LONG-TERM CARE INSURANCE

The Need for Long-Term Care

The primary reason that long-term care (LTC) is a growing market is that our population is aging. The population aged 65 and over is the fastest-growing age group; today it represents about 11 percent of the population, a figure that is expected to increase to between 20 and 25 percent over the next

50 years. The segment of the population aged 85 and over is growing at an even faster rate. While less than 10 percent of the over-65 group is over 85 today, this percentage is expected to double over the next two generations.

Planners should keep in mind that the likelihood of a person needing to enter a nursing home increases dramatically with age. One percent of persons between the ages of 65 and 74 reside in nursing homes, and the percentage increases to 6 percent between the ages of 75 and 84. At ages 85 and over, the figure rises to approximately 25 percent.

Another reason for the rise in popularity of long-term care insurance is cost. Nearly $50 billion is spent each year on nursing home care. This cost is increasing faster than inflation because of the growing demand for nursing home beds and the shortage of skilled medical personnel. The cost of complete long-term care for a client can be astronomical, with annual nursing home costs of $36,000 to $70,000 not unusual.

Characteristics of Individual Policies

For many types of insurance, policies are relatively standardized. For long-term care insurance, the opposite is true. Significant variations (and, therefore, differences in cost) exist from one insurance company to another. State laws also vary, although many have adopted some or all of the provisions in the model NAIC legislation. The model legislation limits provisions somewhat and also limits the way policies can be marketed.

Regardless of the state, a policyowner will typically have options with respect to various policy provisions. The following are a few of the key issues that need to be reviewed for each policy.

Issue Age

Substantial differences exist among insurance companies with respect to the age at which they will issue policies. There is considerably more variation with respect to the youngest age at which coverage will be written. Some companies have no minimum age. Other companies sell policies to persons as young as age 20. Still other companies have minimum ages in the 40-to-50 age range. Most companies also have an upper age of 80 or 85, beyond which coverage will not be issued.

Benefits

Benefits under long-term care policies can be categorized by type, amounts, duration, the ability to restore benefits, and the degree of inflation protection.

Types. There are several levels of care that are frequently provided by long-term care policies:

skilled-nursing care

- *skilled-nursing care,* which consists of daily nursing and rehabilitative care that can be performed only by, or under the supervision of, skilled medical personnel and must be based on a doctor's orders

intermediate care

- *intermediate care,* which involves occasional nursing and rehabilitative care that must be based on a doctor's orders and can be performed only by, or under the supervision of, skilled medical personnel

custodial care

- *custodial care,* which is primarily to handle personal needs, such as walking, bathing, dressing, eating, or taking medicine, and can usually be provided by someone who does not have professional medical skills or training

home health care

- *home health care,* which is received at home and includes part-time skilled-nursing care, speech therapy, physical or occupational therapy, part-time services from home health aides, and help from homemakers

adult day care

- *adult day care,* which is received at centers specifically designed for seniors who live at home but whose spouses or families are not available to stay home during the day. The level of care received is similar to that provided for home health care. Most adult day-care centers also provide transportation to and from the center.

YOUR FINANCIAL SERVICES PRACTICE:
THE BEST TIME TO SELL LTC INSURANCE

Many planners feel the best time to sell long-term care insurance is when clients are in their late 50s. One reason for this is that these clients have often recently undergone the experience of dealing with the long-term care needs of their parents. More important, however, the "numbers" seem to work well for this age group as compared to those who are in their mid- to late 60s, because costs are more reasonable.

Most policies cover at least the first three levels of care, and many cover all five. Some policies also provide benefits for respite care, which allows occasional full-time care at home for a person who is receiving home health care. Respite-care benefits enable family members who are providing much of the home care to take a needed break.

It is becoming increasingly common for policies to contain a bed reservation benefit. This benefit continues payments to a long-term care facility for a limited time (such as 20 days) if a patient must temporarily leave to be hospitalized. Without a continuation of payments, the bed may be rented to someone else and unavailable upon the patient's release from the hospital.

Some newer policies provide assisted-living benefits. These benefits are for facilities that provide care for frail seniors who are no longer able to care for themselves but who do not need the level of care that is provided in a nursing home.

Costs. Benefits are usually limited to a specified amount per day that is independent of the actual charge for long-term care. The insured purchases the level of benefit he or she desires up to the maximum level the insurance company will provide. Benefits are often sold in increments of $10 per day up to frequently found limits of $100 or $150 or, in a few cases, as much as $300. Most insurance companies will not offer a daily benefit below $30 or $50.

Duration. Long-term care policies contain both an elimination (waiting) period and a maximum benefit period. Under an elimination period, benefit payments do not begin until a specified time period after long-term care has begun. While a few insurance companies have a set period (such as 60 days), most allow the policyowner to select from three or four optional elimination periods. Choices may occasionally be as low as 30 days or as high as 365 days. The policyowner is also usually given a choice regarding the maximum period for which benefits will be paid. For example, one insurer offers durations of 2, 3, or 4 years; another makes 3-, 6-, and 12-year coverage available. At the extremes, options of one year or lifetime may be available.

Inflation Protection. Most long-term care policies offer some type of inflation protection that the policyowner can purchase. In some cases, the inflation protection is elected (for a higher premium) at the time of purchase; future increases in benefits are automatic. In other cases, the policyowner is allowed to purchase additional benefits each year without evidence of insurability.

Inflation protection is generally in the form of a specified annual increase, often 5 percent. Some policies limit aggregate increases to a specified multiple of the original policy, such as two times. Other policies allow increases only to a maximum age, such as 85. Inflation protection is usually less than adequate to offset actual inflation. The maximum annual increase in benefits is usually 5 percent. This is significantly below recent annual increases in the cost of long-term care, which have been in the double digits over the last decade.

Eligibility for Benefits

activities of daily living

Almost all insurance companies now use a criterion for benefit eligibility that is related to several so-called *activities of daily living*. While variations exist, these activities often include eating, bathing, dressing, transferring from bed to chair, using the toilet, and maintaining continence. In order to receive benefits, there must be independent certification that a person is totally dependent on others to perform a certain number of these activities. For example, one insurer lists seven activities and requires total dependence for any three of them; another insurer requires dependence for two out of a list of six.

Newer policies contain a second criterion that, if satisfied, will result in the payment of benefits even if the activities of daily living can be performed. This criterion is based on cognitive impairment, which can be caused by Alzheimer's disease, stroke, or other brain damage.

Exclusions

Most long-term care policies contain the exclusions permitted under the NAIC model act. One source of controversy is the exclusion for mental and nervous disorders. Similarly, many policies also use the model act pre-existing conditions limit, excluding benefits within the first 6 months of a policy for a condition for which treatment was recommended or received within 6 months prior to policy purchase.

Underwriting

The underwriting of long-term care policies, like the underwriting of medical expense policies, is based on the health of the insured. However, underwriting for the long-term care risk focuses on situations that will cause claims far into the future. Most underwriting is done on the basis of questionnaires rather than on the use of actual physical examinations. Numerous questions are asked about the health of relatives. Underwriting tends to become more restrictive as the age of an applicant increases.

guaranteed renewable

Renewability

Long-term care policies currently being sold are *guaranteed renewable*, which means that an individual's coverage cannot be canceled except for nonpayment of premiums. While premiums cannot be raised on the basis of a particular applicant's claim, they can (and often are) raised by class.

Deductibility of Premiums and Taxation of Benefits

Starting with a federal statute enacted in August 1996, the tax treatment of long-term care (LTC) policies has become more favorable. Essentially, they are treated like health insurance policies under the federal income tax laws. Employer expenditures on LTC are a deductible business expense, and the employee does not recognize income when the employer pays the premiums. However, the law prohibits individuals from paying LTC premiums through a flexible spending account. This limitation makes it clear that individuals are not allowed to pay the premiums with pretax dollars.

Another limitation in the law prohibits employers from offering LTC policies as a choice under a cafeteria plan for benefits. Employers can provide LTC coverage outside a cafeteria plan. Most existing plans are merely a payroll deduction for premium payments where the employee is paying all of the premium.

Individuals may deduct their LTC premium payments as a medical expense provided they have enough medical expenses to satisfy the 7.5 percent of adjusted gross income threshold. If the threshold is not satisfied, the deduction will be lost.

The 1996 statute specifies that qualified long-term care policies will provide benefits that are generally exempt from federal income taxes. There is an unlimited exclusion from income for benefits that reimburse for actual expenses or do not exceed actual expenses. There is a limit on the amount of benefits exempt from income taxes when the benefit amount exceeds actual expenses. The latter limitation applies to policies that provide a per diem benefit regardless of actual expense.

ADVANCE DIRECTIVES

Individuals by law have the right to make their own medical choices based on their own values, beliefs, and wishes. But what happens if a person has an accident or suffers a stroke and can no longer make decisions? Would the person want to have his or her life prolonged by any means necessary, or would he or she want to have some treatments withheld to allow a natural death? Usually, directives will go into effect only in the event that the person cannot make and communicate his or her own health-care decisions. Preparing an advance directive lets the physician and other health-care providers know the kind of medical care the individual wants (or does not want) if he or she becomes incapacitated. It also relieves family and friends of the responsibility of making decisions regarding life-prolonging actions.

advance directive
living will

do-not-resuscitate orders

The term *advance directive* can describe a variety of documents. A *living will* is a document in which an individual states whether he or she wants his or her life prolonged through medical intervention if he or she has a terminal illness or if her or she is permanently unconscious. *Do-not-resuscitate orders* are more specific and are typically signed by terminally ill patients to address the withholding of CPR (cardiopulmonary resuscitation) or other forms of resuscitation if they would only temporarily prolong life and perhaps increase pain.

health-care power of attorney (HCPOA)

A *health-care power of attorney (HCPOA)* allows an individual to name an agent to make health-care decisions for the person if he or she is unable to do so. The HCPOA is more flexible than a living will and can cover any health-care decision, even if the person is not terminally ill or permanently unconscious. Some states also have a document specifically called an advance health-care directive that addresses all of the issues contained in both a living will and in a health-care power of attorney. The term advance directive may be used to refer to any of these specific documents or to all of them in general.

States differ widely on what types of advance directives they officially recognize. Some states require a specific style for the format and content of the advance directive. Moreover, the laws regarding honoring advance directives from one state to another are not clear. If a person lives in one state but travels to other states frequently, he or she may want to consider having the advance directive meet the laws of other states. A good source of information is the Office of the State Attorney General for each state.

Under the federal Patient Self-Determination Act, hospitals and other health-care providers across the country are required to give patients information about their rights to make their own health-care decisions. This includes the right to accept or refuse medical treatment. If an individual has an advance directive, it is appropriate to provide a copy to relevant health-care providers. These directives are more likely to be followed if a friend or family member becomes an active advocate for the patient.

Individuals should keep a number of issues in mind when considering advance directives. First, no one has to have an advance directive if he or she does not want one. Second, if an advance directive is adopted, it is crucial to do the following:

- Tell family members and make sure they know where it is located.
- Inform the person's lawyer.
- Discuss the advance directive with the family doctor before signing it. It is important that both the patient and the doctor are comfortable with the contents. The doctor may have some additional suggestions that the patient had not thought to include. Make sure the advance directive is part of the patient's medical records.
- If a person has a durable power of attorney, give a copy of the advance directive to the person holding the power of attorney.
- Be sure to comply with the state's signature and witness requirements. States have various requirements about who can be a witness, how many witnesses are needed, and if the directive must be notarized.

- The person should keep a small card in his or her wallet to notify emergency medical services (EMS) providers of his or her wishes. (EMS generally refers to ambulance companies and paramedics.) In an emergency situation, however, EMS staff members do not have much time to look for or to evaluate different types of documentation. They may only acknowledge cards issued by a state's EMS program and only when the cards are signed by a personal physician.

An individual may change or cancel an advance directive at any time. Any change or cancellation should be written, signed, and dated. Copies should be given to the doctor and to anyone else who had a copy of the original. Some states allow a person to change an advance directive by oral statement. Even if the advance directive is not officially withdrawn, a patient with a clear mind who is communicating his or her wishes directly to the doctor carries more weight than a living will or durable power of attorney.

More Information

For more information on options for maintaining individual autonomy in health-care decision making, consider taking advantage of the following resources:

- AARP holds education workshops on medical decision making. Call AARP at 1-800-424-3410.
- Contact Choice in Dying, a national organization providing state-specific advance directive forms and instructions, as well as a number of booklets about health-care powers of attorney and living wills. Call 212-366-5540.
- You also can obtain state forms and literature from local hospitals, nursing homes, state or local offices on aging, state bar associations, or medical associations.

CHAPTER REVIEW

Key Terms

IRC Sec. 121 [23-1]	sale-leaseback [23-3]
downsize [23-2]	reverse mortgage [23-4]
life-care community [23-2]	Medicare Part A [23-5]
age-restricted housing [23-2]	Medicare Part B [23-5]
domicile [23-3]	benefit period [23-5]

lifetime reserve days [23-5]
Medigap insurance [23-5]
skilled-nursing care [23-7]
intermediate care [23-7]
custodial care [23-7]
home health care [23-7]
adult day care [23-7]

activities of daily living [23-7]
guaranteed renewable [23-7]
advance directive [23-8]
living will [23-8]
do-not-resuscitate orders [23-8]
health care power of attorney
  (HCPOA) [23-8]

Review Questions

Review questions are based on the learning objectives in this chapter. Thus, a [23-3] at the end of a question means that the question is based on learning objective 23-3. If there are multiple objectives, they are all listed.

1. Answer the following questions about the exclusion of gain provisions upon the sale of a personal residence. [23-1]
    a. What are the ownership and use requirements?
    b. What is the maximum amount that can be excluded for the sale of a personal residence by a single taxpayer?
    c. What is the maximum amount that can be excluded for the sale of a personal residence by a married taxpayer filing jointly?

2. If a couple is planning to marry, and each owns a home that he or she is planning to sell, what should they do about the two properties? [23-1]

3. Describe the typical fee structure of a life-care community and what the promise of lifetime care can mean for the client. [23-2]

4. Explain the differences between the age-62 restriction and the age-55 restriction to your client, who is interested in an age-restricted housing community. [23-2]

5. What factors should be considered by clients planning to relocate out of state? [23-3]

6. What type of home improvements should a retiree staying in the home typically consider? [23-4]

7. Describe a sale-leaseback arrangement. [23-4]

8. When is a reverse mortgage typically available? [23-4]

9. How are lenders protected under the HECM program? [23-4]

10. How much will the lender be able to borrow under a reverse mortgage? [23-4]

11. What happens under a reverse mortgage if the retiree dies and the amount of the outstanding loan exceeds the value of the home? What if the value of the home exceeds the amount of the outstanding loan? [23-4]

12. Identify who is eligible to receive Medicare benefits. [23-5]

13. Joan (aged 66) is hospitalized for 80 days (January–March), goes home for 6 months, and is hospitalized again in October for an additional 30 days. How will Medicare treat each stay for payment purposes? [23-5]

14. Identify the key benefits that are not covered by Parts A or B of Medicare. [23-5]

15. Ralph has drug costs this year of $2,800. He has enrolled in Part D of Medicare and pays $35 a month in premiums. What are Ralph's total out-of-pocket costs under the program for the year? How much will Part D pay of his drug expenses? [23-5]

16. What benefits are covered under all Medigap policies? [23-5]

17. How does Medicare SELECT differ from the traditional Medigap policies? [23-5]

18. Describe how a managed care plan works under Medicare. [23-5]

19. Discuss how COBRA coverage can help solve the pre-Medicare/postretirement gap. [23-6]

20. In addition to COBRA, what other options are available to people who face pre-Medicare/postretirement problems? [23-6]

21. Briefly discuss the need for long-term care insurance. [23-7]

22. Discuss the following characteristics of long-term care policies: [23-7]
    a. issue age
    b. benefits
    c. costs
    d. duration

23. Describe each of the following: [23-8]
    a. living will
    b. health care power of attorney
    c. advance care directive
    d. do-not-resuscitate order

Distributions from Retirement Plans—Part I

Learning Objectives

An understanding of the material in this chapter should enable you to

24-1. Identify the exceptions to the general rule that distributions from qualified plans, 403(b) annuities, and IRAs are included as ordinary income.

24-2. Clarify the legal limitations and planning strategies for avoiding the Sec. 72(t) early withdrawal penalty tax.

24-3. Identify the various methods for recovering cost basis from qualified and other tax advantaged retirement plans.

24-4. Explain the tax treatment of qualified and nonqualified distributions from a Roth IRA or a Roth account in a 401(k) or 403(b) plan.

24-5. Distinguish between distributions that can be rolled over into other tax-advantaged retirement plans and those that cannot.

24-6. Discuss the special tax rules that may apply to lump-sum distributions from qualified plans.

24-7. Describe when required distributions must begin, and how to calculate the required minimum distributions during the participant's lifetime and after the participant's death.

24-8. Describe the post mortem planning opportunities under the minimum required distribution rules.

Chapter Outline

Planning for the distribution of funds from employer-sponsored retirement plans and IRAs can be one of the most challenging aspects of retirement planning. Any strategy selected must account for the following factors:

- the client's needs and goals
- the variety of distribution options that are available in your client's particular situation
- the implications of choosing one option over another from a tax perspective
- the implications of choosing one option over another from a cash-flow perspective
- the implications of choosing one option over another from a death benefit and estate tax perspective
- the ability to delay the receipt and taxation of a distribution by rolling the distribution over into an IRA or another qualified plan

This chapter examines the tax implications of the withdrawal. The following chapter discusses the nontax rules, typical distribution options, and planning considerations for selecting the appropriate distribution option.

TAX TREATMENT

General

From the employee's perspective, the advantage of tax-sheltered retirement plans (qualified plans, 403(b) plans, IRAs, SEPs, and SIMPLEs) is that taxes are deferred until benefits are distributed—the day of reckoning. Generally, the entire value of a distribution is included as ordinary income in the year of the distribution. If the individual has made after-tax contributions or receives an insurance policy and has paid PS 58 costs, he or she will have a cost basis that can generally be recovered. Taxable distributions from tax-sheltered retirement plans made prior to age 59½ are also subject to the 10 percent Sec. 72(t) penalty tax, unless the distribution satisfies one of several exceptions.

If the benefit is distributed in a single sum, the taxable portion may be eligible for one of several special tax benefits, but only if the distribution is from a qualified plan and satisfies certain lump-sum distribution requirements. Persons born before 1936 may be eligible for 10-year forward averaging or special capital-gains treatment. Any participant who receives employer securities as part of a lump-sum distribution can defer tax on the unrealized appreciation until the stock is later sold.

In many cases, all taxes, including the Sec. 72(t) penalty tax, can be avoided by rolling—or directly transferring—the benefit into an IRA or other qualified plan. Today, most distributions are eligible for rollover treatment. Taxes cannot be deferred indefinitely, however. Under the minimum-distribution rules, distributions generally have to begin at age 70½.

Estate Taxation of Pension Accumulations

Qualified plan and other tax-sheltered benefits payable to a beneficiary at the death of the participant are included in the participant's taxable estate. Benefits payable to beneficiaries are still subject to income tax, although the benefit amount is treated as income in respect of a decedent, meaning the income taxes are reduced by the estate taxes paid as a result of the pension benefit.

Sec. 72(t) Penalty Tax

Sec. 72(t) penalty tax

Distributions prior to age 59½ from all types of tax-advantaged retirement plans are subject to the 10 percent *Sec. 72(t) penalty tax* (unless an exception applies). The 10 percent penalty applies to distributions that are made from a qualified plan, a Sec. 403(b) plan, an IRA, or a SEP. The rule

---

**YOUR FINANCIAL SERVICES PRACTICE:
ASKING THE RIGHT QUESTIONS**

In most cases, taxation of a distribution from a pension plan or IRA is simple. The distribution is fully taxable as ordinary income. However, there are a number of critical exceptions. (This whole chapter is about the exceptions.) Here is a series of questions to ask your client to determine if any of the special rules apply.

1. What type of plan is the distribution from?
   There are some rule differences between the different types of plans. For example, the grandfathered lump-sum distribution rules only apply to qualified plans.
2. Is a portion of the distribution attributable to amounts that have already been taxed?
   After-tax employee contributions or PS 58 costs in a qualified plan or nondeductible contributions to an IRA are treated as cost basis and will not be taxed twice. The methodology for recovering the basis is complicated and depends on the type of plan involved. Form 1099-R, which is provided to the recipient, will reveal such amounts.
3. Is the benefit payable to an individual who has not attained age 59½?
   If the answer is yes, then in addition to income taxes, a 10 percent penalty tax may apply if the recipient is not eligible for one of the exceptions.
4. Is the distribution to a plan participant or to a beneficiary receiving a death benefit?
   If it is a distribution to the death beneficiary, the beneficiary still pays income taxes, but he or she might be entitled to a deduction if the participant had paid federal estate taxes on the value of the pension.
5. Is some or all of the distribution attributable to stock of the sponsoring entity?
   If the distribution is from a qualified plan and it qualifies as a lump-sum distribution, the taxpayer may be entitled to deferral of gain on the unrealized appreciation on the employer stock.
6. Is the distribution from a qualified plan payable as a lump sum to an individual born before 1936?
   If the distribution is from a qualified plan, the recipient may be entitled to a special tax rate using grandfathered 10-year averaging or the grandfathered capital-gains rule.
7. Is the distribution from a Roth IRA or a Roth account in a 401(k) or 403(b) plan?
   The tax treatment of Roth IRAs and Roth accounts is different than other types of tax-advantaged plans. Qualifying distributions are tax free. The tax treatment of nonqualifying distributions depends upon the type of plan involved.

---

also applies to SIMPLEs with a modification. During the first 2 years of plan participation, the early withdrawal penalty is 25 percent instead of 10 percent.

The 10 percent tax applies only to the portion of the distribution subject to income tax. This means the tax does not apply when a benefit is rolled over from one tax-deferred plan into another. It also does not apply to the nontaxable portion of a distribution (which may occur with a distribution of after-tax contributions).

However, a distribution made prior to age 59½ can escape the 10 percent penalty if it qualifies under one of several exceptions. To avoid the 10 percent penalty, the distributions must be

substantially equal periodic payments

- to a beneficiary or an employee's estate on or after the employee's death
- attributable to disability
- part of a series of *substantially equal periodic payments* made at least annually over the life or life expectancy of the employee or the joint lives or life expectancies of the employee and beneficiary. (If the distribution is from a qualified plan, the employee must separate from service.)
- after a separation from service for early retirement after age 55 (not applicable to IRAs, SEPs, or SIMPLEs)
- made to cover medical expenses deductible for the year under Sec. 213 (medical expenses that exceed 7.5 percent of adjusted gross income)

Several additional exceptions apply to IRAs (which include SEPs and SIMPLEs). Distributions from IRAs escape the penalty if the distribution is for the

- purpose of paying health insurance premiums by an individual who is collecting unemployment insurance
- payment of acquisition costs (paid within 120 days of the distribution) of a first home for the participant, spouse, or any child, grandchild, or ancestor of the participant or spouse (with a lifetime limit of $10,000 per IRA participant)
- payment for qualified higher education expenses for education furnished to the taxpayer, the taxpayer's spouse, or any child or grandchild of the taxpayer or taxpayer's spouse at an eligible postsecondary educational institution

Qualified home acquisition expenses are those used to buy, build, or rebuild a first home. To be a first-time homebuyer, the individual (and spouse, if married) must not have had an ownership interest in a principal residence during a 2-year period ending on the date the new home is acquired. Qualified education expenses include tuition, fees, books, supplies, and equipment required for enrollment in a postsecondary education institution. For at least half-time students, room and board are also qualified education expenses.

The following examples should help to illustrate when the Sec. 72(t) 10 percent penalty applies and when it does not.

Example 1:	Greg Murphy, aged 57, takes a $50,000 distribution from his profit-sharing plan. If Greg terminated employment after age 55 and before receiving the benefit, the tax does not apply. If Greg is still employed at the time of the distribution, then the $50,000 lump-sum distribution will be subject to a $5,000 (10 percent) penalty.
Example 2:	Jane Goodall, aged 45, takes a life annuity from Biological Researchers, Inc., when she quits and goes to work for The Primate Institute. Jane's distribution is not subject to penalty because of the substantially equal periodic payments exception.
Example 3:	Ed Miller, aged 35, takes a $10,000 distribution from his 401(k) plan as a downpayment on his first home. Ed's distribution is subject to the 10 percent penalty.
Example 4:	Sandra Smalley, aged 45, takes a distribution from her IRA to pay for her child's college education. Sandra's distribution is not subject to the 10 percent penalty.
Example 5:	Catherine Thegrate, aged 45, withdraws $10,000 from her IRA to make the downpayment on her first home. The distribution is exempt from the 10 percent penalty. However, no additional with-drawals from any of Catherine's IRAs (or Roth IRAs) can qualify for the exception.

Avoiding the Sec. 72(t) Penalty Tax

Clients may need to make withdrawals prior to age 59½ to pay personal or business expenses. Voluntary early retirement, involuntary retirement followed by a period of not working, or leaving a job to start a business are common scenarios. Within the exceptions to the Sec. 72(t) penalty tax, some planning opportunities do exist.

Age 55 Exception. Distributions from a qualified plan or 403(b) plan to a participant who retires after attaining age 55 are exempt from the penalty tax. This exception is useful if the participant wants to take a portion of the distribution into income now and roll over the rest to an IRA. It also works when the participant elects a stream of installment distributions or an annuity payment from the plan. However, if the participant wants more discretion over the timing of the withdrawal then the plan allows, the only option is a rollover into an IRA. Once the distribution is in the IRA, it is no longer eligible for the exception.

YOUR FINANCIAL SERVICES PRACTICE:
TAX FORMS REQUIRED WITH EARLY WITHDRAWALS

When a participant receives a distribution from a pension plan or IRA the payor must provide Form 1099-R, which reports the distribution. If the recipient has not yet attained age 59½, the payor will identify in box 7 of the form whether an exception to the Sec. 72(t) tax applies (in this case, he or she identifies "2", "3", or "4" in the box.) If he or she writes "1" in the box, "no known exception," then the recipient is required to file Form 5329 with his or her tax return. On Form 5329, the taxpayer identifies the taxable amount, but also has the opportunity to identify the applicable exception to the penalty tax.

Education Expenses. For IRA participants (this includes SEPs and SIMPLEs), the exception for educational expenses can also be useful. The education expense exception requires that the taxpayer pay qualified education expenses for the family member, but the expenses do not have to be paid directly from the IRA. The actual education payments can be paid from employment income, loans, gifts, or inheritances. However, education expenses paid with tax-free distribution from a Coverdell education account, tax-free scholarships, Pell grants, employer-provided educational assistance or veterans' educational assistance do not qualify.

Qualified education expenses include tuition, fees, books, supplies, and equipment required for enrollment in a postsecondary education institution. Room and board is also included for students attending school at least half time. An eligible educational institution is any college, university, or vocational school eligible to participate in the student aid programs administered by the Department of Education. It includes virtually all accredited, public, nonprofit, and proprietary postsecondary institutions.

Example: Randolph, aged 56, withdraws $50,000 during the year from his IRA to pay for a new boat (before calling his financial advisor). It is determined that he also took out a second mortgage to pay $25,000 of tuition, $1,000 for books, and $12,000 for room and board for his daughter, a full-time student at Private University. Since Randolph incurred $38,000 of qualified education expenses for his daughter, he only has to pay the 10 percent penalty on $12,000 of the $50,000 withdrawal.

Substantially Equal Periodic Payments. The most helpful exception is the substantially equal periodic payment exception. This exception applies to all types of plans. However, with qualified plans, the participant must separate from service before distributions begin in order to be eligible. Payments can begin at any age, as long as the stream of distributions is set up to last for the life of the participant or the joint lives of the participant and his or her beneficiary. For the individual who needs the withdrawals for ongoing financial needs, periodic distributions may be just right. If, on the other hand, a large single-sum amount is needed, this strategy could still work. The individual can borrow the sum needed and repay the loan from the periodic distributions. The borrower, however, is not allowed to use the pension or IRA account as collateral for the loan.

Under this exception, there is some flexibility in calculating the annual withdrawal amount. Withdrawals must be made at least annually (or more often) and the stream of withdrawals can be calculated under one of three IRS-approved methods. The first is the required minimum-distribution method. Under this approach, the annual payment for each year is determined by dividing the account balance for that year by the number from the chosen life expectancy table for that year. Under this method, the account balance, the number from the chosen life expectancy table, and the resulting annual payments are redetermined for each year.

The second method is the fixed-amortization method. The annual payment for each year is determined by amortizing, in level amounts, the account balance over a specified number of years determined using the chosen life expectancy table and the chosen interest rate. Under this method, the account balance, the number from the chosen life expectancy table, and the resulting annual payment are determined once for the first distribution year, and the annual payment is the same amount in each succeeding year.

The third method is the fixed-annuitization method. The annual payment for each year is determined by dividing the account balance by an annuity factor that is the present value of an annuity of one dollar per year beginning at the taxpayer's age and continuing for the life of the taxpayer (or the joint lives of the individual and beneficiary). The annuity factor is derived by using the mortality table in appendix B of Rev. Rul. 2002-62 and by using the chosen interest rate. Under this method, the account balance, the annuity factor, the chosen interest rate, and the resulting annual payment are determined once for the first distribution year and then the annual payment is the same amount in each succeeding year.

The life expectancy tables that can be used to determine distribution periods are the uniform lifetime table (found in Rev. Rul. 2002-62, a portion of which can be found in the minimum-distribution materials in the next chapter), the single-life table or the joint and survivor table (found in appendix 4). These are the same tables used for determining the required minimum distribution. The number that is used for a distribution year is the number shown from the table for the participant's age on his or her birthday in that year. If the joint and survivor table is being used, the age of the beneficiary on the beneficiary's birthday in the year is also used. In the case of the required minimum-distribution method, the same life expectancy table that is used for the first distribution year must be used in each following year. Thus, if the taxpayer uses the single-life expectancy table for the required minimum-distribution method in the first distribution year, the same table must be used in subsequent distribution years.

The interest rate that may be used is any interest rate that is not more than 120 percent of the federal mid-term rate for either of the 2 months immediately preceding the month in which the distribution begins. For example, 120 percent of the mid-term rate was 6.03 percent for September of 2006.

Example: George, aged 50, has an IRA with an account balance of $500,000. In October 2006 he decides that he wants to take the maximum withdrawals allowed under the substantially equal periodic payment rule. The annuitization and amortization methods give similar results, and the calculation using the amortization method is quite easy to calculate. To get the maximum withdrawal, use the the highest allowable interest rate (6.03% in September 2006) and the single life expectancy table. The life expectancy factor is 34.2 for an individual aged 50. Using a financial calculator with the present value of $500,000, 6.03 (i), and 34.2 (n), the required annual stream of payments is $34,855.

Even though the distribution amount is calculated based on lifetime payments, the rules do not actually require that payments continue for life. Payments can be stopped without penalty after the later of 5 years after the first payment or age 59½. For example, an individual who began distributions in substantially equal payments at age 56 in January 2006 must continue taking the distributions until January 2011. Or, in the case of an individual beginning withdrawals at age 47, the payments must continue until he or she attains age 59½, which is a period of 12½ years.

A client who uses the substantially equal payment exception needs to understand that once payments have begun, they must continue in the exact amount for the required period or the 10 percent penalty will be due on all distributions made before age 59½, as well as interest on the tax obligation that was avoided during the years in which distributions were made.

**YOUR FINANCIAL SERVICES PRACTICE:
THE SUBSTANTIALLY EQUAL PAYMENT EXCEPTION
IN A DOWN MARKET**

The biggest limitation of the substantially equal periodic payment exception is the inability to change the calculation methodology after the first year. With the amortization and annuitization approaches, the amount withdrawn in each and every year must remain the same for the prescribed period. This can cause problems in a down market when the value of the account can drop suddenly. A participant who is concerned about this issue should consider using the required minimum-distribution approach. Under this approach, the required distribution each year is based on the prior year's account balance. Interestingly, in Rev. Rul. 2002-62, the IRS has indicated that anyone who chooses either the amortization or annuitization methods can, after the first year, make a one-time election to change the method to the required minimum-distribution approach. This gives taxpayers a safety net if the value of the account suddenly drops.

Nontaxable Distributions

Most distributions made from qualified plans, IRA accounts, and 403(b) annuities are fully taxable as ordinary income. However, if some of the participant's benefit under the plan is attributable to dollars in the plan that have already been subject to taxation—for example, employee after-tax contributions and amounts attributable to term insurance premiums—then a portion of a distribution may be exempt from tax until the total nontaxable amount has been distributed.

The calculation of the appropriate tax treatment for periodic payments can become quite complex. The rules are different, depending upon the type of plan and type of distribution involved. At the same time, fewer and fewer participant benefits contain nontaxable basis. This is true in part because of law changes that almost eliminated all new after-tax contributions to qualified plans beginning in 1987 (with the exception of a few large 401(k) plans that still allow after-tax contributions). Also, life insurance benefits in qualified plans have become more and more uncommon, thus, reducing the amount of recoverable PS 58 costs. One more complicating factor is that under current rules, participants are allowed to roll nontaxable contributions into an IRA. The tax treatment of withdrawals from the IRA are different than those from a qualified plan. Even though these situations are not that common, they still come up and the financial services professional needs to have a basic understanding of the rules. A summary of the rules follows.

IRA Distributions

Let's begin with the simplest case, the traditional IRA. A participant can accumulate nontaxable amounts (referred to as cost basis) from either nondeductible contributions to the IRA or nontaxable amounts that have been rolled over from qualified plans. The rule is simply that if an individual has unrecovered cost basis, then a portion of each IRA distribution is tax free. The amount excluded from income is

$$\frac{\text{Unrecovered cost basis}}{\text{Total IRA account} + \text{Current year's distribution}} \times \frac{\text{Distribution}}{\text{amount}} = \frac{\text{Tax-free}}{\text{portion}}$$

This calculation is made by looking at all of the IRAs an individual owns—which can have quite a negative impact on the recovery of cost basis if the participant has both nondeductible and deductible IRA contributions. This method applies until the individual has recovered all of his or her nondeductible contributions. After that, any distribution is fully taxable. If the IRA owner dies prior to recovering all nondeductible contributions, the remaining amount can be deducted on the individual's final income tax return.

Example: Julia decides to withdraw $50,000 from her IRA account. After the withdrawal, her account is valued at $750,000 and $50,000 represented after-tax contributions that were rolled over into the IRA. Julia will only recover $3,125 tax free out of the $50,000 withdrawal. The calculation is $50,000/($750,000 + $50,000) x $50,000.

Recovering Cost Basis with a Life Insurance Policy

When a participant has had a life insurance policy as part of his or her benefit in a qualified plan or 403(b) annuity, there is generally an accumulation of cost basis over the years, as the cost of the term insurance portion of the policy is included in income each year (often referred to as PS 58 costs). Note, however, that self-employed persons (sole proprietors and partners) do not technically accumulate PS 58 costs and are, therefore, not allowed to recover them upon distribution.

PS 58 costs can only be recovered if the policy is actually distributed to the participant. However, if a participant does not want to continue the policy, there is a way around this problem. The trustee can strip the policy's cash value (by borrowing) to reduce it to the accumulated PS 58 costs and then distribute the contract and the cash. The participant then cancels the policy and recovers the tax free cost basis. The cash can be rolled to an IRA to avoid all taxation.

If the participant dies and the policy proceeds are paid out to a beneficiary, then the PS 58 costs can again reduce the taxable portion of the distribution to the death beneficiary. When paid out as a death benefit, the death beneficiary pays income tax only on the cash value of the policy less PS 58 costs. The remaining value is income tax free.

Example: Serena dies while still employed. She had a life insurance policy with a face value of $100,000, a cash value of $20,000, and $4,000 of accumulated cost basis. Serena's daughter Tina is the beneficiary and she elects a lump-sum withdrawal of the $100,000 benefit. Tina will pay income tax on $16,000, the difference between the cash value and the unrecovered cost basis; $84,000 is recovered tax free.

Rollovers from Qualified Plans

When a participant receives a distribution from a qualified plan that is eligible to be rolled into an IRA, the whole distribution (including after-tax contributions) may be rolled into an IRA. However, if the after-tax amount is rolled over, it is subject to the IRA recovery rules. As described above, these rules are not very favorable, especially with large rollover accounts. A participant may want to choose instead to roll over all but the nontaxable amount. In IRS Publication 575, *Pension and Annuity Income,* the IRS clarifies that the participant is not required to pay any income taxes if he or she rolls over all of the distribution except for the amount of after-tax contributions.

Example: Assume in the Julia example above that the $800,000 IRA was recently rolled over from a qualified plan. Remember that in the example Julia had $50,000 in after-tax contributions. If at the time of the IRA rollover she would have rolled only $750,000 into the IRA, she would have avoided income taxes on the entire $50,000 amount.

As mentioned above, when a participant receives a life insurance policy from a qualified plan, the PS 58 costs may be recovered tax free if the policy is distributed. Special consideration must be made when the participant wants to receive the policy but minimize the tax consequences by rolling over as much of the benefit into an IRA as possible. Because a life insurance policy may not be rolled into an IRA, the tax consequences of this transaction can be minimized by having the trustee strip the cash value of the policy (by borrowing) to reduce the cash value to the accumulated PS 58 costs. Then the extra cash is distributed as part of the benefit and may be rolled over.

Single-Sum Distributions

If a participant receives the entire benefit and does not roll it into an IRA or other tax-sheltered retirement plan, recovery of basis occurs at the time of the distribution.

Distribution of After-tax Contributions Prior to the Annuity Starting Date

Prior to 1987, an amount up to the participant's cost basis could be withdrawn prior to the annuity starting date (the time periodic retirement benefits begin) without income tax consequences. The Tax Reform Act of 1986 changed this rule significantly. A grandfather provision still allows a participant to withdraw an amount equal to the pre-1987 cost basis as long as the plan provided for in-service distributions on May 5, 1986. Post-1986 amounts attributable to the cost basis, however, are now subject to a pro rata rule. The general rule is that the amount of the distribution that is excluded from tax is based on a ratio, with the numerator being cost basis and the denominator being the total account balance at the time of the distribution. However, when determining the ratio, an individual may treat employee after-tax contributions and the investment experience thereon separately from the rest of the participant's benefit. This rule still allows a participant to withdraw after-tax contributions with limited tax liability. This principle can be best illustrated with an example.

Example: Joe has an account balance of $1,000, $200 of which is attributable to post-1986 employee contributions and

$50 of which is attributable to investment earnings on $200. Joe takes an in-service distribution of $100. The exclusion ratio is $200/$250 or 80 percent. Therefore, Joe will receive $80 income tax free and will owe tax on $20.

> **YOUR FINANCIAL SERVICES PRACTICE:**
> **AFTER-TAX CONTRIBUTIONS**
>
> It is not uncommon for a business owner to have made after-tax contributions prior to 1987. These amounts can be withdrawn tax free, making them an excellent source of funds if the owner has a life insurance need or some other reason to need cash. After 1986, large company 401(k) plans are typically the only plans that still have an after-tax contribution feature.

Periodic Distributions from Qualified Plans and 403(b) Annuities

When the participant has a cost basis and begins to receive periodic annuity payments from a qualified plan or 403(b) annuity, the amount of each distribution that is not subject to income tax is determined by dividing the cost basis by the number of expected monthly annuity payments. When the annuity is on the participant's life only, the number of months are as cited in table 24-1. For a joint and survivor annuity, use the number of months in table 24-2.

TABLE 24-1
Number of Months—Single Life Annuity

Age of Distributee	Number of Payments
55 and under	360
56–60	310
61–65	260
66–70	210
71 and over	160

TABLE 24-2
Number of Months—Joint Annuity

Combined Age of Annuitants	Number of Payments
Not more than 110	410
More than 110 but not more than 120	360
More than 120 but not more than 130	310
More than 130 but not more than 140	260
More than 140	210

The cost basis is the aggregate amount of after-tax contributions to the plan (plus other after-tax amounts such as PS 58 costs and repayments of loans previously taxed as distributions) minus the aggregate amount received before the annuity starting date that was excluded from income.

The distributee recovers his or her cost basis in level amounts over the number of monthly payments determined in the tables above. The amount excluded from each payment is calculated by dividing the investment by the set number of monthly payments determined as follows:

$$\frac{\text{Investment}}{\text{Number of monthly payments}} = \frac{\text{Tax-free portion}}{\text{of monthly annuity}}$$

This amount is excluded from each payment until the entire investment is recovered. After that, each monthly payment is fully taxable.

Example:	John Thomas is about to begin a retirement benefit in the form of a single life annuity. His investment in the contract is $40,000. John is aged 65 at the time benefit payments begin. The set number of months used to compute the exclusion amount is 260 (for age 65 from table 24-1). Because his cost basis is $40,000, the amount excluded from each payment is $154 ($40,000 ÷ 260).

Roth IRAs and Roth Accounts

With the maturation of the Roth IRA and the availability of Roth 401(k) and Roth 403(b) accounts beginning in 2006, tax questions involving these accounts will become more prevalent. Conceptually, with all Roth accounts the participant is forgoing a deduction at the time of the contribution in exchange for tax-free withdrawals. It is true that qualifying distributions are entirely free of federal income tax; however, nonqualifying distributions may or may not be subject to tax. Unfortunately, there also is a difference between the tax treatment of nonqualifying distributions from Roth IRA and Roth 401(k) (or 403(b)) plans. We will first discuss Roth IRAs and then identify the differences that apply to Roth 401(k) and Roth 403(b) accounts.

Tax Treatment of Roth IRA Distributions

Any qualified distribution from a Roth IRA is free from federal income taxes. Qualified distributions must satisfy two requirements. First, the distribution must be made after the 5-tax-year period beginning with the first tax year for which a contribution was made to an individual's Roth IRA (or converted Roth IRA). For an individual with multiple Roth IRAs, the 5-year period begins for all Roth IRAs the first time a contribution is made to any Roth IRA. The 5-tax-year period ends on the last day of the individual's fifth consecutive taxable year beginning with the taxable year described in the preceding sentence (even if the participant dies prior to this date).

Example:	Karen Crumbcake made her first Roth IRA contribution on April 15, 2001, for the year 2000. The 5-year period ended on December 31, 2004, and distributions in 2005 or later have satisfied the 5-tax-year requirement. Because of the aggregation rule, if Karen opened another Roth IRA in 2003, the 5-year period ends at the end of 2004 for that plan as well.

The second requirement is that the distribution must be made after one of the four following events has occurred:

- The participant has attained age 59½.
- The distribution is paid to a beneficiary due to the participant's death.
- The participant has become disabled.
- The withdrawal is made to pay qualified first-time homebuyer expenses.

Qualified first-time homebuyer expenses include acquisition costs of a first home (paid within 120 days of the distribution) for the participant, spouse, or any child, grandchild, or ancestor of the participant or spouse. This exception, however, has a $10,000 lifetime limit per IRA (or Roth IRA) participant.

Distributions that do not satisfy both the 5-year and the triggering event requirements are referred to as nonqualified distributions. Tax treatment of nonqualified distributions from a Roth IRA is still quite favorable. The law allows the withdrawal of the participant's Roth IRA contributions (or converted contributions) first without any income tax consequences. Once all contributions have been withdrawn, any additional amounts withdrawn are subject to both income tax and the 10 percent Sec. 72(t) excise tax. However, all of the exceptions to the premature distributions penalty that apply to traditional IRAs will apply to distributions from the Roth IRA as well.

Example: Sheila made her first Roth IRA contribution on April 15, 1998. As of the end of 2005, her total contributions equaled $14,000 and her total account was valued at $26,000. In 2006, at age 53, she withdrew $18,000 to pay for her son's college education expenses. Although she has met the 5-year requirement, the withdrawal does not match up with any of the specified trigger events. As a nonqualified distribution, $14,000 (her total contribution) can be withdrawn tax-free. She will have to include $4,000 as ordinary income on her tax return. The $4,000 is subject to the Sec. 72(t) 10 percent early withdrawal tax. However, the education expense exception to that tax applies and no penalty tax is due.

There is a special tax rule that applies to Roth IRAs created with a conversion. Under this rule, the Sec. 72(t) early withdrawal penalty tax applies to any distributions from a converted IRA made within the 5-year period starting with the first day of the tax year in which the conversion occurred. This tax rule is necessary to ensure that individuals cannot use the conversion as a way to avoid the Sec 72(t) early withdrawal penalty tax.

Example: Rhonda, currently age 45, converted an IRA on December 31, 2003, to a Roth IRA in the amount of $50,000 (she paid tax in 2003 on the $50,000 converted). In 2007, she takes her first withdrawal from the converted IRA in the amount of $10,000 to purchase a new car. This withdrawal is not treated as ordinary income subject to income tax because it does not exceed the value of the converted amount. However, the $10,000 distribution is subject to the Sec. 72(t) early withdrawal penalty because it is within the 5-taxable-year period subsequent to the conversion. Since none of the exceptions applies, Rhonda is subject to a $1,000 penalty tax.

Tax Treatment of Roth Accounts

As with Roth IRAs, qualifying distributions from Roth 401(k) and Roth 403(b) accounts will not be subject to federal income tax. Because the tax treatment of these two programs is identical, we will refer to them both as Roth 401(k) accounts.

The qualification requirements for tax-free treatment are the same as with a Roth IRA—there is the same 5-tax-year rule and a triggering event requirement. The major difference is in the application of the 5-tax-year requirement. With Roth 401(k) plans, each Roth 401(k) has to satisfy the 5-tax-year rule; plans cannot be aggregated. The only exception is if an individual elects a direct rollover from one Roth 401(k) to another Roth 401(k) plan. In this situation, the time earned under the first plan is aggregated with the years of participation in the second plan.

The second major difference is the tax treatment of nonqualifying distributions. In a Roth IRA, contributions can be withdrawn without income tax consequences. With a Roth 401(k), nonqualifying distributions are subject to the same pro rata requirement that applies to distributions of after-tax contributions made after 1986 (see discussion above). That is, the distribution is taxed using a pro rata rule, looking solely at the value of the Roth account.

Even though Roth accounts are subject to required minimum distributions and a less favorable method of taxing nonqualified distributions, these issues are not likely to cause difficulties for most plan participants. Because the law allows rollovers from a Roth account to a Roth IRA, many participants will roll over their benefits at termination of employment. Once in a Roth IRA, these amounts are subject to the more liberal Roth IRA rules.

Exclusion of Income for Charitable Contributions

If a participant takes a withdrawal from an IRA or other tax-advantaged retirement plan during his or her lifetime and then contributes the amount to a charity, the distribution is treated as a taxable distribution and the participant may also be eligible for a deduction for part or all of the contribution to the charity. There are numerous rules that limit the charitable deduction, one being that an individual must itemize deductions in order to benefit from the contribution. Other complex rules limit the deduction to a specified percentage of income. For these reasons, it is quite possible that the deduction will not equal the amount taken into income.

As an attempt to encourage lifetime gifts to charities, the Pension Protection Act of 2006 allows certain distributions to simply be excluded from the participant's income. However, the exclusion only applies to distributions made on or after the date that the participant attains age 70½, and presently it only applies to distributions in 2006 and 2007. Also, it only applies to distributions from IRAs and Roth IRAs; other types of plans (even SEPs and SIMPLEs) are not included. However, it is expected that charities are likely to exert pressure to extend this provision.

Under the Pension Protection Act, qualified charitable distributions from IRAs or Roth IRAs that would be otherwise taxable are excluded from income. The exclusion may not exceed $100,000 per taxpayer per taxable year. The limit is based on the aggregate amount of a taxpayer's qualified charitable distributions in a year, meaning that an individual's tax-free IRA donations may consist of one or more distributions from one or more IRAs.

Also to be eligible for the exclusion, the distribution must be made from the trustee directly to the charitable organization; the participant cannot receive the funds and later make the donation. Only contributions to public charities are allowed; contributions to donor-advised funds or private foundations are prohibited. Also, the donation must qualify as a deductible contribution under the current rules that apply to charitable deductions.

For the charitably inclined individual, there are several reasons to take advantage of the income exclusion. One reason is that the charitable contribution is fully excluded from income. Second, by avoiding an increase in AGI, other tax problems can be avoided. For example, individuals with AGI that exceed specified thresholds begin to lose the personal exemption and itemized deductions. Another advantage of this strategy is that the distributions count toward satisfying the required minimum distribution rules. Also, the amount contributed to the charity reduces the value of the individual's taxable estate.

ROLLOVERS

When a plan participant retires, changes jobs, or wants to change service providers (in the case of an IRA), in most cases a plan benefit can be rolled out of one plan and into another tax-deferred vehicle without any income tax consequences. Even though the rollover rules are relatively straightforward today, that doesn't mean that things don't go wrong, and a mistake could result in one of the biggest tax problems that an individual will ever encounter.

Distributions from Qualified, Governmental 457, and 403(b) Plans

eligible rollover distribution

The regulatory scheme is virtually the same for distributions from qualified plans, 403(b) annuities, and 457 plans sponsored by a governmental agency. A participant receiving an *eligible rollover distribution* can defer tax on the distribution by rolling it over in total or in part to a qualified plan, 403(b) annuity, 457 governmental plan, or a traditional IRA. Most distributions qualify as eligible rollover distributions with a few limited exceptions. The most common distributions that do not qualify are as follows:

- minimum required distributions
- hardship withdrawals from a 401(k) plan
- distributions of substantially equal periodic payments made
  - over the participant's remaining life (or life expectancy)
  - over the joint lives (or life expectancies) of the participant and a beneficiary
  - over a period of more than 10 years

In addition, certain corrective distributions, loans treated as distributions, dividends on employer securities, and the cost of life insurance coverage are not eligible rollover distributions.

Example: Your client, Jean Jones, calls you to say she is receiving a life annuity from her former employer's defined-benefit plan. This month, Jean does not need the money. She wants to know whether she can roll the benefit into an IRA account. The answer is no. Because it is part of a stream of life annuity payments, it is not an eligible rollover amount.

Rollover

rollover

The term *rollover* is used to describe the situation in which the participant physically receives the distribution and subsequently deposits the amount into an eligible plan. A distribution must be rolled over by the 60th day after the day it is received, or the entire distribution is subject to income tax and, if applicable, the 10 percent Sec. 72(t) penalty tax. The IRS can waive the 60-day requirement when the failure to satisfy that requirement is beyond the individual's reasonable control (discussed further below).

Direct Rollover

Rollovers are problematic because eligible rollover distributions from qualified plans, 403(b) annuities, or 457 governmental plans are subject to 20 percent mandatory income tax withholding. This means that a participant wanting to roll over the benefit only receives 80 percent of the total benefit. The entire benefit could be rolled over, but the other 20 percent would have to be contributed from other funds.

direct rollover

Mandatory withholding is not required if the participant elects a *direct rollover*. Qualified plans, 403(b) plans, and 457 governmental plans are required to give participants the option to elect a direct rollover for eligible distributions to an IRA or other employer-sponsored retirement plans. When a participant elects the direct rollover, instead of receiving the distribution, the funds are paid directly to the trustee of the new plan.

Planning Considerations

For many retiring plan participants, the best strategic decision is to elect a direct rollover of the entire benefit into an IRA. The direct rollover bypasses the 20 percent withholding rules, and once in the IRA the participant has maximum investment and withdrawal flexibility. As discussed in the next chapter, in some cases (especially defined-benefit plans) it might be economically beneficial to take the distribution directly from the employer's retirement plan. As discussed later in this chapter, there is also the occasional situation in which a participant receiving a lump-sum distribution from a qualified plan will want to consider electing one of the special tax rules that applies to lump-sum distributions.

There may also be several good reasons not to elect to roll over the entire distribution. As discussed earlier, the portion of the benefit that represents after-tax contributions should not be rolled over in most cases. Second, if the distribution includes the sponsoring company's stock, then the participant needs to carefully evaluate whether the net unrealized appreciation rules make it advantageous to take the stock portion of the distribution in income.

A participant over age 55 (but not yet age 59½) who needs funds might consider withdrawing the amount of the current need and rolling over the rest to avoid the 10 percent early withdrawal tax.

If the participant is changing jobs, the new employer's qualified plan, 403(b) annuity, or 457 governmental plan may (but is not required to) permit rollovers. Most individuals prefer the investment and withdrawal flexibility of an IRA. Also, if a participant dies while the money is held in the qualified plan (or 403(b) annuity or 457 plan), the death beneficiary will be limited by the distribution options offered by the plan. The plan may require a single sum distribution or limited installment payments. If the benefit was in an IRA, the beneficiary typically can withdraw the funds over his or her entire life expectancy as allowed under the minimum distribution rules. Stretching out the payments defers income taxes, resulting in additional tax deferred growth and a larger after-tax benefit for the heirs.

On the other hand, the ability to borrow, or specialized investment options like a guaranteed investment contract, may create an incentive to choose the new employer's plan instead of an IRA. If the participant is approaching or has attained age 70½ and is continuing to work, the rollover to the new employer's plan can potentially delay the timing of required minimum distributions.

Distributions from IRAs

Rollovers from SEPs and SIMPLEs (as well as traditional IRAs) are somewhat easier to accomplish because the 20 percent mandatory withholding rules do not apply. SIMPLE distributions have the most limitations. They can be rolled into another SIMPLE or, 2 years after the SIMPLE was established, into a traditional IRA. Once in a traditional IRA, in most cases the entire IRA amount can be rolled into another IRA or, for that matter, a qualified plan, 403(b) annuity, or 457 governmental plan. One exception is that required minimum distributions for the year cannot be rolled over.

Even though the mandatory withholding rules do not apply, a participant wishing to roll over a distribution from a SEP, SIMPLE, or IRA should have the assets transferred directly from one trustee to the other. This transaction, referred to as a trustee-to-trustee transfer, ensures that the participant does not violate the 60-day rollover rule. This is an important consideration because failure to meet the 60-day requirement means the entire distribution is subject to income tax and, if applicable, the 10 percent Sec. 72(t) penalty on the entire taxable portion of the distribution.

**YOUR FINANCIAL SERVICES PRACTICE:
CLIENT QUERY**

Question: Your client Rudolph, aged 50, has found out that he is eligible to receive a hardship withdrawal from his profit-sharing plan in the amount of $5,000. The withdrawal is to pay college education expenses for his daughter. He wants to know the withholding rules and income tax consequences of this distribution.

Solution: Because a hardship withdrawal is not an eligible rollover amount, he can receive the entire $5,000—the plan administrator is not required to withhold 20 percent for payment of income taxes. However, at the end of the year, Rudolph will have significant tax consequences. He will have to pay ordinary income taxes and the 10 percent Sec. 72(t) penalty tax. If the withdrawal were from an IRA account instead, the 10 percent penalty would not apply because the withdrawal is to pay for a family member's college education expenses.

Even considering the potential for a tax problem, there will be some occasions in which the participant will want short-term access to an IRA account. It is possible to withdraw some or all of the assets from a plan for 60 days. If a withdrawal is made and then returned within the 60 days, this is considered a rollover; no additional rollover can occur in that plan for one year from the time of the withdrawal. However, this requirement applies to each IRA separately; consequently, a participant with multiple IRAs could have one rollover in each plan annually. For purposes of the one-year rule, trustee-to-trustee transfers and direct transfers from a qualified plan to an IRA are not counted as a rollover.

Rollovers by Beneficiaries

Until this point, we have been discussing rollovers by participants. There are several situations in which other recipients are allowed the rollover option. A beneficiary who is the surviving spouse receiving an eligible rollover distribution may roll it over in total or in part to a qualified plan, 403(b) annuity, 457 governmental plan, or traditional IRA. Similarly, a spouse or former spouse entitled to a payout of benefits under a qualified domestic relations order (QDRO) is also entitled to a rollover.

Distributions in these cases are also subject to the direct rollover requirement and the 20 percent mandatory withholding requirements. When a spouse or former spouse rolls the benefit into an IRA or other plan, the spouse is treated as if he or she were the participant. This characterization is significant. Under the minimum-distribution rules, required distributions are calculated treating the spouse as the participant and not a beneficiary.

A spousal death beneficiary inheriting an IRA can leave the IRA account in the name of the decedent or roll the benefit into an IRA in his or her own name. Technically, the account can be retitled without even changing the IRA vehicle. The decision whether or not to retitle the account in the spouse's name has an impact on several related tax rules. If the spouse has not yet attained age 59½, changing the title could result in penalty taxes if withdrawals are made prior to age 59½. If the account is left in the participant's name, any payments to the spouse are death benefits exempt from the 10 percent penalty tax. On the other hand, retitling typically has advantages under the minimum-distribution rules. Fortunately there is no time limit on the ability to retitle the IRA, so the spousal beneficiary could leave the benefit in the name of the participant until the spouse attains age 59½ and then retitle it in his or her own name.

If a non-spouse is the death beneficiary of an IRA, then the IRA is treated as an inherited IRA. The IRA is generally a flexible vehicle that allows the death beneficiary to take withdrawals as slowly as required under the minimum-distribution rules. As discussed in the minimum-distribution rules, when there are multiple beneficiaries, it may even be possible to separate the inherited IRA into separate accounts to facilitate separate investing and withdrawal plans by the beneficiaries. Beginning in 2007, non-spouse death beneficiaries are allowed to roll distributions from a qualified plan, 403(b) plan, or government-sponsored 457 plan into an inherited IRA.

This again permits the beneficiary to stretch out benefits as allowed under the minimum-distribution rules.

Waivers for the 60-Day Rollover Requirement

Code Section 402(c)(3) provides that the IRS may waive the 60-day rollover requirement when the failure to waive such requirement "would be against equity or good conscience, including casualty, disaster, or other events beyond the reasonable control of the individual subject to such requirement."

When the 60-day rule has been violated, Rev. Proc. 2003-16 clarifies the conditions in which a waiver can be granted. The waiver is automatic (no application to the IRS is required) if a financial institution receives funds prior to the expiration of the 60-day rollover period, the taxpayer follows all procedures for depositing the funds into an eligible retirement plan within the 60-day period, and, solely due to an error on the part of the financial institution, the funds are not deposited into an eligible retirement plan within the 60-day rollover period. Automatic approval is granted only: (1) if the funds are deposited into an eligible retirement plan within one year from the beginning of the 60-day rollover period; and (2) if the financial institution had deposited the funds as instructed.

If an automatic waiver is not available, the taxpayer can file for a waiver using the same procedures for a private letter ruling described in Rev. Proc. 2003-4 and paying the user fee described in Rev. Proc. 2003-8 (generally $90). Rev. Proc. 2003-16 provides that in determining whether to grant a waiver of the 60-day rollover requirement the IRS will consider all relevant facts and circumstances, including: (1) errors committed by a financial institution; (2) inability to complete a rollover due to death, disability, hospitalization, incarceration, or restrictions imposed by a foreign country or postal error, (3) the use of the amount distributed (for example, in the case of payment by check, whether the check was cashed); and (4) the time elapsed since the distribution occurred.

A review of the private letter rulings that have been granted show that the IRS has been quite generous in granting the waiver of the 60-day requirement. Typically, the waiver has been granted when

- the facts and circumstances consisted of an error by the financial institution
- erroneous investment advice was given
- plan administrator errors were made
- the client's medical condition made it difficult to comply with the rules

- client errors occurred that ran contrary to the client's intention to make a rollover
- there was an existence of intervening causes such as the death of a spouse, weather conditions, or fraud by the taxpayer's child

Typically the waiver has been denied in situations where the taxpayer intended to use the amount for personal purposes and could not return it to the IRA before the 60-day time limit.

LUMP-SUM DISTRIBUTIONS

Instead of taking periodic payments from a qualified plan, employees are frequently permitted to receive their retirement benefit in a lump-sum distribution. In the past, participants who received a lump sum from a qualified plan had the opportunity to take advantage of several special tax rules. Most of these rules have been repealed, but several are still grandfathered for certain taxpayers. One rule that continues to be broadly available is the rule that defers the net unrealized appreciation of distributed employer securities. Grandfather rules include 10-year income averaging and a special capital-gains rate available for distributions attributable to pre-1974 participation. These rules are only available to individuals born before 1936.

Net Unrealized Appreciation

net unrealized appreciation (NUA)

Whenever a recipient receives a lump-sum distribution from a qualified plan, he or she may elect to defer paying tax on the *net unrealized appreciation (NUA)* in qualifying employer securities. If the distribution is not a lump-sum distribution, NUA is excludible only to the extent that the appreciation is attributable to nondeductible employee contributions.

lump-sum distribution

To qualify as a *lump-sum distribution,* the participant's entire benefit (referred to as balance to the credit) must be distributed in one tax year on account of death, disability, termination of employment, or attainment of age 59½. For purposes of 10-year forward averaging (but not the NUA rules), the participant also must have 5 years of plan participation to qualify. Under the balance-to-the-credit rules, all pension plans of a single sponsor (defined-benefit, money-purchase, target-benefit or cash-balance plan) are treated as a single plan; all profit-sharing plans (including 401(k)) are treated as a single plan; and all stock-bonus plans are treated as a single plan. This means, for example, that a participant in both a defined-benefit plan and a money-purchase plan would have to receive both benefits in the same year to receive the balance to the credit.

The NUA in the employer's stock that is included in a lump-sum distribution is excluded when computing the income tax on the distribution. NUA is the difference between the stock's value when credited to the participant's account and its fair market value on the date of distribution. The plan provides the participant with the value of the stock when it was credited to the account (referred to as the stock's cost basis). The plan can choose one of several methods for valuing the cost basis as found in Treas. Reg.1.402(a)-1(b)(2)(i).

This NUA is taxable as long-term capital gain to the recipient when the shares are sold, even if they are sold immediately. If the recipient holds the shares for a period of time after distribution, any additional gain (above the NUA) is taxed as long- or short-term capital gain, depending on the holding period (long term if held for one year or more).

To ensure that the participant's unrealized appreciation is taxed at some point, if the stock is left to an heir, the unrealized appreciation is not entitled to a step up in basis, but is treated as income in respect of a decedent (IRD). As with other IRD, the amount retains its character as long-term capital gain, and the beneficiary is entitled to a deduction for the amount of estate taxes paid on the IRD amount.

Taking Advantage of the NUA Rule

Recently, the NUA rule has been receiving more attention in the press. First, it is one of the only remaining special tax rules that apply to qualified plan distributions. Second, with the proliferation of the 401(k) plan, many plan participants are accumulating large employer stock accounts. Many mid-size and large companies provide employer securities as an investment alternative or even make employer-matching contributions in employer stock. Third, the current long-term capital-gains rate of 15 percent (10 percent in some cases) is less than half the top marginal tax rate (35 percent) for ordinary income. Participants receiving lump sums that include a distribution of employer securities should seriously consider taking advantage of this rule versus simply rolling the entire benefit into an IRA or other tax-sheltered retirement plan. Once the benefit is rolled over, future distributions will be subject to ordinary income tax.

Another reason the NUA rule can be quite useful is that a participant may elect to take advantage of the deferral of income recognition on NUA and roll over the remainder of the lump-sum distribution (see private letter ruling 9721036). This means a participant in a 401(k) plan with an employer securities account can elect NUA treatment on the employer stock account and roll over any other investments tax free into an IRA.

Example: Joe retires at age 62 and receives a lump-sum distribution with a current market value of $700,000. The market value of employer securities is $200,000, but the cost basis is $50,000. Joe should consider rolling the cash (worth $500,000) into an IRA but not rolling over the $200,000. At the time of the distribution, Joe will have to pay tax on the $50,000 cost basis. When he sells the stock, he will pay long-term capital gains on the $150,000 NUA, and he will pay long-term gain on any subsequent appreciation (as long as he holds the stock for at least one year). If Joe is in the 35 percent federal income tax bracket, he pays 35 percent on the $50,000 distribution, but he pays only 15 percent on the rest of the gain. If he rolls the employer securities into an IRA, all subsequent distributions will be taxed at 35 percent.

This example illustrates the importance of considering NUA tax treatment. It is the type of situation in which the election may well be the right choice. However, in each individual case, determining whether or not to roll the benefit into an IRA or to take the employer stock in income will not be an easy decision. Factors in the decision-making process include the following:

- The rule only has a positive impact when the cost basis of the securities is significantly lower than the current market value.
- If the participant needs cash in the near future, then taking the stock in income is probably a good idea since it results in a conversion of a portion of the taxable income from ordinary income to capital gains. Also, if the individual is under age 59½, the Section 72(t) tax will only apply to that portion of the income subject to ordinary income tax.
- A younger person receiving a distribution that includes company stock will generally want to sell the stock to diversify his or her retirement portfolio. Because the sale will result in current taxation, the individual is giving up what could be significant income tax deferral if he or she decides not to roll the stock into an IRA. Deferral is very valuable, even if the tax rate in the future is somewhat higher than the rate today.

In addition to the above considerations, the participant's attitude about paying taxes and projections about future tax rates are important considerations. The planner's main objective should be to present all of the alternatives clearly so the participant can make the right election.

Grandfathered Special Tax Rules

Individuals born before 1936 who receive lump-sum distributions from qualified plans may still be eligible for several grandfathered tax rules. (These rules never applied to IRAs, SEPs, SIMPLEs, or 403(b) plans.) Because these rules affect only a small portion of the pension population, they are covered here only briefly.

Ten-Year Averaging

10-year averaging

Ten-year averaging may still be available for individuals born prior to January 1, 1936 if the following conditions are met:

- The distribution qualifies as a lump-sum distribution.
- The election for 10-year averaging has not been made before (only one election per taxpayer).

The tax rate on a lump sum eligible for 10-year averaging depends upon the amount of the lump sum. The tax rate is calculated as follows:

- calculate one-tenth of the distribution (after taking into consideration a minimum-distribution allowance on distributions under $70,000)
- calculate the tax on that amount using 1986 tax rates, considering the lump-sum distribution as the taxpayer's only income
- multiply the result by 10

Because tax rates in 1986 were highly bracketed, the tax rate is generally favorable only when the distribution amount is relatively low. Table 24-3 can be used to determine the tax on a specific distribution. Assume your client receives a lump-sum distribution of $150,000. For simplicity, assume the entire distribution is taxable and there are no plan accumulations attributable to pre-1974 service. Looking at the table, the $150,000 distribution falls in the range between $137,100 and $171,600. Therefore, the tax on the $150,000 distribution is equal to $21,603 plus 23 percent of the excess over $137,100. The excess over $137,100 is $12,900; 23 percent of $12,900 is $2,967. Thus, the total 10-year averaging tax on a $150,000 distribution is equal to $21,603 plus $2,967, or $24,570.

The taxpayer reports the tax on Form 4972, which is filed with the tax return for the year. Form 4972 is quite useful because it includes detailed instructions and a worksheet for making the calculation.

Capital-Gains Election

Clients born before January 1, 1936, can elect to treat the portion of a lump-sum distribution attributable to pre-1974 plan participation as capital gain. If this election is made, the amount subject to capital gain is taxed at a special grandfathered rate of 20 percent (which was the capital gains tax rate in 1974). A recipient may make only one such election.

If the capital-gain provision is elected, the capital gain portion of a lump-sum distribution is then excluded when the person calculates the 10-year averaging tax. Therefore, the total tax payable on a lump-sum distribution when a person elects capital-gains treatment for pre-1974 plan accruals is equal to 20 percent of the portion of the distribution attributable to the pre-1974 plan accruals plus the averaging tax on the remainder. For example, assume that a lump-sum distribution is equal to $150,000, and the capital-gain portion is $33,000. If your client elects capital-gains treatment, only the portion of the distribution not attributable to the capital-gains portion (in this case, $117,000) is included in the adjusted total taxable amount when computing the averaging tax.

Clearly, a client born before January 1, 1936, should elect the capital-gains provision for pre-1974 plan accruals whenever the adjusted total taxable amount after subtracting the capital-gains portion is taxed at an effective rate of more than 20 percent. If we look at table 24-3, we can see that a person who elects 10-year averaging will always benefit by electing the capital-gains treatment for pre-1974 plan accruals if the adjusted total taxable amount after subtracting the capital-gains portion is equal to or greater than $137,100. At that level, each additional dollar of adjusted total taxable amount is taxed at a rate of 23 percent or higher.

Choosing Ten-Year Averaging and the Capital Gains Treatment

When should clients who are still eligible for these grandfathered special tax rules elect to receive lump-sum distributions, rather than periodic payouts from their plans (or from IRA rollover accounts)? First, tax rates in 1986 were quite high and the tax rate with special averaging will not be very attractive unless the distribution is approximately $300,000 or less. If this is the case, it is generally appropriate to explore the decision at least to the point of calculating the tax under the special rules.

TABLE 24-3				
10-Year Averaging (Using 1986 Tax Rates)*				
If the adjusted total taxable amount is				
at least	but not more than	the separate tax is	plus this %	of the excess over
. . .	$ 20,000	0	5.5	0
$ 20,000	21,583	$ 1,100	13.2	$ 20,000
21,583	30,583	1,309	14.4	21,583
30,583	49,417	2,605	16.8	30,583
49,417	67,417	5,769	18.0	49,417
67,417	70,000	9,009	19.2	67,417
70,000	91,700	9,505	16.0	70,000
91,700	114,400	12,977	18.0	91,700
114,400	137,100	17,063	20.0	114,400
137,100	171,600	21,603	23.0	137,100
171,600	228,800	29,538	26.0	171,600
228,800	286,000	44,410	30.0	228,800
286,000	343,200	61,570	34.0	286,000
343,200	423,000	81,018	38.0	343,200
423,000	571,900	111,342	42.0	423,000
571,900	857,900	173,880	48.0	571,900
857,900	. . .	311,160	50.0	857,900

* Persons who elect 10-year averaging must use the 1986 single tax rate schedule regardless of the year in which they actually receive the distribution.

Once the special tax rate is determined, then the client needs to consider whether the tax rate looks attractive or not. This will depend upon several factors, including

- the length of the potential period of additional tax deferral
- the current investment environment
- expected increases (or decreases) in the income tax rates

Estate planning considerations are also crucial in the equation. Sometimes the best way to pass on wealth to the next generation is to defer income taxes as long as possible. (See the discussion in the following chapter.) Other times, concerns about liquidity can weigh in favor of taking a lump sum. In estate planning, the liquidity can be needed for funding a gifting program, retitling assets in the name of the spouse, or funding the purchase of life insurance.

Even when the special tax rate seems quite low, it is appropriate to begin with a healthy skepticism regarding the advantages to paying tax on the lump sum. Tax deferral is hard to beat, especially when the potential distribution stream is going to be 20 years or more—which is the case for most clients.

Ultimately, the decision generally needs to be made only after a lot of fact finding and consideration of the factors mentioned above. Only then can it be determined whether special averaging treatment makes sense for a specific client.

MINIMUM-DISTRIBUTION RULES

The minimum-distribution rules contained in IRC Sec. 401(a)(9) are designed to limit the deferral of taxation on plan benefits. The primary reason for allowing the deferral of taxes is to encourage savings for retirement. This tax-preferred item comes at a great cost to the government; therefore, the minimum-distribution rules have been designed both to ensure that a significant portion of a participant's benefit is paid out during retirement and to limit the period for benefits paid after death.

General

The rules of 401(a)(9) apply in essentially the same way (with a few exceptions) to all tax-preferred retirement plans, including qualified plans, IRAs (including SEPs and SIMPLEs), 403(b) annuity plans, and even IRC Sec. 457 plans. This means that any Roth accounts in a 401(k) plan or 403(b) plan would be subject to the minimum-distribution rules. Roth IRAs are not subject to the rules governing lifetime distributions to the participant, but are required to make minimum distributions to the beneficiary after the death of the participant.

It is important to understand that there are actually two separate minimum-distribution rules. One rule applies to those individuals who live until the required beginning date (generally the April 1 following the year the participant attained age 70½) and a separate rule that applies when the participant dies before the required beginning date.

Another complicating factor is that Code Sec. 402 allows a spouse the option to roll over a benefit received at the death of the participant into an IRA in his or her own name. The rollover is treated as a complete distribution from the participant's plan, meaning that the minimum-distribution rules will have to be satisfied, treating the spouse as the participant. This rule provides planning opportunities, but can also be confusing.

Failing to satisfy the minimum-distribution rules results in an extremely harsh penalty. Under IRC Sec. 4974, if the minimum distributions are not made in a timely manner, the plan participant is required to pay a 50 percent excise tax on the amount of the shortfall between the amount actually distributed and the amount required to be distributed under the minimum-distribution rules. In addition, if the plan is a qualified plan, it may lose its tax-favored status if the minimum-distribution rules are not satisfied.

To help enforce the minimum-distribution rules, IRA trustees are required to report on Form 5498 participants who have a required minimum distribution. At the same time, IRA trustees are also required to notify participants by January 31 that a required distribution is due for that year. Trustees can either provide a calculation of the required minimum distribution or offer to make the calculation at the participant's request. At the present time, there are no similar reporting requirements for qualified plans. The requirement also currently ends at the participant's death; no reporting is required concerning required distributions for death beneficiaries.

Minimum Distributions at the Required Beginning Date

The next several pages describe the minimum-distribution rules that apply when the individual has lived until the required beginning date (generally April 1 of the year following attainment of age 70½). The rules for determining the minimum distribution differ depending on whether the distribution is from an individual account plan or is payable as an annuity—either from a defined-benefit plan or from a commercial annuity. The account plan rules apply to all IRAs, 403(b) plans, SEPs, SIMPLEs, Sec. 457 plans, and qualified plans of the defined-contribution type, unless a commercial annuity is purchased prior to the required beginning date. The account plan rules are reviewed below, followed by a discussion of the annuity distribution rules.

Required Beginning Date

required beginning date

The date benefit payments must begin is called the *required beginning date*. This date is generally April 1 of the year following the calendar year in which the participant attains age 70½. However, there are two important exceptions:

- Any participant in a government or church plan who remains an employee after reaching age 70½ does not have to begin distributions until the April 1 following the later of either the calendar year in which the participant reaches age 70½ or the calendar year in which he or she retires.
- Any qualified plan participant who reaches age 70½ and who is not considered a 5 percent owner of the entity sponsoring the plan does not have to begin distributions until the April 1 following the later of either the year of attainment of age 70½ or the year in which the

participant retires. This exception also applies to 403(b) plans without regard to the 5-percent-owner rule.

Note that there are no exceptions to the required beginning date for IRAs—which also includes SEPs and SIMPLEs. For these plans, the required beginning date is always the April 1 of the year following the calendar year in which the covered participant attains age 70½.

first distribution year

The required beginning date is somewhat of a misnomer because a minimum distribution is required for the year in which the participant attains age 70½ or, if one of the exceptions applies, the year in which the participant retires. Because a distribution must be made for this year, it is referred to as the *first distribution year*. The distribution for the first distribution year can be delayed until the following April 1, but required distributions for all subsequent distribution years must be made by December 31 of the applicable year.

Example: Shelley, who has an IRA, turned 70 on March 15, 2005. On September 15, 2005, she turned 70½. The first required distribution from Shelley's IRA is for the year ending December 31, 2005, but she has the option to take the distribution any time in 2005 or delay it up to the required beginning date of April 1, 2006. However, if she delays the distribution into 2006, she will still have to take a minimum distribution for the second distribution year by December 31, 2006.

As you can see, delaying the first distribution into the second year doubles up the required distribution for that year and increases taxes for that year—not a desirable result in some cases.

Account Plan Distributions During the Participant's Life

Once the participant attains the required beginning date, a minimum distribution is required for each and every distribution year (and no credit is given for larger distributions in prior years) through the year of the participant's death. The required distribution is calculated by dividing the account balance by the applicable distribution period. The participant's benefit in a defined-contribution plan, 403(b) plan, or IRA is based on the participant's account balance. In an IRA account, the benefit for a distribution year is the IRA account balance at the end of the previous calendar year. For qualified plans and 403(b) plans, the employee's benefit is his or her individual account balance as of the last valuation date in the calendar year immediately preceding the distribution year.

The distribution period comes from the Uniform Lifetime table (see table 24-4) and is determined based on the age of the participant at the end of the distribution year. The same methodology is used for every year the participant is alive. Each year the applicable distribution period is determined by simply looking at the uniform table based on the age of the participant during that year.

TABLE 24-4
Uniform Lifetime Table

Age of Participant	Distribution Period	Age of Participant	Distribution Period
70	27.4	93	9.6
71	26.5	94	9.1
72	25.6	95	8.6
73	24.7	96	8.1
74	23.8	97	7.6
75	22.9	98	7.1
76	22.0	99	6.7
77	21.2	100	6.3
78	20.3	101	5.9
79	19.5	102	5.5
80	18.7	103	5.2
81	17.9	104	4.9
82	17.1	105	4.5
83	16.9	106	4.2
84	15.5	107	3.9
85	14.8	108	3.7
86	14.1	109	3.4
87	13.4	110	3.1
88	12.7	111	2.9
89	12.0	112	2.6
90	11.4	113	2.4
91	10.8	114	2.1
92	10.2	115 and older	1.9

Example: Sally, an IRA participant, is aged 71 at the last day of the first distribution year (the year she attains age 70½). Her IRA balance at the end of the preceding year is $200,000. The first year's required distribution is $200,000/26.5 = $7,547 (table 24-4). This is the required minimum regardless of the beneficiary unless Sally's sole beneficiary is her spouse and he is more than 10 years younger than she. For the second distribution year the applicable distribution period is 25.6 (table amount for a 72-year-old participant).

An exception applies if the employee's sole beneficiary is the employee's spouse and the spouse is more than 10 years younger than the employee. In that case, the employee is permitted to use the longer distribution period measured by the joint life and last survivor life expectancy of the employee and spouse (calculated looking at the IRS Joint and Last Survivor Table, a portion of which is reproduced in table 24-5. The complete table appears in appendix 4.) This exception will apply for any distribution year in which the spouse (who is more than 10 years younger than the participant) is the sole beneficiary as of January 1 of the distribution year. This means that if the spouse dies or the couple gets divorced after January 1, the joint life table can still be used for that year.

TABLE 24-5
Joint and Last Survivor Table

Ages	45	46	47	48	49	50	51	52	53	54
68	39.6	38.7	37.9	37.0	36.2	35.3	34.5	33.7	32.9	32.1
69	39.5	38.6	37.8	36.9	36.0	35.2	34.4	33.6	32.8	32.0
70	39.4	38.6	37.7	36.8	35.9	35.1	34.3	33.4	32.6	31.8
71	39.4	38.5	37.6	36.7	35.9	35.0	34.2	33.3	32.5	31.7
72	39.3	38.4	37.5	36.6	35.8	34.9	34.1	33.2	32.4	31.6
73	39.3	38.4	37.5	36.6	35.7	34.8	34.0	33.1	32.3	31.5
74	39.2	38.3	37.4	36.5	35.6	34.8	33.9	33.0	32.2	31.4
75	39.2	38.3	37.4	36.5	35.6	34.7	33.8	33.0	32.1	31.3
76	39.1	38.2	37.3	36.4	35.5	34.6	33.8	32.9	32.0	31.2
77	39.1	38.2	37.3	36.4	35.5	34.6	33.7	32.8	32.0	31.1
78	39.1	38.2	37.2	36.3	35.4	34.5	33.6	32.8	31.9	31.0

*Source: Treas. Reg. Sec. 1.401(a)(9)-9

Example: If Sally's beneficiary in the previous example was her 51-year-old spouse, the minimum distribution would be $200,000/34.2 = $5,848 (table 24-5). In this case, for the second distribution year the applicable distribution period is 33.2—their joint life expectancy calculated at the end of that distribution year.

Death of the Participant after the Required Beginning Date

For the participant who dies after the required beginning date, distributions must continue to satisfy the required minimum-distribution rules. In the year of death, the heirs must take the decedent's required distribution (if this distribution was not taken before death) based on the method under which the decedent had been taking distributions.

In subsequent years, the required distributions will depend upon who is the chosen beneficiary. When the beneficiary is an individual who is not the spouse, the applicable distribution period is that individual's life expectancy (using the IRS Single Life Table [(table 24-6)]) as of the end of the year

TABLE 24-6
Single Life Table *

Age	Multiple	Age	Multiple
40	43.6	66	20.2
41	42.7	67	19.4
42	41.7	68	18.6
43	40.7	69	17.8
44	39.8	70	17.0
45	38.8	71	16.3
46	37.9	72	15.5
47	37.0	73	14.8
48	36.0	74	14.1
49	35.1	75	13.4
50	34.2	76	12.7
51	33.3	77	12.1
52	32.3	78	11.4
53	31.4	79	10.8
54	30.5	80	10.2
55	29.6	81	9.7
56	28.7	82	9.1
57	27.9	83	8.6
58	27.0	84	8.1
59	26.1	85	7.6
60	25.2	86	7.1
61	24.4	87	6.7
62	23.5	88	6.3
63	22.7	89	5.9
64	21.8	90	5.5
65	21.0		

*Source: Treas. Reg. Sec. 1.401(a)(9)-9.

following death. In subsequent years, the applicable distribution period is the life expectancy from the previous year less one. This means that remaining distributions are now made over a fixed period. This is true even if the beneficiary at the time of death subsequently dies and leaves the benefit to another heir.

Example: John dies at age 82 with an $800,000 IRA account (at the end of the previous year). For the year of death, the required minimum distribution is $800,000/17.1 = $46,783. Assuming that, at the end of the year of death, the value of the account is $840,000 and on September 30 of the following year the sole beneficiary is John's daughter, Sarah, who is aged 54 at the end of that year, the minimum distribution is $840,000/30.5 = $27,540. The remaining distribution period is now fixed. In the next year, the applicable distribution period is 29.5 (30.5 – 1), and so on in future years. In total, distributions can continue for 31 years after the death of the participant. This would be true even if Sarah dies before the end of the period and leaves the benefit to her heirs.

If there is no designated beneficiary as of September 30 of the year after the employee's death (which would be the case if a nonperson such as a charity or the estate was the chosen beneficiary), the distribution period is the employee's life expectancy calculated in the year of death, reduced by one for each subsequent year.

Example: Sandra dies at age 80 with her estate as the beneficiary. Her account balance at the end of the year of her death is $240,000, and her life expectancy is 9.2 years (10.2 – 1) in the year following death. The required distribution in the year following death is $26,087 ($240,000/9.2). In each following year, the applicable distribution period is reduced by one, until all amounts are distributed after 10 years.

If the participant's spouse is the chosen beneficiary, there are a number of options. In most cases, the spouse will elect to roll the benefit into his or her own IRA (or, in some cases, treat the account as his or her own). In this case, subsequent distributions (in the year following death) are calculated by using the same methodology as when the participant was alive—with the spouse now treated as the participant.

Example: Rollo dies at age 80; his spouse Cassandra, aged 75, is the beneficiary. Cassandra rolls the benefit into her own IRA and names their only child, Alexis, as beneficiary. During Cassandra's life, the uniform table is still used to calculate the minimum required distribution. For example, in the year following Rollo's death, the applicable distribution period is 22.0 (see table 24-4 for individual aged 76). Assume that Cassandra dies at age 86 and, on the September 30 following the year of her death, her daughter Alexis is the beneficiary. At the end of that year, Alexis is aged 53. The applicable distribution period is 31.4 for that year (see table 24-6). This is now the fixed remaining distribution period, even if Alexis dies prior to the end of that time period. Her beneficiaries could continue distributions over the remaining period. In this example, the minimum distributions are spread over a 50-year period!

If the participant's spouse is his or her sole beneficiary as of September 30 in the year following the year of death, and the distribution is not rolled over, the distribution period during the spouse's life is the spouse's single life expectancy, recalculated each year. For years after the year of the spouse's death, the distribution period is the spouse's life expectancy calculated in the year of death, reduced by one for each subsequent year.

Annuity Payments

When a defined-benefit pension plan pays out a benefit in the form of an annuity, or if a commercial annuity is purchased to satisfy benefit payments in a defined-contribution plan, the regulations provide a method for determining whether the annuity satisfies the minimum-distribution rules. Under these rules, the determination only has to be made one time—when the annuity payments begin.

If the annuity is meant to satisfy the required minimum-distribution rules, it must begin on or before the participant's required beginning date. Most life annuity and joint and survivor annuities will satisfy the rules as long as the payment interval is uniform, does not exceed one year, and the stream of payments satisfies a nonincreasing requirement. The term *nonincreasing* is defined broadly in the regulations, and variable annuities and annuities that increase due to cost-of-living increases fit within the definition. An annuity with a cash-refund feature also qualifies.

Joint and survivor annuities with a survivor benefit of up to 100 percent are generally allowed. The only exception is for nonspousal beneficiaries who are more than 10 years younger than the participant. In this case, the maximum survivor benefit will be something less than 100 percent. To determine the applicable survivor percentage, see the IRS Table reproduced in table 24-7. The example below explains how this works.

TABLE 24-7
Table for Determining the Maximum Applicable Survivor Annuity Percentage

Excess of Age of Employee over Age of Beneficiary	Applicable Percentage	Excess of Age of Employee over Age of Beneficiary	Applicable Percentage
10 years or less	100%	28	62%
11	96	29	61
12	93	30	60
13	90	31	59
14	87	32	59
15	84	33	58
16	82	34	57
17	79	35	56
18	77	36	56
19	75	37	55
20	73	38	55
21	72	39	54
22	70	40	54
23	68	41	53
24	67	42	53
25	66	43	53
26	64	44 years and more	52
27	63		

Source: Proposed Treas. Reg. Sec. 1.401(a)(9)-2

Example: Sandra wants to elect a 100 percent joint and survivor benefit from her company's defined-benefit plan beginning at age 70. She is considering her son, Albert, aged 45, as the contingent beneficiary.

Looking at table 24-7, notice that the maximum survivor benefit for a beneficiary who is 25 years younger than the participant $(70 - 45 = 25)$ is 66 percent.

The life annuity can have a period certain (or the annuity can be a period certain annuity without a lifetime contingency) as long as the period certain does not exceed the joint life expectancy of the participant and beneficiary using the uniform table (or joint and survivor table in the case of a spouse more than 10 years younger than the participant).

Example: Suppose Herb, aged 70 (at the end of the first distribution year), chooses a joint and survivor annuity with Sally, aged 80, as the contingent beneficiary. Herb wants to have a period-certain feature and wants to know if there are limitations on the length of the period certain. Because the joint life expectancy under the uniform table for Herb (age 70) is 27.4, this is the maximum length for period-certain payments for an annuity beginning at age 70.

**YOUR FINANCIAL SERVICES PRACTICE:
ANNUITIZING AFTER THE REQUIRED BEGINNING DATE**

It's quite possible that an IRA participant past the required beginning date would want to purchase an immediate annuity. This transaction is allowed as long as the amount of the distribution satisfies the account plan rules in the year the annuity is purchased, and the annuity purchased satisfies the annuity limitations.

Preretirement Death Benefits

When the participant dies prior to the required beginning date, the general rule is that a participant's entire interest must be distributed by December 31 of the calendar year that contains the fifth anniversary of the date the participant dies. Under this rule, the entire interest could be distributed at the end of the 5-year period.

There are two important exceptions that allow payments over the beneficiary's life expectancy, one that applies to spousal beneficiaries and one that applies to nonspousal beneficiaries. For nonspousal beneficiaries, the minimum-distribution rule is satisfied if distributions are made over the expected lifetime of the beneficiary, as long as the benefit begins by December 31 of the year following the year of death. The calculation of each required distribution is determined using the same methodology as with a nonspousal beneficiary when the participant dies after the required beginning date.

Example:	Suppose that Gilligan dies at age 65 and his daughter Ginger is the beneficiary of his IRA. In the year following death, Ginger is aged 40 and her life expectancy is 43.6 years. If the lifetime exception is used and the account balance is $300,000 at the end of the year in which Gilligan dies, the required distribution in the following year is $300,000/43.6 = $6,880. Note that as long as distributions begin by the end of the year following the year Gilligan died, distributions can continue for 44 years. If this deadline is not met, the entire distribution must be made within 5 years!

When the beneficiary is the participant's spouse, the distribution may be made over the life of the spouse, as long as payments begin on or before the later of (1) December 31 of the calendar year immediately after the calendar year in which the participant dies or (2) December 31 of the calendar year immediately after the year in which the participant would have reached age 70½. However, if the spouse dies prior to the commencement of benefit payments, then benefits may be distributed to his or her beneficiary under the same rules that would apply to the participant. Note that the spousal exception is generally not utilized since the spouse will typically elect to roll the benefit into his or her own account.

If the participant does not have a designated beneficiary, or chooses a nonperson such as a charity or estate, then distributions must be made over a 5-year period. The lifetime exceptions are not available.

Beneficiary Issues

All of the minimum-distribution rules involve the identification of the participant's beneficiary. Under the current regulations, the beneficiary used to determine the required distribution is the beneficiary that actually inherits the benefit. Technically, it is the beneficiary identified as of September 30 of the year following death. (See the discussion of postdeath planning below.)

Generally, a beneficiary must be an individual (that is, not a charity or the participant's estate) in order to take advantage of the ability to stretch out payments over a beneficiary's lifetime. A nonperson beneficiary (estate, charity, trust) is treated as having no beneficiary, unless the beneficiary is a trust and the following requirements are satisfied:

- The trust is irrevocable at death.
- The beneficiaries under the trust are identifiable.
- The trust document or a statement identifying the distribution provisions is provided to the plan's administrator.

In the case of a trust that conforms to the rules, the beneficiaries of the trust will be treated as the beneficiaries for purposes of the minimum-distribution rules. In most cases, the requirement of notifying the plan administrator does not have to occur until the time the beneficiaries have to be identified.

If there are multiple designated beneficiaries on September 30 of the year following death (and separate accounts for each participant have not been established), the life expectancy of the oldest beneficiary (with the shortest life expectancy) is used to determine the required distributions. If one of those beneficiaries is a nonperson, then the participant is deemed to have no designated beneficiary. If there are multiple designated beneficiaries and separate accounts exist, the minimum distributions of his or her separate share are taken by each beneficiary over the fixed-term life expectancy of each respective beneficiary.

Additional Rules

Multiple Plans

With qualified retirement plans, required minimum distributions must be calculated—and distributed—separately for each plan subject to the rules. The rules are more liberal with multiple IRAs or 403(b) plans. With IRAs, the minimum distribution must be calculated separately for each IRA, but then the actual distributions can come from any of the IRA accounts. If, however, an individual has accounts in his or her own name as well as inherited IRAs, he or she cannot aggregate the two groups to determine the required minimum 403(b) plans to be aggregated in a similar way (although IRAs and 403(b) plans may not be aggregated).

Rollovers and Transfers

As we have discussed, liberal rules allow participants the right to roll or transfer benefits from one type of tax-sheltered plan to another. This transaction is relatively simple except in the case of the individual rolling over the benefit after attainment of age 70½. In order to ensure that the minimum distributions are made, the rules clarify what to do in this special situation.

Special rules apply to amounts rolled (or transferred) from one tax-sheltered retirement plan to another. From the perspective of the distributing plan, the amount distributed (to be rolled over or transferred) is credited toward determining the minimum distribution from the plan. However, if a portion of the distribution is necessary to satisfy the minimum-distribution requirements, that portion may not be rolled (or transferred) into another plan.

Example:	Shirley, aged 71½, receives a single-sum distribution from a qualified retirement plan. She intends to roll the distribution into an IRA. She may not roll the portion of the lump-sum distribution that represents the minimum distribution for the current distribution year into the IRA.

After the amount is rolled into the second plan, it will count toward determining the participant's benefit for determining the minimum distribution. However, because the minimum distribution is based on the benefit in the previous year, the amount rolled over does not affect the minimum until the following year.

Spousal Rollovers

When the spouse is the beneficiary of the participant's retirement plan benefit, the spouse has a unique opportunity to roll the benefit into an IRA in his or her own name. Under the minimum-distribution rules, the rollover is treated as a complete distribution of the participant's benefit, satisfying the minimum-distribution rules from the perspective of the participant's plan. After the benefit is in the spouse's name, the minimum-distribution rules have to be satisfied with the spouse treated as the participant. The spouse has the opportunity to name a beneficiary and calculate future minimum distributions based upon the joint life expectancy of the spouse and the beneficiary.

Grandfather Provisions for Qualified Plans and 403(b) Plans

There are two situations in which the current distribution rules do not apply. In a qualified plan, participants with accrued benefits as of December 31, 1983, were allowed to sign an election form (prior to January 1, 1984) to indicate the time and method of distribution of their plan benefit.

The benefit election form had to be specific and had to conform to pre-TEFRA rules, which allowed distributions to be deferred much later than age 70½. These grandfather provisions were contained in Sec. 242(b) of TEFRA and are generally referred to as *TEFRA 242(b) elections.*

The Sec. 242(b) elections continue to be valid if benefits are being paid from the original plan in which the election was made, and if the plan distributions follow the Sec. 242(b) distribution election. If it is not followed exactly with regard to the form and timing of the payments, the election is considered revoked. A substitution or addition of a beneficiary generally does not result in the revocation of the election. If the benefit election is changed or revoked after the individual has reached the required beginning date under the current rules, the participant will be forced to "make up" distributions that would otherwise (absent the Sec. 242(b) election) have been required under the current rules.

Sec. 242(b) elections can delay the timing of required distributions substantially. The retirement planner should be sure to ask if the client has retained an election form in his or her files. As noted above, the election has to be followed exactly in order to avoid having to take a potentially large distribution at some later date.

In a 403(b) plan, a separate grandfathering rule allows the participant to delay the distribution of amounts earned prior to 1987 until the participant attains age 75. There are no special grandfathering exceptions that apply to IRA distributions.

Planning

Under the current rules, the designated beneficiary does not have to be determined until September 30 of the year following the year of the participant's death. This permits some flexibility for determining the postdeath minimum required distributions from the retirement plan or IRA. Of course, the decedent's potential beneficiaries are "carved in stone" at the time of his or her death, because the decedent can no longer make additional beneficiary choices. However, the use of a qualified disclaimer or early distribution of a beneficiary's share could be effective in changing the designated beneficiary to contingent beneficiaries by the time specified to determine such beneficiary.

Example: Helen dies at age 80. At the time of her death, her son, Bud, from her first marriage, The American College, and her second husband, Saul, are each beneficiaries of one-third of the benefit. Before

September 30 of the year following death, Saul rolls his benefit into a spousal IRA, benefits are paid out to The American College, and Bud is the sole beneficiary. This means subsequent required distributions will be based on Bud's life expectancy. If Helen had also named a contingent beneficiary for Bud's benefit (for example, Bud's child, Kelly), Bud could disclaim his benefit in favor of Kelly and the distribution could continue over Kelly's longer life expectancy.

Another way to limit problems that could arise with multiple beneficiaries is to divide benefits into separate accounts. The regulations define acceptable separate accounting to include allocating investment gains and losses, and contributions and forfeitures, on a pro rata basis in a reasonable and consistent manner between such separate portion and any other benefits. If these rules are followed, the separate beneficiary of each share determines his or her minimum required distribution based on his or her life expectancy according to his or her age on the birthday that occurs in the year following the year of the decedent's death. The final regulations clearly state that the account can be divided into a separate account for each beneficiary up to the end of the year following the death of the participant.

**YOUR FINANCIAL SERVICES PRACTICE:
BENEFICIARY ELECTIONS**

Under the final regulations, taking advantage of maximum deferral is an option that remains open even after the death of the participant, but only if the beneficiary election contains the appropriate list of contingent beneficiaries and qualified disclaimers are made. For example, with a married person with children, the following beneficiary and three layers of contingent beneficiary elections may be an appropriate choice:

- payable to the spouse and if disclaimed
- payable to a credit-shelter trust with the spouse as income beneficiary and the children as remainder beneficiaries, and if disclaimed
- payable directly to the children, and if disclaimed
- payable to a trust with the grandchildren as beneficiaries

Because of the ability to disclaim benefits, pay them out, or establish separate accounts after the death of the participant, postmortem planning is possible. However, to effectively use these tools, the participant should give careful consideration to the beneficiary election form. For many individuals, this means the establishment of multiple layers of contingent beneficiaries on the designation form in order to provide the most flexibility after the participant's death.

CHAPTER REVIEW

Key Terms

Sec. 72(t) penalty tax [24-2]   lump-sum distribution [24-6]
substantially equal periodic   10-year averaging [24-6]
   payments[24-2]   required beginning date [24-7]
eligible rollover distribution[24-5]   first distribution year [24-7]
rollover [24-5]   TEFRA 242(b) elections [24-7]
direct rollover [24-5]
net unrealized appreciation (NUA)
   [24-6]

Review Questions

Review questions are based on the learning objectives in this chapter. Thus, a [24-3] at the end of a question means that the question is based on learning objective 24-3. If there are multiple objectives, they are all listed.

1. Describe the federal income tax treatment of benefit distributions to a participant from a tax-advantaged retirement plan. [24-1]

2. Describe the estate tax treatment of an accumulated qualified plan or IRA account and how this affects the income tax treatment of a distribution to a death beneficiary. [24-1]

3. Which of the following plan distributions is subject to the 10 percent Sec. 72(t) penalty? [24-2]
    a. a death benefit from a defined-benefit plan payable to a beneficiary upon the death of an employee aged 52
    b. a lump-sum benefit from a money-purchase pension plan payable to a disabled employee aged 57
    c. a distribution from a 401(k) plan to an employee aged 52 who qualifies under the plan's "financial hardship" distribution provision
    d. an in-service distribution made to an employee aged 63 from a profit-sharing plan
    e. a $10,000 distribution from a SIMPLE to pay for qualifying acquisition costs of a first home for the participant

4   Ralph withdraws $100,000 from his IRA for start-up costs for his new business. In the same year, he pays $40,000 in tuition, $12,000 in room, board, and fees, and $2,000 for books for his two daughters, who are full-time students at Haverford College. What is the applicable Sec. 72(t) penalty tax? [24-2]

5.   What method for avoiding the 10 percent early-withdrawal penalty is the most useful and flexible for planning purposes? [24-2]

6.   What are the risks of relying on the substantially equal payment exception? [24-2]

7.   Ralph has two IRAs, one created with nondeductible contributions (contributions total $12,000 and current value is $43,000) and one created by a rollover from a qualified plan ($357,000). He has not taken any previous withdrawals. Ralph withdraws $12,000 from the nondeductible IRA, thinking this transaction will have no income tax ramifications. In reality, how much of the distribution is taxable? [24-3]

8.   Your client, Cherie Reisenberg, is single and plans to retire at age 62. Payments from her employer's qualified plan will start at the end of the first month after her 62nd birthday. The monthly retirement benefit that will be paid to Cherie in the form of a single-life annuity without any guaranteed payments is $1,000. Her cost basis in the plan is $72,900. What portion of her first distribution will be nontaxable? [24-3]

9.   Mick Jagner (aged 60 in 2007) made his first Roth IRA contribution on January 20, 2002, for the 2001 tax year. On February 1, 2007, he withdraws $19,000 from the Roth IRA to help purchase a new car. This is the first withdrawal from the plan that he has taken. As of February 1, the value of the account is $24,000 and $15,000 represents Roth IRA contributions. [24-4]
   a.   Based on these assumptions, what is the tax treatment of the withdrawal?
   b.   Now assume that Mick is aged 55, not aged 60. What is the tax treatment of the withdrawal?

10.   Sally is receiving a life annuity from her former employer's defined-benefit pension plan. Sometimes she doesn't need the money for day-to-day expenses. Can she roll over some of the payments into an IRA? [24-5]

11.   Carole Gumley, aged 54, is retiring early and has a profit-sharing balance of $150,000. She receives a notice of the right to receive a direct rollover, but she hasn't yet decided where she would like to invest her retirement money so she receives the distribution from the plan directly. Answer the following questions. [24-5]
   a.   How much will Carole actually receive from the plan?
   b.   Can Carole roll over the entire benefit?

c.   What are the tax ramifications if she doesn't get around to rolling over the benefit for 75 days?

d.   Would the situation be different if the reason that she waited 75 days is that a financial advisor told her that she had 90 days to accomplish the rollover?

12.   In what situations is it more prudent to take some or all of a distribution into income instead of rolling the benefit into an IRA? [24-5]

13.   What conditions must a lump-sum distribution meet in order to qualify for special tax treatment? [24-6]

14.   Andrew Fiddler, aged 45, receives a distribution of $400,000 in cash and $100,000 of company stock from his employer's 401(k) plan. Andrew rolls over the cash portion of the distribution and elects to take the stock portion into income. The company tells him that the cost basis for the stock is $25,000. Andrew sells the stock 3 years later for $125,000. What are the tax ramifications of these two transactions? [24-6]

15.   What special tax treatment is available for qualifying lump-sum distributions if the client was born before January 1, 1936? [24-6]

16.   William Nims receives a lump-sum distribution of $250,000 from his company's profit-sharing plan (the only plan that William participated in). William was born in 1934 and has not elected grandfathered 10-year averaging before. It turns out that $40,000 of the benefit is eligible for the 20 percent grandfathered capital gains provision. How much tax will William have to pay if he elects both 10-year averaging and the capital gains provision? [24-6]

17.   What types of plans are subject to the required minimum-distribution rules? [24-7]

18.   Sara Stewart is required to take a minimum distribution of $2,000 from a qualified retirement plan at the required beginning date. The distribution does not occur. What penalties arise from this failure? [24-7]

19.   James Daniel was born on July 15, 1934. State his required beginning date in the following situations: [24-7]
a.   He is a participant in an IRA.
b.   He is an employee of Alpha Corp. and he is a participant in a 401(k) plan. He is not a 5-percent owner. He plans to terminate employment on June 1, 2008.

20.   Distributions for the first two distribution years have to be made by when? [24-7]

21.   Joe is aged 70 at the end of the first distribution year. His IRA account balance was $250,000 at the end of the previous year. His beneficiary is his

65-year-old spouse, Jenny. What is the required minimum distribution for the first distribution year? [24-7]

22. Taking the facts from the previous question, what is the required distribution for the second distribution year if the account balance is $265,000? [24-7]

23. Joe is aged 70 at the end of the first distribution year. His IRA account balance was $250,000 at the end of the previous year. His beneficiary is his 52-year-old spouse, Jenny. What is the required minimum distribution for the first distribution year? [24-7]

24. Sally dies at age 75 and leaves her benefit to her 48-year-old son. How is the required minimum distribution calculated in the year of her death and for subsequent years? [24-7]

25. If a participant dies at age 55 and has named a 30-year-old child as beneficiary, what must happen to ensure distributions can be made over the child's life expectancy? [24-7]

26. Will an individual with two IRA accounts satisfy the minimum-distribution rules by taking a distribution from only one plan? [24-7]

27. Describe four important planning tools that can be used to maximize the potential deferral period after the participant's death under the minimum-distribution rules. [24-8]

25

Distributions from Retirement Plans—Part II

Learning Objectives

An understanding of the material in this chapter should enable you to

---

25-1.   Review the types of benefit distribution options that are available in qualified plans, IRAs, and 403(b) plans.

25-2.   Identify the key distribution issues for the middle-class client who is concerned about financing retirement needs.

25-3.   Identify the key distribution issues for the wealthier client who is concerned about both financing retirement needs and building an estate for his or her heirs.

Chapter Outline

CHOOSING A DISTRIBUTION OPTION

Choosing the best distribution at retirement can be a complex decision that involves personal preferences, financial considerations, and interplay between tax incentives and tax penalties. Planners must keep a myriad of factors in mind in order to render effective advice.

For example, typical considerations include whether

- the periodic distribution will be used to provide income necessary for sustaining the retiree or whether the distribution will supplement already adequate sources of retirement income
- the client has properly coordinated distributions from several different qualified plans and IRAs
- the retiree will have satisfactory diversification of his or her retirement resources after the distribution occurs
- the client has complied with the rules for minimum distributions from a qualified plan

The first step in making a choice is to fully understand the available options. Following is a discussion of the options that are available from qualified plans, SEPs, SIMPLEs and 403(b) plans. Of course, the only way to understand the options for a plan is to read the appropriate documents.

Benefits Available from the Plan

When discussing the options available in tax-advantaged retirement plans, it is important to distinguish qualified plans from those that are funded with IRAs (SEPs and SIMPLEs) and 403(b) plans. Qualified plans are subject to a significant number of limitations, while the others are more open-ended.

Qualified Plans

Every qualified retirement plan specifies when payments may be made and what benefit options are available. Each plan also has a default option if the participant fails to make an election. The distribution options are generally quite limited in a qualified plan. This is because any option that is available must be available to all participants. Also, under the anti-cutback rules, options generally cannot be taken away once they are in the plan. To find out when benefits are payable and what the optional forms of benefit are requires a careful review of the plan's summary plan description and, in some cases, a review of the actual plan document.

A qualified plan is allowed to defer the payment of distributions until participants attain normal retirement age, but much more typically, the plan will also allow payment upon attainment of early retirement age, death, or disability. Today, most plans also make distributions available to employees who terminate employment (prior to retirement age) with vested benefits. This is almost always the case in defined-contribution plans, but is increasingly common in defined-benefit plans as well. Plans in the profit-sharing category can also allow in-service withdrawals after a stated amount of time or upon a stated event.

involuntary cash-out option

When the participant terminates employment with a vested benefit of $5,000 or less, the plan can provide that such small benefits will be cashed out in a lump sum—without giving the participant any choice in the timing or form of benefit. Most plans choose this *involuntary cash-out option* to simplify plan administration. A recipient of an involuntary cash out retains the right to elect a direct rollover to an IRA or to receive the distribution directly. If the involuntary cash out is $1,000 or more and the participant fails to make an affirmative election, the plan administrator is required to roll the involuntary cash out directly to the designated IRA. When the benefit exceeds $5,000, participants must be given all the benefit options allowed under the plan as well as the right to defer receipt of payment until normal retirement age.

In some cases, a plan will also allow withdrawals prior to termination of employment. As discussed in chapter 3, this type of provision is generally not allowed from plans in the pension category, which includes defined-benefit, cash-balance, target-benefit, and money-purchase pension plans. However, distributions may be available even from these types of plans at the earlier of age 62 or the plan's normal retirement age.

In-service withdrawals are allowed in profit-sharing-type plans (including profit-sharing, 401(k), stock bonus, and ESOP plans) even though many plans do not elect to have such a provision. A special rule applies to the salary deferral account in a 401(k) plan—the withdrawals cannot be made prior to age 59½ unless the participant has a financial hardship (see chapter 5). Because in-service withdrawals result in taxable income, some plans (especially 401(k) plans) also provide for participant loan programs (see chapter 9). All types of qualified plans may allow distributions at the attainment of normal retirement age, even if the participant is still working.

The normal form of benefit for a married individual—in qualified plans that are subject to the qualified joint and survivor annuity rules—must be a joint and survivor benefit of not less than 50 percent or greater than 100 percent and a life annuity for a single participant (see chapter 10). Beginning in 2008, in addition to the required form for married participants, the plan must give married participants the option to elect a 75-percent survivor option (if the normal form has a survivor benefit of less than

75 percent) and a 50-percent option (if the normal form is more than 75 percent).

In qualified plans, not subject to the rules (generally, profit-sharing, 401(k), and stock bonus plans), the normal form of payment is usually a single-sum payment. Regardless of the plan's normal form of benefit payment, participants frequently choose one of the alternative forms of distribution allowed under the plan. Options for distributions may include

- annuity payments
- installment payments
- lump-sum distributions

Let's take a closer look at some of the more common options available.

Life Annuity. A life annuity provides monthly payments to the participant for his or her lifetime. Payments from a life annuity stop when your client dies and no other benefit is paid to any beneficiary. A life annuity can be an appropriate option for individuals who want the guarantee of lifetime payments but who have no need to provide retirement income to a spouse or other dependent.

Joint and Survivor Annuity. A joint and survivor annuity provides monthly payments to the participant during his or her lifetime and if, at the participant's death, the beneficiary is still living, a specified percentage of the participant's benefit continues to be paid to the beneficiary for the remainder of his or her lifetime. The plan will specify the survivor portion and may allow the participant to choose from a 50-percent to a 100-percent survivor portion. Joint and survivor annuities can be appropriate if there is a need to provide for the continuation of retirement income to a spouse or other beneficiary who outlives the participant.

Life Annuity with Guaranteed Payments. A life annuity with guaranteed payments (sometimes referred to as a life annuity with a period-certain guarantee) provides monthly benefit payments to the participant during his or her lifetime. Payments are made for the longer of the life of the participant or some specified period of time. The plan may offer a 5-year, 10-year, or other specified guarantee period.

Example: Sandy has elected a life annuity with a 10-year certain in the amount of $1,000 a month. If Sandy dies after 8 years, her designated beneficiary will continue to receive a $1,000 a month for 2 years. If,

> instead, Sandy dies 12 years after payments begin, there are no additional payments.

Participants with no real income concern for a beneficiary may still elect guaranteed payments to ensure that, at least, minimum payments are made in case of an untimely death. (*Planning Note:* If a client outlives the guarantee period, he or she has, in effect, gambled and lost, because lower monthly benefits will be paid under a life annuity with guaranteed payments than under a straight life annuity.) Also, guaranteed payments can be a good option when the spouse (or some other beneficiary) is ill and has a short life expectancy. For example, if a retiring husband expects to outlive his wife who is in relatively poor health, then a life annuity with a minimum guarantee might be purchased to protect against the unlikely case of the husband predeceasing the wife. The period chosen should reflect, to some extent, the planner's best estimate of the wife's maximum life expectancy and, if applicable, the client's desire to pass on wealth.

Annuity Certain. This annuity provides the beneficiary with a specified amount of monthly guaranteed payments, after which time all payments stop (for example, payments for 20 years). An annuity certain continues to be paid whether the participant survives the annuity period or not. If the client dies prior to 20 years, payments will be made to the client's beneficiary. This type of annuity can be appropriate when the participant's income need has a predictable period, such as for the period prior to beginning Social Security payments.

Lump-sum Distribution. This is what it sounds like—the entire benefit is distributed at once in a single sum. A participant interested in rolling the benefit into an IRA will elect the lump-sum distribution option. Some individuals elect this option from qualified plans in order to take advantage of the special tax treatment (10-year averaging for those born before 1936) and deferral of gain for those who receive a portion of their benefit in qualifying employer securities.

Installments. The installment option is similar to, but definitely different from, a term-certain annuity. With installment payments, the participant elects a payout length and, based on earnings assumptions, a payout amount is also determined. Payments will be from the account, not an insurance carrier, and there are no guaranteed payments. If the funds run out before the period is over, payments will stop. If the assumptions are exceeded, the participant typically gets a refund with the remaining account at the end of period. This option would not be available in a defined-benefit plan because there is no individual account.

Value of the Benefit

To understand the value of the benefit provided by the plan, it is important to discuss defined-contribution plans and defined-benefit plans separately. In a defined-contribution plan, the benefit is always based on the value of the account balance. If the participant elects a lump-sum withdrawal, it will represent the entire value of the vested account balance. If installment options are elected, the account balance (along with continued investment return) is simply liquidated over the specified time period. If the participant elects an annuity option, the plan will purchase the annuity from an insurance company. Depending upon the service providers involved in investment of plan assets, the plan may be able to get a favorable annuity purchase rate.

actuarial equivalent

In a defined-benefit plan, the value of each benefit is almost always the *actuarial equivalent* of a specified form of payment—most typically a single life annuity. For example, if the participant chooses a lump-sum benefit, the amount of the lump sum is based on the single-sum value of a life annuity using the actuarial assumptions prescribed in the plan. Under current law, actuarial assumptions must be tied to the PBGC long-term rate, which is reassessed each month. This means that over time the value of the lump sum may go up or down as the PBGC interest rate changes.

To get a sense of the relative values of different distribution options, table 25-1 provides an example based on a $1,565 monthly life annuity. The other annuity options pay less than the life annuity because of the longer guaranteed payout period.

TABLE 25-1
Comparison of Optional Benefit Forms **(Defined-benefit plan with a monthly life annuity payment of $1,565;** **assume both participant and spouse are aged 65)**

Annuity Form	Monthly Benefit
Life	$ 1,565
Life annuity/10-year guarantee	$ 1,494
Life annuity/20-year guarantee	$ 1,360
Joint and survivor (50 percent)	$ 1,418
Joint and survivor (66 2/3 percent)	$ 1,375
Joint and survivor (100 percent)	$ 1,296
Lump-sum payment	$ 200,000

subsidized benefits

Occasionally, in a defined-benefit plan, all forms of benefit will not be the actuarial equivalent. Forms of payment that are more valuable than the standard form of payment are referred to as *subsidized benefits*. Some plans provide an unreduced qualified joint and survivor benefit. For example, a single participant would be entitled to a $1,000 a month life annuity and a married participant with the same benefit accrual would be entitled to a $1,000 a month qualified joint and survivor annuity (a more valuable benefit). It is also not uncommon to see early retirement benefits that are subsidized. For example, the plan may allow an individual aged 60 with 30 years of service to receive the full normal retirement benefit payable at age 65 at the earlier age of 60.

IRAs

Typically, form-of-distribution options from IRAs are much more flexible than qualified plans because the individual is the owner and beneficiary. Withdrawals can be made on a discretionary basis or the participant can purchase any of the types of annuities discussed above. In addition, the participant can purchase an immediate variable annuity contract, which can guarantee lifetime payments while allowing some potential upswing in monthly payments.

Variable Annuities

A variable immediate annuity is one in which the periodic payments received from the contract vary with the investment experience of the underlying investment vehicle. The variable immediate annuity was developed to answer the problem of a fixed-payment immediate annuity's purchasing power being eroded by inflation. The variable immediate annuity can often accomplish this objective, but not without risk to the annuity owner that the payments can decrease as well as increase.

With fixed immediate annuities, the insurance company accepts the mortality risk, the expense risk, and the interest rate risk. The contract owner accepts the liquidity and the purchasing power risks. With the variable annuity, the contract owner trades guarantees and unwavering income for variable payments. The mortality and expense risks stay with the insurance company.

Currently, the market for variable immediate annuities is small, but it is expected to increase as baby boomers deal with retirement. Trying to live for several decades on money from a 401(k) plan can be stressful and difficult. It is likely that those with extreme longevity in their families will opt to have some portion of their income guaranteed for life while still being able to withstand inflation.

Operation of a Variable Annuity

In the process of implementing a variable immediate annuity, the annuity owner selects from among the various subaccounts offered in the contract to create a diversified portfolio and a suitable asset allocation. In most cases, this asset allocation can be changed among the subaccounts offered within the contract. The annuity owner may also select automatic rebalancing within most variable immediate annuity contracts. The proceeds to be immediately annuitized buy units of the selected subaccounts on the date of purchase; future changes in value of the selected subaccounts will determine the amount of the future annuity payments.

assumed investment return (AIR)

The amount of the two initial monthly annuity checks will be determined based on the *assumed investment return (AIR)*. The contract owner may be given a choice of AIRs, such as 3 percent, 5 percent, or 7 percent. After the two initial checks, the underlying investment accounts have to exceed the AIR to increase the amount of future checks. If the subaccount performance is below the chosen AIR, future checks will decrease. Accepting a low AIR increases the chances of receiving higher future checks, whereas accepting a high AIR increases the chances of receiving lower future checks.

403(b) Annuities

Withdrawal flexibility from 403(b) plans generally falls somewhere between the limited options in a qualified plan and the more open-ended options of the IRA. As discussed in chapter 6, 403(b) plans have some restrictions on withdrawals prior to termination of employment. Also, if the plan contains an employer contribution, it is subject to ERISA fiduciary rules and can even be subject to qualified joint and survivor annuity rules.

Still, the participant may have more distribution options than with a qualified plan, especially if the benefit is funded with an annuity. Here, the participant may have virtually any annuity option commercially available from the insurance carrier, including an immediate variable annuity.

One item that is different for a 403(b) plan than a qualified plan is that the participant can, in many cases, simply maintain the account after termination of employment without selecting a specific cash-out option. This is similar to an IRA. Of course, the participant could also roll the benefit into an IRA account. There are two good reasons to leave the account in the 403(b) vehicle versus an IRA rollover. First, if the participant has accumulated a significant pre-1987 account balance, these amounts are not subject to the normal minimum-distribution rules (payments generally do not have to begin until the participant attains age 75). Second, many carriers will continue to allow participant loans from the 403(b) plan, even after termination of service.

PUTTING IT ALL TOGETHER

Throughout the text, we have discussed rules that affect pension distributions. Learning this information and integrating it into a cohesive package can be highly difficult. To help with these concerns, we will first review the rules as they apply to qualified plans, IRAs, and 403(b) annuities. Then we will examine common issues that can arise when you are working with different types of clients.

Qualified Plans

Qualified plans must have clear and precise rules regarding the amount, timing, and form of available benefits. The following discusses the tax treatment of these distributions and summarizes the rules that affect qualified plan distributions:

- Distributions are taxed as ordinary income unless the distribution is a lump sum and one of the special tax rules applies (the deferral of gain on employer securities and the grandfathered 10-year averaging and capital gains rules), or unless the participant has basis. Basis includes after-tax contributions and PS 58 costs.

- The 10 percent premature distribution excise tax applies to the taxable portion of a distribution made prior to age 59½. Exceptions apply if the distribution is made because of death or disability, to pay for certain medical expenses, or if substantially equal periodic payments are withdrawn (after separation from service). Another exception (that does not apply to IRAs) is that of distributions to a terminating participant after attainment of age 55.

- If a participant has a qualified plan balance payable to a beneficiary at his or her death, the value of the benefit is included in the taxable estate. Payments to beneficiaries are treated as income in respect to a decedent—meaning that beneficiaries who receive benefit payments pay income tax but may get a deduction for any estate taxes paid because of the value of the pension.

- In-service distributions are subject to limitations. No in-service withdrawals are allowed from plans categorized as pension plans. Profit-sharing-type plans may allow distributions upon a stated event; 401(k) plans are subject to more limiting hardship withdrawals.

- In lieu of taxable in-service withdrawals, plans may offer participant loan programs. Loans within prescribed limits are not subject to income tax.

- Distributions from most plans are subject to the qualified joint and survivor annuity (QJSA) requirements. A limited exception applies for certain profit-sharing plans.

- Distributions are subject to the minimum-distribution rules. The distribution can be made under the pre-TEFRA (Tax Equity and Fiscal Responsibility Act) distribution rules, if the participant made a written election in 1983. Participants (except for 5-percent owners) who continue working until they are past age 70 can defer the required beginning date until April 1 of the year following the year in which they retire.

- Distributions other than certain annuities, hardship withdrawals from 401(k) plans, and required minimum distributions can be rolled over into another qualified plan, 403(b) plan, 457 plan, or IRA.

- Qualified plans are required to give participants the option to directly roll over distributions to an IRA or other qualified plan. Distributions that are not directly rolled over are subject to a 20 percent mandatory income tax withholding.

IRAs

The following is a brief review of the distribution rules that apply to IRAs. With one exception (described below), these rules apply to regular IRAs or IRAs associated with SEPs or SIMPLEs.

- Distributions are always taxed as ordinary income unless the participant has made nondeductible IRA contributions (or rolled over after-tax contributions from a qualified plan). None of the special tax rules that apply to qualified plans apply here.

- The 10 percent premature distribution excise tax applies to the taxable portion of a distribution made prior to age 59½. Exceptions apply if the distribution is made because of death or disability, to pay for certain medical expenses, or if substantially equal periodic payments are withdrawn (after separation from service). With IRAs, there are three additional exceptions: withdrawals to cover medical insurance premiums for certain unemployed individuals, withdrawals to cover post-secondary education expenses, and withdrawals of up to $10,000 for first-time homebuyer expenses.

- With SIMPLE IRAs, the 10 percent penalty tax becomes a 25 percent penalty if withdrawals are made in the first 2 years of participation. So this tax cannot be avoided, SIMPLE IRAs cannot be rolled over or transferred into a regular IRA in the first 2 years of participation.

- If a participant has an IRA account payable to a beneficiary at his or her death, the value of the benefit is included in the taxable estate.

Payments to beneficiaries are treated as income in respect to a decedent—meaning that beneficiaries who receive benefit payments pay income tax but may get a deduction for any estate taxes paid because of the value of the pension.

- Participants can make withdrawals from IRAs (as well as SEPs and SIMPLEs) at any time, without limitation. No participant loans are available, however.
- Distributions are subject to the minimum-distribution rules under which the required beginning date is always the April 1 following the year of attainment of age 70½.
- The QJSA rules do not apply to IRAs.
- The 20 percent mandatory withholding rules do not apply to IRAs.
- Except for amounts that satisfy the required minimum-distribution rules, distributions can be rolled over or transferred to another IRA, qualified plan, 403(b) annuity, or 457 plan.

403(b) Plans

The following is a brief review of the distribution rules that apply to 403(b) plans:

- Distributions are generally taxed as ordinary income. Although there are no after-tax contributions, it is possible for the participant to have basis due to the PS 58 costs that may be recovered tax free.
- The 10 percent premature distribution excise tax applies in the same way as it does to qualified retirement plans.
- If a participant has a 403(b) account payable to a beneficiary at his or her death, the value of the benefit is included in the taxable estate. Payments to beneficiaries are treated as income in respect to a decedent—meaning that beneficiaries who receive benefit payments pay income tax but may get a deduction for any estate taxes paid because of the value of the pension.
- In-service distributions are subject to limitations. When a plan (funded with annuity contracts) contains a salary-deferral feature, contributions attributable to the deferral election may not be distributed until the employee attains age 59½, separates from service, becomes disabled, becomes a hardship case, or dies. When the plan is funded with mutual fund shares, the special distribution requirements apply to all contribution amounts. 403(b) plans can have participant loan programs.
- Distributions are subject to the minimum-distribution rules. An exception applies to the portion of the benefit that accrued prior to 1987. That amount can generally be deferred until age 75. In

addition, participants (except for 5-percent owners) who continue working past age 70 can defer the required beginning date until the April 1 following the year in which they retire.

- Distributions (other than required minimum distributions and certain annuity payments) from a 403(b) plan sponsored by a governmental entity can be rolled over into another 403(b) annuity, qualified plan, 457 plan, or IRA. Distributions from nongovernmental 403(b) plans can be rolled to another 403(b) plan or IRA.

- A participant can generally keep the 403(b) vehicle even after termination of employment. This may be a better option than rolling the benefit into an IRA because of the pre-87 exception to the minimum-distribution rules and the ability to continue to take a loan from the 403(b) plan.

- Participants must be given the option to directly rollover distributions to a new trustee or custodian. Distributions that are not directly rolled over are subject to a 20 percent mandatory income tax withholding.

- In some cases, distributions are subject to the qualified joint and survivor annuity (QJSA) requirements.

Working with Clients

Financial services professionals work with a wide variety of clients, and each of their needs is unique. The checklist in table 26-2 identifies typical client issues. Generally, the specific issues that need to be addressed can be anticipated based on the client's economic status. There are two general groups: clients with limited resources who are trying to make those resources last throughout the retirement years, and wealthier individuals who will not use up all of their assets during their own lifetime. The latter group faces the dual concern of financing retirement and maximizing the after-tax estate that they leave to their heirs. We will address each of these situations.

Primary Concern: Funding Retirement Needs

For most of us, accruing adequate retirement resources is a daunting task. In many cases, the most significant retirement asset is the company pension. For this reason, it is imperative that the distribution decisions maximize the family's available after-tax dollars. The following materials address the vital issues that apply to clients whose primary concern is affording retirement.

TABLE 25-2
Checklist of Issues and Decisions at Retirement

1. Do you want an annuity for all or part of your funds?
2. What type of annuity is best for your situation?
3. Can you maximize the monthly payment of your annuity by rolling it into an IRA or another qualified plan—in other words, shop your annuity?
4. Should you delay taxation of a distribution by rolling it into an IRA or another tax-deferred plan?
5. Is a rollover possible from a cash-flow perspective?
6. Is a direct rollover to the new trustee preferable to a rollover?
7. Do you want a lump-sum distribution for part or all of your funds?
8. Can you elect the grandfathered 10-year averaging or capital-gains treatment for pre-'74 income?
9. Should you elect 10-year averaging or the capital-gains treatment?
10. What is the best tax strategy for dealing with the distribution of employer stock?
11. Has the client complied with the rules for minimum distributions from the qualified plan?
12. When do distributions have to begin?
13. Have the beneficiary forms been carefully selected?
14. In what order should assets be cashed in order to maintain optimum tax-shelter and proper asset allocation ratios?
15. Has there been proper coordination of distributions from qualified plans and IRAs?
16. Will distributions be used to provide necessary income for sustaining your client, or will they supplement already adequate sources of retirement income?
17. Did you meet the need to provide for surviving dependents?
18. Has your client integrated his or her retirement planning with proper estate planning?

Preretirement Distributions. The major concern for the individual who receives a pension distribution prior to retirement is ensuring that pension accumulations are used to finance retirement and are not spent beforehand. In this regard, participants must satisfy rollover rules so inadvertent taxes do not have to be paid. Meeting the rollover requirements has become much easier now that participants in qualified plans and 403(b) annuities must be given the option to transfer benefits directly to an IRA or other qualified plan. Note that these direct rollover rules do not apply to IRA-funded plans, including SEPs and SIMPLEs. However, when a participant leaves an IRA-funded plan, there is generally no reason for a rollover.

Still, some clients are tempted to spend preretirement pension distributions. If you have clients in this position, showing them the power of the compounding return sometimes convinces them otherwise.

Example: Sonny Shortview, aged 40, is changing jobs. He will be receiving a much higher salary in his new job and he is feeling quite well off. Sonny has the opportunity to receive a pension distribution from his old company in the amount of $35,000. Even though he does not really need the funds, the amount seems small enough to Sonny that he is considering paying taxes and using the after-tax proceeds for an auto upgrade. Hopefully, Sonny will change his mind when he learns that if he rolls the distribution into an IRA and earns a 10 percent rate of return, his $35,000 distribution would grow to $367,687 by the time he reaches age 65.

Another difficult situation arises in the case of involuntary dismissal. An employee who is terminated due to downsizing or other reasons may experience a prolonged period of unemployment. In this case, the individual may need to tap into his or her pension. If the participant is younger than age 59½, he or she must pay the 10 percent premature distribution excise tax unless one of the exceptions applies. The substantially equal periodic payment exception is one way to avoid this tax, but the problem is that distributions must be made for the longer of 5 years or until attainment of age 59½, and this period will probably be much longer than the period of unemployment. This problem can be mitigated somewhat by dividing assets into a number of IRAs. For example, part of the need can be met by using a periodic payment from one IRA and simply paying the excise tax for certain short-term needs from another IRA. If a lump sum is needed, the individual could consider borrowing from another source and repaying the loan with periodic distributions.

Form of Retirement Distribution. For the client living on his or her pension distribution, the two most important decisions are usually when to retire and the form of payment that should be received. As we discussed previously in this book, the effect of early retirement can be quite profound, especially in defined-benefit plans. Even if the plan subsidizes some part of the early retirement penalty, there is always a cost for early retirement. Other timing issues that need to be understood are the consequences of delaying payments to some time after retirement and of retiring after the plan's normal retirement age. Spend time with your clients to make sure they understand these important timing issues—it is rare that a plan participant will fully understand them without your help. Of course, the answers always depend upon the specific terms of the plan, so be sure to review the summary plan description.

Once the client has a full understanding of the timing issues, the next decision is choosing the form of retirement benefits. Almost all individual account-type plans (including qualified plans of the defined-contribution type, SEPs, SIMPLEs, and 403(b) annuities) give the participant the option to receive a lump-sum distribution, which can be rolled into an IRA without tax consequences. This benefit option affords the participant the most flexibility because he or she can take money out as slowly or as quickly as it is needed.

Defined-benefit plans may or may not have a lump-sum option, depending upon the terms of the plan. Also note that a lump sum from a defined-benefit plan is based on the actuarial equivalent of a normal form of payment, usually a life annuity. If the lump sum is calculated with unfavorable assumptions, this option may not be advisable. One way to test the value of the lump sum is to compare the amount payable as a life annuity from the plan to the amount that would result from taking a lump sum, rolling it into an IRA, and then buying a life annuity at commercially available prices.

Many participants will be satisfied with the IRA rollover approach because it provides both investment and withdrawal flexibility. However, this method does not ensure that the participant will not outlive pension distributions. Even with careful distribution planning, investment performance may not meet expectations, or the individual may live too long. To protect against this contingency, retirees should consider having at least a portion of their retirement income payable as some form of life annuity. We reviewed the advantages and disadvantages of various annuity options in the earlier part of this chapter. Participants can generally receive the type of annuity that they want, even if it is a not offered by the particular plan involved. They can accomplish this by electing a lump-sum option, rolling the benefit into an IRA, and then purchasing the annuity. Variable annuities should be considered because they can combine the promise of lifetime benefits with the possibility of increasing payments over time to offset the effects of inflation.

Qualified Joint and Survivor Considerations. A married participant who receives a pension distribution in a form other than a qualified joint and survivor annuity generally must have his or her spouse sign a waiver. Unless there is marital discord, the receipt of an alternate form of benefit generally poses no special concerns. In fact, the disclosure and paperwork involved probably ensure that the participant is carefully considering all the available distribution options. Still, this is a matter that retirees may not understand.

Explaining the effect of the joint and survivor form of payment is an excellent way to provide service to the client and solidify the advisory relationship.

Tax Issues

For the individual who receives a distribution from a qualified plan and qualifies for special tax treatment, an issue will be the decision of whether or not to elect special averaging treatment. With smaller distribution amounts, the tax rate using special averaging treatment can look quite attractive; it is possible that the effective rate can be 20 percent or less. Even though this rate is low, remember it must be compared to the individual's marginal tax rate. The effect of deferring taxes is quite powerful, and taking the benefit as a lump sum should be examined thoroughly.

If the client receives a lump-sum distribution but does not elect special averaging treatment, then the lump sum should generally be rolled directly into an IRA. As discussed in the previous chapter, it often is appropriate not to roll over the portion of the benefit that represents after-tax contributions. If the distribution includes employer stock, the effect of the net unrealized appreciation rules should be considered before making the rollover election.

To maximize the benefit of tax deferral, once the rollover occurs, amounts should be distributed only when needed (unless, of course, the minimum-distribution rules require a larger distribution).

Another concern is whether the retiree should elect to convert his or her pension distribution to a Roth IRA. To do this, the distribution first must be rolled or transferred to an IRA and then converted to a Roth IRA. Only single individuals or marrieds filing jointly who have an adjusted gross income of under $100,000 for the year are allowed to convert. As discussed in chapter 18, conversion results in taxable ordinary income in the amount of the conversion. Once in the Roth IRA, growth is tax free as long as the distribution meets certain eligibility requirements. The determination of whether to convert or not is a complex issue that requires a full understanding of the participant's retirement and estate planning concerns. However, there are some general considerations that will affect the participant's decision.

- The Roth IRA conversion becomes more appropriate the longer the period of distributions is stretched out. The individual who is struggling to meet retirement needs will probably require early withdrawals, which means the Roth IRA will not have time to generate substantial tax-free accumulations.
- The Roth IRA conversion is more appropriate when the income tax rate is the same or higher at the time of distribution than at the time of conversion. For the average person, the post-retirement income

tax rate is probably lower than the rate at the time of distribution. This factor weighs against conversion.

- Any portion of an IRA can be converted to a Roth IRA. This means the retiree who has all of his or her retirement income may still want to convert some of it as a hedge against future tax rate increases.

YOUR FINANCIAL SERVICES PRACTICE:
CLIENT QUERY

Question: Your client Wanda is single, aged 73, and has an IRA worth $150,000. Because she does not need to take distributions from the plan to live on, she asks you whether she can avoid taking minimum distributions from the plan. Upon further inquiry, you find out she has three adult children who are all successful financially and six grandchildren. Her goal is to leave the IRA money to her family. You also find out that she has an income of $120,000 a year, but only has AGI of $85,000, because some of her income is from tax-free municipal bonds.

Solution: Wanda sounds like a great candidate for a conversion to a Roth IRA. Once the assets are in a Roth IRA, she can avoid minimum distributions during her lifetime. She will have to pay income taxes at the time of conversion—but the prepaid income taxes also reduce her taxable estate. If she names her six grandchildren as the beneficiaries, at Wanda's death, this account can be divided into six accounts and distributed over the lifetime of each grandchild.

- For retirees who are struggling to meet their retirement needs, converting and paying taxes does not seem like an appropriate choice. For this group, it may be more appropriate to put away the maximum amount in a Roth IRA each year to accumulate amounts in this vehicle prior to their retirement years.

Primary Objective: Maximizing the Estate

When examining your clients' needs, you will find there is a distinct difference between those who will probably spend most of their assets over retirement and those who can afford to leave an estate to their heirs. Nonetheless, it is impossible to divide the world into two distinct client groups, and the issues will certainly be different for the person with a $20 million estate than for the person with a $2 million estate. Even for wealthier clients, the first and foremost concern is retirement security, with estate planning as a secondary objective.

However, simply having significant assets in a tax-preferred retirement plan can pose serious problems. As we have learned in the last two chapters, lifetime distributions can be subject to income tax and the 10 percent premature distribution excise tax. If money that is still in the plan is left to heirs, the amount is included in the taxable estate, and distributions are still subject to federal income taxes. If assets are distributed at death, a large portion of the pension asset can be confiscated by taxes. The following example shows the devastating effect that these taxes can have.

Example:	Oliver, aged 80, died (without a surviving spouse) with $2 million in his IRA account. Assume Oliver's other assets are large enough that his pension is taxed at the highest marginal estate tax rate of 46 percent (the maximum estate tax rate in 2006). Also assume that after Oliver's death, the entire IRA is distributed to his beneficiary, who is in the 35 percent income tax bracket. Looking just at federal taxes, the benefit will be taxed as follows:

Federal estate tax	$920,000
46% of $2,000,000	
Income tax on IRA	$378,000
35% of ($2,000,000 – $920,000)	
Total reduction $1,298,000	
Net value of IRA for heirs	$702,000
Percentage of IRA passing to heirs	35.1%

Fortunately, there are a number of ways to minimize the tax threat at the time of the participant's death. Under the minimum-distribution rules, it is possible to distribute assets over the remaining life expectancy of the beneficiary after the death of the participant. This strategy spreads out the payment of income taxes, meaning that the pension asset can continue to generate significant income for the beneficiaries. However, in order to take advantage of the extra deferral period, the pension plan assets cannot be used to pay estate taxes. Readers familiar with estate planning know that the pension asset problem is similar to problems that can arise with other illiquid assets. In many cases, the solution to the illiquid asset problem is to purchase life insurance—usually using an irrevocable life insurance trust—because the insurance proceeds will not be subject to estate taxes. This approach generates capital for paying estate taxes. In fact, the pension problem is often less difficult to solve than the problem of illiquid assets because distributions from the plan can function as a source of insurance premiums. In many cases, the premiums are simply paid out of distributions that are already required under the minimum-distribution rules.

When the participant is uninsurable or unwilling to purchase insurance, the problem becomes more difficult to solve. One option is to use pension distributions to fund a family gifting program—taking advantage of the ability to give away $12,000 per year (as indexed for 2007) to a beneficiary without estate or gift tax consequences. Another solution for the charitably inclined is to leave the benefit to charity. When the charity receives the benefit, it pays no income taxes and the estate receives an estate tax deduction for the amount of the contribution.

This type of client also needs to consider whether or not to convert some or all of his or her pension assets to a Roth IRA. The major conversion impediment for wealthier clients is that they will earn more than the $100,000 cap. Some advisors are so enthusiastic about the conversion idea that they look for ways to reduce the individual's income for a year so the conversion can occur. The reason conversion can be so valuable for the wealthier client is that there are no required minimum distributions during the participant's lifetime. If the spouse is the beneficiary, no distributions have to be made over the spouse's lifetime either. After the spouse's death, distributions must be made over the life expectancy of the beneficiaries at that time. This may mean that even if the conversion occurs at age 65, the Roth IRA will grow income tax free for possibly 25 or more years, followed by distributions that can be spread over the next 30 to 40 years (the life expectancy of the beneficiaries). Similar to planning for distributions from traditional IRAs, the Roth IRA conversion works best when estate taxes are not withdrawn from the Roth IRA. Once again, life insurance can be the appropriate means to prepare for this contingency.

Form of Distribution Option. For a client with substantial assets, the IRA rollover option is generally the appropriate choice. This type of client can afford to self-insure against the contingency of living a long life and, therefore, will generally not want to annuitize the benefit. The IRA provides both investment and distribution flexibility. This strategy is also necessary if the individual wants to convert some or all of the distribution to a Roth IRA.

As discussed in the previous chapter, individuals with large pension benefits generally will not elect lump-sum averaging treatment. The effective tax rate is not that attractive for large distributions. Sometimes electing lump-sum averaging is appropriate when an individual is a participant in multiple plans. If, for example, an individual has accumulated benefits of $250,000 in a profit-sharing plan and $1 million in a pension plan, choosing lump-sum tax treatment for the profit-sharing distribution may be appropriate. This strategy should be evaluated carefully because there are a number of traps regarding the aggregation of multiple distributions. Also, remember that averaging is available only to those born before 1936.

MINI-CASES

Case One—Facts

Jerry Jobchanger, aged 32, terminated employment with Midsize Corporation in order to take a job with Mega Corporation as a systems analyst. He was in both a defined-benefit plan and a 401(k) plan at Midsize Corporation. The present value of his accrued benefit in the defined-benefit plan is $4,200, and the 401(k) account balance is $9,500. He has come to you to discuss what he should do with his pension distributions from Midsize. He also has told you that he will not be eligible for Mega Corporation's pension plans for one year. He is thinking about withdrawing both benefits and buying a car better suited for his position as a young executive. Discuss his options with him.

Case Two—Facts

Joseph Professional is 55 years old and has accumulated $1.3 million in his company's profit-sharing plan. That is good news, but the trouble is that this asset represents 80 percent of his net worth. He is a dentist and does not expect to be able to sell his practice for a large sum. He has a house, some other personal property, and little other savings. Joseph is married and his wife is aged 52. He has two children, ages 24 and 27. His first concern is his retirement security, but he is also concerned about passing on wealth to his children. He enjoys his work and intends to continue working until age 70. After he retires, he anticipates withdrawing his current salary, $150,000 a year, from the IRA (in today's dollars).

Case Three—Facts

Mary Middle Class is single (divorced) and works for ABCD University as an administrator. Her current income is $42,000. She is aged 62 and is thinking of retiring in the near future. The university has a defined-benefit pension plan and a 403(b) plan. The benefit formula in the defined-benefit plan is one and one-half percent of final-average compensation times years of service (limited to 30 years). Mary currently has 12 years of service. She has an account balance of $95,000 in her 403(b) plan.

Mary has come to you to help her determine whether she can afford to retire now and, if so, how she should take her distributions from her qualified plans.

After asking Mary more about her retirement planning goals, you find out that Mary was married for 15 years (to a well-paid lawyer) and several years ago she got a large house in the divorce settlement. The house has a small mortgage payment, high taxes, and a significant amount of equity buildup. Other than the house, she has no significant investments. You also find that she would like to live closer to her adult children so that she can spend more time with the grandchildren. She has little interest in travel, but would like to get additional education.

Case Four—Facts

Barney Businessowner turns 70½ this year. He has a profit-sharing benefit of $250,000 and a money-purchase pension benefit of $900,000. He is retiring and his daughter has purchased the business. The plans only allow for distributions in the form of a lump sum or in installments, and plan assets are invested by the trustees (there is no participant investment direction). Barney has a lot of additional income, including installment payments, from the sale of the business for the next 20 years. He sees the pension benefits as assets that he does not need to live on and that he wants to leave to his family. His first concern is his wife, then his adult children and grandchildren.

CHAPTER REVIEW

Key Terms

involuntary cash-out option [25-1]
actuarial equivalent [25-1]

subsidized benefits [25-1]
assumed investment return (AIR) [25-1]

Review Questions

Review questions are based on the learning objectives in this chapter. Thus, a [25-3] at the end of a question means that the question is based on learning objective 25-3. If there are multiple objectives, they are all listed.

1. What considerations affect an individual's decision concerning the appropriate form of pension distribution? [25-1]

2. When do qualified plans typically allow for benefit payments? [25-1]

3. What options does a participant have with regard to the timing and form of payment of benefits? Is there any situation in which the participant does not have these same rights? [25-1]

4. What is the major limitation of a life annuity? [25-1]

5. Why can a life annuity with guaranteed payments be used to provide for the income needs of a beneficiary? [25-1]

6. Describe an installment payment option from a defined-contribution plan. [25-1]

7. In a defined-benefit plan, what does it mean to say that if a participant elects a life annuity with 10-year-certain payments the amount of the distribution is the actuarial equivalent to a life annuity? [25-1]

8. In a defined-benefit plan, what does it mean to say that a benefit is subsidized? [25-1]

9. What is the impact on the benefit payments in an immediate variable annuity contract when the actual rate of return exceeds the assumed investment return? [25-1]

10. Explain the following: [25-1]
    a. Are distributions from qualified plans always taxed as ordinary income?
    b. What exception to the 10 percent Sec. 72(t) excise tax applies to qualified plans and 403(b) plans, but does not apply to IRAs?
    c. What is the exception that applies to the minimum-distribution rules for qualified plans?
    d. Do the 20 percent mandatory income tax withholding rules apply to distributions from IRAs?
    e. In an IRA, is the required beginning date ever later than the April 1 following the year in which the participant attained age 70½?

11. Sheila, single and aged 50, is laid off from her job. She receives a $150,000 distribution from a 401(k) plan that she rolls directly into an IRA. She decides to take some well-deserved time off and plans to go back to work in about a year. She needs living expenses for the current year. How could she make withdrawals from her IRA that would avoid the 10 percent penalty tax? [25-1]

12. Why is choosing the right distribution option so important for someone with a relatively small account balance? [25-2]

13. Explain the estate tax threat that faces those with significant retirement plan balances and the strategies to minimize its effect. [25-2]

14. Can the Roth IRA conversion be used as an effective tax planning strategy for the wealthier individual? [25-2]

Appendix 1

Post-ERISA Legislation

Below is description, law by law, of legislation affecting the pension field. Following that is a table identifying the laws for those interested in researching them further.

In 1981, the ***Economic Recovery Tax Act (ERTA)*** expanded the retirement market by breathing new life into old retirement products. ERTA lifted the prohibition against employees who were active participants in employer-sponsored plans having an individual retirement account (IRA) and opened the door for widespread sales of IRAs. The public response was tremendous as millions flocked to save for retirement. ERTA also contributed to the success of stock option plans by liberalizing the rules for deducting leveraged employee stock ownership plans (ESOPs) and creating payroll-based stock option plans (PAYSOPs). PAYSOPs, phased out in 1987, allowed for an income tax credit that benefited certain corporations. Finally, ERTA started the trend of making the rules for retirement plans for the self-employed (Keogh plans) similar to those for corporate plans.

The Tax Equity and Fiscal Responsibility Act of 1982 (TEFRA) created plan parity between Keogh plans and corporate plans, finishing the job started by ERTA. The major emphasis of TEFRA, however, was on stopping tax abuses, primarily loopholes used by small-employer plans. TEFRA created special rules for plans that unduly benefit key employees—if a plan inordinately favors the privileged few, restrictive "top-heavy" rules take effect. The top-heavy rules guarantee minimum benefits for rank-and-file employees and restrict benefits available for key employees. TEFRA also closed other loopholes: it stopped plan loan abuses, limited contributions to the plan and distributions from the plan by reducing the maximum contributions or distributions allowed, and forced plan distributions to be used for retirement purposes, as opposed to sheltering the money for the beneficiary.

The Retirement Equity Act of 1984 (REA) shifted Congress's focus from tax abuses by small employers to perceived mistreatment of women under pension rules. REA helps people (male or female) who do not fit the standard work pattern, especially those who interrupt or stop their career for children, by reducing the age required to participate in a retirement plan. REA makes it harder to lose pension benefits because of career interruptions. REA also protects the rights of a plan participant's spouse or ex-spouse by ensuring that the spouse has some say in how retirement money is distributed and by allowing retirement funds to be part of a divorce settlement.

The Tax Reform Act of 1986 (TRA '86) represented the biggest shake-up since ERISA. A need for revenue was the motivation for TRA '86 rules that cut back salary reduction contributions previously allowed under some types of plans (401(k)s, tax-sheltered annuities) and restricted the deductibility of contributions made to individual retirement accounts. A second target of TRA '86 was the discrimination in favor of officers and key employees. Existing discrimination restrictions were tightened, and some plans that had previously escaped nondiscrimination coverage were brought under a new, tougher nondiscrimination umbrella. Other tax reform changes were also included:

- modifications to the profit-sharing rules, which permit profit-sharing contributions when the employer has no profits (this was a response to the trend of using profit-sharing plans as a major source of pension benefits)
- amendments liberalizing ERISA's vesting schedules
- creation of a 10 percent premature distribution penalty tax for most plan distributions prior to age 59½
- minimum distribution requirements and restrictive changes in the taxation of retirement distributions

The Omnibus Budget Reconciliation Act of 1987 (OBRA '87) focused on yet another legislative target—underfunded pension plans. OBRA '87 tightened ERISA's funding requirements in an effort to prevent plans from being inadequately funded and consequently reneging on the pension-benefit promises that they made. OBRA '87 took away some of the leeway actuaries had concerning the amount and timing of plan contributions and forced employers to meet stricter funding requirements. In addition to tightening funding standards, the Revenue Act of 1987 also increased insurance premiums that are owed the PBGC from $8.50 to $16 per participant per year. Under the higher premium schedules, underfunded plans were subject to a variable rate greater than $16, depending on the amount by which they were underfunded.

The Revenue Reconciliation Act of 1989 represented yet another legislative change to pension law. This act focused on, among other things, restructuring the rules governing employee stock ownership plans (ESOPs). Specifically, the act abolished many of the special tax advantages that an ESOP had, such as the estate tax reduction brought about by selling employer stock back to the ESOP after an employee's death.

The Revenue Reconciliation Act of 1990 dramatically changed the rules governing an employer's ability to acquire an asset reversion from a terminating defined-benefit plan (see chapter 13). In addition, the new law enhanced an employer's ability to prefund retiree health benefits in a so-called 401(h) account by allowing excess pension assets to be transferred to the 401(h) account without the employer having to pay either regular income tax or a pension reversion excise tax on the amount transferred. Finally, the new law increased annual PBGC premiums for covered defined-benefit plans from $16 to $19 per participant.

The Emergency Unemployment Act of 1992 changed several of the rules governing distributions from qualified plans. Apparently the policy behind the changes was to encourage employees to save preretirement distributions for their retirement needs. The new rules, effective for distributions after December 31, 1992, liberalize the rollover rules (allowing most preretirement distributions to be rolled into a tax-sheltered IRA or qualified plan); require mandatory 20 percent federal income tax withholding on most distributions made directly to participants; and require qualified plans to allow participants the option to have distributions transferred directly to another tax-sheltered vehicle. (Transferred amounts are not subject to the 20 percent withholding requirements.)

The Omnibus Budget Reconciliation Act of 1993 targeted the benefits of the highly compensated by capping the amount of compensation that could be taken into account for determining contributions or benefits to $150,000.

The Retirement Protection Act of 1994 (RPA '94) made significant changes in the funding rules for single-employer defined-benefit plans, the cash-out provisions for lump sums, and the PBGC premium structure for underfunded defined-benefit plans. The primary focus of the legislation was to give employers added incentive to fund underfunded defined-benefit plans and to put the PBGC in a better financial position.

The Small Business Job Opportunities Act of 1996 was the most sweeping legislation in the pension area in years. Believe it or not, the new law actually simplifies the pension rules. For example, the law creates a less complicated definition of highly compensated employees, simplifies the nondiscrimination testing in a 401(k) plan, and even eliminates nondiscrimination testing in 401(k) plans that comply with certain safe harbors. In the distribution area, the law simplifies the annuity taxation rules and eliminates special 5-year averaging. To provide a 401(k) look-alike savings plan for small employers, the law establishes a SIMPLE (savings incentive match plan for employees).

The Economic Growth and Tax Relief Reconciliation Act of 2001 (EGTRRA) is the most positive pension law in years. It increased many pension limits. For example, the $35,000 limit on annual additions in a defined- contribution plan for each participant increased to $40,000 and the defined-benefit annual benefit limit increased from $140,000 a year to $160,000. All maximum salary deferral limits increased as well. Limits for Sec. 401(k) plans and Sec. 403(b) plans will increase over the next several years to $15,000 (up from $10,500); the SIMPLE limit will increase from $6,500 to $10,000 over the next several years as well. Even IRA limits were increased, going from $2,000 in 2001 up to $5,000 in 2008. Participants over age 50 can also make additional catch-up contributions to 401(k), 403(b), and even to IRA plans.

Many other changes in the law were intended to encourage small business owners to establish plans. This was done in a number of ways, from eliminating IRS user fees for new plan sponsors to tax credit, to eliminating some of the complexity of maintaining a plan. For example, the top-heavy rules were simplified and the prohibition against certain owners borrowing from the plan was removed. Also, the maximum deductible contribution to a profit-sharing plan went up to 25 percent of compensation, so a sponsor can maximize contributions to a defined-contribution plan with just one plan.

Other provisions provided simplification for both plan sponsors and plan participants. The most important change was allowing participants to roll over pension benefits between qualified plans, IRAs, 403(b) plans, and Sec. 457 plans.

The Katrina Emergency Tax Relief Act of 2005 (KETRA) was passed in response to the hurricane that devastated New Orleans and other Gulf Coast cities. This law provided for penalty-free withdrawals for people under age 59½ in the affected areas. It also provided for tax relief by taxing withdrawals using 3-year averaging and waiving income tax if withdrawals were returned within 3 years. Also it allowed for participant loans of up to $100,000.

The Deficit Reduction Act of 2005 made three important PBGC premium changes. First, it increased the PBGC's premiums from $19 to $30 per participant in single employer plans. Second, it increased the premiums from $2.60 to $8 per participant in multiemployer plans. Finally, it established an employer paid termination premium for companies that terminate their pension plans after 2005 and before 2011.

The Pension Protection Act of 2006 was a sweeping law that started as a plan funding statute and expanded into much more. Some of the key changes to the plan funding rules include:

- A complete revision of the minimum funding requirements for defined-benefit plans
- Changes in how lump-sum distributions are calculated (which will reduce the value of the lump-sum in many cases)
- Replaces the summary annual report with a notice to participants about plan funding
- Provides for additional consequences for severely underfunded plans referred to as "plans at risk"

Other changes in the Pension Protection Act included amending the fiduciary provisions of ERISA to allow more investment advice to participants, validation for cash balance plans, and strengthening of the automatic enrollment rules. In addition, it made permanent some EGTRRA provisions, liberalized payout and rollover rules, and allowed tax-free distributions from an IRA to a charity in certain situations.

The Tax Increase Prevention and Reconciliation Act of 2006 (TIPRA) included one important pension change. Beginning in 2010, the law eliminated the income limitations for individuals seeking to convert a traditional IRA into a Roth IRA.

Appen

Pension Acronyms

ADP test	actual deferral percentage test
AGI	adjusted gross income
AIR	assumed investment return
Automatic J&S	automatic joint and survivor annuity
CODA	cash or deferred arrangement
COLA	cost-of-living adjustment
DA contract	deposit-administration contract
DB	defined benefit
DBO plan	death benefit only plan
DC	defined contribution
DOL	Department of Labor
ERIC	ERISA Industry Committee
ERISA	Employee Retirement Income Security Act of 1974
ESOP	employee stock ownership plan
FASB	Financial Accounting Standards Board
FSA	flexible spending account
GIC	guaranteed-investment contract
IG contract	investment-guarantee contract
IPG contract	immediate-participation-guarantee contract
IRA	individual retirement account

IRC	Internal Revenue Code
IRD	income in respect of a decedent
IRS	Internal Revenue Service
ISO	incentive stock option
LSD	lump-sum distribution
MPPAA	Multiemployer Pension Plan Amendments Act
NRA	normal retirement age
NRD	normal retirement date
PBGC	Pension Benefit Guaranty Corporation
PC	professional corporation
PLR	private-letter ruling
PTE	prohibited-transaction exemption
QDRO	qualified domestic relations order
QPAM	qualified professional asset manager
QPSA	qualified preretirement survivor annuity
QVEC	qualified voluntary employee contribution
SAR	summary of annual reports
SARSEP	salary reduction simplified employee pension
SEP	simplified employee pension plan
SERP	supplemental executive retirement plan
SIMPLE	savings incentive match plan for employees
SMM	summary of material modifications
SPAC	single-premium annuity contract

SPD	summary plan description
TDA	tax-deferred annuity
TPA	third-party administrator
TSA	tax-sheltered annuity
VDEC	voluntary deductible employee contribution
VEBA	Voluntary Employee's Beneficiary Association
401(a)(4)	discrimination rule
401(k) plan	cash or deferred arrangement
403(b) plan	tax-deferred annuity
410(b)(1)	discrimination rule
457 plan	state or local government plan
501(c)(3)	charitable organizations
5500s	pension forms filed with IRS

Appendix 3

Average Life Expectancies

1983 Individual Annuity Table (1971–1976)*				
	Male		Female	
Age	Deaths per 1,000	Expectation of Life (Years)	Deaths per 1,000	Expectation of Life (Years)
30	.76	49.83	.44	54.75
31	.79	48.87	.46	53.77
32	.81	47.91	.48	52.80
33	.84	46.95	.50	51.82
34	.88	45.99	.52	50.85
35	.92	45.03	.55	49.87
36	.97	44.07	.57	48.90
37	1.03	43.11	.61	47.93
38	1.11	42.15	.65	46.96
39	1.22	41.20	.69	45.99
40	1.34	40.25	.74	45.02
41	1.49	39.30	.80	44.05
42	1.67	38.36	.87	43.09
43	1.89	37.43	.94	42.12
44	2.13	36.50	1.03	41.16
45	2.40	35.57	1.12	40.20
46	2.69	34.66	1.23	39.25
47	3.01	33.75	1.36	38.30
48	3.34	32.85	1.50	37.35
49	3.69	31.96	1.66	36.40
50	4.06	31.07	1.83	35.46
51	4.43	30.20	2.02	34.53
52	4.81	29.33	2.22	33.59
53	5.20	28.47	2.43	32.67
54	5.59	27.62	2.65	31.75
55	5.99	26.77	2.89	30.83
56	6.41	25.93	3.15	29.92
57	6.84	25.09	3.43	29.01
58	7.29	24.26	3.74	28.11
59	7.78	23.44	4.08	27.21
60	8.34	22.62	4.47	26.32

	Male		Female	
1983 Individual Annuity Table (1971–1976) (Continued)*				
Age	Deaths per 1,000	Expectation of Life (Years)	Deaths per 1,000	Expectation of Life (Years)
61	8.98	21.80	4.91	25.44
62	9.74	20.99	5.41	24.56
63	10.63	20.20	5.99	23.69
64	11.66	19.41	6.63	22.83
65	12.85	18.63	7.34	21.98
66	14.20	17.87	8.09	21.14
67	15.72	17.12	8.89	20.31
68	17.41	16.38	9.73	19.49
69	19.30	15.66	10.65	18.67
70	21.37	14.96	11.70	17.87
71	23.65	14.28	12.91	17.07
72	26.13	13.61	14.32	16.29
73	28.84	12.96	15.98	15.52
74	31.79	12.33	17.91	14.76
75	35.05	11.72	20.13	14.02
76	38.63	11.13	22.65	13.30
77	42.59	10.56	25.51	12.60
78	46.95	10.00	28.72	11.91
79	51.76	9.47	32.33	11.25
80	57.03	8.96	36.40	10.61
81	62.79	8.47	40.98	9.99
82	69.08	8.01	46.12	9.40
83	75.91	7.57	51.89	8.83
84	83.23	7.15	58.34	8.28
85	90.99	6.75	65.52	7.77
86	99.12	6.37	73.49	7.28
87	107.58	6.02	82.32	6.81
88	116.32	5.69	92.02	6.38
89	125.39	5.37	102.49	5.98
90	134.89	5.07	113.61	5.60
91	144.87	4.78	125.23	5.26
92	155.43	4.50	137.22	4.94
93	166.63	4.24	149.46	4.64
94	178.54	3.99	161.83	4.37
95	191.21	3.75	174.23	4.12
96	204.72	3.51	186.54	3.88
97	219.12	3.29	198.65	3.65
98	234.74	3.07	211.10	3.44
99	251.89	2.86	224.45	3.22
100	270.91	2.66	239.22	3.01

1983 Individual Annuity Table (1971–1976) (Continued)*				
	Male		Female	
Age	Deaths per 1,000	Expectation of Life (Years)	Deaths per 1,000	Expectation of Life (Years)
101	292.11	2.46	255.95	2.80
102	315.83	2.26	275.20	2.59
103	342.38	2.08	297.50	2.38
104	372.09	1.90	323.39	2.18
105	405.28	1.73	353.41	1.98
106	442.28	1.57	388.11	1.79
107	483.41	1.41	428.02	1.60
108	528.99	1.27	473.69	1.43
109	579.35	1.13	525.66	1.26
110	634.81	1.01	584.46	1.11
111	695.70	.89	650.65	.97
112	762.34	.78	724.75	.83
113	835.06	.70	807.32	.71
114	914.17	.67	898.89	.60
115	1,000.00	.50	1,000.00	.50

*These figures come from annuity tables which typically assume a longer life expectancy than other tables that can be used.

Joint and Last Survivor Table*

Ages	0	1	2	3	4	5	6	7	8	9
0	90.0	89.5	89.0	88.6	88.2	87.8	87.4	87.1	86.8	86.5
1	89.5	89.0	88.5	88.1	87.6	87.2	86.8	86.5	86.1	85.8
2	89.0	88.5	88.0	87.5	87.1	86.6	86.2	85.8	85.5	85.1
3	88.6	88.1	87.5	87.0	86.5	86.1	85.6	85.2	84.8	84.5
4	88.2	87.6	87.1	86.5	86.0	85.5	85.1	84.6	84.2	83.8
5	87.8	87.2	86.6	86.1	85.5	85.0	84.5	84.1	83.6	83.2
6	87.4	86.8	86.2	85.6	85.1	84.5	84.0	83.5	83.1	82.6
7	87.1	86.5	85.8	85.2	84.6	84.1	83.5	83.0	82.5	82.1
8	86.8	86.1	85.5	84.8	84.2	83.6	83.1	82.5	82.0	81.6
9	86.5	85.8	85.1	84.5	83.8	83.2	82.6	82.1	81.6	81.0
10	86.2	85.5	84.8	84.1	83.5	82.8	82.2	81.6	81.1	80.6
11	85.9	85.2	84.5	83.8	83.1	82.5	81.8	81.2	80.7	80.1
12	85.7	84.9	84.2	83.5	82.8	82.1	81.5	80.8	80.2	79.7
13	85.4	84.7	84.0	83.2	82.5	81.8	81.1	80.5	79.9	79.2
14	85.2	84.5	83.7	83.0	82.2	81.5	80.8	80.1	79.5	78.9
15	85.0	84.3	83.5	82.7	82.0	81.2	80.5	79.8	79.1	78.5
16	84.9	84.1	83.3	82.5	81.7	81.0	80.2	79.5	78.8	78.1
17	84.7	83.9	83.1	82.3	81.5	80.7	80.0	79.2	78.5	77.8
18	84.5	83.7	82.9	82.1	81.3	80.5	79.7	79.0	78.2	77.5
19	84.4	83.6	82.7	81.9	81.1	80.3	79.5	78.7	78.0	77.3
20	84.3	83.4	82.6	81.8	80.9	80.1	79.3	78.5	77.7	77.0
21	84.1	83.3	82.4	81.6	80.8	79.9	79.1	78.3	77.5	76.8
22	84.0	83.2	82.3	81.5	80.6	79.8	78.9	78.1	77.3	76.5
23	83.9	83.1	82.2	81.3	80.5	79.6	78.8	77.9	77.1	76.3
24	83.8	83.0	82.1	81.2	80.3	79.5	78.6	77.8	76.9	76.1
25	83.7	82.9	82.0	81.1	80.2	79.3	78.5	77.6	76.8	75.9
26	83.6	82.8	81.9	81.0	80.1	79.2	78.3	77.5	76.6	75.8
27	83.6	82.7	81.8	80.9	80.0	79.1	78.2	77.4	76.5	75.6
28	83.5	82.6	81.7	80.8	79.9	79.0	78.1	77.2	76.4	75.5
29	83.4	82.6	81.6	80.7	79.8	78.9	78.0	77.1	76.2	75.4
30	83.4	82.5	81.6	80.7	79.7	78.8	77.9	77.0	76.1	75.2
31	83.3	82.4	81.5	80.6	79.7	78.8	77.8	76.9	76.0	75.1
32	83.3	82.4	81.5	80.5	79.6	78.7	77.8	76.8	75.9	75.0
33	83.2	82.3	81.4	80.5	79.5	78.6	77.7	76.8	75.9	74.9
34	83.2	82.3	81.3	80.4	79.5	78.5	77.6	76.7	75.8	74.9
35	83.1	82.2	81.3	80.4	79.4	78.5	77.6	76.6	75.7	74.8
36	83.1	82.2	81.3	80.3	79.4	78.4	77.5	76.6	75.6	74.7
37	83.0	82.2	81.2	80.3	79.3	78.4	77.4	76.5	75.6	74.6
38	83.0	82.1	81.2	80.2	79.3	78.3	77.4	76.4	75.5	74.6
39	83.0	82.1	81.1	80.2	79.2	78.3	77.3	76.4	75.5	74.5

*Source: Treas. Reg. 1.401(a)(9)-9.

Joint and Last Survivor Table (Continued)

Ages	0	1	2	3	4	5	6	7	8	9
40	82.9	82.1	81.1	80.2	79.2	78.3	77.3	76.4	75.4	74.5
41	82.9	82.0	81.1	80.1	79.2	78.2	77.3	76.3	75.4	74.4
42	82.9	82.0	81.1	80.1	79.1	78.2	77.2	76.3	75.3	74.4
43	82.9	82.0	81.0	80.1	79.1	78.2	77.2	76.2	75.3	74.3
44	82.8	81.9	81.0	80.0	79.1	78.1	77.2	76.2	75.2	74.3
45	82.8	81.9	81.0	80.0	79.1	78.1	77.1	76.2	75.2	74.3
46	82.8	81.9	81.0	80.0	79.0	78.1	77.1	76.1	75.2	74.2
47	82.8	81.9	80.9	80.0	79.0	78.0	77.1	76.1	75.2	74.2
48	82.8	81.9	80.9	80.0	79.0	78.0	77.1	76.1	75.1	74.2
49	82.7	81.8	80.9	79.9	79.0	78.0	77.0	76.1	75.1	74.1
50	82.7	81.8	80.9	79.9	79.0	78.0	77.0	76.0	75.1	74.1
51	82.7	81.8	80.9	79.9	78.9	78.0	77.0	76.0	75.1	74.1
52	82.7	81.8	80.9	79.9	78.9	78.0	77.0	76.0	75.0	74.1
53	82.7	81.8	80.8	79.9	78.9	77.9	77.0	76.0	75.0	74.0
54	82.7	81.8	80.8	79.9	78.9	77.9	76.9	76.0	75.0	74.0
55	82.6	81.8	80.8	79.8	78.9	77.9	76.9	76.0	75.0	74.0
56	82.6	81.7	80.8	79.8	78.9	77.9	76.9	75.9	75.0	74.0
57	82.6	81.7	80.8	79.8	78.9	77.9	76.9	75.9	75.0	74.0
58	82.6	81.7	80.8	79.8	78.8	77.9	76.9	75.9	74.9	74.0
59	82.6	81.7	80.8	79.8	78.8	77.9	76.9	75.9	74.9	74.0
60	82.6	81.7	80.8	79.8	78.8	77.8	76.9	75.9	74.9	73.9
61	82.6	81.7	80.8	79.8	78.8	77.8	76.9	75.9	74.9	73.9
62	82.6	81.7	80.7	79.8	78.8	77.8	76.9	75.9	74.9	73.9
63	82.6	81.7	80.7	79.8	78.8	77.8	76.8	75.9	74.9	73.9
64	82.5	81.7	80.7	79.8	78.8	77.8	76.8	75.9	74.9	73.9
65	82.5	81.7	80.7	79.8	78.8	77.8	76.8	75.8	74.9	73.9
66	82.5	81.7	80.7	79.7	78.8	77.8	76.8	75.8	74.9	73.9
67	82.5	81.7	80.7	79.7	78.8	77.8	76.8	75.8	74.9	73.9
68	82.5	81.6	80.7	79.7	78.8	77.8	76.8	75.8	74.8	73.9
69	82.5	81.6	80.7	79.7	78.8	77.8	76.8	75.8	74.8	73.9
70	82.5	81.6	80.7	79.7	78.8	77.8	76.8	75.8	74.8	73.9
71	82.5	81.6	80.7	79.7	78.7	77.8	76.8	75.8	74.8	73.8
72	82.5	81.6	80.7	79.7	78.7	77.8	76.8	75.8	74.8	73.8
73	82.5	81.6	80.7	79.7	78.7	77.8	76.8	75.8	74.8	73.8
74	82.5	81.6	80.7	79.7	78.7	77.8	76.8	75.8	74.8	73.8
75	82.5	81.6	80.7	79.7	78.7	77.8	76.8	75.8	74.8	73.8
76	82.5	81.6	80.7	79.7	78.7	77.8	76.8	75.8	74.8	73.8
77	82.5	81.6	80.7	79.7	78.7	77.7	76.8	75.8	74.8	73.8
78	82.5	81.6	80.7	79.7	78.7	77.7	76.8	75.8	74.8	73.8
79	82.5	81.6	80.7	79.7	78.7	77.7	76.8	75.8	74.8	73.8

Joint and Last Survivor Table (Continued)

Ages	0	1	2	3	4	5	6	7	8	9
80	82.5	81.6	80.7	79.7	78.7	77.7	76.8	75.8	74.8	73.8
81	82.4	81.6	80.7	79.7	78.7	77.7	76.8	75.8	74.8	73.8
82	82.4	81.6	80.7	79.7	78.7	77.7	76.8	75.8	74.8	73.8
83	82.4	81.6	80.7	79.7	78.7	77.7	76.8	75.8	74.8	73.8
84	82.4	81.6	80.7	79.7	78.7	77.7	76.8	75.8	74.8	73.8
85	82.4	81.6	80.6	79.7	78.7	77.7	76.8	75.8	74.8	73.8
86	82.4	81.6	80.6	79.7	78.7	77.7	76.7	75.8	74.8	73.8
87	82.4	81.6	80.6	79.7	78.7	77.7	76.7	75.8	74.8	73.8
88	82.4	81.6	80.6	79.7	78.7	77.7	76.7	75.8	74.8	73.8
89	82.4	81.6	80.6	79.7	78.7	77.7	76.7	75.8	74.8	73.8
90	82.4	81.6	80.6	79.7	78.7	77.7	76.7	75.8	74.8	73.8
91	82.4	81.6	80.6	79.7	78.7	77.7	76.7	75.8	74.8	73.8
92	82.4	81.6	80.6	79.7	78.7	77.7	76.7	75.8	74.8	73.8
93	82.4	81.6	80.6	79.7	78.7	77.7	76.7	75.8	74.8	73.8
94	82.4	81.6	80.6	79.7	78.7	77.7	76.7	75.8	74.8	73.8
95	82.4	81.6	80.6	79.7	78.7	77.7	76.7	75.8	74.8	73.8
96	82.4	81.6	80.6	79.7	78.7	77.7	76.7	75.8	74.8	73.8
97	82.4	81.6	80.6	79.7	78.7	77.7	76.7	75.8	74.8	73.8
98	82.4	81.6	80.6	79.7	78.7	77.7	76.7	75.8	74.8	73.8
99	82.4	81.6	80.6	79.7	78.7	77.7	76.7	75.8	74.8	73.8
100	82.4	81.6	80.6	79.7	78.7	77.7	76.7	75.8	74.8	73.8
101	82.4	81.6	80.6	79.7	78.7	77.7	76.7	75.8	74.8	73.8
102	82.4	81.6	80.6	79.7	78.7	77.7	76.7	75.8	74.8	73.8
103	82.4	81.6	80.6	79.7	78.7	77.7	76.7	75.8	74.8	73.8
104	82.4	81.6	80.6	79.7	78.7	77.7	76.7	75.8	74.8	73.8
105	82.4	81.6	80.6	79.7	78.7	77.7	76.7	75.8	74.8	73.8
106	82.4	81.6	80.6	79.7	78.7	77.7	76.7	75.8	74.8	73.8
107	82.4	81.6	80.6	79.7	78.7	77.7	76.7	75.8	74.8	73.8
108	82.4	81.6	80.6	79.7	78.7	77.7	76.7	75.8	74.8	73.8
109	82.4	81.6	80.6	79.7	78.7	77.7	76.7	75.8	74.8	73.8
110	82.4	81.6	80.6	79.7	78.7	77.7	76.7	75.8	74.8	73.8
111	82.4	81.6	80.6	79.7	78.7	77.7	76.7	75.8	74.8	73.8
112	82.4	81.6	80.6	79.7	78.7	77.7	76.7	75.8	74.8	73.8
113	82.4	81.6	80.6	79.7	78.7	77.7	76.7	75.8	74.8	73.8
114	82.4	81.6	80.6	79.7	78.7	77.7	76.7	75.8	74.8	73.8
115+	82.4	81.6	80.6	79.7	78.7	77.7	76.7	75.8	74.8	73.8

Joint and Last Survivor Table (Continued)

Ages	10	11	12	13	14	15	16	17	18	19
10	80.0	79.6	79.1	78.7	78.2	77.9	77.5	77.2	76.8	76.5
11	79.6	79.0	78.6	78.1	77.7	77.3	76.9	76.5	76.2	75.8
12	79.1	78.6	78.1	77.6	77.1	76.7	76.3	75.9	75.5	75.2
13	78.7	78.1	77.6	77.1	76.6	76.1	75.7	75.3	74.9	74.5
14	78.2	77.7	77.1	76.6	76.1	75.6	75.1	74.7	74.3	73.9
15	77.9	77.3	76.7	76.1	75.6	75.1	74.6	74.1	73.7	73.3
16	77.5	76.9	76.3	75.7	75.1	74.6	74.1	73.6	73.1	72.7
17	77.2	76.5	75.9	75.3	74.7	74.1	73.6	73.1	72.6	72.1
18	76.8	76.2	75.5	74.9	74.3	73.7	73.1	72.6	72.1	71.6
19	76.5	75.8	75.2	74.5	73.9	73.3	72.7	72.1	71.6	71.1
20	76.3	75.5	74.8	74.2	73.5	72.9	72.3	71.7	71.1	70.6
21	76.0	75.3	74.5	73.8	73.2	72.5	71.9	71.3	70.7	70.1
22	75.8	75.0	74.3	73.5	72.9	72.2	71.5	70.9	70.3	69.7
23	75.5	74.8	74.0	73.3	72.6	71.9	71.2	70.5	69.9	69.3
24	75.3	74.5	73.8	73.0	72.3	71.6	70.9	70.2	69.5	68.9
25	75.1	74.3	73.5	72.8	72.0	71.3	70.6	69.9	69.2	68.5
26	75.0	74.1	73.3	72.5	71.8	71.0	70.3	69.6	68.9	68.2
27	74.8	74.0	73.1	72.3	71.6	70.8	70.0	69.3	68.6	67.9
28	74.6	73.8	73.0	72.2	71.3	70.6	69.8	69.0	68.3	67.6
29	74.5	73.6	72.8	72.0	71.2	70.4	69.6	68.8	68.0	67.3
30	74.4	73.5	72.7	71.8	71.0	70.2	69.4	68.6	67.8	67.1
31	74.3	73.4	72.5	71.7	70.8	70.0	69.2	68.4	67.6	66.8
32	74.1	73.3	72.4	71.5	70.7	69.8	69.0	68.2	67.4	66.6
33	74.0	73.2	72.3	71.4	70.5	69.7	68.8	68.0	67.2	66.4
34	73.9	73.0	72.2	71.3	70.4	69.5	68.7	67.8	67.0	66.2
35	73.9	73.0	72.1	71.2	70.3	69.4	68.5	67.7	66.8	66.0
36	73.8	72.9	72.0	71.1	70.2	69.3	68.4	67.6	66.7	65.9
37	73.7	72.8	71.9	71.0	70.1	69.2	68.3	67.4	66.6	65.7
38	73.6	72.7	71.8	70.9	70.0	69.1	68.2	67.3	66.4	65.6
39	73.6	72.7	71.7	70.8	69.9	69.0	68.1	67.2	66.3	65.4
40	73.5	72.6	71.7	70.7	69.8	68.9	68.0	67.1	66.2	65.3
41	73.5	72.5	71.6	70.7	69.7	68.8	67.9	67.0	66.1	65.2
42	73.4	72.5	71.5	70.6	69.7	68.8	67.8	66.9	66.0	65.1
43	73.4	72.4	71.5	70.6	69.6	68.7	67.8	66.8	65.9	65.0
44	73.3	72.4	71.4	70.5	69.6	68.6	67.7	66.8	65.9	64.9
45	73.3	72.3	71.4	70.5	69.5	68.6	67.6	66.7	65.8	64.9
46	73.3	72.3	71.4	70.4	69.5	68.5	67.6	66.6	65.7	64.8
47	73.2	72.3	71.3	70.4	69.4	68.5	67.5	66.6	65.7	64.7
48	73.2	72.2	71.3	70.3	69.4	68.4	67.5	66.5	65.6	64.7
49	73.2	72.2	71.2	70.3	69.3	68.4	67.4	66.5	65.6	64.6

Joint and Last Survivor Table (Continued)

Ages	10	11	12	13	14	15	16	17	18	19
50	73.1	72.2	71.2	70.3	69.3	68.4	67.4	66.5	65.5	64.6
51	73.1	72.2	71.2	70.2	69.3	68.3	67.4	66.4	65.5	64.5
52	73.1	72.1	71.2	70.2	69.2	68.3	67.3	66.4	65.4	64.5
53	73.1	72.1	71.1	70.2	69.2	68.3	67.3	66.3	65.4	64.4
54	73.1	72.1	71.1	70.2	69.2	68.2	67.3	66.3	65.4	64.4
55	73.0	72.1	71.1	70.1	69.2	68.2	67.2	66.3	65.3	64.4
56	73.0	72.1	71.1	70.1	69.1	68.2	67.2	66.3	65.3	64.3
57	73.0	72.0	71.1	70.1	69.1	68.2	67.2	66.2	65.3	64.3
58	73.0	72.0	71.0	70.1	69.1	68.1	67.2	66.2	65.2	64.3
59	73.0	72.0	71.0	70.1	69.1	68.1	67.2	66.2	65.2	64.3
60	73.0	72.0	71.0	70.0	69.1	68.1	67.1	66.2	65.2	64.2
61	73.0	72.0	71.0	70.0	69.1	68.1	67.1	66.2	65.2	64.2
62	72.9	72.0	71.0	70.0	69.0	68.1	67.1	66.1	65.2	64.2
63	72.9	72.0	71.0	70.0	69.0	68.1	67.1	66.1	65.2	64.2
64	72.9	71.9	71.0	70.0	69.0	68.0	67.1	66.1	65.1	64.2
65	72.9	71.9	71.0	70.0	69.0	68.0	67.1	66.1	65.1	64.2
66	72.9	71.9	70.9	70.0	69.0	68.0	67.1	66.1	65.1	64.1
67	72.9	71.9	70.9	70.0	69.0	68.0	67.0	66.1	65.1	64.1
68	72.9	71.9	70.9	70.0	69.0	68.0	67.0	66.1	65.1	64.1
69	72.9	71.9	70.9	69.9	69.0	68.0	67.0	66.1	65.1	64.1
70	72.9	71.9	70.9	69.9	69.0	68.0	67.0	66.0	65.1	64.1
71	72.9	71.9	70.9	69.9	69.0	68.0	67.0	66.0	65.1	64.1
72	72.9	71.9	70.9	69.9	69.0	68.0	67.0	66.0	65.1	64.1
73	72.9	71.9	70.9	69.9	68.9	68.0	67.0	66.0	65.0	64.1
74	72.9	71.9	70.9	69.9	68.9	68.0	67.0	66.0	65.0	64.1
75	72.8	71.9	70.9	69.9	68.9	68.0	67.0	66.0	65.0	64.1
76	72.8	71.9	70.9	69.9	68.9	68.0	67.0	66.0	65.0	64.1
77	72.8	71.9	70.9	69.9	68.9	68.0	67.0	66.0	65.0	64.1
78	72.8	71.9	70.9	69.9	68.9	67.9	67.0	66.0	65.0	64.0
79	72.8	71.9	70.9	69.9	68.9	67.9	67.0	66.0	65.0	64.0
80	72.8	71.9	70.9	69.9	68.9	67.9	67.0	66.0	65.0	64.0
81	72.8	71.8	70.9	69.9	68.9	67.9	67.0	66.0	65.0	64.0
82	72.8	71.8	70.9	69.9	68.9	67.9	67.0	66.0	65.0	64.0
83	72.8	71.8	70.9	69.9	68.9	67.9	67.0	66.0	65.0	64.0
84	72.8	71.8	70.9	69.9	68.9	67.9	67.0	66.0	65.0	64.0
85	72.8	71.8	70.9	69.9	68.9	67.9	66.9	66.0	65.0	64.0
86	72.8	71.8	70.9	69.9	68.9	67.9	66.9	66.0	65.0	64.0
87	72.8	71.8	70.9	69.9	68.9	67.9	66.9	66.0	65.0	64.0
88	72.8	71.8	70.9	69.9	68.9	67.9	66.9	66.0	65.0	64.0
89	72.8	71.8	70.9	69.9	68.9	67.9	66.9	66.0	65.0	64.0

Joint and Last Survivor Table (Continued)

Ages	10	11	12	13	14	15	16	17	18	19
90	72.8	71.8	70.9	69.9	68.9	67.9	66.9	66.0	65.0	64.0
91	72.8	71.8	70.9	69.9	68.9	67.9	66.9	66.0	65.0	64.0
92	72.8	71.8	70.9	69.9	68.9	67.9	66.9	66.0	65.0	64.0
93	72.8	71.8	70.9	69.9	68.9	67.9	66.9	66.0	65.0	64.0
94	72.8	71.8	70.8	69.9	68.9	67.9	66.9	66.0	65.0	64.0
95	72.8	71.8	70.8	69.9	68.9	67.9	66.9	66.0	65.0	64.0
96	72.8	71.8	70.8	69.9	68.9	67.9	66.9	66.0	65.0	64.0
97	72.8	71.8	70.8	69.9	68.9	67.9	66.9	66.0	65.0	64.0
98	72.8	71.8	70.8	69.9	68.9	67.9	66.9	66.0	65.0	64.0
99	72.8	71.8	70.8	69.9	68.9	67.9	66.9	66.0	65.0	64.0
100	72.8	71.8	70.8	69.9	68.9	67.9	66.9	66.0	65.0	64.0
101	72.8	71.8	70.8	69.9	68.9	67.9	66.9	66.0	65.0	64.0
102	72.8	71.8	70.8	69.9	68.9	67.9	66.9	66.0	65.0	64.0
103	72.8	71.8	70.8	69.9	68.9	67.9	66.9	66.0	65.0	64.0
104	72.8	71.8	70.8	69.9	68.9	67.9	66.9	66.0	65.0	64.0
105	72.8	71.8	70.8	69.9	68.9	67.9	66.9	66.0	65.0	64.0
106	72.8	71.8	70.8	69.9	68.9	67.9	66.9	66.0	65.0	64.0
107	72.8	71.8	70.8	69.9	68.9	67.9	66.9	66.0	65.0	64.0
108	72.8	71.8	70.8	69.9	68.9	67.9	66.9	66.0	65.0	64.0
109	72.8	71.8	70.8	69.9	68.9	67.9	66.9	66.0	65.0	64.0
110	72.8	71.8	70.8	69.9	68.9	67.9	66.9	66.0	65.0	64.0
111	72.8	71.8	70.8	69.9	68.9	67.9	66.9	66.0	65.0	64.0
112	72.8	71.8	70.8	69.9	68.9	67.9	66.9	66.0	65.0	64.0
113	72.8	71.8	70.8	69.9	68.9	67.9	66.9	66.0	65.0	64.0
114	72.8	71.8	70.8	69.9	68.9	67.9	66.9	66.0	65.0	64.0
115+	72.8	71.8	70.8	69.9	68.9	67.9	66.9	66.0	65.0	64.0

Joint and Last Survivor Table (Continued)

Ages	20	21	22	23	24	25	26	27	28	29
20	70.1	69.6	69.1	68.7	68.3	67.9	67.5	67.2	66.9	66.6
21	69.6	69.1	68.6	68.2	67.7	67.3	66.9	66.6	66.2	65.9
22	69.1	68.6	68.1	67.6	67.2	66.7	66.3	65.9	65.6	65.2
23	68.7	68.2	67.6	67.1	66.6	66.2	65.7	65.3	64.9	64.6
24	68.3	67.7	67.2	66.6	66.1	65.6	65.2	64.7	64.3	63.9
25	67.9	67.3	66.7	66.2	65.6	65.1	64.6	64.2	63.7	63.3
26	67.5	66.9	66.3	65.7	65.2	64.6	64.1	63.6	63.2	62.8
27	67.2	66.6	65.9	65.3	64.7	64.2	63.6	63.1	62.7	62.2
28	66.9	66.2	65.6	64.9	64.3	63.7	63.2	62.7	62.1	61.7
29	66.6	65.9	65.2	64.6	63.9	63.3	62.8	62.2	61.7	61.2
30	66.3	65.6	64.9	64.2	63.6	62.9	62.3	61.8	61.2	60.7
31	66.1	65.3	64.6	63.9	63.2	62.6	62.0	61.4	60.8	60.2
32	65.8	65.1	64.3	63.6	62.9	62.2	61.6	61.0	60.4	59.8
33	65.6	64.8	64.1	63.3	62.6	61.9	61.3	60.6	60.0	59.4
34	65.4	64.6	63.8	63.1	62.3	61.6	60.9	60.3	59.6	59.0
35	65.2	64.4	63.6	62.8	62.1	61.4	60.6	59.9	59.3	58.6
36	65.0	64.2	63.4	62.6	61.9	61.1	60.4	59.6	59.0	58.3
37	64.9	64.0	63.2	62.4	61.6	60.9	60.1	59.4	58.7	58.0
38	64.7	63.9	63.0	62.2	61.4	60.6	59.9	59.1	58.4	57.7
39	64.6	63.7	62.9	62.1	61.2	60.4	59.6	58.9	58.1	57.4
40	64.4	63.6	62.7	61.9	61.1	60.2	59.4	58.7	57.9	57.1
41	64.3	63.5	62.6	61.7	60.9	60.1	59.3	58.5	57.7	56.9
42	64.2	63.3	62.5	61.6	60.8	59.9	59.1	58.3	57.5	56.7
43	64.1	63.2	62.4	61.5	60.6	59.8	58.9	58.1	57.3	56.5
44	64.0	63.1	62.2	61.4	60.5	59.6	58.8	57.9	57.1	56.3
45	64.0	63.0	62.2	61.3	60.4	59.5	58.6	57.8	56.9	56.1
46	63.9	63.0	62.1	61.2	60.3	59.4	58.5	57.7	56.8	56.0
47	63.8	62.9	62.0	61.1	60.2	59.3	58.4	57.5	56.7	55.8
48	63.7	62.8	61.9	61.0	60.1	59.2	58.3	57.4	56.5	55.7
49	63.7	62.8	61.8	60.9	60.0	59.1	58.2	57.3	56.4	55.6
50	63.6	62.7	61.8	60.8	59.9	59.0	58.1	57.2	56.3	55.4
51	63.6	62.6	61.7	60.8	59.9	58.9	58.0	57.1	56.2	55.3
52	63.5	62.6	61.7	60.7	59.8	58.9	58.0	57.1	56.1	55.2
53	63.5	62.5	61.6	60.7	59.7	58.8	57.9	57.0	56.1	55.2
54	63.5	62.5	61.6	60.6	59.7	58.8	57.8	56.9	56.0	55.1
55	63.4	62.5	61.5	60.6	59.6	58.7	57.8	56.8	55.9	55.0
56	63.4	62.4	61.5	60.5	59.6	58.7	57.7	56.8	55.9	54.9
57	63.4	62.4	61.5	60.5	59.6	58.6	57.7	56.7	55.8	54.9
58	63.3	62.4	61.4	60.5	59.5	58.6	57.6	56.7	55.8	54.8
59	63.3	62.3	61.4	60.4	59.5	58.5	57.6	56.7	55.7	54.8

Joint and Last Survivor Table (Continued)

Ages	20	21	22	23	24	25	26	27	28	29
60	63.3	62.3	61.4	60.4	59.5	58.5	57.6	56.6	55.7	54.7
61	63.3	62.3	61.3	60.4	59.4	58.5	57.5	56.6	55.6	54.7
62	63.2	62.3	61.3	60.4	59.4	58.4	57.5	56.5	55.6	54.7
63	63.2	62.3	61.3	60.3	59.4	58.4	57.5	56.5	55.6	54.6
64	63.2	62.2	61.3	60.3	59.4	58.4	57.4	56.5	55.5	54.6
65	63.2	62.2	61.3	60.3	59.3	58.4	57.4	56.5	55.5	54.6
66	63.2	62.2	61.2	60.3	59.3	58.4	57.4	56.4	55.5	54.5
67	63.2	62.2	61.2	60.3	59.3	58.3	57.4	56.4	55.5	54.5
68	63.1	62.2	61.2	60.2	59.3	58.3	57.4	56.4	55.4	54.5
69	63.1	62.2	61.2	60.2	59.3	58.3	57.3	56.4	55.4	54.5
70	63.1	62.2	61.2	60.2	59.3	58.3	57.3	56.4	55.4	54.4
71	63.1	62.1	61.2	60.2	59.2	58.3	57.3	56.4	55.4	54.4
72	63.1	62.1	61.2	60.2	59.2	58.3	57.3	56.3	55.4	54.4
73	63.1	62.1	61.2	60.2	59.2	58.3	57.3	56.3	55.4	54.4
74	63.1	62.1	61.2	60.2	59.2	58.2	57.3	56.3	55.4	54.4
75	63.1	62.1	61.1	60.2	59.2	58.2	57.3	56.3	55.3	54.4
76	63.1	62.1	61.1	60.2	59.2	58.2	57.3	56.3	55.3	54.4
77	63.1	62.1	61.1	60.2	59.2	58.2	57.3	56.3	55.3	54.4
78	63.1	62.1	61.1	60.2	59.2	58.2	57.3	56.3	55.3	54.4
79	63.1	62.1	61.1	60.2	59.2	58.2	57.2	56.3	55.3	54.3
80	63.1	62.1	61.1	60.1	59.2	58.2	57.2	56.3	55.3	54.3
81	63.1	62.1	61.1	60.1	59.2	58.2	57.2	56.3	55.3	54.3
82	63.1	62.1	61.1	60.1	59.2	58.2	57.2	56.3	55.3	54.3
83	63.1	62.1	61.1	60.1	59.2	58.2	57.2	56.3	55.3	54.3
84	63.0	62.1	61.1	60.1	59.2	58.2	57.2	56.3	55.3	54.3
85	63.0	62.1	61.1	60.1	59.2	58.2	57.2	56.3	55.3	54.3
86	63.0	62.1	61.1	60.1	59.2	58.2	57.2	56.2	55.3	54.3
87	63.0	62.1	61.1	60.1	59.2	58.2	57.2	56.2	55.3	54.3
88	63.0	62.1	61.1	60.1	59.2	58.2	57.2	56.2	55.3	54.3
89	63.0	62.1	61.1	60.1	59.1	58.2	57.2	56.2	55.3	54.3
90	63.0	62.1	61.1	60.1	59.1	58.2	57.2	56.2	55.3	54.3
91	63.0	62.1	61.1	60.1	59.1	58.2	57.2	56.2	55.3	54.3
92	63.0	62.1	61.1	60.1	59.1	58.2	57.2	56.2	55.3	54.3
93	63.0	62.1	61.1	60.1	59.1	58.2	57.2	56.2	55.3	54.3
94	63.0	62.1	61.1	60.1	59.1	58.2	57.2	56.2	55.3	54.3
95	63.0	62.1	61.1	60.1	59.1	58.2	57.2	56.2	55.3	54.3
96	63.0	62.1	61.1	60.1	59.1	58.2	57.2	56.2	55.3	54.3
97	63.0	62.1	61.1	60.1	59.1	58.2	57.2	56.2	55.3	54.3
98	63.0	62.1	61.1	60.1	59.1	58.2	57.2	56.2	55.3	54.3
99	63.0	62.1	61.1	60.1	59.1	58.2	57.2	56.2	55.3	54.3

Joint and Last Survivor Table (Continued)

Ages	20	21	22	23	24	25	26	27	28	29
100	63.0	62.1	61.1	60.1	59.1	58.2	57.2	56.2	55.3	54.3
101	63.0	62.1	61.1	60.1	59.1	58.2	57.2	56.2	55.3	54.3
102	63.0	62.1	61.1	60.1	59.1	58.2	57.2	56.2	55.3	54.3
103	63.0	62.1	61.1	60.1	59.1	58.2	57.2	56.2	55.3	54.3
104	63.0	62.1	61.1	60.1	59.1	58.2	57.2	56.2	55.3	54.3
105	63.0	62.1	61.1	60.1	59.1	58.2	57.2	56.2	55.3	54.3
106	63.0	62.1	61.1	60.1	59.1	58.2	57.2	56.2	55.3	54.3
107	63.0	62.1	61.1	60.1	59.1	58.2	57.2	56.2	55.3	54.3
108	63.0	62.1	61.1	60.1	59.1	58.2	57.2	56.2	55.3	54.3
109	63.0	62.1	61.1	60.1	59.1	58.2	57.2	56.2	55.3	54.3
110	63.0	62.1	61.1	60.1	59.1	58.2	57.2	56.2	55.3	54.3
111	63.0	62.1	61.1	60.1	59.1	58.2	57.2	56.2	55.3	54.3
112	63.0	62.1	61.1	60.1	59.1	58.2	57.2	56.2	55.3	54.3
113	63.0	62.1	61.1	60.1	59.1	58.2	57.2	56.2	55.3	54.3
114	63.0	62.1	61.1	60.1	59.1	58.2	57.2	56.2	55.3	54.3
115+	63.0	62.1	61.1	60.1	59.1	58.2	57.2	56.2	55.3	54.3

Joint and Last Survivor Table (Continued)

Ages	30	31	32	33	34	35	36	37	38	39
30	60.2	59.7	59.2	58.8	58.4	58.0	57.6	57.3	57.0	56.7
31	59.7	59.2	58.7	58.2	57.8	57.4	57.0	56.6	56.3	56.0
32	59.2	58.7	58.2	57.7	57.2	56.8	56.4	56.0	55.6	55.3
33	58.8	58.2	57.7	57.2	56.7	56.2	55.8	55.4	55.0	54.7
34	58.4	57.8	57.2	56.7	56.2	55.7	55.3	54.8	54.4	54.0
35	58.0	57.4	56.8	56.2	55.7	55.2	54.7	54.3	53.8	53.4
36	57.6	57.0	56.4	55.8	55.3	54.7	54.2	53.7	53.3	52.8
37	57.3	56.6	56.0	55.4	54.8	54.3	53.7	53.2	52.7	52.3
38	57.0	56.3	55.6	55.0	54.4	53.8	53.3	52.7	52.2	51.7
39	56.7	56.0	55.3	54.7	54.0	53.4	52.8	52.3	51.7	51.2
40	56.4	55.7	55.0	54.3	53.7	53.0	52.4	51.8	51.3	50.8
41	56.1	55.4	54.7	54.0	53.3	52.7	52.0	51.4	50.9	50.3
42	55.9	55.2	54.4	53.7	53.0	52.3	51.7	51.1	50.4	49.9
43	55.7	54.9	54.2	53.4	52.7	52.0	51.3	50.7	50.1	49.5
44	55.5	54.7	53.9	53.2	52.4	51.7	51.0	50.4	49.7	49.1
45	55.3	54.5	53.7	52.9	52.2	51.5	50.7	50.0	49.4	48.7
46	55.1	54.3	53.5	52.7	52.0	51.2	50.5	49.8	49.1	48.4
47	55.0	54.1	53.3	52.5	51.7	51.0	50.2	49.5	48.8	48.1
48	54.8	54.0	53.2	52.3	51.5	50.8	50.0	49.2	48.5	47.8
49	54.7	53.8	53.0	52.2	51.4	50.6	49.8	49.0	48.2	47.5
50	54.6	53.7	52.9	52.0	51.2	50.4	49.6	48.8	48.0	47.3
51	54.5	53.6	52.7	51.9	51.0	50.2	49.4	48.6	47.8	47.0
52	54.4	53.5	52.6	51.7	50.9	50.0	49.2	48.4	47.6	46.8
53	54.3	53.4	52.5	51.6	50.8	49.9	49.1	48.2	47.4	46.6
54	54.2	53.3	52.4	51.5	50.6	49.8	48.9	48.1	47.2	46.4
55	54.1	53.2	52.3	51.4	50.5	49.7	48.8	47.9	47.1	46.3
56	54.0	53.1	52.2	51.3	50.4	49.5	48.7	47.8	47.0	46.1
57	54.0	53.0	52.1	51.2	50.3	49.4	48.6	47.7	46.8	46.0
58	53.9	53.0	52.1	51.2	50.3	49.4	48.5	47.6	46.7	45.8
59	53.8	52.9	52.0	51.1	50.2	49.3	48.4	47.5	46.6	45.7
60	53.8	52.9	51.9	51.0	50.1	49.2	48.3	47.4	46.5	45.6
61	53.8	52.8	51.9	51.0	50.0	49.1	48.2	47.3	46.4	45.5
62	53.7	52.8	51.8	50.9	50.0	49.1	48.1	47.2	46.3	45.4
63	53.7	52.7	51.8	50.9	49.9	49.0	48.1	47.2	46.3	45.3
64	53.6	52.7	51.8	50.8	49.9	48.9	48.0	47.1	46.2	45.3
65	53.6	52.7	51.7	50.8	49.8	48.9	48.0	47.0	46.1	45.2
66	53.6	52.6	51.7	50.7	49.8	48.9	47.9	47.0	46.1	45.1
67	53.6	52.6	51.7	50.7	49.8	48.8	47.9	46.9	46.0	45.1
68	53.5	52.6	51.6	50.7	49.7	48.8	47.8	46.9	46.0	45.0
69	53.5	52.6	51.6	50.6	49.7	48.7	47.8	46.9	45.9	45.0

Joint and Last Survivor Table (Continued)

Ages	30	31	32	33	34	35	36	37	38	39
70	53.5	52.5	51.6	50.6	49.7	48.7	47.8	46.8	45.9	44.9
71	53.5	52.5	51.6	50.6	49.6	48.7	47.7	46.8	45.9	44.9
72	53.5	52.5	51.5	50.6	49.6	48.7	47.7	46.8	45.8	44.9
73	53.4	52.5	51.5	50.6	49.6	48.6	47.7	46.7	45.8	44.8
74	53.4	52.5	51.5	50.5	49.6	48.6	47.7	46.7	45.8	44.8
75	53.4	52.5	51.5	50.5	49.6	48.6	47.7	46.7	45.7	44.8
76	53.4	52.4	51.5	50.5	49.6	48.6	47.6	46.7	45.7	44.8
77	53.4	52.4	51.5	50.5	49.5	48.6	47.6	46.7	45.7	44.8
78	53.4	52.4	51.5	50.5	49.5	48.6	47.6	46.6	45.7	44.7
79	53.4	52.4	51.5	50.5	49.5	48.6	47.6	46.6	45.7	44.7
80	53.4	52.4	51.4	50.5	49.5	48.5	47.6	46.6	45.7	44.7
81	53.4	52.4	51.4	50.5	49.5	48.5	47.6	46.6	45.7	44.7
82	53.4	52.4	51.4	50.5	49.5	48.5	47.6	46.6	45.6	44.7
83	53.4	52.4	51.4	50.5	49.5	48.5	47.6	46.6	45.6	44.7
84	53.4	52.4	51.4	50.5	49.5	48.5	47.6	46.6	45.6	44.7
85	53.3	52.4	51.4	50.4	49.5	48.5	47.5	46.6	45.6	44.7
86	53.3	52.4	51.4	50.4	49.5	48.5	47.5	46.6	45.6	44.6
87	53.3	52.4	51.4	50.4	49.5	48.5	47.5	46.6	45.6	44.6
88	53.3	52.4	51.4	50.4	49.5	48.5	47.5	46.6	45.6	44.6
89	53.3	52.4	51.4	50.4	49.5	48.5	47.5	46.6	45.6	44.6
90	53.3	52.4	51.4	50.4	49.5	48.5	47.5	46.6	45.6	44.6
91	53.3	52.4	51.4	50.4	49.5	48.5	47.5	46.6	45.6	44.6
92	53.3	52.4	51.4	50.4	49.5	48.5	47.5	46.6	45.6	44.6
93	53.3	52.4	51.4	50.4	49.5	48.5	47.5	46.6	45.6	44.6
94	53.3	52.4	51.4	50.4	49.5	48.5	47.5	46.6	45.6	44.6
95	53.3	52.4	51.4	50.4	49.5	48.5	47.5	46.5	45.6	44.6
96	53.3	52.4	51.4	50.4	49.5	48.5	47.5	46.5	45.6	44.6
97	53.3	52.4	51.4	50.4	49.5	48.5	47.5	46.5	45.6	44.6
98	53.3	52.4	51.4	50.4	49.5	48.5	47.5	46.5	45.6	44.6
99	53.3	52.4	51.4	50.4	49.5	48.5	47.5	46.5	45.6	44.6
100	53.3	52.4	51.4	50.4	49.5	48.5	47.5	46.5	45.6	44.6
101	53.3	52.4	51.4	50.4	49.5	48.5	47.5	46.5	45.6	44.6
102	53.3	52.4	51.4	50.4	49.5	48.5	47.5	46.5	45.6	44.6
103	53.3	52.4	51.4	50.4	49.5	48.5	47.5	46.5	45.6	44.6
104	53.3	52.4	51.4	50.4	49.5	48.5	47.5	46.5	45.6	44.6
105	53.3	52.4	51.4	50.4	49.4	48.5	47.5	46.5	45.6	44.6
106	53.3	52.4	51.4	50.4	49.4	48.5	47.5	46.5	45.6	44.6
107	53.3	52.4	51.4	50.4	49.4	48.5	47.5	46.5	45.6	44.6
108	53.3	52.4	51.4	50.4	49.4	48.5	47.5	46.5	45.6	44.6
109	53.3	52.4	51.4	50.4	49.4	48.5	47.5	46.5	45.6	44.6

Joint and Last Survivor Table (Continued)

Ages	30	31	32	33	34	35	36	37	38	39
110	53.3	52.4	51.4	50.4	49.4	48.5	47.5	46.5	45.6	44.6
111	53.3	52.4	51.4	50.4	49.4	48.5	47.5	46.5	45.6	44.6
112	53.3	52.4	51.4	50.4	49.4	48.5	47.5	46.5	45.6	44.6
113	53.3	52.4	51.4	50.4	49.4	48.5	47.5	46.5	45.6	44.6
114	53.3	52.4	51.4	50.4	49.4	48.5	47.5	46.5	45.6	44.6
115+	53.3	52.4	51.4	50.4	49.4	48.5	47.5	46.5	45.6	44.6

Joint and Last Survivor Table (Continued)

Ages	40	41	42	43	44	45	46	47	48	49
40	50.2	49.8	49.3	48.9	48.5	48.1	47.7	47.4	47.1	46.8
41	49.8	49.3	48.8	48.3	47.9	47.5	47.1	46.7	46.4	46.1
42	49.3	48.8	48.3	47.8	47.3	46.9	46.5	46.1	45.8	45.4
43	48.9	48.3	47.8	47.3	46.8	46.3	45.9	45.5	45.1	44.8
44	48.5	47.9	47.3	46.8	46.3	45.8	45.4	44.9	44.5	44.2
45	48.1	47.5	46.9	46.3	45.8	45.3	44.8	44.4	44.0	43.6
46	47.7	47.1	46.5	45.9	45.4	44.8	44.3	43.9	43.4	43.0
47	47.4	46.7	46.1	45.5	44.9	44.4	43.9	43.4	42.9	42.4
48	47.1	46.4	45.8	45.1	44.5	44.0	43.4	42.9	42.4	41.9
49	46.8	46.1	45.4	44.8	44.2	43.6	43.0	42.4	41.9	41.4
50	46.5	45.8	45.1	44.4	43.8	43.2	42.6	42.0	41.5	40.9
51	46.3	45.5	44.8	44.1	43.5	42.8	42.2	41.6	41.0	40.5
52	46.0	45.3	44.6	43.8	43.2	42.5	41.8	41.2	40.6	40.1
53	45.8	45.1	44.3	43.6	42.9	42.2	41.5	40.9	40.3	39.7
54	45.6	44.8	44.1	43.3	42.6	41.9	41.2	40.5	39.9	39.3
55	45.5	44.7	43.9	43.1	42.4	41.6	40.9	40.2	39.6	38.9
56	45.3	44.5	43.7	42.9	42.1	41.4	40.7	40.0	39.3	38.6
57	45.1	44.3	43.5	42.7	41.9	41.2	40.4	39.7	39.0	38.3
58	45.0	44.2	43.3	42.5	41.7	40.9	40.2	39.4	38.7	38.0
59	44.9	44.0	43.2	42.4	41.5	40.7	40.0	39.2	38.5	37.8
60	44.7	43.9	43.0	42.2	41.4	40.6	39.8	39.0	38.2	37.5
61	44.6	43.8	42.9	42.1	41.2	40.4	39.6	38.8	38.0	37.3
62	44.5	43.7	42.8	41.9	41.1	40.3	39.4	38.6	37.8	37.1
63	44.5	43.6	42.7	41.8	41.0	40.1	39.3	38.5	37.7	36.9
64	44.4	43.5	42.6	41.7	40.8	40.0	39.2	38.3	37.5	36.7
65	44.3	43.4	42.5	41.6	40.7	39.9	39.0	38.2	37.4	36.6
66	44.2	43.3	42.4	41.5	40.6	39.8	38.9	38.1	37.2	36.4
67	44.2	43.3	42.3	41.4	40.6	39.7	38.8	38.0	37.1	36.3
68	44.1	43.2	42.3	41.4	40.5	39.6	38.7	37.9	37.0	36.2
69	44.1	43.1	42.2	41.3	40.4	39.5	38.6	37.8	36.9	36.0
70	44.0	43.1	42.2	41.3	40.3	39.4	38.6	37.7	36.8	35.9
71	44.0	43.0	42.1	41.2	40.3	39.4	38.5	37.6	36.7	35.9
72	43.9	43.0	42.1	41.1	40.2	39.3	38.4	37.5	36.6	35.8
73	43.9	43.0	42.0	41.1	40.2	39.3	38.4	37.5	36.6	35.7
74	43.9	42.9	42.0	41.1	40.1	39.2	38.3	37.4	36.5	35.6
75	43.8	42.9	42.0	41.0	40.1	39.2	38.3	37.4	36.5	35.6
76	43.8	42.9	41.9	41.0	40.1	39.1	38.2	37.3	36.4	35.5
77	43.8	42.9	41.9	41.0	40.0	39.1	38.2	37.3	36.4	35.5
78	43.8	42.8	41.9	40.9	40.0	39.1	38.2	37.2	36.3	35.4
79	43.8	42.8	41.9	40.9	40.0	39.1	38.1	37.2	36.3	35.4

Joint and Last Survivor Table (Continued)

Ages	40	41	42	43	44	45	46	47	48	49
80	43.7	42.8	41.8	40.9	40.0	39.0	38.1	37.2	36.3	35.4
81	43.7	42.8	41.8	40.9	39.9	39.0	38.1	37.2	36.2	35.3
82	43.7	42.8	41.8	40.9	39.9	39.0	38.1	37.1	36.2	35.3
83	43.7	42.8	41.8	40.9	39.9	39.0	38.0	37.1	36.2	35.3
84	43.7	42.7	41.8	40.8	39.9	39.0	38.0	37.1	36.2	35.3
85	43.7	42.7	41.8	40.8	39.9	38.9	38.0	37.1	36.2	35.2
86	43.7	42.7	41.8	40.8	39.9	38.9	38.0	37.1	36.1	35.2
87	43.7	42.7	41.8	40.8	39.9	38.9	38.0	37.0	36.1	35.2
88	43.7	42.7	41.8	40.8	39.9	38.9	38.0	37.0	36.1	35.2
89	43.7	42.7	41.7	40.8	39.8	38.9	38.0	37.0	36.1	35.2
90	43.7	42.7	41.7	40.8	39.8	38.9	38.0	37.0	36.1	35.2
91	43.7	42.7	41.7	40.8	39.8	38.9	37.9	37.0	36.1	35.2
92	43.7	42.7	41.7	40.8	39.8	38.9	37.9	37.0	36.1	35.1
93	43.7	42.7	41.7	40.8	39.8	38.9	37.9	37.0	36.1	35.1
94	43.7	42.7	41.7	40.8	39.8	38.9	37.9	37.0	36.1	35.1
95	43.6	42.7	41.7	40.8	39.8	38.9	37.9	37.0	36.1	35.1
96	43.6	42.7	41.7	40.8	39.8	38.9	37.9	37.0	36.1	35.1
97	43.6	42.7	41.7	40.8	39.8	38.9	37.9	37.0	36.1	35.1
98	43.6	42.7	41.7	40.8	39.8	38.9	37.9	37.0	36.0	35.1
99	43.6	42.7	41.7	40.8	39.8	38.9	37.9	37.0	36.0	35.1
100	43.6	42.7	41.7	40.8	39.8	38.9	37.9	37.0	36.0	35.1
101	43.6	42.7	41.7	40.8	39.8	38.9	37.9	37.0	36.0	35.1
102	43.6	42.7	41.7	40.8	39.8	38.9	37.9	37.0	36.0	35.1
103	43.6	42.7	41.7	40.8	39.8	38.9	37.9	37.0	36.0	35.1
104	43.6	42.7	41.7	40.8	39.8	38.8	37.9	37.0	36.0	35.1
105	43.6	42.7	41.7	40.8	39.8	38.8	37.9	37.0	36.0	35.1
106	43.6	42.7	41.7	40.8	39.8	38.8	37.9	37.0	36.0	35.1
107	43.6	42.7	41.7	40.8	39.8	38.8	37.9	37.0	36.0	35.1
108	43.6	42.7	41.7	40.8	39.8	38.8	37.9	37.0	36.0	35.1
109	43.6	42.7	41.7	40.7	39.8	38.8	37.9	37.0	36.0	35.1
110	43.6	42.7	41.7	40.7	39.8	38.8	37.9	37.0	36.0	35.1
111	43.6	42.7	41.7	40.7	39.8	38.8	37.9	37.0	36.0	35.1
112	43.6	42.7	41.7	40.7	39.8	38.8	37.9	37.0	36.0	35.1
113	43.6	42.7	41.7	40.7	39.8	38.8	37.9	37.0	36.0	35.1
114	43.6	42.7	41.7	40.7	39.8	38.8	37.9	37.0	36.0	35.1
115+	43.6	42.7	41.7	40.7	39.8	38.8	37.9	37.0	36.0	35.1

Joint and Last Survivor Table (Continued)

Ages	50	51	52	53	54	55	56	57	58	59
50	40.4	40.0	39.5	39.1	38.7	38.3	38.0	37.6	37.3	37.1
51	40.0	39.5	39.0	38.5	38.1	37.7	37.4	37.0	36.7	36.4
52	39.5	39.0	38.5	38.0	37.6	37.2	36.8	36.4	36.0	35.7
53	39.1	38.5	38.0	37.5	37.1	36.6	36.2	35.8	35.4	35.1
54	38.7	38.1	37.6	37.1	36.6	36.1	35.7	35.2	34.8	34.5
55	38.3	37.7	37.2	36.6	36.1	35.6	35.1	34.7	34.3	33.9
56	38.0	37.4	36.8	36.2	35.7	35.1	34.7	34.2	33.7	33.3
57	37.6	37.0	36.4	35.8	35.2	34.7	34.2	33.7	33.2	32.8
58	37.3	36.7	36.0	35.4	34.8	34.3	33.7	33.2	32.8	32.3
59	37.1	36.4	35.7	35.1	34.5	33.9	33.3	32.8	32.3	31.8
60	36.8	36.1	35.4	34.8	34.1	33.5	32.9	32.4	31.9	31.3
61	36.6	35.8	35.1	34.5	33.8	33.2	32.6	32.0	31.4	30.9
62	36.3	35.6	34.9	34.2	33.5	32.9	32.2	31.6	31.1	30.5
63	36.1	35.4	34.6	33.9	33.2	32.6	31.9	31.3	30.7	30.1
64	35.9	35.2	34.4	33.7	33.0	32.3	31.6	31.0	30.4	29.8
65	35.8	35.0	34.2	33.5	32.7	32.0	31.4	30.7	30.0	29.4
66	35.6	34.8	34.0	33.3	32.5	31.8	31.1	30.4	29.8	29.1
67	35.5	34.7	33.9	33.1	32.3	31.6	30.9	30.2	29.5	28.8
68	35.3	34.5	33.7	32.9	32.1	31.4	30.7	29.9	29.2	28.6
69	35.2	34.4	33.6	32.8	32.0	31.2	30.5	29.7	29.0	28.3
70	35.1	34.3	33.4	32.6	31.8	31.1	30.3	29.5	28.8	28.1
71	35.0	34.2	33.3	32.5	31.7	30.9	30.1	29.4	28.6	27.9
72	34.9	34.1	33.2	32.4	31.6	30.8	30.0	29.2	28.4	27.7
73	34.8	34.0	33.1	32.3	31.5	30.6	29.8	29.1	28.3	27.5
74	34.8	33.9	33.0	32.2	31.4	30.5	29.7	28.9	28.1	27.4
75	34.7	33.8	33.0	32.1	31.3	30.4	29.6	28.8	28.0	27.2
76	34.6	33.8	32.9	32.0	31.2	30.3	29.5	28.7	27.9	27.1
77	34.6	33.7	32.8	32.0	31.1	30.3	29.4	28.6	27.8	27.0
78	34.5	33.6	32.8	31.9	31.0	30.2	29.3	28.5	27.7	26.9
79	34.5	33.6	32.7	31.8	31.0	30.1	29.3	28.4	27.6	26.8
80	34.5	33.6	32.7	31.8	30.9	30.1	29.2	28.4	27.5	26.7
81	34.4	33.5	32.6	31.8	30.9	30.0	29.2	28.3	27.5	26.6
82	34.4	33.5	32.6	31.7	30.8	30.0	29.1	28.3	27.4	26.6
83	34.4	33.5	32.6	31.7	30.8	29.9	29.1	28.2	27.4	26.5
84	34.3	33.4	32.5	31.7	30.8	29.9	29.0	28.2	27.3	26.5
85	34.3	33.4	32.5	31.6	30.7	29.9	29.0	28.1	27.3	26.4
86	34.3	33.4	32.5	31.6	30.7	29.8	29.0	28.1	27.2	26.4
87	34.3	33.4	32.5	31.6	30.7	29.8	28.9	28.1	27.2	26.4
88	34.3	33.4	32.5	31.6	30.7	29.8	28.9	28.0	27.2	26.3
89	34.3	33.3	32.4	31.5	30.7	29.8	28.9	28.0	27.2	26.3

Joint and Last Survivor Table (Continued)

Ages	50	51	52	53	54	55	56	57	58	59
90	34.2	33.3	32.4	31.5	30.6	29.8	28.9	28.0	27.1	26.3
91	34.2	33.3	32.4	31.5	30.6	29.7	28.9	28.0	27.1	26.3
92	34.2	33.3	32.4	31.5	30.6	29.7	28.8	28.0	27.1	26.2
93	34.2	33.3	32.4	31.5	30.6	29.7	28.8	28.0	27.1	26.2
94	34.2	33.3	32.4	31.5	30.6	29.7	28.8	27.9	27.1	26.2
95	34.2	33.3	32.4	31.5	30.6	29.7	28.8	27.9	27.1	26.2
96	34.2	33.3	32.4	31.5	30.6	29.7	28.8	27.9	27.0	26.2
97	34.2	33.3	32.4	31.5	30.6	29.7	28.8	27.9	27.0	26.2
98	34.2	33.3	32.4	31.5	30.6	29.7	28.8	27.9	27.0	26.2
99	34.2	33.3	32.4	31.5	30.6	29.7	28.8	27.9	27.0	26.2
100	34.2	33.3	32.4	31.5	30.6	29.7	28.8	27.9	27.0	26.1
101	34.2	33.3	32.4	31.5	30.6	29.7	28.8	27.9	27.0	26.1
102	34.2	33.3	32.4	31.4	30.5	29.7	28.8	27.9	27.0	26.1
103	34.2	33.3	32.4	31.4	30.5	29.7	28.8	27.9	27.0	26.1
104	34.2	33.3	32.4	31.4	30.5	29.6	28.8	27.9	27.0	26.1
105	34.2	33.3	32.3	31.4	30.5	29.6	28.8	27.9	27.0	26.1
106	34.2	33.3	32.3	31.4	30.5	29.6	28.8	27.9	27.0	26.1
107	34.2	33.3	32.3	31.4	30.5	29.6	28.8	27.9	27.0	26.1
108	34.2	33.3	32.3	31.4	30.5	29.6	28.8	27.9	27.0	26.1
109	34.2	33.3	32.3	31.4	30.5	29.6	28.7	27.9	27.0	26.1
110	34.2	33.3	32.3	31.4	30.5	29.6	28.7	27.9	27.0	26.1
111	34.2	33.3	32.3	31.4	30.5	29.6	28.7	27.9	27.0	26.1
112	34.2	33.3	32.3	31.4	30.5	29.6	28.7	27.9	27.0	26.1
113	34.2	33.3	32.3	31.4	30.5	29.6	28.7	27.9	27.0	26.1
114	34.2	33.3	32.3	31.4	30.5	29.6	28.7	27.9	27.0	26.1
115+	34.2	33.3	32.3	31.4	30.5	29.6	28.7	27.9	27.0	26.1

Joint and Last Survivor Table (Continued)

Ages	60	61	62	63	64	65	66	67	68	69
60	30.9	30.4	30.0	29.6	29.2	28.8	28.5	28.2	27.9	27.6
61	30.4	29.9	29.5	29.0	28.6	28.3	27.9	27.6	27.3	27.0
62	30.0	29.5	29.0	28.5	28.1	27.7	27.3	27.0	26.7	26.4
63	29.6	29.0	28.5	28.1	27.6	27.2	26.8	26.4	26.1	25.7
64	29.2	28.6	28.1	27.6	27.1	26.7	26.3	25.9	25.5	25.2
65	28.8	28.3	27.7	27.2	26.7	26.2	25.8	25.4	25.0	24.6
66	28.5	27.9	27.3	26.8	26.3	25.8	25.3	24.9	24.5	24.1
67	28.2	27.6	27.0	26.4	25.9	25.4	24.9	24.4	24.0	23.6
68	27.9	27.3	26.7	26.1	25.5	25.0	24.5	24.0	23.5	23.1
69	27.6	27.0	26.4	25.7	25.2	24.6	24.1	23.6	23.1	22.6
70	27.4	26.7	26.1	25.4	24.8	24.3	23.7	23.2	22.7	22.2
71	27.2	26.5	25.8	25.2	24.5	23.9	23.4	22.8	22.3	21.8
72	27.0	26.3	25.6	24.9	24.3	23.7	23.1	22.5	22.0	21.4
73	26.8	26.1	25.4	24.7	24.0	23.4	22.8	22.2	21.6	21.1
74	26.6	25.9	25.2	24.5	23.8	23.1	22.5	21.9	21.3	20.8
75	26.5	25.7	25.0	24.3	23.6	22.9	22.3	21.6	21.0	20.5
76	26.3	25.6	24.8	24.1	23.4	22.7	22.0	21.4	20.8	20.2
77	26.2	25.4	24.7	23.9	23.2	22.5	21.8	21.2	20.6	19.9
78	26.1	25.3	24.6	23.8	23.1	22.4	21.7	21.0	20.3	19.7
79	26.0	25.2	24.4	23.7	22.9	22.2	21.5	20.8	20.1	19.5
80	25.9	25.1	24.3	23.6	22.8	22.1	21.3	20.6	20.0	19.3
81	25.8	25.0	24.2	23.4	22.7	21.9	21.2	20.5	19.8	19.1
82	25.8	24.9	24.1	23.4	22.6	21.8	21.1	20.4	19.7	19.0
83	25.7	24.9	24.1	23.3	22.5	21.7	21.0	20.2	19.5	18.8
84	25.6	24.8	24.0	23.2	22.4	21.6	20.9	20.1	19.4	18.7
85	25.6	24.8	23.9	23.1	22.3	21.6	20.8	20.1	19.3	18.6
86	25.5	24.7	23.9	23.1	22.3	21.5	20.7	20.0	19.2	18.5
87	25.5	24.7	23.8	23.0	22.2	21.4	20.7	19.9	19.2	18.4
88	25.5	24.6	23.8	23.0	22.2	21.4	20.6	19.8	19.1	18.3
89	25.4	24.6	23.8	22.9	22.1	21.3	20.5	19.8	19.0	18.3
90	25.4	24.6	23.7	22.9	22.1	21.3	20.5	19.7	19.0	18.2
91	25.4	24.5	23.7	22.9	22.1	21.3	20.5	19.7	18.9	18.2
92	25.4	24.5	23.7	22.9	22.0	21.2	20.4	19.6	18.9	18.1
93	25.4	24.5	23.7	22.8	22.0	21.2	20.4	19.6	18.8	18.1
94	25.3	24.5	23.6	22.8	22.0	21.2	20.4	19.6	18.8	18.0
95	25.3	24.5	23.6	22.8	22.0	21.1	20.3	19.6	18.8	18.0
96	25.3	24.5	23.6	22.8	21.9	21.1	20.3	19.5	18.8	18.0
97	25.3	24.5	23.6	22.8	21.9	21.1	20.3	19.5	18.7	18.0
98	25.3	24.4	23.6	22.8	21.9	21.1	20.3	19.5	18.7	17.9
99	25.3	24.4	23.6	22.7	21.9	21.1	20.3	19.5	18.7	17.9

Joint and Last Survivor Table (Continued)

Ages	60	61	62	63	64	65	66	67	68	69
100	25.3	24.4	23.6	22.7	21.9	21.1	20.3	19.5	18.7	17.9
101	25.3	24.4	23.6	22.7	21.9	21.1	20.2	19.4	18.7	17.9
102	25.3	24.4	23.6	22.7	21.9	21.1	20.2	19.4	18.6	17.9
103	25.3	24.4	23.6	22.7	21.9	21.0	20.2	19.4	18.6	17.9
104	25.3	24.4	23.5	22.7	21.9	21.0	20.2	19.4	18.6	17.8
105	25.3	24.4	23.5	22.7	21.9	21.0	20.2	19.4	18.6	17.8
106	25.3	24.4	23.5	22.7	21.9	21.0	20.2	19.4	18.6	17.8
107	25.2	24.4	23.5	22.7	21.8	21.0	20.2	19.4	18.6	17.8
108	25.2	24.4	23.5	22.7	21.8	21.0	20.2	19.4	18.6	17.8
109	25.2	24.4	23.5	22.7	21.8	21.0	20.2	19.4	18.6	17.8
110	25.2	24.4	23.5	22.7	21.8	21.0	20.2	19.4	18.6	17.8
111	25.2	24.4	23.5	22.7	21.8	21.0	20.2	19.4	18.6	17.8
112	25.2	24.4	23.5	22.7	21.8	21.0	20.2	19.4	18.6	17.8
113	25.2	24.4	23.5	22.7	21.8	21.0	20.2	19.4	18.6	17.8
114	25.2	24.4	23.5	22.7	21.8	21.0	20.2	19.4	18.6	17.8
115+	25.2	24.4	23.5	22.7	21.8	21.0	20.2	19.4	18.6	17.8

Joint and Last Survivor Table (Continued)

Ages	70	71	72	73	74	75	76	77	78	79
70	21.8	21.3	20.9	20.6	20.2	19.9	19.6	19.4	19.1	18.9
71	21.3	20.9	20.5	20.1	19.7	19.4	19.1	18.8	18.5	18.3
72	20.9	20.5	20.0	19.6	19.3	18.9	18.6	18.3	18.0	17.7
73	20.6	20.1	19.6	19.2	18.8	18.4	18.1	17.8	17.5	17.2
74	20.2	19.7	19.3	18.8	18.4	18.0	17.6	17.3	17.0	16.7
75	19.9	19.4	18.9	18.4	18.0	17.6	17.2	16.8	16.5	16.2
76	19.6	19.1	18.6	18.1	17.6	17.2	16.8	16.4	16.0	15.7
77	19.4	18.8	18.3	17.8	17.3	16.8	16.4	16.0	15.6	15.3
78	19.1	18.5	18.0	17.5	17.0	16.5	16.0	15.6	15.2	14.9
79	18.9	18.3	17.7	17.2	16.7	16.2	15.7	15.3	14.9	14.5
80	18.7	18.1	17.5	16.9	16.4	15.9	15.4	15.0	14.5	14.1
81	18.5	17.9	17.3	16.7	16.2	15.6	15.1	14.7	14.2	13.8
82	18.3	17.7	17.1	16.5	15.9	15.4	14.9	14.4	13.9	13.5
83	18.2	17.5	16.9	16.3	15.7	15.2	14.7	14.2	13.7	13.2
84	18.0	17.4	16.7	16.1	15.5	15.0	14.4	13.9	13.4	13.0
85	17.9	17.3	16.6	16.0	15.4	14.8	14.3	13.7	13.2	12.8
86	17.8	17.1	16.5	15.8	15.2	14.6	14.1	13.5	13.0	12.5
87	17.7	17.0	16.4	15.7	15.1	14.5	13.9	13.4	12.9	12.4
88	17.6	16.9	16.3	15.6	15.0	14.4	13.8	13.2	12.7	12.2
89	17.6	16.9	16.2	15.5	14.9	14.3	13.7	13.1	12.6	12.0
90	17.5	16.8	16.1	15.4	14.8	14.2	13.6	13.0	12.4	11.9
91	17.4	16.7	16.0	15.4	14.7	14.1	13.5	12.9	12.3	11.8
92	17.4	16.7	16.0	15.3	14.6	14.0	13.4	12.8	12.2	11.7
93	17.3	16.6	15.9	15.2	14.6	13.9	13.3	12.7	12.1	11.6
94	17.3	16.6	15.9	15.2	14.5	13.9	13.2	12.6	12.0	11.5
95	17.3	16.5	15.8	15.1	14.5	13.8	13.2	12.6	12.0	11.4
96	17.2	16.5	15.8	15.1	14.4	13.8	13.1	12.5	11.9	11.3
97	17.2	16.5	15.8	15.1	14.4	13.7	13.1	12.5	11.9	11.3
98	17.2	16.4	15.7	15.0	14.3	13.7	13.0	12.4	11.8	11.2
99	17.2	16.4	15.7	15.0	14.3	13.6	13.0	12.4	11.8	11.2
100	17.1	16.4	15.7	15.0	14.3	13.6	12.9	12.3	11.7	11.1
101	17.1	16.4	15.6	14.9	14.2	13.6	12.9	12.3	11.7	11.1
102	17.1	16.4	15.6	14.9	14.2	13.5	12.9	12.2	11.6	11.0
103	17.1	16.3	15.6	14.9	14.2	13.5	12.9	12.2	11.6	11.0
104	17.1	16.3	15.6	14.9	14.2	13.5	12.8	12.2	11.6	11.0
105	17.1	16.3	15.6	14.9	14.2	13.5	12.8	12.2	11.5	10.9
106	17.1	16.3	15.6	14.8	14.1	13.5	12.8	12.2	11.5	10.9
107	17.0	16.3	15.6	14.8	14.1	13.4	12.8	12.1	11.5	10.9
108	17.0	16.3	15.5	14.8	14.1	13.4	12.8	12.1	11.5	10.9
109	17.0	16.3	15.5	14.8	14.1	13.4	12.8	12.1	11.5	10.9
110	17.0	16.3	15.5	14.8	14.1	13.4	12.7	12.1	11.5	10.9
111	17.0	16.3	15.5	14.8	14.1	13.4	12.7	12.1	11.5	10.8
112	17.0	16.3	15.5	14.8	14.1	13.4	12.7	12.1	11.5	10.8
113	17.0	16.3	15.5	14.8	14.1	13.4	12.7	12.1	11.4	10.8
114	17.0	16.3	15.5	14.8	14.1	13.4	12.7	12.1	11.4	10.8
115+	17.0	16.3	15.5	14.8	14.1	13.4	12.7	12.1	11.4	10.8

Joint and Last Survivor Table (Continued)

Ages	80	81	82	83	84	85	86	87	88	89
80	13.8	13.4	13.1	12.8	12.6	12.3	12.1	11.9	11.7	11.5
81	13.4	13.1	12.7	12.4	12.2	11.9	11.7	11.4	11.3	11.1
82	13.1	12.7	12.4	12.1	11.8	11.5	11.3	11.0	10.8	10.6
83	12.8	12.4	12.1	11.7	11.4	11.1	10.9	10.6	10.4	10.2
84	12.6	12.2	11.8	11.4	11.1	10.8	10.5	10.3	10.1	9.9
85	12.3	11.9	11.5	11.1	10.8	10.5	10.2	9.9	9.7	9.5
86	12.1	11.7	11.3	10.9	10.5	10.2	9.9	9.6	9.4	9.2
87	11.9	11.4	11.0	10.6	10.3	9.9	9.6	9.4	9.1	8.9
88	11.7	11.3	10.8	10.4	10.1	9.7	9.4	9.1	8.8	8.6
89	11.5	11.1	10.6	10.2	9.9	9.5	9.2	8.9	8.6	8.3
90	11.4	10.9	10.5	10.1	9.7	9.3	9.0	8.6	8.3	8.1
91	11.3	10.8	10.3	9.9	9.5	9.1	8.8	8.4	8.1	7.9
92	11.2	10.7	10.2	9.8	9.3	9.0	8.6	8.3	8.0	7.7
93	11.1	10.6	10.1	9.6	9.2	8.8	8.5	8.1	7.8	7.5
94	11.0	10.5	10.0	9.5	9.1	8.7	8.3	8.0	7.6	7.3
95	10.9	10.4	9.9	9.4	9.0	8.6	8.2	7.8	7.5	7.2
96	10.8	10.3	9.8	9.3	8.9	8.5	8.1	7.7	7.4	7.1
97	10.7	10.2	9.7	9.2	8.8	8.4	8.0	7.6	7.3	6.9
98	10.7	10.1	9.6	9.2	8.7	8.3	7.9	7.5	7.1	6.8
99	10.6	10.1	9.6	9.1	8.6	8.2	7.8	7.4	7.0	6.7
100	10.6	10.0	9.5	9.0	8.5	8.1	7.7	7.3	6.9	6.6
101	10.5	10.0	9.4	9.0	8.5	8.0	7.6	7.2	6.9	6.5
102	10.5	9.9	9.4	8.9	8.4	8.0	7.5	7.1	6.8	6.4
103	10.4	9.9	9.4	8.8	8.4	7.9	7.5	7.1	6.7	6.3
104	10.4	9.8	9.3	8.8	8.3	7.9	7.4	7.0	6.6	6.3
105	10.4	9.8	9.3	8.8	8.3	7.8	7.4	7.0	6.6	6.2
106	10.3	9.8	9.2	8.7	8.2	7.8	7.3	6.9	6.5	6.2
107	10.3	9.8	9.2	8.7	8.2	7.7	7.3	6.9	6.5	6.1
108	10.3	9.7	9.2	8.7	8.2	7.7	7.3	6.8	6.4	6.1
109	10.3	9.7	9.2	8.7	8.2	7.7	7.2	6.8	6.4	6.0
110	10.3	9.7	9.2	8.6	8.1	7.7	7.2	6.8	6.4	6.0
111	10.3	9.7	9.1	8.6	8.1	7.6	7.2	6.8	6.3	6.0
112	10.2	9.7	9.1	8.6	8.1	7.6	7.2	6.7	6.3	5.9
113	10.2	9.7	9.1	8.6	8.1	7.6	7.2	6.7	6.3	5.9
114	10.2	9.7	9.1	8.6	8.1	7.6	7.1	6.7	6.3	5.9
115+	10.2	9.7	9.1	8.6	8.1	7.6	7.1	6.7	6.3	5.9

Joint and Last Survivor Table (Continued)

Ages	90	91	92	93	94	95	96	97	98	99
90	7.8	7.6	7.4	7.2	7.1	6.9	6.8	6.6	6.5	6.4
91	7.6	7.4	7.2	7.0	6.8	6.7	6.5	6.4	6.3	6.1
92	7.4	7.2	7.0	6.8	6.6	6.4	6.3	6.1	6.0	5.9
93	7.2	7.0	6.8	6.6	6.4	6.2	6.1	5.9	5.8	5.6
94	7.1	6.8	6.6	6.4	6.2	6.0	5.9	5.7	5.6	5.4
95	6.9	6.7	6.4	6.2	6.0	5.8	5.7	5.5	5.4	5.2
96	6.8	6.5	6.3	6.1	5.9	5.7	5.5	5.3	5.2	5.0
97	6.6	6.4	6.1	5.9	5.7	5.5	5.3	5.2	5.0	4.9
98	6.5	6.3	6.0	5.8	5.6	5.4	5.2	5.0	4.8	4.7
99	6.4	6.1	5.9	5.6	5.4	5.2	5.0	4.9	4.7	4.5
100	6.3	6.0	5.8	5.5	5.3	5.1	4.9	4.7	4.5	4.4
101	6.2	5.9	5.6	5.4	5.2	5.0	4.8	4.6	4.4	4.2
102	6.1	5.8	5.5	5.3	5.1	4.8	4.6	4.4	4.3	4.1
103	6.0	5.7	5.4	5.2	5.0	4.7	4.5	4.3	4.1	4.0
104	5.9	5.6	5.4	5.1	4.9	4.6	4.4	4.2	4.0	3.8
105	5.9	5.6	5.3	5.0	4.8	4.5	4.3	4.1	3.9	3.7
106	5.8	5.5	5.2	4.9	4.7	4.5	4.2	4.0	3.8	3.6
107	5.8	5.4	5.1	4.9	4.6	4.4	4.2	3.9	3.7	3.5
108	5.7	5.4	5.1	4.8	4.6	4.3	4.1	3.9	3.7	3.5
109	5.7	5.3	5.0	4.8	4.5	4.3	4.0	3.8	3.6	3.4
110	5.6	5.3	5.0	4.7	4.5	4.2	4.0	3.8	3.5	3.3
111	5.6	5.3	5.0	4.7	4.4	4.2	3.9	3.7	3.5	3.3
112	5.6	5.3	4.9	4.7	4.4	4.1	3.9	3.7	3.5	3.2
113	5.6	5.2	4.9	4.6	4.4	4.1	3.9	3.6	3.4	3.2
114	5.6	5.2	4.9	4.6	4.3	4.1	3.9	3.6	3.4	3.2
115+	5.5	5.2	4.9	4.6	4.3	4.1	3.8	3.6	3.4	3.1

Joint and Last Survivor Table (Continued)

Ages	100	101	102	103	104	105	106	107	108	109
100	4.2	4.1	3.9	3.8	3.7	3.5	3.4	3.3	3.3	3.2
101	4.1	3.9	3.7	3.6	3.5	3.4	3.2	3.1	3.1	3.0
102	3.9	3.7	3.6	3.4	3.3	3.2	3.1	3.0	2.9	2.8
103	3.8	3.6	3.4	3.3	3.2	3.0	2.9	2.8	2.7	2.6
104	3.7	3.5	3.3	3.2	3.0	2.9	2.7	2.6	2.5	2.4
105	3.5	3.4	3.2	3.0	2.9	2.7	2.6	2.5	2.4	2.3
106	3.4	3.2	3.1	2.9	2.7	2.6	2.4	2.3	2.2	2.1
107	3.3	3.1	3.0	2.8	2.6	2.5	2.3	2.2	2.1	2.0
108	3.3	3.1	2.9	2.7	2.5	2.4	2.2	2.1	1.9	1.8
109	3.2	3.0	2.8	2.6	2.4	2.3	2.1	2.0	1.8	1.7
110	3.1	2.9	2.7	2.5	2.3	2.2	2.0	1.9	1.7	1.6
111	3.1	2.9	2.7	2.5	2.3	2.1	1.9	1.8	1.6	1.5
112	3.0	2.8	2.6	2.4	2.2	2.0	1.9	1.7	1.5	1.4
113	3.0	2.8	2.6	2.4	2.2	2.0	1.8	1.6	1.5	1.3
114	3.0	2.7	2.5	2.3	2.1	1.9	1.8	1.6	1.4	1.3
115+	2.9	2.7	2.5	2.3	2.1	1.9	1.7	1.5	1.4	1.2

Joint and Last Survivor Table (Continued)

Ages	110	111	112	113	114	115+
110	1.5	1.4	1.3	1.2	1.1	1.1
111	1.4	1.2	1.1	1.1	1.0	1.0
112	1.3	1.1	1.0	1.0	1.0	1.0
113	1.2	1.1	1.0	1.0	1.0	1.0
114	1.1	1.0	1.0	1.0	1.0	1.0
115+	1.1	1.0	1.0	1.0	1.0	1.0

Glossary

accrued benefit • the amount of benefit earned as of a given date

accumulated earnings tax • penalty tax for C corporations that attempt to reduce shareholders' tax burden by accumulating earnings instead of paying them out to shareholders

active participant • an individual who is covered by an employer plan and actually receives a benefit or contribution from the employer under the plan. An active participant cannot have a deductible IRA unless he or she has an adjusted gross income below prescribed limits.

activities of daily living (ADLs) • activities such as eating, bathing, and dressing. The inability to perform a specified number of these activities triggers eligibility for benefits in a long-term care insurance contract.

actual contribution percentage (ACP) test • an annual mathematical nondiscrimination test that applies to matching contributions and/or employee after-tax contributions in a qualified plan. The mathematical test works in essentially the same manner as the ADP test.

actual deferral percentage (ADP) test • an annual mathematical nondiscrimination test that applies to salary deferrals in a 401(k) plan. The test compares the level of salary deferrals of highly compensated employees with those of nonhighly compensated employees. In order to pass the ADP test, one of two requirements must be satisfied:

    (1) *the 1.25 requirement*—The actual deferral percentage for highly compensated employees for the current year cannot be more than 125 percent of the actual deferral percentage for nonhighly compensated employees for the previous year.

    (2) *the 200 percent/2 percent difference requirement*—The actual deferral percentage for highly compensated employees for the current year cannot be more than 200 percent of the actual deferral percentage for nonhighly compensated employees for the previous year, and the spread between the two cannot be more than 2 percent.

actuarial assumptions • assumptions that are made about investment return, mortality, turnover, and other factors concerning the employee group to determine the annual funding required in a defined-benefit plan

actuarial cost methods • methods used to determine the annual employer contribution to a defined-benefit plan

actuarial equivalent • a term indicating that one form of payment is equivalent to another, based on a specified set of actuarial assumptions

adoption agreement • the vehicle used for choosing from the various optional provisions provided in a master or prototype plan. The adoption agreement lists the various design choices that are available, and employers then pick from the menu of provided options.

adult day care • care that is provided at centers specifically designed for seniors who live at home but whose spouses or families are not able to be home during the day. The level of care received is similar to that provided by home health care. Most adult day-care centers also provide transportation to and from the center.

advance-determination letter • a letter from the IRS stating that a plan meets the qualification standards

advance directive • a document that identifies the medical treatment an individual would like to receive at a time when he or she is no longer competent to make health care decisions

advisory opinion • an opinion, issued by the Department of Labor, regarding the legality of a given situation. An advisory opinion can be sought before a client enters a transaction in which the ERISA consequences are unknown.

affiliated service group • two or more organizations that are aggregated for purposes of the qualified plan requirements. There are actually several different affiliation rules—all were promulgated to ensure that employees who worked together to produce a single product could not be divided into separate entities to avoid the qualified plan coverage requirements.

age-restricted housing • under federal law, a housing community may legally limit the age of the residents as long as the provision meets one of two federal exemptions to the equal housing law. The community can either require all residents to be aged 62 or over or it can limit the age to 55 and still allow up to 20 percent of the residents to be younger than age 55.

age-weighted formula • a defined-contribution method that allocates contributions to participants in such a way that when contributions are converted to equivalent benefit accruals (stated as a percentage of compensation), each participant receives the same rate of benefit accrual

aggregation rules • rules that determine whether affiliated companies will be considered the same entity for purposes of conducting qualified pension plan tests such as the nondiscrimination test

AIME (average indexed monthly earnings) • the term used to describe the indexed earnings figure used to calculate Social Security retirement benefits. AIME represents the 35 highest years of wages earned by the individual.

allocated • when contributions are assigned to provide benefits for specific employees, such as individual insurance or annuity contracts

allocation formula • a formula used to determine the amount of profits distributed to each participant in a profit-sharing plan. Allocation formulas can divide the profit-sharing "pie" to favor employees with higher salaries and longer service.

annuity • the distribution or liquidation of a sum of money on an actuarial basis. The amount paid to an annuitant is typically paid monthly and is determined by such factors as the annuity purchase price, the client's age, the number of lives covered by the annuity, the number of guarantees that are offered, and the interest assumption used.

annuity certain • provides an annuitant or his or her beneficiary with a specified number of monthly guaranteed payments, after which time all payments stop

anticutback rules • rules that state that once a participant has accrued a benefit or has received a contribution, the benefit or contribution cannot be reduced. Future reductions in accruals or contributions (prospective reductions), however, can be made.

assumed investment rate • the rate assumed in a variable annuity that the investment portfolio must earn in order for benefit payments to remain level. If the experience rate or actual investment rate is higher than the assumed investment rate, then annuity payouts will be higher. Conversely, if the experience or actual investment rate is lower than the assumed rate, annuity payouts will be lower.

average-benefit-percentage test • one of the nondiscrimination rules established under Code Sec. 410(b). The average benefit of nonhighly compensated employees must be 70 percent of the average benefit of highly compensated employees, and a fair cross section of employees must be covered.

average indexed monthly earnings • *See* AIME

baby-boom generation • the generation of Americans born from 1946 to 1964

backloading • the prohibited practice of accruing excessive benefits in later years. The accrued-benefit rules make backloading impossible in a qualified plan.

benefit period • a key Medicare concept that is measured beginning the first time a Medicare recipient is hospitalized and ending only after the recipient has been out of a hospital or skilled-nursing facility for 60 consecutive days. A hospitalization after that 60-day period then begins a new benefit period.

blue book • books published after a tax law change by the joint committee on taxation that help to explain the legislative history behind the tax law. The blue book can be quite informative, but is not considered a primary source of law.

break in service • a technical pension term used to describe a measured absence from employment for vesting and eligibility purposes. A break in service occurs when the individual has fewer than 500 hours in a year.

business risk • the type of investment risk that is the result of consumer preference, ineffective management, law changes, or foreign competition that affects the performance of a particular business

buy-and-hold strategy • a retirement planning strategy under which the client buys securities, bonds, mutual funds, and so on, and holds them until restructuring is required—the opposite of market timing

cafeteria plan • a plan that provides flexible benefit dollars that an employee can allocate to pay for certain benefits from a menu of benefit choices (such as life insurance, health insurance, or child care) and/or place in a 401(k) plan

capital-gains election • a portion of a participant's benefit earned prior to 1974 that may be entitled to capital-gains treatment. The amount subject to capital-gains tax is determined by dividing the amount of months prior to 1974 into the total months the participant worked under the plan. The subsequent ratio is then multiplied by the amount of distribution to determine the portion that is subject to the favorable capital-gains tax rate.

career-average compensation • a definition of average compensation in defined-benefit plans that either uses the entire salary history in the definition of average compensation or accrues a benefit each year based on that year's compensation

cash-balance plan • a defined-benefit plan that is designed to look like a defined-contribution plan in that the benefit grows based on contribution and investment credits. As a defined-benefit plan, it has some level of funding flexibility and is subject to minimum funding requirements and the PBGC insurance program.

cash equivalents • an investment, such as a Treasury bill, that either has no specified maturity date or has one that is one year or less in the future

cash or deferred arrangement (CODA) • a feature of a profit-sharing or stock bonus plan that allows participants to defer a portion of their compensation on a pretax basis

catch-up provision • a provision that allows employees covered by a 403(b) plan to make larger than typically permitted contributions to the plan

cliff vesting • a vesting schedule under which an employee is not entitled to any percentage of his or her retirement benefit until he or she is fully vested after the attainment of a specific number of years of service. The maximum amount of years of service that an employee can be forced to wait in a qualified plan is 5 years.

CODA • *See* cash or deferred arrangement

collectibles • items such as antique cars, precious metals, stamps, coins, and Persian rugs. Individual retirement accounts cannot invest in collectibles.

common trust fund • a commingled trust fund that combines assets from a number of trusts

conduit IRA • a rollover from a qualified plan into a new separate IRA. By making a conduit rollover, the benefit can later be rolled into another qualified plan.

constructive receipt • when an employee has the opportunity to control the timing of the receipt of a payment from the employer (can take it now or later), the employee is deemed to be in "constructive receipt" and will incur current taxation

controlled group rules • rules that require companies with a sufficient amount of common control to be tested as a single employer for purposes of the qualified plan requirements

controlled groups • aggregations of employers who share a sufficient amount of common ownership. There are three types of controlled groups: parent-subsidiary, brother-sister, and combined.

covered compensation • the average of the maximum Social Security wage bases for the number of years of earnings used to calculate the Social Security benefit for the 35-year period ending with the year the employee reaches the Social Security retirement age. Covered compensation is the integration level used in most defined-benefit plans.

cross-testing • a qualified plan that tests whether its contribution formula discriminates in favor of highly compensated employees by converting contributions made for each participant into equivalent benefit accruals

currently insured • a status under Social Security that means that the worker's decedents are eligible for certain survivors' benefits. To be currently insured, it is only necessary to have credit for 6 quarters of coverage out of the 13-quarter period ending with the quarter in which death occurs.

custodial care • a level of care described in a long-term care insurance policy that provides care to handle activities of daily living such as walking, bathing, dressing, eating, or taking medicine, and can usually be provided by someone who does not have professional medical skills or training

deemed IRA • separate IRA or Roth IRA accounts that are established on a voluntary basis in qualified plans, 403(b) annuities, and government 457 plans

deferred compensation • an agreement that states that compensation for services rendered is postponed until sometime after the services in question have been performed

deferred retirement age • any retirement age beyond the normal retirement age. In a defined-contribution plan, contributions will continue to be made after the normal retirement age until the deferred retirement age. In a defined-benefit plan, unless there is a years-of-service cap on the benefit formula, benefit accruals will continue until the deferred retirement age.

defined-benefit plan • a retirement plan that specifies the benefits that each employee receives at retirement. The employer is responsible for making contributions necessary to pay the promised benefit.

defined-contribution plan • a retirement plan in which the employer contributions are allocated to participants' accounts. The participant's benefit is leased on the account balance, which consists of the employer's contributions and investment experience.

direct rollover • a rollover directly from the trustee of a qualified plan to an IRA or other qualified plan

direct rollover rule • qualified plans are required to offer direct rollovers, and these transactions avoid the 20 percent income tax withholding that generally applies to distributions from qualified plans

disability insured • the term used to describe an individual who is eligible to receive Social Security disability benefits. Disability-insured status requires that a worker (1) be fully insured and (2) have a minimum amount of work under Social Security within a recent time period.

discretionary contributions • profit-sharing-type plans that provide the employer with discretion as to how much of a contribution will be made each year

distress termination • a plan termination that is allowed because the employer is experiencing financial difficulties

diversification requirement • an affirmative fiduciary duty that requires the fiduciary to diversify assets to guard against large losses

dollar cost averaging • a system for timing investment transactions that has a fixed dollar amount being invested in a particular security in each time period

domicile • an individual's intended permanent home that is determined by such factors as where the client spends time, is registered to vote, has a driver's license, and where his or her will is executed

do-not-resuscitate orders • documents in which an individual states he or she would like to have CPR (cardiopulmonary resuscitation) or other forms of resuscitation withheld if they would only prolong death and perhaps increase pain

double-bonus plan • a Sec. 162 life insurance program in which the employer pays both the life insurance premium and a bonus to the executive to cover the taxes resulting from the employer's payment of the life insurance premium

downsize • to purchase a retirement residence that costs less than the one being sold in order to transfer a portion of the gain (enhanced by tax breaks) into cash for retirement

early-retirement age • the age at which, if the plan permits, employees are permitted to retire and receive benefits prior to the normal retirement age. Typical early-retirement ages are 55, 60, and 62.

earnings test • a participant receiving Social Security benefits prior to his or her Social Security full retirement age will have a reduction in benefits if his or her earnings from employment exceed a specified level. In 2007, Social Security benefits are reduced one dollar for every $2 earned in excess of $$12,960. There is an exception in the calendar year when the individual attains the full retirement age; in that year, the reduction is only one dollar for every $3 of earnings in excess of $34,440. Under the exception, earnings include only amounts earned before the month the individual reaches full retirement age.

economic benefit • a tax concept that states that employment income is subject to income tax at the time the employee is deemed to receive an economic benefit

elapsed-time method • the computation of credit for plan service that is measured from date of employment to date of severance

eligible rollover distribution • distributions from qualified plans, 403(b) annuities, and 457 plans sponsored by a governmental agency that are allowed to be rolled over to qualified plans, 403(b) annuities, 457 governmental plans, or traditional IRAs. Most distributions qualify as eligible rollover distributions with a few limited exceptions including certain annuity payments, required minimum distributions, and hardship withdrawals from 401(k) plans.

Employee Retirement Income Security Act (ERISA) • the act that laid the foundation for modern pension law. ERISA established the nondiscrimination requirements, reporting and disclosure requirements, plan funding standards, vesting and participation requirements, and fiduciary responsibilities.

employee stock ownership plan (ESOP) • a profit-sharing type plan that invests primarily in employer stock. ESOPs are usually leveraged by borrowing from a bank to fund the plan.

enrollment meeting • a meeting during which employees may sign up to be covered by the employer's plan. An enrollment meeting is typically held to get proper enrollments in salary reduction plans, such as 401(k) and 403(b) plans, and also to get adequate participation in a contributory plan.

entry date • a sign-up time at which an employee becomes a participant under the plan. An employee must first satisfy the plan's eligibility requirements to be admitted as a participant on the next plan entry date.

ERISA Sec. 404(c) (individual account plan exception) • a provision of ERISA that relieves fiduciaries from liability for the investment decisions of plan participants

excess contribution • a contribution to an IRA or Roth IRA that exceeds the allowable limits

exclusion for the sale of a home • an exclusion from federal income taxation of up to $250,000 ($500,000 for married taxpayers filing jointly) of any capital gain realized from the sale of an individual's primary residence. This exclusion applies to individuals who have owned and used the property as a personal residence for at least 2 years.

exclusive-benefit rule • a rule that prevents misuse of the retirement plan. A fiduciary is required to discharge all duties solely in the interest of plan participants and their beneficiaries.

family maximum • a Social Security term referring to the maximum benefit payable when there are three or more family members (including a retired or disabled worker) eligible for benefits based on a single worker's wages

FASB 106 • an accounting rule that requires recognition on the company's books of the cost of future retiree medical expenses

fiduciaries. *See* fiduciary.

fiduciary • a person or corporation that exercises any discretionary authority or control over the management of the plan or plan assets, renders investment advice for a fee, or has any discretionary authority or responsibility in the administration of the plan

final-average compensation • a definition of average compensation used in many defined-benefit plans. Final-average compensation generally means the highest 3 to 5 years of a participant's compensation. It may also be limited to the final years of participation, for example, the average of the highest 3 years of compensation earned during the final 5 years of participation.

final regulations • regulations that explain and interpret the various sections of the Internal Revenue Code. Final regulations are legally enforceable, and the Internal Revenue Service is bound by them.

financial hardship • a financial need that is "necessary in light of immediate and heavy financial needs of an employee" and no other resources can be reasonably available to meet this end

first distribution year • under the minimum-distribution rules, the first year for which a distribution is required. For example, when the required beginning date is the April 1 following the year of attainment of age 70 1/2, the first distribution year is the year when the participant attained age 70 1/2.

fiscal welfare • an indirect payment made to individuals through the tax system

501(c)(3) organizations • certain tax-exempt organizations as specified in the Internal Revenue Code section that can have a 403(b) plan. A corporation, community chest, fund, or foundation that is organized and operated exclusively for religious, charitable, scientific, public safety, testing, literary, or educational purposes; for fostering national or international amateur sports competition; or for the prevention of cruelty to children or animals will probably qualify for 501(c)(3) status.

flat-amount formula • a formula for determining benefits that does not take into account an employee's service or salary

flat-amount-per-year-of-service formula • a benefit formula that relates the pension benefit solely to service and does not reflect an employee's salary

flat-percentage-of-earnings formula • a benefit formula that is related solely to salary and does not reflect an employee's service

forfeiture • an amount that is lost when a participant terminates employment before being fully vested under the plan's vesting schedule

401(a)(4) rule • a rule that forbids disparity in the amount of contributions or benefits that can be provided for highly compensated employees as compared with those provided for the rank-and-file employees

401(a)(26) minimum-participation rule • a rule that requires that defined-benefit plans cover the lesser of 50 employees or 40 percent of the workforce

401(k) plan • a defined-contribution profit-sharing plan that gives participants the option of reducing their taxable salary and contributing the salary reduction on a tax-deferred basis to an individual account for retirement purposes

403(b) plan • a retirement plan similar to a 401(k) plan that is available to certain tax-exempt organizations and to public schools

457 plan • all nonqualified salary reduction plans sponsored by a governmental or non-church-controlled tax-exempt organization are subject to the rules in Code Sec. 457

full retirement age • the age at which an individual is entitled to full retirement benefits from Social Security. The age is currently transitioning from age 65 to age 67. Individuals born in 1960 and after will have a full retirement age of 67.

fully insured • a qualified plan that is completely funded with life insurance or annuity contracts

fully insured status • the term used to describe an individual who is eligible to receive Social Security benefits. A person is fully insured for retirement benefits if he or she has 40 quarters of coverage.

funding instrument • the type of legal entity used to fund a retirement plan including trusts, insurance contracts, and annuities

funding policy • a stated strategy for ensuring that the plan has sufficient assets to pay promised benefits

funding standard account • the account used to determine if the minimum funding standards are being satisfied

general-counsel memorandum • a legal memorandum relied on by IRS personnel when deciding disputes with taxpayers

golden handshakes • additional benefits paid to employees to induce early retirement

golden parachutes • substantial payments made to corporate executives who are terminated upon change of ownership or corporate control

graded vesting • a vesting schedule under which the participant gradually becomes fully vested over time. The statutory 3-through-7 graded schedule requires 20 percent vesting after 3 years of service and an additional 20 percent for each additional year of service.

group-deposit administration contract • an unallocated group pension contract funded by a series of employer contributions made throughout the year. Contributions are accounted for under two different systems—one that reflects investment guarantees that are given (the active-life fund) and one that reflects the actual investment experience.

guaranteed-investment contract (GIC) • a group insurance investment product in which the insurance company guarantees both principal and rate of return

guaranteed renewable • in long-term care policies currently being sold this means that an individual's coverage cannot be canceled except for nonpayment of premiums. While premiums cannot be raised on the basis of a particular applicant's claim, they can (and often are) raised by class.

hardship withdrawal • a withdrawal permitted under a 401(k) plan or 403(b) plan if the participant has a hardship and no other resources available to meet the financial hardship. Under regulations, a hardship has been described as payments for a college education, for a residence, and for medical bills.

health care power of attorney (HCPOA) • a document in which an individual names someone (an agent) to make health care decisions if he or she is unable to do so

highly compensated employees (HCEs) • individuals who are 5 percent owners in the current or previous year as well as individuals who earned over $100,000 (the limit for both 2006 and 2007). The employer can elect to limit this second category to employees whose compensation puts them in the top 20 percent of payroll.

holistic retirement planning • a way of looking at retirement planning that considers all aspects of the person, not just his or her financial picture

home health care • care that is received at home and includes part-time skilled-nursing care, speech therapy, physical or occupational therapy, part-time services from home health aides, and help from homemakers

hour of service • any hour for which a participant is paid or entitled to be paid

immediate-participation-guarantee contract • an unallocated funding instrument that holds benefit amounts in a commingled fund. At retirement, either the fund is charged directly with benefit payments or the fund is charged with a single annuity premium.

incentive stock options (ISOs) • options to purchase shares of company stock at a stated price over a specified period of time. Different from nonqualified stock options in that the rules governing ISOs are quite strict and the tax treatment is more favorable to the executive. The executive pays no tax at the time options are exercised, only when shares of stock are sold.

incidental-death-benefit rules • ERISA rules that limit the amount of life insurance that can be used in a qualified plan

income-replacement ratio • the amount of gross income that is replaced by the retirement plan

individual retirement account. *See* IRA.

individual retirement annuity • an individual retirement account that is funded with an annuity contract

inflation • an increase in the general (average) level of prices

in-service withdrawals • withdrawals taken from the qualified plan while the participant is still employed. No in-service withdrawals are permitted from a pension plan.

installment payout • the periodic payout of funds from a qualified plan

integration with Social Security • a method of dovetailing a qualified plan with Social Security benefits. Because Social Security does not provide benefits on earnings above the taxable wage base, an integrated plan is allowed to provide additional benefits on those earnings to make up the difference.

integration level • the dividing line between the base and excess percentages in an integrated plan. The integration level for a defined-benefit plan is typically covered compensation; the integration level for a defined-contribution plan is typically the taxable wage base.

interest-rate risk • the type of investment risk that results from changes in interest rates in the market

intermediate care • a level of care described in a long-term care insurance policy that requires occasional nursing and rehabilitative care that must be based on a doctor's orders and can be performed only by, or under the supervision of, skilled medical personnel

investment-guarantee contract (IG) • a group insurance investment product similar to a GIC. The major difference is that contributions are received over a number of years, and the guarantee rate for the later years is only a floor with the investor receiving the actual rate if higher.

investment guidelines • a set of written instructions that provide guidance and structure for those involved in investing plan assets

investment policy • a statement concerning the investment of plan assets that addresses the appropriate degree of risk and yield for the trust and the importance of yield in relation to safety of principal and the plan's cash flow needs

investment risk • the variability in the value of an investment

involuntary cash-out option • a rule that gives the plan administrator the option to distribute benefits valued at less than $5,000 from a qualified plan without giving the participant an election with regard to the timing or form of payment

involuntary terminations • terminations that are called for by the PBGC when a plan is seriously unfunded and the PBGC would be liable for continuation of unfunded benefits. (An involuntary termination can also be called for by the IRS if plan contributions cease and no provision is made for plan continuance.)

IRA (individual retirement account) • a trust or custodial account established by an individual that allows for saving for retirement in a tax-advantaged manner

IRC Sec. 121 • code provision that allows taxpayers who sell their principal residence to exclude up to $250,000 of their gain ($500,000 for married taxpayers filing jointly) if certain qualification requirements have been satisfied

IRS news releases • announcements about forthcoming regulations and information about statistical and survey results

IRS publications • general reviews of retirement topics provided by the IRS to aid individuals in filing their tax returns

joint and survivor annuity • an annuity for a participant's life that terminates at the participant's death. If, however, at the participant's death his or her spouse is still alive, annuity payments in a predetermined amount will continue for the life of the surviving spouse. A joint and survivor annuity is the normal form of benefit for married individuals in a qualified plan.

Keogh plans • qualified plans for unincorporated businesses

key employee • an employee who owns more than 5 percent of the business, an officer who earns over $145,000 (as indexed for 2007), or a one percent owner who earns over $150,000

leased employee • a term, under the pension rules, that describes an individual who is leased on a full-time, ongoing basis. The rules require that such leased employees be generally treated as employees for purposes of the qualified plan coverage requirements.

level annual funding • a schedule to save funds for a specific dollar retirement goal where the same level investment is made each year until retirement age

leveraged ESOP • in order to have the funds to purchase large blocks of stock, an ESOP can borrow the funds and repay the loan with the contributions (deductible) that the employer makes to the plan each year

life annuity • an annuity that pays income for the participant's life and stops payments at the participant's death. No survivor or additional death benefits are payable. It will yield the largest monthly payment per given purchase price of all the annuity types, because there are no residual benefits.

life annuity with guaranteed payments • an annuity that pays benefits for a participant's life and stops when a participant dies. If, however, a participant dies before the guaranteed payments are made, payments are made to the participant's beneficiary for the remainder of that period. The longer the stipulation or guaranteed period, the smaller the monthly amount for a given dollar figure. Conversely, the shorter the stipulated or guaranteed period, the larger the monthly amount for a given dollar figure.

life-care community • a retirement community that offers to its residents a range of housing options (depending on needs), meals, and a variety of other services, generally including nursing care

life-care retirement communities • organizations that provide housing and services to retired parties in exchange for up-front and/or monthly fees

lifetime reserve days • if a Medicare recipient runs out of hospital coverage during a benefit period, he or she will be able to receive benefits for a total of an additional 60 days—which, when used, are no longer available

living will • a document in which individuals state whether they want their lives prolonged through medical intervention, if they will soon die from a terminal illness or if they were to become permanently unconscious

long-term accumulation period • the stage in an individual's investment program that begins when funds are first accumulated for retirement and is phased out with the onset of the portfolio restructuring period

loose-leaf services • publications that describe the legal and administrative framework of pensions in an up-to-date manner

lump-sum distribution • a distribution from a qualified plan that represents the participant's entire account balance. In order to be considered a qualified lump-sum distribution, the distribution must meet the following conditions:

– The client must have been a plan participant for at least 5 years.
– The funds must be distributed to the client within one taxable year.
– The distribution must represent the entire account balance or benefit.
– The amount distributed must be payable only upon death, attainment of age 59 1/2, separation from service, or disability.

market risk • the type of investment risk due to changes in political, economic, demographic, or social events that have an impact on the market as a whole

master and prototype plans • standardized plans approved and qualified in concept by the Internal Revenue Service that the insurance companies make available for their agents. Although these plans must go through qualification procedures, a favorable result is more predictable. The master or prototype plan offers an employer fewer choices in plan design and, thus, can be installed very easily.

matching contribution • a plan feature in which the plan sponsor agrees to match employee savings to a certain extent. For example, the sponsor might agree to contribute 50 cents to the plan for each dollar that the employee saves, up to the first 6 percent of compensation that the participant saves.

maximum insured benefits • the maximum amount that the PBGC will insure. This amount is approximately $4,000 per month.

Medicare, Part A • the hospital portion of Medicare. It provides benefits for expenses incurred in hospitals, skilled nursing facilities, and hospices with various limits and restrictions, and for home health care for a condition treated in a hospital or skilled nursing facility. It is available at no monthly cost to any person aged 65 or older who is entitled to monthly retirement benefits under Social Security.

Medicare, Part B • the supplementary medical insurance portion of Medicare. It provides benefits for physicians' and surgeons' fees, diagnostic tests, certain drugs and medical supplies, rental of certain medical equipment, and home health service when prior hospitalization has not occurred. With some exceptions, Part B pays 80 percent of the approved charges for covered medical expenses after the satisfaction of an annual deductible. Any person eligible for Part A is eligible for Part B and is automatically enrolled. A monthly premium is charged for Part B, which is adjusted annually to reflect the cost of the benefits provided.

G.14 *Planning for Retirement Needs*

medigap • a common term used to describe private insurance that is purchased to supplement Medicare coverage

minimum-distribution rules • set procedures for determining the minimum required distributions from qualified plans, 403(b) plans, SEPs, and IRAs when a person reaches age 70 1/2

minimum-participation rule • a coverage requirement for defined-benefit plans whereby an employer's plan must cover (1) 50 employees or (2) 40 percent of the employer's employees, whichever is less

modified cash-refund annuity • an annuity that provides payments for a person's life and stops payment at a person's death. If, however, a stipulated amount of the annuity purchase price has not been received by the annuitant, then that portion will be refunded to the annuitant's beneficiary. It is typically the normal form of benefit for single individuals in a contributory pension plan, thus returning any contributions they made to the plan.

money-purchase pension plan • a defined-contribution plan that specifies a level of contribution (for example, 10 percent of salary) to each participant's account each year

net unrealized appreciation (NUA) • the name given to the rule that allows deferral of the tax on the unrealized gain when a lump-sum distribution from a qualified plan includes employer securities

new comparability • another name for a defined-contribution plan that tests whether its contribution formula discriminates in favor of highly compensated employees by converting contributions made for each participant into equivalent benefit accruals; also referred to as cross testing

nonqualified plan • a flexible retirement plan that can be established for executives only, but is not eligible for the special tax benefits available for qualified or other tax-advantaged retirement plans

nonqualified stock options (NQSOs) • options granted by the company to the executive to purchase shares of company stock at a stated price over a specified period of time. The employee pays tax (as ordinary income) on the difference between the market value and the option price at the time the options are exercised.

normal form of benefit payment • a distribution from a qualified plan that for a married individual is a joint and survivor annuity of at least 50 percent. For a single individual, the normal form of benefit is typically a life annuity, or in a contributory plan, a modified cash-refund annuity.

normal retirement age • the age at which a participant can retire and receive the full, specified retirement benefit

notice to interested parties • part of the process of applying to the IRS for an advance determination letter is to notify participants of that submission

Office of Pension and Welfare Benefit Plans (OPWBP) • the branch of the Department of Labor responsible for overseeing retirement plans

offset integration • a method of integrating defined-benefit plans by subtracting out a specified amount from the benefit formula that represents a percentage of the participant's Social Security benefits

partial plan termination • a termination in which part of the plan continues for a smaller group of participants and part of the plan ceases to exist

parties-in-interest • persons who have a relationship to the qualified plan. Parties-in-interest include plan fiduciaries, plan counsels, persons providing services to the plan, employers connected with the plan, employees in the plan, employee organizations whose members are covered by the plan, relatives of any of the above, and shareholders, officers, and directors who have a 10-percent-or-more ownership interest in any of the above.

past service • service prior to the inception of the plan. In a defined-benefit plan, the employer has the option of funding for past service.

Pension Benefit Guaranty Corporation (PBGC) • an organization that oversees defined-benefit plans and provides insureds protection in case a defined-benefit plan cannot pay promised benefits to participants

pension-funding contract • an unallocated group insurance product that evolved from the IPG contract but which contains no guarantees; no annuity purchases are made; and no funds are earmarked for retired employees

pension plan category • four of the qualified plans (defined-benefit, cash-balance, money-purchase, and target-benefit) are categorized as pension plans. Pension plans are subject to an annual funding requirement, a prohibition from distributing assets prior to termination of employment, and a limitation on investments to 10 percent of employer stock.

percentage test • one of the nondiscrimination tests established under Code Sec. 410(b). Under this test, the plan must benefit at least 70 percent of employees who are not highly compensated employees.

permanency requirement • a requirement that all qualified plans must be intended to be permanent

phantom stock • an executive incentive pay program that grants units analogous to company shares to executives. Phantom units mature at a fixed date. On the maturation date the company may pay the executive the difference between the initial value of the units and the current value of the units based on the stock's current market price.

PIA (primary insurance amount) • Social Security retirement benefits are based on a formula that is a function of the worker's average indexed monthly earnings (AIME)

piggybacking • a method that combines a money-purchase and profit-sharing plan. Piggybacking also refers to combining a qualified and nonqualified plan.

plan administrator • the person who administrates the plan

plan termination • the means by which the employer can discontinue his or her obligation to make contributions to participant accounts in a defined-contribution plan or to fund a promised benefit in a defined-benefit plan

portfolio restructuring period • the investment stage during which an individual's portfolio composition shifts from growth orientation to income orientation prior to retirement

preservation and current-income period • the retirement period when portfolio management objectives focus most heavily on the preservation of capital and high current income and only to a limited degree on long-term growth

primary sources • the actual text of statutory and regulatory law when discussing legal research

private-letter rulings • IRS interpretations of the law in light of a specific set of circumstances that face a taxpayer; also, a method by which a taxpayer can inquire about the acceptability of a specific transaction in which he or she is engaged

profit-sharing plan • a defined-contribution plan structured to offer an employee participation in company profits that he or she may use for retirement purposes

profit-sharing plan category • four of the qualified plans (profit-sharing, 401(k), ESOP, and stock-bonus) are categorized as profit-sharing plans. In contrast to plans categorized as pension plans, these plans can have discretionary employer contributions, in-service withdrawals, and can invest up to 100 percent of the plan's assets in employer stock.

prohibited transactions • disallowed dealings between the plan and a party-in-interest

prohibited-transaction exemptions • exemptions from the prohibited-transaction rules that allow a transaction that would otherwise be disallowed

projected benefit • the participant's benefit projected to normal retirement age, assuming the individual will continue working until that date

proposed regulations • regulations often issued after major legislation so practitioners can receive guidance on complex provisions of new laws. Unlike final regulations, proposed regulations have no legal force or effect (unless specifically stated in the proposed regulations).

provisional income • a technical term to describe the income counted when determining whether or not Social Security benefits are taxed.. Provisional income includes adjusted gross income, tax-free municipal bond earnings, and one-half of the Social Security benefits received.

prudent-fiduciary rule • a rule that states a plan fiduciary must perform his or her functions as a prudent person would perform them under like circumstances or else legal liability will be incurred. A prudent fiduciary must use the care, skill, prudence, and diligence under the circumstances then prevailing that a prudent fiduciary acting in like capacity would use.

PS 58 rule • a present benefit received by a participant in the form of current life insurance protection that must be included in taxable gross income for that year. The cost attributable to this pure life protection will be the lower of the actual cost as provided by the carrier or the rates supplied by the so-called PS 58 table.

purchasing power risk (inflation risk) • the investment risk associated with the loss of purchasing power due to inflation

qualified domestic relations order (QDRO) • a decree under state law that assigns a participant's plan benefits to a spouse or other designated party

qualified joint and survivor annuity (QJSA) • the normal form of benefit distribution offered to a married participant at retirement

qualified plans • retirement plans that are eligible for favorable tax status under Internal Revenue Code Sec. 401(a). There are eight types of qualified plans including defined-benefit pension plans, cash-balance plans, money-purchase pension plans, target-benefit plans, profit-sharing plans, 401(k) plans, stock bonus plans, and ESOPs.

qualified preretirement survivor annuity (QPSA) • death benefit given to a surviving spouse following the death of a participant prior to retirement. For a defined-benefit plan, the amount of the survivor annuity is basically equal to the amount that would have been paid under the qualified joint and survivor annuity. To determine this amount, the plan administrator assumes the participant had retired the day before death or, if the participant was not yet able to retire, he or she had left the company the day prior to death, survived until the plan's earliest retirement age, and then retired with an immediate joint and survivor annuity. For a defined-contribution plan, the qualified preretirement survivor annuity is an annuity for the life of the surviving spouse that is at least actuarially equivalent to 50 percent of the participant's vested account balance as of the date of death.

quarters of coverage • the method of determining eligibility for Social Security benefits. For 2007, a worker receives credit for one quarter of coverage for each $1,000 in annual earnings on which Social Security taxes are paid. A total of four quarters of coverage can be earned in one year.

rabbi trust • a trust established and funded by the employer that is subject to the claims of the employer's creditors (thus avoiding current taxation for the employee), but the funds in the trust cannot be used by, or revert to, the employer

ratio test • one of the nondiscrimination tests established under Code Sec. 410(b). A plan must benefit a percentage of nonhighly compensated employees that is at least 70 percent of the percentage of highly compensated employees benefited under the plan.

reallocated forfeiture • an amount forfeited by employees leaving prior to full vesting that is distributed to the remaining plan participants

replacement-ratio method • the percentage of preretirement income replaced in the postretirement period. For example, a qualified defined-benefit plan typically replaces between 40 and 60 percent of a person's final-average salary.

required beginning date • the date when distributions from qualified plans, 403(b) TDAs, SEPs, and IRAs must commence under the uniform minimum-distribution rules. In most cases, this date is April 1 of the year after a person reaches age 70 1/2.

restricted stock • an executive incentive pay program in which shares of company stock are titled in the participant's name but are subject to forfeiture upon the occurrence of a specific event.

revenue procedures • statements concerning the internal practices and procedures of the IRS

revenue rulings • the IRS's interpretations of the provisions of the Internal Revenue Code and regulations as they apply to factual situations presented by taxpayers. Revenue rulings may be used as precedents.

reverse annuity mortgage • a life or term annuity in the form of a loan, paid to an individual and secured by the individual's ownership of his or her residence

reverse mortgage • a loan against an individual's home that requires no repayment for as long as the individual continues to live in the home

risk tolerance • the degree to which an investor can accept risk and uncertainty in either the performance and/or the value of his or her investments

rollover • a way to delay taxation by transferring funds from one IRA or qualified plan to a second IRA or qualified plan

Roth IRA • an individual retirement account in which contributions are made on an after-tax basis and qualifying distributions are made tax free

salary reduction agreement • the form that authorizes the employer to reduce an employee's salary and make plan contributions to a 401(k) or a 403(b) plan in the amount of the reduction

salary reduction plans • nonqualified plans that give executives the opportunity to defer compensation until termination of employment as a way to lower current income and to save for retirement

sale-leaseback • occurs when an individual sells his or her house to an investor and then rents it back from the investor under a lifetime lease

sale-leaseback agreement • the sale of a property ownership interest in real estate (or other asset) and the immediate leasing of the property by the seller for either a specified or an indefinite term

savings incentive match plan for employees (SIMPLE) • a simplified retirement plan that allows employees to save on a pretax basis, with limited employer contributions

Sec. 72(t) penalty tax • Section 72(t) generally imposes a 10 percent penalty tax on premature withdrawals from qualified plans, 403(b) TDAs, SEPs, and IRAs prior to age 59 1/2

Sec. 501(c)(3) organizations • employers that are exempt from tax under Code Sec. 501(c)(3) or educational institutions of a state or political subdivision of a state

Sec. 401(a)(4) nondiscrimination rule • a qualified plan cannot discriminate in favor of highly compensated employees (HCEs) with regard to benefits or contributions

Sec. 423 stock purchase plan • a Code section that provides for special tax rules for employee stock purchase programs that satisfy certain requirements. Generally, the plan must be available to full-time employees. The plan can allow a discount of up to 15 percent on the purchase price of the stock.

Sec. 162 bonus plan • also referred to as an executive-bonus life insurance plan, this is a program in which the corporation pays a bonus to the executive for the purpose of purchasing cash-value life insurance. The executive is the policyowner, the insured, and the person who designates the beneficiary. This type of plan can be limited to certain executives and does not provide any deferral of income. The executive pays taxes at the time the premium is paid.

Sec. 121 • This code section provides that capital gains on the sale of a personal residence of up to $250,000 ($500,000 for married couples filing jointly) can be excluded from income as long as 2-year ownership and use requirements are satisfied.

secular trust • a funding instrument for nonqualified plans in which the assets typically are irrevocable, meaning that they can only be used to pay benefits for participants and cannot revert to the employer or be accessed by the employer's creditors

self-directed IRAs • IRAs in which the taxpayer is able to shift investments between general investment vehicles offered by the trustee

separate-investment accounts contract • under the separate-investment accounts contract, the plan fund manager can invest in one of several separate accounts (similar to mutual funds) offered by the insurance company

separate lines of business • a term used under the minimum-coverage rules that allows a company that operates a separate line of business and has at least 50 employees to treat that entity as a separate company under the qualified plan rules

simplified employee pension (SEP) • a retirement plan that uses an individual retirement account (IRA) as the receptacle for contributions. A SEP is a simplified alternative to a profit-sharing or 401(k) plan.

single-premium annuity contract (SPAC) • a product sold when a plan terminates that transfers the employer's liability under the plan to an insurer. SPACs require the payment of a single premium by the employer in return for which the life insurance company issues paid-up annuities to all former participants.

skilled-nursing care • a level of care described in a long-term care insurance policy that requires daily nursing and rehabilitative care that can be performed only by, or under the supervision of, skilled medical personnel and must be based on a doctor's orders

social assistance • a type of social benefit that contains eligibility criteria designed in part to encourage the able-bodied poor to work by providing minimal benefits

Social Security • the old-age, survivors, disability, and health insurance (OASDHI) program of the federal government

split-funded plan • a term that describes a retirement plan that is funded with both a trust fund and life insurance contracts

split-interest purchase • the acquisition of property by two parties whereby one party owns certain rights to the property, such as lifetime use, and the other party owns the remaining rights, such as full ownership upon the death of the lifetime-use owner

spousal consent • the protection generally afforded by qualified plans for a spouse's interest in a participant's qualified plans by automatic provision of a qualified preretirement survivor annuity (QPSA) in the event the participant dies before retirement and a qualified joint and survivor annuity (QJSA) as the normal benefit when the participant retires. Elections to waive QPSA or QJSA benefits and to elect some other form of benefit or to designate some other beneficiary are not valid unless the participant's spouse consents in writing to the election.

spousal IRA • a traditional IRA or a Roth IRA for a nonworking spouse .

stand-alone plan • a 401(k) plan that only provides for employee pretax contributions. The employer does not make any matching contributions or profit-sharing contributions.

standard-hours counting method • a way to compute the hours of service an employee has for plan purposes by counting each hour the employee works and each hour for which the employee is entitled to be paid

standard termination • a voluntary termination of a qualified defined-benefit plan in which the plan sponsor has sufficient assets to pay its benefit commitments

stepped-up annual funding • a schedule to save funds for a specific dollar retirement goal in which the level of contributions is increased (stepped up) each year

stipulated annuity • *See* life annuity with guaranteed payments.

stock bonus plans • defined-contribution profit-sharing-type plans in which the participants have the right to receive distributions in the form of employer stock

stock appreciation right (SAR) • an arrangement under which an executive has the right to receive the amount of the increase in the value of employer stock during a specified period

subsidized benefits • a term used to describe benefits (such as an early retirement benefit) that are actuarially more valuable than the normal form of payments

substantially equal periodic payments • an exception to the Sec. 72(t) penalty tax

summary annual report (SAR) • a summary of the 5500 forms filed with the IRS that is provided to plan participants every year

summary of material modification (SMM) • an explanation given to plan participants that informs them about major changes in their plan

summary plan description (SPD) • an easy-to-read booklet that explains the retirement plan to participants

superannuated employees • older employees whose productivity levels are lower than their salary levels

supplemental executive retirement plan (SERP) • a nonqualified plan that provides additional retirement benefits (paid for by the employer) for executives and is used to attract and retain management personnel

surety bond • a third-party promise guaranteeing that a nonqualified plan benefit will be paid

Table 2001 • IRS table used for determining the current cost of the "pure insurance" protection that is subject to taxation when life insurance is purchased in a qualified plan. It replaced the P.S. 58 table.

target-benefit pension plan • a hybrid retirement plan that uses a benefit formula like that of a defined-benefit plan and the individual accounts like that of a defined-contribution plan. The contribution is derived from the benefit formula in a target-benefit plan, but once determined, the plan resembles a money-purchase plan in all other ways.

tax-advantaged retirement plans • employer-sponsored retirement plans that are eligible for special tax treatment. These plans include qualified plans, SEPs, SIMPLEs, and 403(b) plans.

technical-advice memorandum • a private ruling on a completed transaction issued by the national office of the IRS

TEFRA 242(b) elections • grandfather elections made before 1984 that allowed participants to elect out of the current minimum-distribution rules

temporary regulations • regulations issued immediately after major legislation so practitioners can receive guidance on complex provisions of new laws. Temporary regulations have legal force and effect until withdrawn.

10-year averaging • a preferential method for computing the tax on a qualifying lump-sum distribution from a qualified plan that has been grandfathered for certain taxpayers born before January 1, 1936

1099-R forms • the IRS forms that report distributions from pension plans

terminal funding approach • funding a plan as benefits are due instead of putting money aside over time. Qualified plans must be funded over time (prefunded) but nonqualified plans can still use the terminal funding approach.

third-party administrators (TPAs) • organizations that offer design consulting, record-keeping, legal, and actuarial services to either support plan administrators (the sponsors or employees of the sponsor) or stand in as the plan administrator

top-hat exemption • An ERISA exemption for unfunded, nonqualified plans maintained by an employer, primarily for the purpose of providing deferred compensation for a select group of management and/or highly compensated employees

top-heavy plan • a plan that unduly favors key employees by providing 60 percent or more of the benefits or contributions to these employees. These plans are subject to additional restrictions.

trustee-to-trustee transfer • a transfer of an IRA or tax-advantaged retirement plan directly from the trustee of the plan to the trustee of another IRA or tax-advantaged retirement plan

21-and-one rule • a rule stating that to be eligible for participation in the plan, an employee must have one year of service and be at least 21 years of age

2-year/100 percent rule • a term used to describe a special qualified plan participation rule that allows the sponsor to exclude employees who have earned less than 2 years of service as long as the participants are 100 percent immediately vested

unallocated group pension contract • a method by which contributions are assigned to a general pool and specifically allocated to employees only at retirement—for example, deposit-administration contracts and immediate-participation-guarantee contracts

unit-benefit formula • a formula that accounts for both service and salary in determining the participant's benefit in a defined-benefit plan

valuation date • the date when investment earnings, gains, and losses are allocated to participants' accounts

variable annuity • an annuity with an equity-based component. It is designed to provide fluctuating benefit payments over the payout period that may provide increasing benefits during periods of inflation.

vesting • the acquisition by an employee of his or her right to receive a present or future pension benefit

vesting schedules • methods of determining the portion of the accrued benefit that a participant will receive if he or she terminates employment prior to normal retirement age

voluntary after-tax employee contribution • a contribution that does not result in matching employer contributions

withdrawal rate • the amount of cash withdrawn from the portfolio during the year, divided by the portfolio's market value at the start of the year

year of service • a 12-month period in which the participant has 1,000 hours of service

Index

THE AMERICAN COLLEGE
ALUMNI
ASSOCIATION

Your Bridge to a Lifetime of Professional Achievement

We encourage you to take advantage of knowing more about The Alumni Association. Together we can create a stronger community and explore new opportunities for professional success.

Call us at (610) 526-1200

e-mail: russell.figueira@theamericancollege.edu